D1823161

Urban and Regional Economics

Urban and Regional Economics

John P. Blair
Wright State University

Homewood, IL 60430
Boston, MA 02116

© RICHARD D. IRWIN, INC., 1991

All rights reserved. No part of this publication may be reproduced, stored in a retrieval system, or transmitted, in any form or by any means, electronic, mechanical, photocopying, recording, or otherwise, without the prior written permission of the publisher.

Sponsoring editor: Gary L. Nelson
Project editor: Waivah Clement
Production manager: Ann Cassady
Cover designer: Michael Finkelman
Compositor: Bi-Comp, Incorporated
Typeface: 10/12 Times Roman
Printer: The Book Press, Inc.

Library of Congress Cataloging-in-Publication Data

Blair, John P.
   Urban and regional economics / John P. Blair.
      p.   cm.
   ISBN 0-256-06147-5
   1. Urban economics.   2. Regional economics.   I. Title.
HT321.B63   1991
330.9173'2—dc20   90–36270
                                                      CIP

Printed in the United States of America
1 2 3 4 5 6 7 8 9 0 BP 7 6 5 4 3 2 1 0

TO MY SONS AND THEIR PLACE IN THE WORLD

Preface

This book has three general purposes. First, it provides a framework for understanding how spatial relationships affect economic behavior. Familiar economic concepts are recast in a spatial setting to spark fresh insights. Second, theory is applied to real-world situations. Both conceptual and quantitative applications are presented, thereby providing students with a solid professional orientation. Finally, policy issues are presented so that controversies and trade-offs are confronted.

The motivation for writing an urban and regional economic text emerged slowly. After 15 years of teaching as well as serving as a consultant to cities, states, and private developers, I perceived a widening gap between urban economics texts and the practice of urban economics. In class, I tried to help my students develop tools needed to understand issues of today and tomorrow, but I sometimes felt I was "fighting" the textbook. Discussions with urban and regional economists convinced me that many others experienced similar problems.

Urban economics attracted me because the field addresses issues as if people matter. While some economic models represent individuals as abstractions (and there are often good reasons for doing so), urban and regional economics has a tradition of maintaining a focus on flesh-and-blood people. I have tried to write in this tradition.

This book is geared to students who have had an introduction to economics but who may have forgotten some of the details. Students with strong theoretical and quantitative backgrounds in economics should breeze through much of the material. The book is intended primarily for advanced undergraduate or first-year graduate students in economics. However, it will also be useful in planning and public affairs programs as well.

There are many routes to understanding urban and regional economics. The book avoids devoting separate chapters to theory and policy issues in order to facilitate integration and avoid duplication. However, there is more material in the text than can be easily covered in a one-semester course. I believe that the scope of the material will allow instructors substantial flexibility to tailor their courses to the needs and interests of their students. Numerous springboards for discussion have been incorporated in each chapter to encourage student discussions and to provide an opportunity to discuss issues in the context of areas they know. Occasional freewheeling discussions will enrich the academic experience. The book also reflects the fact that the field of urban and regional economics lacks definitive boundaries. Consequently, material from other disciplines, principally political science, planning, geography, and sociology, is incorporated throughout the text in the tradition of urban economics. These disciplinary overlaps are necessary in developing a well-rounded perspective on urban and regional economics.

ACKNOWLEDGMENTS

This book would not have been written without help from many people. The support, understanding, and encouragement of my wife, Joyce, was essential and appreciated. William Miernyk is the professor who first introduced me to the field and has greatly influenced my thinking. I've noticed that after my students integrate an idea into their worldview, they cease saying, "Blair said . . ." and simply state the idea as an obvious truth. I'm sure I have internalized many of my previous teachers' ideas and presented them as my own.

Colleagues at Wright State who helped me clarify issues through lively and interesting discussions are too numerous to name, but I am grateful to them for specific assistance and for maintaining a stimulating intellectual atmosphere.

Penny Stacy and Norma Adams helped in manuscript preparation. As anyone with a good secretary knows, their help goes well beyond typing.

Finally, I am grateful to teachers and scholars who read and commented on early drafts.

Joseph Alexander	Babson College
Daniel R. Blake	California State University at Northridge
David E. Clark	Marquette University
Joyce Cooper	University of Iowa
Rudy Fichtenbaum	Wright State University
Arthur E. Kartman	San Diego State University
Charles L. Leven	Washington University
Michael I. Luger	University of North Carolina at Chapel Hill
Robert Premus	Wright State University
Roger Riefler	University of Nebraska
Steve Ross	Wright State University

Larry D. Singell	University of Colorado
Timothy Treganther	University of Colorado at Colorado Springs
Kay Unger	University of Montana
Harold F. Williamson	University of Illinois at Urbana

John P. Blair

Contents

Chapter One

Introduction to Urban and Regional Economics

Urban and regional economics concern interactions between the spatial environment and economic activity. Urban and regional economics are often treated separately. They are important fields to study because all economic activity takes place somewhere, and unless the spatial dimension is recognized, economics will always be an abstraction that is difficult to relate to where people live and work. Urban economics has traditionally focused upon urban problems and land-use issues; whereas, questions of interregional resource flows, industrial location, and regional growth have been central concerns of regional economists. However, the topics are so closely related that it is appropriate to treat them together and insights from both areas are necessary to a comprehensive understanding of spatial economics.

This book has three primary goals: theory, applications, and public policy.

First, this text is designed to help readers understand how economic theory can be modified to reflect spatial considerations. Economic theory tends to ignore the impact of space and density on economic activity even though the most fundamental economic concepts are influenced by location. For example, both a company's costs and demand will depend upon where it is located. One of the purposes of this book is to show how fundamental economic concepts are affected by distance and density. Familiar economic concepts such as supply and demand will be recast in a spatial setting. The inclusion of spatial concepts enriches traditional economic theory.

The second goal is to show how theory can be applied in a spatial setting. Urban and regional economics traditionally has had a strong applied orientation. In that tradition, both conceptual and quantitative applications will be presented. The discussions of applications will provide a professional orientation. An understanding of urban and regional economics is an asset in many careers. Fields that frequently require the use of urban and regional economic concepts include corporate and public planning, economic development, housing and community development, transportation, land-use planning, real estate marketing and property development.

The third goal is to examine public policy issues. Public policy issues are a special type of application. Many social problems are inextricably linked to location, so policies designed to alleviate these problems should be informed by spatial economics. Urban and regional economists are normally attuned to public issues. In fact, many urban economics books revolve around a "litany of urban problems," such as housing and the homeless, crime, education, fiscal crisis, unemployment, poverty, segregation, slums, and so forth. Public policy issues are important to the study of urban and regional economics because there is an inescapable spatial dimension to most policy issues. People see problems in the context of where they live. However, the spatial setting of a policy issue may shift from a neighborhood, city, state, multistate area or group of nations depending upon the problem and the concerned agency. In addition, solutions to policy issues generally target particular places.

The policy orientation encourages an interdisciplinary approach. Many problems may be examined from a variety of perspectives. Although this text stresses the economic perspective, insights from a variety of disciplines, including geography, political science, sociology, and planning, have been incorporated into policy discussions.

A ROAD MAP OF THE BOOK

Organizing a textbook as well as learning the principles of urban and regional economics is a bit like piecing together a jigsaw puzzle. There is no single best starting place. Even after the first few pieces are in place, the sequences that follow may vary. The best path will depend upon the perspective of the person solving the puzzle. But unlike a puzzle, the field of urban and regional economics lacks clear boundaries. Thus, there is ample room for disagreement about what should be included. Although there is no single best way to organize most textbooks, the choice of organization is not arbitrary. In general, this book progresses from the classical theoretical core to issues of policy and practice.

Chapters 2 and 3 describe the location of economic activity. First, individual location decisions are discussed, including institutional factors that influence decisions and key locational factors. Central-place theory is the heart of Chapter 3, which builds from location decisions of individual establishments to locational patterns of a variety of activities. Chapter 3 emphasizes dispersive forces, particularly the tendency for firms to seek unique markets. Chapter 4 describes forces that encourage activities to locate together. A knowledge of these cohesive and adhesive forces is essential to understand the characteristics of a major metropolitan area. After comparing Chapters 3 and 4, a picture of location as a balancing of dispersive and uniting forces will emerge.

Urban and regional growth are examined in Chapters 5, 6, and 7. First, fundamental theories of growth, including historical perspectives and the export-base theory are discussed in Chapter 5. Somewhat more sophisticated models and empirical tools for analyzing growth are discussed in the next chapter. The "Practice of Economic Development" is the focus of Chapter 7. The chapter presents a practitioner's perspective of economic development, including a discussion of relevant tools, programs, and policy issues. The sections on urban and regional growth are particularly useful to individuals contemplating careers in public economics or with local planning agencies or chambers of commerce (Watkins, 1980). Issues of poverty are closely associated with labor market opportunities which, in turn, are influenced by local job growth. Therefore, "Poverty and Antipoverty Program," Chapter 8, follows the chapters on urban and regional growth.

Local economies are open to numerous external influences. Chapter 9, "Interregional Resource and Commodity Flows," explores the nature of an open region and describes mechanisms whereby economic events in one region influence another. The chapter is important to students interested in national urban policy. It bridges the fields of regional and international economics by exploring flows of capital, labor, and ideas. Therefore, this chapter is of special interest to students interested in international economics.

Issues concerning land use and urban form are discussed in Chapters 10, 11, and 12. An understanding of these issues is the foundation for careers in land development, community organizing, urban planning, and related fields (Blakely, 1989). First, the fundamental theoretical positions regarding the use of a parcel of land area are described, followed by an analysis of land-use patterns and urban form—cities as systems. Neighborhoods constitute the building blocks of metropolitan regions and are often identified by their housing. Neighborhood change is reflected in the housing stock. Thus, Chapter 11 examines the basics of housing markets, housing policies, and residential choice. Transportation is an additional factor that affects urban form and locational choice. Chapter 12 discusses the economics of urban transportation, including alternative pricing methods and other policy changes that could enhance the efficiency of urban transit.

Urban finance is a broad field. Chapter 13, "Metropolitan Government and Finance," addresses some public finance issues that are necessary for an introduction to urban and regional economics. The discussion of the appropriate functions and size of government, intergovernmental grants and spillovers, and tax criteria will be useful to anyone with an interest in government employment.

The final chapter is prospective. It discusses alternative urban futures and the perspectives of urban planners and futurists. Because of the rapidly changing world, students with a variety of interests should benefit by understanding alternative future possibilities.

However, before launching into a discussion of location theory, it may be helpful to first provide an introduction to the nature of regions and sketch how economists approach the study of urban and regional issues. The discussion of the economic approach to issues will be particularly interesting to students with modest backgrounds in economics.

THE NATURE OF REGIONS

"Region" refers to a part of an area. In practice, the term "region" is a chameleon, taking meaning from the context of use. For instance, the statement, "the region around my house" normally connotes a neighborhood region. However, if someone were to say they lived in a cold region, the phrase would connote a multistate area. As trade between nations increases, international regions are becoming more important and economists are more concerned with multinational regions. In fact, international economics is becoming more like regional and urban economics because resources flow between some nations as easily as they do between some regions within a nation. In keeping with common usage, both large and small regions will be examined in this text.

The concept of international regions also suggests that regions do not necessarily have to be contiguous. The Oil Producing and Exporting Countries (OPEC) and the North Atlantic Treaty Organization (NATO) are examples of organizations whose names refer to regions consisting of parts that are separated by areas that do not belong to these regions.

"Urban" is also a term that has different meanings. An urban area, no matter how it is defined, is a region. Urban areas are normally associated with large, high population density cities. Yet, some places with populations as small as 2,500 are considered urban by the Census Bureau. Thus, small villages with only a few stores could be considered urban by the census bureau, although such a place might not be considered an urban area as used in everyday conversation.

Many social scientists define "urban" in terms of lifestyle rather than density. Urban society is often contrasted with traditional society. In this sense, urbanization reflects a social change in which diversity, rationality, tolerance, impersonality, functional relationships, and bureaucratic organizations become important characteristics. According to the perspective of the social scientist, the farmer who uses a variety of advanced technologies in production, has major capital investments, buys and sells grain futures in a world market, and watches TV broadcasts from around the world via satellite, is in the urban sector.

Functional Regions

Functional regions are distinguished by the degree to which they are integrated or the extent that their component parts interact. If interaction of components within a region is significant compared to interaction with other places, the basis for a functional economic region exists. An area in which local businesses trade with each other more than they trade with the rest of the world would constitute a functional area.

Nodal Regions.   Nodal regions are an important type of functional area. A nodal region is based primarily upon a hierarchical system of trade relationships. Small business centers may depend upon large centers, and both small centers and large centers may depend upon a still larger business center for specialized economic goods. The area served by a business center is often referred to as a hinterland, and the larger the hinterland, the larger the business center tends to be. The concept of a nodal region implies that there are regions within regions in the sense that a medium-sized city may have a hinterland of its own while it is part of the hinterland of a larger city.

Metropolitan Statistical Areas.   Metropolitan areas exhibit hierarchical patterns that characterize nodal regions. Specifically, employment and retail activity tend to be concentrated in the central business district and other subcenters throughout the metropolis. The nodes of concentrated economic activity contrast with residential areas where the extent of business activity is small. However, the business concentrations and residential areas are dependent upon each other. Many regional policies are best implemented at the metropolitan level because of the interdependence within the region.

The concept of a functional economic area has been operationalized in the statistical construct of Metropolitan Statistical Areas (MSAs).[1] Because of the importance of MSAs to analysis and policy, it may be useful to describe their structure in detail. Central cities are the heart and node of the MSA. Each MSA must include one city with 50,000 or more residents or a Census Bureau-defined urbanized area of at least 50,000 inhabitants and a total MSA population of at least 100,000 (75,000 in New England).

---

[1] The term "Metropolitan Statistical Area" replaced the term "Standard Metropolitan Statistical Area" (SMSA). However, they are conceptually the same.

Counties are the big building blocks of MSAs. The central county(ies) containing the central city and all contiguous counties that have close economic ties to the central county and are metropolitan in character are included in the MSA. The extent of economic linkage among counties is measured by commuting patterns. The metropolitan character is measured by population density and the percentage of the population that is urban. MSAs in New England are based upon groups of cities and towns because there are no counties in New England. However, the intent is to operationalize the same concept of urbanization and integration.

MSAs contain suburbs, or urban communities that are closely linked to the central city. Suburbs include satellite communities and bedroom suburbs. Satellite communities normally have an active local economy, often including a substantial manufacturing base. Frequently, businesses in satellite communities developed independently of the central city. Bedroom suburbs lack an independent economic base. While a few retail and service stores may be located in bedroom communities, their primary function is to provide a residence for individuals who work elsewhere. Because bedroom communities often provide an environment sheltered from many urban problems, an anonymous wit referred to bedroom communities as a "womb with a view." In addition, there is usually some agricultural activity within most MSAs because parts of farms are located in the outlying counties. Figure 1–1 presents a stylized picture of an MSA.

An advantage of collecting MSA data by county only rather than by cities or by the urbanized portion of an MSA is that the geographic boundaries of a county seldom change. Although counties may be added or dropped from particular MSAs, it is relatively easy to establish a consistent time series by aggregating data collected for individual counties. In contrast, when city boundaries change or an urbanized area increases, it is usually very difficult or impossible to reconstruct a consistent time series. However, the use of counties as the units from which MSAs are built results in more diversity with the MSA than would be the case if only the most urbanized areas were included.

Figure 1–2 shows the major MSAs in the United States.

The rapid growth of metropolitan areas is one of the most important features of economic geography. In the 1950s, about 55 percent of the U.S. population lived in metropolitan areas and they accounted for only about 5 percent of the land area. During the 1960s, metropolitan populations grew about seven times as fast as nonmetropolitan populations. The pattern was reversed during the 1970s as nonmetropolitan areas grew faster than metropolitan areas. During the period 1980–88, the pattern again reversed with metropolitan populations increasing almost twice as fast as nonmetropolitan populations. However, central-city populations have been declining or growing very slowly throughout the 1970s and 1980s. (U.S. Department of Commerce, 1986, Table A). Currently, about

FIGURE 1–1   A Metropolitan Statistical Area

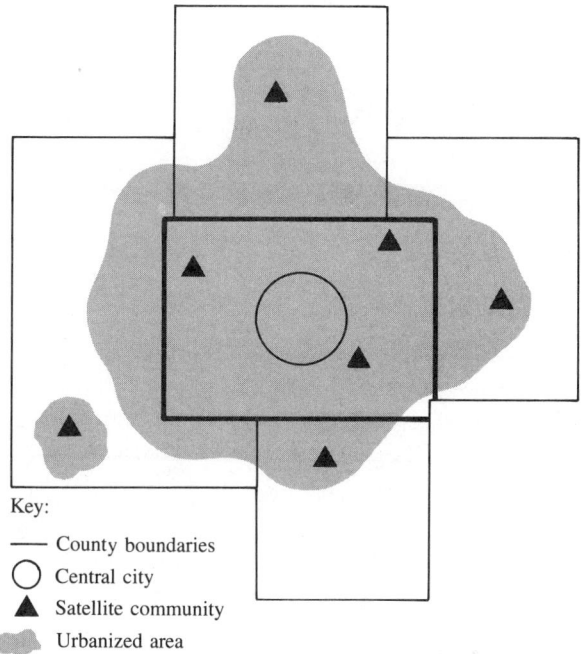

Key:

—— County boundaries
○ Central city
▲ Satellite community
🔘 Urbanized area

An MSA contains a central city and an urbanized area around the central city that often includes satellite communities. Most MSAs also include rural areas on the fringe.

75 percent of the population of the United States reside in MSAs, and these account for about 16 percent of the land area. (President's National Urban Policy Report, p. 11.) The growth of metropolitan areas is even more rapid in many developing countries where only one or two metropolitan areas absorb a huge proportion of the population growth. Mexico City, for example, is growing so rapidly that it absorbs most of Mexico's capital and other resources. Greater Mexico City contains about 50 percent of the nation's population and may already be the largest city in the world.

Many urban complexes have grown to a population of over 1 million, in large part because metropolitan areas have grown together. As urban areas have overlapped, commuting and other economic relationships have extended beyond the original metropolitan area.

A Consolidated Metropolitan Statistical Area (CMSA) is a combination of contiguous metropolitan areas. It is defined as a metropolitan area

FIGURE 1-2 Major Metropolitan Areas

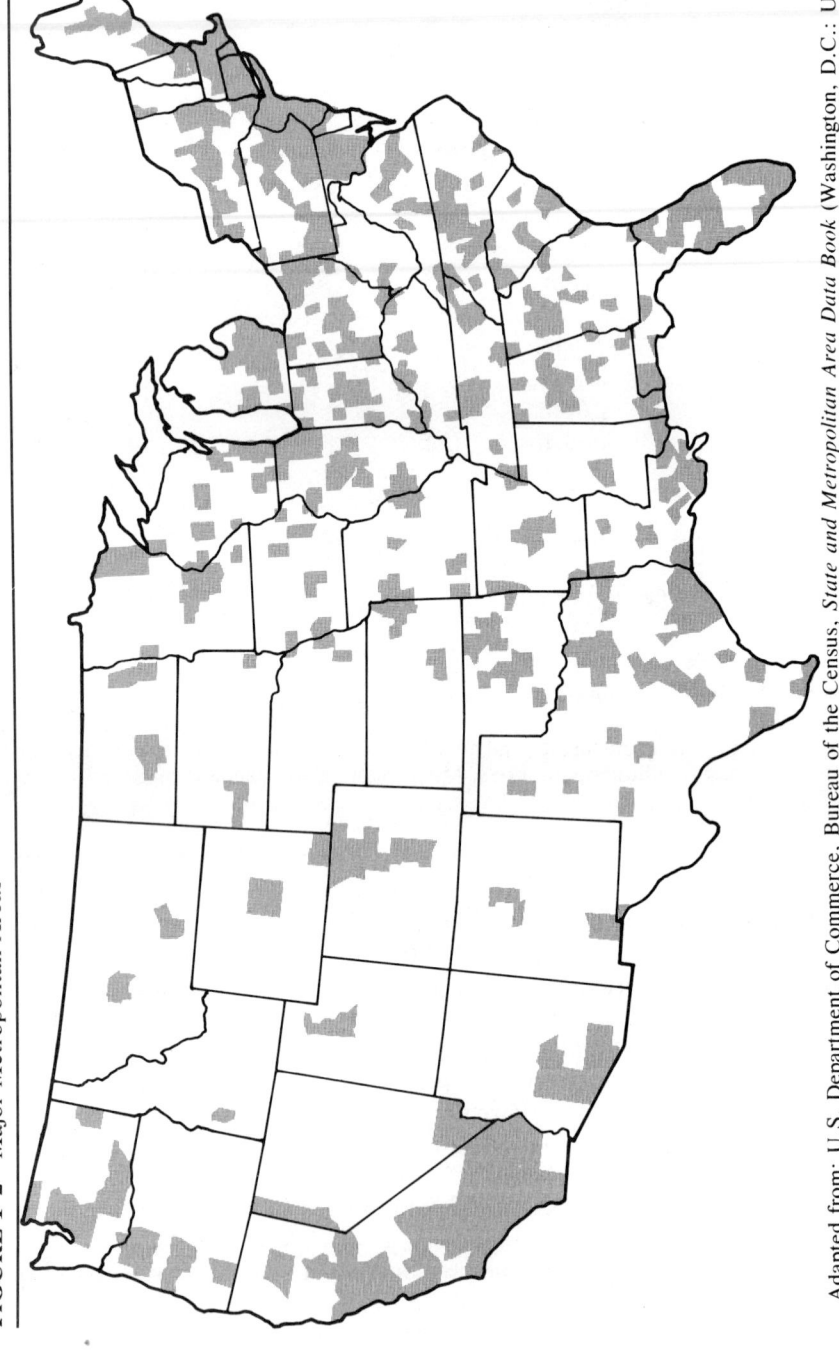

Adapted from: U.S. Department of Commerce, Bureau of the Census, *State and Metropolitan Area Data Book* (Washington, D.C.: U.S. Government Printing Office, 1986).

which has a population of at least 1 million. The metropolitan components of CMSAs are designated as Primary Metropolitan Statistical Areas (PMSAs). For instance, the Cleveland-Akron-Lorain CMSA is composed of the Akron, Cleveland, and Lorain-Elyria PMSAs. PMSAs are similar to MSAs except for their inclusion in a larger metropolitan complex. Table 1–1 shows Consolidated Metropolitan Statistical Areas and their major components.

Metropolitan growth has also resulted in significant diversity within metropolitan areas. Almost three quarters of the U.S. population lives in metropolitan areas. About 30 percent of metropolitan residents live in central cities, 45 percent live in suburbs, and, surprisingly, almost one quarter live in areas classified as rural by the Census Bureau. In addition, nearly 40 percent of nonmetropolitan residents live in areas defined as urban by the Census Bureau. The diversity of living arrangements within these two areas shows a further need to unify urban and regional economics.

TABLE 1–1 Supercities: Consolidated Metropolitan Statistical Areas

	1986 Population (000s)
Boston–Lawrence–Salem, Massachusetts	4,056
Buffalo–Niagara Falls, New York	1,182
Chicago–Gary–Lake County, Illinois–Indiana–Wisconsin	8,116
Cincinnati–Hamilton, Ohio–Kentucky–Indiana	1,690
Cleveland–Akron–Lorain, Ohio	2,766
Dallas–Ft. Worth, Texas	3,665
Denver–Boulder, Colorado	1,847
Hartford–New Britain–Middletown, Connecticut	1,044
Houston–Galveston–Brazorio, Texas	3,634
Los Angeles–Anaheim–Riverside, California	8,269
Miami–Fort Lauderdale, Florida	2,912
New York–Northern New Jersey–Long Island, New York–New Jersey–Connecticut	17,968
Philadelphia–Wilmington–Trenton, Pennsylvania, New Jersey, Delaware, Maryland	5,833
Pittsburgh–Beaver Valley, Pennsylvania	2,316
Portland–Vancouver, Oregon–Washington	1,364
Providence–Pawtucket-Fall River, Rhode Island–Massachusetts	1,108
San Francisco–Oakland–San Jose, California	5,876
Seattle–Tacoma, Washington	2,284

Homogeneous Regions

Homogeneous regions are defined on the basis of internal similarity. The many so-called belt regions—corn, Bible, rust, sun, snow, and so forth—are homogeneous regions characterized by common activities, cultures or climates. The Appalachian region, on the other hand, is a homogeneous region distinguished by common economic development problems.

Many neighborhoods are distinguished by ethnic or economic similarity and, hence, are basically homogeneous regions. The Census Bureau provides data on census tracts which are small areas consisting of several blocks. While the census tracts are not necessarily established on the basis of homogeneity, data on homogeneous neighborhoods are often derived from census tract information.

The U.S. Department of Commerce has developed a set of regions based upon relative homogeneity. Figure 1–3 shows the major census divisions and regions of the United States.

Administrative Regions

Administrative regions are formed for managerial or organizational purposes. Both private organizations and governments find administrative regions useful. Administrative regions are normally more clearly delineated than either functional or homogeneous regions because administrative regions are formed to clarify spheres of activity for businesses or governments. Administrative regions are also important because they frequently become the basis for policy. Cities, states, and counties are important administrative regions.

Administrative regions may not be distinct from homogeneous or functional regions. For instance, a company may establish a set of sales districts based upon similar tastes for product lines within each district. If regional offices provide support services for local sales offices, the administrative region will assume characteristics of a functional area as well. Furthermore, once an administrative region is formed, the various components may develop commonalities that make the region more homogeneous, and/or chains of communication, trade, and control that are characteristic of functional regions may emerge.

The number of governmental regions is large. There are approximately 85,000 units of local government in the United States. Within the Chicago metropolitan area, for example, there are 1,214 units of local government ranging from well-known governments such as cities, counties, and school districts to many special-purpose districts that are nearly unknown to average citizens, such as water-control districts, lighting districts, and recreation districts. With so many districts, it is rare that

FIGURE 1–3 Map of the United States Showing Major Census Divisions and Regions

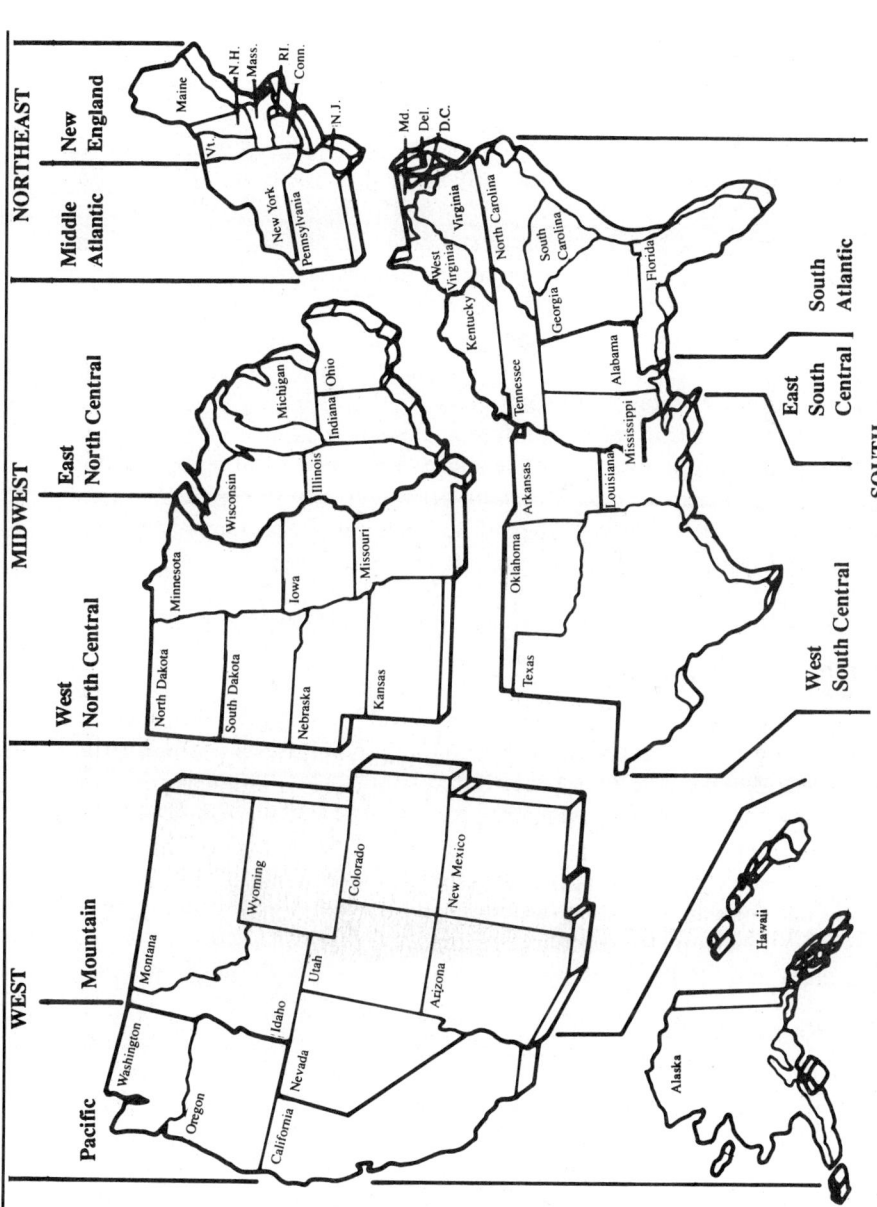

SOURCE: From Statistical Abstract of the United States U.S. Department of Commerce, Bureau of the Census 1989.

workers in an urban business will have the same district profile. In the Chicago area, there are 1.7 units of local government per 100,000 people. Many observers believe that political fragmentation is a major impediment to good government while others believe that a diversity of governmental units contributes to wise decision making.

The European Economic Community is an increasingly important administrative region. It was originally formed on the basis of weak commonalities between the countries of western Europe. It is in the process of reducing trade and migration barriers between nations within the Common Market, and by 1992, most governmental barriers to trade and population mobility are scheduled to be removed. Common trade barriers with the rest of the world have also been established. It has been anticipated that as time goes by the region will assume characteristics of a single nation—a united states of Europe.

Once administrative regions are established, they tend to be self-perpetuating. Many observers have suggested that state boundaries could be redrawn to be made more efficient. It is interesting to speculate about what state or city boundaries would be if they were developed today on the basis of functional or homogeneous regions. However, in practice, it is very difficult to change well-established political regions.

ECONOMIC PERSPECTIVES

The previous section provided an introduction to the nature of regions. This section sketches the economic perspectives on urban policy issues. Economists often disagree. This diversity of opinion has given rise to numerous jokes about how many economists it takes to reach a conclusion. The public attention given to disagreements among economists reflects the importance of economic issues. Consequently, disagreements among economists are sometimes newsworthy. Although economists do disagree about important policy issues, there are also broad areas of agreement about what questions are important and how to examine those questions.

A paradigm is a widely accepted approach to solving particular problems in a scientific discipline (Kuhn, 1970, chapters 1–2). Economists generally agree about the broad outlines of appropriate methods and approaches to problems, although they may disagree regarding specific details and policy implications. In other words, there is general agreement about the appropriate paradigm but some disagreement at the operational level. Students who have not studied economics extensively sometimes fail to understand the role of models and assumptions in economic analysis, the economist's view of individual behavior, and how disagreements about policy can arise. A sketch of these important aspects of the economic paradigm will set the stage for analysis of urban and regional phenomena.

FIGURE 1–4 The European Community

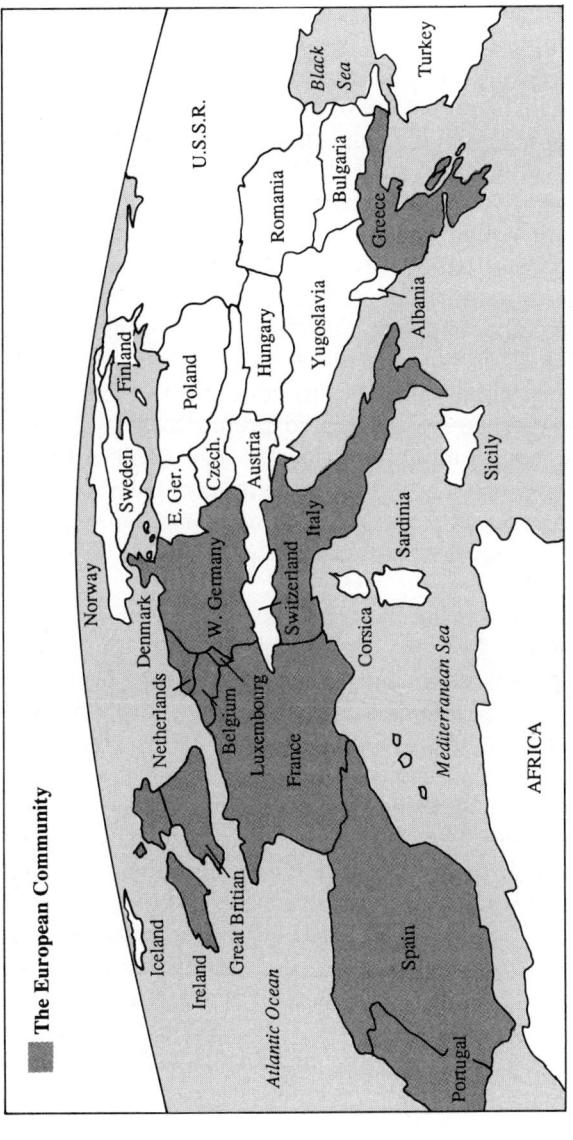

■ The European Community

SOURCE: *Dayton Daily News,* May 22, 1989.

Models and Assumptions

Economists often build deductive models to help understand economic processes. A model is a simplification of reality to help analysts focus on important components. Most economic models consist of premises or assumptions about a situation and a series of deductions about what behavior will flow from the assumptions.

Analysis is the process of breaking a problem into its components. In the process of analysis, it is important to examine the effect of one or two independent variables on a dependent variable. In order to see how a few variables interact, it is necessary to assume that other variables do not change and thus alter the relationship between the dependent and independent variables that are the focus of the analysis. This is the well-known "ceteris paribus" or, "other things equal" assumption.

A widely known application of the "other things equal" assumption is the law of demand. It states that if the price of a good falls, the quantity individuals are willing and able to consume will increase, other things being equal. Changes in tastes and preferences, incomes, the price of other goods, expectations, and market size could result in a situation where price could change but the quantity demanded could stay the same. Therefore, in order to express the law of demand properly, it is necessary to make explicit the assumption that everything stays the same except price and quantity.

Students often resist the many assumptions that are incorporated in economic models because the assumptions are unrealistic. In reality, other things do not remain equal, so why do economists assume that they do? The value of the assumptions is that they provide a systematic framework for analysis. The assumptions may be relaxed so the impact of changing assumptions may be analyzed. For instance, the assumptions that incomes do not change may be replaced by the assumption that incomes increased. Then it can be shown that increases in income may increase demand. In other words, changing the assumptions of a model provides insights about the variable that was being held constant.

Urban and regional models are often predicated upon unrealistic assumptions, such as perfect knowledge, profit-maximizing behavior, uniform transportation costs, consumers with identical tastes, and homogeneous space. The insights gained from these models can be increased if consideration is given to how the model will be affected if the assumptions were changed.

Individual Behavior

For most economists, individuals are the building blocks of group actions. Let's examine how individual decisions are viewed. First, economists are careful not to assign to groups motives that reside in individuals.

Phrases such as "the city believes in liberty" may be a shorthand way of expressing the idea that many or perhaps the majority of individuals in the city believe in liberty. At the same time, economists are aware that collective actions are more than the sum of the parts. For instance, it may be true that anyone may become a millionaire if they work hard enough and/or are lucky enough. However, it is not true that everyone can become a millionaire.

Economists also believe that individuals behave so as to maximize their utility, and out of this drive to maximize utility come benefits for others. Adam Smith expressed this concept as well as anyone when he said:

> It is not from the benevolence of the butcher, the brewer, or the baker, that we expect our dinner, but from their own self-interest. We address ourselves, not to their humanity but to their self-love, and never talk to them of our own necessities but of their advantages.

Unfortunately, it is impossible to determine directly whether an individual is trying to maximize utility, because actions that bring satisfaction to one person may not provide satisfaction for another. Activities that provide satisfaction or utility include acquiring money, gaining prestige, helping others, and so forth. Consequently, economists usually assume that individuals try to maximize utility by trying to achieve an optimal work-leisure balance, maximize profits, make wise consumption choices and so forth.

Economists also assume that individuals are rational in their efforts to maximize utility. The rationality assumption is essential if economic models are to predict behavior. If individuals did not act rationally, then all behavior could be explained as the result of irrational actions.

Students sometimes object to the concept of *utility-maximizing man.* One type of objection is based on the mistaken idea that utility-maximizing behavior is selfish. In fact, economists recognize that altruistic behavior can provide satisfaction to some individuals. The second type of objection to the economic-man construct is that it does not examine how tastes and preferences are formed or why individuals differ in how they attain satisfaction. Economists tend to assume that individuals have a set of preferences, but little attention is given to how preferences are formed. It is likely that if economic and social life were different individuals would have a different set of preferences. Urban and regional economists often rely upon the work of sociologists and planners who are often more informed about questions of preference formation.

Efficiency, Equity and Welfare

Equity and efficiency are the principal criteria economists use to evaluate change. Efficiency refers to the ability to use resources to produce something of value. If resources are used to produce more goods and

services using the same level of inputs, the economy may be characterized as more efficient. Likewise, efficiency may be enhanced if a given
level of resources are used in a different way so that the value of output is
increased.

Benefit-cost comparisons are sometimes used to evaluate the efficiency of a change. In a competitive market, the costs of undertaking an
activity will reflect the value of resources used in their next best opportunity (opportunity cost). The monetary value of the benefits reflect the
value individuals place on the new output. Hence, if the benefit-cost ratio
is greater than one, the monetary value of the goods and services created
will exceed the momentary value of the resources used to produce those
goods and services. Thus, when a public policy change is being evaluated,
the benefit-cost comparison provides an indication of efficiency for a
given distribution of income.[2]

Externalities are activities that provide costs or benefits outside the
market system. Externalities are a major source of inefficiency because
individuals do not consider the full costs or benefits of their actions in
situations where externalities exist. For instance, there may be too much
pollution because some producers do not pay for the damage they commit
when they pollute. In a high-density, urban environment, externalities are
an important source of inefficiency because so many more people tend to
be affected. While driving a noisy, oil-burning motorcycle down a country
road may result in almost no externalities, the same activity on a Manhattan street could impose significant external costs.

Efficiency is often described as a static or comparative static concept. Sometimes, policy makers are more concerned with economic
growth than static efficiency. A society that operates with a little inefficiency but grows rapidly may be better off in the long run than a society
that maintains a high level of static efficiency but does not grow rapidly.

Equity usually refers to fairness. When a policy change hurts some
individuals but benefits others, questions of fairness arise. Ultimately, the
appropriateness of most changes must be decided on normative grounds.

Policy Debates

Finally, economists explore two distinct types of questions. On the
one hand, positive questions inquire into why things are the way they are.
They are concerned with describing the world as it is. On the other hand,

---

[2] The monetary value of costs and benefits cannot be determined in the absence of a set of
distribution of income because the distribution of income affects valuation. For instance, the
monetary value of inner city beautification would probably be larger if inner city residents
were richer.

normative questions inquire into how things should be or ought to be and involve value judgments. It is often useful to determine whether the source of a disagreement is based on different analyses, different values, or both. Economists may disagree about appropriate policies either because of different analyses about how the economy operates or because they have different values.

An example of an agreement about positive analysis, but a disagreement regarding values, would exist if economists agree about how the economy operates but disagree about the actions that should be taken. For instance, most urban and regional economists agree that if the population density of an area increased and everything else remained the same, rents would increase. However, they may disagree about whether rents should increase. Some economists might say rents should increase because high rents will efficiently ration a scarce resource. Others might oppose rent increases because of adverse effects on the poor. Those who believe rents should not increase may suggest that the government should intervene in the economy to prevent rents from increasing.

An example of normative agreement and positive disagreement could arise if economists shared the normative opinion that it is unfortunate that rents increase but disagree about consequences of government intervention. One group may argue that government attempts to lower rents will decrease the supply of housing and hurt the poor while another group may believe intervention will successfully shield the poor from paying more rent.

In practice, it is sometimes difficult to distinguish between differences in analysis and differences in values because it is not always possible to determine whether individuals choose their analysis to fit their values. There are two alternative perspectives on economic policy that are within the framework of the traditional economic paradigm—conservative and liberal.

The conservative perspective places a high value on individual freedom, particularly economic freedom, and economic efficiency. Many conservatives agree with Friedman (1962) that capitalism is necessary for political freedom. The analyses of conservative economists tend to show that the laissez-faire market works well. When competitive market conditions exist, individuals seeking their own self-interest act in the social interest. Consequently, conservatives tend to oppose government involvement in regional and urban problems. Even when their analysis leads them to believe that the market outcomes are imperfect, conservatives tend to believe that the imperfect market outcome is preferable to government-imposed solutions.

Liberal economists tend to place a high value on economic equity while viewing market operations as sometimes both inefficient and inequitable but still useful. Blinder (1987) referred to the liberal philosophy as combining respect for the free market with concern for those the market leaves behind. Consequently, liberals tend to believe that government action is important to solving urban problems and securing a more equitable distribution of income. Fundamentally, liberals want to maintain the basic framework of market decision making, but they believe there is substantial potential for government actions to improve market outcomes. In particular, government may help reduce the impacts of externalities through taxes, regulation, and other actions.

Conservatives and liberals constitute the mainstream of economic thinking. Both perspectives rely upon the market to provide information and establish the basic incentives that encourage socially desirable behavior. Most of the policy issues discussed in this text are within the liberal-conservative framework.

Radical economic analysis is outside the traditional economic paradigm and often provides interesting challenges to traditional economic thinking. Radical economists are distrustful of the market. Many radical economists believe the market is not an impartial mechanism that helps organize economic activities. Rather, the market is a means of social control. They are less concerned with whether market mechanisms are efficient than whose interests the market serves. Government programs that affect economic outcomes often do not significantly help the express beneficiaries because the same interests that control the market also control government. Radicals tend to see urban problems as a reflection of class conflicts. Greater government involvement in the economy, including direct ownership of productive resources, is seen by radicals as a more preferable solution to problems than either a policy of laissez-faire or government modification of market outcomes.

SUMMARY

Three main purposes of this book are to describe spatial theory, show how spatial economics can be applied, and discuss public policy issues.

Although the term "region" is vague, economists distinguish among types of regions. Functional areas are distinguished by the degree that they are integrated or the extent that their component parts interact. Nodal and metropolitan areas are types of functional areas. The concept of functional areas has been operationalized through such concepts as Metropolitan Statistical Areas (MSAs) and Consolidated Metropolitan Statistical Areas (CMSA). About 75 percent of the U.S. population live in MSAs. Homogeneous regions are defined on the basis of internal similarity. Administrative regions are formed for organizational purposes.

Economists rely upon a variety of assumptions to build models. The assumptions may be relaxed so the impact of changing assumptions may be analyzed. They are also careful to distinguish between normative (value judgments) and positive (factual) analyses.

The three principal schools of economics differ in how they view the market: (1) the conservative school relies primarily on the market, (2) the liberal school relies on the market but recognizes the frequent need for government involvement, and (3) the radical school distrusts the market.

REFERENCES

Blakely, J. Edward. *Planning Local Economic Development: Theory and Practice*. Newbury Park, California: Sage Publications, 1989.

Blinder, Alan S. *Hard Heads Soft Hearts: Tough-Minded Economics for a Just Society*. New York: Addison-Wesley Publishing, 1987.

Friedman, Milton. *Capitalism and Freedom*. Chicago: The University of Chicago Press, 1962.

Kuhn, Thomas S. *The Structure of Scientific Revolutions,* 2nd ed. Chicago: University of Chicago, 1970.

U.S. Department of Commerce, Bureau of the Census. *State and Metropolitan Area Data Book*. Washington, D.C.: U.S. Government Printing Office, 1986.

U.S. Department of Housing and Urban Development. *1982 President's National Urban Policy Report*. Washington, D.C.: U.S. Government Printing Office, 1982.

Watkins, Alfred J. *The Practice of Urban Economics*. Beverly Hills, Calif.: Sage Publications, 1980.

Chapter Two

Locational Decisions of the Firm

How do firms decide where to locate their facilities? The answer to this question is important to establishment planners, who want to make the appropriate locational choice, as well as to real estate and community development officials, who hope to attract businesses to their areas. The purpose of this chapter is to develop a preliminary perspective on the firm's locational decision. Although the chapter emphasizes profit-oriented firms, the discussion also considers the locational choices of nonprofit organizations. The discussion of household locational decisions is deferred until Chapters 10 and 11.

The first section examines major locational factors, including inertia, transportation costs, and production costs. The variety of locational factors discussed is extensive, reflecting diverse locational orientations of a variety of organizations. The second section describes the locational decision-making process and the various motives that influence locational choice. The final section describes the relative importance of locational factors and shows that the number of important factors has increased during the 1970s and 1980s.

LOCATIONAL FACTORS

This section describes the major factors that influence locational choice. Every organization will be influenced by many of the locational factors discussed below. However, the degree of influence will differ depending upon the organization's needs. When selecting a location, organizations are generally required to make trade-offs among desired locational features. The trade-offs will differ depending upon an establishment's characteristics. For instance, profit-making organizations will be influenced by bottom-line considerations; political institutions will be influenced by public opinion; and charitable organizations will be influenced by particular aspects of their mission. Although the focus of this section is on business locations, the analysis is relevant to nonprofit organizations as well.

Inertia

Inertia is perhaps the strongest locational factor, yet it is often unrecognized. Once a firm is established at a location, many forces operate to keep it there, even when a new facility is required. First, the reasons for the initial location may not have changed. The same factors that supported the original choice could cause a firm to select that location again. This is particularly true if success has made a new facility necessary to increase capacity.

Second, the economic and social structure of an area may evolve to reinforce the initial choice. In a symbiotic or "coevolutionary" relationship, the firm supports the community and the community develops in ways that support the firm (Norgaard, 1984); they evolve in ways that support (or use) each other. In concrete terms, a firm will develop ties to other producers, buyers, and employees. These ties may be severed or at least not function as effectively if the firm relocates. For instance, a firm may have a local supplier that can accommodate unusual fabrication requirements. The business ties may even be cemented by personal friendships. Although similar types of firms may be located in other cities, the reliability and adaptability of alternative suppliers may be uncertain. Thus, there is some relocation risk. Likewise, a firm that relocates will lose some of its workers. While such a loss may not be critical to firms in some activities, certain skilled workers may be essential to some operations. For instance, a research facility may be hesitant to relocate to another region for fear of breaking up a research team. Key researchers may not choose to move if they like the local environment. The local environment, in turn, may have developed a set of amenities that appeal to researchers. Of course, particular workers' decisions will be influenced by the availability of similar jobs in the area. Schmenner (1982, p. 91) reported that over 60 percent of plant expansions were motivated, in part, by the desire to keep the management team together rather than risk separations if a larger facility were built elsewhere. Many companies have remained in the area in which they initially located, even though the nature of their products has changed radically. For instance, NCR Corporation has remained in Dayton, Ohio, even though it is now a computer company and no longer produces mechanical cash registers.

Transportation-Cost-Minimizing Models

Transportation costs are the most thoroughly analyzed location factor because manufacturing activities are sensitive to transportation costs and they are relatively easy to quantify. Transportation-cost models fit the tools economists have. Products that have high shipping costs (for either inputs or outputs) relative to the value of the final product tend to be sensitive to transportation costs or "transportation oriented."

Transferable and Localized Inputs and Outputs.   Localized inputs are ones that cannot be economically transported, so they must be used at the source where they are found. Climate is a purely localized input because it cannot be transported at any cost (although some might argue that air conditioners make climate within a building transportable). However, most localized inputs can be transported under some circumstances. Labor is a relatively localized input because the cost of transporting a worker from one region to another is normally too expensive even though it is physically possible to do so. However, firms do pay relocation costs for some workers, so labor can be considered transportable rather than localized under some circumstances. When localized inputs are important cost factors, production tends to take place near the inputs because costs of transporting the input to another site are too expensive.

Likewise, localized outputs cannot easily be shipped; therefore, activities producing localized outputs normally locate near their market. Examples of localized outputs include construction, performing arts, and most medical services. The ability to absorb waste by-products may also be considered localized, so some firms must locate near disposal sites.

Transferable inputs and outputs can be transported relatively cheaply, so they are the opposite of localized inputs and outputs. Of course, the distinction between localized and transferable items is not sharp. Under some circumstances, an input may be transferable and under some circumstances not.

Total transportation costs will equal the costs of shipping the material inputs to the production point (assembly cost) plus the cost of shipping the output to the market (distribution cost). The less costly the inputs are to transfer, the more likely the activity will locate near a market; the less costly the output is to transfer, the more likely the activity will locate near an input source.

Ubiquity.   Ubiquitous inputs are a special type of localized input because they are available everywhere. Therefore, ubiquitous inputs are not transported from one place to another. Perhaps there are no pure ubiquitous inputs, although air and water are often used as examples. (Not, however, in places like New Mexico or Arizona where water for industrial or agricultural purposes is sometimes prohibitively expensive.) Clean air is also becoming less ubiquitous as industrialized regions become more polluted. Because of their prevalence, ubiquitous inputs do not usually favor one site over another.

A One-Input, One-Market Model.   In order to focus on transportation costs, let us examine a locational decision for a firm wishing to minimize transportation costs. For simplicity, assume: (1) the product is produced with one material input and the output is sold at only one

FIGURE 2–1   A Simple Transportation-Cost Model

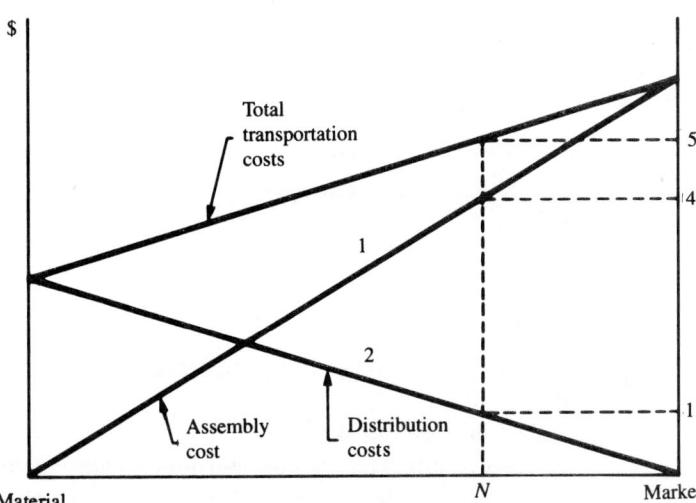

1. Cost of transporting the raw material from the material source to the production point (assembly costs).
2. Cost of transporting output from the production site to the market (distribution costs).

Total transportation costs are the sum of distribution and assembly costs. The above illustration excludes terminal costs or long-haul economies. The tendency for costs to be lowest at either the market or the material source should be recognized.

market, (2) transportation costs are proportional to distance, and (3) neither the demand nor the costs of production are affected by location.

Figure 2–1 illustrates costs involved in the decision. The firm may locate at the source of the material inputs, the market, or at any point in between, such as N, depending upon where transportation costs are lowest. Total transportation costs are the sum of the cost of shipping the material to the production site (assembly costs) and the cost of shipping the finished product from the production site to the market (distribution costs). Thus, an establishment located at N would have per unit transfer costs of $5 ($4 to ship the input to the production site and $1 to transport the output from the production site to the market). Transportation costs start at zero because it is assumed that there are no loading or unloading costs. In the case illustrated by Figure 2–1, the least-cost location is the material site because it is more expensive per mile to ship the raw material needed to produce the one-unit final product than to the ship the final product.

The simple model may be expressed as:

$$TTC_q = K_{mk} + K_m \tag{1}$$

$$K_{mk} = W_o \cdot R_o \cdot (D - q) \tag{2}$$

$$K_m = W_i \cdot R_i \cdot (q) \tag{3}$$

where: TTC_q = Total transportation costs for a plant located at q distance from the material site,

K_{mk} = Cost of transporting the final product to the market from the production site,

K_m = Cost of transporting a unit of material to the production site,

W_o = Weight of a unit of output,

R_o = Transportation rate per mile per unit weight of output,

W_i = Weight of materials needed to produce a unit of output,

R_i = Transportation rate per mile per unit weight of shipping materials needed to produce a unit of output,

D = Distance between the materials and the market site, and

q = Distance from materials site to plant.

Ideal Weights.[1]   The model expressed in Equations 1–3 is useful in understanding the concept of ideal weight. The weight of one unit of output times the transportation-cost rate (i.e., $R_o W_o$) is the ideal weight of the output. Similarly, the weight of the amount of materials needed to produce one unit of output times the transportation-cost rate ($R_i \cdot W_i$) is the ideal weight of the input. Ideal weights represent the strength of the opposing locational pulls. In the simple one-input, one-market model, production will take place at the market if the ideal weight of the final product is greater that the ideal weight of the material. Location will be at the material site if the ideal weight of the material is greater than the ideal weight of the final product. If the ideal weights were equal, any location would be equally desirable. In general, the greater the ideal weight of an input (or output), the greater the locational pull towards the source of the input (or the market).

Market and Material Orientation.   Market-oriented producers tend to locate near the market. Material-oriented activities tend to locate near

---

[1] Since there is nothing "ideal" about the term "ideal weight," some scholars prefer the term "locational weight."

materials. Orientation implies a tendency that could be altered by other considerations. Equation 1 suggests that market-oriented activities would be characterized by $W_o \cdot R_o > W_i \cdot R_i$. Conversely, material-oriented activities are characterized by $W_o \cdot R_o < W_i \cdot R_i$. This section describes characteristics of market- and materials-oriented activities.

Activities that add a resource that is more or less equally available everywhere (ubiquitous) are weight gaining. For instance, soft drinks are considered weight gaining because the materials, glass, syrup, and so forth, are shipped to the bottler where water, the ubiquitous input, is added. Thus, by locating near the market rather than near the bottle supplier, or some other supplier, the producer avoids shipping the water all the way to market. Final products that are hazardous to transport, bulky, perishable, or fragile also tend to be market oriented because of the relatively expensive cost of shipping to the market.

Materials-oriented activities tend to be weight losing. It makes sense for a sawmill to locate near the forest because, in the process of milling, the inputs lose weight. Likewise, chemical producers that use coal in their production process locate in coal-producing regions because most of the coal burns during production. It is less expensive to ship the chemicals than to transport the tons of coal necessary to produce the chemicals. Many canneries are material oriented, particularly when the product being canned is fragile or perishable prior to canning. Likewise, meat packing is material oriented because it is cheaper to ship the butchered meat than live cattle. In addition to weight-losing products, activities tend to locate near the inputs when the inputs are bulky, heavy, fragile, hazardous, or otherwise expensive to transport relative to the final product.

Endpoint Locations.   The model illustrated by Figure 2–1 implies that a midpoint location between the market and the material site would be unlikely. Given the restrictive assumption implicit in Figure 2–1, only if by coincidence the ideal weights of the market pull and the material pull were equal (i.e., $W_o \cdot R_o = W_i \cdot R_i$) would a midpoint location be competitive with the endpoints.

The strength of endpoint locations is bolstered by two additional factors—extra handling costs and nonlinear rate structures. First, a midpoint location would require extra terminal (loading and unloading) costs (unless the midpoint location is a necessary break in the transportation grid as discussed below). If the production site were located between the material site and the market, the inputs would have to be (1) loaded at the material site, (2) transported to the production site, and (3) unloaded, processed, and reloaded at the production site, and then the final product would have to be (4) transported to the market and (5), unloaded at the market. Thus, a midpoint location requires extra handling processes. The extra transfers also involve extra supervision and paperwork expenses.

TABLE 2–1   Loading and Unloading Costs at Three Locations

If the Plant Is Located	Material Site	*Where Loading and Unloading Occur**		Market
		Midpoint		
a. Material site	Load final product	$\left\{\begin{array}{l}\text{Transport}\\\text{final}\\\text{product}\end{array}\right\}$		Unload final product
b. Midpoint	Load material $\left\{\begin{array}{l}\text{Transport}\\\text{material}\end{array}\right.$	$\left\{\begin{array}{l}\text{Unload}\\\text{material}\\\text{and load}\\\text{final}\\\text{product}\end{array}\right\}$	$\left\{\begin{array}{l}\text{Transport}\\\text{final}\\\text{product}\end{array}\right\}$	Unload final product
c. Market	Load material	$\left\{\begin{array}{l}\text{Transport}\\\text{final}\\\text{product}\end{array}\right\}$		Unload material

* An extra loading and unloading occur if a midpoint location is chosen rather than the material site or market.

Frequently, the extra terminal costs can be avoided at endpoint locations. Table 2–1 compares loading, unloading, storage, and processing at both endpoints and a midpoint location. Terminal costs are particularly expensive for rail and water transporters.

A second factor that favors endpoint rather than midpoint locations is that transportation systems frequently charge customers less per mile for long hauls than for short hauls. It costs less than twice as much to travel 200 miles as it does to travel 100 miles, even after accounting for loading-unloading costs. Thus, it is less expensive to transport a product or input the entire distance between the material site and the market than to make two short trips.

Long-haul economies may be attributed to two factors. First, individuals shipping long distances will be more sensitive to price than individuals shipping short distances because transportation costs will account for a higher portion of total costs. Consequently, persons shipping a product a long distance will be more sensitive to price (have more price elastic demands) than short-haul shippers, who will have more inelastic demands. Accordingly, if the transport company were able to price discriminate, it would charge less to the long-haul shippers since the quantity of their business is sensitive to price and more to short-haul shippers.

Second, intermodal competition will occur over longer distances. More competition may directly result in lower long-haul rates as various

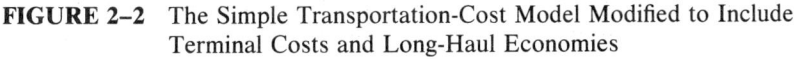

FIGURE 2–2   The Simple Transportation-Cost Model Modified to Include Terminal Costs and Long-Haul Economies

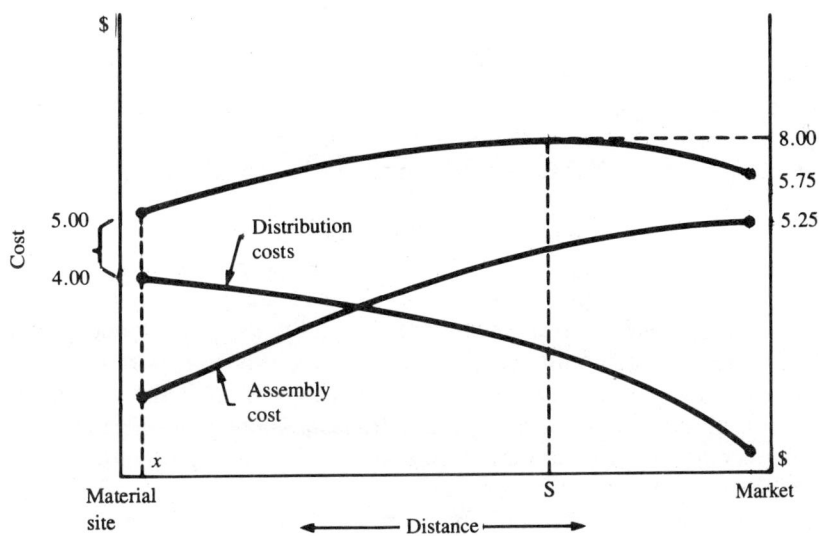

1. Cost of transporting raw material from the material site to the production site (assembly costs).
2. Cost of transporting output from the production site to the market (distribution costs).

Terminal costs and long-haul economies reinforce the advantages of endpoint locations.

modes of transport compete with each other. For instance, truckers may have to lower their long-haul rates to compete with trains. Furthermore, someone shipping a product may be able to switch transportation modes to achieve the lowest overall rate.

Figure 2–2 illustrates how both terminal costs and long-haul economies strengthen the transportation-cost advantages of endpoint locations. Assembly costs would be zero if the establishment is located exactly at the material site because (it is assumed) there would be no need to load materials. The finished product, however, would have to be loaded so there would be some terminal costs. If the inputs are transported even a short distance from the material site, assembly expenses jump by $1 due to terminal costs. Thus, a location at site x would increase per unit costs by at least $1. Likewise, if the production facility were located at the market, the output would not have to be loaded or unloaded; so, similarly, terminal costs for the output would be reduced, but a plant located even a slight distance from the market would increase the terminal costs by 50 cents per unit.

Long-haul economies are also illustrated in Figure 2–2 above. The transportation costs for both the material and the output increase with distance but at a decreasing rate. A firm would be unable to take full advantage of an endpoint location if a midpoint location such as S were selected. A location at S would involve higher terminal costs and would not allow the producer to take advantage of long-haul economies.

Transshipment Points.   Transshipment points represent an important exception to the general advantage of endpoint locations. They are junctures in the transportation network where loading and unloading cannot be avoided. For instance, before the technology developed to construct bridges that could span major rivers, goods transported by land routes had to be unloaded and placed on barges to cross the rivers. Frequently, cities developed near these transshipment points. Since shipments would have to be interrupted in any event, production locations at transshipment points may not increase transportation costs. This transportation cost advantage could be represented in Figure 2–2 by a drop in the transportation costs at the transshipment point. The drop would reflect the fact that, if production were to occur at any point other than the material site (the transshipment point or market), an extra loading/unloading cost would be incurred.

Buffalo and St. Louis were important transshipment points. Coastal cities such as New York, New Orleans, and San Francisco also perform transshipment functions. Transshipment centers could offer economies of scale in loading, unloading, storage, and so forth by providing specialized loading, unloading, packaging, and storage facilities that serve a variety of users. Such economies can reinforce the transshipment points' desirability as production centers. Once cities started to develop around transshipment functions, their economies diversified. When more than one market is being served or when more than one material input is required or when the input can be purchased from different places, then transshipment points can be particularly desirable locations. Cities with major airports are in a good position to attract additional economic activity because of the transshipment point.

The Principle of Median Location.   The tendency for establishments that produce outputs with high ideal weights to locate at the market has been discussed. But what if the market itself is dispersed? In that case, such establishments tend to locate in the center of their market. This tendency is known as the principle of median location. An example will illustrate the principle. Assume that the production costs, quantity de-

FIGURE 2–3   The Principle of Median Location

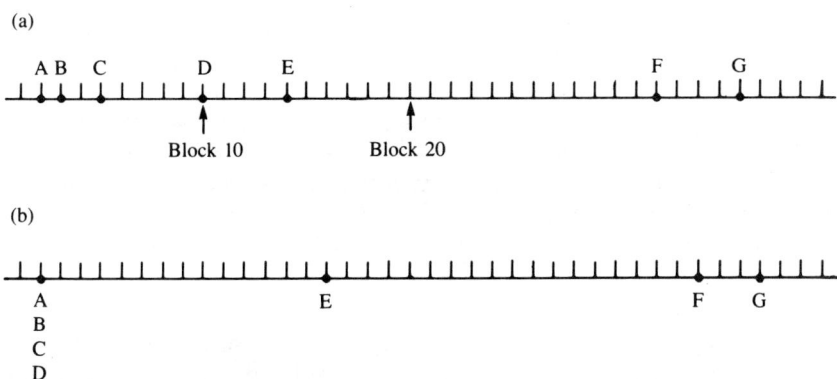

The principle of median location illustrates the tendency of market-oriented activities to locate at the point where half of the customers are on either side.

manded, and price are not affected by location. Distribution costs (including terminal costs) are assumed to be proportional to distance. This might be approximated by the case of a pizza parlor that delivers at a uniform price anywhere in an area. Assume the customers, denoted by letters, are distributed as shown in Figure 2–3(a) and each customer requires one delivery per week. Each dot indicates a block. Further assume that each delivery requires one trip—doubling up to serve both A and B in one trip is not allowed.

Where should the market-oriented activity locate? Intuitively, many people believe a location on block 20 would be the best choice because it is about in the middle of the market. But that solution is incorrect. Block 10 would be the transportation-cost-minimizing location.

In order to see why 10 is optimal, suppose the firm relocated from 10 to 13. On the one hand, the shift would save three blocks travel when serving customers E, F, and G or a total saving of nine blocks traveled. On the other hand, an extra 3 blocks of movement would be added for customers A, B, C, and D or a total of 12 travel blocks. Thus, the travel costs would increase by the move from six to nine. Likewise, any move from block 10 to lower-numbered blocks would increase total travel costs. In general, market-oriented block activities will tend to locate at the median (where half of the customers are on one side and half are on the other side) rather than in the geographic middle of a market.

Figure 2–3(b) shows the same locational problem, but a "city" exists at block three. Again, it might seem as though 20 would be the most appropriate location. However, the same reasoning used in the previous paragraph indicates that block three, the median location, would be the transportation-cost-minimizing point for this market-oriented commodity. Large cities tend to be the median location of customers and, hence, are the locational preference for distribution-oriented firms.

The principle of median location is useful for illustrating locational tendencies of market-oriented firms. However, it is not relevant to some situations because factors such as material inputs and multiple markets are not considered. The case of multiple markets and material sites can be useful in such situations.

Location on a Two-Dimensional Surface. The case of one-input, one-market results in a location along a line. Location along a line was also used to illustrate the principle of medium location. However, when there are multiple resources or markets, they will seldom form a line. Therefore, we must build models that describe locational choices on a two-dimensional surface. For instance, the production of iron requires limestone, ore, and coal. Both the ore and coal needed to produce a ton of iron are expensive to transport. Limestone is relatively ubiquitous. Less than 50 percent of the ore is iron, and the coal is burnt in the production process. Thus, iron production is a weight-losing activity, because about half of the ore and none of the coal will be physically embodied in the product. But where will the mill tend to locate?

If the sources of the ore and coal and the market were located along a line, the tendency would be to produce at the middle site unless the ideal weight of one of the factors was greater than the sum of the other two ideal weights. Notice the similarity to the principle of median location. Given the ideal weights (the cost of transporting enough material to produce one unit of the product one mile or the cost of transporting one unit of the final product one mile) shown in Figure 2–4, location will occur at the ore mine. If the production point were moved towards the coal mine, the savings from shipping the coal a shorter distance ($5 per unit per mile) would be offset by the extra $8 per unit per mile for shipping the ore to the production site and the finished product the extra distance to the market.

A locational triangle can be used to analyze situations where key points are not located on a line. If there are neither terminal costs nor economies of distance, the locational pull of each factor would equal the ideal weight of that factor. Suppose the material sites and market are distributed as shown in Figure 2–5. Notice that the ideal weights are the same as those in Figure 2–4. The transportation-cost-minimizing location would have to be somewhere inside the locational triangle because total distance needed to transport the inputs and outputs could always be reduced by moving from a point outside the triangle to a point on or within the triangle. However, where inside the triangle will the mill locate?

FIGURE 2–4   Location along a Line

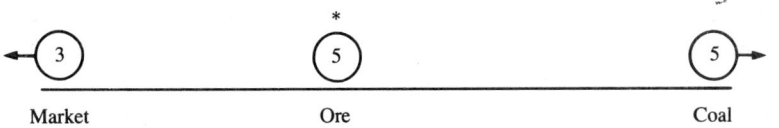

Market   Ore   Coal

○ = Ideal weight

*| = Cost minimizing location

The establishment will locate at the ore mine. A location one mile closer to the market would require an extra weight movement of 10 to save only 3. A location 1 mile closer to the coal mine would require an extra ideal weight movement of 8 to save only 5.

The location with the lowest transfer cost is where the three pulls balance each other—a move towards any point would increase total ideal-weight miles. For instance, if L is the least-cost location, a movement to A would increase total cost by 8 units per mile (the sum of the ideal weights of the ore and the final product) but save only the ideal weight for

FIGURE 2–5   A Locational Triangle

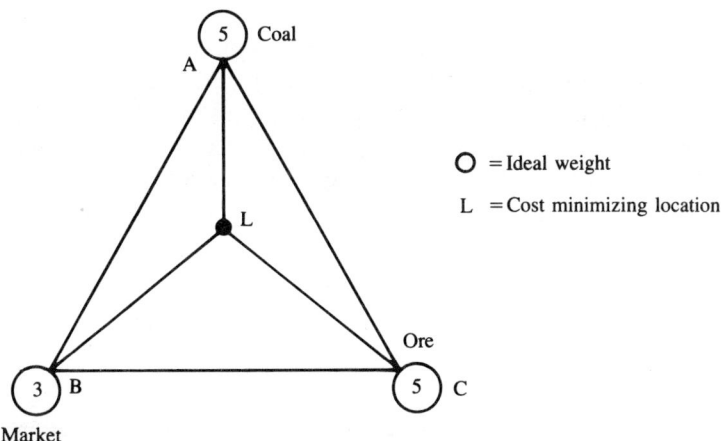

When the important locational points are not in a line, ideal weights still exert locational pulls.

coal of 5.[2] Suppose the ideal weight of resource at A were 20. In this case, it would be cheaper to ship the resource located at B to A, produce the product at A, and ship the output to the market. The resource at A would be the dominant weight.

The above discussion assumed that transportation costs were uniform throughout the triangle. But, if there were no roads to L, it would not be a feasible site for production. Therefore, it is quite reasonable to assume location will occur only on an established road. Figure 2–6 illustrates several possible road systems and shows how the concept of ideal weight can be used to analyze various situations.

Case A is an instance where the firm would locate in the middle of the end pulls even though the ideal weight of the input or output (if the minimum transportation cost point represents the market) is only $3 per unit per mile. Moving north of the transportation-cost-minimizing point would increase transportation costs per unit by $8 ($5 + $3) per mile while saving only $7 per unit per mile. In contrast, case B illustrates an instance where the ideal weight at the endpoint offsets the counterpulls. Moving away from the endpoint would save only $8 ($5 + $3) while costing an extra $10 per unit per mile. Case C shows how a midpoint location may minimize transportation costs if the other weights pull in opposite directions. Case D illustrates the effects of a dominant weight even though there are several small inputs or markets.

Case E is interesting because it represents a classic locational triangle with roads connecting only the tips. In this case, the largest weight, 7, would be sufficient to attract production to that site. In contrast, as a triangle flattens to approach a line as in case F, the situation becomes more like case A, and the midpoint location tends to minimize transportation costs.

Of course, reality presents even more complicated problems than those addressed in Figure 2–6. In practice, a locational planner may have to choose between good and bad roads, alternative routes, and so forth. Nevertheless, the kind of analysis shown in Figure 2–6 provides a foundation for understanding more complicated situations.

Production Costs

Transportation costs have traditionally received more attention than other locational factors because of their importance to many critical manufacturing processes, such as iron and steel production. The early studies

---

[2] A "Varignon Frame" has been used to estimate the least-cost location for transportation-oriented establishments. It is a triangle that sits on a pedestal. A map of the area is placed over the frame, and three strings tied together. The string-ends run over pulleys at each angle, and weights proportional to the ideal weights are attached to the string-ends. They will exert pulls on the center knot. The location where the notch is at physical equilibrium will be the transportation-cost-minimizing point.

FIGURE 2–6   Alternative Transportation Systems

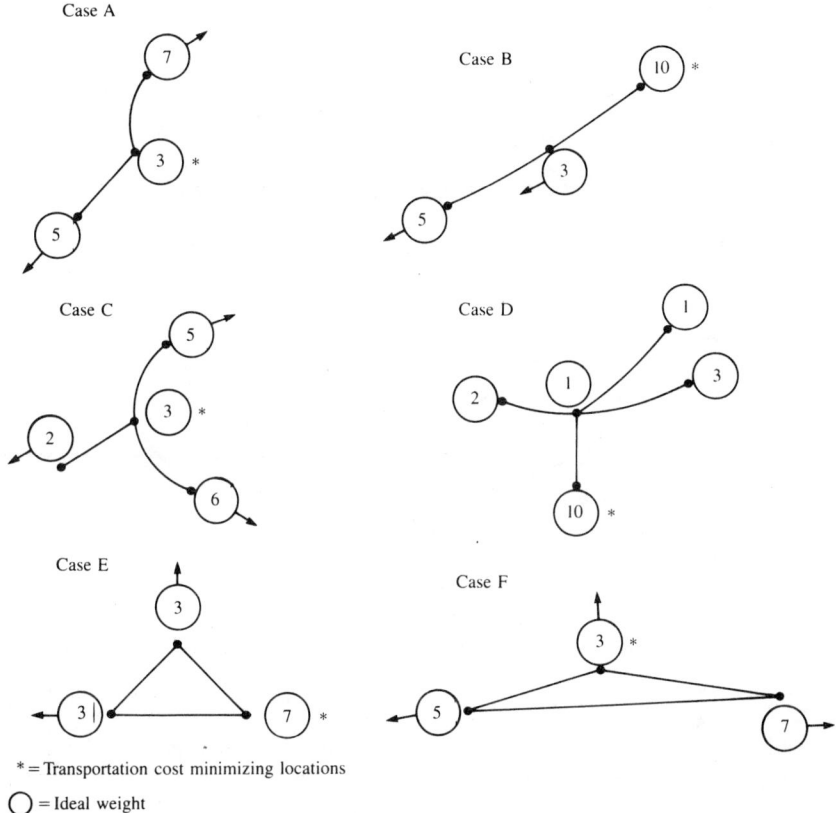

Case A

Case B

Case C

Case D

Case E

Case F

* = Transportation cost minimizing locations

○ = Ideal weight

A fixed transportation system limits possible locations, but ideal weights are still important in determining the transportation-cost-minimizing locations.

of location placed primary emphasis upon the need to minimize transportation costs. However, transportation costs are becoming relatively less important for three reasons. First, manufacturing has decreased in importance. Manufacturing tends to be more transportation oriented than service activities. Second, technology has lowered the cost of transportation compared to other imputs. Transportation costs have fallen dramatically in the past 50 years. Also, products have higher value per pound of raw

FIGURE 2–7   The Transportation Cost—Production Cost Trade-offs

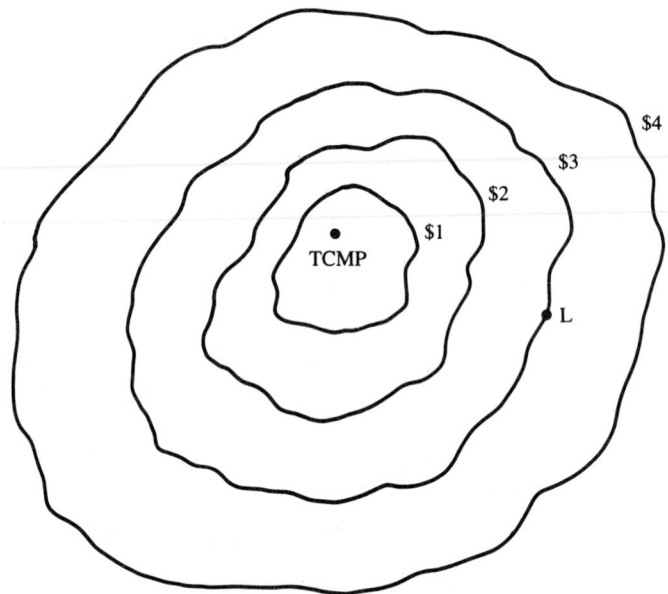

Isodopanes show equal transportation-cost points above the transportation-cost-minimizing site. If production costs can be reduced by more than the increased transportation costs, the alternative location rather than TCMP will be the production site.

materials today than in the past. The higher the value compared to the cost of shipment, the less importance will be attached to shipping costs relative to other costs. Finally, the range of variance in other costs of production, particularly localized inputs, has become more widely recognized. We have assumed that production costs are equal everywhere except for the costs of transportation. However, localized inputs, inputs that are impractical to transport, have become more important in production costs.

Production-cost differentials have traditionally been analyzed by examining the trade-off between the cost reductions from locating at the least-cost production point on the one hand and the increased transportation costs that such a location would entail on the other. Will the production-cost differential offset the higher transportation costs? In Figure 2–7, the transportation-cost-minimizing point is shown as "TCMP." Around TCMP are lines that show the increased transportation cost associated with moving away from the transportation-cost-minimizing point. These lines are known as isodopanes ("iso" means equal and "dopane" means cost) or isocost lines. Let point L be a low-cost production point. Perhaps energy is cheaper at L. If the per unit cost savings are greater than $3, the establishment should locate at L rather than TCMP. If the savings are less than $3, then TCMP is the most profitable location.

The inclusion of production cost variations in the locational decision requires analysts to calculate both production and transportation costs at each location to determine the least-cost location. Let us briefly examine some of the important factors that influence production-cost differentials. The appendix to this chapter shows how localized inputs and other complicating factors affect locational choice.

Labor Costs

Firms that have significant labor costs relative to the value of the final product tend to be labor oriented. Leather, insurance services, and furniture are examples of labor oriented industries. Currently, many office activities are relocating from the central city to the suburbs in order to gain access to the "pink collar" work force that has developed due to the rise of the two-wage-earner families.

The Prevailing Wage. A region's prevailing wage rates are an important indicator of labor costs. They represent the wage of a typical worker in a given job category. An area has many prevailing wage rates because there are many different labor markets within the area depending on the category of labor. A firm employing unskilled workers would be interested in a different prevailing wage than a firm employing typists. However, within a geographic area, labor markets are not usually segmented geographically. Therefore, the prevailing wage for a particular labor type will be the same throughout the metropolitan area. Accordingly, prevailing wage rates affect the choice of region or metropolitan area, but they are not important determinants of the site within the area.

Wage rates alone do not accurately reflect labor costs for several reasons. First, locational decision makers are concerned with fringe-benefit costs as well as hourly wages. Therefore, locational planners are concerned with the entire compensation package. Second, productivity differences can cause labor costs to differ between regions even when hourly compensation is equal. If workers in area A produce twice the hourly output of workers in area B while using equal amounts of other inputs, the compensation rate in A could be higher than in B and yet labor cost per unit of output could be cheaper in A. Some analysts would argue that labor in some cities is paid more than elsewhere because workers are more productive. Education, work habits, and willingness to cooperate with management are elements of productivity. Although it is important, labor productivity is difficult to measure. The Department of Commerce publishes data showing total output divided by the size of the labor force. While this information can be used to approximate labor productivity, it does not account for different amounts of capital used in production.

Since value-added (the difference between the cost of an industry's inputs and the value of the output) data is published, some indication of productivity differentials is available. But if a region's high productivity is due to better management rather than a capable work force, a company might be better off locating in a low-wage region and applying productivity-increasing management techniques. Productivity in the service sector is very difficult to measure. For example, an accounting office for a manufacturing company has no direct output.

A third difficulty in using prevailing wage rates as a measure of labor costs is that employers may be able to hire workers at amounts substantially below an area's prevailing wage rate. A study by White (1987) found that workers in Milwaukee who had experienced substantial spells of unemployment were willing to work for wages substantially below their previous wage and below the prevailing wage in the area. A firm that measures labor costs by the prevailing wage in the industry would overlook the fact that unemployed workers will take substantially less pay. The weakening of unions in recent years has enhanced the ability of new firms to hire at below the local union wage. Two-tier wage systems in which new workers have much lower wages than workers employed before the two-tier system also reduce the usefulness of the prevailing wage as an indication of what the employers must pay. Of course, some employers may fear that workers may not remain satisfied with wages below the local prevailing rate. Therefore, firms may choose to assume that wages will increase to the prevailing level. Considerations of future wage levels cannot be rigorously quantified, but neither can they be ignored.

Unionization.   Unionization is often mentioned as a locational factor related to labor cost. The common perception is that unions increase compensation and promote work rules that reduce productivity. Both factors increase labor costs. States with right-to-work laws (laws allowing employees not to join unions) have experienced more rapid employment growth than those without right-to-work laws in recent years. This has been interpreted as indicating that employers believe unionization causes labor costs to increase. In light of several empirical studies, Schmenner (1981, p. 7) concluded that "right to work laws . . . are often the most effective public policies" for attracting new firms. Unionization may be particularly detrimental to branch plant locations where a skilled, flexible, but highly paid work force is considered less important than a cooperative, low-paid work force that can provide routine work. Bartik (1984, p.

19) found that "a 10 percent increase in the percentage unionization of a state's labor force is estimated to cause a 30–45 percent decrease in the number of new branch plants."

Quality of Life

Increasingly, economic development officials believe that if the local quality of life could be improved, economic development would be enhanced. Amenities refer to quality-of-life-enhancing features. Regional amenities include good weather, museums, sunshine, good roads, schools, and other public services, and a variety of other factors that may only indirectly influence production costs. Universities are an especially notable source of life-quality improvement by providing cultural, sports, and educational outlets.

Amenities have become more important because many industries, particularly in high-tech sectors, have become more "footloose" or freed from traditional, cost-oriented locational pulls. A locational decision maker may choose a site with more amenities or a better quality of life if other direct cost factors are about equal, and many firms will select amenity-rich environments even when other things are not equal. If the firm is not in a competitive industry, a more costly but amenity-rich site may be chosen. The firm may be able to pass costs forward to consumers in the form of higher prices or pass them backwards to stockholders in the form of lower profits. Quality of life may also influence decision makers who want to start or relocate a business to an area they would enjoy. However, even firms in competitive industries may also believe that profits will be enhanced from amenity-rich environments.

Amenities may also enter into the locational decision in a more traditional way. They may allow firms to recruit more productive workers or recruit workers at lower costs. Technically skilled researchers and creative employees value communities with a good quality of life. Since individuals at the top of their professions can often obtain jobs almost wherever they choose to live, they would work in an area with a poor quality of life only if the wage compensation were substantially higher than elsewhere or if the job were particularly challenging. Furthermore, some workers at the very top of their professions may already be earning so much money that they are relatively insensitive to jobs offering "only" more money. A good quality of life may help attract and retain less-skilled workers at lower wage rates as well.

There is considerable uncertainty regarding who captures the benefits of local amenities. On the one hand, many economists believe that firms located in amenity-rich areas benefit because they are able to recruit more productive workers at a lower cost than in an amenity-poor environment. They suggest firms that locate in amenity-rich areas reduce labor costs. On the other hand, amenity-rich areas may experience increases in the demand for property, causing real estate values and rents to rise. In this case, production costs may increase because the company's land rents will increase and because employees may demand higher wages to compensate for better amenities. Roback (1982) used weather-related variables such as the number of cloudy days and the number of heating degree days (i.e., days that are cold and require heating) to measure quality of life. She concluded that amenities both lower wages and increase rents.

Taxes

There are a variety of taxes that influence where a business will locate. Personal income taxes may indirectly affect labor costs as workers require higher compensation to offset higher taxes. Perceived taxes may directly affect the locational decision by influencing the preferred location of high-paid executives who influence the location decision. Wasylenko (1984) and Romans and Sabrahmanyan (1979) have both shown that high personal tax rates have detrimental effects on regional growth.

Corporate income taxes directly affect after-tax profits and so may be a more direct locational factor. Bartik (1984) found that capital-intensive industries were particularly sensitive to state corporate profits taxes.

The real estate property tax is an especially important intraregional locational factor because there are substantial variations in property tax rates within a region (Charney, 1983). Most states and metropolitan regions include both high and low property tax areas.

Business taxes, per se, are usually a minor portion of overall business costs so some analysts believe they are not major locational factors. However, taxes are easy to quantify, and sometimes things that can be counted receive more consideration than more important considerations that cannot be counted. Examinations of where establishments locate provide some evidence regarding the importance of taxes. Most facilities that relocated chose a new site where site taxes were equal to or greater than the previous location (Schmenner, 1981). However, plants that move long distances (over 20 miles) generally select lower-tax locations. Thus, taxes appear to be at least a moderately important locational factor. Papke (1987) examined regional tax differentials and found that tax burden differentials are statistically significant and negatively related to the size and location of capital investment.

Government Incentives

Governments provide a variety of special incentives or subsidies to business to encourage location in an area. Examples of special governmental incentives include: state interest subsidies, loan guarantees, regulatory exemptions, sale of land at below market prices, tax credits, and special infrastructure constructed at public expense. About three fourths of manufacturing locational decisions involve some type of governmental assistance. Figure 2–8 shows the most popular types of incentives. The availability of special incentives is offered by so many places that they are almost a ubiquity. Major downtown hotels or office projects almost always receive special governmental incentives, often from more than one level of government. Like taxes, government incentives are both an intra-

FIGURE 2–8   Public Assistance Used by New and Relocating Plants

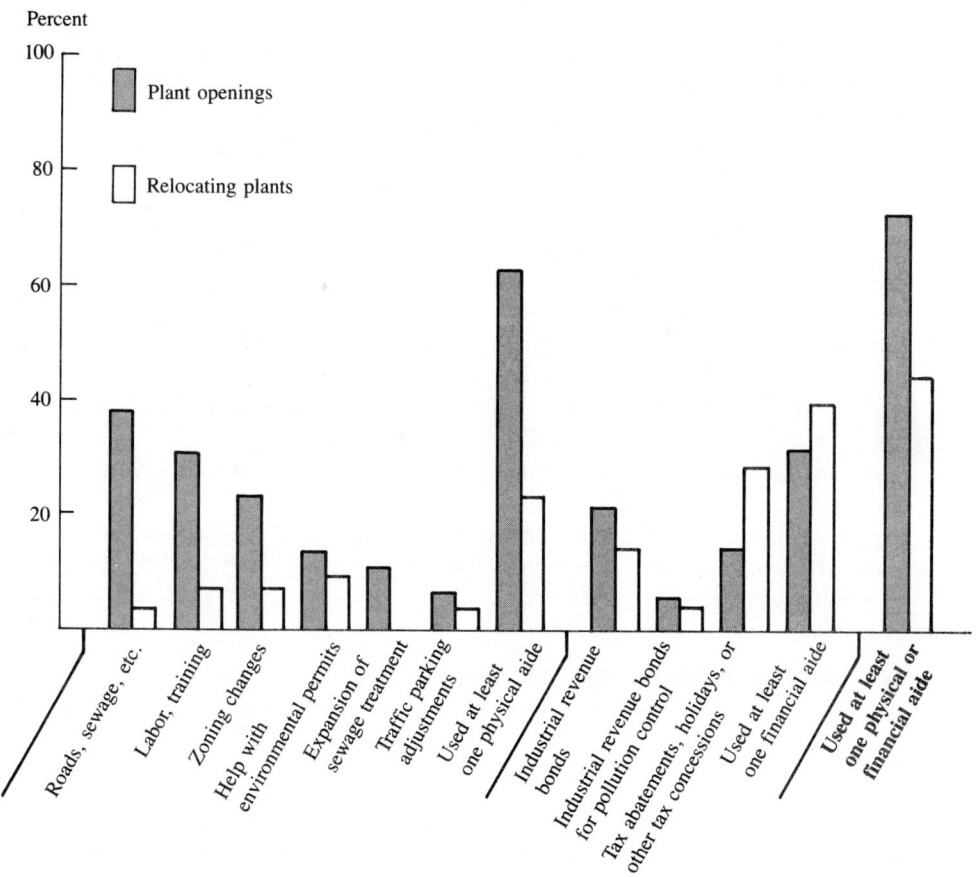

Government incentives for new and relocating plants are important and varied.

SOURCE: Roger W. Schmenner, "Location Decisions of Large Firms: Implications for Public Policy," Commentary, January 1981, p. 6.

and interregional locational factor. However, there is no strong empirical evidence regarding the effectiveness of direct business subsidies, although most economic development practitioners consider them essential.

Local Business Climate

Recently, business climate has been identified as an important locational factor. Business climate is a somewhat slippery concept because it is intended to include not only tax and expenditure programs but also the less tangible aspects of a community's attitude towards business. Do public officials make substantial efforts to accommodate business? Are regulations detrimental to business kept to a minimum? Are business executives accorded a place of respect in the community? Does the community want business development? The above questions indicate some of the less quantifiable aspects of attitude towards business.

Site Costs

The cost of a particular site may be expressed in terms of rents or purchase price of a building. Site costs include the cost of land and building. Site costs are not an important interregional locational factor because almost all regions offer a variety of sites at a wide range of prices, but site costs are a major factor in the competition among jurisdictions within a region. Warehouses and office facilities are particularly sensitive to site costs.

This section has been oriented to activities in search of a location. However, owners of sites are also seeking businesses to locate on their property. For instance, the owners of industrial land may advertise or attempt to find intended developers for the property. The searches complement one another.

National Political Climate and Stability

Political climate is a regional locational factor that is generally the same in regions throughout a nation. As the world economy becomes increasingly interdependent, establishments are considering sites throughout the world. One of the most important considerations a foreign investor has is whether the government is stable and the political climate compatible with a satisfactory return on investment. The political stability of the United States and Canada partly explains the dramatic increase of foreign investment flowing into these countries during the 1980s.

Political factors may also help one area within a country compete with other regions, particularly for establishments that do business with the federal government. In such cases, the strength of the region's congressional delegation may be a very important factor, since businesses that deal with the government have occasion to request assistance in obtaining government business. The choice of Texas as the site for the $4–6 billion supercollider has been attributed to the political strength of Texas.

Energy Costs

Energy prices directly affect transportation costs and, consequently, affect the location of transportation-oriented activities. Energy is also a direct input in the production process. Carlton (1983) examined births of new firms at branch plant locations and concluded that electricity prices were a major locational factor.

Energy costs are highly regulated, and many development officials hope to attract business by keeping costs as low as possible. However, there are important quality dimensions to energy that should also be addressed. For instance, businesses may be concerned with the availability of some energy sources. Can they get natural gas, or will they be subject to blackouts or brownouts? As businesses rely increasingly on computers, the quality of electrical energy, including the minimization of surges, is an important locational consideration.

THE DECISION-MAKING PROCESS

The locational choice can be complex, because the decision may involve a variety of motives and affect a substantial portion of the work force. This section first examines the motives of locational decision makers and then the corporate decision-making process.

Motivations

In economics, the most widely used motivational assumption is that businesses behave to maximize profits. Profit maximization is derived from the assumption of individual utility maximization. The intermediate assumption that bridges utility and profit maximization is that money buys things that provide utility. Since profit maximization is a cornerstone for understanding behavior, it is appropriate, at least as a first approximation, to assume it is the main criterion in choosing a location. However, it will be useful to sketch instances where profit-maximizing explanations will fail or provide only part of the explanation.

The profit-maximizing assumption fails to account for choices of nonprofit institutions. Fire stations and other public facilities are located on the basis of quick service and the political pulls of citizens in various parts of the city. Politics can be a very important locational determinant for many facilities such as military bases.

Profit-maximizing behavior also fails to account for occasional conflicts of interests that can occur between the owners of corporations—the stockholders—on the one hand and the individuals who make the locational decisions on the other. Many corporate officers may own such a small amount of their company's stock in proportion to their overall personal portfolio that a profit-maximizing location may not significantly enhance their wealth compared to a second- or third-best location. Consequently, some managers may choose to locate a facility in an area that has a good climate, low personal tax rates, or other advantages that would appeal to the decision maker. Alternative locations that would return more profits to stockholders might be overlooked. In other words, managers may place their personal interests above stockholder interests, which is not surprising if you believe managers maximize utility and have some insulation from being fired if profits are not maximized.

Since locational analysis involves numerous trade-offs, it may be difficult to identify the *one* best location. Managers may, therefore, identify several locations that are roughly equal. Such a circumstance makes it easy to tilt the choice towards the area where they personally wish to live. Managers may also prefer to recommend safe locations (a high probability of generating satisfactory profits) rather than high-risk, high-return locations; if the high-risk location fails, the managers may be fired.

Uncertainty and Alternative Motives. The complexity of motivations that affect locational choice can be understood with the aid of Table 2–2. It shows four possible entrepreneurial actions: (1) locate a large facility in California, (2) locate a large facility in Texas, (3) locate two small facilities, one in California and one in Texas, or (4) do not establish a facility; buy AAA bonds. Each of the four actions carries a risk. Assume the investor is most concerned about possible state tax increases in California, Texas, or both states. Thus, there are four possible "states of the world": (1) tax increase only in California, (2) tax increase only in Texas, (3) tax increase in both states, or (4) no tax increase in either state. The appropriate payoffs are shown in the cells of Table 2–2. The payoff represents not just one year's return but the present value of all future returns.

What outcome will result? It depends upon the subjective goals of the entrepreneur and the probability of various outcomes (Isard, 1975). Suppose the entrepreneur believed he or she would be lucky. Whatever the decision, events will be favorable to that choice. In this case, a plant would be established in Texas. The decision maker would believe there would be no tax increase in Texas but there would be a tax increase in California. Total anticipated profits would be $101. In the terminology of game theory, this would be a maxi-max strategy because the decision maker maximizes the likelihood of the maximum payoff.

TABLE 2-2 Potential Outcomes and Payoffs

| | Outcomes | | | |
Entrepreneurial Action	No Tax Increase	Tax Increase California Only	Tax Increase Texas Only	Tax Increase Texas and California
Plant in California	$60	$ 15	$100	$45
Plant in Texas	55	101	−10	50
Plant in both	55	40	40	20
No plant, buy bonds	30	30	30	30

Payoffs for four mutually exclusive actions by the entrepreneur depend upon what "state of the world" occurs after the investment. To illustrate, the entrepreneur could earn $101 if a plant in Texas were built and a tax increase were passed only in California.

If the entrepreneur were pessimistic or totally averse to risk, he would attempt to maximize the minimum possible gain. This strategy is a maxi-min approach. The entrepreneur would not build a plant and would buy bonds instead. The smallest possible gain would be $30 regardless of which possible event occurred.

By estimating the probability of various outcomes, the entrepreneur can project the probable return from each possible action. For instance, if each potential event were equally likely to occur, then the expected return from a plant in California would equal ($60 · .25 + $15 · .25 + $100 · .25 + $45 · .25) or $55. An expected return could be calculated for other actions similarly. Construction of the California plant is the decision that maximizes the expected return.

Of course, other motives and outcomes are also rational. Suppose the decision maker's subjective goal is to maximize benefits subject to the constraint that the return be no less than $20 and equal probabilities be assigned to each outcome. In that case, the two plant locations would be selected. Such a situation occurs if management's main goal is to generate a high enough return to satisfy stockholders or the governing board, and to minimize the risk of displeasing the stockholders. Satisfying behavior occurs when managers attempt to earn a particular level of profits rather than maximize profits.

Limitations of the Theoretical Model. The extensive knowledge of likely future events described in the theoretical model represented by the exact values shown in Table 2-2 is not realistic. Few decision makers list or even know all possible "potential outcomes and payoffs" or the probabilities of their occurrence. In practice, the locational decision involves more guesswork and digging up scraps of data than is indicated by the game-theory model.

The amount of time and study devoted to locational decisions varies drastically. At one extreme, an individual may open a business after comparing rents among few buildings and making sure there are no competitors in the area. It may be rational not to devote much time, effort, or money to a locational decision if the profitability of the enterprise is not sensitive to location. After all, even profit maximizers want to maximize profits *net* of locational search costs. However, other locational decisions involve extensive analysis. The location of retail chain stores and large manufacturing plants usually involves substantial analysis. Activities that require large, long-term investments generally devote substantial resources to determine the most appropriate location. However, even in cases that are studied intensively, the final decision normally requires substantial judgment on the part of the decision makers. Locational analysis is far from a pure science because of the complexity of factors that must be considered, the uncertainty of the future, and the variety of motives.

New businesses are less likely than branch plants to engage in careful, profit-maximizing analysis of locational choice. New businesses often locate where the founder lives, which suggests that personal factors may be as important as factors that might increase profits. However, a successful and enduring business site may have attributes of a profit-maximizing location, even if it was initially selected based upon personal factors. Locations based upon purely personal choices in areas that cannot support satisfactory profits will perish. As Hoover (1948, p. 211) put it:

> A good analogy is the scattering of certain types of seeds by the wind. These seeds may be carried for miles before finally coming to rest, and nothing makes them select spots particularly favorable for germinations. . . . Because of the survival of those which happen to be well located, the resulting distribution of such plants from generation to generation follows closely the distribution of favorable growing conditions.

Steps in the Corporate Site-Selection Process

Although there are a variety of motives involved in selecting a location, large businesses tend to follow similar steps in the site-selection process. Schmenner (1982) has identified five basic steps.

Need Recognition.   Locational decisions are seldom *only* location decisions. They are usually part of a broader corporate planning process and occur at critical junctures in a firm's life cycle. The search for a new location may be due to an abrupt change in corporate strategy, say a decision to abandon one product line and enter another. The search could also be prompted by a routine process, such as accommodating projected increases in demand.

A corporate planning office or a division of a multidivision firm may begin the locational process with a forecast of future demand. The forecast may be ad hoc or, more typically, part of a company's ongoing corporate planning process, such as a rolling five-year plan. If a capacity shortage is anticipated, officials must decide how to address the issue. Expansion at one or more of the company's existing sites normally will be one option. Increasing the product price or subcontracting work to other producers could be other options. If a new facility is determined to be the best way to address the projected capacity shortage, a site-selection team will be formed.

Establishing the Selection Team.   The organization of the company affects the nature of the site-selection process. Corporations with a centralized staff will generally form a team at the corporate level. Members of the team will include representatives from key corporate departments, such as transportation, distribution, personnel, engineering, real estate, and planning. Decentralized companies, such as loosely organized conglomerates with relatively strong divisions or subsidiaries and weaker corporate staffs, may carry out the locational study at the divisional level. In this case, the head office will provide a supervisory role. Small companies usually have a clear top-down decision-making process. The CEO is more directly involved in the decision because the small company cannot afford a team of in-house specialists. Small companies also normally search within short distances of their existing plants so information costs may not be as significant.

Several consulting firms specialize in locational decisions. They can often conduct a site analysis cheaper than in-house staffs because they have access to data on a great many sites throughout the United States. Consulting firms are used in about one third of the locational decisions of *Fortune* 500 companies. The proportion may be even higher for small and medium-sized firms that do not have the internal staff needed to conduct a locational study. Consulting firms may work with the corporate locational team or they may work independently, reporting directly to a CEO. Additional advantages of employing consulting firms rather than doing the work in-house include the insulation of the site-selection team from internal pressure and greater anonymity for the company. Companies usually do not reveal that they are seeking an alternative location until they are far enough into the selection process to start negotiating the specific terms on land, locational incentives, and so forth. Secrecy will deter company officials from lobbying for their personal choices, and representatives of local areas will be less likely to intervene in the corporate selection process.

Developing Criteria.   The site-selection team will develop a list of important locational "must have/want" characteristics for the new facility. Many large companies already have lists that have been used in other studies, but criteria might be modified depending upon the circumstances. The role of the proposed facilities in the overall corporate strategy will be considered in developing and revising the list of criteria. Desires to penetrate new markets, to segregate or integrate corporate functions, or to increase a firm's visibility may be important elements in the locational decision. The must have/want list will include both quantitative and qualitative locational factors. The locational factors may be weighted to indicate which locational features are most important.

Some trade-off occurs in developing criteria between information that is ideally desired and information that is available. No firm can use a locational model that includes every factor that could possibly influence profits. The information needed to make such a model operational would be too costly. Consequently, much of the data needed to make informed locational decisions is unpublished and must be gathered from expensive site visits. Secondary data already collected by governmental agencies or by local chambers of commerce is usually inexpensive but may only approximate the specific information decision makers require. Secondary data may also be several years old by the time it is collected and disseminated. Therefore, most firms focus on a few important factors that are necessary and a few additional desirable factors.

Winnowing and Focusing.   Once the criteria have been established, the search for a site will begin. The search is normally made sequentially. The first stage involves the choice of a multistate, state, or urban region. Over half of all locational studies make their "first cut" at a multistate level, although the first cut is often at the metropolitan level. Once a region or state has been selected, a more microgeographic focus will be taken culminating in the short list of one or a few communities. At this stage, the search for an exact site will begin. Individual suburban and central-city jurisdictions within a metropolitan area often compete with one another as well as with sites in other regions.

In selecting a broad region, the site-selection team will focus on labor, state taxes, climate, proximity to customers and suppliers, and other features that may have significant interregional variation, but are similar almost everywhere within the region.

Locational factors that are similar within large regions are termed macrolocational factors. Locational factors that vary at the microgeographic level of detail, such as land costs, access to major roads, and good local schools, are less important in the initial winnowing stage because satisfactory accommodations can generally be found somewhere within all major regions. Hence, microlocational factors become more important when selecting a specific community within a region or a specific site within the metropolitan area.

Several consulting firms use large-scale computer models to aid in the winnowing process, particularly in ranking states and metropolitan areas. In constructing such a model, weights are first assigned to the must have/ want list of characteristics—the more important the attribute, the higher the weight. A score for each locational factor is also assigned to each region—the better the regional attribute, the higher the score. By multiplying the weight times the region's location score and summing the results, an overall desirability index can be obtained. A computerized score for each region can be generated by this process.

Grant Thornton, a well-known locational consulting firm, developed the weighted list of important locational criteria shown in Table 2–3. Locational factors and their weights represent the combined judgment of members of state manufacturing associations.

Figure 2–9 shows the ranking of states and regions that resulted when relative positions of individual states were compared. Each state's score is the sum of the state's measure on each factor (in terms of number of standard deviations from the mean) times the factor score.[3] The states that had favorable scores on highly weighted factors accordingly received the higher manufacturing climate score.

The large-scale, computer-generated, site-selection method has been criticized for three reasons. First, it creates a false sense of rigor (Erickson, 1987). The very concept of business climate is vague, and a good business climate for one industry may not be a good business climate for another. Furthermore, even a state with a very low business-climate rating may include regions that are ideal for certain businesses. Second, Skoro (1988) showed that rankings of business climate fail to predict where state growth will occur. If the measure of business climate is unrelated to growth, an analyst must question how well business climate is measured. Third, only easy-to-quantify data is generally used in the early stages; thus, locational factors that may be important to particular firms may be ignored. Nevertheless, large-scale computer winnowing is an accepted practice and is utilized to some degree, even among individuals who recognize the limitations.

Once a few regions have been identified, a specific site must be found. At this stage, computer models are less useful than the telephone and legwork. Information costs limit the number of sites that can be examined in detail. Normally, a firm making a major locational decision will gather detailed information on 10 to 25 specific sites. A company may make its requirements or needs known to state or local agencies and let

---

[3] If a low factor score is desirable, the state's score is multiplied by -1.

TABLE 2–3   Ranking of Most Desirable Locations, 1984

Rank	Factors	1984 Factor Weight
1	Energy costs	7.78%
2	Wages	7.05
3	Unionization	6.56
4	Man-hours lost	5.58
5	Unemployment compensation rates*	5.55
6	Taxes*	5.06
7	Value added	5.04
8	Expenditure versus revenue growth*	4.76
9	Change in wages	4.70
10	Unemployment compensation benefits*	4.38
11	Unemployment compensation worth	4.37
12	Change in taxes*	4.21
13	High school–educated adults*	4.14
14	Maximum workers' compensation payment*	4.04
15	Environment control*	3.94
16	Voc-Ed enrollment*	3.87
17	Change in unionization	3.84
18	Debt*	3.71
19	Hours worked	3.24
20	Welfare expenditure*	2.93
21	Population change	2.71
22	Population density	2.50

The important location factors for manufacturing were rated by leaders of trade associations.

* Indicates factor is controlled or strongly influenced by state or local governments.
SOURCE: Alexander Grant and Co. *General Manufacturing Climate of Forty-Eight Contiguous States* (Chicago: Alexander Grant, 1985) p. 3.

them respond by describing the assets of particular communities. Regional and city planning agencies, local utilities, banks, railroads, and chambers of commerce are all sources of information. Features of each site will be compared against the must have/want list. Sites will be eliminated as more detailed and difficult-to-obtain information is gathered on remaining sites after each elimination round. Site visits and collections of nonstandard or unpublished data will help narrow the number of sites.

Discussions with local public officials regarding potential problems and incentives may begin as the locational choices are narrowed. Most communities are anxious to attract new economic activity because they believe it will create jobs and increase the tax base. The firm may require

FIGURE 2–9 1984 Manufacturing Climates Study (state ranks and regional averages)

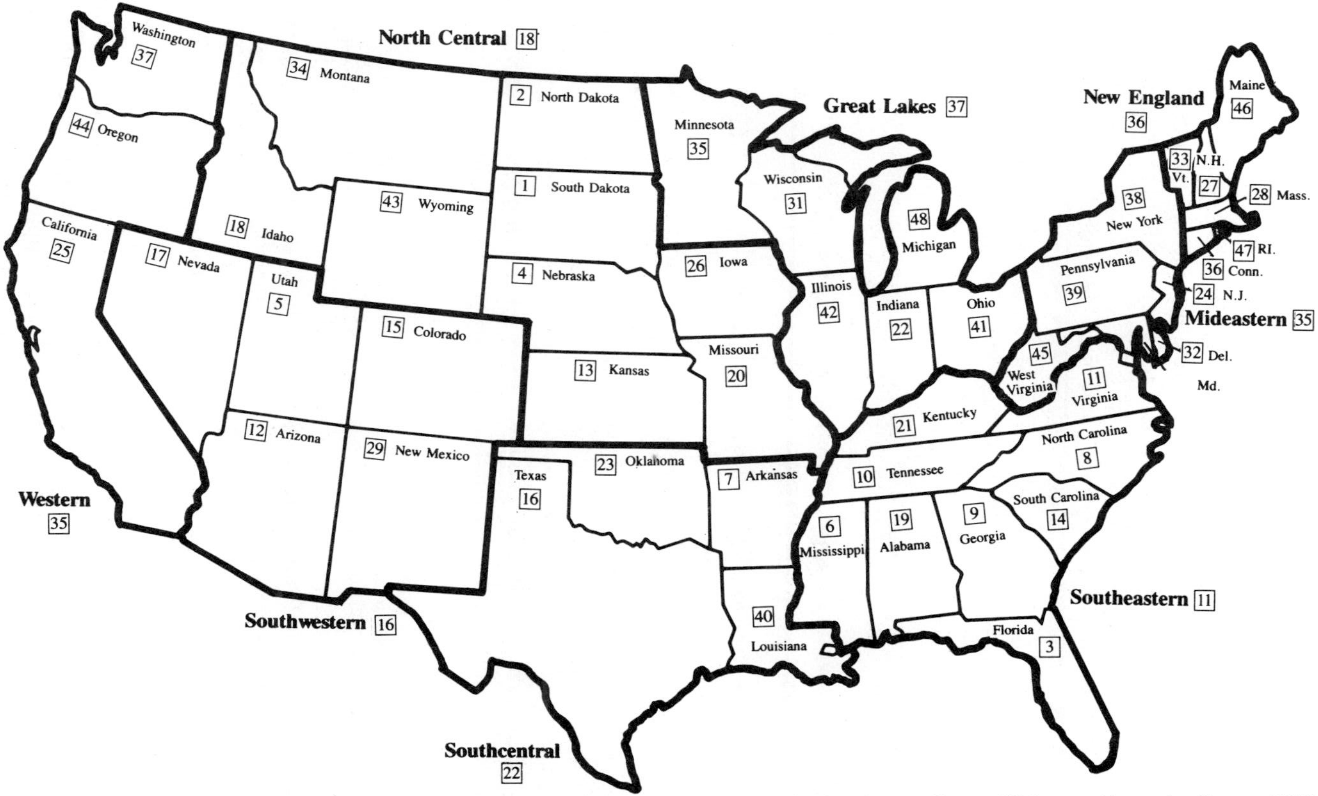

SOURCE: Alexander Grant and Co., *General Manufacturing Climate of Forty-Eight Contiguous States* (Chicago: Alexander Grant, 1985) p. 5.

assurances from local officials that zoning or other land-use regulations will not become impediments if it decides to locate in the area. The firm's consultants may also want to feel that they will be welcome members of the community. Increasingly, firms are asking for and receiving special incentives to locate in a particular area. Incentives include tax abatements, below-market-price land, and a variety of indirect subsidies.

Reaching a Final Decision. The final decision is normally formalized in the firm's capital budget. Preliminary estimates of land acquisition and construction costs will be developed for inclusion in the corporation's capital budget. In a large corporation with several divisions, each unit may have to compete with other divisions for a share of the capital budget. A feasibility analysis must normally show that the proposed facility will earn a sufficient rate of return to justify the construction costs.

CHANGING RELATIVE IMPORTANCE OF LOCATIONAL FACTORS

Various locational factors were discussed previously, but their relative importance was not assessed. Numerous scholars have questioned corporate decision makers to determine the most important locational factors. It is difficult to generalize from these studies because each study used a different research design. The differences in the studies include the types of locational factors examined, the time period examined, the types of businesses analyzed, and the techniques used to draw a conclusion. Nevertheless, a useful perspective on the relative importance of various locational factors can be gained by reviewing previous surveys.

The Use of Surveys

Before reviewing the results of surveys, some methodological problems regarding their use should be sketched. Surveys are frequently used to determine why firms locate where they do. Surveys allow researchers to probe the significance of long lists of variables, some of which may be qualitative and thus difficult to measure. For instance, quality of life is important to many decision makers, but it is difficult to measure. Thus, quality of life may be found to be important, but the researcher may not know what quality of life is. Also, questions must be designed carefully to avoid ambiguous responses. For instance, suppose a survey found that unionization was an important locational factor. One might still be unclear whether unionization impeded or stimulated location change.

Three additional problems of survey-based research that are of special concern to studies of locational determinants should be pointed out. First, respondents may provide answers that they believe will influence policy in their favor or that they believe the surveyor wants to hear. Taxes, for instance, are often ranked high on surveys even though they are not a major cost element for most activities. This is possibly because respondents believe that, if taxes are considered important, governments will reduce taxes. Second, only existing firms can be surveyed. Firms that made bad choices and went out of business cannot be contacted. Suppose proximity to recreational facilities was important to firms in selecting a site, but such criteria were unrelated to potential success. In that case, the firms that selected a site based upon recreational facilities could be defunct by the time the survey was taken. Finally, the choices given by the survey researcher can affect the response. Suppose all the labor-related locational factors—labor cost, productivity, cost of skilled labor, fringe benefits, changes in the wage rate, presence of clerical workers, unionization, right-to-work laws—were listed in great detail. Possibly no single factor would be considered important by more than a few respondents. However, every firm might respond that "labor" was an important factor if labor were a choice by itself. This problem makes comparison of findings very difficult.

Survey Findings: Past to Present

Early location theory treated transportation costs as the dominant locational factor. Later, Morgan (1964) examined the results of 17 locational studies conducted prior to 1963. He found four significant factors: (1) markets, (2) labor, (3) raw materials, and (4) transportation. Other factors, such as taxes, quality of life and financial incentives, were not found to be significant. The direct, cost-oriented locational factors exerted the dominant influence on industrial location. Morgan's study is dated, but it provides an excellent reference point for examining how locational factors have changed since the mid-1960s.

More recent surveys (*Fortune,* 1977; Hekman, 1985; Alexander Grant, 1985; Kieschnick, 1981; Schmenner, 1982; Premus, 1982) indicate that many additional factors affect locational choices. The most important locational determinants, based upon recent surveys, are shown in Table 2–4. Several important generalizations can be made by contrasting the findings in Table 2–4 with surveys conducted prior to 1970.

First, the traditional economic factors of location—labor, markets, transportation, and, to a lesser extent, access to raw materials—remain the most important influence in industrial location studies, but the relative rankings of these traditional locational factors vary in more recent studies.

Second, the traditional economic factors of location are becoming less important as a group in relation to other locational factors. For example, unlike studies in the 1940s and 1950s, most of the recent locational

TABLE 2–4 Summary of Recent Surveys' Findings regarding Locational Determinants

	Fortune— Future	Fortune— Past	Hekman	Industry Week	Alexander Grant	Kieschnick— New.	Kieschnick— Expansion	Schmenner	Premus
Labor force	2[a]	1[a]	4[c]		1[c]	2[i]	1[i]	1[k]	1[m]
Transportation	3	2	3	1[d]		5		3[j]	5
Markets	1	3				1[h]	2[h]	2	4
Raw materials							3		
Energy	4	4			2		4		
Productivity			2	2	5[g]				2
Taxes	5	4.5	5	3[f]	3[e]			4	
Education									3[h]
Unionization				4	4				
Personal reasons						3	5		

Attitudes toward business	5[b]	4.5[b]	1	5		5[1]
Familiar with economy					4	

Recent surveys of locational determinants indicate a wide variety of factors are rated as important.

Factors include:

a. availability of (1) unskilled or semiskilled, (2) skilled workers, and (3) clerical workers
b. (1) state and/or local attitude and (2) community receptivity
c. wage rate, change in wages
d. (1) land transportation, (2) air transportation, (3) rail transportation, and (4) sea transportation
e. (1) WCI rates, (2) taxes, (3) UC benefits, and (4) change in taxes
f. (1) state and local government, (2) tax exemptions, and (3) tax credits
g. (1) man-hours lost and (2) value added
h. (1) access to present customers and (2) access to growing markets
i. (1) supply of skilled labor, (2) cost of skilled labor, (3) supply of unskilled labor, and (4) cost of unskilled labor
j. (1) expressway, (2) rail service, and (3) air transportation
k. (1) favorable labor climate and (2) low wage rate
l. (1) college, (2) government help with roads, etc., and (3) government financing
m. (1) availability of skilled-labor—technicians, engineers, and scientists and (2) cost of labor
n. proximity to academic institutions, such as universities and colleges

SOURCE: John P. Blair and Robert Premus, "Major Factors in Industrial Location: A Review," *Economic Development Quarterly* 1, February 1987, p. 81.

studies found noneconomic factors to have at least some influence on location. Education, unionization, personal reasons, business climate, energy, and familiarity with local conditions have been added to the must have/want list. In contrast, in his review of 17 locational studies conducted prior to 1963, Morgan (1964) found the traditional locational factors to be practically the only factors that mattered.

Third, the primary impact of technological change is the reduced significance of proximity to raw materials as a locational factor. Technology increased the number of steps in the production process, reduced the importance of raw materials, and lowered transportation costs. One consequence has been a shift in the growth of manufacturing activities from the resource-rich Midwest to areas of the country where markets are expanding, such as the Southwest and Far West.

Fourth, studies have found that, in recent years, state and local taxes have had an important effect on business location, particularly within metropolitan areas where business property taxes can vary substantially among jurisdictions. Thus, contrary to what the earlier literature suggested, it would be imprudent to ignore taxes as one of the important factors that influence the industrial development of regions (Hekman, 1985; Grant, 1985). Nevertheless, the preponderance of evidence suggests that state and local tax policies *alone* will do little to change the economic fortune of regions.

Fifth, there are many more locational factors today than in the 1960s. Four different factors received a ranking of "most important" in one or more of the nine studies conducted since 1975.

Typically, recent studies found that markets and availability of labor were still the most important locational factors (Premus, 1982; Schmenner, 1982; Kieschnick, 1981; *Fortune,* 1977). However, personal preferences of company executives were considered to be important in corporate headquarters decisions (Kieschnick, 1981). Central cities were unlikely to be considered as locational sites except for corporate headquarters. Finally, *Fortune* (1977) found that western Europe and Latin America, particularly Brazil, were likely overseas locations. Companies look for political calm and stability, but possible locations can no longer be automatically limited to one country.

Future Locational Factors

The corporate facility planner is dealing with issues that will influence his company's assets 30 years in the future—well into the 21st century. Many loans taken in 1995 to finance new facilities will mature after 2020. Major downtown developments have even longer expected economic lives. This means that facility planners are today planning for events years in the future.

TABLE 2–5   Factors Influencing Future Locational Choices

Most Significant before 2000	*Most Significant after 2000*
(1) Transportation	
• Piggyback services between trucks, trains, ships, and freight helicopters	• 30 minutes air service between United States, Europe and the Far East
• Corporate internal airlines	• Private commercialization of space
• Collision-avoidance avionics will reduce airport congestion	• Computer-controlled cars driven on selected express freeway routes
• Computer controlled sails on ocean-going vessels	• Newspapers will be delivered by facsimile printing in home
• Government-subsidized tax: fleets as feeders to rapid transit systems	
(2) Political-Legislative	
• Global agreements to allow more data and information transfer	• Laws may regulate use and behavior of robots
• International agreements regarding control of multinational corporations	• A world monetary unit will be adopted to facilitate international trade
• Water conservation legislation will limit development prospects	• Leading cities will be multiloop cities, having two or more perimeter routes
• A national land-use policy will be enacted	• Urban parks will be enclosed and climate controlled
• No urban or industrial construction on prime agricultural land will be permitted without state or federal approval	
(3) Technology	
• Permanently manned space stations will be in orbit	• A child will be born in space
• A process for economically desalting sea water will be possible	• Energy will be plentiful and inexpensive
• Product life cycle will get shorter, requiring shorter amortization periods	• The human brain will be linked to a computer
• Acquisition, strategy, and distribution of body parts will be a fast-growth industry	• Large-scale agriculture using untreated sea water will be possible

SOURCE: McKinley Conway, *A Technology Review and Forecast for Development Strategists* (Atlanta, Ga.: Conway Publishing, 1986).

The speed with which locational factors can emerge as important can be understood by examining changes that occurred between 1956 and 1986. During that period, the interstate highway system was developed and jet aircraft began scheduled air routes. The super airports such as Dallas–Ft. Worth and Atlanta emerged. In the realm of policy, numerous states passed right-to-work legislation and states strengthened the economic development efforts through a variety of assistance programs. The research park, the urban highway loop, metropolitan government, and other planning and zoning concepts were implemented. Technological changes, such as inexpensive air conditioning, the microchip, global satellite communication, and mass transit technologies have also influenced locational choice. Clearly, the list of factors that affect the desirability of locational choices can be greatly expanded.

In the future, rapid changes in important locational determinants can be similarly anticipated. But it is more difficult to anticipate what the changes will be. Table 2–5 summarizes well-informed speculation about some transportation, political, and technological factors that will influence future locational choices. Clearly, no one can anticipate all potential changes that can affect a locational choice. But some potential changes will be critical to firms in industries that will be directly affected. It is an interesting exercise to ask how different industries will be affected by each of the changes. Because of the long-term nature of facility location, locational planners are more future oriented than professionals in many other occupations.

SUMMARY

Many motives may influence a decision maker. Profit maximization is the behavioral assumption used most frequently to explain industrial location. However, utility maximization may diverge from profit maximization under certain circumstances. Uncertainty and high decision-making costs also make pure profit maximization difficult to operationalize.

The site-selection process may be divided into five steps: (1) need recognition, (2) forming the selection team, (3) developing criteria, (4) winnowing and focusing, and (5) reaching a final decision.

Inertia may be one of the strongest locational factors—once a firm is established at a location, many factors operate to keep it there. Minimizing transportation costs was once considered the primary location factor. Firms located away from the transportation-cost-minimizing point only if savings in the form of lower production costs could offset the higher transportation costs.

Labor, quality of life, taxes, government incentives, business climate, site costs, energy, and political stability are among the other important locational factors.

Surveys indicate that the most important traditional locational factors—markets, labor, raw materials, and transportation—continue to be important, but recent evidence indicates that other factors, such as education, quality of life, and business climate, have become relatively more important. There are many more locational factors considered by corporate planners today than in the 1950s. Continuing change in the technological, legal, and economic environment can be expected to influence locational choice.

APPENDIX: AN EXTENDED EXAMPLE AND SOME GENERALIZATIONS

An exercise will help illustrate how localized inputs and other complicating factors affect locational decisions. It is not a difficult exercise, but, because of the numerous variables that must be considered, it is long. One by one, several important assumptions are relaxed and some useful generalizations are shown.

The example is premised upon the following assumptions:

1. A fixed-proportion production function exhibiting neither economies nor diseconomies of scale is assumed. That is, per unit costs do not change with output. Land and labor are the only inputs. The total- and average-cost functions are:

$$TC = q(AC) \tag{1}$$

$$AC = 10\,W + 20\,R \tag{2}$$

where TC = total costs,
   q = Quantity of output,
   W = Wage rate per unit of labor,
   R = Cost of land per unit, and
   AC = Average cost.

2. Labor and land are localized inputs that can be purchased at each of the three cities shown in Figure 2A–1, but cannot be transported. Costs at each of the three locations differ as indicated in Table 2A–1.

3. The cost of transporting the output to the market is zero. (Assuming the transportation costs are equal for all possible locations would have the same consequence.)

4. There are no transferable inputs.

5. The firm's objective is to maximize profits.

6. The firm is a price taker. Prices are equal at all three markets, and the quantity sold at each market will not be altered by location.

All of the above assumptions will be relaxed later in the example so that the effect of different situations on the locational choice can be analyzed.

FIGURE 2A–1   Abstract Map of Locational Choices: Three Cities, Two
Material Sites

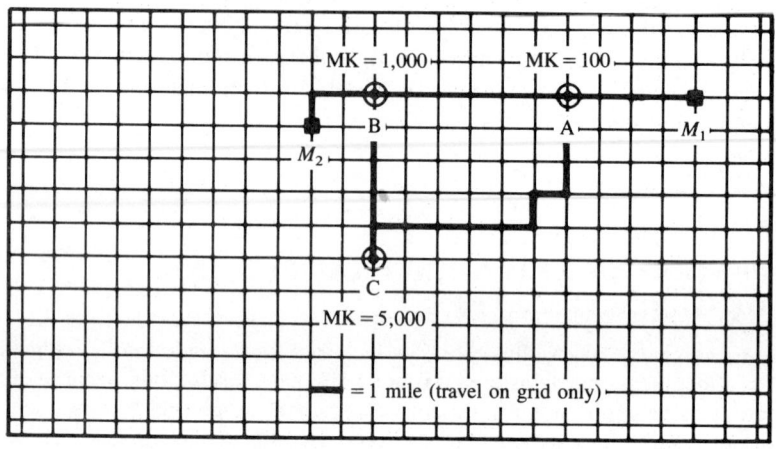

A, B, and C are possible production sites. M_1 and M_2 are sources of coal. A road
system is indicated by the grid lines.

Where Will a Single Plant Firm Locate?

If labor, a localized input, can be purchased in only one of the three places,
production must occur in A, B, or C. Since, according to assumption (6), price
and quantity will not be altered by location, production will take place at the least-
cost site. The least-cost location can be determined by "plugging-in" the costs of
labor and land at each location. Therefore, the least-cost location is B where the
per unit cost of production is $40.[4]

Technological Changes.   What would be the impact of a change in technology that reduces the importance of land in the production process? Rather than
using 20 units of land per unit of output, suppose a new production technique
allows a unit of output to be produced using only 10 units of land. Because land is
used in many other production processes, we will assume that the price of land
does not fall in response to the technological change. The pull of land would be

---

[4] $C_a = (\$1 \cdot 10) + (\$2 \cdot 20) = \$50.$

$C_b = (\$1 \cdot 10) + (\$1.50 \cdot 20) = \$40.$

$C_c = (\$.75 \cdot 10) + (\$1.75 \cdot 20) = \$42.50.$

TABLE 2A–1   Costs per Unit of Input at Three Locations

	City A	City B	City C
Cost per unit of labor	$1.00	$1.00	$ .75
Cost per unit of land	2.00	1.50	1.75

reduced since land will account for a smaller portion of costs. Place B would no longer be the least-cost production point. Rather, the firm located at C would produce at an average cost of $24.50, lower than the other two locations.[5]

In general, the fewer the units of an input needed to produce the output, the smaller the locational pull of that factor and the less important a low price for that factor will be in the locational decision.

Decreased Input Costs.   Suppose the wage rate decreased by 50 percent in all three locations, possibly because of a nationwide increase in labor supply or an across-the-board decrease in labor demand. The shift would diminish the relative attractiveness of location C. The savings per unit of labor from locating in C compared to either A or B would drop from $.25 to $.125. Since 10 units of labor are required to produce a unit of output, the savings from locating at C due to cheaper labor would drop from $2.50 to $1.25 per unit of output.

In general, price reductions will decrease the relative cost advantages of locations with that low-cost resource. Conversely, proportional cost increases will enhance the locational advantage of places with relatively low-priced inputs.

Transferable Inputs.   Next, let us add a transferable input to the initial set of assumptions. Assume five tons of coal are required per unit of output. Coal can be purchased from either of two locations, M_1 or M_2 in Figure 2A–1. Coal costs $3 per ton at both material sites and costs $.25 per ton per mile to transport. There are no terminal costs or long-haul economies. The revised cost function would become:

$$c_i = 10\ W + 20\ R + 5(k) + (.25)(5)(d) \tag{3}$$

where d = distance from the coal mine to the production site, k is the price of coal, and all other symbols are as in equation 5.

---

[5] Given $c_i = 10\ W + 10\ R$, the cost at each location now becomes:

$$C_a = 10\ (\$1) + 10\ (\$2) = \$30.$$

$$C_b = 10\ (\$1) + 10\ (\$1.50) = \$25.$$

$$C_c = 10\ (\$.75) + 10\ (\$1.70) = \$24.50.$$

Assuming the plant purchases coal from the nearest mine, the cost per unit would be $70.00 at A, $58.75 at B, and $66.50 at C.[6] Thus, B would be the least-cost location. Notice that the cost of coal was equal at the two mines. If there were a cost differential, then the decision maker would purchase from the source with the lowest delivered price.

Suppose the cost of transporting the coal increases from $.25 per mile to $3 per mile. Of course, costs will increase at all locations, but location C will be most disadvantaged from such a change because C is furthest from a source of coal and, therefore, uses more transportation inputs.

The discussion of transportation-oriented production processes concluded that, as the ideal weight (transport cost per unit of output) of a material increased, the locational pull of that input would increase. In this example, location at the material source is not possible because localized inputs are necessary. The transportation costs of these localized inputs are prohibitive. However, the effect of increasing the ideal weight of coal is to tilt the locational decision closer to the material source. If the ideal weight of coal had been increased by increasing the quantity of coal necessary to produce a unit of output (a change in technology), the result would also be to increase the pull of transferable input. In general, when the transportation cost of an input increases, locations near the source of that input will benefit relative to locations further from that source.

Output Transfer Costs. Next, the costs of transporting output to the market can be examined. Let the annual size of each market be as indicated in Figure 2A–1. Perhaps the market size was estimated based upon a target price, or perhaps the extent of market penetration was estimated by the company's marketing department. Further, assume there are no terminal costs. Transportation costs are $2 per mile per unit of output. There are no shipping costs for units sold in the city where production occurs.

In this case, if the production is at C, 100 units must be shipped to A and 1,000 units must be transported to B. Hence, transport costs will equal $10,000 (1,000 units at $2 per mile for 5 miles) to ship from C to B and $2,200 to ship from C to A. Since average costs of the total output are being compared, the total cost must be spread over the total quantity produced, including the output sold locally.[7]

In general, the greater the ideal weight of the output, the stronger the locational pull of the largest market.

---

[6] $C_a = 10\ (\$1) + 20\ (\$2) + 5\ (\$3) + (\$.25)(5)(4) = \$70.00.$

$C_b = 10\ (\$1) + 20\ (\$1.50) + 5\ (\$3) + (\$.25)(5)(3) = \$58.75$

$C_c = 10\ (\$.75) + 20\ (\$1.70) + 5\ (\$3) + (\$.25)(5)(8) = \$66.50.$

[7] $C_a = 10(\$1) + 20(\$2) + (((6)(\$2)(.1000) + (11)(\$2)(5000))/6100) = \$70.00.$

$C_b = 10(\$1) + 20(\$1.50) + (((6)(\$2)(100) + (5)(2)(5000))/6100) = \$48.39.$

$C_c = 10(\$.75) + 20(\$1.75) + (((5)(\$2)(1000) + (11)(\$2)(100)/6100) = \$44.50.$

An implicit assumption of this approach is that the seller must absorb the costs of transporting the output. If the transportation costs could be passed on to consumers in the form of higher prices, transportation costs would not be of concern. The assumption that the producer absorbs transportation costs is appro- priate if the firm sells in a competitive market with an already established price.

But what if the firm were able to pass on some of the transportation costs to consumers by charging different prices in different cities? If so, the firm can no longer simply minimize average cost to determine profits. The quantity to be sold in each city would be a function of price.

Multiple Locations and Scale Economies

If there are three markets, why not locate a facility in each city and avoid the costs of shipping the output? This outcome depends upon the potential to achieve economies of scale in production.

Figure 2A–2 illustrates three average-cost curves. The flat curve (a), ex- hibits no economies or diseconomies of scale; it is similar to the cost curve represented in equation 1. In this case, it would make sense to construct three separate facilities. However, under other circumstances, it may be more econom- ical to have only one plant.

Figure 2A–2(b) represents a cost curve that might have been estimated with engineering data. Optimum plant capacity can be considered to be between a and b. On the one hand, if each market could support a facility with a capacity of at least a units, then a firm could develop three separate facilities—one in each city. Possibly more than one facility could be located in a large city to avoid producing beyond output b. On the other hand, if the market for the three cities combined

FIGURE 2A–2   Three Typical Cost Curves

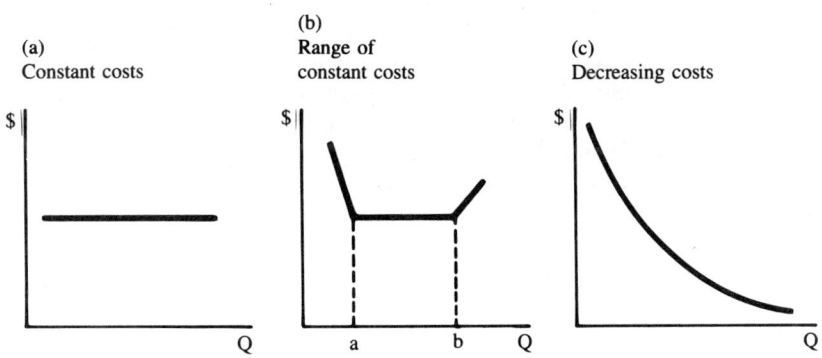

The number of locations is affected by the nature of costs. Constant costs for the plant result in many locations. Production processes with significant decreasing costs tend to result in only a few locations.

were only large enough to provide a market for a units, then a single facility would be indicated, allowing fixed costs to be spread over larger units of output. (Although, if transportation costs were high enough, a facility in all three locations could be efficient even if fewer than a units could be sold.) In order for a single facility to serve all three markets, the transportation costs of the output must not exceed the savings from the economies of plant size at a single location. Similarly, a continually declining average-cost curve shown in Figure 2A–2(c) tends to encourage the firm to have one facility to take advantage of the plant's internal economies of scale. But again, transportation costs must be low enough to allow the output to be shipped to other markets without offsetting the savings from lower average costs.

In general, few economies of scale to the plant and high ideal weights of the output orient production towards many markets. Significant economies of scale and low-output transfer costs mitigate towards production at one site.

Input Substitution

Throughout this exercise, we have assumed only one recipe for producing the product. In reality, a producer may substitute a relatively cheaper input for a more expensive one. Given the original price ratios described in the second assumption, a plant located at B might use more land (the relatively cheaper input) and less labor (the relatively expensive input) than if it were to be located at A or C, assuming, of course, that an alternative production process were available. Suppose an alternative way of producing the product existed with an associated cost function of:

$$c = 6\,W + 22.5\,R \tag{4}$$

In this case, the average cost of producing at B would equal \$39.75 (based upon the original assumptions), so a firm located at B would use the alternative production technique. However, if the firm at A switched to the alternative technology, its average costs would increase. Thus, the possibility exists that firms will produce the same output using different input mixes depending upon location. Changes in the quantity of output or the scope of output (multiple products) may also alter the optimum recipes. In general, the more production recipes, the weaker the locational pull of any particular site.

Many theoretical production functions tacitly assume a smooth ability to substitute one input for another. However, most engineering-based production functions assume limited substitution of inputs. Thus, most locational decisions are analyzed around one or two relatively linear, fixed-proportion production functions.

REFERENCES

Alexander Grant and Co. *General Manufacturing Climate of the Forty-Eight Contiguous States of America.* Chicago: Alexander Grant, January–February 1985, pp. 1–12.

Bartik, Timothy. "Business Locational Decisions in the U.S.: Estimates of the Effects of Unionization, Taxes and Other Characteristics of the States." *Journal of Business and Economic Statistics* 3, 1984, pp. 14–22.

Blair, John P., and Robert Premus. "Choosing a Location for an Industrial Facility: What Influences the Corporate Decision Maker?" *Perspective* 14, 1987, pp. 1–12.

Carlton, D. "The Location and Employment Choices of New Firms: An Econometric Model with Discrete and Continuous Endogenous Variables." *Review of Economics and Statistics* 65, 1983, pp. 440–49.

_____. "Why New Firms Locate Where They Do: An Econometric Model in Interregional Movements and Regional Growth." ed. W. Wheaton. Washington, D.C., The Urban Institute, 1979.

Charney, A. H. "Intraurban Manufacturing Locational Decisions and Local Tax Differentials." *Journal of Urban Economics* 14, 1983, pp. 184–205.

Erickson, Rodney A. "Business Climate Studies: A Critical Evaluation." *Economic Development Quarterly* 1, no. 1, 1987, pp. 62–72.

"Facility Location Decisions." New York: *Fortune,* 1977.

Hekman, John S. "Survey of Locational Decisions in the South." *Economic Review,* June 1982, pp. 6–19.

Hoover, Edgar M. *The Location of Economic Activity.* New York: McGraw-Hill, 1948.*

Hoover, Edgar M., and Frank Giarratani. *An Introduction to Regional Economics.* 3rd ed. New York: Alfred A. Knopf, 1984.

Isard, Walter. *Introduction to Regional Science.* Englewood Cliffs, N.J.: Prentice Hall, 1975, chapters 6 and 7.

Kieschnick, Michael. *Taxes and Growth: Business Incentives and Economic Development.* Washington, D.C.: Council of State Planning Agencies, 1981.

Losch, August. *The Location of Economic Activity.* New York: McGraw-Hill, 1948.*

Morgan, W. *The Effects of State and Local Tax and Financial Incentives on Industrial Location.* Ph.D. dissertation, University of Colorado, 1964.

Norgaard, Richard. "Coevolutionary Development Potential." *Land Economics* 60, 1984, pp. 159–167.

Papke, Leslie E. "Subnational Taxation and Capital Mobility: Estimates of Price Elasticities." *Motivational Tax Journal* 40, no. 2, June 1987, pp. 141–203.

Premus, Robert. "Locational High-Technology Firms and Regional Economic Development." Washington, D.C.: U.S. Congress, Joint Economic Committee, 1982.

Roback, Jennifer. "Wages, Rents, and the Quality of Life." *Journal of Political Economy* 90, no. 6, 1982, pp. 1257–78.

Romans, T., and G. Sabrahamanyan. "State and Local Taxes, Transfers, and Regional Economic Growth." *Southern Economic Journal* 46, 1979, pp. 435–44.

Schmenner, Roger W. "Locational Decisions of Large Firms: Implications for Public Policy." *Commentary,* January 1981, pp. 3–7.

————. *Making Business Location Decisions.* Englewood Cliffs, N.J.: Prentice Hall, 1982.

Skoro, Charles L. "Ranking of State Business Climates." *Economic Development Quarterly* 2, no. 2, May 1988, pp. 138–52.

Stevens, Benjamin H. "Location of Economic Activities: The JRS Contribution to the Research Literature." *Journal of Regional Science* 25, no. 4, November 1985, pp. 663–85.

Thisse, Jacques-Francois. "Location Theory, Regional Science and Economics." *Journal of Regional Science* 27, no. 4, November 1987, pp. 519–28.

Wasylenko, Michael. "The Effects of Business Climate on Employment Growth in the States between 1973 and 1980." Report for the Minnesota Tax Study Commission, 1984.

White, Sammis B. "Reservation Wages: Your Community May Be Competitive." *Economic Development Quarterly* 1, no. 1, February 1987, pp. 18–29.

* Classics.

Chapter Three

Market Areas and Urban Systems

The previous chapter discussed individual location decisions. This chapter shows how individual locational choices of firms may result in the formation of cities and networks of cities. The logic of a system of cities will be built based solely upon economic concepts. A wide range of topics, from spatial demand to market areas to a hierarchy of cities, will be covered as this system of cities is constructed. The urban patterns that result from the theoretical approach sometimes differ from observed patterns because the assumptions set forth in the model may not square with reality. Nevertheless, the chapter describes important tendencies that influence urban development.

First, demand is presented in a spatial context. The analysis is different from traditional discussions of demand that ignore the spatial dimension. Spatial variations in demand give rise to market areas. The further a consumer is from the producer, the more costly the delivered price and, hence, the smaller the quantity demanded. Competition among producers also affects the size of market areas. Central-place theory is described in the second section. It shows how producers, who locate in the center of their particular market areas, contribute to the development of a hierarchial system of cities. An evaluation of central-place theory is presented in the third section. The final section describes some techniques that can be used to measure the extent of market areas.

DEMAND AND MARKET AREAS

A market area is the region in which a product is sold. This section examines the nature of market areas. In order to focus on the principal economic forces that shape a product's market area, it is useful to assume an economy existing on a homogeneous plain. In other words, natural resources and other locational features such as climate and population density are the same. Assume further that the plain is initially populated by self-sufficient families. That is, they produce all their own food, clothing and do not rely on outside producers. Let transportation costs be equal in all directions and proportional to distance. After developing this restrictive model, assumptions may be relaxed. As the assumptions are relaxed, a framework will exist to help understand the importance of geographic irregularities.

Under the above conditions, production would concentrate at particular places due to economies of scale in production. Some of the original self-sufficient families would specialize, producing products at lower costs than their neighbors. The area in which they sold their output would constitute their market area. Producers would be the only sellers within their area. The market area would be limited because the larger the area serviced, the greater the transportation costs at the market fringe. Thus, unless economies of scale were substantial, transportation costs would prevent one family from servicing the entire nation. In order to see how the above implications are derived from economic principles, it is useful to first understand price funnels.

Price Funnels and Demand Cones

The nature of market areas can be better understood by examining demand in a spatial setting. Traditional demand analysis as described in most economics textbooks states that the demand curve shows the quantity of a good consumers would be willing and able to buy at each price in a range of prices during a given time period. The stability of the demand curve depends upon (1) consumer tastes, (2) income, (3) prices of related products (complements and substitutes), (4) market size, and (5) expectations. When any one of these factors change, the entire demand curve shifts. Furthermore, the value of a product is understood to have time and place utility. For example, a consumer might pay five dollars for a pencil if she is in class and a final exam is being given. Regional economists make the spatial dimension explicit by showing how location influences product demand.

Price Funnels. Suppose a producer operating on the "uniform plane" initially priced a product at P_1 in Figure 3–1. The price represents the selling price at the establishment (called the FOB price for "free on board"). A consumer buying the product must pay the FOB price plus the transfer costs. Transportation costs include monetary and nonmonetary costs. Thus, time and aggravation are "transportation costs" just as gasoline and automobile depreciation are transportation costs. There are two important implications of the existence of transfer costs. First, transportation costs drive a wedge between the cost to consumers (the price plus

FIGURE 3–1   Demand with and without Transportation Costs

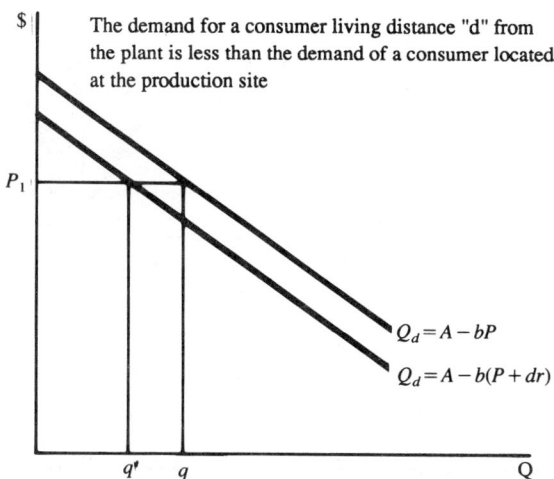

transportation costs) and the revenues received by producers. Figure 3–1 compares an individual's demand for a product, assuming no transportation costs ($Q_d = A - bP$), and the demand when transportation costs are included ($Q_d = A - b(P + dr)$). The spatial demand equation assumes that transportation costs are proportional to distance since transportation costs are equal to a uniform rate, r, times the distance, d. The transport-adjusted demand curve is below the demand curve that ignores transport costs, reflecting the fact that if the transportation costs are borne by consumers, they will purchase less.

Second, the cost to consumers will differ depending on how near to the producer they live even though the FOB price may be equal for everyone. This aspect of cost is illustrated in Figure 3–2(a). The FOB price is P_1 and transportation costs are r per round-trip mile. (Assume ½ r transportation costs to the factory and ½ r from factory to home.) A consumer located d miles from the establishment would pay P_1 for the product and dr in transport costs. If the price-distance line is spun to reflect consumers located in all directions, a price funnel is derived.

Demand Cones.   The concept of a price funnel can be used to derive a distance demand curve—a curve that shows the quantity that would be purchased by consumers living various distances from the factory. There will be a different distance demand curve for each FOB price. In order to

FIGURE 3–2   Price Distance Relationships

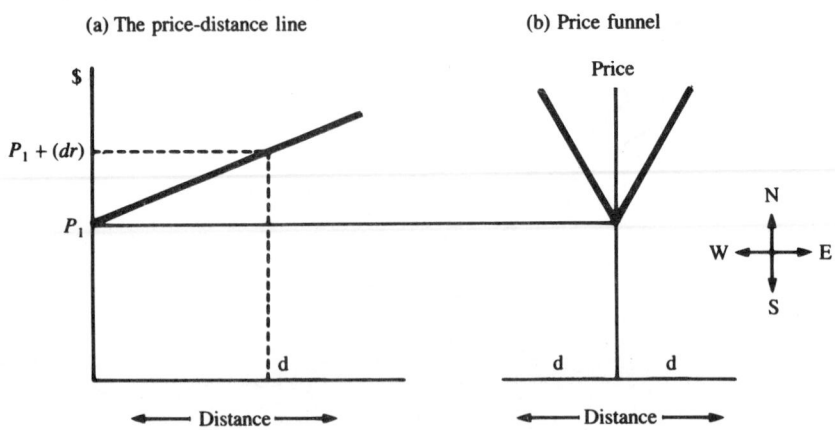

The price-distance line shows that for an FOB priced P_1, the effective price to the customer increases with distance. By spinning the price-distance line in all directions, a price funnel can be derived.

understand the distance demand curve, assume consumers have identical preferences and the FOB price is established at P_1. Panel (a) of Figure 3–3 shows part of a price funnel; cost to the consumer increases with distance from the factory. The transport costs, *dr,* constitute the difference between the delivered cost and the FOB price. Panel (b) is the demand curve of a representative consumer. It shows the quantity demanded at each delivered price paid by the consumer. Panel (c) is simply a mapping graph that relates quantity to quantity. Panel (d) shows the quantity-distance curve. It shows that quantity demanded will decrease with distance. Consumers living next to the producer will buy most at each FOB price because they face the lowest cost. Beyond d_2, price to the consumer is so high that no units will be purchased. Notice that the quantity-distance function is valid only for a given FOB price. If the FOB price were increased, the quantity-distance function would decrease (shift to the left).

The quantity-distance relationship represents demand extending in one direction from the factory. The total demand along that "road" would equal the sum of the height of the demand curve times the population density at each point. Since it was assumed that demand density was equal in all directions, the total quantity demanded at P_{FOB} could be

FIGURE 3–3   Derivation of a Distance Demand Curve

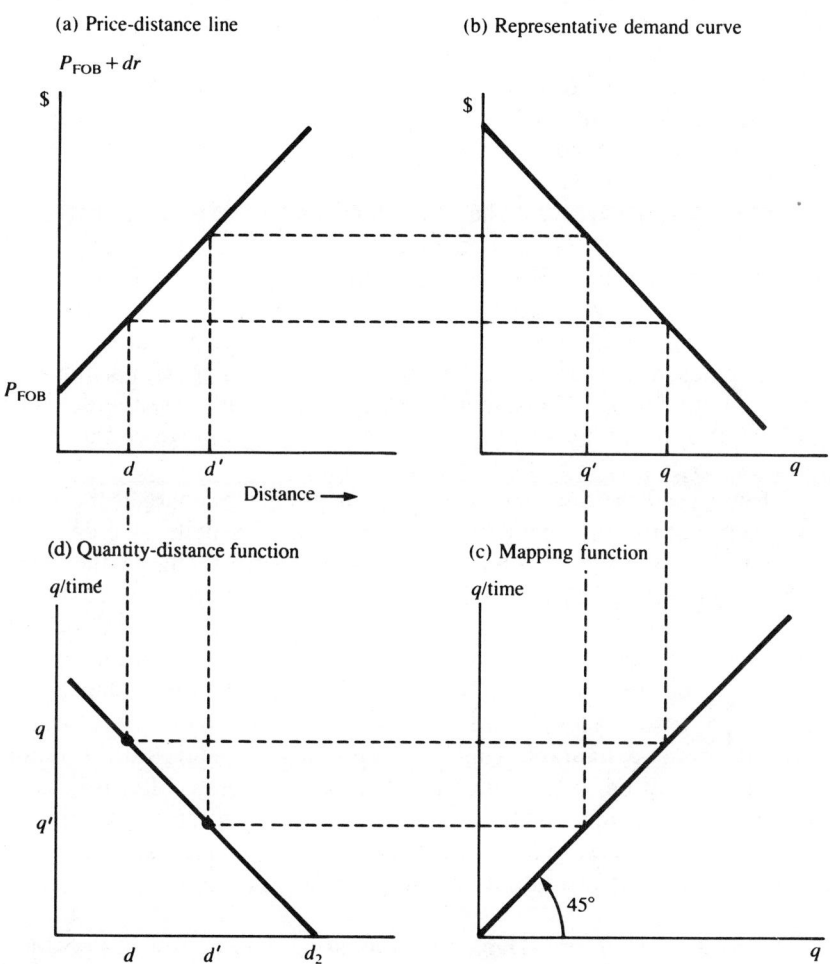

(a) Price-distance line

$P_{FOB} + dr$

(b) Representative demand curve

(d) Quantity-distance function

(c) Mapping function

The quantity-distance function can be derived from a price-distance line and a traditional demand curve.

Adapted from Edgar M. Hoover and Frank Giarratani, *An Introduction to Regional Economics,* 3rd ed. (New York: Alfred A. Knopf, 1984).

pictured by rotating the quantity-distance curve. The result is a demand cone.

Figure 3–4 represents a demand cone. The height of the demand cone at any point represents the quantity demanded at that location. The volume of the demand cone represents the total quantity demanded at the FOB price, p.[1] Figure 3–4 shows the quantity demanded for two individuals, one located at distance d and the other d' from the factory; they will consume q and q' units, respectively. Of course, a separate demand cone should be constructed for each FOB price. Notice that for any given FOB price the demand cone indicates the geographic market size as well as the total quantity demanded.

Who Pays Delivery?   The preceding analysis assumed that consumers paid different prices depending on where they live. Most retail products have uniform FOB prices regardless of where the consumer lives; consumers pay the cost of travel to and from the store. Wholesale products are generally priced in the same way. Some producers charge the consumer for delivery with delivery prices increasing with distance in discontinuous blocks. Consumers directly or indirectly pay the delivery costs in all of the above cases. There are many ways in which the transportation costs can be shifted to consumers.

How would the analysis be affected if producers charged the same delivered price to consumers? A pizza parlor with free delivery is an example of the alternative possibility in which producers charge the same delivered price to everyone. A furniture store that offers free delivery is another example. In these cases, a producer would be concerned about *net price*—revenue received minus delivery cost. As a customer's distance from the store increases, net revenue decreases. For instance, the pizza parlor receives less net revenue when it sells to consumers located further from the restaurant. Thus, when producers absorb transportation costs, they may be able to increase their market areas. Regardless of whether the consumer or the producer directly pays the transportation costs, there is a decrease in the quantity producers can sell at various net revenues as distance from the production point increases.

Derivation of a Firm's Demand: Summary.   We are now in a position to summarize our understanding of the spatial demand curve. The quantity demanded can be conceptualized as the area under the demand cone at each FOB price. Thus, each point on a traditional demand curve can be derived as follows:

---

[1] The total quantity demanded represented by Figure 3–4 is:

$$Q = \pi D((a - bp)^3/(3(br))$$

Where D = population density j per unit of area, $a - bp$ = quantity demanded by individuals who do not pay transport costs, and r = transportation costs per unit.

FIGURE 3–4   A Demand Cone

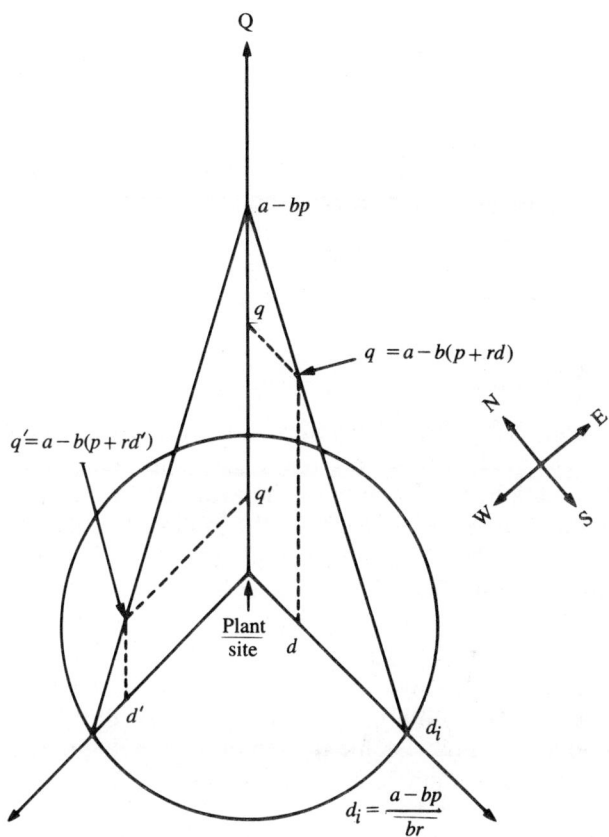

A demand cone shows the quantity sold at each location at a given FOB price. The area under the demand cone represents total quantity demanded at each FOB price.

1. Generate a price funnel (Figure 3–2(b)) for an FOB price. The price funnel shows the delivered price for consumers located at various distances from the plant.
2. Examine individual demand to determine quantity demanded for each delivered price associated with the FOB price.
3. Construct a quantity-distance function (Figure 3–3(d)) from the information in the first two steps.
4. "Spin" the quantity-distance function to create a demand cone (Figure

3–4). The volume of the demand cone represents one point on the market demand curves.

5. Repeat the process for each FOB price to derive a complete demand curve.

Two factors explain the slope of the spatial demand curve. First, an increase in FOB price normally will cause consumers who remain in the market to purchase fewer units. Second, consumers on the market fringe will no longer purchase the product. The total market will shrink both in numbers of consumers and in area. Thus, as price increases, the spatial aspect of demand will cause quantity demanded to drop more rapidly than the nonspatial case due to geographic market shrinkage.

Pricing Decisions

We have described how demand is derived in a spatial context. All of the factors discussed in basic economics are important determinants of demand. In addition, the location of the producer relative to customers affects demand. This section describes the pricing decision. Thus far, we have assumed the producer is a monopolist. There may be other producers of the same product, but for now let's assume that they are far enough apart that they do not infringe on each other's customers. As long as customers have a preference for nearby producers, there will always be some product differentiation. Hence, the perfectly competitive demand curve (completely horizontal) will not exist. Although the model insures that all producers will have some degree of monopoly power, some producers may price discriminate and others may not.

Nonprice Discrimination.   Assume that a producer will sell the product to all customers for the same price or, if there are price differences, they reflect cost differences. A spatial monopolist, like all profit maximizers, will set an FOB price that equates marginal cost and marginal revenue (MC = MR). Figure 3–5 illustrates the pricing decision of a producer. Price is set at $7. Profits are 12,000 × ($7 − $6.50), or $6,000. If firms were free to enter the market, the above-normal profits would not be sustainable. At the same time that price is established, the geographic market area will be determined. If the firm were to lower its price, it would expand the geographic market area, but profits would decrease. The additions to total revenue (MR) would be less than the additions to cost (MC). If there were no quantity at which price was greater than average cost, the product would not be produced.

Price Discrimination.   Price discrimination occurs when a product sells for a higher price in one location or market than in another location

FIGURE 3–5   Profit-Maximizing Monopolist: No Price Discrimination

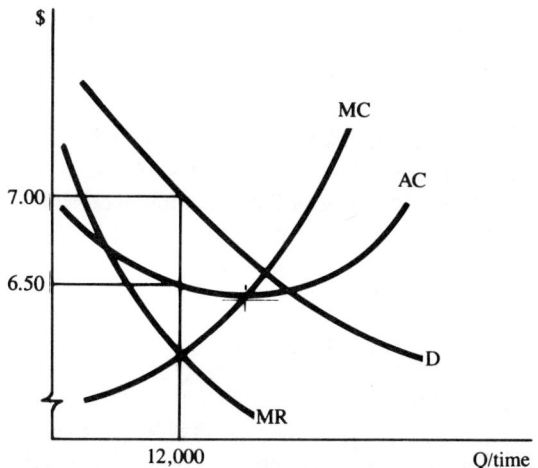

A profit-maximizing firm will produce the level of output where MC = MR. At that point, 12,000 units will be sold at a price of $7.00 each. Average costs will be $6.50. Total profits will equal $6,000.

or market and price differences cannot be explained by cost factors. Some monopolists have opportunities to price discriminate. In order to price discriminate, three conditions must be met: (1) The seller must be able to separate markets; otherwise, some individuals would purchase the product in the lower-price market and resell it in the higher-price market. Arbitrage would iron out price differences. (2) The costs of separating the markets must not be prohibitive. (3) The elasticities of demand must be different among the markets if the price discrimination is to be profitable. In other words, some consumers must be more sensitive to price increases than others. Consequently, a producer may charge a higher price to customers who are less price sensitive with less fear that consumers will reduce the quantity demanded. Sellers want to discriminate in favor of customers with elastic demands because they are most sensitive to price.

Spatial monopolists frequently have opportunities to price discriminate because customers are geographically separated. Furthermore, the more distant customers are likely to have more elastic demands—that is, they will be more sensitive to a change in price. There are two reasons why more distant customers will be more sensitive to price. First, nearby customers pay a lower price and, therefore, the price is a lower portion of their income. Second, distant customers are closer to other firms, so they have alternative suppliers. Since nearby customers are less sensitive to price (have more inelastic demands), price discrimination will tend to favor distant consumers.

"Dumping" is an example of spatial price discrimination. Dumping occurs when products are sold in distant markets at cut-rate prices. Foreign markets are separated from domestic markets by transportation costs, tariffs, and other institutional barriers. Thus, arbitrage is difficult. Furthermore, a domestic monopolist may have competitors in international markets. Therefore, the demand in foreign markets is likely to be more elastic than in the domestic market.

Competition for Markets

Suppose a producer is successful and earns economic profits as shown in Figure 3–5. Will the excess profits remain in the long run? Assuming that other potential producers have knowledge of market opportunities and freedom of entry, new producers will enter the industry in search of profits. Producers will locate away from each other to avoid competition. Thus, new producers will carve out their own market areas and earn profits similar to the representative firm shown in Figure 3–5. The market areas for the group of spatial monopolists are shown in panel (a) of Figure 3–6. In Figure 3–6(a), the producers are separated so each establishment is a monopolist in its own market areas. Each producer earns excess profits. However, the excess profits will encourage still more producers, and the landscape will become increasingly crowded as shown in Figure 3–6(b). A point may be reached where no new firms can enter the market without directly competing with an existing producer; hence, new firms take customers from existing firms and market areas shrink. However, in the situation illustrated in 3–6(b), some unserved areas exist. If still more firms entered the market, hexagonal market areas as shown in panel (c) might result.

Hexagons are an efficient shape for filling an area. However, they are not the only possible outcome of spatial competition. Suppose every firm were earning slightly above-normal profits when the market areas were tightly packed but still circular as shown in Figure 3–6(b). In that case, an additional producer may not be able to operate profitably while some consumers would be unserved. Tightly packed circles with some unserved areas could represent an equilibrium. Therefore, there is a degree of indeterminacy about market size. The important point is that, as firms enter the industry in search of profits, profits of existing firms drop and market areas shrink.

The equilibrium shown in Figure 3–7(c) is similar to the outcome suggested for firms in monopolistically competitive industries. Even if all

FIGURE 3–6   Market Areas of Spatial Markets

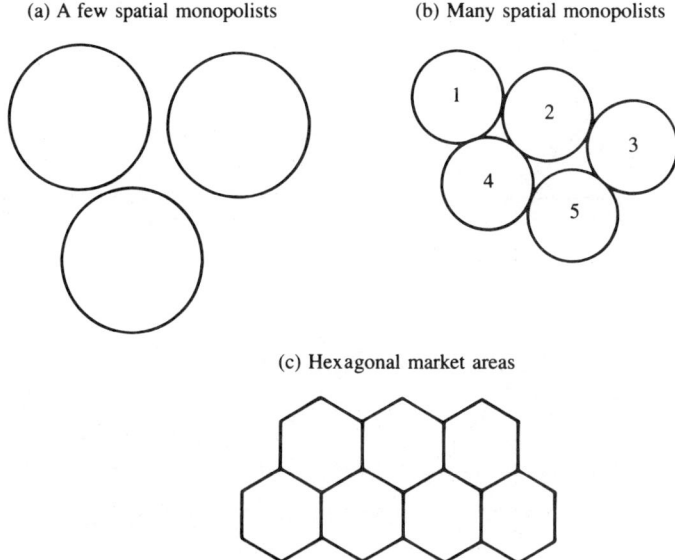

(a) A few spatial monopolists

(b) Many spatial monopolists

(c) Hexagonal market areas

If monopolists earn profits, competitors will enter the industry, decreasing profits and market areas.

producers sold identical products, the spatial perspective indicates that demand for the product would be downsloping—not horizontal as suggested in the traditional discussions of the purely competitive industry. The spatial analysis indicates that monopolistic competition may better depict markets that would otherwise be classified as competitive. Essentially, producers are differentiated by location. Consumers have preferences for producers' locations just as they have preferences for particular brands of very similar products.

Extent of Market Areas

The geographic size of a product's market area is of interest to regional economics. Products with large market areas will have fewer production centers and will be further apart than establishments with small market areas. The spacing of production centers has important implications for the development of cities.

Threshold Demand and Range.   "Threshold" and "range" are useful concepts for understanding market areas. The threshold demand is the

FIGURE 3–7   Equilibrium of Spatial Producers

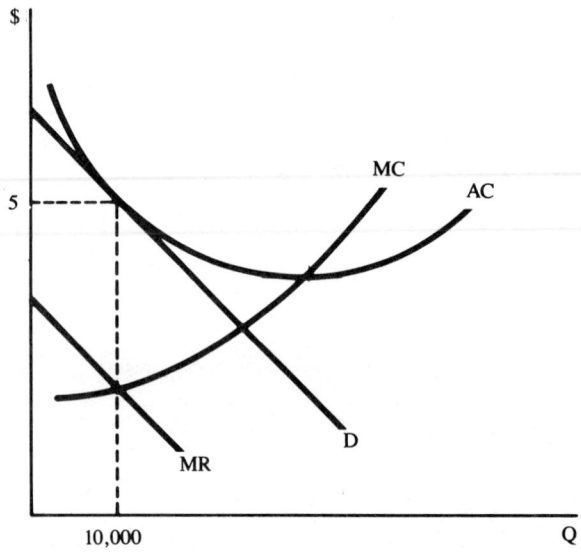

When revenue is just sufficient to cover costs, the firm will earn only normal profits as shown. Market areas may shrink, and as that happens, the demand curve will decrease.

minimum quantity a producer must sell in order to earn at least normal profits. It may be thought of as the break-even quantity. Figure 3–8 shows the geographic threshold associated with a quantity demanded of 10,000 units (the break-even quantity in Figure 3–7). Assuming individuals consume roughly equal amounts regardless of where they live, the threshold quantity can be associated with a threshold population. For instance, if the typical individual consumes 10 units per year at a price of $5, the threshold population associated with Figure 3–8 would be 10,000/10, or 1,000. The threshold population is also associated with a threshold geographic market often called the inner range. For a firm that is producing an amount just sufficient for the inner range, price, average total cost, and average revenue are equal.

Variations in threshold size explain why some economic activities are more common than others. Activities with very low demand thresholds such as filling stations, food stores, churches, and restaurants are more common than activities with high thresholds such as undertakers, public accountants, and physicians.

FIGURE 3–8   Threshold and Range

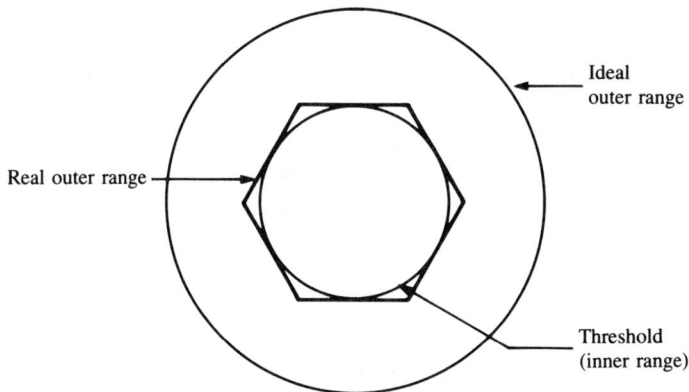

The threshold is the market size that will allow a firm to break even. The ideal outer range is the distance at which the transportation cost makes the product prohibitively expensive. The actual outer range represents the actual market area.

The "ideal outer range" of a good is the maximum distance individuals are willing to travel to purchase a good at the lowest possible average cost. It is the location where consumer cost is so high that demand for the product is zero. Competition from other producers normally reduces the distance a consumer will travel below the ideal outer range. The "real outer range" is the maximum distance a customer will travel in a competitive environment. It is the actual market area of a firm.

The real outer range describes the firm's actual market area. In Figure 3–8, the firm has an opportunity to make excess profits because the real outer range is larger than the threshold level. Of course, if the producer is inefficient and produces at above the minimum necessary average costs, the opportunity to earn excess profits will be lost. When threshold and real outer range are equal, only normal profits (normal return to owner) are possible even if the producer operates efficiently.

Determinants of Market Size.   Three factors determine the size of the market area for a particular product: (1) If *economies of scale* are significant, producers will be able to offset some or all of the additional transportation costs of serving distant markets. Thus, establishments in industries with significant economies of scale will have large market areas. Economies of scale are often associated with high fixed costs. (2) *Demand density* is the quantity demanded per unit of land area or the quantity demanded per person times the population density. The larger the demand density the greater the number of producers that can operate in a given area. Hence, high demand-density products will have smaller market areas. (3) The effect of *transportation costs* on market size is ambiguous. Lower transport costs could cause market size to increase for some products but decrease for others. On the one hand, if scale economies exist and transportation costs decline, the product could be provided cheaper everywhere including beyond the market fringe. Thus, the decreased transportation costs would allow firms and consumers to take advantage of both scale economies and lower transportation costs by expanding the market. On the other hand, if the representative firm faces increasing cost conditions, a decrease in transportation costs will increase profits initially and may eventually attract more firms into the industry. In this case, the combination of increasing production costs may offset the lower transportation costs so that it becomes more expensive per unit to serve an expanded market. Accordingly, smaller market areas may result.

Pressures are operating to change the size of the market areas. For instance, there has been a long-term tendency for incomes and population to increase. As a result, market areas for some products, particularly retail goods, have become more dense. At the same time, economies of scale have increased in some manufacturing industries, creating a countervailing tendency.

THE URBAN HIERARCHY AND URBAN SYSTEMS

The previous section described the formation of market areas. This section shows how market areas combine to form cities and systems of cities. Once production becomes concentrated at the center of a particular market area, the economic landscape will no longer consist of families distributed evenly over a homogeneous plane. Cities will form. Some cities will be small because they are the production points of only a few products with few economies of scale. Furthermore, economic forces will impose an order on the size of, spatial distribution of, and relationships among cities. This section shows how a hierarchy of central places will develop and a system of cities will emerge.

Central Places

In order to understand the development of central places, it is necessary to recognize the economic advantages that accrue when two or more plants locate together. These advantages are termed "agglomeration economies" (see Chapter 4). Economies of agglomeration strongly influence where plants locate. Producers will trade off some of the advantages of locating near their customers in order to gain advantages from locating near other producers. Examples of agglomeration economies include shared parking among retail stores, shared roads, and other shared public infrastructures. Two different activities may have similar, but not identical, market areas. Because of agglomeration economies, they may find it advantageous to locate together. If there were no competitors, the establishments could still have market areas of different sizes. However, as other firms enter the landscape, the real outer range of the two market areas will tend to become identical. Fixed transportation systems and geopolitical barriers will reinforce the tendency of establishments to share market areas. Thus, there will be fewer market areas than products; producers with similar threshold market sizes will find it advantageous to serve the same market areas.

Assume there is a fixed number of different market sizes reflecting the trade-off between ideal market areas and agglomeration economies. Market sizes will range from small areas for convenience goods to markets that include the entire region or multiregion areas. Commodities or service providers with similar threshold markets will locate together, and market areas will be standardized. Furthermore, assume that some of the producers with small market areas locate in the same place as producers serving large market areas. This assumption will economize on the number of cities, reduce infrastructure needs, and make other agglomeration economies possible.

A hierarchy of central places will result from the sharing of common locations. Many cities will be the site of only a few producers serving small market areas. These first-order central places—hamlets—will provide services such as grocery, drug store, church, and so forth. The rural population is the hinterland (market area) for the first-order central places. Second-order central places will provide all of the services provided by first-order central places because residents and the rural population near the second-order central places represent an effective demand. In addition, second-order central places will provide services that have larger threshold markets. Clothing and furniture stores are examples of additional functions that might be offered by second-order central places. The market area of the second-order goods and service producers will include several first-order central places. For example, if a resident of a first-order central place needed a new suit, it might be purchased in the nearest second-order city. First-order places are part of the second-order city's hinterland.

Second-order cities will be part of the hinterland of third-order cities, and so on, up the hierarchy. The largest cities will be the production centers for establishments with the largest market areas, but they will also provide lower-order functions. A functional regularity exists in the system of cities. Higher-ordered cities will provide some services to lower-ordered places in their hinterland. Figure 3–9, a scalogram, illustrates a hypothetical distribution of activities according to the rank of the central place. Of course, in reality, the functional separations will not be so regular. Some higher-ordered cities might have missing functions; say, they may lack a grain elevator and some lower-ordered cities might have functions that particular larger cities do not have. A listing such as Figure 3–9 is useful in identifying activities that might be appropriate for development in an area. For instance, if a function is unexpectedly absent and a more detailed study fails to uncover any reasonable explanation for the absence, that activity might be a successful new business possibility.

There will be a spatial regularity to city systems as well as a functional regularity. If establishments in first-order towns have market areas of radius r, then first-order towns will be $2r$ apart. Higher-ordered places will be further apart than first-order places because some of the producers

---

Perspectives on Market Size

The geographic size of markets was examined empirically by Leonard W. Weiss. He defined a market area as the radius from a plant within which 80 percent of a plant's output was shipped.

Weiss concluded that:

1. There are wide variations in market size depending upon the product.
2. Manufacturing goods generally have large, multistate market areas.
3. Only a minority of markets are unequivocally national in scope.

Radius of Market Areas
(product [radius in miles])

Soft drinks (68)	Soap and detergents (572)
Concrete products (144)	Flour and grain products (682)
Ice cream (158)	Truck trailers (780)
Bricks (200)	Fertilizers (828)
Metal cans (362)	Tires and inner tubes (833)
Malt liquors (370)	Cigarettes (1108)
Railroad cars (542)	

Berry and Garrison examined market size in terms of the minimum population needed to support an economic activity in Snohomish County, Washington. They defined threshold size as the smallest population size of a community in which the function exists. Their findings are summarized below:

Perspectives on Market Size (*concluded*)

Function (threshold size)	Function (threshold size)
Filling station (196)	Furniture store (542)
Church (256)	Veterinarian (579)
Tavern (282)	Apparel store (590)
Elementary school (322)	Bank (616)
Appliance store (385)	Florist (729)
Auto dealer (398)	Local taxi (762)
Dentist (426)	Shoe repair shop (896)
Drug store (458)	Sheet metal work (10176)
Meeting hall (525)	Hospital (1159)

SOURCES: Leonard W. Weiss, "The Geographic Size of Markets in Manufacturing," *Review of Economics and Statistics* 54 (1972), pp. 255–57; and Bert L. Berry and W. L. Garrison, "Functional Bases of the Central-Place Hierarchy," *Economic Geography* 34 (1958), pp. 304–22.

in these places serve larger market areas. Furthermore, each second-order city includes some first-order cities in its hinterland. Likewise, since first-order cities have smaller market areas, more first-order places will exist than second-order places.

Figure 3–10 (p. 81), is a stylized map of a system of cities in our theoretical urban hierarchy. It shows villages, towns, metropolitan areas, and one capital. In other words, there are only four different market sizes, and producers locate according to the size of the area they serve. The market areas of higher-order places are also identified. Each town has six villages in its hinterland; each metropolis has six towns and thirty-six villages in its hinterland. The largest city is the "capital" of the region. Its hinterland includes 6 metropolitan areas, 36 (6 × 6) towns, and 216 (36 × 6) villages (not all of the villages are pictured).

Population size can also be understood within the framework of the central-place model by assuming that local population is a function of employment; employment depends upon output; output in turn is determined by the size of the market served by the central place. First-order cities will serve themselves and their hinterland. Since higher-order cities serve several lower-order cities, market size increases exponentially up the urban hierarchy. Hence, so does population. This intuitive description of the size distribution of cities is developed more rigorously in the appendix.

Central-place theory emphasizes trading patterns to explain the large number of small places compared to the number of large places. Evans

FIGURE 3–9   Hypothical Hierarchy of Urban Functions

Level of Convenience	Economic Functions	Order of Central Places					
		6	5	4	3	2	1
Minimum	Filling stations	x	x	x	x	x	x
convenience	Grocery	x	x	x	x	x	x
Full	Eating places	x	x	x	x	x	
convenience	Hardware store	x	x	x	x	x	
	Drug store	x	x	x	x	x	
	Laundry	x	x	x	x		
	Clothing store	x	x	x	x		
Low-order	Appliances	x	x	x	x		
specialty	Hotel, motel	x	x	x			
	Shoe store	x	x	x			
	Sporting goods	x	x	x			
	Radio	x	x				
High-order	Paint store	x	x				
specialties	Music store	x	x				
	Antique store	x	x				
	Lumber supplies	x					
	Professional service						
Wholesale	equipment	x					
	Wholesale groceries	x					
	Bulk oil	x					
Number of cities in class		1	3	9	27	81	243

Higher-order cities have more functions than lower-order central places.

Nesting factors = 3.

(1985, p. 74) developed an alternative explanation for the size distribution of cities based upon manufacturers' preferences for cities of various sizes. It takes a large number of firms to form a large city but very few, possibly only one establishment, to employ the whole labor force of a small town. If the number of firms preferring to locate in a small town is the same as the number wishing to locate in a large city, there would be many small towns but very few large cities. Note, however, that Evans's explanation does not account for the spatial distribution of cities.

Changing Urban Patterns

The concepts of central-place theory have been used to analyze the history of the development of urban systems. Berry et al. (1988, p. 105) described two ways the urban hierarchy may have developed—from the top down or bottom up. The bottom-up possibility is that an urban system

FIGURE 3–10   Spatial Distribution of Cities

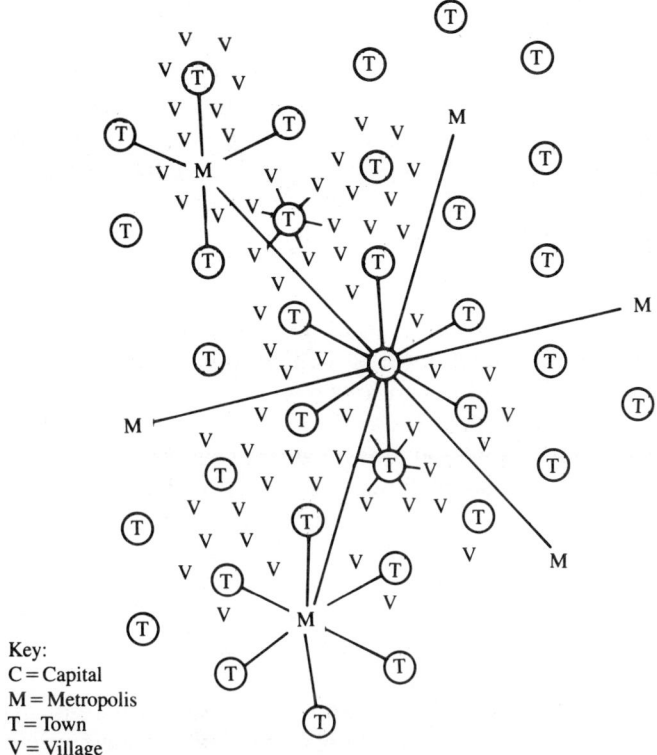

Key:
C = Capital
M = Metropolis
T = Town
V = Village

Central-place theory describes an ordered region with snowflakelike symmetry.

might have developed starting with small villages followed by towns and, eventually, metropolitan areas as larger places were added to the base of lower-order places. Parr (1978) developed a bottom-up model that might represent the development of older regions such as Europe. Alternatively, a hierarchy of urban places might grow from the top down (Vance, 1970). Top-down development represents patterns experienced by colonized areas such as the United States and Canada. In these cases, the first settlements tended to be centers of trade and administration. Settlements that developed later depended upon the original settlements for higher-order goods and services.

Once an urban system has developed, the central-place model can be used to examine forces that cause it to change. Since the system of cities is based upon market systems, the same factors that cause market areas to change will cause the hierarchial structures of cities to change. Thus, changes in transportation costs, in the scale economies of production, and in demand density are important influences on the urban hierarchy.

In general, when the optimum size of a market area declines because of increases in income, increases in population density, decreases in optimum plant size, or increased transportation costs, activities will shift towards lower-order central places. Economic activities will shift down the hierarchy, and goods previously provided exclusively by larger places will now be provided by lower-order places. In effect, the dominance of higher-order urban places will be weakened. For instance, when video cameras were introduced, they could be purchased only in specialty shops located in large metropolitan areas. As consumer acceptance increased (increasing demand density), they became available in lower-order central places. When market areas increase, possibly due to improved transportation or increases in economies of scale, the site of services will shift upward and lower-order central places will be weakened compared to larger cities.

When one or a few functions become available at a different level of the hierarchy, the economic functions of central places will change. But if the location of a large number of economic activities shifts upward or downward, an entire category of central places could disappear. Stabler and Williams (1973) documented the disappearance of some intermediate places that lost their role in serving smaller areas in the Saskatchewan area. Hence, the number of categories of central places decreased. The rural ghost towns—or near–ghost towns—apparent in many parts of the Midwest may be attributable to the tendency of farmers to bypass groceries and other service establishments in small hamlets, preferring the greater variety and other advantages of shopping in towns only slightly further away. Improved transportation and the mechanization of agriculture (lowering demand density) probably contributed to this phenomenon.

The changes discussed above should not obscure the overall stability of the urban hierarchy. If we examine a region over a period of one or two years, we would find little change in the relationship among central places. It is unlikely that a central place would disappear or that a new place would emerge. Although cities will grow at different rates, it is very rare that the primary or highest-ranking city will change. The system of cities changes slowly, partly because of inertia and the long economic life of capital investment, particularly infrastructure, and partly because new activity will have incentives to fit the existing urban grid.

The stability of places in the urban hierarchy may also be explained by the establishment of channels of interdependence. Once urban or regional linkages are created, they transmit growth from one place to another. Cities lower in the hierarchy may grow; but as they do, opportunities for growth among linked cities within the hierarchy will be created. Roads and wire connections (telegraph and telephone) are important

TABLE 3–1   A Ranking of U.S. Cities: Hierarchy of U.S. Cities 1881, 1910, 1967 and 1980

1881	*1910*	*1967*	*1980*
First Rank	*First Rank*	*First Rank*	*First Rank*
New York	New York	New York	New York
Second Rank	*Second Rank*	*Second Rank*	*Second Rank*
Philadelphia	Philadelphia	Philadelphia	Philadelphia
Chicago	Chicago	Chicago	Chicago
Boston	Boston	Boston	Boston
St. Louis	St. Louis	Washington	Washington
Baltimore	Baltimore	Los Angeles	Los Angeles
San Francisco	Pittsburgh	San Francisco	San Francisco
Cincinnati	Detroit	Detroit	Detroit
New Orleans	Cleveland		Houston
			Atlanta
Third Rank	*Third Rank*	*Third Rank*	*Third Rank*
Detroit	San Francisco	St. Louis	St. Louis
Washington	Washington	Pittsburgh	Pittsburgh
Rochester	Rochester	Dallas–Ft. Worth	Dallas–Ft. Worth
Albany	Los Angeles	Buffalo	Buffalo
Buffalo	Buffalo	Tampa	Tampa
New Haven	New Haven	Miami	Miami
Louisville	Louisville	Indianapolis	Indianapolis
Indianapolis	Indianapolis	Milwaukee	Milwaukee
Milwaukee	Milwaukee	Minneapolis–	Minneapolis–
Pittsburgh	Minneapolis–	St. Paul	St. Paul
Cleveland	St. Paul	Kansas City	Kansas City
	Kansas City	Seattle	Seattle
	Seattle	Denver	Denver
	Denver	Portland	Portland
	Portland	Cincinnati	Cincinnati
	Cincinnati	New Orleans	New Orleans
	New Orleans	San Diego	San Diego
		Baltimore	Baltimore
		Cleveland	Cleveland
			Nashville
			Des Moines
			Phoenix

SOURCE: M. Conzen, "The Maturing Urban System in the United States, 1840–1910," *Annals of the Association of American Geographers,* 1977, pp. 88–108; and J. R. Borchert, "America's Changing Metropolitan Regions," *Annals of the Association of American Geographers* 62, 1972, pp. 352–73, and author.

physical linkages that support economic linkages. The hierarchy of cities was less stable in the Southeast than in other regions both before and after the Civil War. Pred (1977) attributed the lack of stability to the fact that southeastern cities were not yet members of a regional city-system. Most southeastern cities were linked directly to New York or Philadelphia, so southern cities lacked established hinterlands. Consequently, growth opportunities occurred without going through channels of the urban hierarchy so cities in the South did not benefit from growth of other southern cities.

Table 3–1 provides an indication of the urban hierarchy and changes that have occurred. Perhaps the most notable feature is the development of more third-rank cities. Another important change (not evident in the table) is that the area represented by each city has increased. In 1881, Philadelphia represented a city. Today, it represents a multicounty urban area.

A ranking of urban areas depends upon judgment as well as data. Some analysts might argue that Los Angeles is a first-rank metropolis due to the influence of Hollywood, TV, and movie productions on American culture. Isard (1975, p. 29) has taken a more global view of the urban hierarchy. He suggested that, after WW II, London lost its dominant position in the world to the megalopolis that centers around New York and included Boston and Washington. Today, Moscow, Beijing, and Tokyo vie with New York for status as the highest-order central place in the world.

AN EVALUATION OF THE CENTRAL-PLACE APPROACH

The patterns generated by the central-place model are highly regular. There are as many size classes of cities as market sizes. Cities of the same order have equal hinterlands, offer the same services, and have the same population size. Higher-order cities provide all of the goods and services that lower-order cities provide, plus functions of producers serving the next-larger size market. Smaller cities with smaller hinterlands are more numerous and closer together than larger cities. Central places of the same order will be equal distances from one another. While residents of lower-order cities may purchase goods and services from producers located in higher-order cities, commodities will not flow from lower-ordered places up the urban hierarchy.

Considerations Extraneous to Central-Place Theory

The above sketch of the conclusions of central-place theory described a well-ordered region with snowflakelike symmetry that does not exist in reality. The conclusions, however, follow from the model's initial assumptions: (1) Economic activity occurs on a homogeneous plain (implying that production costs are not affected by natural resources); (2) Transportation costs are equal in all directions; (3) Rural markets are evenly distributed; and (4) Noneconomic factors (defense, culture, etc.) are not important to the development of cities. The combined results of these assumptions are market-oriented locational decisions by firms. Accordingly, cities are also market oriented. This section will describe some factors that alter the shape of trading areas from the idealized model. When market areas lose their symmetry, the patterns described by central-place theory will not match reality.

Spatial Differences in Production Costs.   The abstract central-place model implicitly assumed that all locations provide the same resource-cost opportunities. Therefore, firms located primarily to be near their markets. In fact, as discussed in Chapter 2, some areas are more suitable as production sites than others. Production processes requiring raw materials may tend to locate near the materials, firms may locate near suppliers or purchasers, and land has different levels of productivity.

Some producers of products having large market areas may operate most profitably in small towns because of lower labor costs, access to raw materials, and so forth. In this case, goods will travel up the urban hierarchy. Manufacturing activities are particularly sensitive to spatial cost variations. Richardson (1978, p. 81) described the location of manufacturing activities as "wild cards" within the hierarchy because large manufacturers may locate in small towns as well as major cities. Central-place theory is more applicable to activities that are market oriented in location than activities that are cost oriented. Thus, central-place models describe the location of service centers (where activities such as retailing, wholesaling, and business services dominate) much better than the site selection of manufacturing.

The locational factors excluded from central-place theory can create a situation where two towns have similar hinterlands and similar functions except that one of the towns may be the site of a manufacturing plant with a very large market area. Thus, the manufacturing town will be larger than the other place, even though, with the one exception, they are similarly situated in the urban hierarchy.

Transportation Costs.   The central-place model included the assumption that transportation costs are uniform in all directions. In reality, transfer costs are cheaper along established routes. Thus, market areas will be extended along transportation routes. Discontinuities in transportation costs will arise due to disruptions in the transportation system caused by rivers, mountains, and other geographic features. For instance,

FIGURE 3–11 Block Rates and Market Overlap

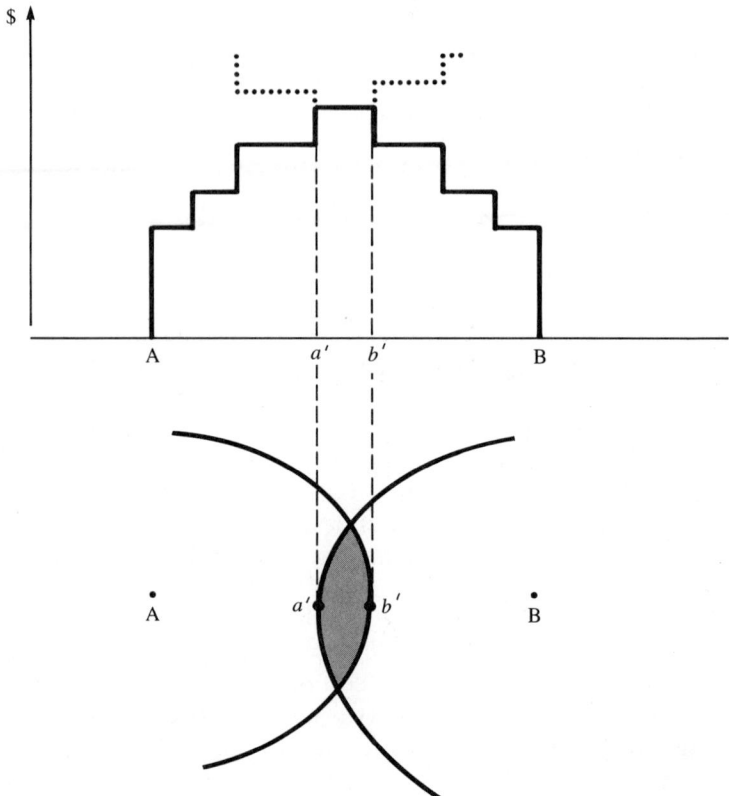

Block rates create situations where producers may have equal prices in a particular area. Market overlap may result as is the case between $a'-b'$.

a mountain may raise transportation costs and cut off part of what would otherwise have been part of a city's hinterland. Accordingly, urban systems will be distorted from the ideal central-place pattern.

Transport companies often charge block rates rather than continuously increasing rates. This can lead to market overlap and indeterminate market boundaries because two producers may deliver a product at the same price. Figure 3–11 illustrates market overlap. It shows a price funnel which assumes that freight rates increase in a block fashion. Consumers between A, the point of production, and a' will purchase from the firm located in A because the delivered price is less. Likewise, B's market area

FIGURE 3–12   Market Areas with Different Production Costs and Long-Haul Economies

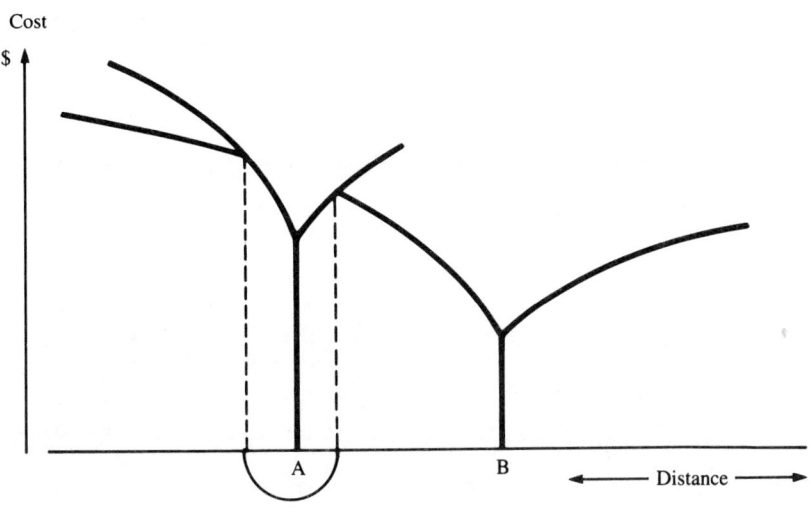

Long-haul economies may result in a high-production-cost firm such as A being surrounded by a lower-cost competition.

will include the region in which the firm in B can deliver at a lower price. The area between a' and b', however, is contested.

Long-haul economies exist when the per mile cost of transferring a good or service decreases with distance. Most transportation systems exhibit long-haul economies. Long-haul economies coupled with different production costs at alternative sites can result in surrounded markets. Figure 3–12 illustrates the case where the transportation costs of both firms are identical but the concave shape shows long-haul economies. The firm located at B is able to produce the product at a lower cost, possibly because important inputs are available cheaply at the site. The firm located at A is the higher-cost producer. Thus, the market of the firm located at A will be surrounded.

Seller Rate Absorption.   Sellers may absorb some of the transfer costs themselves in order to extend their markets. An example of rate absorption would be a producer who sold a product at a uniform delivery price to all customers in the region instead of charging an FOB price plus delivery. A seller could use this technique to price discriminate against nearby customers in order to offer lower prices to distant customers. In a more dynamic setting, there may be promotional or advertising advantages to offering uniform prices to all customers. A furniture store may offer free delivery anywhere in a metropolitan area in order to attract distant customers even though some very distant customers may have delivery costs so high as to make the sale unprofitable. When many firms practice freight absorption, market overlap may occur.

Institutional Factors.   Numerous political factors can affect the urban networks. Liquor stores may be underrepresented in a state with stringent laws or high liquor taxes, whereas a cluster of similar stores may be found on the other side of the state border. Interstate commerce within the United States is relatively free of barriers to trade, but not entirely. Buy-at-home campaigns, tax policies, licensing, and inspection regulations are a few institutional impediments that affect market area.

Institutional factors are more important in international commerce. Languages, tariffs, quotas, customers, and differences in legal systems are just a few impediments that prevent a firm located in one country from extending its market area abroad. Some regions, such as the European Economic Community countries, are trying to reduce institutional impediments. However, progress is slow. There is a tendency for products with larger market areas and export impediments to locate near the center of a country's population to avoid border problems.

Product Differentiation.   The abstract model included the assumption that products were undifferentiated, so it was reasonable to assume consumers would buy the least-cost item. If all firms charged the same FOB price, the nearest producer would be the least-cost supplier. However, if consumers have a preference for one brand over another, some customers would be willing to pay a premium to purchase the brand preferred. Thus, market overlap is likely to occur. The more intense brand loyalty is, the greater the extent of market overlap.

Nonemployment Residential Locations and Commuting.   The previous variations in central-place theory described deviations from ideal market areas that, in turn, could influence the urban system. The factors were related to production and employment. However, cities can grow for reasons unrelated to employment. Retirement and amenity-oriented communities in the South and Southwest are examples of growth outside the central-place framework. Likewise, bedroom communities can grow without local employment increases because residents can work in other places.

An implicit assumption in the central-place model is that individuals live where they work. While this may be roughly true when central places are widely dispersed, it is not true in urbanized areas. Central-place theory does not explain the distribution of economic activity within metropolitan regions.

Empirical Evidence

Does the empirical evidence support central-place theory? There are many more small cities than large as suggested by central-place theory. (See the discussion on the rank-size rule below.) Larger cities are further apart and provide a greater variety of services than smaller places. These observations support central-place theory. However, whether the theory explains economic geography sufficiently depends upon individual judgment rather than a definitive statistical test.

One of the first empirical tests was undertaken by A. Losch (1954), who used 1930 census data to analyze urban places in Iowa. He divided cities into various orders and found that the central-place model predicted the number of places in each order, the size of centers, and the distances between places. Since Losch, numerous other empirical studies of central-place theory have been reported. Central-place theory even explains settlement patterns in communist (Skinner, 1964) and traditional economies (Steponaitis, 1981). The consensus of these studies is that:

1. Central-place theory explains the size and spatial distribution of cities in homogeneous agricultural regions such as the Midwest. It does less well in explaining urban patterns in complex regions, such as the megalopolises of New York and Washington, D.C., because places of work are often separated from places of residence.

2. The distribution of service activities can be explained by central-place theory reasonably well. Manufacturing, extractive, and governmental activities are not explained by central-place theory. These goods and services are likely to move up as well as down the urban hierarchy.

3. The central-place model has also been tested using data from shopping centers in metropolitan areas (West, Von Hohenbalken, and Kroner, 1985; Morrill, 1987). The authors obtained the expected hierarchies of shopping centers although they observed stores of the same type replicated in the same centers. This finding is outside the traditional central-place finding although it may be explained by economics of comparison shopping. When similar stores are located together, consumers may economize on trips by comparison shopping in an area with many competing stores.

The Rank-Size Rule

A discussion of urban systems would be incomplete without a discussion of the rank-size rule. The rule states that the rank of a city times its population equals a constant:

$$C = P_r R \tag{1}$$

where C = A constant, equal to the population of the largest city.
P_r = Population of city of rank r (largest city, smaller rank).
R = City rank (larger city, smaller rank).

Notice that when discussing the rank-size rule, the largest city is the first rank. In terms of the central-place theory, the first rank city is the highest-order city.

The rank-size rule fits the size distribution of cities in the United States and other developed countries quite well, particularly when the population of the entire metropolitan area (rather than the central-city population) is used as the indicator of size. Metropolitan areas better reflect the economic unit than the political concept of city. However, at the upper end of the distribution there is not as much difference in size as would be implied by the rank-size rule. For instance, the New York metropolitan agglomeration is not twice the size of Los Angeles. But, the rule fits well for many regions within the United States (Berry, Parr et al. 1988, ch. 1). Regions in less-developed countries do not fit the rank-size generalization. They tend to have a primate city much larger than the next largest city. In fact, in some less-developed countries, the largest city becomes a growth magnet attracting economic activities to an extent that may be detrimental to the rest of the country.

Central-place theory provides one explanation for the rank-size rule. If factors exogenous to central-place theory are assumed to vary randomly, then cities could form a smooth distribution (rather than all cities of the same order having the same population size). Furthermore, population size would increase exponentially.[2]

A second explanation of the rank-size rule is stochastic. If growth is proportional to size, then the rank-size distribution could be the result of chance or a variety of factors operating randomly. The strength of the stochastic explanation is that it recognizes, at least implicitly, the complexity of factors that determine urban size. Furthermore, the "many factors operating in many ways" explanation would not be as applicable to many underdeveloped countries because they have simpler economic

---

[2] If k (see Appendix, equation 7) were assumed to approach 0, then the rank-size rule could be derived from central-place theory. Thus, the rank-size rule could be used as further empirical evidence in support of central-place theory.

structures. Hence, a random process would be less likely to generate the rank-size rule. It is precisely in less-developed countries that the rank-size rule does not fit the population pattern.

The usefulness of central-place theory lies in the fact that it gives important insights into forces that influence regional and urban development. It shows that urban places are linked by trade flows forming a "system of cities." It provides a framework for understanding how development in one system can affect other places in the system. It describes economic tendencies rather than actual outcomes. The factors that are isolated in the central-place model are not the only forces operating. Frequently, the effects of factors extraneous to central-place theory dominate. Nevertheless, the concept of city systems based upon market areas is essential to understanding the development of regions and cities.

HOW TO MEASURE AREAS OF INFLUENCE

The concepts of market area and hinterland are similar. Market area refers to the region in which a particular product is sold. The size of a market area, of course, depends upon the product. An urban hinterland refers to the areas in which one central place dominates other cities. In addition to hinterland, the general area of dominance for a central place has been referred to a sphere of influence, urban field, market area, umland, and tributary area. Just as the distribution point of a product tends to be near the center of its market area, the city is near the center of the region it dominates (or serves), and the city's influence weakens the farther the hinterland area is from the central place. It is sometimes useful to measure a city's hinderland as distinct from the market for an individual product.

Survey Techniques

There have been numerous attempts to measure the range of a city's hinterland. Early efforts examined the circulation of major daily newspapers between New York and Boston, reasoning that newspapers accurately reflect retail trade patterns and social orientation among the cities between New York and Boston. Thus, a city could be placed in New York's hinterland if a New York paper had a larger circulation than Boston papers. Today, television coverage may be as good an indicator as newspapers.

Green (1959) also examined the border between New York and Boston. In addition to newspaper circulation, he examined other indicators of influence, such as railroad-ticket purchases, freight movement, telephone calls, origin of vacationers, addresses of directors of major firms, and associations of hinterland banks. Green found that the various indicators did not give a constant definition of the urban field. For instance, Springfield would have been classified in Boston's hinterland when newspaper circulation was the criterion but was in New York's sphere of influence when freight movement was the basis of classification. A generalized sphere of influence does exist, but it should be considered a composite of a variety of indicators.

Shopping patterns are an important indicator of the hinterland. Surveys have also been used to determine shopping patterns within a metropolitan region or for specific products. The market area for single products or shopping centers can also be found directly by examining sales patterns. Direct measurement is particularly easy when producers have records of their customers' addresses.

Several generalizations can be drawn from the direct empirical studies reviewed by Berry and Parr (1988).

1. The proportion of consumers shopping at a central place varies with distance from the shopping area. The closer individuals are to a shopping area, the greater the proportion of individuals who will shop there.
2. The proportion of consumers varies with the size of the shopping area.
3. The distances that consumers travel vary for different types of products.
4. The pull of any shopping area is influenced by the nature of competing shopping areas (Huff, 1963).

The first generalizations—that the proportion of customers decreases with distance and increases with the size of the shopping area—are similar to the law of gravitational attraction. The pull of gravity decreases with distance and increases with the size of the object. This similarity has given rise to gravity models of spatial interaction.

Reilly's Law

W. J. Reilly was the first to apply a gravity model to determine the scope of a city's hinterland. Although Reilly's Law is dated, the initial formulation serves as the basis for modern techniques for measuring spheres of influence. Simply stated, the model postulates that an individual's proclivity to stop at center A will increase as the size of place A increases and will decrease as the square of the distance between the customer and center A increases. Reilly's Law of Retail Gravitation states that the point where trade is equally divided between two cities runs through a point where the ratio of the distances squared equals the

FIGURE 3–13   Generalized Sphere of Influence

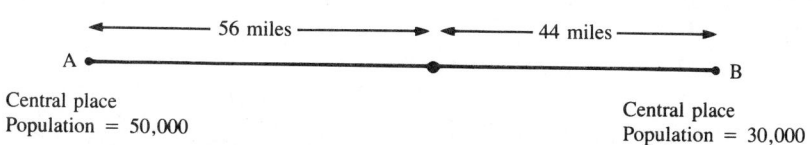

The attraction of an area increases with size and decreases with distance. Using Reilly's "Law of Retail Gravitation," the point at which half the trips are to *A* and half are to *B* can be estimated.

population ratio:

$$\frac{P_a}{P_b} = \frac{D_a{}^2}{D_b{}^2} \tag{2}$$

where P_i = Population of major city and
   D_i = Distance from major city to intermediate place.

   The breaking point is where the influence of the two cities are equal. On one side of the breaking point City *A* will dominate. Beyond that point, City *B* will account for the majority of purchases. If Reilly's Law were applied to the situation depicted in Figure 3–13, the breaking point would be about 56 miles from *A* (rounded to nearest mile).
   Reilly's Law may be restated to express the distance between a major city, say *A*, and the outer limit of its trading area.

$$Sh^a = D_{ab}/(1 + \sqrt{P_a/P_b}) \tag{3}$$

where Sh^a = Scope of *A*'s hinterland (distance from A to the breaking point)
   D_{ab} = Distance from *A* to *B* where *B* is the nearest competing city.
   $P_{a,b}$ = Population in City *A* and *B*

In terms of the hypothetical cities shown in Figure 3–13, the breaking point for *A*'s sphere of influence would be:

$$56 \text{ miles} = 100 \text{ miles}/(1 + \sqrt{30,000/50,000})$$

   The breaking point is closer to *B* than *A* because *A* is the larger city. Thus, individuals equidistant between *A* and *B* would make most of their trips to *A*. After all, consumers could probably purchase anything in *A* that they could purchase in *B* and purchase some things in *A* that could not be purchased in *B*. Reilly's Law has been applied principally to determine the breaking point between cities of approximately the same order within the urban hierarchy. Thus, Reilly used his law to test the breaking points between Pittsburgh and the following major cities: Cleveland, Youngstown, Canton, and Steubenville, in Ohio; Wheeling and Clarksburg, in West Virginia; Cumberland in Maryland; Erie, New Castle, Johnstown, and Altoona, in Pennsylvania; and Buffalo in New York. Obviously, there were small cities that have market areas within Pittsburgh's larger hinterland. However, Reilly's study focused on Pittsburgh's hinterland for higher-order services.

The label, "Law of Retail Gravitation," implies that Reilly's formula is almost universal in applicability and generates highly accurate results. This is not the case. Although Reilly's approach has been widely used to estimate market areas for a variety of retail goods, it does not have the precision of a physical law. Furthermore, three shortcomings weaken the model's practical use. First, the model does not provide estimates of market attraction at above or below threshold levels. In reality, a central place's influence tapers off and hinterlands overlap. Second, the distance parameters (the squares of distance) may not be the same for all types of shopping trips. Third, travel time or cost may be more appropriate than miles as a measure of trade barriers. Some of these criticisms have been addressed by the development of more sophisticated statements of Reilly's Law.

Probabilistic Models

Without modification, Reilly's Law is limited by the inherent uncertainty of consumer behavior. Huff (1963) developed a probabilistic model to determine the influence of shopping areas within metropolitan regions. He estimated the likelihood that an individual in place i would shop at a particular central place. The probability depended upon (1) the distance (usually expressed in time) between the consumer and the destination, j, (2) the number of competing central places, and (3) the size of the central place, j. The measure of size is not necessarily population. Because Huff's model is often used to measure the attractive pull of a retail shopping center within a metropolitan area, the number of square feet of shopping space may be a better size indicator. His formulation may be expressed as:

$$P_{ij} = \frac{S_j/(T_{ij})^b}{\sum_{j=1}^{n} (S_j/(T_{ij})^b)} \qquad (4)$$

where P_{ij} = Probability of an individual in i shopping at j
S_j = Size of central place j

FIGURE 3–14   Retail Trade Areas Determined by Probability Contours

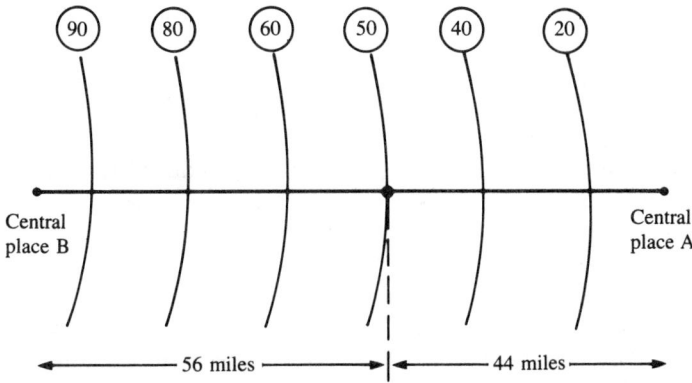

Probability contours show the probability that a shopping trip for a resident located anywhere on the "map" will be to A. The closer to A the shopper is, the higher the probability of shopping at A.

T_{ij} = Distance between i and j expressed in time

b = An exponent (similar to the squared term in Reilly's Law but allowed to vary depending upon what exponent will provide the best fit).

Ideally, a survey of customers should be conducted in order to determine the value of b, depending upon the particular type of goods available in the central place. The need for a survey is a major impediment because of the extra time and cost. However, for most general-merchandise goods, studies have found that b equals about 2. Goods and services for which individuals are willing to travel longer distances will have lower coefficients (lower distance discounts). Often, distance is measured in terms of time rather than miles because time is more relevant in travel decisions. In empirical studies, time is usually measured by dividing the hinterland into five-minute time zones. Within five minutes, $T = 1$, between 5 and 10 minutes, $T = 2$, and so forth. Huff's probabilistic model results in retail trade areas defined in terms of probability contours as shown in Figure 3–14. The point of 50 percent probability is the same as Reilly's break-even point.

Retail Spending.   The model is often extended to estimate total retail spending that would occur at a shopping center. Thus, it is an important tool for commercial developers and planners. In order to understand how a real estate planner might use the model, assume the number of potential customers at each location, POP_i, is known (locations are often defined as census-track areas within an MSA, so the data is available). Assume also that the annual available expenditures per person per year for the types of goods sold by the center equals E. These variables can be determined from surveys or published sources. Estimates on annual household budget by product category for various levels of income are available from data published by the U.S. Bureau of Labor Statistics. "Survey of Buying Power" published by Sales Management has similar data. Total spending of individuals located at i, at shopping area j, would equal the probability of shopping at i, P_{ij} times total spending:

$$TS_{ij} = P_{ij} \times POP_i \times E \qquad (5)$$

By summing the total spending for all areas, i, an estimated total spending at a particular location may be derived. Thus, gravity models are useful for market-oriented locational decisions.

An Example.   In order to see how the model can be applied, assume a developer is planning to construct a small neighborhood shopping strip of 10,000 square feet in census tract j as shown in Figure 3–15. There are two existing centers, A and B. What is the likelihood that an individual located in census tract i will shop at the proposed center? Assume the distance measure, T_{ij}, increases by 1 for each 5-minute distance increase. Applying the probabilistic gravity model yields:

$$P_{ij} = (10{,}000/2^2)/((10{,}000/2^2) + (15{,}000/3^2) + (20{,}000/4^2))$$

Thus, the probability of an individual in area i shopping at the proposed center is .46. We may interpret this result as 46 percent of the population in i shopping only at the proposed center, or more realistically, the average shoppers will make 46 percent of their trips to the proposed center in i. (We are assuming that the point in the center of the customer area represents the location of all consumers in i.)

The estimate of the likelihood of shopping at the proposed center must be supplemented with additional data before the volume of retail trade can be calculated. Specifically, we would need to know (1) the population size of area i (POP_i) and (2) the annual expenditures per capita (E).

In order to estimate retail trade at the proposed center, assume that the population of census track i is 8,000 and the average family in i spends $700 per year on the type of retail goods anticipated for the proposed center. Then, the amount of trade estimated for the proposed center from area i would equal:

$$.46 \times 700 \times 8{,}000 = \$2{,}576{,}000$$

FIGURE 3–15   Location of Customers and Competitors

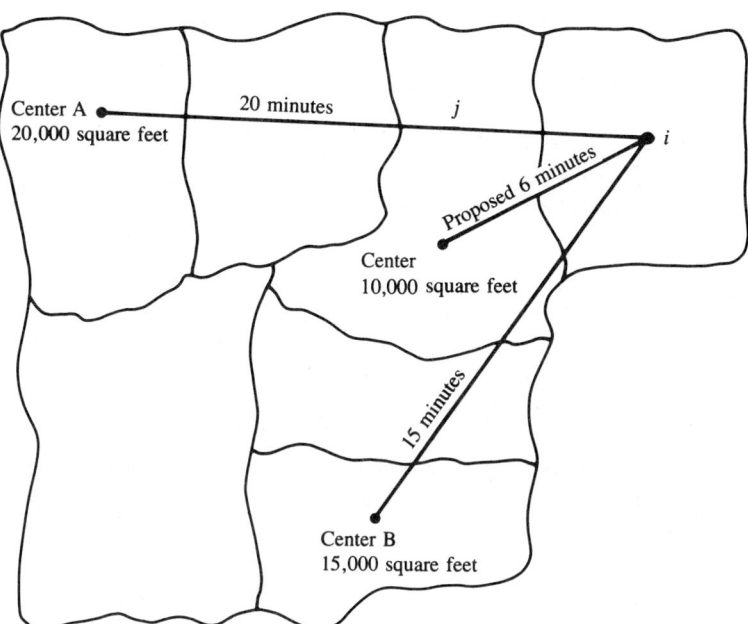

The size and location of other establishments should be considered when estimating the likelihood that a resident located at *i* will shop at the proposed center.

The above example indicates only the sales likely to come from individuals in area *i*. In order to develop an estimate of total sales, the same procedure would have to be followed for every area in the region.

SUMMARY

This chapter described spatial interactions among economic units. An understanding of how the familiar concept of demand can be integrated into a spatial setting is a prerequisite to understanding spatial interactions. Even if all consumers have equal demand determinants, the quantity demanded would be less for more distant buyers because of the transportation costs. Total product cost is the sum of the actual price plus delivery cost.

Firms tend to locate away from each other to avoid competing for customers. However, if above-normal profits are being earned, additional producers will enter the industry. As more firms enter the industry, geographic market areas will shrink and profits will fall. Market areas for producers of different products may overlap and producers with similar market areas will tend to locate near each other to capture agglomeration economies. Central places are centers of one or more market areas. Larger cities will be the site of many market centers, including the production site of some products that have very large market areas. A hierarchy of cities will develop. Factors that tend to change the size of market areas will alter the system of cities.

The central-place model was derived theoretically from a few abstract assumptions. As these assumptions were relaxed, the effect on the distribution of central places was examined. Empirical evidence showed that the predictions of central-place theory are most accurate for rural areas and services and poor for large metropolitan regions and manufacturing.

The rank-size rule is often used to summarize the city-size distribution. The rule states that the rank of a place times its size is a constant. The rank-size rule holds for developed regions better than regions in underdeveloped countries. Also, the place of a city within the hierarchy is stable after the region has become economically integrated.

The final section describes empirical techniques for determining the scope of a market area. The market areas for higher-order services correspond roughly to a city's general hinterland. Models similar to those used for determining hinterlands may be used to determine trade areas within a metropolitan region.

APPENDIX: SIZE OF DISTRIBUTION OF CITIES[1]

The size distribution of cities resulting from the central-place model can be derived from two assumptions. First, let city size be proportional to the population it serves.

$$P_i = kM_i \tag{1}$$

where P_i = Population of a central place of the ith order (the higher the order the longer the place).

M_i = The market served by a city of the ith order.

k = Proportion of the market located in an ith-order central place ($0 < k < 1$ because the central place itself is part of the city's market area).

Second, assume each central place serves a fixed number of satellites of the next-smaller size category. For instance, if third-order cities each have six second-order satellites, then each fourth-order city will have six third-order satel-

---

[1] This section is complex and may be skipped without loss of continuity.

lites. The fixed number of satellites is called a nesting factor. The constant nesting-factor assumption is not necessary to central-place theory, but it simplifies the presentation. Thus, the market served by a city is the city itself plus the population served by the lower-order cities in its hinterland.

$$M_i = P_i + sM_{i-1} \tag{2}$$

where s = the number of satellites served by the higher-order city (nesting factor). If the market size of each of the lower-order places were 100 (i.e., $M_{i-1} = 100$) and the nesting factor were 6, then the market area of the ith-order city would equal its own population plus 600. Combining equations 1 and 2 yields:

$$M_i = \frac{s}{1 - k} M_{i-1} \tag{3}$$

Since market size is determined by the size of the markets of the lower-order cities being served, $M_{i-1} = (s/1 - k)(M_{i-2})$. Therefore, equation 3 may be rewritten:

$$M_i = \frac{s}{1 - k} \frac{s}{1 - k} M_{i-2} = \frac{s^2}{1 - k} M_{i-2} \tag{4}$$

and so on down the hierarchy. The market area may therefore be expressed as an exponential function of the market served by the first-order city,

$$M_i = \frac{s^{i-1}}{1 - k} M_1 \tag{5}$$

Equation 5 indicates that market size increases exponentially, because each city's market area includes a constant number of satellite cities and their hinterlands.

Since markets served by cities increase exponentially moving up the hierarchy and city size is a fixed proportion of market size, it follows that city size also increases exponentially. In order to show this, let the smallest-order city serve itself and the rural population, r. Then:

$$M_1 = P_1 + r = kM_1 + r = \frac{r}{1 - k} \tag{6}$$

Substituting (6) into (5) yields

$$M_i = \frac{s^{i-1}}{(1 - k)} r \tag{7}$$

Substituting (7) into (1) shows

$$P_i = k \frac{s^{i-1}}{(1 - k)} r \tag{8}$$

Thus, population also increases exponentially. The first-order place has a population of $(k/1 - k)(r)$. The second-order city's population is $(ks/(1 - k)^2)(r)$ [or $(s/1 - k)(k/1 - k_r)$] and so forth. Each order city is $(s/1 - k)$ times the lower-ordered central place.

The model expresses the size of any city within the hierarchy as a function of: (1) rural population served by the smallest city, r, (2) the number of satellites served by higher-order cities, s, (3) k, the proportion of the market located in the city, and (4) the order of the place, i.

REFERENCES

Berry, Brian, John B. Parr et al. *Market Centers and Retail Locations.* Englewood Cliffs, N.J.: Prentice Hall, 1988.

Christaller, Waller. *Central Places of Southern Germany.* Englewood Cliffs, N.J.: Prentice Hall, 1966.*

Evans, Alan W. *Urban Economics: An Introduction.* London: Basil Blackwell, 1985.

Green, Howard L. "Hinterland Boundaries of New York City and Boston in Southern New England." In *Readings in Urban Geography,* ed. H. M. Mayer and C. F. Kohn. Chicago: University of Chicago Press, 1959.

Heilbrun, James. *Urban Economics and Public Policy.* 2nd ed. New York: St. Martin's Press, 1981, chapter 5.

Huff, David L. "A Probabilistic Analysis of Shopping Center Trade Areas." *Land Economics* 39, 1963, pp. 81–90.

Isard, Walter. *Introduction to Regional Science.* Englewood Cliffs, N.J.: Prentice Hall, 1975, chapter 12.

Losch, August. *The Economics of Location.* New Haven: Yale University Press, 1954.*

Mills, Edwin S., and M. R. Lau. "A Model of Market Areas with Free Entry." *Journal of Political Economy* 72, 1964, pp. 278–88.

Morrill, R. L. "The Structure of Shopping in a Metropolis." *Urban Geography* 8, 1987, pp. 97–128.

Neenan, William B. *Urban Public Economics.* Belmont, Calif.: Wadsworth, 1981, chapter 3.

Parr, J. B. "Models of the Urban Systems: A More General Approach." *Urban Studies* 15, 1978, pp. 35–49.

Pred, Allen. *City-Systems in Advanced Economics.* New York: John Wiley & Sons, 1977, chapter 1.

Reilly, William J. *The Law of Retail Gravitation.* New York: Pillsbury Publishers, 1931.*

Richardson, Harry W. *Urban Economics.* Hinsdale, Ill.: The Dryden Press, 1978.

Sales and Marketing Management, "Survey of Buying Power," July issue, published annually.

Skinner, G. W. "Marketing and Social Structures in Rural China—I." *Journal of Asian Studies* 24, 1964, pp. 3–33.

Stabler, J. C., and P. R. Williams. "The Changing Structure of the Central-Place Hierarchy." *Land Economics* 49, 1973, pp. 454–58.

Steponaitis, V. P. "Settlement Hierarchies and Political Complexity in Nonmarket Societies: The Formative Period of the Valley of Mexico." *American Anthropologists* 83, 1981, pp. 320–65.

Valevanis, Stephen. "Losch on Location." *American Economic Review* 45, 1955, pp. 637–44.

Vance, J. E. *The Merchant's World: Geography of Wholesaling.* Englewood Cliffs, N.J.: Prentice Hall, 1970.

West, Douglass; Balder Von Hohenbalken; and Kenneth Kroner. "Tests of In terurban Central-Place Theories." *Economic Journal* 95, March 1985, pp. 101–17.

Yeates, Maurice, and Berry Garner. *The North American City.* New York: Harper & Row, 1980, chapter 4.

* Classics.

Chapter Four

Agglomeration and Economic Structure

Repulsion among competing firms was a principal economic force described in the discussion of market areas. However, cohesive forces also operate in regional and metropolitan economies. Production and marketing interdependencies, which tend to attract firms toward each other, are critical to urban development. This chapter examines relationships among the components of a local economy and describes important factors that unify such an economy.

The concept of agglomeration economies—benefits achieved from spatial concentration of economic activity—is discussed first. Agglomeration economies range from benefits that accrue to a single, specific establishment to benefits so diffuse that they affect many diverse firms within an area. The conditions under which agglomeration will accrue and some possible impediments to agglomeration are also discussed. External-economy industries are described in the second section. These activities have particularly strong locational attractions to sites that offer agglomeration economies. The next section describes tools for measuring and analyzing economic structure. Location quotients are widely used measures of industrial structure and can also be used to estimate the extent of export activity. The concept of economic structure is broadened to include political and social factors as well as traditional economic variables in the next section. Finally, the issues of regional convergence and divergence are discussed.

AGGLOMERATION ECONOMIES

Agglomeration economies are cost reductions that occur because economic activity is carried on at one place. Isard (1975, p. 113) stressed the importance of agglomeration economies: "An understanding of the development of cities and regions cannot be acquired without a full appreciation of the forces of agglomeration and deglomeration that are at play."

But, while acknowledging the importance of agglomeration economies, economists generally agree that agglomerative forces are not well understood (Bergsman et al. 1973). This section will focus on the importance of agglomeration economies, but will also discuss some conceptual ambiguities. There are several types of agglomeration economies, ranging from savings that accrue to only one establishment to agglomeration economies that spread throughout the entire region. Insights into the nature of agglomeration economies can be gained by examining several types of agglomeration economies discussed in the literature.

Internal Agglomeration Economies

Internal agglomeration economies are per unit cost reductions that accrue to a firm that expands its activity at a particular point. Since the firm that expands also receives the benefits of the expansion, the agglomeration economies are "internal"; that is, the benefits are captured by the firm engaging in the activity. There is a subtle distinction between internal agglomeration economies and the well-known microeconomic concept of economies of scale. Economies of scale refers to per unit cost savings a firm achieves when it increases output and it is free to increase any or all inputs. (Scale economies are represented by a movement down an average-cost curve.) If a firm lowered its average costs by establishing a second or third plant in areas where it previously had no facilities, a traditional internal economy of scale would be achieved. However, for an internal agglomeration economy to result, the cost savings must be due to location or extension of establishments in proximity to an existing facility. The spatial aspect is essential to the concept of agglomeration economies.

Cost reductions achieved by the expansion of an existing plant would represent both an internal economy of scale and an internal agglomeration economy. However, if a firm consolidated the activities of two separate facilities into a single plant and, thereby, lowered costs, an internal agglomeration economy would occur without a traditional internal economy of scale.

Economies of scope refers to decreases in production costs from expansion into new product lines. For instance, if the average cost to a firm of producing toothpaste fell because the firm decided to produce shaving cream also, then an economy of scope would be achieved. In a spatial setting, an increase in one activity that lowers the cost of producing another product at that location is also an internal agglomeration economy.

The spreading of fixed costs over a larger output is an important reason for internal agglomeration economies. Other sources of internal agglomeration economies include greater division of labor, potential for using alternative technologies, and saving through bulk purchases. Many separate operations normally occur within a plant. Better use of a manager's time or better use of specialized machinery can result in lower average costs as output increases. The concentration of General Motors' headquarters activity in Detroit undoubtedly allows a substantial internal agglomeration economy.

Interindustry Linkages

The tendency for firms that trade with each other to locate in the same region is one of the most important causes of industrial agglomeration. Interindustry agglomeration occurs through forward and backward linkages. A forward linkage involves suppliers attracting buyers; a backward linkage involves buyers attracting suppliers. For instance, if a metal-fabricating plant were located in an area and a farm implement manufacturer decided to operate nearby to be close to its suppliers, a forward linkage would be the dominant locational factor. Conversely, a backward linkage would exist if the metal facility were attracted to the farm implement producer.

When two firms trade with each other, there are usually mutual benefits from locating together, such as transportation and communications cost savings. However, the pull is likely to be stronger for one of the firms than for the other. The effectiveness of the agglomeration pull depends upon the importance of proximity to the respective establishments relative to other locational factors. For example, a lumberyard would not attract a mill because the location of a mill does not significantly depend upon buyers and because one mill supplies many lumberyards. The mill's locational pull is towards forests.

The question of whether forward or backward linkages are generally more influential is important to development planners. If forward linkages are more important, then a regional policy maker might choose to concentrate on development of primary production activities such as oil, raw materials, and agriculture. The primary activities could then be expected to attract establishments that will use their inputs. If backward linkages are more effective, then an economic strategy might focus first on the development of final products such as apparel or food canning. Once established, these activities would induce further growth through backward linkages.

Hirshman (1972) argued that underdeveloped countries (and by implication, underdeveloped regions) are characterized by weak interdependencies and linkages. That is, firms in the underdeveloped countries do not trade with each other. Agriculture and extractive activities, which are major sectors in less developed countries, have few backward linkages almost by definition. Furthermore, Hirshman argued that the few forward linkages—principally, refining of raw materials—that might be generated by these activities do not encourage significant development that spreads elsewhere. Therefore, oil, mineral, and agricultural products are often exported without encouraging additional local economic activity. Likewise, activities that merely put finishing touches on imported products— packaging or making minor modifications—have ineffective backward linkages. Hirshman recommended governmental activity to encourage the development of large-scale industries with significant backward linkages. Forward linkages were not ignored, but they were not considered as effective in inducing further growth as backward linkages.

Hirshman's analysis might favor the establishment of an automobile assembly facility in a less developed region. Initially, engines, tires, chassis, and other inputs in the assembly process would have to be imported. But Hirschman suggested that some of the imports would eventually be replaced by local products. Locally produced inputs would have a competitive advantage over imported inputs because transportation costs would be less and proximity to the purchaser could improve communications. Locally produced inputs could be more responsive to the needs of the assembly plant. This approach is consistent with an import-substitution development strategy.

Most economists now believe that generalizations about whether forward or backward linkages are more effective are inadequate. Whether forward linkages are more powerful than backward linkages depends upon the industry pairs and the specific sets of circumstances. The issue of how to use linkages in the development process calls for additional empirical research.

Localization Economies

Interindustry linkages among direct trading partners are a special type of localization economy, but locationalization economies can encompass much broader-based agglomeration economies. Localization economies occur when increases in the output of an entire group of firms at a particular place result in lower costs for firms in that industry at that location.[1]

Localization economies are similar to what Alfred Marshall called economies external to the firm, but internal to the industry. Marshall pointed out that when output in an entire industry increased, supporting activities such as trade organizations and specialized suppliers could

---

[1] One of the problems in the agglomeration literature is that the concept of an industry is vague. For practical purposes, it is best to think of an industry as a group of firms related by similarity of output, production process, or inputs rather than in terms of a formal definition such as the Department of Commerce's Standard Industrial Classification (SIC).

emerge. The presence of new activities, in turn, could help lower costs to all firms in the industry. Marshall's analysis applies to firms in the same (or closely related) industries regardless of where located. Localization economies refers to a similar concept, but it applies to firms located in the same place.

Bergsman et al. (1982) studied the formation of localized clusters in urban areas. They examined 186 detailed industries and found evidence of clustering among many industries in widely separate sectors of the economy. Many of the clusters were suppliers or customers of each other, which suggests that interindustry linkages existed. However, their analysis identified clusters that arose for reasons other than agglomeration economies. Some clusters were due to political or other institutional factors. Thus, not all local concentrations of economic activity are due to economies of agglomeration. Furthermore, they found that many activities were part of more than one cluster. For instance, the metal-containers sector was part of several clusters. The overall conclusion of their work is that agglomeration economies extend beyond firms in a single industry and even beyond a small cluster of closely related industries. Clustering may occur among industries in widely separated sectors of the economy possibly because interdependencies that link firms can be subtle.

An enhanced labor pool, specialized machinery, imitation, and the chance to comparison shop are important sources of localization economies.

Labor Pool.   First, if many firms in the same industry locate together, they may contribute to the development of a skilled labor pool. The relocation of the American Society of Personnel Administrators (ASPA) headquarters from Berea, Ohio, to Washington, D.C., is an example of the importance of specialized labor pools. An ASPA official explained the decision by pointing out that "There's a special work force available in Washington, D.C. You can find people with association backgrounds." In other words, the society could operate more efficiently because it was easier to hire more people with complex sets of skills needed by a nonprofit organization.

Labor-market advantages from agglomeration are particularly useful when firms have unstable labor demands as in the case of many consulting firms concentrated in New York, Boston, Washington, and the Silicon Valley. If such firms are in a large center of qualified labor, they can expand their work force quickly, even when skill requirements are specialized.

Fluxuations in employment demand may contribute to agglomeration economies. If only one or two firms in an industry were located in the same region, they might have difficulty hiring specialized workers during periods of peak demand, particularly if both firms had simultaneous increases in demand. Hiring peaks might level, however, if many firms in similar and competitive businesses were located together. Firms that do business with the Department of Defense often swap staff when one firm wins several contracts at the expense of its competitors. The employment process is much smoother, cheaper, and more efficient if the employees do not have to change residence each time they change jobs. Furthermore, if a local industry had unique skill requirements that were sufficiently large, it might even be feasible to develop a school to train workers. Such schools or training programs would not only improve the quality and availability of labor, but could also enhance the ability of workers to adapt to industrial change. Thus, junior colleges often have excellent training programs designed to meet unique local labor-market requirements in their districts.

Specialized Machinery.   The ability to share specialized machinery and other factors of production is another source of localization economies. For example, an area may start developing as a distribution and warehousing center. When the area attains a large enough volume of activity, the market may be sufficient to support a distribution-equipment firm that sells, produces, or modifies loading and handling equipment. (Notice the backward linkage effect.) As a consequence of the improved availability of specialized distribution equipment, all distribution and warehousing firms in the area may operate more efficiently. In this example, the specialized distribution-equipment firm could not have achieved sufficient size to operate efficiently in an area that had only a few distribution and warehousing establishments. Thus, an external economy to the industry (the presence of the distribution-equipment manufacturer) can be explained by an internal economy (the distribution-equipment establishment can be large enough to achieve economies of scale).

Imitation, Modification, and Innovation.   Firms in the same industry may be able to imitate and copy one another more readily if they are located together. Therefore, they may be able to respond to changes in their industry quicker than if they were isolated from their competitors. Of course, the firm that is copied may be harmed, so it would be better off in an isolated location where copying would be more difficult. However, managers may not know which firm will develop leading innovations. Therefore, the cluster of firms as a whole may benefit from locating together even though individual firms may be disadvantages. In industries with numerous and scattered innovations, such as the fashion industry, all firms may be better off if they have locations that allow them to imitate quickly. Furthermore, a firm that copies two changes is in a better position to innovate yet another change, perhaps by combining or modifying changes that were taken from other firms. Thus, particularly in fast-changing industries, economies from industrial imitation, modification, and innovation tend to be important sources of localization economies.

Comparison Shopping.   Another localization economy can be traced to the desire of individuals to compare products. Individuals may prefer to shop for shoes in a regional shopping mall because they can compare the merchandise in four or five different stores. Firms selling similar products may repel one another under most circumstances, but when consumers have a demand for display variety, similar competing establishments may agglomerate. An additional shoe store in a regional shopping mall may actually benefit all the shoe stores by making the mall a more desirable place to shop for shoes. The additional store may lower the percentage of mall shoe shoppers who purchase at each existing store, but total sales may increase due to the greater number of shoppers.

Households are the direct beneficiaries of display variety because their shopping costs are reduced. But some of these advantages may be captured by retailers due to greater sales. Shopping center owners may also benefit if they can charge retailers higher rents because of the popularity of the shopping center.

Display-variety agglomeration is most likely to occur for products that are differentiated and have price variations sufficient to make comparison shopping worthwhile. Few of us would comparison shop for oatmeal or other grocery items, so grocery stores do not tend to agglomerate. Automobile alleys and urban restaurant areas are examples of agglomerations based on display variety. Centers of agglomeration that are national or international in scope include sales conventions (i.e., television executive meetings are often buying conventions for TV programs), New York's Fifth Avenue jewelry stores, and Kentucky horse auctions. Individuals come to these events from around the world to comparison shop.

Retail establishments selling complementary products also tend to cluster. For instance, a theater and restaurant often locate together reflecting the fact that people like to eat out before or after seeing a movie. Yet, are the theater and restaurant in the same industry? Perhaps if the "industry" is defined as an "evening's entertainment," they could be considered to be in the same industry. Industry is a slippery concept. Where does primary-metal production end and fabricated metals begin? Should a manufacturer of plastic caps for shoes be classified as part of the shoe or plastics industry? The Standard Industrial Classifications (SIC) used in most statistical studies are somewhat arbitrary. Agglomeration clusters may have similar outputs, similar production techniques (but different outputs), or similar input requirements.

Division of Labor, Agglomeration Economies, and the Extent of the Market

Adam Smith said that, "the division of labor is limited by the extent of the market." Stigler asked how such a dictum is compatible with a competitive market structure:

> Either the division of labor is limited by the extent of the market and, characteristically industries are monopolized, or industries are competitive, and therefore the theorem is false or of little significance. Neither alternative is inviting.

To reconcile the seemingly divergent principles, a product that requires three separate processes or functions for its completion was considered. The output of each process is unrelated to the level of output of the others (i.e., there are no externalities among processes), and all inputs are used in constant proportion. Figure 4–1 shows the average-cost curves associated with each of processes 1, 2, and 3 as well as the average total-cost curve that would exist if all processes were conducted internally.

FIGURE 4–1   Specialization and Agglomeration

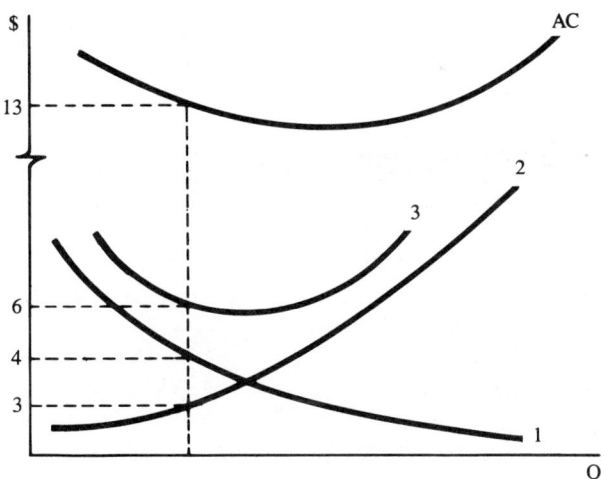

Three production processes are involved in the production process. If process 1 is performed by a large specialty firm and process 2 is undertaken by small specialty shops, the industry will be more efficient. The specialization may cause agglomeration.

SOURCE: Edgar M. Hoover and Frank Giarratani, *An Introduction to Regional Economics*, 3rd ed. Copyright 1984. Reprinted with permission of McGraw-Hill Inc.

Division of Labor, Agglomeration Economies, and the Extent of the Market (*concluded*)

Stigler argues that process 1 will tend to be performed by a specialty firm that can achieve full economies of scale if total industry output is large enough. This firm might indeed be a monopolist, but it would be prevented from fully exploiting a monopolist's position for it could not charge a price higher than the final producer's average cost of carrying out the process internally. Process 2 will tend to be performed by small specialty firms, with the final producer carrying out the function internally only so long as the cost is lower than that of purchasing the intermediate product.

The major implication of Stigler's analysis is that when industries are small, firms must locate together in order to achieve an agglomeration economy. One firm will carry out process 1 as a constrained monopolist, but firm purchasing, or selling to the firm engaged in process 1, must be in the same area to achieve agglomeration economies. As an industry becomes larger, it will disperse geographically: "geographic dispersion is a luxury that can be afforded by industries only after they have grown large (so that even the smaller production centers can reap the major gains of specialization)."

SOURCE: George Stigler, "The Division of Labor Is Limited by the Extent of the Market," *Journal of Political Economy* 59, no. 3 (June 1951), pp. 185–93.

Urbanization Economies

Urbanization economies, the most diffuse type of agglomeration economy, are cost savings that accrue to a wide variety of firms when the volume of activity in an entire urban area increases. The firms that share in urbanization economies may be unrelated. Urbanization economies may result from several sources.

Infrastructure.   First, urbanization economies may result from economies of scale in public infrastructure. Most publicly provided goods, such as roads, sewers, and fire protection, as well as some private goods, such as recreation and health facilities, can be included in the concept of urban infrastructure. Components of a region's infrastructure become inputs into a wide variety of production and consumption activities. When significant economies of scale exist in infrastructure provision, an increase in the size of an urban area will allow lower per unit infrastructure costs. These cost savings may be passed on to producers and consumers. However, as discussed more fully in Chapter 13, there need not necessarily be a fixed relationship between the size of an urban area and the size of the units producing the infrastructure. A small area may, in some cases, purchase infrastructure from larger producers to achieve the necessary economies of scale.

The transportation sector is an important component of the urban infrastructure. Firms using transportation facilities will benefit from locating near transportation modes. The larger the number of establishments, the better the transportation facilities are likely to be, and all firms using those facilities will benefit. For instance, as the number of air passengers increases, the number and diversity of flights will increase and almost all air travelers will benefit. Likewise, as more highways are constructed, transportation costs will fall for firms shipping by truck, salespeople travelling by car, and tourists visiting regional attractions.

Division of Labor.   Urbanization economies may also result from a more extensive division of labor made possible by greater size and activity. In a small town, many aspects of production and distribution must be carried out within the plant because the local market cannot support specialty firms. Activities that cannot be carried out within the plant must be purchased from elsewhere or not performed at all. The extra costs of importing will tend to place the firm at a competitive disadvantage relative to other producers.

Internal Economies.   Establishments that sell to a variety of firms and households may also achieve cost reductions as the urban area expands because larger markets will allow firms to achieve internal economies of scale. Internal economies may be passed forward to customers or backwards to the factors of production.

Averaging of Random Variations.   Larger urban markets allow for an averaging of variations in economic activity. A drop in sales to one customer or groups of customers may be offset by new orders from other customers. Mills and Hamilton (1984, p. 18) summarized this aspect of agglomeration economies:

> [The] most important of such agglomeration economies is statistical in nature and is an application of the law of large numbers. Sales of outputs and purchases of inputs fluctuate . . . for random, seasonal, cyclical and secular reasons.

Thus, to the extent that business ups and downs are uncorrelated, a firm in an urban area will have fewer scheduling production problems than if it were located in a smaller place. Similarly, labor changes can be accommodated more easily in a large urban area. If a chief financial officer or a tax accountant quits, finding a replacement will be a more significant problem in a small town than in a metropolitan area.

Urban Diseconomies. As the size of an economic concentration increases, diseconomies appear. Urbanization economies may be partially offset by urban diseconomies. Some social scientists believe crime, anxiety, and loneliness are personal costs of high-density living. Examples of urban diseconomies are the inconvenience, delay, and aggravation associated with congestion in metropolitan regions. Competition for locations near the center of large agglomerations increases rents, which, in turn, repel some firms. The higher wages paid in large cities may reflect compensation necessary to offset negative psychological costs of work in congested areas. Businesses are unequally affected by urban diseconomies so some firms are repelled from large cities before others.

However, there does not appear to be a size so large that overall urban diseconomies outweigh the economies associated with size. For instance, productivity generally increases as metropolitan size increases. Therefore, urbanization economies tend to outweigh urban diseconomies over the range of city sizes observed in the world today.

Recap

The impacts of agglomeration economies range from specific to diffuse. The most specific agglomeration economies accrue to a plant. Agglomeration economies affecting pairs of firms are also rather specific. Economies that result when an industry or an industrial cluster expands are slightly more diffuse. Urbanization economies are the most diffuse type of agglomeration economy. They depend upon the size of the entire urban area, and the benefits of the agglomeration are shared by a wide variety of businesses.

How Centers of Agglomeration Develop

Agglomeration economies are important cohesion forces in regional development. However, potential agglomeration economies can be realized only if firms locate in proximity to one another. This section examines the process that may encourage or impede agglomeration.

In order for agglomeration to occur, it must be profitable for the establishment to move away from what otherwise would have been its profit-maximization location. Figure 4–2 helps illustrate this aspect of agglomeration economies in four different cases. Suppose two firms are located at what would be their profit-maximizing locations if agglomeration economies were ignored. Costs of moving from the profit-maximizing point will increase production, assembly, and distribution costs or decrease revenues. Normally, the further the plant moves from the profit-maximizing location, the greater these costs will be. The circle around each location in Figure 4–2 represents the maximum distance the firm would be willing to move in order to achieve agglomeration economies. This distance is determined by the trade-off between increased operating

FIGURE 4–2   Agglomeration Potential

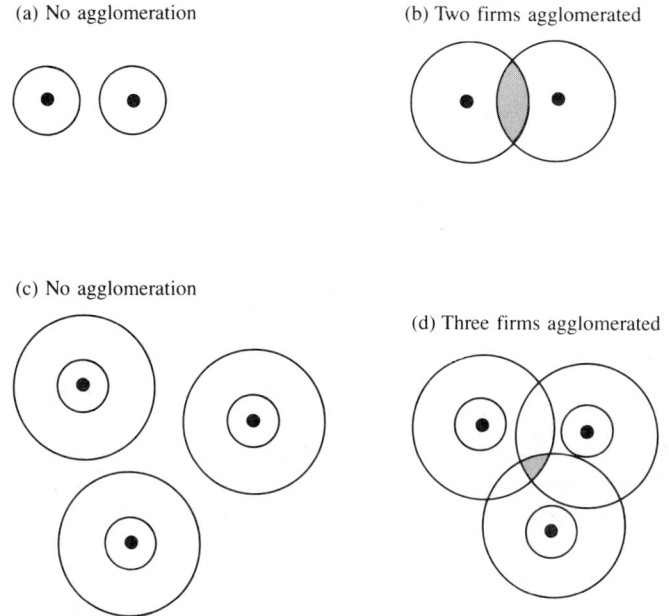

(a) No agglomeration

(b) Two firms agglomerated

(c) No agglomeration

(d) Three firms agglomerated

Agglomeration will occur when the benefits from agglomeration outweigh the costs of moving from the otherwise optimum site.

SOURCE: Based on Walter Isard, "Game Theory, Location Theory and Industrial Agglomeration," *Papers and Proceedings of the Regional Science Association* 18, 1960, pp. 1–11.

and transportation costs on the one hand and the benefits from agglomeration economies on the other. In panel (a) of Figure 4–2, agglomeration would not occur because the extra cost of operating at the site of agglomeration is greater than the benefits from agglomeration. However, agglomeration of firms could occur within the shaded area of panel (b) because the cost reductions from agglomeration economies more than offset the extra costs from moving away from the location that would maximize profits in the absence of agglomeration economies. Panels (c) and (d) show situations involving more than two firms. The larger circle around each firm indicates the maximum distance they would move if the unit of agglomeration were large enough to encompass three firms. In other words, for these establishments, the economies from agglomeration increase with the size of the agglomeration. Notice that in panel (c) there is no potential for agglomeration because the costs of relocating are not justified by the agglomeration economies. In panel (d), all three firms could locate together and form a higher-order agglomeration.

Point of Agglomeration.   Figure 4–2 suggests that agglomeration could occur anywhere within the shaded region. Is there a way to narrow the location to a particular point? Some sites within the area of potential agglomeration may offer special locational advantages, such as cheap inputs or proximity to other firms. However, if the area of potential agglomeration is homogeneous, the exact point of location may be indeterminate. Each firm may want to remain as close as possible to its own original profit-maximizing point. Perhaps firms will bargain over the appropriate site, and the relative bargaining strengths of the firms will determine the exact site.

The Spatial Scope of Agglomerations.   How close must establishments be in order to achieve agglomeration economies? The discussion above assumed a point of agglomeration. In fact, some agglomeration economies require almost immediate proximity. Internal economies of scale normally require plants of the same firm to be at least next to each other. This is particularly true if plant management is one of the functions to be shared among the numerous plant activities. Shopping centers offering display variety are another instance where stores must be relatively close together—within a few blocks—in order to achieve agglomeration economies. However, other agglomeration economies may be attainable when firms are further apart. A metal-fabricating facility may benefit from a railhead, even if the fabricating plant were 20 miles away from the railhead.

Most research on agglomeration economies has examined the tendency of firms to cluster within metropolitan areas or within neighborhoods such as industrial parks or central business districts. However, some agglomeration economies may be effective over longer distances, perhaps encompassing states or even multistate areas. Agglomeration economies that span large regions have not received adequate theoretical or empirical attention.

Institutions of Agglomeration.   Figure 4–2 illustrates conditions under which agglomeration could occur, but it does not provide a realistic analysis of the process of agglomeration. How do firms agree to locate together? Obviously, one firm would be reluctant to move into the area of potential agglomeration unless the other firm also agrees to do so.

Consider the payoff matrix shown in Figure 4–3. Firms x and y have two locational choices: inside or outside the area of agglomeration. Agglomeration economies will occur only if the firms locate together in the area of agglomeration. The figures in the cells represent net profits, appropriately discounted, for firm y (lower left part of each cell) and firm x (upper right part of each cell). Firm x is adversely affected by a location in the area of agglomeration as indicated by the fact that its profits decrease by $200 compared to profits from a location outside the area of agglomera-

FIGURE 4–3   A Locational Payoff Matrix

Firm y's Location	*Firm x's Location*	
	*In Area of Agglomeration**	*Outside Area of Agglomeration*
In Area of Agglomeration	3,800 x / 5,000 y	4,000 x / 1,000 y
Outside Area of Agglomeration	3,800 x / 2,000 y	4,000 x / 2,000 y

In the absence of coordinating mechanisms, if firm x located in the area of agglomeration, firm y would locate outside of the area of agglomeration. The combined payoff would be reduced.

* The shaded area in Figure 4–2(b).

tion. (Perhaps relocation costs are high for firm x, and that accounts for the lower present value of future profits.) Clearly the combined optimum location would be for both firms to locate in the area of agglomeration where combined profits are $8,800. However, firm x must receive an incentive to locate in the area of agglomeration. In other words, some institutional device to allow side payments must be developed if agglomeration is to occur. Possible inducements include locational grants from cities hoping to encourage agglomeration or the operation of an industrial park that sells land at below market prices. Both of these techniques might be motivated by groups hoping to develop a major center of agglomeration. Mergers between firms would also help ensure that the establishments would act to maximize combined profits by both establishments locating in an area where agglomeration economies could be obtained. Long-term contracts are also a possible device for reducing risk, thus encouraging linked industries to locate together. For instance, firm y might agree (implicitly or explicitly) to purchase output from firm x at an agreed price. Because of the assured market, firm x may agree to relocate to the agglomeration area. Thus, the benefits of agglomeration may be shared.

Figure 4–3 was constructed on the premise that only one firm benefitted from agglomeration. Even in cases where both firms received some benefits from agglomeration, the issue of how the benefit should be split is important. A third party such as an industrial-park developer could bring the firms together and capture some of the benefits of agglomeration in the form of higher rent.

Relocation costs are a significant impediment to agglomeration. Suppose, with reference to Figure 4–3, that firm y had already located outside the area of potential agglomeration and the cost of relocating was $5,000. Under these circumstances, agglomeration would not occur.

Relocation costs explain the tendency of current centers of agglomeration to become self-participating and reinforcing. Once an establishment has selected a location, other firms will probably move to it if agglomeration is to occur, because relocation costs may prohibit relocation of the original establishment. Therefore, an evolutionary perspective is important to understand the development of urban and regional agglomeration economies. We could easily conceive of a better system of cities and agglomeration networks than now exists, if we could start with a systematic master plan and no relocation costs. The author would place the capital, Washington, D.C., near the center of the United States, for instance, but such changes are precluded by relocation costs of physical and, perhaps more important, social infrastructure.

EXTERNAL-ECONOMY INDUSTRIES

Industries composed of firms that are dependent upon many diffuse agglomeration economies with nearby establishments are referred to as external-economy industries. Firms in external-economy industries receive spillover benefits when related establishments locate in the area. Examples of external-economy industries include the fur-goods, handbags, children's coats, dresses, and book-publishing industries. These are generally rapid-change industries. In each case, firms in these industries must purchase a variety of inputs from other firms. The inputs must be obtained quickly, and rapid changes in the product, such as style changes, make flexibility important.

External-economy industries tend to concentrate in large urban areas because of the diversity of products and information available. Over 90 percent of all U.S. jobs in paints and varnishes, periodicals, security and commodity brokerage, millinery, and aircraft are in large urban areas. The concentration in production in such activities is much greater than could be explained based upon market orientation.

Lichtenberg (1960) examined industries that he considered to be highly dependent on external relationships. He found that nearly all of the external-economy industries were overrepresented in the New York area. (The high location quotients for New York in publishing and apparel (see Table 4–1) indicate that Lichtenberg's findings are still relevant.) New York accounted for about 10 percent of all national employment at the time of his study, but the region accounted for a much higher percentage of employment in the external-economy industries. Furthermore, he found that firms in the external-economy industries tended to be smaller when they were located in New York than similar firms located elsewhere. Lichtenberg attributed this size difference to the ability of the New

York–based firms to purchase inputs and obtain services quickly at reasonable costs outside the firm. Similar firms located in smaller cities were more likely obligated to produce inputs internally rather than purchasing from vendors. Therefore, external-economy firms located in smaller cities require more "in-house" capacity.

COMPARATIVE MEASURES OF ECONOMIC STRUCTURE

While agglomeration economies is an important theoretical concept for understanding regional economic structure, we also need means to measure and analyze economic activities. This section describes some of the important empirical tools used by applied urban and regional economists. We start by describing a widely used way of categorizing industries. Next, location quotients are explained, and then techniques for using location quotients for estimating exports are illustrated. Coefficients of specialization and the industrial concentration index, additional tools that can be useful to regional economists, are the final topics discussed in this section.

Standard Industrial Classifications

The Standard Industrial Classification (SIC) system is the most commonly used means of labeling economic activities. It is a uniform identification procedure used by most U.S. agencies that collect and analyze data on economic activity. Industries in Table 4–1 are identified by a numerical SIC code as well as industry name. A SIC code is assigned to each business establishment. The code reflects the specific activity at that site and places the establishment within a larger industrial group. For instance, a meat-packing plant would have a SIC number of 2011. The first two digits indicate that it is a food-processing establishment. All meat products establishments are in SIC 201. Thus, the meat-packing designation indicates that it is part of the meat products industries, which are themselves part of the food products group.

The major industrial categories (sometimes referred to as "one-digit industries") are (1) agriculture, forestry and fisheries, (2) mining, (3) construction, (4) manufacturing, (5) wholesale and retail trade, (6) finance, insurance and real estate, (7) services, (8) transportation, communication, electric, gas, and sanitary services, and (9) government.

A firm may have several plants or establishments producing a variety of products. The Standard Industrial Classification system classifies establishments rather than firms or companies. In most instances, the establishment is a facility at a single location. Thus, if a diversified company makes several different products at different sites, it will have plants in different SIC categories.

If a single plant makes more than one product, the establishment is classified according to the dominant product. For example, suppose a plant produced construction machinery (SIC 3531) and mining machinery (SIC 3532). The first two digits indicate that the establishment is in the "machines, except electrical category." The first three digits indicate "construction and related machinery." If over half of the output (in terms of sales) were in construction machinery, the entire activity would be considered in SIC 3531.

Because more than one product can be produced by a single establishment, the SIC system may lead to an underestimation of the variety of goods and services produced in a region. Furthermore, changes in the internal operations of a plant can cause an establishment to be reclassified by a different four-digit code. Consequently, it is sometimes difficult to distinguish between an internal change in production on the one hand and the death of one firm and the establishment of another on the other.

Although the four-digit code provides considerable detail, a variety of separate activities are still lumped together within one four-digit designation. For instance, SIC 3729, "aircraft engines and engine parts," includes about 50 separate manufactured items, such as "starting vibrators" and "rocket motors."

Information on community economic activity is limited by the disclosure rule. Data will usually not be released if it can be traced to a particular establishment. For instance, if there is only one bakery (SIC 205) in a county, no information on that industry will be disclosed. However, bakery information may be included in the description of the food products sector (SIC 20). The disclosure rule is a particular problem for small regions. Even in large regions, disclosure problems will occur at the three- and four-digit level of detail.

Location Quotients

The location quotient (LQ) is a technique for assessing a region's specialization in an industry or some other activity. The industrial composition of a local economy may be better understood by comparing the local industrial structure with other cities or with the country as a whole than by examining a local economy in isolation. For instance, suppose it were determined that fabricated metals accounted for 12 percent of total employment in a community. While this information may be useful for some purposes, it does not tell us whether the economy is highly concentrated in metal fabrication compared with other cities.

The employment location quotient is the ratio of (a) the percentage of regional employment in a particular industry to (b) the comparable percentage in a benchmark area. The country is usually the benchmark area, although states or similar regions may also be used as reference points. Accordingly, the location quotient for industry i is generally expressed as:

$$LQ_i = (e_i/e_t) \div (US_i/US_t) \qquad (1)$$

where LQ_i = Location quotient for industry i,
$\quad\;\; e_i$ = Local employment in industry i,
$\quad\;\; e_t$ = Total local employment,
$\quad\;\, US_i$ = National employment for industry i, and
$\quad\;\, US_t$ = Total national employment.

Quotients can vary among regions due to differences in consumption and production. A $LQ = 1$ for a particular industry means that the region has the same percentage of employment in that industry as the nation. A $LQ < 1$ implies that the area has a less than proportionate share of employment in a particular industry while a $LQ > 1$ implies a greater than proportionate concentration of employment.

Location quotients can be useful tools for identifying industries in which a region has a disproportionate level of employment. The reasons for a community having concentrations of employment in particular industries can often be traced to a current or historical locational advantage. The specific locational advantages often have economic development implications that warrant more detailed study. Likewise, if an industry is underrepresented locally, a development planner might investigate why employment is low and what can be done to increase it. This is not to say that communities should strive to develop economies with structures that are identical to the U.S. average. It would be silly to suggest that Manhattan should have a little piece of the nuclear waste disposal industry. Therefore, good judgment is important in determining how to interpret location quotients.

Table 4–1 shows the location quotients for several major metropolitan regions. They are roughly consistent with our casual knowledge of these regions. For instance, New York has high location quotients in apparel, printing, and FIRE (finance, insurance, and real estate). The Los Angeles location quotient in transportation equipment reflects the area's heavy concentration in aerospace production. The dominance of petroleum and chemicals in Houston is consistent with our perception of the Texas economy.

The picture of industrial structure given by the location quotient can change depending upon the level of industrial detail used in the calculations. For instance, the data in Table 4–1 reflect the two-digit level of industrial detail. Houston is obviously highly concentrated in the chemical industry when the classification is limited to two digits. However, Houston does not have high concentrations in all aspects of chemical

TABLE 4-1 Location Quotients in Four Major Urban Regions: 1980

SIC	New York	Los Angeles	Chicago	Houston
Manufacturing				
20 Food products	.46	.77	1.07	.45
23 Apparel	2.92	1.55	.29	.03
24 Lumber or wood	.19	.43	.27	.34
25 Furniture, fixtures	.68	1.85	.99	.20
26 Paper and allied products	.74	.61	1.17	NA
27 Printing and publishing	2.29	.98	1.67	.64
28 Chemicals	.61	.68	1.13	1.90
29 Petroleum or coal	NA	1.49	.77	4.90
30 Rubber and plastic	.47	1.04	1.23	.54
32 Stone, clay, glass	.25	.87	.80	.72
33 Primary metals	.23	.60	1.06	.66
34 Fabricated markets	.47	1.19	1.62	1.36
35 Machinery except electrical	.24	.83	1.20	1.46
36 Electronic equipment	.45	1.33	1.46	.50
37 Transportation equipment	.15	2.31	.38	.17
38 Instrument and related	.68	1.00	1.12	.38
Transportation, etc.	1.2	.92	1.12	1.14
Wholesale	1.36	1.07	1.18	1.25
Retail	.72	.79	.90	.84
FIRE	2.17	1.04	1.24	.98
Services	1.36	1.27	1.05	1.14

production. If the chemical industry were divided into more narrowly defined sectors, Houston would be seen to have LQs significantly less than 1 for many chemical activities and a very high LQ for petrochemicals.

Location quotients are a versatile tool. While employment is the most frequently used measure of the extent of economic concentration, value added, sales, and other measures of activity have also been used. The formula shown in equation 4–1 used industrial employment as the specialization variable and total employment as the reference variable. However, the specialization variable need not even be the same as the reference variable. For instance, employment in teaching occupations could be used as an indication of specialization with reference to population:

$$LQ = (t/p) \div (T/P) \qquad (2)$$

where p = Local population,
t = Number of teachers locally,

P = U.S. population, and

T = Number of teachers in the United States.

Such a location quotient would indicate whether the region has a typical proportion of teachers per capita compared to the United States as a whole. Thus, the location quotient may be an indication of service adequacy or local need. Similarly, a variant of the location quotient could compare cubic feet of grain storage facilities (specialization variable) to grain production (reference variable). In this case, a very low location quotient could (but would not necessarily) indicate a shortage of grain storage facilities.

How to Estimate Export Employment

The difference between export activities and activities that serve local consumers is an important structural distinction.[2] According to the export-base theory discussed in Chapter 5, export industries are the engines of economic growth. The purpose of this section is not to explore the role of exports in the growth process but to show how understanding an area's exports is a key element in understanding its structure and how location quotients can be used to measure regional exports.

In order to understand the link between the location quotient in a particular industry and export employment, the following assumptions are necessary: (1) the output employment ratio is identical in all regions, (2) consumption patterns throughout the country are identical, and (3) the product of each SIC industry is identical in each region. Under these circumstances, a $LQ > 1$ means that the region has more individuals employed in the particular industry than would be expected based upon benchmark patterns. A possible explanation for a higher than average proportion of regional employment in a particular sector is that some of the sector's workers are producing exports—products that are sold outside the region. If this explanation is valid, a $LQ > 1$ means that some portion of the employees in that industry is producing for export. Conversely, a $LQ < 1$ means that the product is underproduced locally and, hence, must be imported. Exact self-sufficiency is signified by a $LQ = 1$.

Export employment can be estimated using a variant of location quotient. If a $LQ = 1$ means exact self-sufficiency, then export employment in an industry would be the excess employment above the number necessary to satisfy local needs. Self-sufficient employment would be the number required to bring the location quotient to 1. Let s_i equal the self-sufficient

---

[2] In urban and regional economics, the term "export" normally means that the product is sold outside the area, not outside the country.

employment level. Then

$$1 = (s_i/e_t) \div (US_i/US_t) \text{ or} \tag{3}$$

$$s_i = (US_i/US_t) \cdot e_t \tag{4}$$

where US_i represents United States employment in industry i, US_t is the total employment in the country, and e_t equals total local employment. Equation 3 may be modified to estimate export employment in industry i, x_i:

$$x_i = e_i - s_i, \text{ or} \tag{5}$$

$$x_i = e_i - e_t(US_i/US_t). \tag{6}$$

Total export employment is the sum of the export employment in the individual sectors. Therefore, total regional export employment x_t may be expressed as:

$$x_t = \Sigma x_i. \tag{7}$$

Critique.   Unfortunately, the location quotient is not a precise indicator of the extent of importing and exporting. There are several possibilities that break the link between the value of the location quotient and the level of exports.

1. When analysts assume that a LQ of 1 implies exact self-sufficiency, they overlook the possibility of cross-hauling (simultaneously importing and exporting the same product). Since cross-hauling is generally ruled out by assumption, gross and net exports are therefore assumed to be identical for each sector.

2. If workers in a region are more productive than workers elsewhere, a $LQ_i < 1$ might be appropriate for a community, even though the industry was an exporter of the product. Conversely, an unproductive sector could have a high LQ_i, even though it produced only for local consumption. In order to minimize the problem of worker productivity differences, value-added or total output could be used to develop the location quotient.

3. If there are significant regional variations in the level of demand, the location quotient will not necessarily reflect the extent of exports or imports. For instance, southern cities have had a disproportionate level of employment in air-conditioning maintenance. However, this difference is due to greater local demand compared to the rest of the United States rather than significant exportation of such goods and services.

4. The estimated level of exports depends upon the level of industrial detail and product differentiation. As pointed out previ-

ously, when broad industrial categories are examined, the *LQ*s tend to be closer to 1 than when more-detailed industries are examined. A region could have a low location quotient in manufacturing, indicating no exports, but some sectors within manufacturing may be exporters. Similarly, Detroit is a net exporter of automobiles, but it also imports models of cars not made in Detroit due to product differentiation. Because of the existence of cross-hauling, the volume of exports estimated by the *LQ* technique will be subject to error. Generally, the more detailed the industrial breakdown, the greater the exporting sector will appear. Thus, the direction of bias due to the failure to disaggregate completely or due to product differentiation is predictable.

5. A *LQ* of 1 indicates self-sufficiency only in a closed national economy. However, the United States imports products from the rest of the world. Hence, the average community with a *LQ* of 1 for a particular good or service may still be exporting or importing some of the commodity.

Rebuttal.   The criticisms above suggested that the location quotient approach to determining exports would not result in an exact estimate of export activity. Empirical studies indicate that the number of individuals in the export sector is normally underestimated when location quotients are used to estimate exports. However, the technique has three important advantages that are responsible for its continued popularity.

First and foremost, location quotients are an inexpensive way to describe a region's exports because they can be constructed from published data. Second, location quotients can help estimate indirect exports. For instance, a city that exports computers may have a high location quotient in molded plastic parts because the plastic is embodied in the computer and indirectly exported. If the plastic parts manufacturers were asked directly, they might respond that their products were sold within the local economy and not exported. However, they are, in fact, indirect exports. Unfortunately, the *LQ* technique does not allow determination of whether products like molded plastics are exported as part of computers or whether they are exported in some other form. Third, the *LQ* technique applies equally to commodities and services. How can a service be exported? A service can be considered an export when nonresidents enter the region to purchase a service. In this sense, Orlando, Florida, is an exporter of entertainment services because the vacationers go to Disney World.

The Minimum-Requirements Technique.   Some analysts believe a more accurate picture of local export sectors can be obtained by the minimum-requirements technique. Whereas the *LQ* technique normally uses the entire national economy as a benchmark, the minimum-requirements approach bases the self-sufficient employment level upon analysis of similar areas. For instance, suppose you wish to determine the export employment for a region with a population of 100,000. The minimum-requirements approach could involve examination of, say, 20 cities of similar size. The cities might be selected based on other common characteristics such as location or per capita income. The city with the smallest location quotient in an industry (i.e., smallest percentage employment) would be presumed to represent the minimum requirement needed by a city to satisfy its domestic needs. Thus, it represents the self-sufficient level. The minimum-requirements approach normally results in a higher level of estimated exports than the *LQ* technique. A variant of the minimum-requirements technique might use some other threshold, such as the fifth smallest location quotient, as the minimum requirement for self-sufficiency. Export employment would be all employment above the minimum-requirement threshold.

Coefficient of Specialization

The coefficient of specialization measures the extent that a region's industrial structure differs from some standard such as the national industrial structure. Table 4–2 indicates the coefficient of specialization for the Great Lakes and the Far West regions in terms of income earned from major industrial categories. In 1986, the Great Lakes region was the most specialized (due largely to the high concentration in manufacturing) and the Far West was the least specialized.

The first three columns show the percentage of income from each of the sectors. The fourth and fifth columns show the differences between the proportion of U.S. income from each sector and the comparable regional percentage. For each region, the positive differences in some sectors must be offset by a negative percentages in other sectors. The sum of the positive differences (or the absolute value of the negative differences) is the coefficient of specialization. The more detailed the industrial structure, the larger the coefficient of specialization will be.

A coefficient of zero would indicate that the region had exactly the same percentage of income or other variable from each sector as the nation. The maximum coefficient would approach 100; for instance, residents of a region might receive all of their income from sources not available elsewhere in the United States. A coefficient of specialization is high or low by comparison with other areas.

Like location quotients, the coefficient of specialization is a versatile tool. It can be used to examine employment, value-added sales, and so forth. The coefficient of specialization could be used to determine the extent to which the demographic pattern of a region—age, sex, and/or race—fits the national average.

TABLE 4–2 1986 Coefficient of Specialization in the Great Lakes and Far West Region

	Percentage of Income			Difference from United States	
Source of Income	United States	Great Lakes	Far West	Great Lakes	Far West
Agriculture	1.78	1.65	2.0	− .13*	.25
Mining	.93 ·	.37	.69	− .55	− .24
Construction	6.68	6.25	6.63	− .43	− .05
Manufacturing	22.21	36.41	19.32	14.20	−2.89
Wholesale/Retail	14.93	5.42	16.52	− 9.51	1.60
FIRE	7.42	7.09	7.11	− .32	− .30
Transportation, Commerce, and Public Utility	6.42	2.49	6.47	− 3.92	.05
Services	23.58	24.79	25.31	1.21	1.73
Government	16.04	15.51	15.88	− .53	− .16
Coefficient of specialization				15.41	3.63

* A negative number indicates the United States has a larger percentage than the region. Totals may differ slightly due to rounding.

SOURCE: Calculated from *Survey of Current Business*, U.S. Department of Commerce, Bureau of Economic Analysis, August 1970 and August 1987.

Industrial Concentration Index

The *LQ* helps answer the question: To what extent is a particular area's economic structure concentrated in a particular activity? An analogous but subtly different question is: To what extent is a particular industry concentrated in a city type? For instance, we might want to determine whether firms in a group of advanced-technology industries tend to locate in metropolitan regions with populations of over 5 million. A measure of the tendency for firms in industry i to locate facilities in regions of type t could be derived as follows:

$$ICI_{it} = (e_{it}/US_i) \div (e_{tt}/US_t) \qquad (8)$$

where ICI_{it} = Industrial concentration index for industry i in city type t,
  e_{it} = Total employment in industry i in city type t.
  US_i = Total U.S. employment in industry i,
  e_{tt} = Total employment in cities of type t, and
  US_t = Total U.S. employment.

According to equation 8, if 10 percent of an industry's employment is located in regions of a particular type, say in cities with 10,000–20,000 people, while 5 percent of the nation's employment is concentrated in cities of that type, then the ICI would be 2. An analyst could conclude that employment tends to concentrate in the type of places being examined.

The industrial concentration index is not a measure of the economic structure of a particular area. It measures the locational pull of types of cities for particular industries. Nevertheless, the ICI can be useful in understanding the industrial composition of an area. The ICI is also of use to development planners who seek to direct development efforts towards industries likely to locate in the region.

OTHER ASPECTS OF REGIONAL STRUCTURE

Thus far, we have viewed regional economic structure primarily in terms of industrial composition. This perspective is traditional and appropriate among regional economists. However, the structure of a local economy includes more than industrial composition. A detailed understanding of an area's structure might include social and political factors as well as the traditional economic variables. The purpose of this section is to sketch some of the important structural features that can influence local development as much as industrial composition.

Occupational Structure

Imagine two economies with very similar industrial structures as indicated by similar local quotients. This similarity could mask important occupational differences. For instance, both areas could be dominated by employment in the steel industry. But, in one city, the employees could be primarily production workers while the other city could be the corporate home office where the employees are primarily managers, accountants, scientists, secretaries, or other related white- and pink-collar workers. In fact, the home office community may produce no steel directly and yet have significant employment in the steel industry.

It is as important to observe changes in the regional occupational structure as it is to monitor changes in the industrial structure. Some economists contend that part of the economic development process is a movement from goods-producing to knowledge-producing activities. This shift requires a change in the occupational structure. Many large cities have gone through a transformation from goods to service production without drastically changing their occupational mix. Akron, Ohio, for instance, was once the site of almost all tire production in the world. Now, no tires are made in Akron, but it remains the corporate headquarters for major rubber companies and is a center for polymer research. In this case, the region's revitalization was reflected in the changing occupation structure even though the principal corporate employers did not change.

Ownership Structure

Are the major establishments owned primarily by local residents, or are they branches of other corporations? When local residents are the primary owners of major corporations, they may be in a position to provide community leadership and are often big contributors to local philanthropic causes. In contrast, if the major businesses were owned by individuals or corporations located outside of the area, local executives may have less interest, experience, or incentive to become involved in local affairs. For instance, a manager of a major General Motors plant is unlikely to have known about the needs of an area before being transferred. It may take several years to learn enough about a community to be an effective leader. Yet, most ambitious managers hope for transfers up the corporate ladder; they may hope to leave the community. Such attitudes and incentives are likely to deter community involvement.

The ownership structure may also affect the growth prospects of local establishments. However, the effect on growth could be good or bad depending upon the circumstance. On the one hand, the nonlocal owners could treat local branches as cash cows, depriving the firm of the investment needed to expand. On the other hand, the outside owners could provide financing that may be needed for expansion. Perhaps, in a pure economic world, the separation of ownership and location would not be an important determinant of investment. However, in practice, noneconomic considerations sometimes influence investment decisions. Smith (1979) found that external takeovers generally harm the growth prospects of acquired firms.

Local economies may experience leadership voids when the managers of the major employers are temporary residents on rotation among various corporate facilities or where they hope to eventually be relocated to the home office. Furthermore, areas have had their philanthropic base weakened as founding families have sold locally based businesses to larger firms with professional managers based in distant locations. The descendants of the company founders eventually leave the area, further weakening the philanthropic and leadership base.

Market Structure

The nature of the markets in which firms buy and sell can affect the economic well-being of a community. For instance, if a community's base is composed primarily of vertically integrated large businesses, there may be fewer opportunities for new ventures that can sell to the dominant companies. The entrepreneurial climate may be dampened. The few producers may act as monopsonists in the labor market, thus keeping the wage rate lower than it would otherwise be. If the dominant firms sold their output in oligopolistic commodity markets, the price of the output may be inflexible downward because each firm would fear a price war if any firm first lowered price. Therefore, when demand for output falls as in a recession, more local unemployment would result than would have been the case had the industry been competitive. Consequently, regions with a high proportion of oligopolitic firms are likely to be more sensitive to national business cycles.

Political and Social Structure

Political scientists often distinguish between communities with pluralistic power structures where decision making is widely shared among most groups and elite power structures where participation is closed or dominated by one or a few groups at the exclusion of others. Of course, the economic structure of an area affects the political structure. The nature of the political structure also affects economic growth and development prospects and strategies. For instance, many retirement and resort communities are dominated by real estate–related interests that are usually progrowth. When these interests conflict with a no-growth/quality-of-life perspective, the economic future of an area may depend upon the political structure.

Demographic Structure

The age, gender, and educational composition of a region influences economic development prospects in many ways. In some communities, the retired and near retired make up an exceedingly large part of the population. Such communities are often dependent upon transfers from the government, interest payments, and private pensions. Economic activity is likely to be oriented towards providing services for the retired population. Other communities may have a highly mobile population that makes it difficult to retain employees or a young population that creates major demand upon schools and other public infrastructures. Certainly, an economic development official should be aware of how the demographic structure affects community needs and prospects.

Many experts believe that the 1990s will be a period of urban labor shortages because the rate of growth of the work force will decrease. Furthermore, the aging of the baby boom may increase productivity. Both of these demographic factors may increase incomes; hence, higher living standards are predicted.

REGIONAL CONVERGENCE AND DIVERGENCE

Many economists believe that regional economies are becoming more alike, an observation called the convergence thesis. However, the process of increasing similarity is not universal. Although convergence appears to be the more powerful of the trends, it is important to examine instances of divergence as well.

The major regions of the United States have become more alike in several important respects. New England, the Middle Atlantic, and the East–North Central were the most industrialized and urbanized areas in the United States at the start of the 20th century, and they continue to be. In contrast, the West, West–South Central, and the mountain states have been the most rural and agriculture-based regions. However, throughout the century, regional structures have been changing so as to narrow the difference. Convergence in poverty rates and per capita incomes has also occurred. Gold (1987) even found evidence of convergence in the progressivity of the tax system.

Table 4–3 provides an indication of the extent of convergence among major regions in the United States by showing regional coefficients of specialization for 1967 and 1986. Convergence is indicated by the fact that the coefficient of specialization decreased between the two years for all regions except the Great Lakes region. The highest specialization coefficient was 16.55 in 1967 (Rocky Mountain region) compared to 15.41 in the Great Lakes region in 1986. The average coefficient of specialization also declined substantially. Thus, evidence indicates that the sources of income are becoming more similar among regions.

TABLE 4–3   Coefficients of Specialization: 1967–1986 (by region)

Region	1967	1986
New England	10.65	6.89
Mideast	7.42	5.75
Great Lakes	10.43	15.41
Plains	10.25	7.67
Southeast	6.27	5.86
Southwest	11.70	8.19
Rocky Mountains	16.55	11.43
Far West	5.82	3.62
Average	9.88	8.10

SOURCE: Calculated from *Survey of Current Business,* U.S. Department of Commerce, Bureau of Economic Analysis, August 1970 and August 1987.

Undoubtedly, the movement of labor and other factors of production towards regions where the rate of return is highest has contributed to convergence. As resources move from surplus to scarce regions, the regions become more alike in terms of the relative abundance of those resources. These resource and commodity movements are discussed in detail in Chapter 9 and help explain the economic factors that contribute to convergence. International evidence obtained by using countries as regions also indicates that convergence is a powerful force. Dollar and Wolff (1988) showed evidence of convergence in productivity among industrialized countries. In particular, they found productivity increases were higher in countries that initially had the lowest productivity levels. Baumal (1986) showed that convergence among industrialized regions holds for planned and unplanned economies alike, but not for less developed nations. Thus, some level of development appears necessary to the establishment of economic linkages that will allow the process of convergence to operate.

National and international convergence in tastes and the way economic activity is organized have also been discussed in the literature. Not only are many individual business organizations within capitalist economies becoming more alike, but many observers believe that communist and socialist nations will become more capitalist while capitalist nations will increase regulations and strengthen the "social safety net" so as to become more socialist. In this ideological context, the most recent movements of socialist countries to introduce elements of capitalism into their system are most noticeable. Most capitalist or "free enterprise" economies include substantial components of regulation and welfare spending that are not consistent with the pristine notions of pure capitalism.

Whether divergence or convergence dominates regional process is an important issue. Neither process is either universal or inevitable. Hoover and Giarratani (1984, p. 335) pointed out that during periods of rapid economic change, such as the periods of development of the railroads or the disruptions caused by the Civil War, divergence in regional structure (particularly income) occurred. Thus, major shocks to an economy may cause one region to jump ahead or fall behind other regions for several decades.

In recent years, several economists have been concerned with uneven economic growth between different regions. North (1979) found that regions experience "long waves" of growth and decline. Accordingly, divergence in regional development could occur if one region were in the up cycle of a long wave while another region was declining.

Booth (1986) suggested that the main cause of regional growth-rate disparities is the industrial mix of the area. Some areas have new, fast-growth industries while regions in the retardation stage of the long wave have a high percentage of large, older businesses that are past the rapid-growth phase of their life cycles. Such businesses and managerial orientation contrast with the entrepreneurial orientation of fast-growth business in rapid-growth regions. The main barrier to new business formation in older regions is the existence of established industries that divert potential entrepreneurs from new business activities. Disparities between regions in such things as unionization, labor costs, and taxes are also the result of regional differences in their long wave cycles.

Furthermore, increasing similarities among some broad economic variables at the state or regional level may mask divergent tendencies that are apparent at a more detailed level of analysis. For instance, within metropolitan areas, poverty and the pathologies associated with poverty are increasingly concentrated in fewer neighborhoods. Further, some differences attributed to disparity in natural resource endowments are likely to continue as are differences attributable to economies of scale. However, the prospects are for increasing convergence in regional economic structure.

Some observers suggest that regions are becoming more alike in respects other than economic structure. For instance, television and mass advertising have made our values, behavior, language, and consumption patterns more alike. Increased travel among regions also has a homogenizing effect. Thus, not only are regional economic structures becoming more alike but other distinctive regional traits are weakening.

SUMMARY

Cost reductions due to spatial concentration of economic activity are termed agglomeration economies. There are several types of agglomeration economies. Internal agglomeration economies are due to increases in a single firm's activities in a region. Furthermore, establishments that trade with one another may receive benefits from locating together, even if they are unrelated in any other way. Localization economies are internal to a particular industry, but external to the firm. Since industry can be a fuzzy concept, localization economies should be interpreted to include benefits that accrue to clusters of related activities. Urbanization economies are the most diffuse type of agglomeration economy and result from an expansion in overall economic activity in an area.

Agglomeration will occur only when the benefits of moving to the site of agglomeration outweigh the costs. Therefore, agglomeration sometimes requires coordination among firms in order to determine where they will locate and how the benefits of agglomeration will be divided. If institutions for coordination are lacking, agglomeration economies may not occur. Impediments to agglomerations are greater for relocating establishments than for newly formed establishments because of relocation costs. Cities can become self-reinforcing points of agglomeration. Once economic activity reaches a sufficiently high level, activities that will add to the agglomerative strength are attracted to the area.

External-economy industries are particularly sensitive to agglomeration economies. Generally, such activities must respond quickly to changes in the business environment in order to succeed. They often require flexible suppliers. External-economy industries are a significant part of the economy of large cities, and the linkages in the urban environment are important to the successful functioning of firms in external-economy industries.

There are several important techniques for measuring economic structure. Location quotients are the most widely used measure. The employment location quotient is the percentage of local employment in a region compared to the percentage of national employment in the same industry. A $LQ = 1$ means that local employment in the industry is proportional to national employment. Besides employment, sales, value added, payrolls, and other indicators may be used to measure activity. Location quotients are useful in estimating local export activity. Coefficients of specialization and industrial concentration indexes are also useful tools.

Interindustry relationships were the primary focus of this chapter. Other important aspects of a region's economic structure include the occupational mix, type of ownership, and nature of firms. The political and social structure of a region also influence the economy.

The convergence hypothesis suggests that regions are becoming more alike. The evidence indicates that differences in regional economic structure are diminishing. However, the convergence hypothesis is a generalization with many exceptions. Many parts of central cities, for instance, have become increasingly different from the rest of the metropolitan region in terms of important variables such as industrial and demographic structures.

REFERENCES

Baumal, William J. "Productivity Growth, Convergence, and Welfare." *American Economic Review* 76, no. 5, December 1986, pp. 1072–85.

Bergsman, Joel; Peter Greenston; and Robert Healy. "The Agglomeration Process in Urban Growth." *Urban Studies* 9 October 1972, pp. 263–88.

Booth, Douglas E. "Long Waves and Uneven Regional Growth." *Southern Economic Journal* 53, no. 2, October 1986, pp. 448–60.

Dollar, David, and Edward N. Wolff. "Convergence of Labor Productivity among Advanced Economies 1963–1982." *Review of Economics and Statistics* 70, no. 4, 1988, pp. 549–58.

Gold, Steven D. "State Government Response to Federal Income Tax Reform" *National Tax Journal* 40, no. 3, September 1987, pp. 431–43.

Goldstern, D. "The State Government Response to Federal Income Tax Reform: Indications from the States that Completed Their Work Early." *National Tax Journal* 40, issue 3, September 1987, pp. 431–43.

Henderson, William L., and Larry C. Ledabur. *Urban Economics: Processes and Problems*. New York: John Wiley & Sons, 1972, chapter 4.

Hirshman, A. O. *Strategies of Economic Development: Processes and Problems*. New York: John Wiley & Sons, 1972, chapter 4.*

Hoover, Edgar M. *Location Theory and the Shoe and Leather Industry*. Cambridge, Mass.: Harvard University Press, 1937.

Hoover, Edgar M., and Frank Giarratani. *An Introduction to Regional Economics,* 3rd ed. New York: Alfred A. Knopf, 1984, chapter 5.

Isard, Walter. "Game Theory, Location Theory, and Industrial Agglomerations." *Papers and Proceedings of the Regional Science Association* 18, 1966, pp. 1–11.*

Lichtenberg, R. M. *One-Tenth of a Nation*. Cambridge, Mass.: Harvard University Press, 1960.*

Mills, Edwin S., and Bruce W. Hamilton. *Urban Economics,* 3rd ed. Glenview, Ill.: Scott, Foresman, 1984, chapter 1.

North, R. D. *City Life-Cycles and American Urban Policy*. New York: Academic Press, 1979.

Smith, Ian J. "The Effect of External Takeovers on Manufacturing Employment Change in the Northern Region between 1963 and 1973." *Regional Studies* 13, 1982, pp. 421–37.

Streit, M. E. "Spatial Associations and Economic Linkages between Industries." *Journal of Regional Science* 9, no. 2, 1969, pp. 177–88.

* Classics.

Chapter Five

Regional Growth and Development: Fundamental Perspectives

Previous chapters have not addressed the issue of economic growth directly, although the implications of various models for urban and regional growth have been very near the surface. Local growth is affected by locational decisions of firms, the area's place in the system of cities, and its economic structure. This chapter presents fundamental theories of urban and regional growth. The following chapter builds on the fundamentals by developing additional models and perspectives.

The first section of this chapter compares the stages and epochal historical models of growth. The stages model suggests that areas experience similar growth stages. The epochal model attributes growth to the interaction between local economies and national economies in different eras. The second section presents a simple circular-flow model of a local economy, setting the stage for a description of the export-base theory in section three. This theory implies that regions grow because of their ability to sell products to individuals living outside the area. The next section is an evaluation of the export-base approach. The export-base model is a demand-side approach because it suggests that the foundation of regional growth is external demand for the region's products. In contrast, the final section describes the supply-side approach. From this perspective, increases in local factors of production cause growth.

HISTORICAL PERSPECTIVES

Perhaps the most direct way to address the issue of why cities grow is to form generalizations based on history. Using the stages-of-growth approach, individual cities from different countries and different historical periods can be examined to determine whether they passed through common stages in the course of their development. Additionally, a location's potential contribution to national economic growth during various historical periods can be described. For instance, during the early period of industrial production, cities with environments favorable to industrialization, such as waterway locations, grew rapidly. This second approach is termed the epochal model.

Stages of Growth

Thompson (1965) and Jacobs (1969) both observed that cities pass through stages as they develop. Although there are differences in the terminology, emphasis, and details, the similarities between their descriptions are striking. Table 5–1 summarizes the stages of growth described by Thompson and Jacobs.

The stages of growth indicate that metropolitan areas initially export one or a few products. The initial export becomes the foundation for additional activities. During the second and third stages of the development process, the local economy becomes more complex. Exports become more diversified, and goods previously imported into the area may

TABLE 5–1   Stages of Urban Growth

Thompson's Stages of Growth	*Jacobs's Stages of Growth*
1. Export Specialization: "The local economy is the lengthened shadow of a single, dominant industry."	1. Expanding market for a few exports and suppliers of the exports.
2. Export Complex: "Local production broadens and/or deepens by extending forward or backward."	2. Suppliers begin exporting directly.
3. Economic Maturation: "The principal expansion is in the direction of replacing imports."	3. Goods initially imported into the area are produced and sold locally.
4. Regional Metropolis: "The local economy becomes a node connecting and controlling neighboring cities."	4. The city's enlarged and diversified local economy becomes a potential source of exports. The exports increase the volume of imports.
5. Technical-Professional Virtuosity: "National eminence in some specialized economic function is achieved."	5. New work is constantly developed. An "economic reciprocating system" results in new skills or businesses.

Adapted from: Jane Jacobs, *The Economy of Cities* (New York: Random House, 1969); and Wilbur R. Thompson, *A Preface to Urban Economics* (Baltimore: The Johns Hopkins Press, 1965).

be produced internally (import substitution). For instance, Chicago's manufacturing activities began as small operations designed to serve the local market. Products originally intended to satisfy local customers may make the product unique and help establish an export demand. Also, the increases in the variety of goods that the locality exports may cause the number of suppliers to the dominant exporter to increase. Development of new economic activities is a critical element for continued growth. In the fourth stage, the area becomes a regional center by developing a hinterland that depends upon the city for a variety of goods and services. As cities grow, they improve their ability to develop or improve products and production processes as well as to copy what others have done. The service sectors such as education, banking, and real estate become important in generating new products and attracting new industry. This innovative and imitative ability contributes to further growth in the fifth stage.

Once an area reaches a critical mass, the local economy has resources to develop new work. Thompson referred to an "urban-size ratchet," because he believed that once a threshold was reached, urban areas could muster the resources—public and private—to maintain their local economies:

> If the growth of an urban area persists long enough to raise the area to some critical size, power, huge fixed investments, a rich local market, and a steady supply of industrial leadership may almost ensure its continued growth and fully ensure against absolute decline. (p. 24)

The strength of the urban-size ratchet can be overstated. During recent years, many cities and even some metropolitan areas have declined, even after attaining dominance within a region. The point that larger and more complex cities have abilities to generate new economic activity is important to understanding the development process.

Industrial Filtering: Life-Cycle Model.   The theory of industrial filtering helps explain the necessity for metropolitan areas to generate new exports. In Thompson's view, metropolitan areas have a pioneering role in the development process. Larger urban areas tend to be the location of firms when their industries are in the early stages of their life cycle. Activities eventually filter down from their urban birthplace to the less urban hinterland. During the early stages of industrial development, firms often require advanced technical skills, support of other business, and production flexibility. Later, after the production process has become more routine, the need for skills, business support, and flexibility may decrease and other locational factors become more important. Firms engaged in routine work may relocate or expand in less-urban areas in search of lower production costs. Thus, urban areas are on a treadmill, developing new economic activities as old activities filter down to lower-production-cost areas. Also, larger metropolitan areas may retain control of research and development functions within an industry even as the routine functions are dispersed to low-production-cost sites.

Adding New Work to Old.   Jacobs used the phrase "adding new work to old" to describe what she believed was a key element in the movement through the developmental stages. Cities do not grow by simply doing more of what they have done previously. Economies expand by developing new kinds of work. New work results in more diversified export products, many of which started production simply to replace imports; but new work is usually an extension or modification of previous activities. The process of adding new work to old is so pervasive that it is often overlooked—as when a day-care center offers a "sick-child care service" in addition to normal service. The cumulative impact of such activities is vital to development. New work often increases the specialization of labor. A manufacturer of kitchen equipment, a delicatessen, a cheese importer, and a night club might all have resulted from new work being added to an original restaurant. Creating new work also helps conserve old work. As a product spins off from an old activity, the new product may be a supplier or a purchaser supporting the "mother" activity.

Jacobs indicated that larger areas have an edge in the ability to add new work to old:

> The greater the sheer numbers and varieties of division of labor already achieved in an economy, the greater the economy's inherent capacity for adding still more kinds of goods and services. Also, the possibilities increase for combining the existing divisions of labor. (p. 59)

Many instances of service duplication and congestion that urban critics claim are inefficiencies of large places are defended by Jacobs, because she believed they contribute to the innovative climate that encourages new products and processes. Thus, the analysis of how new work develops contributes to our understanding of the process of urban innovation.

Movement between Stages.   How do cities move from one stage to the next? Many theories regarding stages of growth (including the theories of Jacobs and Thompson) are weak in answering this question. To Jacobs, the key is the ability to add new work to old. But why do some areas move to the next stage and others not? According to Thompson, momentum gained during an early stage of development may help propel an area to the next stage. At each stage, the growth stimulus must be sufficient to lift an area to a level complex and large enough so that additional products can be developed and produced locally. In order to continue to move up the urban hierarchy, momentum must be considered relative to other cities, particularly for areas striving towards the regional metropolis stage.

Epochal Models

One of the criticisms of the developmental-stages approach is the assumption that cities pass through similar stages regardless of the historical era in which the major development spurts occurred. In fact, urban development depends upon the historical, cultural, and economic environment of the time (Watkins, 1980).[1] Therefore, another historical approach is to describe important growth attributes during various historical periods. Complete descriptions of urban development may combine concepts of developmental stages with particular historical epochs in which local growth spurts occurred.

Trade Centers. During the Middle Ages, great cities arose as centers of trade and centers of political, social, cultural, and religious life. Transportation was important because it allowed cities to increase their hinterland. Location on one or more trade routes was a major growth determinant. A city's "economic policy" was to prevent the existing hinterland from trading with other towns and to expand the hinterland if possible. Although commerce was important in defining the scope of urban hinterland, so were political, religious, and cultural activities. Some historians have noted that early cities exported "order" and protection. They were military centers that collected tribute in the form of taxes from residents in the hinterland. The central-place model (see chapter 3) is especially helpful in understanding the spatial relationship during this era.

Industrial Era. Somewhere between 1840 and 1860, the industrial era began. Markets became more specialized; a city could develop national or international markets for a single manufactured good, while maintaining a much smaller hinterland for retail and wholesale activities. Access to raw materials and agglomeration economies were key growth components during the industrial era. Technology greatly increased the minimum efficient size of plants. Accordingly, areas that had locational attributes favorable to large manufacturing experienced growth during the industrial era.

The era of the industrial revolution included advances in agriculture and transportation as well as in direct production techniques. Agricultural changes enabled fewer workers to produce a given quantity of food. The

---

[1] For an alternative set of development stages, see Rostow (1966).

advances in agriculture contributed to the dislocation of many rural residents, forcing them into cities and creating conditions for a low-paid manufacturing work force. The era of industrialization also included advances in transportation so that a particular facility could serve a larger market. Adam Smith, writing when portents of the industrial revolution could be observed, stated that "the division of labor is limited by the extent of the market." As transportation improved, the extent of the market increased, making possible large plants where production was divided into very specialized tasks.

The industrial era was vital to the rapid growth of urban areas. Many historians refer to a period of urban industrialization because the processes of urbanization and industrialization are so closely associated. Mills and Hamilton (1989) observed that urbanization "proceeded very rapidly . . . when industrial output and employment were increasing very rapidly" (p. 55), but "since about 1920, there has been a deceleration of growth in manufacturing employment. One consequence has been a deceleration in the growth of urban areas" (p. 57). Additionally, since the 1930s, urban employment in manufacturing has grown less rapidly than employment in other sectors. Especially during the last two decades, urban employment has grown in services, finance, and knowledge based activities. This shift has led analysts to conclude that our economy has entered a postindustrial era of development.

Postindustrial Era.   Today, many economists believe the industrial period is over. Unfortunately, those who argue that we are in a postindustrial era disagree about how to characterize the current development epoch. However, several characteristics do seem critical. These include:

1. Knowledge based.   Knowledge has always been an important urban resource. Today, the more rapid rate of knowledge diffusion has made the generation of new products and processes important to the growth of many places.

2. Global interdependence.   Worldwide markets and production networks have resulted in more local specialization. Headquarters, research and development, and precision operations are increasingly important in major cities throughout the world. Multinational corporations are outsourcing routine manufacturing operations to less-developed countries.

Garnick (1985) has shown that manufacturing jobs, particularly those that have filtered to nonmetropolitan areas, were exposed to much greater import competition in the 1980s than previously. Many areas have become much more sensitive to variations in the exchange rate and to international economic cycles as a result of global interdependence.

3. Intentional cities.   Urban growth is determined by planning more than ever before. Most large regions have several different planning boards, and analytical as well as legal planning tools are more powerful than previously. Thus, communities have a better opportunity to guide regional development toward intended outcomes. Of course, there will be a gap between what is envisioned by planners and other policy makers and the result. But there can be little doubt that deliberate policies are shaping local economics more than previously—for better or worse.

4. Cultural and amenity based.   In more affluent societies, many cities attract residents and businesses on the basis of their cultural resources and other amenities. Social trends, such as longer retirement periods, increased leisure, the footlooseness of many businesses and creative freelancers, and improved communications, contribute to the importance of cultural amenities. Benjamin (1984) used the phrase ''waterways to waterfronts'' to highlight the shift in locational importance from low-cost travel on canals to amenity-rich waterfronts that provide nice settings for relaxation, recreation, and shopping.

Alternative classifications of historical periods that influence urban and regional development have been developed, and historical periods discussed here can be broken down further to provide more detail. However, the trade-center, industrial, and postindustrial periods adequately illustrate how aggregate economic circumstances influence local growth.

In addition, a variety of other factors are always operating to stimulate development in every epoch. For instance, governmental activities have always been a boost to particular cities. Furthermore, manufacturing and mercantile activities are important aspects of urban economies today. Perhaps it is more accurate to envision new functions being grafted onto old functions during successive epochs. The existing functions are not totally replaced by new activity. Hicks (1985) showed that the current era of postindustrial development is associated with the spatial rearrangement of firms and industries. Such a perspective would help bridge the epochal approach by adding the concepts of industrial filtering and adding new work to old.

A Note on Less-Developed Countries

The stages and epochal models are based primarily on the urbanization process in the Western world. Many cities in less-developed countries are in the initial stages of growth where exports are the dominant source of growth. However, the type of export is influenced by the world economy today more than in the past. For instance, when Western cities were primarily engaged in manufacturing, the exports from cities in less-developed countries were primarily related to agricultural and mineral products. Although the urban areas in less developed countries did not produce a significant amount of primary material, they provided related services to both the hinterland and the countries receiving the exports. Unfortunately only a few of the urban areas in less-developed countries that provided services to extractive industries generated new activity necessary to evolve to higher stages.

Currently, the economies of many developed nations are shedding manufacturing activities to lower-labor-cost areas in less-developed countries. Since manufacturing activities have a greater variety of linkages, it will be interesting to observe whether cities in less-developed countries are better able to add new work to old and generate stronger linkages.

CIRCULAR-FLOW DIAGRAM

A circular-flow diagram is illustrated in Figure 5–1. The circular flow is not a theory of *how* a region grows because it implies no causal relationships. Rather, it is a stylized picture of some important linkages and money flows and is the basis for several important theories of growth, which will be discussed later.

A national circular-flow model is a standard feature in most introductory economics principle texts. The circular-flow diagram for an area is similar to the circular-flow diagram for a nation. However, there is an important difference between the national model and the regional model. Exchanges with the "rest of the world" are a smaller portion of national economic activity than of a region's activity. Interactions with the rest of the world are often ignored in treatments of a national economy, although, as the world becomes more interdependent, it is more difficult to ignore outside trade. (As national macroeconomic models reflect the importance of international trade, they will become more like regional models.) One of the keys to understanding the regional circular-flow model and urban growth in general is to understand linkages between the region and the rest of the world.

Elements of the Circular-Flow Model

In the highly simplified circular-flow model, the economy is divided into households and businesses. These categories overlap because the same person can be in the household category while also fulfilling a business role. Specifically, the same individual may be in the business sector when purchasing factors of production and in the household role when purchasing goods and services.

There are five important types of markets in the circular-flow model:

FIGURE 5–1 A Regional Circular-Flow Model

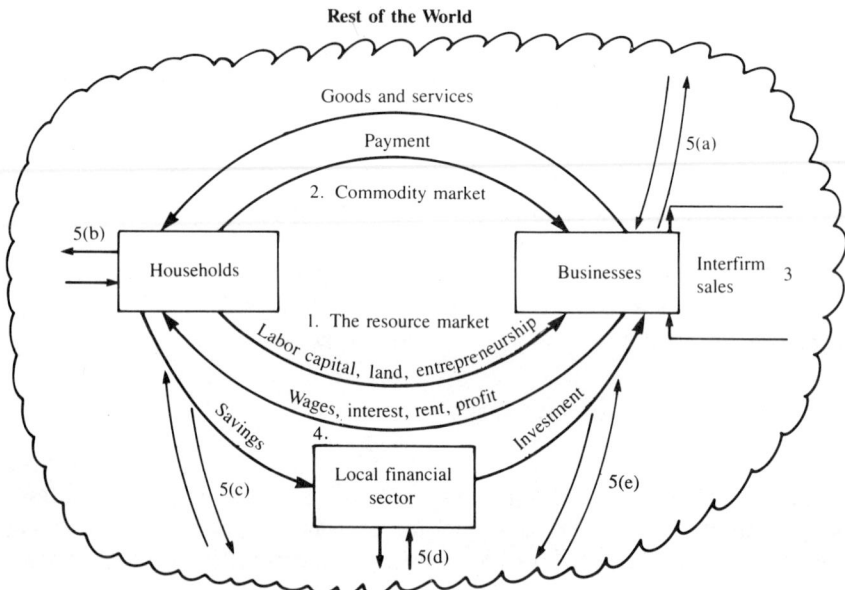

The circular flow diagram shows major sectors of an economy and how they interact. The main difference between a national and a regional economy is the importance of monetary inflow, resulting from exports and other factors, and outflows, resulting from imports and other factors (5).

Resource Market (1). The lower portion of the diagram, the resource market, shows that businesses purchase factors of production from households. In return for the factors of production, households receive wages, rents, interests, and profits. Notice that profits are not retained by businesses in this model. If none of the households earns income outside of the community, the sum of payments received by households from area businesses would equal total regional income.

Commodity Market (2). The local commodity market is the second subsector of the model regional economy. In this market, households purchase goods and services from local businesses. If we assume no nonlocal customers, local-household spending will account for all net (excluding local firms selling to each other) business receipts.

Interfirm Sales (3).   Interfirm sales are an important category of local transactions. Establishments within an area sell intermediate goods and services to each other. The role of interindustry transactions will be described in detail in the discussion of input-output analysis in Chapter 6.

Local Financial Sectors (4).   The fourth set of transactions occur within the local financial sector. Some local-household savings flow into the local financial sector. In Figure 5–1, all savings is by households, implying that businesses do not retain earnings. Even if a household saves by putting money in a sock, rather than an established savings institution, that transaction is considered savings in the local financial sector. Household savings take two forms. A part of the local savings is invested locally. Other savings flow out of the area and are presumably deposited in outside financial institutions or invested directly in outside business ventures by local households. Savings invested outside the area are treated as monetary outflows.

Exchanges with the Rest of the World (5).   The fifth set of transactions is necessary because of the region's interaction with the rest of the world. Exchange with the rest of the world—other regions within and outside the country—are important to the local-economy model. Some aspects of an open economy were previously described in the discussion of financial transactions. Monetary inflows and outflows constitute a relatively small, but growing, percentage of economic activity for the United States, as a whole. Exports constitute about 10 percent of the U.S. GNP. However, for a region, monetary inflows may account for well over half of business receipts or, expressing the idea in real terms, exports may account for over half of business sales. Normally, the smaller the region, the more open the economy and the more important money inflows and outflows are. Notice that households, businesses, and the local financial sector are all shown to interact with the rest of the world. These interactions result in monetary inflows and outflows.

Transaction 5(a) represents business sales to nonresidents that result in a counterflow of money into the area. Businesses also make purchases outside the area. Transaction 5(b) represents household transactions outside the area, such as the direct purchase of goods from other regions or the direct export of labor as would be the case of someone working outside the area. Transaction 5(c) represents direct investment or savings placed outside the area. The return on such investments constitutes a counterflow. Transaction 5(d) represents financial exchanges with the rest of the world that flow through the local financial sector. Outside investments made directly to local businesses and the return on such investments are represented by 5(e).

Money flows into a region for a variety of reasons: gifts from relatives, payments for services performed for nonresidents, payment for goods sold to nonresidents, governmental transfer payments, interest on nonlocal investments made outside the area, and so forth. A portion of the monetary inflows would go directly to households, immediately increasing household income. Another portion accrues to businesses. This would be the case when businesses sell goods and services to nonresidents. Businesses also receive money inflows when nonresidents make investments in local businesses.

Money inflows that accrue to local business may become income to households as businesses pay the households for the factors of production used in producing the goods and services.[2] However, only a portion of business sales becomes income to local residents. Suppose a nonresident purchased a $3,000 stamping machine from a local business. How much income will accrue to households? If the machine were produced entirely within the area, then the full $3,000 would flow to households in the form of wages, rents, interest, and profits. But it is unrealistic to suppose the entire machine was produced locally. More realistically, some of the materials necessary for the production of the stamping machine were purchased from another area outside the region. In this case, the firm making the stamping machine might spend a portion of the $3,000 purchase price, say $1,000, to replenish the inventories used in production. Only $2,000 would accrue to local households. Local households may be perceived as receiving the value added locally, not the total value of exports. Accordingly, the sale of an item for export may be viewed as a net monetary inflow equal to the total value of the product less the cost of the components purchased from outside the community.

Monetary outflows refer to money that leaves the local economy. Monetary outflows occur when households purchase goods or services from outside the area, pay taxes to nonlocal governments, make interest payments to nonresidents, invest in business outside the area, and so forth. Many consumer imports are indirect. For instance, if a person purchased a hat from a local haberdasher, a portion of that expenditure may be attributed to the import of the hat that was made elsewhere. Only the local value added will accrue to household income. As described in the above discussion of the stamping machine, businesses contribute to monetary outflows when they purchase inventories and parts from outside the area.

---

[2] The payments may accrue to households before the export sale or investment is actually made if business increases production in anticipation of export sales.

Complicating the Model

A model is intended to simplify reality. It is tempting to add details in order to make the model more realistic. However, too much added complexity defeats the purpose of a model, which is to highlight key factors. Perhaps Figure 5–1 may already be too complicated to be a good model. Nevertheless, it is usually a worthwhile exercise to examine what has been excluded from models and to ask whether the simplifications seriously distort the reality the model seeks to represent. For instance, one important exclusion from the circular-flow model is the absence of government. Thus, taxes, transfer payments, and government purchases are excluded. However, the exclusion does not distort the analysis of private-sector interactions. Furthermore, monetary inflows and outflows lump together many types of spending. The model would be more realistic if the flows were disaggregated, but it would be messy. Inventions and technological change also affect regional income. It is interesting to imagine how a technology sector could be incorporated into the model. Although it might be possible to do so, it would clearly complicate the model. The process of asking how the model could incorporate these sectors can show the strengths and weaknesses of the circular-flow model.

Equilibrium and Change

The difference between the size of monetary inflows and outflows is critical to local economic growth. Monetary inflows can cause the entire volume of resources circulating within a city to increase. This, in turn, increases employment.

Payments for goods produced in the area and sold elsewhere are a major source of income for the community. For example, when a Detroit-made automobile is sold to a resident of Chicago (or more accurately, when the Detroit-made automobile is sold to an auto dealer who expects to sell it to a Chicago resident), money flows into the Detroit area and becomes income. The inflow of money does not by itself increase real output. However, monetary inflows increase the ability of residents to command additional goods and services and may attract additional resources to the area or stimulate the use of previously unemployed local resources. Sales of goods and services to nonlocal customers are often referred to as "exports." Other nonlocal sources of community income include interest payments from outside corporations, government transfers such as Social Security, gifts received, and investments by nonresidents.

Monetary outflows shrink an area's circular flow and consequently decrease local income and employment. For example, when residents of one area increase their purchases from neighboring regions, the outflow represents foregone income to local business—money that could have been paid to local households in subsequent transactions. Purchases of goods and services from nonlocal sources are called "imports." The term "imports" applies to all purchases made outside the city and not just to international transactions. Thus, the resident of Chicago who purchases a car from Detroit causes an outflow of funds from Chicago and an inflow of dollars to Detroit (assuming auto retailers maintain their inventories by replacing the car they sold).

What is the equilibrium condition of the model represented in Figure 5–1? When monetary outflows equal monetary inflows, the community income level will remain constant. The equilibrium condition can be proven mathematically, but it can also be grasped intuitively by using the bathtub analogy. The amount of water in the tub will remain constant only when the water flowing from the faucet equals the amount that leaves through the drain.

The condition of equilibrium in the circular-flow model does not imply stagnation. The composition of the inflows and outflows can change and new products may be exported or imported. The mix of jobs can change, and some families can enter and others can leave the city. But as long as these changes do not alter the size or velocity of monetary exchanges, the size of the circular flow will remain constant.

The Multiplier

Economic growth in both income and employment results from increases in the volume of transactions. As the volume of business begins to expand, there will be multiplier or ripple effects that will further increase the amount of activity. In order to illustrate the multiplier, suppose a business increases its sales by increasing exports to a business in a nearby state. A portion of the increase will accrue to households as payment for labor and other services involved in producing the output. Households will spend a fraction of the increased earnings in local establishments, thereby expanding the local consumer market and allowing businesses to purchase additional factors of production. However, businesses and households will also purchase from outside the area and cause monetary outflows. Therefore, the process of local spending and respending will not continue indefinitely.

Figure 5–2 illustrates what might happen if a major convention were held in a city. Suppose the convention resulted in increased spending by nonresidents of $260,000. Assume that of the $260,000 in increased spending, $160,000 went to outside suppliers and to a nonlocal corporation that owns the major hotel. Consequently, $100,000 of the initial spending would go to residents who provided services for the conventioneers. Of the $100,000, local residents might spend $80,000 locally. The remainder,

FIGURE 5–2   A Community Income/Expenditure Pattern

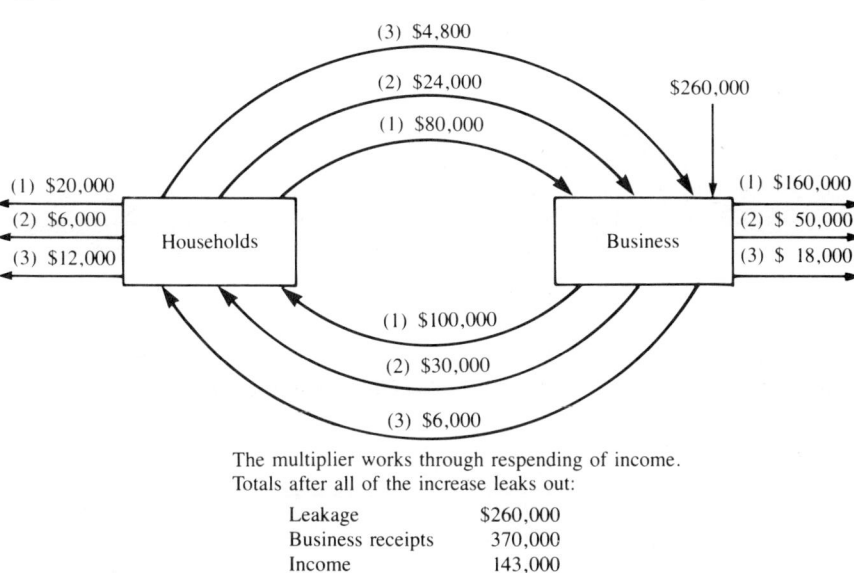

The multiplier works through respending of income.
Totals after all of the increase leaks out:

Leakage	$260,000
Business receipts	370,000
Income	143,000

$20,000, would flow outside the city as households spent or invested outside the local area. Carrying the process further, of the $80,000 spent at local businesses, $50,000 might be used by local businesses to replace inventories (purchased outside the city) and $30,000 may be returned to residents in the form of wages, rent, interest, and profits. Thus, the $260,000 of additional spending resulted in an increase of $100,000 in local income initially and $30,000 of income in a second round of spending. In this instance, because of imports of local businesses, the marginal propensity to consume locally would be ($30,000/$100,000) or .3. If the process were to continue, after a few rounds the original $100,000 would leak out of the community in the form of business and consumer spending. Because of successive rounds of local spending, about $43,000 of household income would be created in addition to the initial $100,000.[3] The larger the leakages per transaction, the smaller the total increase in household income.

---

[3] For reasons explained more thoroughly later, this figure was derived by using a multiplier of 1.43. This was derived as $1/1-$ (marginal propensity to consumer locally) = $1/1-$ .3 = 1.43. The initial $100,000 of locally created income was multiplied by 1.43.

The multiplier has a different effect if the monetary inflow occurs in a single period compared to a permanent increase in income. In order to distinguish between temporary and permanent increases in exports, assume local convention business increased permanently by $260,000 annually. An extra $100,000 would be earned by households every period. Community income would be increased by $130,000 in the second period—the $30,000 second round increase shown in Figure 5–2 plus the extra $100,000 earnings from the first round spending of the second year. In the third period, total income would rise to the sum of (1) first-round, year three spending, (2) second-round, year two spending, and (3) third-round, year one spending or $136,000 (100,000 + 30,000 + 6,000). Thus, the permanent increase in inflows would cause annual community income to rise permanently by $143,000. Figure 5–3 compares the income effects of a temporary and permanent increase in monetary inflows.

FIGURE 5–3   Income Paths from Temporary and Permanent Increases in Monetary Inflows

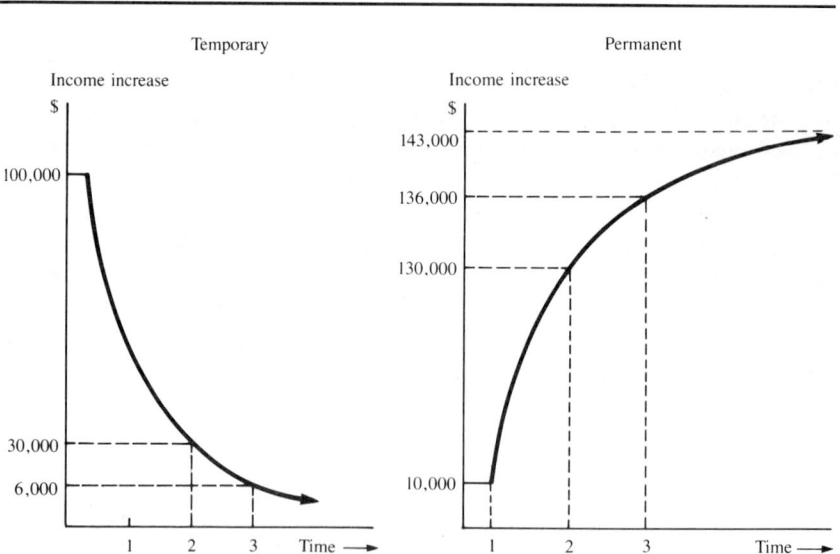

A temporary increase in monetary inflows will increase income by successively smaller amounts. A permanent increase in monetary inflows will permanently increase income by a multiple of the original increase.

The fact that households receive only temporary increases in income from "one-shot" money inflows indicates that many public construction projects and other temporary infusions will not be a source of a long-run increase in incomes. Of course, even a temporary increase in income is nice. However, a business that permanently increases its exports will increase community income to a new, higher equilibrium.

THE EXPORT-BASE THEORY OF GROWTH

The export-base theory of growth is grounded in the idea that a local economy must increase its monetary inflows in order to grow and the only effective way to increase monetary inflow is to increase exports.

Tiebout (1962, p. 10) described the fundamental relationships posed by the export-base theory:

> Export markets are considered the prime movers of the local economy. If employment serving this market rises or falls, employment serving the local market is presumed to move in the same direction. When the factory (export) closes, retail merchants (local) feel the impact as laid-off factory workers have less to spend. Because of the prime mover role, export employment is considered as "basic." Employment which serves the local market is considered adaptive and is titled "non-basic."

The export-base theory may be expressed in terms of either income or employment:

$$\Delta T = k\Delta B \tag{1}$$

$$\Delta Y = k\Delta E \tag{1'}$$

where T = Total employment,
Y = Total income,
B = Basic (export) employment,
E = Export earnings,
k = Export-base multiplier, and
Δ = Change.

The key concept of the economic-base theory is that the export activity is the engine of growth. Income originally earned by the export sector is spent and respent locally, creating additional income through the multiplier. Export industries generate the money that flows into the city. A portion of the export-earned dollars is spent locally by the export workers, creating local service jobs. Employees serving the local economy, in turn, spend much of their earnings locally, thus supporting additional jobs. The size of the multiplier depends upon the propensity of individuals to spend money in the local economy rather than spending it outside of the local area.

It is vital to distinguish between two meanings of "services." Services are a type of economic output as in the phrase "goods and services." In the export-base literature, "local service activities" refer to economic activities that serve local residents. Sometimes students confuse the two meanings and assume that activities in the service sector cannot generate exports. This conclusion is wrong.

Services can be a source of export earnings and a part of the region's basic activities. Services can be exported from the region either when local residents travel outside the area to provide the service or when nonresidents come from outside the area to purchase services, as when individuals travel to Williamsburg, Virginia, for a vacation. When sales by the local service sector bring outside dollars into the local economy, they are basic and should be considered as sources of economic growth (Gillis, 1987).

Recent studies have documented the extent that service activities are export earners. Ashton and Sternal (1978) found that 20 percent of New England's service-producing industries export more than half of their sales to individuals outside the region. Similarly, Beyers and Alvine (1985) found that about 40 percent of the services originating in the Puget Sound region in Washington are sold outside the state. Keil and Mack (1986) identified 22 out of 53 service categories as having strong or moderate export potential. Accordingly, service activities can be a source of export earnings and an important part of an area's economic base. Table 5–2 shows export employment for several metropolitan areas using a location-quotient technique similar to that described in Chapter 4. Exports employment was estimated as all employment over 120 percent of the national average. (The authors justified using the 120 percent cut-off rather than 100 percent on the grounds that residents of major metropolitan areas had above average service demand.)

Proponents of the export-based theory recognize that many businesses serve both local customers and nonresidents. The use of location quotients to determine the export and service sector are discussed in Chapter 4. For the remainder of this section, we will simply assume that we can distinguish between exporting and activities serving the local economy.

The Formal Income Model

The export-base theory can be derived from the circular-flow model. Income rather than employment is usually the focus of formal presentations of the export-base theory. Income may be expressed as:

$$Y = C + MI - MO \qquad (2)$$

TABLE 5–2   Estimated Export Employment in Broad Service Industries

SMSA	Service Export Employment 1985	Rank	Change in Export Employment 1974–1985 (percent)
New York, New York	646,324	1	13.6
Washington, D.C., Maryland	228,010	2	63.4
Los Angeles, California	172,057	3	39.5
San Francisco, California	148,016	4	17.3
Boston, Massachusetts	140,242	5	15.8
Chicago, Illinois	109,415	6	−12.0
Philadelphia, Pennsylvania	96,075	7	38.2
Las Vegas, Nevada	82,525	8	78.4
Atlanta, Georgia	74,870	9	32.8
Miami, Florida	73,806	10	−8.1
Pittsburgh, Pennsylvania	54,742	15	65.7
Detroit, Michigan	38,569	22	57.3
Indianapolis, Indiana	21,336	46	26.6
Milwaukee, Wisconsin	16,726	61	44.9
Dayton, Ohio	8,455	78	350.7
Erie, Pennsylvania	6,571	85	59.3

Notes: Export employment is calculated as employment exceeding the employment associated with a location quotient 20 percent above the average location quotient. The location quotient for an industry is defined as local employment share for that industry, divided by national employment share. National rank refers to the 89 SMSAs studied. Data from: U.S. Department of Commerce, Bureau of the Census, *County Business Patterns*, 1974 and 1985.

Analysis by: The Center for Regional Economic Issues, Weatherhead School of Management, Case Western Reserve University.

SOURCE: Ziona Austrian and Thomas J. Zlatoper, "The Role of Export Services," *Regional Economic Issues Review,* Fall 1988, pp. 24–29.

where Y = Total income,
MI = Monetary inflows,
C = Consumption spending by local residents, and
MO = Monetary outflows.

Equation 2 states that income of local residents is equal to consumption (C) plus net monetary inflows. Notice that consumption of goods or services purchased from outside the area would increase C and MO by equal amounts, so Y would not be changed when local residents spend outside the region.

Consumption.   Consumption has two components. One component is independent of the level of income. Even if residents had no income, consumption might be financed from previous savings, for instance. But most consumption depends upon the level of income. The marginal propensity to consume is the fraction of an increase in income that is spent. If the marginal propensity to consume is .80, then 80 cents of each dollar increase in income will be spent. Thus,

$$C = A + bY \tag{3}$$

where A = Consumption that is unrelated to income, and
   b = The marginal propensity to consume.

Monetary Inflows.   Proponents of the export-base theory argue that exports are the prime source of monetary inflow. Exports are determined by outside demand for goods and services produced in the region. Since the extent of outside demand is beyond the area's control, it is considered "exogenous." Although other sources of monetary inflows have been identified, for the moment assume that monetary inflows are not related to the size of regional income. Alternatives to this assumption will be discussed later. Accordingly, exports are the only source of monetary inflows. Therefore,

$$MI = E_o \tag{4}$$

where E_o = Exogenously determined export income.

Monetary Outflows.   Monetary outflows are determined by the extent to which residents spend outside the area. As local incomes increase, the level of imports will increase. Therefore, monetary outflows are determined by the level of local income. Purchases of goods and services from nonresidents, imports, are the primary source of monetary outflows. For simplicity, assume that all monetary outflows are related to the level of income. Savings that are not reinvested in the local economy are another form of leakage. The greater the savings, the lower will be the marginal propensity to consume, b. However, to avoid complicating the model, the role of financial institutions in the recycling of savings will not be addressed directly. Thus,

$$MO = iY \tag{5}$$

where i = the marginal propensity to import (create monetary outflows).

The Unified Model.   Equations 3–5 can be inserted into equation 2:

$$Y = A + bY + E_o - iY \tag{6}$$

or

$$Y = [1/(1 - b + i)] \times (A + E_o) \tag{7}$$

Based upon equation 7, the factors that determine regional income can be summarized. The first term represents the tendency for dollars to recirculate within the circular flow. The larger the marginal propensity to consume and the smaller the marginal propensity to import, the larger income will be. The second term represents autonomous spending. That is, spending unrelated to the level of regional income. A minimum level of consumption, A, and the level of exports, E, are not affected by income.

Changes in the various parameters of the model such as b, i, and A are determined by institutional, physical, and political factors beyond the scope of the export-base model. Therefore, according to the logic of the strict export-base model, income will increase only if exports, E, change. Setting ΔA to zero[4] and allowing the change in exports to equal ΔE_o, the change in income is:

$$\Delta Y = (1/(1 - (b - i)) \times \Delta E_o \qquad (8)$$

Equation 8 indicates that a change in export income will change total income by $(1/(1 - (b - i)))$ times ΔE_o. Notice that $(b - i)$ is the marginal propensity to spend locally—the marginal propensity to consume minus the propensity to consume from outside the area. Thus, the export-base multiplier is conceptually similar to the Keynesian multiplier used in macroeconomic analysis. The multiplier effect occurs because the initial increase in export income is spent and respent, thus creating additional income. However, some of the additional spending "leaks" from the circular flow in the form of monetary outflow.

A Graphical Approach.   The equilibrium level of regional income is illustrated in Figure 5–4. The vertical axis shows the value of purchases from the region—consumption plus export spending minus monetary outflows. These purchases create income for residents. The horizontal axis shows the value of regional output. Since output creates income for residents, the horizontal axis also shows regional income. The economy will be in equilibrium only when the value of desired purchases from the region equals the regional output. The 45° line shows the possible points of equilibrium.

The spending line, $C + E - MO$, shows the demands for the region's resources at various levels of regional income. The slope of the spending line is equal to the marginal propensity to spend locally. The spending line

---

[4] Let a new level of exports equal $E_o + \Delta E_o$ and the resulting level of income equal $Y + \Delta Y$. Hence, the new income level will be:

$$Y + \Delta Y = (1/(1 - b + i) \times (A + E_o + \Delta E_o).$$

Subtracting equation 7 from the new income level results in equation 8.

will shift upward if exports increase. For instance, if regional export income increases by $50 from $0 to $50, the value of purchases from the region will increase by $75. Increases in exports will shift the $C + E - MO$ line upward.

If the region's output (horizontal axis) exceeds the demand for its product (vertical axis), production will decrease in subsequent periods. Therefore, points on the $C + E - MO$ line to the right of $175 represent situations where regional output exceeds purchases from the region. In such a situation, regional output can be anticipated to fall. Conversely, if the current region's output is insufficient to satisfy the demand for that output, regional output will increase. This case would be represented by points on $C + E - MO$ to the left of $175. Only at level $175 does the amount that individuals are willing and able to spend on products produced with resources within the region equal regional income. Hence, it is an equilibrium point.

The export-base approach is popular for at least two reasons. First, it has a straightforward policy implication—increase exports and grow. Second, it is relatively easy to operationalize.

FIGURE 5–4   Regional Output and Demand

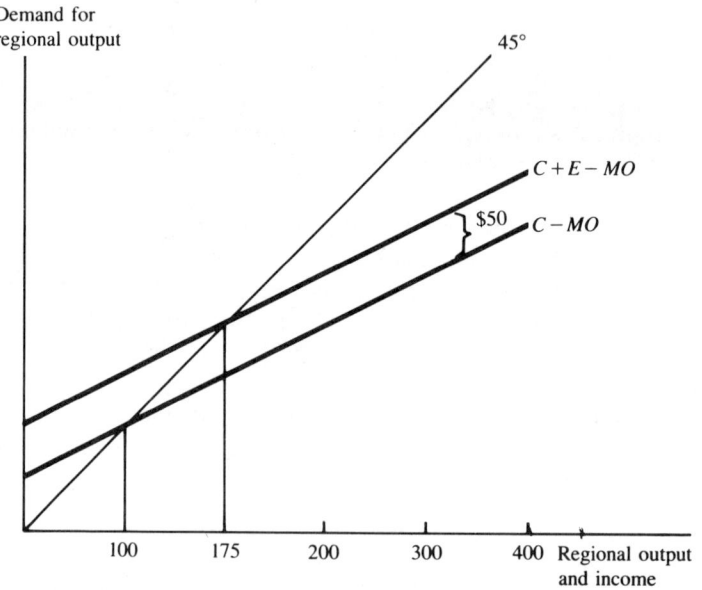

A local economy will be in equilibrium when the value of the desired purchases that create demands on the region's resources equals regional income. In this example, a $50 increase in export income results in a $75 increase in total income.

How to Operationalize the Export-Base Approach

Data on small areas are difficult to obtain, particularly information on marginal propensities to consume and marginal propensities to import. Surveys of local spending habits have been made. But such surveys are expensive and difficult to design. A survey would have to determine both consumer and business spending patterns in order to have a complete measure of imports. In order to avoid the need for surveys, practitioners have developed a technique to estimate the local multiplier using readily available employment data. Employment is used as a proxy for income because of the lack of regional income data. Thus, while the formal model was concerned with income, employment will be used to operationalize the model. On the basis of location quotients, surveys, or other techniques, local employment is split into the number of workers producing for export and the number producing for local consumption.

Key Assumptions. Two assumptions are useful in operationalizing the export-base model. The first assumption is that income is proportional to employment. Therefore, nonbasic income as a proportion of total income will equal nonbasic employment divided by total employment. This assumption is important because it supports the use of employment data as a measure of income changes. In the short run, it is likely that incomes could increase without employment increasing. In this case, per capita income would increase. However, it is reasonable to suppose that higher incomes would attract additional workers to the area. Hence, the link between income and employment can be supported by the movement of labor from lower to higher wage areas. The second assumption is that the ratio of export employment to total employment is constant. Each new export job creates the same number of nonbasic jobs. This implies that as the number of export workers (income) increases, the number of nonbasic employees (income) will increase in the same proportion as the existing export to total employment ratio. The assumption is important because when combined with the first assumption, it allows the estimation of $(b - i)$. With reference to equation 7, $(b - i)$ is the proportion of an income increase spent locally. Therefore, $(b - i)$ will be the same as the nonbasic employment to total employment ratio. Accordingly, the export-base multiplier (equation 1) can be expressed as:

$$k = 1/1 - (b - i) = 1/1 - (NB/T) = 1/(T/T - NB/T) = 1/(B/T) = T/B \tag{9}$$

where T = Total employment,
$\quad\ B$ = Export (or basic) employment, and
$\ NB$ = Nonbasic employment (serving the local market).

Therefore, equation 1 may be expressed as:

$$\Delta T = (T/B) \times \Delta B \tag{10}$$

where ΔT = Change in total employment,
   T = Total employment, and
   B = Basic employment.

Given an understanding of the theory that underlies the export-base approach, the multiplier can be easily calculated. If total employment is 2,000 and export employment is determined to be 1,000, then the employment multiplier would be 2.

Steps in an Export-Base Forecast.   Export-base studies are used for a variety of purposes, and each study is normally tailored to specific circumstances. However, export-base studies tend to have similar structures. The steps in an export-base forecast may be summarized in five stages.

1. The first step in an export-base forecast is to determine the appropriate geographic area for study. The appropriate area is sometimes a compromise between the area relevant for the purpose of the study and the area for which data is available. A neighborhood or small town may be too small an area for a successful study because employment data on such areas is often not available. Furthermore, small neighborhoods or suburban communities have extremely high degrees of interdependence within the larger metropolitan economy. Such subareas do not have a sufficiently integrated internal circular flow, and the service workers are often not even local residents. The export-base concepts may have less meaning in such a very small area. Consequently, studies of very small areas are often undertaken in conjunction with larger studies of integrated areas. While the appropriate area depends upon the purpose of the study, cities, counties, or metropolitan statistical areas are generally chosen for analysis because such areas are integrated economies, export similar items, and are affected by the same trends.

2. The second step is to describe the local economy and determine the sources of export employment. This step sets the stage for deriving the multiplier. A table showing location quotients for each industry is useful for identifying export sectors. Equation 7 in Chapter 4 is one tool that can be used to calculate export (basic) employment. However, determining the level of exports is often difficult, given the lack of detailed data.

3. The third step in an export-base study is to determine k, the local multiplier. The question to be answered is: If basic employment increases by a given amount, how many additional jobs will be created in the region as a whole? As explained above, the multiplier may

be expressed as total employment divided by export employment. Since export employment was estimated in step two and total employment is readily available, this step can be less complicated.

4. The fourth step is to forecast exogenous changes in the local export sector. A frequently employed estimating technique is to apply national trends, appropriately modified to account for the local environment, to current employment levels in order to estimate the change in basic employment. Opinions of experts could be used to estimate possibilities of the development of new export sectors. This step can be quite complicated. However, the end result will be an estimate of the change in export employment (ΔB in equation 1).

5. Once the export employment has been forecast, the multiplier can be used to determine total employment changes. For instance, if the multiplier is 2 and the export sector is estimated to increase by 75 jobs, then the total estimated increase in employment would be 150.

Since it was implicitly assumed that employment is proportional to income, the same multiplier can be used to estimate the change in total income given an initial change in export income.

The forecasting process need not stop at step 5. In fact, the purpose of this section was to describe the bare bones of a typical study rather than to delve into the many complications that can arise in practice. The new level of employment may be used as information to forecast other variables such as income, population, housing demand, and traffic congestion.

Employment-Impact Studies

Urban and regional economists are occasionally asked to estimate the impact of an event, such as the opening of a new plant or the closing of a military base. The impacts of major changes may be wide ranging, including impacts on local fiscal capacity and cultural opportunities. Employment impacts are a major focus of most economic-impact studies. The export-base methodology can be used to estimate the impact of a known or anticipated employment change. For instance, an analyst may be required to estimate the total impact on the economy if a local firm that exported its output and employed 200 people were to close. The initial change in export employment, -200, could be multiplied by the multiplier to estimate the total employment impact.

Of course, many of the techniques for estimating employment changes and for estimating the multiplier can be refined for an important forecast. The purpose of the above discussion was to present the essentials. Determining how to approach more complicated situations is a useful exercise.

Many observers are justifiably skeptical of employment-impact studies because the authors or sponsors of the study often have an interest in exaggerating the size of the impact. For instance, the managers of a facility might hope to exaggerate its importance in the regional economy in order to increase their influence or to strengthen their ability to seek government assistance.

Local impacts of a plant opening or closing may be exaggerated by overestimating the size of the local multiplier or by exaggerating the size of the change in export employment. Small regions normally have significant monetary outflows, and, consequently, the local multipliers are often between 1 and 2. However, in an effort to increase the size of the total employment impact, blatantly unrealistic multipliers have been used. Another way to exaggerate the local impact of an employer is to assume that all the employment in a particular facility is devoted to export. For instance, if a local university that employed 600 people were to close, an inaccurate analysis might assume that 600 jobs would be lost locally. In fact, some of the university students would probably transfer to another local university, junior college, or trade school, and as a result, other local institutions would increase their employment. Hence, not all of the 600 teaching jobs would be lost to the local economy.

CRITIQUE OF THE EXPORT-BASE APPROACH

In recent years, export-base studies have been criticized. It is important to review the criticisms in order to avoid misinterpretations of other studies and to understand the limits of the approach. In general, objections can be divided into those that concern theory and those that concern technique. The criticisms of export-base theory form the basis for recently popular supply-side theories of urban and regional growth. The criticisms of technique suggest that more detailed analysis of the local economy is necessary. However, in spite of the following criticisms, the export-base approach remains one of the principal theories underlying policies of many development officials and urban planners.

Primacy of Exports

Critics contend that the export-base theory places too much emphasis upon exports and overlooks other important factors that can lead to growth. Regions may experience increases in income through increases in the productivity of resources and increases in investment from outside the region or by substituting domestic production for goods and services that were previously imported.

"Reductionism" is an attempt to reduce a complex situation to one cause or to one explanation. The export-base approach is a reductionist analysis. Are exports the only source of monetary inflows? No.

The formal model can be adjusted to incorporate other sources of monetary inflows. For example, investment can be considered an additional inflow. When investment (I) is included, the new definition of income will become:

$$Y = A + bY + I + E_o - iY \qquad (11)$$

or

$$Y = 1/(1 - b + i) \times (A + E_o + I) \qquad (12)$$

Additional leakages can also be included in the model. More leakages will result in a smaller multiplier. An example of an additional leakage might include higher tax payments as the level of local income increases. Obviously, the more factors we include in the formal model, the greater the divergence from the pure export-base theory. Models that could be considered export-base oriented could include investment and other sources of monetary inflows and outflows. These more sophisticated options are in the export-base genre because it is implicitly or explicitly assumed that exports are the main variables that cause change.

Import Substitution

Import substitution is an alternative development strategy that some communities have used to encourage growth without expanding exports. Rather than increasing exports, it may be useful to produce locally what otherwise would have been imported. Such a strategy would result in fewer leakages; each dollar that enters the circular flow would create more income. For instance, if the local multiplier were 2 and export and other autonomous income were $250, the level of income would be:

$$\$500 = k \times (A + E) = 2 \times \$250$$

A successful import substitution strategy would increase the multiplier to, say, 2.25. Therefore, if k were increased through import substitution, the level of income would increase to $562.50 with no increase in exports.

An advantage of import substitution is that many products currently being imported into the area can be identified easily. If that product could be produced locally, it might have a cost advantage in the local market compared to similar imported products because the local product would probably require lower transportation costs. Of course, import substitution may be more difficult than it first appears because the local community may not be able to produce many products economically. Raw materials may not be available, or the most economical scale of production may be too large to justify production for just the local market. In such cases, the imported items could still undersell the locally produced items in the local market.

Both Wilbur Thompson (1968) and Jane Jacobs (1969) emphasized the import replacement role in a region's evolution (see Table 5–1). Thompson suggested that an economy may be positioned to produce goods that were previously imported after the export sector had diversified. Import replacement often requires that the new producer modify the production process or product in some way. The case of Los Angeles shows how import replacement can enhance an economy. At the end of World War II, Los Angeles lost much of its export business because the economy was heavily engaged in the production of war materials. The export-base approach could lead to the conclusion that Los Angeles would experience significant contraction, but this did not happen. Instead, Los Angeles firms started producing to satisfy local demand which had grown substantially during the war. Firms that formerly exported to Los Angeles opened branch plants in the area to serve that market. Thus, the economy grew while exports declined. Eventually, export earnings stopped declining and, in fact, started to increase again. However, growth from import replacement as exports decline is an exceptional situation and it is unlikely that such a process could continue indefinitely.

Many items that eventually become export leaders for a city began as import replacements. For example, one of the products produced originally to replace imports in Los Angeles was the glass door. Glass doors fit the California lifestyle and climate better than the previously imported doors. Eventually, the glass doors caught on and were exported throughout the United States. Many Los Angeles door firms originally produced for the local market but later expanded their operations to include exports. When import replacement occurs simultaneously with an expanding export base, explosive growth occurs (Jacobs, 1969, p. 57).

Productivity

Improving labor productivity and the productivity of other resources can also increase the level of income without increasing the level of exports. Suppose productivity increases in the nonbasic or service sector of the economy. The level of real income in the community could increase, but the level of exports remain the same.

Productivity increases could also cause exports to increase if the improvement in productivity were in the export sector. In this instance, exports are associated with growth yet causal relationship is different from the export-base theory. The increased exports were not exogenous, such as an increase in outside demand. The increase in exports was caused by productivity-increasing forces inside the region, such as local research or education activities.

Exports Not Always Exogenous

The export-base theory includes the implicit assumption that the demand for exports originates outside the area. Several analysts believe that the ability to develop and produce exports may, in fact, rest with the quality of local services within the economy. Service firms play a role in building the export sector. A particular financial institution may provide capital needed to start an export business, a university may provide an idea that results in an innovation, or a land developer may create an attractive industrial park. Collectively, the service sector may provide an overall environment conducive to export development. Most large cities have development councils dedicated to encouraging economic growth. The most active members normally include bankers, real estate developers, brokers, university officials, and public utility planners. These individuals represent the service sector, but they play major roles in encouraging the location and growth of export firms.

In a related vein, Chinitz (1961) asked why some areas are able to rebound after losing their export base while other cities experience long periods of stagnation when they lose their base. He concluded that resilience depended on the structure of the local economy, especially the availability of intermediate services. Chinitz's analysis contributed to the development of the supply-side approach discussed in the next section.

Small versus Large Regions

The export-base theory may be more applicable to small regions, such as MSAs, than to large regions, such as state or multistate areas. At one extreme, an individual will sell services outside the household in order to increase income because the opportunities to increase by home production (i.e., import substitution) are limited to backyard gardens, do-it-yourself projects, and so forth. As the size of the community increases, opportunities to increase income by internal production increase. At the other extreme, the world, a region in the cosmic scheme, has grown without exports. Clearly, the scope for growth through internal production is greater the larger the region. Thus, the larger the region, the less important exports are and the less adequate the export-base theory is in describing growth.

Feedbacks

Feedbacks are a function of interdependence and regional size. Actions of large regions may create feedback effects from other large regions, and the extent of the feedback will depend upon the strengths of the economic linkages between the regions. When a major region such as the European Economic Community (EEC) increases its purchases from the United States, incomes in the exporting region in the United States will increase. The United States may in turn increase its imports from the EEC, a major trading partner. Thus, one reason for the EEC exports is the extent of their imports. When the region is small or has weak linkages, these feedbacks can be ignored because income increases in a small region will have only negligible feedbacks. But, if the region is large, the feedbacks can be significant.

Automatic Inducement of Nonbasic Activities

The export-base multiplier is predicated on the assumption that when the export sector expands, the demand for local services increases and the increase in demand will be sufficient to bring forth an increase in supply of such services. However, some local services, such as those requiring large capital investment or highly skilled (or scarce) labor, may not be easily expanded. Many small towns have difficulty attracting physicians, for example. Likewise, nonbasic employment may remain constant for some time after a decrease in export employment if the providers of local services are not mobile.

If exports increase (decrease) but the nonbasic sector does not increase (decrease), then the multiplier (total employment/basic employment) will not adequately reflect the impact of changes in exports. The usefulness of the export-base approach for forecasting and impact analysis would be correspondingly weakened. Supporters of the export-base theory may admit that there are some lags between an increase in exports and a change in nonbasic employment but claim that it is simply a problem of delayed adjustment. They might argue that short-run impacts of an increase in exports could be determined if only the appropriate lags were known. Given ample time, the "true" total employment/basic employment ratio will be reestablished. However, this defense is complicated by concerns about the long-run stability of the multiplier.

Long-Run Instability of the Multiplier

In the long run, most of the "other things equal" assumptions that underlie most economic models will change. With regard to the export-base approach, changes in the fundamental economic relationships will alter the relationship between the export and nonbasic sectors. Hence, the multiplier will change over time. The marginal propensity to consume and, more importantly, the marginal propensity to import will change as the economy changes.

The marginal propensity to import is particularly sensitive to three variables: (1) the size of the economy, (2) per capita income, and (3) the degree of spatial isolation. The smaller the economy of the region, the fewer the opportunities to purchase goods locally. For example, if you live in a small town and want a meal in a four-star restaurant, the service would have to be "imported," thus increasing the leakages. Higher-income individuals have greater propensity to purchase specialized goods that need to be imported. So, as per capita income increases, the marginal propensity to import increases. Finally, proximity to other communities will increase the variety of competing goods and services. Thus, residents will have a greater tendency to shop outside the community and areas within metropolitan areas will have smaller ratios of total employment to basic employment.

Excessive Aggregation

The assumption that the impact of all exports is the same is embedded in the use of the export-base multiplier. The likelihood that some types of exports may have a greater impact upon the economy than other exports is ignored. In reality, some export businesses have many local suppliers, whereas other exporters may purchase almost all of their inputs from outside. When exports are produced by a firm that is economically integrated with other local firms, the repercussions will be felt in the form of increased orders from other local firms. This contrasts with the impact of increased exports produced by a firm that imports all required intermediate inputs from nonlocal suppliers. In the latter instance, there may be no second-order consequences. Accordingly, the export-base approach discussed in this chapter may be more useful in predicting the effects of a 10 percent increase in average exports than an increase in a particular sector. In the next chapter, the use of input-output analysis to desegregate the impact of growth is explained.

SUPPLY-SIDE APPROACHES

Supply-side theories of economic development are partly an outgrowth of criticisms of demand-dominated approaches, such as the export-base theory, and partly an extension of neoclassical economic theory to regional production. The heart of regional supply-side growth theories is the idea that regions grow because the internal supply of available resources increases or the existing resources are used more effectively. The supply-side approach may be summarized by a regional production function:

$$0 = f(f_1 \ldots f_r) \tag{13}$$

where 0 = Regional or urban output, and
$\quad f_i$ = The ith factor of production.

Before "supply-side economics" became an approach to national economic growth, it was widely recognized as a path to local development. However, like proponents of national supply-side strategies, regional economists have done a better job developing hypotheses about what factors might affect the local supply of productive resources than they have been in developing workable ways to stimulate the supply side. The current industrial structure of an area may "explain" the supply of some factors of production. The current set of resources, in turn, shapes the future development of an area. Such an explanation is circular but probably contains some truth. A sketch of some potentially important determinants of supply would include intermediate inputs as well as the primary factors of production—land, labor, capital, and entrepreneurship.

Intermediate Inputs

The availability of intermediate inputs is an important supply factor. On the one hand, communities with economic bases dominated by large, vertically integrated firms may have fewer intermediate inputs available to new businesses. On the other hand, new businesses in communities with many small interdependent firms may have access to a variety of intermediate inputs through other local firms. Consequently, it would be harder for a fledgling new business to obtain legal, trucking, and other services in a city like Pittsburgh than in a city like New York. In Pittsburgh, a high percentage of the trucking and legal services are inside large existing companies, so they are not available to small businesses.

Entrepreneurship

Almost every development economist has stressed the importance of the entrepreneur in risk taking and bringing factors of production together. The centrality of the entrepreneur to the development process has

---

The Chinitz Hypothesis

Chinitz (1961) compared the economies of New York and Pittsburgh. He hypothesized that Pittsburgh would be less likely to spin off new businesses because (1) its economy was less diversified and (2) it was dominated by a few large industries that carried out many operations in-house. New York, on the other hand, had an industrial structure that was diversified and where many small and midsize firms served each other. Therefore, New York would generate new activity more quickly than Pittsburgh because:

1. Large firms neither buy nor sell externally. Therefore, there are few markets and services available to small firms.
2. Banking activity will be less oriented towards small entrepreneur-oriented firms.
3. Entrepreneurship is less visible in a large corporation-dominated city.

Carlino (1980) provided partial support for the Chinitz theory. He found that "the external economies of scale (agglomeration) are an important force in understanding agglomeration economies for manufacturing establishments." A large number of small firms increases the agglomerative attraction of an area. However, Carlino did not find evidence that diversification by itself contributed to the agglomeration pull. Thus, the number of firms is more significant than the extent of diversification.

---

been stressed at national, regional, and local levels. Storey and Johnson (1987) attributed regional differences in birth rates of new firms to differences in entrepreneurship, while Booth (1986) attributed long waves of regional decline to the absence of entrepreneurial activity needed to stimulate employment growth.

In spite of the generally recognized importance of entrepreneurship, economists know very little about factors that contribute to the development of entrepreneurship. The importance of risk taking, creativity and the presence of role models are among the factors that have been mentioned in the diverse and multidisciplinary literature that has attempted to understand entrepreneurship. There are no schools that can teach entrepreneurship in the same sense that other professions can be taught. If the essence of entrepreneurship could be taught, it would become a technical skill. The heart of entrepreneurship is an ability to respond to unique opportunities. Even though schools cannot teach entrepreneurship, many of the skills needed to become an entrepreneur can be taught, such as accounting, finance, and communications.

The interest in entrepreneurship has been spiked by findings that firms employing less than 20 people account for about half of all new jobs created. Small firms have more entrepreneurship per employee than large firms and are often associated with the early stage of a product's life cycle where percentage growth is rapid. Thus, entrepreneurship has been seen as a key to developing fast-growth firms.

Several observers have suggested that a region dominated by large corporations will not nurture entrepreneurship because large corporations may attract young, talented individuals who might otherwise attempt to start their own businesses. They have suggested that graduating students in communities dominated by a few major companies may see a job in the corporate bureaucracy as the choicest position because of the greater security, clearly defined job ladders, and high visibility of the corporate executives. Therefore, entrepreneurial career paths will not be favored. Similarly, bankers in corporate-dominated cities may feel less secure when making loans to small entrepreneurial firms. Thus, it may be more difficult for entrepreneurs to survive in such a financial atmosphere. In fact, in corporate-dominated cities, the entire social system may be oriented to supporting large firms, giving their executives places of honor. Such an environment would probably not encourage entrepreneurship.

Observers tend to conclude that areas that have a high percentage of entrepreneurs will be able to perpetuate that strength because entrepreneurship is learned through the family and other role models and because an entrepreneurial environment is conducive to new entrepreneurs. While there is no evidence that any policy or set of policies can improve the supply of entrepreneurial talent in an area, communities have adopted policies such as business incubators (discussed in Chapter 7) and loan programs to more effectively use existing entrepreneurial talent.

Capital

Capital is often considered the most mobile factor of production because of the existence of national and international capital markets. As a result, capital is available on roughly equal terms in various regions. For instance, an automobile loan may be secured in Chicago or Phoenix on approximately the same terms. Large corporations borrow in the national market, so the availability of capital to firms with access to national capital markets is not influenced by location. However, capital may not be totally ubiquitous for small firms or for unique purposes. In many instances, a business's location may affect capital cost or availability.

It has been hypothesized that small firms may have more difficulty obtaining capital in some regions than in others. For small firms, the capital markets tend to be local. Often, large institutional investors are limited in the degree of risk or type of project they may undertake. Thus, they shy away from small firms. Governmental regulations, internal rules, and the desire of portfolio managers to earn at least satisfactory returns (rather than the highest returns) for their clients tend to make some organizations risk adverse. However, traditional lenders in some areas may be more willing to lend to new ventures than in other areas. For instance, bankers in Detroit tend to be more willing to lend to the established automobile manufacturers than to new ventures.

Individuals are important sources of capital, especially equity capital. Through various types of joint ventures, wealthy residents may provide funds for new enterprises. Venture capitalists specialize in identifying small, high-growth-potential companies and providing them with funds for projects that commercial banks and other traditional lenders consider too risky or unorthodox. The venture capitalists normally take an equity position in the company (i.e., they will earn a share of the profits) and often provide business advice as well as money. Government and quasi-government agencies, such as community development corporations, have recognized the need that small firms have for local capital and have developed programs to increase the supply of funds to smaller companies.

Land

Land is defined as a natural resource in the broadest sense. "Land" includes all factors of production endowed by nature. Location or ground and climate are part of land. They may be characterized as the most fundamental resources from a regional perspective since they are the only immobile factor of production. If nonland factors of production were perfectly mobile, land would be the only resource that would differentiate areas.

Resources such as mineral deposits, natural harbors, topography, and the agricultural fertility of the hinterland have played an important role in the historical development of cities. Although land is probably not as significant an urban growth component currently as it was in the past, land continues to exert an influence on development. For example, processed food is an important part of the economic base of many midwestern cities and the location of food processors is influenced by the production of agricultural land. Topography can affect building costs and, hence, growth prospects in specific parts of a metropolitan region.

In recent years, climate has been cited as an important determinant of urban growth. The rise of "sunbelt cities" and the amenity orientation of advanced-technology firms have contributed to the perception that climate is an important growth determinant. Several econometric models have included variables such as average temperature and average number of days with sunshine as independent variables in employment growth models.

Labor

The size of the labor force is largely determined by population size. The quality of the labor force is more difficult to define than size, although it is probably more important than size in determining an area's growth or revitalization prospects.

Past industrial activities help shape the skills of the current work force. Not only are skills an important element of labor quality, but work habits and attitudes may also be shaped by the industrial structure. Individuals in industries subject to regular or long spans of unemployment may develop savings and other habits that contribute toward the maintenance of a stable work force. For instance, families in the eastern coal area developed savings plans so that when a lay-off or strike occurred, the family would not be forced to leave the area. Thus, the supply of skilled miners remained stable. Educational institutions also contribute to an area's labor quality and adaptability. The adaptability of the work force is important to an area's ability to develop new economic activities.

Extensive unionization has been hypothesized to affect the labor supply adversely by raising wages, encouraging strikes, and supporting work rules that restrict what a particular category of workers can do. The percentage of the labor force that is unionized has decreased nationwide. However, the willingness of union representatives to consider new work rules, encourage training, and otherwise accommodate change can affect the quality of the local labor pool. Currently unions are attempting to work more closely with management to enhance productivity.

Supply and Demand Approaches Compared

Economists recognize that both supply and demand are necessary to induce production. Thus, neither the supply- nor the demand-side approaches should be rejected. There is, however, disagreement regarding which approach has the greatest predictive power under particular circumstances. On the one hand, if supply is responsive to increases in demand (elastic supply), then demand-side approaches such as the export-base theory will have significant predictive power. On the other hand, if demand for the region's output is responsive to changes in local supply, then supply-side theories will have predictive power.

Implicit in the supply-side approach is the assumption that the demand for the region's output will be sufficient to employ additional resources. Increases in supply will more easily translate into increases in output if resource prices are flexible downward, so that if unemployed resources existed, price decreases would enable the increased output to be offered at market-clearing prices. If a region already has unemployed resources, then increasing the quantity of the region's resources could aggravate the unemployment problem without causing output to increase. Increases in the supply of resources will also tend to translate into increased output when there is increasing or unsatisfied demand for the region's products. Furthermore, the availability of many resources, particularly those highlighted in Chapter 2, are important determinants of firm location. Firms create demand for additional local resources and often have established marketing contacts needed to sell what they produce.

SUMMARY

Viewing the historical record is the most direct way to examine urban and regional growth. Stage theories describe the key stages that cities pass through as they develop. Initially, a region may export one or only a few products. As regions develop, they achieve the ability to generate new products. Epochal models describe important growth attributes during various historical periods. Currently, a knowledge base, global linkages, planning abilities, and a supply of amenities are important growth attributes.

The circular-flow diagram is a simplified model of how an economy operates. Five important subsectors of a local economy are: (1) the resource market, (2) the local consumer market, (3) interfirm sales, (4) the local financial sector, and (5) the import and export sector. The circular-flow model can be used to illustrate equilibrium—when monetary inflows equal monetary outflows—and the local multiplier.

The export-base theory of growth claims that exports are the dominant source of monetary inflows and, hence, the main source of growth. The export-base approach may be operationalized by assuming that income is proportional to employment and that the ratio of export employment to total employment is constant. Hence, an export multiplier can be derived as the ratio of total employment to export employment. The export-base approach has straightforward policy implications and is relatively easy to operationalize.

There are several criticisms of the export-base theory. First, it may place too much emphasis on exports. Import substitution is an alternative development strategy. Second, productivity is another source of growth. Third, exports may not always be exogenous, particularly in the long run.

Fourth, the theory may have more explanatory power for small regions than for large regions. Fifth, it ignores interregional feedback. Sixth, the export-base theory implies that additional local services will respond to an increase in local demand. Seventh, the value of the export-base multiplier will change over time. Finally, the assumption that all exports affect the local economy alike is an oversimplification. In spite of the criticisms, the export-base theory remains the dominant theory of regional growth.

Supply-side theories emphasize the availability of inputs as principal growth determinants. The presence of intermediate inputs as well as the primary factors of production—land, labor, capital, and entrepreneurship—contribute to the ability of a region to produce. Supply-side factors may also account for the ability of a region to generate new sources of export demand. Although demand-side and supply-side approaches are sometimes presented as alternative theories, economists recognize that both supply and demand are necessary for profitable production and economic growth.

Both supply of resources and export demand are potential constraints on growth. At any given time, one of the two constraints is likely to dominate. For instance, if a region has substantial unemployment, the constraint on growth is likely to be demand. If the economy is at or near full employment, the constraint is likely to be supply.

REFERENCES

Ashton, D. J., and B. K. Sternal. *Business Services and New England's Export Base*. Boston, Mass.: Federal Reserve Bank of Boston, 1978.

Austrian, Ziona, and Thomas J. Zlatoper. "The Role of Export Services." *Regional Economic Issues Review,* Fall 1988, pp. 24–29.

Benjamin, Robert. "From Water Ways to Water Fronts," in Bingham and Blair, eds., *Economic Development*. Beverly Hills, Calif.: Sage, 1984.

Beyers, W. B., and M. J. Alvine. "Export Services in Post Industrial Society." *Papers of the Regional Science Association* 57, 1985, pp. 33–45.

Booth, Douglas E. "Long Waves and Uneven Regional Growth," *Southern Economic Journal* 53, no. 2, October 1986, pp. 448–460.

Carlino, G. A. "Contrasts in Agglomeration: New York and Pittsburgh Reconsidered." *Urban Studies* 17, 1980, pp. 343–51.

Chinitz, R. "Contrasts in Agglomeration: New York and Pittsburgh." *American Economic Review* 51, May 1961, pp. 1–12.

Garnick, Daniel H. "Patterns of Growth in Metropolitan and Nonmetropolitan Areas: An Update." *Survey of Current Business* 65, no. 5, May 1985, pp. 33–38.

Gillis, William. "Can Service-Producing Industries Provide for Regional Economic Growth?" *Economic Development Quarterly* 1, no. 3, August 1987, pp. 249–55.

Hicks, Donald A. *Advanced Industrial Development: Restructuring, Relocation, and Renewal.* Boston: Olegeschlager, Gunn and Hain.

Jacobs, Jane. *The Economy of Cities.* New York: Random House, 1969.*

Keil, Stanley R., and Richard S. Mack. "Identifying Export Potential in the Export Sector." *Growth and Change* 55, 1986, pp. 1–10.

Mills, Edwin S., and Bruce E. Hamilton. *Urban Economics.* 4th edition. Glenview, Ill.: Scott, Foresman, 1989.

Morse, Hugh O. *Regional Economics.* New York: McGraw-Hill, 1968, chapter 5.

Rostow, W. W. *The Stages of Economic Growth.* Cambridge: Cambridge University Press, 1966.

Storey, David J., and Steven G. Johnson, "Regional Variations in Entrepreneurship in the U.K." *Scottish Journal of Political Economy* 34, no. 2, May 1987, pp. 161–73.

Thierry, J. Noyelle, and Thomas M. Stanback, Jr. *The Economic Transformation of American Cities.* Totowa, W. G.: Littlefield, Adams; Rowman and Allanheld, 1984.

Thompson, Wilbur R. *A Preface to Urban Economics.* Baltimore: The Johns Hopkins Press, 1965.*

Tiebout, Charles. *The Community Economic Base Study.* New York: The Committee for Economic Development, 1962.

Watkins, Alfred J. *The Practice of Urban Economics.* Beverly Hills, Calif.: Sage, 1980, chapter 6.

* Classics.

Chapter Six

Regional Growth and Development: Advanced Perspectives

The previous chapter provided an introduction to urban and regional growth, including a discussion of demand- and supply-side approaches. However, except for some very broad distinctions, such as the basic and nonbasic categories or the various factors of production, Chapter 5 did not explore relationships among specific subcomponents of an area's economy. This chapter extends the analysis begun in Chapter 5 by presenting perspectives and tools that view local economies in a more disaggregated fashion.

The first section describes the input-output model and shows how it may be used in growth analysis by providing detailed information on the interdependence among economic sectors. Next, shift-share analysis, a frequently used method of classifying the sources of growth for various industrial sectors, is presented. Econometric models are currently the most popular regional forecasting technique. The third section presents econometric and simulation methods that are used to forecast and describe the relationships among parts of a local economy. Disequilibrium perspectives are discussed in the fourth section. It shows that components of a regional economy may interact in a way that may prevent a new regional equilibrium from being attained. The final section examines which groups are most likely to gain from local economic growth and which groups may not benefit or may actually be harmed.

INPUT-OUTPUT ANALYSIS

Input-output analysis is a versatile tool because it enables us to examine linkages among sectors. Input-output tables may be used to simply describe a regional economy or to analyze and forecast. First, we show how input-output analysis can contribute to an understanding of interindustry linkages and regional structures. Next, the model's usefulness in understanding the growth process will be presented.

TABLE 6–1 The Transaction Table

Supplied by	Sold to			Final Demand		Total Gross Output
	Agriculture	Manufacturing	Service	Household	Exports	
Agriculture	$ 300	$ 350	$ 300	$1,000	$ 700	$ 2,650
Manufacturing	50	150	600	600	1,400	2,800
Service	500	800	800	700	1,050	3,850
Primary Supply						
Households	1,100	300	100	30	20	2,450
Imports	700	1,200	115	120	0	3,170
Total	2,650	2,800	3,850	2,450	3,170	14,920

The Transactions Table

The first step to understanding input-output analysis is to understand the transactions table. It shows annual sales and purchases for each sector in a regional economy (see Table 6–1). The interpretation of the transactions table is straightforward. Each row shows the annual dollar value of output that each sector listed in the left-hand column sold to each of the sectors listed across the top. For instance, Table 6–1 indicates that agriculture sold $300 of output to itself, $350 to firms in the manufacturing sector, $300 to firms in the service sector, $1,000 directly to local households, and $700 to businesses and households in the rest of the world as exports.

The columns show where the sectors listed across the top purchased their inputs. In this example, local manufacturing firms purchased $350 from agriculture, $150 from each other, $800 from local service firms, $300 from local households (factors of production, especially labor), and $1,200 in the form of imports from individuals and businesses outside the area.

There is significant double counting in the transactions table because intermediate products are counted each time they are resold. Thus, total gross output is different from gross regional production or regional income. Total household income is $3,170. Table 6–1 contains only three producing sectors—agriculture, manufacturing, and services. Actual input-output tables may contain hundreds of producing sectors to enhance detailed analysis.

In addition to the interindustry sectors, what agriculture, manufacturing, and service sell to each other, two final-demand sectors are shown in Table 6–1. The household column reflects purchases of residents of the region, and the export column reflects goods and services that are sold to nonresidents. Two primary-supply sectors are also shown—household and imports. Households provide labor, entrepreneurship, capital, and land as inputs, and each of the values in the household row reflects compensation for these services. The import row shows the dollar value of all commodities imported yearly. The manufacturing sector was the largest importer, importing $1,200 worth of goods.

The final-demand (in this case representing sales outside the region) and primary-supply sectors are often further disaggregated in more detailed input-output models than Table 6–1. Exports and imports could be disaggregated to specify exactly who purchased the exports and who sold the imports. A sector for government purchases and gross capital formation could also be included. However, for our purposes, the number of sectors has been restricted for easier exposition. Since the total value of output must be paid to intermediate suppliers or to the primary factors of production, total gross output must equal the value of the inputs used in production.

The basic transactions table provides detailed information about the local economic structure. However, the table can be rearranged to show the linkages between sectors more directly. A table of direct coefficients can be constructed to show the amount each sector listed across the top will purchase per dollar of output from the sectors listed on the left.

The Table of Direct Coefficients

Table 6–2 is a table of direct coefficients. Each coefficient was derived by dividing the amount that each sector purchased from each of the economy's subcomponents by the total gross output of each of the three producing sectors and the household sector. For instance, the manufacturing sector purchased $800 of inputs from the service sector in order to produce $2,800 of total gross output (see the transaction table). Thus, for each dollar of output, the manufacturing firms purchased $.286 (800/2800) from firms in the service sector. The direct coefficient for the manufacturing column and service row, $.286, is the strongest linkage among the three industries in the model economy. Agriculture requires the most resources from local households; $.415 of household inputs is required for each dollar of agricultural output.

The table of direct coefficients implies a "fixed-input production function." In other words, there is only one recipe for producing the output of each sector; inputs cannot be substituted. If the price of a commodity increased or decreased, the total amount spent on the commodity per dollar of output would remain constant. In reality, most production processes allow for some substitution, such as substituting capital for labor if the price of labor increases.

The table of direct coefficients illustrates interindustry linkage. For instance, if the agricultural sector were to produce an extra dollar of output, using the same input proportions that were used when the input-output table was constructed, it would need to purchase $.113 from other agriculture producers (i.e., when a hog producer purchases corn or feed),

TABLE 6–2   Table of Direct Coefficients (purchases over dollar of output)

Supplied by	Sold to			
	Agriculture	*Manufacturing*	*Service*	*Households*
Agriculture	$.113	$.125	$.078	$.408
Manufacturing	.019	.053	.156	.245
Service	.189	.286	.208	.286
Households	.415	.107	.259	.012
Imports	.264	.429	.299	.048

$.019 from the manufacturing sector, and $.189 from services. In addition, $.415 would go to households to pay for inputs such as labor and $.264 would be spent on imported inputs of all types. All manufacturing goods, services, agricultural products, and direct inputs from households that are purchased outside the region are included in the $.264 of imports.

The Table of Direct and Indirect Coefficients

Regional multipliers can be obtained from the table of direct coefficients. However the table of direct coefficients shows only partial multipliers because they account for only first-round spending effects. Sectors providing inputs to manufacturing will require additional output from their suppliers; suppliers of suppliers will purchase more from their suppliers and so forth. For instance, Table 6–2 shows that, if the manufacturing sector increases its output by $1, $.1250 of additional output will be required from the local agricultural sector. But, if agriculture is to increase its output by $.125, agricultural firms must purchase $.0141 (.113 × $.1250) from other agricultural firms, $.0024 (.0189 × $.1250) from manufacturing firms, and $.0236 (.189 × $.1250) from service firms. Household income will increase by $.0134 ($.125 × .107) because of the primary factors of production needed to produce the extra output required by manufacturing. But household income will also increase because of the increases in agricultural and service output created by the initial increase in manufacturing output. The household income will be spent according to the coefficients in the household column of Table 6–2, if consumption patterns remain constant. Obviously, we can only scratch the surface of the various feedbacks before the calculations become very awkward.

In theory, these ripples would continue forever. However, each round of spending results in successively smaller amounts of induced output. The cumulative size of the various rounds of spending can be calculated mathematically.[1] The results are shown in Table 6–3. It shows the total dollar amount of output that would be required from each sector listed on the left in order to accommodate a dollar's increase in output from each sector listed across the top. In other words, if manufacturing increased its output by $1, the total effect on the agricultural sector would be to increase output by $.373. The total effect is the sum of:

1. Direct effects. The first-round increase shown in the table of direct coefficients.

---

[1] The table of direct and indirect coefficients is $[I - A]^{-1}$ where A is the matrix of direct coefficients and I is an identity matrix of equal dimensions.

TABLE 6–3 Table of Direct and Indirect Coefficients

Supplied by	Sold to			
	Agriculture	Manufacturing	Service	Household
Agriculture	1.570	0.373	0.255	0.815
Manufacturing	0.342	1.250	0.298	0.538
Service	0.757	0.651	1.490	0.907
Households	0.717	0.310	0.179	1.440

2. Indirect effects. The interindustry effects as local industries purchase from one another.
3. Induced effects. The additional increases in output due to household spending and the indirect effects of household respending.

Endogenous and Exogenous Activity. Many applications of input-output analysis require that a distinction be made between exogenous (outside system) and endogenous (inside system) activity. Exogenous activities are determined by forces outside the region. Exports for each of the sectors within the economy are normally the major exogenous component. In our little model, they are the only exogenous component. The assumption that exports are the only exogenous factor is consistent with the export-base theory.

The endogenous sectors respond to changes in exogenous activity. Accordingly, when the export requirements are known, the value of the output required from the endogenous sectors can be determined. In fact, the table of direct coefficients can be thought of as a system of equations. Total output of each sector is equal to the export demand from other local sectors plus the demand for intermediate inputs. Thus, the output of the agricultural sector may be expressed as:

$$A = .113\,A + .125\,M + .078\,S + .408\,HH + Ax \qquad (1)$$

where: A = The total output of agriculture,
M = Total output of manufacturing,
S = Total output of services,
HH = Household income, and
Ax = Agricultural exports.

The equation may be interpreted as meaning that the output of the agricultural sector is determined by the amount agriculture sells to itself, to local manufacturing firms, to local service firms, to local households, and to firms and individuals in other regions. Sales to local sectors depend upon the extent of output by the local sector.

Similar equations can be written for each of the other sectors where Mx, Sx, and HHx represent manufacturing, service, and household exports, respectively. The input-output system of equations reads:

$$A = .113\ A + .125\ M + .078\ S + .408\ HH + Ax, \qquad (2)$$

$$M = .019\ A + .053\ M + .156\ S + .245\ HH + Mx, \qquad (3)$$

$$S = .189\ A + .286\ M + .208\ S + .286\ HH + Sx, \text{ and} \qquad (4)$$

$$HH = .415\ A + .107\ M + .259\ S + .012\ HH + HHx. \qquad (5)$$

Since exports are determined by forces outside the region, they can be treated as given. In other words, the volume of exports is "known" for purposes of the above set of equations. Therefore, the system of five equations has five unknowns. Since the number of equations equals the number of unknown variables, the system of equations may be soluble. By increasing the export sales of a sector by $1, the total change in output of the other sectors can be derived. Thus, a unique set of multipliers showing how a dollar of extra final demand produced by one sector will affect each sector can be derived. In practice, solving even a small system of equations becomes messy and unwieldy. Thus, high-speed computers and techniques of matrix algebra, as described in Footnote 1, are used to derive the value of total outputs of each sector.

The Treatment of Households.   The above discussion of input-output analysis treated households as just another producing sector. The value of household income depended upon the amount of labor and other primary factors of production that were sold to the endogenous sectors, as well as factors of production sold as exports to individuals and firms in other regions. The compensation for the use of these factors constituted household income. Households were assumed to spend their income in fixed proportions for both local and imported consumption. For instance, for each $1 increase in household income, $.2442 would be spent on local manufacturing.

Should households be included with the endogenous sectors? In calculating Table 6–3, household consumption was considered to be determined by the amount of spending within the system. Thus, household spending was endogenous. Such a treatment was consistent with the export-base theory of growth, which claims that all local economic activity is supported by exports. However, some input-output analyses have treated household consumption as independent of the level of exports; in other words, household spending has been treated as exogenous. Clearly, some consumption would occur even if households had no income. The consumption could be financed from past savings. Thus, to some extent, household consumption is exogenous.

When household consumption is treated as independent of the level of exports, the size of the multiplier is smaller than when household consumption is considered to be induced by the level of exports. When consumption is induced by exports, an increase in exports will not only stimulate industry trade, but also local consumption; hence, the multiplier will be larger when household consumption is considered to be dependent upon exports.

Government and Investment.   Government outlays and investments are other spending sources normally included in detailed input-output tables. Realistically, part of the spending of these sectors is endogenous and part of the spending is exogenous. The shorter the time period under consideration, the more likely that spending will be independent of other aspects of the local economy. In the long run, government spending would probably increase if exports increased because of greater demands for infrastructure and other public services. But the increase in government spending would not be proportionally tied to the size of the expansion of the export sector. Likewise, investment may be partly determined by outside forces and partly created by the increased demand for capital that could result from an economic expansion. However, in practice, government and investment are usually treated as exogenous sources of spending. Clearly, distinctions between what is endogenous and exogenous are somewhat arbitrary.

Uses of Input-Output Tables for Growth Analysis

Both the tables of direct coefficients (see Table 6–2) and direct and indirect coefficients (see Table 6–3) have many uses in growth analysis and economic development policy. This section shows how input-output tables can be used to (1) assess local economic structure, (2) estimate imports, (3) inform locational decisions and industrial targeting, (4) forecast and determine economic impacts, and (5) simulate technological change.

Assessing Regional Structure.   Comparing one region's direct and indirect coefficients with those of another area can provide a useful perspective on its internal structure. Underdeveloped regions normally have few internal interindustry linkages, because they lack an integrated economic structure. The lack of internal linkages can be an impediment to development because, if a firm increases its output, few of the benefits will ripple through the rest of the economy; the local multiplier will be smaller. Likewise, small regions will have fewer internal linkages than larger regions because small regions are more likely to import required inputs. Interindustry linkages will be larger for a nation as a whole than for a region, because a smaller portion of a nation's input requirements are imported while imports for a region include goods purchased from other regions.

Suppose regions A and B are similar in size, produce a similar output, and use identical production techniques. Therefore, the input requirements of the regions are the same. However, suppose region A is well-integrated internally and region B has only a few significant interindustry linkages. There would be many more gaps—entries of $0 or very small amounts—in region B's input-output table, implying that its economy is less integrated. Consequently, intermediate inputs would have to be imported into the region. When an industry expands, it will have a bigger impact on other industries in region A because of strong linkages.

Estimating Imports.   It is also useful to compare local input-output coefficients with national coefficients to estimate imports. Suppose that, nationally, the electrical-machinery sector sells .10 cents to the motor-vehicles sector per dollar of motor-vehicle output. Furthermore, suppose the corresponding coefficient for a locality is .04 cents as indicated by a local table of direct coefficients. Also, assume that (1) the national economy is closed, so there is no international trade, and (2) the production technology locally is the same as the national level. The difference in coefficients implies that for every dollar of output by the regional motor-vehicle sector, .06 cents worth of electrical machinery is imported. If the motor-vehicle sector is large, the dollar value of imported electronic equipment may be large. The total value of the imports of electrical machinery for motor vehicles could be estimated by multiplying .06 times the value of automobile output. Consequently, a development planner may wish to determine whether there was potential for growth in the electrical-machinery sector based upon the potential for import substitution through sales to motor-vehicle establishments. Of course, there are other locational requirements, besides the presence of a buyer, that a community must satisfy if it is to attract electrical-machinery producers. However, the structural perspective given by comparing the national and local table of direct coefficients can be a useful starting point for analysis.

Informing Locational and Targeting Decisions.   The identification of imports by comparing national and regional coefficients can assist in locational decisions. A firm may wish to locate near potential customers. A firm located near its customers may be able to undersell competitors because of lower transportation costs, provide better service, or cultivate contacts that could enhance future sales. Hence, some firms may choose to seek locations where imports of their products are substantial.

Urban and regional planners may also use input-output analysis to help target the types of industries they would like to attract. Development officials may wish to recruit industries that strengthen interindustry linkages in order to build a more substantial agglomeration in a particular industrial cluster. For instance, a food-processing plant might be attracted to an area that produces a type of agricultural product. This strategy may involve attempting to attract buyers of products already produced in the region or sellers of products that other industries purchase. Another development strategy might be to target high–value-added industries, activities that purchase a large portion of inputs directly from households.

Economic development officials might reasonably believe that local subsidies are easier to justify if the benefits flow to a large portion of the economy, help clusters they wish to nurture, or require large inputs from households, thus, creating household income. Since input-output tables indicate how each sector impacts every other sector and households, they can be very useful in industrial targeting.

Conducting Impact Studies. The multipliers can be used to make forecasts and to perform impact analysis. An input-output forecast would normally first require an estimate of final demand (export levels) for each sector. Since final demand is exogenous, estimates of final demand must come from outside the input-output model. The endogenous sectors could then be confronted with the set of final demands, and the output of each industry as well as its transactions with every other industry could be calculated. In terms of equations 2–5, when exports are determined, the total output of each sector can be calculated. When the total output of each sector is known, the value of interindustry transactions can be determined. Essentially, a new transactions table could be created reflecting alternative levels of exports.

Impact analysis is similar to other projections, except that the impacts are usually special events rather than a general change in export demand. The impact of closing a university, for example, could be simulated using input-output analysis. In this case, the external demand for services (or education, if a very detailed model were being used) would decrease by the amount of outside funds going to the university (state and federal funds plus tuition paid by nonresident students). The direct, indirect, and induced declines in output due to the university closing would constitute the impact. In all probability, all of the sectors in the input-output model would be affected although some would be affected more than others.

Stimulating Technological Change. Input-output analysis has also been used to simulate technological change. Suppose a panel of engineering experts reported that new technology would reduce the dependence of manufacturing on the agricultural sector by 10 percent. In economic terms, the impact could be expressed as: For each dollar of manufacturing productions, manufacturing firms will purchase 10 percent less from agriculture. But, if less per dollar of output is spent on agriculture, another sector's sales to manufacturing will have to increase, because the value of total output must equal the value of the inputs. Perhaps the household sector would "sell" more entrepreneurial services to manufacturing on the assumption that the lower agricultural requirement would flow to households in the form of higher profits. Alternatively, perhaps service firms will replace the agricultural input. Perhaps the savings from lower agricultural requirements will be distributed evenly among the other sectors. In any event, a new set of direct input requirements reflecting the most likely repercussions of technological change can be developed.

In order to simulate the impact of the technological change, the existing set of final-demand requirements can be applied to the (assumed) new set of direct requirements. A new set of outputs for the local sectors could be derived. As a result of the simulation, the level of total output and the distributions of output among the sectors can be calculated.

Advantages and Limitations

One of the most obvious and important advantages of input-output analysis is that the export-base theory can be operationalized in a manner that shows the interindustry repercussions in detail. The effects of, say, a $10,000,000 increase in manufacturing exports can be differentiated among the component sectors of the economy. Since an input-output table will show which activities will expand most in order to support an increase in exports from a particular sector, it can be a useful tool for urban planners. If the input-output table were detailed enough to include categories for specific public services, planners could determine which public services would be required if particular sectors increased their exports.

Not only can the differential effects of an increase in the output of one sector be shown, but the sectors with the largest local-multiplier effects can be determined. Thus, input-output analysis could also help a community determine which industries it should promote in order to maximize the total economic impact. Thus, if a community wanted to encourage exports, it might consider focusing efforts on those sectors that have substantial interindustry effects.

Data Collection.   The most notable difficulty with the input-output approach is the cost of collecting data. Surveys are necessary to accurately determine interindustry trade flows, and surveys are costly. Therefore, it is seldom feasible to use input-output analysis for a single, one-shot study. Multiple and continuing use of input-output tables helps to justify the initial cost of developing the table by spreading the cost over several projects.

In order to reduce survey costs, some analysts have used a "rows only" approach to data collection. Local firms are asked only who their customers are—not their suppliers. Firms normally have better records of customers than suppliers. The transactions table can be developed by filling in the rows only. A second way to lower the cost of developing an input-output table is to adjust the direct coefficients from the national input-output table. The regional direct coefficients have been predicted by assuming local firms use the same input proportions as indicated by the national input-output table. Purchases among local firms are estimated using regression techniques and information about the relative size of local sectors (such as location quotients). Proponents of nonsurvey estimation techniques claim that when coefficients derived by using estimation techniques are compared with coefficients derived by surveys, the differences are small. If the accuracy of estimated regional coefficients can be established, the use of local input-output analysis will expand. Multipliers based on accurate estimated coefficients would certainly be preferable to the simple export-base multiplier.

Static Analysis.   Another group of criticisms of input-output analysis involves the static nature of the direct coefficients. This criticism takes two forms: (1) inputs do not increase in fixed proportions as output increases and (2) the coefficients change over time. The input-output model includes the assumption that as the output increases, the ratio of inputs will remain constant. But there are a number of reasons why direct coefficients may vary as output changes. Relative price changes may encourage an establishment to substitute a relatively cheaper input for a more expensive one. Technological change can also affect the production technique. The development of hard plastics has reduced the dependence of the automobile sector on metals. Such changes would be reflected by a change in the technical coefficients.

Empirical evidence has indicated that the coefficients in the national input-output table change very slowly, particularly for broad sectors, suggesting that the coefficients are durable. However, regional coefficients probably change more rapidly than national, technical coefficients because in addition to the factors that affect national coefficients, area coefficients will be affected by changing regional trade patterns. For instance, a chemical plant might locate in an area where none existed before. The new firm would likely sell some chemicals locally, while previously all chemical products had been imported. This change in trade patterns would increase local interindustry linkages. At the national level, the new chemical firm's sales would be more likely to replace sales of other U.S. firms, so the national coefficients would not change significantly. Likewise, regional price changes could create a situation where local suppliers sold more or less of their output to local producers, thus changing local interindustry trade but leaving national linkages unaffected.

Export-Base Orientation. Finally, input-output models are based on the export-base theory of growth, so many of the criticisms that have been levied against the export-base approach can also be levied against most applications of input-output analysis. Specifically, changes in output are normally driven by exogenous changes in exports. Internal improvements in productivity, technology, and other sources of growth are usually ignored.

SHIFT-AND-SHARE ANALYSIS

Shift-and-share analysis provides a retrospective view of the causes of growth. It is a technique for dividing an area's growth into three components. First, an area's growth can be attributed to national economic growth. Growth at the national average rate is termed the national growth component. If a locality grew at the national average, it would have maintained its share of national employment, hence the "share" of shift-and-share analysis. Second, an area may grow faster (slower) than the national average if it has a disproportionate level of employment in industries that grew fast (slow) nationwide. For instance, financial services were a fast-growth activity during the 1980s. One would expect that if an area had a large employment base in financial services, it would grow more rapidly than the national average. Growth that differs from the national average because of the initial employment composition of an area is termed the mix component. Third, an area may have a competitive advantage (disadvantage) compared to other areas because its environment is conducive (an impediment) to growth of particular industries. Growth differentials due to the nature of the local environment are termed the competitive component. The mix and competitive components account for regional growth that differs from the national level. The mix and competitive components account for the "shift" term.

An important feature of shift-and-share analysis is that the growth components for individual sectors can be added to provide an aggregate description of growth. Thus, the competitive (or mix) component for each individual sector can be added to determine the aggregate competitive (or mix) component.

The formula for calculating the shift-and-share components for a single industry can be expressed as:

$$\Delta e_i = e_i((US^*/US) - 1) + e_i((US_i^*/US_i) - (US^*/US)) \qquad (6)$$
$$+ e_i((e_i^*/e_i) - (US_i^*/US_i)).$$

where: Δe_i = The change in local employment in industry i,

$\quad e_i$ = Local employment in industry i at the beginning of the period,

$\quad e_i^*$ = Local employment in industry i at the end of the period,

$\quad US^*$ = Total U.S. employment at the end of the period,

$\quad US$ = Total U.S. employment at the beginning of the period, and

$\quad i$ = As subscript, indicates reference to industry i.

The first term $e_i(US^*/US) - 1)$ indicates growth that would occur if local industry i grew at the national average rate. The second term $e_i((US_i^*/US_i) - (US^*/US))$ indicates extra (reduced) growth because a particular industry grew more (less) rapidly than the overall national average growth rate. The third term $e_i((e_i^*/e_i) - (US_i^*/US_i))$ indicates that local industry grew more (less) rapidly than the national rate for industry i. The shift-and-share components for individual local industries can be summarized to provide an overall description of growth components. Table 6–4 shows the data and the results of a small shift-and-share analysis for a local economy.

An Application

How would an economic planner or analyst interpret the findings shown in Table 6–4? Star City had a total employment increase of 100 workers during the 10-year period. If Star City had grown as rapidly as the nation as a whole, 122 jobs should have been added. Agriculture, manufacturing, and services would have added 16, 41, and 65 jobs, respectively. Therefore, there was a loss of 22 jobs in Star City's share of national employment. This negative shift of 22 jobs can be accounted for by the negative mix component. If Star City had an industrial base proportionate to the rest of the United States, the mix component would have been zero. In the example, agriculture and manufacturing grew faster than the U.S. average and Star City had some employment in these nationally fast-growing industries; hence, the positive mix components for these sectors. However, the service sector was a slow-growth industry nationwide and Star City had a disproportionate concentration of employment in that slow-growth sector. Therefore, the mix component for service was −99 and the overall mix effect for Star City was −81 jobs.

TABLE 6–4   Shift-and-Share Analysis for a Local Economy

(a)   Data

Sector	Star City 1970	Star City 1980	United States (in $ millions) 1970	United States (in $ millions) 1980
Agriculture	50	100	7	10.5
Manufacturing	125	175	4	5.6
Service	200	200	3	2.5
Total	375	475	14	18.6

(b)   Shift-and-Share Results

Sector	Share	Components Mix (Shift)	Components Competitive (Shift)
Agriculture	16	9	25
Manufacturing	41	9	0
Service	65	−99	34
Total	122*	−81	59

Actual change = 100

* If the share component were calculated by multiplying the total 1970 job level by the national growth rate a share component of 123 jobs would be indicated. The difference of one job is due to rounding.

The actual shift was 22 jobs—Star City had 22 fewer jobs than antici-pated based on the national share. The mix component by itself would have resulted in a shift of −81 jobs, but Star City appeared to be a particularly good environment for agriculture and services. Both activi-ties grew more rapidly in Star City than they did nationwide. Thus, the region recorded a positive competitive component of 59.

The actual employment change was equal to the sum of the share (122), mix (−81), and competitive (59) components.

The positive competitive components in agriculture and services may indicate a potential building block for future growth. For instance, a de-velopment official might try to determine exactly why local service firms maintained their employment levels while service employment declined nationwide. If one or two favorable aspects of the local environment could be identified, they could be used to help market the community to other service firms that might consider locating in the area. The shift-and-share approach can also be used to help spot weaknesses in the competitive environment that may require corrections.

Although the shift-and-share formula is expressed in terms of employment, the technique can be applied to changes in other variables, such as income, government spending, and productivity changes.

Table 6–5 shows the results of a shift-and-share analysis for the Great Lakes region between 1979 and 1988. This was a period in which the region lagged substantially behind most of the United States in employment growth. The shift-and-share analysis can help economists understand the extent and structure of the growth lag.

Overall, the region would have gained 3,100,500 jobs if it grew at the national rate, but it actually gained only 482,800 jobs. Industries grew slower than their national counterparts. The only sectors that registered positive competitive components were the two government sectors. The difference is accounted for almost entirely by negative competitive components. The mix component is not exactly zero but was rounded to zero during the calculations. The zero mix component reflects the diversity of the region's economy.

TABLE 6–5   Shift-and-Share Analysis of Employment 1979–1988 for the Great Lakes Region (in 000s)

Industry	Share	Mix	Competitive	Change in Employment 1979–1988
Durable	688.2	−1,050.3	−501.6	−863.7
Nondurable	262.3	−306.5	−25.1	−69.3
Construction	128.9	0.5	−123.3	6.1
Transport	274.9	−87.1	−873.7	−797.0
Finance	155.7	132.5	−90.9	197.3
Wholesale	177.2	−2.0	−108.9	66.4
Retail	528.2	275.0	−334.3	468.9
Service	562.4	921.3	−402.7	1,081.0
Federal	51.5	−31.6	41.3	61.2
State & Local	382.2	−187.1	136.8	331.9
Total	3,100.5	0.0	−2,617.7	482.8

SOURCE: Derived from *Employment and Earnings, 1979 and 1988.* U.S. Department of Labor, Washington, D.C.

Critique

Shift-and-share analysis has been widely used by planners and economic development officials to help them understand economic performance. It is relatively easy to use and understand. The data required to perform the analysis are readily available. However, the technique has some legitimate criticisms.

One criticism of shift-and-share analysis is that the components are frequently misinterpreted. Some critics have charged that shift-and-share analysis implies that industries should grow at the aggregate national rate. The national growth rate is used as a point of comparison, but there is no theoretical reason to believe that local employment growth should match the national rate. Likewise, the mix component should not be interpreted as implying that local industries should expand at the same rate as their nationwide counterparts. The national and mix components serve only as comparative benchmarks.

A second criticism is that the shift-and-share components may change depending upon the level of industrial detail. For instance, if industries were greatly disaggregated so that, at the extreme, each plant constituted its own industry, the competitive component would be zero (the plant's growth would equal the national industry growth rate); therefore, the total shift should be attributable to the mix component. Defenders of shift-and-share analysis recognize this problem but reply that selecting the appropriate level of industrial detail is a problem common to most industry studies.

Third, although the competitive component may be useful in explaining what has happened, its ability to predict the future course of development has been questioned. The competitive component has been combined with national projections of the growth of a particular industry to improve forecasting. By using a top-down forecasting technique, for instance, a national forecast of growth in a particular industry could be adjusted up or down depending upon an area's competitive component. However, critics of such forecasting techniques claim that the competitive component changes too frequently and rapidly in response to a variety of forces, such as local taxes, resource availability, and technology. Therefore, a competitive component for one historical period may be a poor guide for future competitive components for the same sector.

Finally, critics have pointed out that, although the competitive component can be an indicator of where to look for local strengths and weaknesses, it does not identify *why* a particular sector may have a positive or negative competitive component. In fact, the competitive component is a residual and may not necessarily reflect what most of us envision when we talk about a good competitive environment. Thus, analysts must go beyond the model to explain positive or negative competitive effects. For instance, suppose the steel industry in a particular region grew more rapidly than the industry did nationwide. A positive competitive component for that sector would result, but how would it be explained? Perhaps something about the local environment permitted lower-cost steel production, and firms took advantage of the lower-cost environment by expanding output. Alternatively, maybe a steel executive made a *bad* decision to expand steel employment in that area. Both possibilities could explain a positive competitive component. More in-depth study would be required to distinguish between these and numerous other potential explanations of the competitive component.

ECONOMETRIC AND SIMULATION MODELS

Econometric models combine statistical techniques and economic theory to estimate relationships among variables. Simulation models answer "what if" questions. For instance, a simulation model may be used to forecast the impact of a particular policy or the absence of policy. A simulation model would allow a researcher to estimate the path of a community's development if current trends persist or if new trends develop. Both econometric and simulation models have a variety of uses, although this section focuses on how they are used to understand the growth process.

Many simulation models use econometric techniques, such as regression, to establish relationships among variables. Once the relationships have been established, the simulation may involve asking what would happen if one or more of the variables changed or what would happen if the relationship among variables changed. For instance, an econometric model might show that for each 1 percent increase in the property tax rate, property values decrease by one tenth of 1 percent. A simulation model could show how property values would be affected by a 3 percent tax increase. However, as will be detailed later, not all simulation models are based upon econometric relationships.

The purpose of this section is to impart a sense of how econometric and simulation models can be used to understand the growth process and describe some of the potential pitfalls of their use. Our purpose is not to describe how to build such models. Such a task would be well beyond the scope of this book.

Econometric Models

Econometric models are perhaps the most widely used tool for analyzing regional growth. Econometric models are more flexible than input-output models because input-output models rely upon the assumption of fixed-proportion production functions. Econometric models normally combine both supply- and demand-side approaches. Furthermore, while changes in production or employment are the primary outcomes of input-output forecasts, econometric models can include equations to estimate changes in other variables, such as prices, tax revenues, and fiscal impacts. A final advantage of econometric models is that they can be modified. If an unanticipated question arises, new equations may be added to the core model. For instance, if a city official wanted to know how a change in federal tax policies would affect the local economy, new equations could be estimated that feed into the core model.

Good econometric models are informed by economic theory. Theory normally specifies what variables are important and the causal relationship among them. Three major uses of econometric models are to test the validity of theoretical relationships, to specify the magnitude of the relationships, and to assist forecasting. For instance, theory might indicate that migration into an area occurs when the local employment rate is less that the nation's. Statistical analysis might confirm the proposition and demonstrate that migration increases by, say 3 percent a year for each percentage point difference between the national and local unemployment rate. A planner might then use the quantitative relationship between unemployment and migration to help forecast the future population.

There are two important kinds of variables in econometric models. On the one hand, independent variables are not estimated by the model; they are taken as given. On the other hand, the value of dependent variables can be predicted by the model. Often, independent variables can be thought of as the "cause" and dependent variables as the "effects."

Parameters are a third important component of econometric models. They show the magnitude of the relationship between the dependent and independent variables. For instance, suppose a $1 million increase (decrease) in regional exports resulted in an employment increase (decrease) of 5 persons. This relationship could be described by the equation:

$$LE = 25,000 + 150\ E_x \tag{7}$$

where LE = Local employment, and
E_x = Local exports in $1,000,000 s.

Econometric models may be estimated using cross-sectional data or time-series data. Cross-sectional studies examine relationships that exist based on a variety of observations at a single time. Time-series studies show relationships within a particular set of variables during various periods of time.

Bolton (1985) described three types of regional forecasting methods frequently used in local forecasting. Top-down models use national inputs often gathered from national econometric forecasters as independent variables to the regional model. For example, the value of national output in the steel industry may be taken from a national study and 10 percent of national steel output allocated to the region. Of course, other variables could be included in the equation that allocated national production to a given region. A regional model of Alaska allocated shares of international activity in certain sectors to the state (Kresge, 1984). In contrast, bottom-up models may estimate national output (or the output of a large region) as the sum of forecasts for subregions. Multiregional models are an additional way to structure an econometric model. Such models include feedbacks describing how activity in one industry of a region affects various sectors in other regions. Multiregional models require information on trade flows among regions. Because of the complexity and substantial data requirements, most bottom-up and multiregional models focus on only a few regions.

An Export-Base Example.   Weiss and Gooding (1970) used an econometric equation to examine growth in the Portsmouth area. Although their study is dated, its simplicity and relationship to the export-base theory, described in the previous chapter, make it useful for study. Weiss and Gooding postulated that service employment should grow when export employment grows. However, one of the problems with the export-base approach is that it lumps together all export sectors, even though changes in some sectors may have a bigger impact than changes in others. Accordingly, a theoretical model was specified that divided the export sector into three categories reflecting the employment patterns in Portsmouth:

$$S = Q + b_1X_1 + b_2X_2 + b_3X_3 \tag{8}$$

where S = Service employment,
   X_1 = Private export employment,
   X_2 = Civilian employment at Portsmouth shipyard, and
   X_3 = Employment at Pease Air Force Base.

Q and b_i are parameters that can be estimated statistically using multiple regression. A time-series data set was collected for each of the independent variables, and their relationship to service employment was estimated. The statistical results yielded the following equation:

$$S = -12,905 + .78\ X_1 + .55\ X_2 + .35\ X_3 \tag{9}$$
$$(t = 2.5)\ (t = 2.4)\ (t = 2.5)$$

$$R^2 = .78.$$

Statistical tests were performed to provide a confidence level in the findings. The R^2 of .78 indicates that 78 percent of the variance in service employment (the dependent variable) was accounted for by the independent variables, X_1, X_2, and X_3. The "t" values indicate that the coefficients for each dependent variable are statistically different from zero.

The econometric findings could be used to simulate the impact of a change in employment in one of the three export sectors. Suppose, for example, that employment at Pease Air Force Base (X_3) was projected to increase during the next year by 100 employees. What would the total impact on the economy be? Assuming all other variables remained unchanged, the change in service employment would be:

$$S = .35 \, X_3 = .35(100) = 35. \tag{10}$$

Since the change in service employment is 35 and the change in export employment is 100, the total employment change due to the increase in export employment is 135. The multiplier for X_3 is 1.35 (135/100). For similar reasons, the multipliers for X_1 and X_2 equal 1.78 and 1.55, respectively.

The econometric model depends upon the export-base theory. If, for instance, an observer believed that service employment significantly influenced private export employment, then causation runs both ways: S determines X_1, and X_1 determines S. In this case, a simultaneity bias would exist. Consequently, the estimate of b_1, the parameter that links service and private employment, may be inaccurate.

More-Complicated Models. The model described had only one equation, and there was only one "outcome"—service employment. Urban econometric models are usually much more complex. The ability to add additional equations to existing econometric models provides them with flexibility. Once a model is established, it may be extended or modified to address other questions. Suppose the developers of the model described above later wanted to estimate total regional income. Using similar econometric techniques, an additional equation could have been developed relating total income to employment in the service sector and the three export sectors. After estimating the parameters, the income equation might be:

$$Y = 700 + 10175 \, S + 12542 \, X_1 + 17159 \, X_2 + 15445 \, X_3. \tag{11}$$

Notice how the outcome of the original model, service employment, feeds into the determination of total income. The model might be further expanded by including an equation relating both income and employment to changes in construction and another equation showing the link between the federal defense budget and employment in sectors X_2 and X_3. (Thus, X_2 and X_3 will no longer be exogenous or taken as a given to the econometric model, although they will still be independent variables in the local employment equation.)

Time lags could also be introduced so that the model predicts one period's "feedback" and determines outcomes in later periods. For instance, a statistical relationship might be established between expenditures (E) in period "t" and taxes (T) in period $t + 1$; $T_{t+1} = a(E_T)$. By (1) determining how key economic variables are linked theoretically and then (2) using statistical techniques (primarily regressions) to quantify the relationships, large and complicated models containing hundreds of equations may be constructed. The Milwaukee model illustrates an outcome of this process.

The Milwaukee Model

Rubin and Erickson (1980) developed a comprehensive forecasting model for Milwaukee that included over 97 statistical equations, definitions, and identities. Describing the entire economic model is well beyond the scope of this section. However, examining a few of the equations may provide the flavor of their approach and that of similar models.

Employment, output, and wage rates were forecast for 16 economic sectors. Other outcomes of the model were personal income, productivity, government expenditures, and relative unit-labor costs in several sectors.

The equation for output in the leather and leather-products sector was:

$$Q31 = -62.108 + 24.77 \ USQ31 + 0.055 \ POP \qquad (1)$$
$$(2.74) \qquad\qquad (2.68)$$

$$R^2 = 769$$

where $Q31$ = Output in leather and leather products (in dollars),
$USQ31$ = U.S. output in leather and leather products (in millions of dollars), and
POP = Population in the urban region.

A separate equation was estimated for each sector based upon the variables with the best predictive power consistent with theoretical relationships. The leather and leather-products sector shows that output is influenced by national events ($USQ31$) as well as the size of the local market, as measured by population (POP). This result is consistent with the theory that part of the sector's export is dependent upon outside demand and part depends upon local demand.

Population was estimated separately:

$$POP = 388.157 + 14.672 \ NTINC + 0.091 \ GRP \qquad (2)$$
$$(4.97) \qquad\qquad (10.88)$$

$$R^2 = .941$$

where $NTINC$ = Natural increase in 1,000s (births − deaths) and
GRP = Gross regional product.

The Milwaukee Model (concluded)

The natural increase was determined from outside forecasts and was, there-fore, exogenous to the model.

Gross regional product was defined as:

$$GRP = QMN + QCC + QSU + QWR + QF1 + QTR + QGU \quad (3)$$

where QMN = Output in manufacturing,
QCC = Output in construction,
QSU = Output in services,
QWR = Output in wholesale and retail trade,
$QF1$ = Output in finance, insurance and real estate,
QTR = Output in transportation, and
QGU = Government expenditures.

Each of the components of gross regional product was determined by other equations in the model. The output of the leather and leather-products sector, $Q31$, along with the output of other two-digit industries were used to estimate total output in manufacturing, QMN.

In order to test the entire model, predicted outcomes were compared to actual outcomes. The mean absolute percentage error for gross regional product was 3.49, and for manufacturing it was 2.21 percent. There is no standard for acceptable errors in econometric modeling, although errors below 5 percent are considered good and errors of 10 percent are accept-able. By these standards, the Milwaukee model is successful.

SOURCE: Barry M. Rubin and Rodney A. Erickson, "Specification and Perfor-mance Improvements in Regional Econometric Forecasting Models: A Model for the Milwaukee Metropolitan Area," *Journal of Regional Science* 20, no. 1, 1980, pp. 11–35.

Caveats. Econometric models are an established part of the re-gional economist's tool kit. However, anyone applying econometric find-ings to policy problems should be aware of two general types of limita-tions—measurement errors and specification errors. One measurement problem is that the values of parameters are based upon past observa-tions. Relationships among variables may change in such a way that a model that worked well in the past can no longer serve as a good predictor of the future. This is particularly likely to happen when large or abrupt changes occur. For instance, many economists believe that the major oil-price increases that occurred in the 1970s rendered previously estimated relationships inaccurate. Most economic models are much better at "predicting" the past than the future. Severe critics of econometric modeling would argue that, in reality, the "other things equal" assumptions that are needed to maintain stable relationships change too rapidly to allow good forecasts. In a related vein, Klaasen and Pawlowski (1982) pointed out that a model that predicts the future on the basis of current trends is bound to fail, because current trends will change.

A second measurement problem involves data requirements. Even the best data collected from well-established sources, such as Census data, are subject to significant measurement errors. (Officials in many cities believed that the Census of Population underestimated the number of city residents by failing to account for the homeless, families that were doubled up, the large portion of transients living in parts of major cities, and illegal immigrants. Since many intergovernmental funding programs are linked to population, the issue was vital to the size of urban grants.) Many governmental statistics are published as estimates first and later revised for better accuracy. Consequently, model builders sometimes must choose between using the most recent data or using older, but more accurate data. Furthermore, data for large, comprehensive econometric models are seldom available from published sources, so proxy variables are often required. The use of changes in employment to reflect changes in output is an example of the use of proxy variables. Sometimes the use of proxy variables is benign, but sometimes the practice can reduce the accuracy of the model.

Specification errors arise from theoretical misunderstandings or deliberate simplification. Suppose a regression model attempted to show that the local unemployment rate was a function of job growth. Since other factors that are practically impossible to measure, such as labor skills and migration patterns, are also important determinants of the unemployment rate, such a model is likely to exclude theoretically important variables and, hence, be misspecified. Often, models are knowingly misspecified, while sometimes inaccurate theoretical understanding of the process being modeled results in misspecifications.

Both measurement and specification errors can be compounded when equations have multiplicative or exponential forms. If there were a ± 10 percent error in measuring X, the problem would be greater if the equation to estimate Y were $Y = X^2$ than if the equation were $Y = 2X$ or $Y = 12 + X$. An additional type of error compounding can arise when long chains of logic are employed. If a logical chain has four steps from beginning to end (if A, then B, then C, then D) and if each step is 80 percent certain, then the certainty of the conclusion would be less than 50 percent. This type of problem arises when the results of one equation feed into another and is common to econometric models and other models, such as the input-output model.

Local Leading Economic Indicators

Leading economic indicators are designed to anticipate turning points in economic activity rather than to forecast values of particular variables. The index of 12 leading economic indicators is a staple of national business-cycle analysis. When the index of leading indicators declines for several periods in a row, a decline in output is normally anticipated. The longer and deeper the decline, the more likely a recession will occur. Regional economists have designed indexes of leading economic indicators similar to the national index. While indexes of leading indicators are not strictly econometric models, econometric techniques are used in their development.

An index of leading economic indicators may be expressed as:

$$I = \sum_{i=1}^{n} w_i X_i \qquad (12)$$

where I = Index value,
  w_i = The weight assigned to the ith indicator, and
  X_i = The value of the ith time-series indicator.

The construction of an index requires both that the variables used in the index be identified and that an appropriate weight be assigned to each data series.

Kozlowski (1987) pointed out that regional economists have less choice in building an index of leading economic indicators than economists engaged in similar activity at the national level, because they have fewer time-series data sets to incorporate into an index. In fact, the problem in constructing leading indicators at the national level is to filter out data series while regional economists normally seek to expand the set of leading indicators. Table 6–6 shows the variables that compose the index of leading economic indicators for seven areas.

Kozlowski evaluated the accuracy of regional economic indicators. He found that they were accurate in forecasting peaks of economic activity. However, they were less reliable when used as independent variables in models that predicted levels of economic activity. Kozlowski's findings are not surprising because indicators normally require less data than econometric models and they reveal less about the nature of changes.

Simulation and Urban Dynamics

Simulations are models that allow an individual to observe how a system might react to certain events. There can be a close link between econometric and simulation models because most simulation models use econometric techniques to establish the relationships among the variables concerned. However, not all simulation models use econometric techniques. Since econometric models have already been discussed, this section deals primarily with nonstatistical simulations.

Board games have been used to simulate urban change. One of the most widely used urban simulations, *CLUG: The Community Land Use Game,* is a board game that simulates urban development. It is predicated on the export-base theory. Exports directly or indirectly affect land-use patterns, public-sector decisions, and numerous other parts of the urban network. Participants in CLUG and other simulations assume roles of various actors and make decisions as they believe their characters would act. The outcomes of the game depend upon the decisions the participants make. The development of home computers have expanded the potential use of urban simulations. SIM City is a computer game based upon a similar land-development process that allows a player to simulate urban development.

Urban Dynamics.   One of the most complex models of urban growth was developed by Jay Forrester in his influential book, *Urban Dynamics* (1969). Forrester's background as an electrical engineer coupled with his interest in cities led him to think in "systems" terms about the city. He developed a set of equations and simulated the development of a hypothetical city over a 250-year period. In his model, the city grew rapidly for the first 100 years or so (depending upon the parameters selected). Then the growth rate declined and the city moved towards an equilibrium.

The parameters of Forrester's model were not derived empirically. They were based upon conversations with experts in urban development. However, the imprecision of the parameters was not considered a major problem. As Forrester put it, "Any reasonably consistent set of coefficients could be used as the basis for this model. . . . Most of the values are not critical in determining the behavior of the system (p. 50)." Sensitivity analysis—changing the value of certain parameters to determine whether the outcome changes appreciably—was employed to prove that the specific value of most parameters was not important in determining the path of development.

Forrester believed that the model generated a reasonably accurate development path consistent with historical observation (although many economists disagreed) and the fact that it was not sensitive to small changes in the values of parameters was evidence that the model was accurate. The use of sensitivity analysis to avoid the need to test relationships statistically was seen by many as a major advantage of Forrester's approach.

Structure of Urban-Dynamics Model.   A brief description of the city described by Forrester's equations will help clarify how the model works.

TABLE 6–6 Components of Indexes of Leading Indicators

Series	Detroit	Fort Wayne	Memphis	Nebraska	South Carolina	Texas	Toledo
1. Residential housing units authorized by building permit	x	x	x	x	x	x	x
2. Average weekly initial claims for unemployment insurance	x	x		x	x	x	x
3. Average workweek—manufacturing workers	x				x	x	x
4. Total deposits at financial institutions (deflated)	x	x				x	x
5. New business incorporations					x	x	
6. Change in credit outstanding							x
7. Average weekly earnings—manufacturing workers (deflated)			x	x			
8. Index of prices of farm products				x			
9. Ratio of coincident to lagging indexes			x				

10. Percent of industries reporting employment increases		x					
11. Nonfarm job openings—unfilled					x		
12. Unemployment rate					x		
13. Ratio—average weeks claimed to insured employment					x		
14. Unemployment insurance benefits (current dollars)					x		
15. Money stock—M2 (deflated)			x				
16. Standard & Poor's Index of 500 Stock prices				x			
17. New car inventories—U.S. dealers days supply	x						
18. Index of consumer sentiment (University of Michigan)	x						
Number of components	6	4	4	5	8	5	5

SOURCE: Paul J. Kozlowski, "Regional Indexes of Leading Indicators: An Evaluation of Forecasting Performance," *Growth and Change*, Summer 1987, p. 65.

The urban-dynamics model was predicated upon a city in a "limitless" surrounding region. The city interacted with the external region but did not alter it. Differences in attractiveness between the urban area and its surrounding region are primary causes of population movements into or out of the area. But migration occurs only with a lag to reflect the time it takes for individuals to become aware of and act on differences in attractiveness.

The city contained three systems—population, housing, and business. The businesses were assumed to go through stages from new business to mature business to declining industry. The particular stages of the local businesses determined urban employment. The rate of business aging depended in part upon conditions elsewhere in the city. There were three types of housing—premium housing, worker housing, and housing for the underemployed. The housing stock was determined by the demand for housing and deterioration rates. The population system was composed of three "classes" that were defined according to job status. People could enter each category by moving into or out of the area or by socioeconomic mobility within the city.

Feedback loops are essential building blocks of the system. Figure 6–1 illustrates a feedback loop linking the city to the limitless regional hinterland. The flow rate is controlled by the level of the variable. However, information on the level of the variable may be fed back into the model with time lags or in other imperfect ways. For instance, suppose the feedback system represented housing. The rate of new construction would be determined by the level of existing housing. However, overbuilding could occur before the message to slow housing construction was received by housing developers. Thus, the market may already have been overbuilt before housing starts decrease. Likewise, the surplus may be eliminated and a shortage may occur before the rate of new construction increases. Clearly, imperfect information negates the possibility of a perfectly functioning market. Notice that since the flow is linked with an unlimited environment, the size of the flow will be influenced by conditions in the environment, but the city cannot affect the limitless environment.

Generalizations.   Several important generalizations emerged from the simulation study. Cities were described as complex systems or systems with many interdependent, nonlinear feedbacks. Cities, like most complex systems, are described as:

1. Counterintuitive. The outcome from a particular intervention is often the opposite of what would be expected. For example, attempts to reduce poverty may attract more poor to the city from the limitless environment, thus increasing the rate of poverty. Since ur-

FIGURE 6–1   Feedback Loop

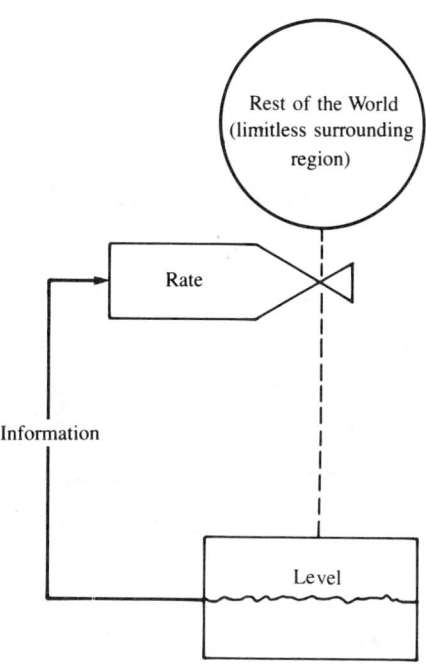

The simplest possible feedback loop has one rate, one level, and one channel for conveying information.

SOURCE: Adapted from Jay W. Forrester, *Principles of Systems,* Cambridge, Mass. Wright Allen Press, 1971, pp. 1–8.

ban policies normally have intuitive appeal for political reasons, policies are likely to fail (see point 3).

2. Insensitive to parameter changes. Sensitivity analysis (changing the assumed value of parameters) indicated that major changes in many parameters did not significantly change the equilibrium outcome in the long run.

3. Resistant to policy change. This conclusion is implied by the first two points and is partly the result of the free migration from the "rest of the world." For instance, suppose the local government transfers a given amount of money from rich to poor. The initial impact would be to increase incomes of lower-income households. But, other low-income families would move into the area to take advantage of the program. As the number of recipients increases,

benefits diminish until equilibrium is reestablished. In equilibrium, the poor in the city would have incomes equal to households with similar skills in the "rest of the world."

4. Containing influential pressure points. In spite of point 3, changes at critical pressure points can result in major changes in outcomes. But such pressure points are not easily determined. In fact, they are also often counterintuitive. Thus, simulation models can be useful policy tools by helping determine what changes will result in desired outcomes. For instance, in the urban-dynamics model, a reduction in worker housing would decrease the underemployed population and increase the managerial population and new business.

5. Differing in short- and long-run consequences. Short-term reactions to a policy change are often what one would intuitively expect. But in the long run, the reactions will be the opposite. For instance, the simulation of the effects of an employment and training program first reduced the number of unemployed, but later resulted in slightly higher levels of unemployment that otherwise would have occurred.

Evaluation of Simulation Approaches.   The urban-dynamics model was influential for at least two reasons. First, it came out at a time when many policy makers were puzzled as to why urban policies had not worked as well as they had hoped, and so the concept of cities as counterintuitive systems provided an explanation for the apparent failure of direct policies. Second, the simulation method provided a relatively cheap analytic tool that had fewer data requirements than econometric models.

However, as economists analyzed the model carefully, they became very critical of Forrester's approach and dubious about the usefulness of large-scale simulations in general. One set of criticisms of the urban-dynamics model and other simulation models is that the parameters were not realistic. Rather than using statistical methods to establish relationships between variables, Forrester based his parameters on his own opinions and on conversations with others. Sensitivity tests indicated that the major conclusions were insensitive to the particular parameters. However, while outcomes may not have been affected significantly given Forrester's centuries-long time frame, policy makers may be more interested in short or intermediate effects. As Keynes quipped, "In the long run we're all dead." Accurate estimates of short- and intermediate-term policy impacts usually require accurate estimates of parameters rather than hunches.

Another group of criticisms charges that the model's conclusions followed from its structure, which, in turn, depended upon an underlying theory that was simplistic. In particular, Forrester assumed a "limitless" environment outside of the city and migration into or out of the city depended upon the advantages of each of the two locations. Given this structure, there is little surprise in finding that if a city increased benefits to the poor, then more poor would migrate from the limitless environment into the city. But in reality, migration decisions are much more complex, as explained in Chapter 9. There are many cities with diverse policies and opportunities. The assumption of the "unlimited regional hinterland" appears to have oversimplified the situation. If the purpose of the simulation is to formulate national urban policy, one must consider the effects of many cities seeking to improve local conditions.

The serious shortcomings of Forrester's approach to simulation illustrates potential problems of simulation modeling. However, urban simulations continue to be used, and the increasing use of computers will probably contribute to their continued use. However, recent simulations have been more careful in both theoretical structure and the use of empirical relationships (Van den Berg, 1986).

DISEQUILIBRIUM PERSPECTIVES

Most economic-growth models are structured so that an economy starts at equilibrium, experiences a change, and returns to equilibrium at the end of analysis. This is the outcome of the great majority of input-output, econometric, and simulation models. A change in export demand is an example of an exogenous change that could move the economy towards a new equilibrium. Figure 5–3 in Chapter 5 illustrated two typical adjustment paths. While equilibrium models may represent the normal case, many observers have noted that sometimes economies may not have a structure that quickly and automatically leads to a new, stable equilibrium. At least over a range of income, growth may contribute to further growth or decline may contribute to additional decline. This section examines situations in which growth and decline may be cumulative.

Cumulative Causation

Cumulative causation refers to the process in which a change in one direction may reinforce other tendencies for change in the same direction. Myrdal (1957) believed that disequilibrium growth and development paths were common:

> In the normal case, there is no tendency towards automatic self-stabilization in the social system. The system is not by itself moving towards any sort of

balance between forces, but is constantly on the move away from such a situation. In the normal case, a change does not call forth countervailing changes, but, instead, supporting changes which move the system in the same direction as the first change but much further. Because of such circular causation, a social process tends to become cumulative and often to gather speed at an accelerating rate (p. 13).

Although Myrdal was primarily considering underdeveloped regions when he discussed the process of circular causation, the concept has been applied to urban systems. The selective nature of outmigration can contribute to cumulative decline. For instance, in a metropolitan environment, higher-income families tend to move into the suburbs. As the affluent families leave the central city, families with greater public-service needs and lower capacities to pay taxes are left behind. The resulting fiscal mix increases the tax burden of remaining high-income families and reinforces the tendency towards outmigration of even more upper-income families. The decline may be reinforced because the outmigration that results in lower income and lower fiscal capacity may, in turn, contribute to other types of deterioration, such as crime, urban ugliness, and fewer amenities. The population-income decline may also contribute to the movement of retail and other service jobs to the suburbs. The job shift will be particularly significant to the extent that higher-income families (which account for a disproportionate amount of spending) lead the exodus.

Similarly, when an area starts to prosper, self-reinforcing factors may tend to cause cumulative growth. Higher incomes allow for more amenities, attract businesses, and increase agglomeration economies. An area that has a growth reputation may attract additional investment that will, in turn, contribute to growth.

Of course, a new equilibrium will ultimately be established. A city will not increase or decline forever because countervailing forces such as higher or lower land prices will eventually become increasingly powerful. In this sense, most phenomena are equilibrating in the long run. But the disequilibrium models have the advantage of highlighting the potential for cumulative change that may occur over some portion of a community's adjustment path.

The Baumol Model

Baumol (Baumol, 1963; Oates, Howrey and Baumol, 1971) developed a model that illustrates how a negative (positive) change could initiate a cumulative downward (upward) growth path. The Baumol model employs the abstract concept of deterioration. Deterioration represents a variety of urban problems, including crime, pollution, congestion, and taxes, that may cause incomes to fall. The higher the level of deterioration in any given year, the smaller the regional income will be in succeeding years. This idea is expressed in the equation:

$$Y_{t+1} = r - sD_t \qquad (13)$$

where Y_t = Income in period t,
$\quad Y_{t+1}$ = Income in period $t + 1$,
$\quad D_t$ = The level of deterioration in period t, and
$\quad r, s$ = Parameters.

The level of deterioration is determined by the level of income in the community. Higher levels of income decrease the level of deterioration because the community's increased income provides resources to correct problems, purchase more amenities, and provide additional services. Thus:

$$D_t = u - vY_t \qquad \text{where } u, v = \text{parameters.} \qquad (14)$$

The circularity of this model can be seen by the fact that income affects deterioration and deterioration affects income. Substituting equation 14 into 13 yields:

$$Y_{t+1} = r - su + sv(Y_t) \qquad (15)$$

or $\qquad\qquad\qquad Y_{t+1} = g + hY_t \qquad\qquad\qquad\qquad (16)$

where $g = r - su$, and
$\quad h = sv$.

The equilibrium level of income Y_e is found when $Y_e = Y_t = Y_{t+1}$ or when:

$$Y_e = g/(1 - h). \qquad (17)$$

The model simplifies to the proposition that income in one period determines future income. Although it undoubtedly oversimplifies (like most models) the circularity process, the model does have some intuitive appeal and it reflects part of the problem policy makers face.

Whether or not the model will predict a cumulative decline or a process of growth, on the one hand, or a convergence toward a stable equilibrium, on the other, depends upon the values of g and h. If $g < 0$ and $h > 1$, then cumulative change will occur as illustrated in Figure 6–2(a). If $g > 0$ and $h < 1$, then growth will converge towards an equilibrium as illustrated in Figure 6–2(b).

Figure 6–2 illustrates the cumulative decline or explosive growth nature of equation 16. For instance, suppose some force knocked the level of income from Y_e to Y_1. Thus, income in the current year, Y_t, would be Y_1. In the next year, Y_{t+1}, income would be Y_2 (read from the $Y_{t+1} = g + hY_t$ line). As time passed, Y_2 would become the current year's income and reading the $Y_{t+1} = g + hY_t$ line indicates that next year's income will fall again to Y_3. Thus, income would decline continually. Likewise, if

FIGURE 6–2 The Baumol Model

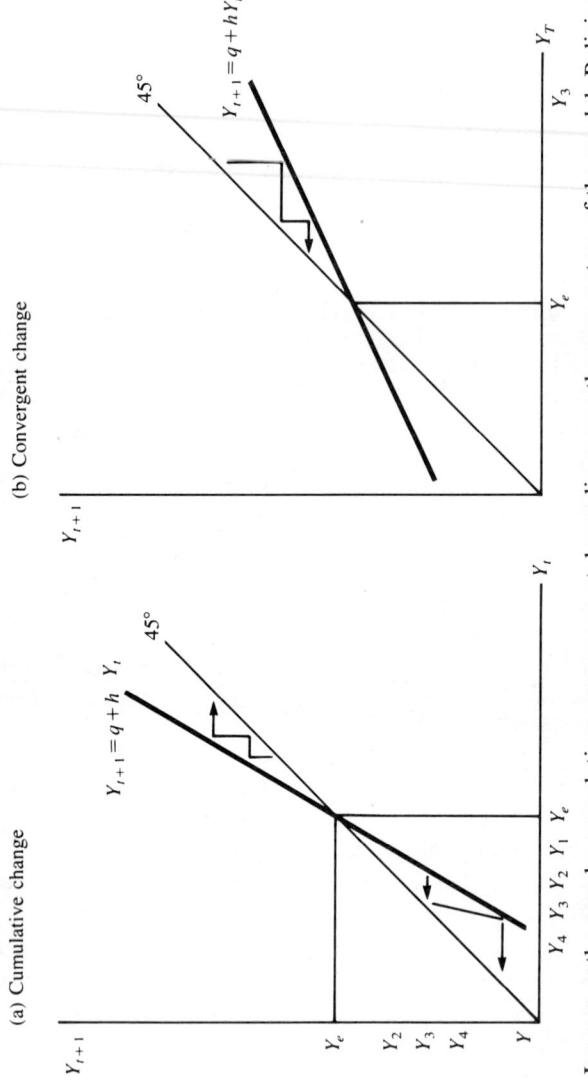

(a) Cumulative change

(b) Convergent change

Income paths may be cumulative or convergent depending upon the parameters of the model. Policies that directly affect income may fail to move an economy towards a new equilibrium.

income were to increase above the initial equilibrium due to some external shock, income could grow explosively.

The Baumol model is more than a set of equations—it has important policy implications. Suppose the relationship between income and deterioration is such that decline is cumulative as indicated by Figure 6–2(a). If income is falling from Y_e to Y_1 to Y_2 and so forth, a direct policy action might be to increase the level of income through government transfers. Income could be increased directly through a cash transfer or indirectly through the provision of government services. However, if incomes are increased from Y_2 to, say, Y_1, the city would experience a temporary rebound, but would eventually continue its cumulative decline as soon as the transfers ceased. On the other hand, if incomes were boosted to Y_e, equilibrium could be maintained without further assistance. Boosting income beyond Y_e could put the city on a cumulative-growth path. In other words, policies sometimes must be of sufficient scope or size to boost a community past a particular threshold. Policies that are insufficient may provide temporary assistance, but fail to generate a permanently higher level of welfare.

If the relationships between income in one period and income in succeeding periods were such that a movement away from equilibrium results in a convergent path back to the original equilibrium level (a more traditional adjustment path), policies to help a community by directly boosting income would succeed only for a short period of time. For instance, Figure 6–2(b) illustrates a situation in which an exogenous increase of income to Y_3 will establish an income-adjustment path from Y_3 back to the initial equilibrium. The convergent-growth path that can be generated by Baumol's model has implications similar to Forrester's urban-dynamics approach without the need for the "limitless region" assumption. Forrester noted that urban systems are complex and intuitive approaches to increasing income may not work. In the context of Baumol's formulation, a direct approach to increasing income might be a grant from outside the region. Although such an action would increase incomes given the model's parameters, income would tend to return to the initial equilibrium level. Under these circumstances, the Baumol model implies that the best way to permanently increase income would be to alter the relationship between income and deterioration so that an increase in deterioration will not cause income to decrease as much as previously or so that a given level of income will result in less deterioration. In equation 13, for instance, an increase in r would cause future income to be higher for any given level of deterioration while an increase in s would reduce the impact of a change in the level of deterioration on future income.

Bradford and Kelejian (1973) provided empirical evidence that strongly supports the idea that urban decline can be cumulative over a particular range. Specifically, they found that middle-class families were more likely to reside in suburbs, (1) the higher the percentage of poor persons residing in the central city 10 years ago and (2) the lower the fiscal surplus generated for middle-class families by the central-city budget.

Policies that change the relationship between income and the rate of deterioration are difficult to formulate, partly because the concept of deterioration is abstract. A policy maker may not know how to effectively slow or stop aspects of deterioration. However, policies that do affect the income-determination process may be preferable to actions that temporarily increase income, but fail to do so enough to establish conditions for cumulative growth. A marketing campaign that convinces people of the advantages of urban living in a particular city and better urban design that reduces the annoyances of a high-density population are examples of actions that could permanently increase the equilibrium income by altering the relationships between deterioration and income.

WHO BENEFITS FROM GROWTH?

The previous sections of this chapter, as well as Chapter 5, focused upon tools and theories that help economists analyze the process of urban and regional development. This section steps back from technical consideration and asks: "Who benefits from growth?"

The beneficiaries of urban growth can be determined most accurately if specifics such as which industries are growing and what areas within the region will experience the development are known. However, aggregate growth will normally benefit some segments of the population more than others. Some groups may even be harmed by growth. The purpose of this section is to make some generalizations about groups of individuals who will probably be harmed by growth and groups that will likely benefit.

Local growth will increase the demand for products and services that are normally considered part of the nonbasic sector serving the local population, such as brokerage services, groceries, retail activities, and newspapers. Demand for output of the export sector is not likely to be altered by growth of the local economy because demand for exports is determined outside the area.[2] Increased demand for local services will, in turn, tend to increase the price of resources used to produce nonbasic goods. Hence, owners of resources that produce for local consumption may experience increases in income as the result of regional growth.

---

[2] An increase in export demand will stimulate the local economy and the demand for labor. However, feedback effects are not likely except when the region is large and closely linked with another area.

Not all of the owners of resources serving local markets will benefit from growth, however. If resource supplies are elastic, the benefits for current resource owners will be limited, because the increase in demand will not translate into higher factor prices. The elasticity of supply for locally sold goods and services, in turn, depends upon how easily such goods can be imported into the area and whether additional resources can be obtained without substantially increasing their price. Furthermore, some resources may shift from the export sector to the nonbasic sector in response to changes in resource demand. The size of the annual benefits from growth will probably diminish in the long run for owners of resources with elastic supplies. The longer the time period, the greater the likelihood that resources can be bought from outside the area. Thus, the supply of locally available resources is more elastic in the long run than in the short run. Owners of monopoly resources, however, may experience permanent increases in income from local growth.

Figure 6–3 illustrates three possible resource-supply situations. In the first case, the supply of the resources to the local economy, S, is perfectly elastic. Thus, an increase in demand for the resource will not cause the price of the resource to increase. This case may approximate the actual situation for many factors of production in the long run or for regionally mobile factors of production even in the short run. Figure 6–3(b) represents a situation where an increase in the price of the resource will be required to affect an increase in supply. Figure 6–3(c) illustrates a perfectly inelastic supply so that the total impact of the demand increase is absorbed in the form of a higher price.

Benefits to Factors of Production

The supply of capital to most sectors of local economies is very elastic. If the expected rate of return on newly invested capital increases in these local sectors, investment from outside will very quickly flow into the area, thus reducing the interest disparity.

Owners of capital invested prior to local economic growth may earn above-normal rates of return, at least on a temporary basis, depending on where their capital was invested. Individuals who purchased buildings may find that their rent receipts increased due to local growth. Therefore, the rate of return on capital may be greater than would have been anticipated. Similarly, owners of local service businesses may experience increased rates of return. The ability to maintain above-normal rates will depend upon how quickly investors realize that above-normal returns can be earned and how quickly the knowledge is acted upon.

Some members of the labor force may also earn above-normal income due to local growth. Imagine an automobile salesperson whose income increased because of larger sales attributed to the stronger local

FIGURE 6–3 Elasticities Determine Response to Increased Demand

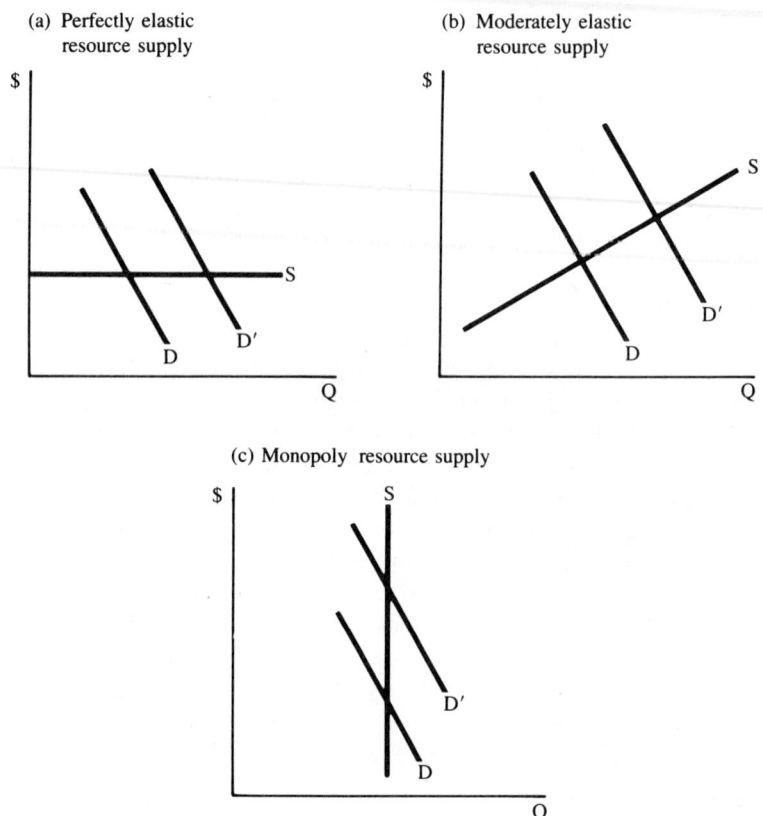

The increase in demand will increase resource prices only if the resource-supply curve is not totally elastic.

economy. Thus, the salesperson could be a beneficiary of local growth. However, the salesperson's increased compensation is likely to be only temporary. The owner of the dealership may realize that the income of the sales staff has increased and cut commission rates accordingly. Alternatively, other dealerships may enter the area, thus reducing sales at the original dealership. The income increase to the automobile salesperson may be substantial, even if it was only temporary; and "temporary" in economic terms may translate into many years. If individuals and institutions are slow to respond to changes in the economic environment, the present value of the increased earnings could be substantial.

If wages in some sectors go up initially, wages in related sectors may also tend to increase. For instance, if automobile exports expand, automobile firms may attempt to hire more employees. Perhaps wages in the automobile sector are fixed by union contract so they do not increase, but because such manufacturing jobs are considered good jobs they may attract labor from other sections. Therefore, wages in competing industries may increase. Furthermore, an increase in the wage rate among one skill group may ripple through the economy and affect other labor markets. If pay differentials increase between a high-wage and a low-wage occupation, workers will have an incentive to obtain the necessary skills to qualify for employment in the higher-skill labor market. Conversely, demand increases in low-skill occupations could narrow wage differentials. Incentives for new workers in the labor market to attain extra skills could be reduced.

Unemployed workers have opportunities to benefit from the increased jobs associated with growth. In fact, an expanding facility is likely to directly and indirectly create jobs that will be filled by unemployed residents. However, in the long run, growth may attract unemployed workers from elsewhere into the local area and the previous unemployment rate may be reestablished. Yet some of the original residents may have obtained permanent employment as the economy grew. Similar benefits may accrue to underemployed residents who secure better jobs during the transition.

Potential employment advantages may not accrue to those among the unemployed who lack skills to obtain and hold jobs. Many unemployed individuals who have physical, mental health, and/or attitudinal problems may not fit into the labor market. Such individuals may not benefit from regional employment expansion. The same inability to participate in the mainstream economy has prevented many women with small children from benefiting from growth. In fact, if an expanding economy raises rents or other prices to increase the cost of living, the unemployable or those on fixed incomes may suffer from growth.

Owners of local monopoly resources are likely to benefit from growth, even in the long run. Landowners do not have to worry about an increased supply of land coming into the area. Since the supply of land is fixed and each site has slight monopoly power, landowners will maintain benefit from growth even in the long run. It is not surprising that individuals involved in land development are usually prominent progrowth advocates. Similarly, some franchise owners may have been granted licenses to serve a region and they can maintain that "monopoly" as the region grows.

The lumpy nature of much economic activity can contribute to the perpetuation of monopolies. Suppose a shoe-repair shop requires a population of at least 10,000 to provide sufficient demand to earn normal profits. If an area grows from 10,000 to 15,000 people, the owner of the shoe-repair store could earn above-normal profits because of the 50 percent increase in the market size. Yet, there would not be room for another store owner. A second shop would face the possibility of splitting a 15,000-person market. (And a new shop might not even be able to capture half the market.) Therefore, a population of 15,000 is not large enough to support two shops. However, if growth continues to 20,000, the market might be large enough to support a second shoe-repair shop. The excess profits made by the original owner could disappear with the opening of the competitor.

In many activities, new firms enter the industry only after substantial time lags, and even after a new enterprise enters the area, it may take a long time for it to get established. It may take years for a second newspaper or bank in a town to gain the air of respectability held by the senior institutions. The lumpy nature of economic activity and the time lags that characterize new-business formation help explain why small retailers tend to be progrowth advocates.

In a sense, local celebrities have monopoly power since a community can only recognize a limited number of personalities. Inability to achieve recognition limits the number of celebrities. Thus, a top TV anchorperson may receive an income increase because of larger audiences due to local growth, although he may not have gotten any better looking and his voice may not have gotten deeper. In other words, his higher ratings are not attributable to changes in appeal. The increase can be attributed solely to general, local economic growth.

In the long run, the larger market size may cause better-looking anchorpersons to compete for the job. The management may have decided that the original anchorperson was adequate for a small market, but not good enough for a big market. Thus, the advantages of growth may turn to a disadvantage for some. However, incumbents usually have an advantage in retaining jobs against new job seekers, since managements would normally prefer to stick with the current personnel. Even if the original anchorperson is unseated, temporary gains will have occurred. Notice that if a new anchorperson were hired, the new employee would not receive an "excess" wage due to growth, because his or her talents are more suitable to larger markets. A new anchorperson would presumably have been able to obtain employment in other large markets.

In general, unless we are concerned with a pure monopoly resource, competition and migration will eliminate or greatly reduce transitory gains. However, it may take years, perhaps generations, before the transitory gains attainable from short-run monopolies are eliminated.

Opponents of Growth

The benefits discussed above were primarily concerned with household income. Growth can affect many characteristics of an area. Many individuals oppose growth because they believe it makes the area less attractive. Higher prices, particularly in resource-inelastic sectors, are a cost of growth that may be imposed upon many residents. An individual living on a fixed income may be disadvantaged due to higher prices that may accompany growth. Furthermore, additional production tends to be associated with more pollution and population growth is associated with greater congestion. Individuals who do not receive substantial growth benefits may feel they are losers from growth. The extent of negative growth spillovers and the inability of everyone to share fully in the benefits of growth explain why some communities have instituted no-growth campaigns. However, many individuals will benefit from the increased amenities, shopping choices, and other opportunities that will become available as their community grows. Hence, not all of the indirect effects of growth are negative. Nevertheless, many individuals seek to protect their immediate neighborhood from negative growth consequences (the "NIMBY" or "Not in my backyard" phenomenon) while benefiting from growth in other parts of the area.

States and regions are much more receptive to growth than they were in the late 1960s when the slow-/no-growth advocates had substantial influence. Most regional communities realize that some economic growth is necessary to provide jobs for current residents and their children. If no new jobs are being created, some outmigration would be forced simply due to natural population increases. The strongest antigrowth coalitions tend to be within suburbs or neighborhoods of metropolitan areas. Some suburban residents may hope to share in the benefits of metropolitan growth while maintaining the current character of their immediate area. The prevalence of such attitudes often brings suburbs in conflict with each other.

SUMMARY

Several empirical and theoretical approaches to urban and regional growth were described in this chapter. Input-output analysis can be used to determine the impact that an increase in the output of one sector will have on all sectors of the economy. The total impact is the result of direct, indirect, and induced effects. Input-output analysis has several uses, including forecasting and simulation. One of the major advantages of input-output analysis is that the results provide substantial industrial detail. The most noticeable difficulties of the input-output approach include the high cost of data collection and the static nature of the model.

Shift-and-share analysis is a technique for dividing an area's growth into various components. First, the share component is growth equal to the national average growth rate. Second, an area may grow differently from the national average due to its mix of industries. Third, an area may have a growth environment. Shift-and-share analysis has been criticized because the components are frequently misinterpreted and because the competitive component is a residual that can be attributed to a variety of other factors.

Econometric models use statistical techniques and economic theory to estimate relationships among variables. Simulation models answer "what if" questions such as the change in key social indicators if a particular policy were implemented. Many simulation models use econometric techniques, such as regression, to establish relationships among variables.

One of the most complex simulation models is the urban-dynamics model. The model's parameters are based upon conversations with experts and are not derived empirically. Urban systems were found to be counterintuitive, insensitive to parameter changes, resistant to policy changes, containing influential pressure points, and having different consequences in the long run compared to the short run.

Most economic models are designed to show the economic system returning to a new equilibrium after a change in the initial state. However, a disruption could set off a cumulative expansion or contraction. Disequilibrium models have been particularly useful in helping us understand the development process in poor regions of the world, but they have also been applied to urban areas.

Not all residents benefit equally when an area grows. Some residents will be harmed, some will benefit only temporarily, and some will capture permanent benefits. The extent of benefits depends upon the long-run elasticity of the supply of resources. Owners of resources with inelastic supply will benefit most from growth.

REFERENCES

Baumol, William J. "Interaction of Public and Private Decisions." In *Public Expenditure Decisions in the Urban Community,* ed. H. S. Schaller. Baltimore: The Johns Hopkins Press, 1963, pp. 1–18.

Bolton, Roger. "Regional Econometric Models." *Journal of Regional Science* 25, no. 4, 1985, pp. 495–518.

Booth, Douglas E. "Long Waves and Uneven Regional Growth." *Southern Economic Journal* 53, no. 2, October 1986, pp. 448–60.

Bradford, D. F. and Kelejian, H. "An Econometric Model of the Flight to the Suburbs." *Journal of Political Economy* 81, 1973, pp. 566–89.

Carlino, G. A. "Contrasts in Agglomeration: New York and Pittsburgh Reconsidered." *Urban Studies* 17, no. 3, 1980, pp. 343–51.

Carlino, Gerald, and Edwin S. Mills. "The Determinants of County Growth." *Journal of Regional Science* 27, no. 1, February 1987, pp. 39–54.

Chinitz, R. "Contrasts in Agglomeration: New York and Pittsburgh." *American Economic Review* 51, no. 2, May 1961, pp. 279–89.*

Forrester, Jay. *Urban Dynamics.* Cambridge, Mass.: MIT Press, 1969.

James, Jan B.; C. F. Lee; and C. F. Sirmans. *Urban Econometrics: Model Development and Empirical Results.* Greenwich, Conn.: JAI Press, 1986.

Klaasen, L. H., and A. Pawlowski. "Long-Term Forecasting; Meditations of Two Pitfall Collectors." *Man, Environment, Space and Time* 2, no. 1, 1982, pp. 17–28.

Kozlowski, Paul J. "Regional Indexes of Leading Indicators: An Evaluation of Forecasting Performance." *Growth and Change,* Summer 1987, pp. 62–73.

Kresge, David. *Regions and Resources.* Cambridge, Mass.: MIT Press, 1984.

Leven, Charles L. "Regional Development Analysis and Policy." *Journal of Regional Science* 25, no. 4, November 1985, pp. 569–92.

Myrdal, Gunnar. "Rich Lands and Poor: *The Road to World Prosperity,*" New York: Harper & Row, 1957.*

Oates, W. E., Howrey, E. P., and Baumol, W. J. "An Analysis of Public Policy in Dynamic Urban Models." *Journal of Political Economy* 79, 142–53.

Rubin, Barry M., and Rodney A. Erickson. "Specification and Performance Improvements in Regional Econometric Forecasting Models: A Model for the Milwaukee Metropolitan Area." *Journal of Regional Science* 20, no. 1, 1980, pp. 11–35.

Storey, David J., and Steven G. Johnson. "Regional Variations in Entrepreneurship in the U.K." *Scottish Journal of Political Economy* 34, no. 2, May 1987, pp. 161–73.

Van den Berg, Leo. *Urban Systems in Dynamic Society.* London: Gower Publishing Company, 1986.

Weiss, Steven J., and Edwin C. Gooding. "Estimation of Differential Employment Multipliers in a Small Regional Economy." In *Regional Economics: A Reader,* ed. H. Richardson. London: Macmillan, 1970, pp. 55–67.

* Classics.

Chapter Seven

The Practice of Economic Development

Previous chapters described theories and tools that help analyze local development. Economic development officials must use theories and empirical evidence to formulate action plans. This chapter examines local economic development policies and programs. Policies represent broad approaches to issues. They provide the basis for developing programs. Programs, in turn, can be implemented in a variety of ways, and the same program may be implemented differently in different areas. Although specific programs are discussed, the theoretical basis for local economic development activity is also of concern. However, program development and implementation, and theoretical perspectives often play only a supporting role. Actions are often driven by economic interests, politics, and other factors, rather than by the theoretically correct action.

The first section of this chapter provides a historical perspective on economic development and discusses some of the motives that drive the process. The second section describes major tools that have been used to stimulate local economies. Programs that draw upon one or more of the economic tools are discussed next. The fourth section presents a theoretical perspective on local job-creation programs that allows us to evaluate the appropriateness of local intervention in market decisions. Several development policy issues are discussed next. The efficiency and effectiveness of local development programs are of special concern. The final section examines the similarities between regional development policy and industrial development policy.

PERSPECTIVES ON ECONOMIC DEVELOPMENT POLICY

Urban and regional economic development is a hot topic, but it is not a new one. Public policies designed to strengthen local economies have long been a major theme in U.S. economic history. Yet the purposes and policies included under the term "economic development" have changed over time. This section reviews local economic development approaches and describes current motives for local economic development.

A Brief History

Even in the early history of the United States, competition among regional economic interests was shaping national policy. Regional conflicts were often expressed in disagreements over tariff policies. Five distinct periods of local development activity can be described: (1) the canal and railroad period, 1815–1870, (2) the great city-building era, 1870–1929, (3) the disruptions of depression and war, 1929–1947, (4) federal-led development efforts, 1947–1980, and (5) state- and local-led development efforts, 1980–present. However, there is considerable overlap among these historical periods because regions differed in the timing of their economic development efforts. In each of these historical periods, it is critical to remember that public policy may have channeled development in certain ways, but the amount of public spending was always much less than private spending. Therefore, the development process should not be viewed as totally determined by public policy.

The Canal and Railroad Period. During this period, economic development efforts centered on building interregional transportation routes linking cities with markets and materials. The predominant local development policy was to influence the construction of canals and railroads. The rewards to communities that first tapped interior markets are illustrated by the advantages that accrued to New York City with the construction of the Erie Canal. After the success of the Erie Canal, local governments vigorously competed with each other for access, first to canals and later to railroads.

State and local governments offered subsidies to influence the routes selected by private railroad and canal companies. Subsidies became so significant that they distorted the economics of route selection. The New York and Oswego Midland Railroad illustrates route distortion. The railroad was financed largely by municipal bonds issued by cities that felt the need for rail access. As a result, the railroad zigzagged across New York without passing through a major city or tapping significant new markets. It is not surprising that the railroad company went bankrupt, because it did not have a viable customer base. The biggest losers were the citizens of communities that helped finance the railroad.

During the latter part of this period, local incentives were overshadowed by federal decisions about route selection. Federal land grants influenced the paths of railroads. Consequently, the nature of the competition shifted from direct economic subsidies to political lobbying. State and local governments lobbied fiercely to influence federally selected routes.

The City-Building Era.   By the latter part of the 19th century, the major rail and water transportation systems were in place, except in the West. The economic development focus turned towards providing the infrastructure needed to support an expanding manufacturing sector and the urban population attracted to manufacturing jobs. The core cities were the recipients of investments often financed by city borrowing, land grants, and tax concessions to transportation and utilities companies. Road, sewer, and water systems were constructed so as to expand the scope of the central city beyond the core. Public buildings were also ,important to local economic development efforts. Major landmarks of today were constructed during the city-building era. Later in this period, the City Beautiful Movement shifted the construction from public building and utilities projects toward parks, monuments, and boulevards.

The principal economic development strategy during this period was that public infrastructure would support and encourage private investment. Political patronage was also supported by the jobs that were created by the high levels of construction in many cities. In fact, the city-building era is often associated with a period of corrupt urban policies.

Disruptions of Depression and War.   Between about 1929 and 1947, economic development efforts were overshadowed by two national crises. The Great Depression effectively halted the city-building era. Economic concerns were focused on providing employment. Cities were financially unable to support recovery programs. Federal programs provided some funding to continue city building, but these efforts were not viewed as local economic development but as part of a national recovery effort. In addition, major regional development efforts, such as the Tennessee Valley Authority, were initiated.

World War II reestablished full employment, but public policy was dominated by the effort to win the war. There was little concern about local economic development, except as it related to the war effort. Then, in the immediate postwar era, economic concern was with the readjustment to a peacetime economy and fear of another depression. Urban policies were not a high public priority.

Federal-Led Programs.   After World War II ended, urban and regional development issues reemerged. The Depression and World War II had disrupted investment in cities, particularly in the housing stock. The problem of urban blight emerged. At the same time, the family formation ("baby boom") that followed the war contributed to a perceived housing shortage. The Federal Housing Act and the construction of major highways, including the interstate highway system, contributed to the suburbanization of the United States. During the first phase of the federal-led development efforts, economic development generally meant housing improvement.

Federal housing insurance and guarantee programs, such as FHA and VA programs, stimulated housing construction, particularly in the suburbs. At the same time, the phenomenon of urban slums was an increasing source of concern. Migration of families from the rural South to the urban North aggravated the problem. The National Housing Act of 1949 provided assistance for cities to clear blighted areas and redevelop land for a variety of purposes. The federal government used the powers of eminent domain to obtain land in blighted areas for profitable development, such as office buildings, as well as for traditional public uses, such as public plazas. This process became known as urban renewal.

Urban-renewal programs were criticized because they destroyed the housing of the poor but did not alleviate the underlying problem of poverty. Urban-renewal programs treated a symptom (slum housing) rather than a cause (poverty). When low-income housing was replaced by more affluent middle-class land uses, the poor were forced to move somewhere else in the city, and new slums followed. Urban renewal was viewed as destroying the housing stock of the poor without providing them with the means to obtain better housing.

Urban-renewal programs were replaced by a series of increasingly "people-oriented" programs during the 1960s that were designed to help the poor. Thus, economic development policy took an antipoverty focus. The Economic Opportunity Act, numerous manpower programs, the Model Cities Program, and the Better Neighborhoods Act refocused economic development toward poverty alleviation. The problem of rural poverty in areas such as Appalachia also become a federal priority. Federal programs to strengthen the infrastructure, particularly highways and water projects, were important elements of rural development efforts.

The urgency of urban problems was spiked by civil disruptions during the 1960s. The Commission on Civil Disorder (cited in Blair and Nachmias, 1979) described the high priority of urban development:

> These programs will require unprecedented levels of funding and performance. . . . There can be no higher priority for national action and no higher claim on the nation's conscience. (p. 14)

However, federal programs failed to generate enough popular support to ensure continued funding. Toward the end of the 1970s, the focus of economic development shifted away from problems of the urban poor towards a stronger business orientation. Programs such as the Urban Development Action Grants (UDAG) emphasized attracting private investment to downtown areas through the construction of hotels and office buildings. Establishing "public-private partnerships" and "leveraging" private funds became key elements in economic development strategies.

State and Local Predominance.   The era of federal initiatives faded for two primary reasons. First, there were few widely recognized successes. Second, there was strong pressure to cut federal spending programs in order to reduce the federal deficit. The *President's National Urban Policy Report,* published by the Department of Housing and Urban Development (1988), reflected the diminishing role of federal programs in regional (1988) economic development:

> State and local governments are increasingly sophisticated in managing their own economies, and the federal government should in most cases avoid interfering. Although well intentioned, market intervention by the federal government has often had unforeseen negative consequences. (pp. 110–11)

State and local communities were given more discretion in how to spend shrinking federal grant money. Accordingly, the focus of economic development varied depending upon local circumstances. Today, it is generally recognized that fewer federal funds will be forthcoming and that state and local governments by themselves lack the resources necessary for revitalization. Governments are attempting to play a catalytic role in attracting private investment.

Currently, the number of state and local programs is huge and ubiquitous. A recently published reference manual providing an overview of state-by-state business incentives was 652 pages long (National Association of State Development Agencies, 1983). The October 1988 issue of the Directory of Business Incentives identified 51 development incentive programs. The average state had 31 incentive programs to assist business by providing direct financial assistance, tax incentives, or special services. Texas had only 18 such programs, the fewest of any state. Connecticut, with 41, had the greatest number of programs.

Motives Underlying Economic Development

Although the objectives of economic development programs are not always stated explicitly, most have three objectives: (1) job creation, (2) fiscal improvement, and (3) physical improvements. In addition to public objectives, public officials and private investors engaged in economic development efforts have their own aspirations for success, recognition, and wealth. However, for each objective, it should be recalled that benefits of local growth will not be shared evenly among local residents.

Job Creation.   Communities with loose labor markets are characterized by high unemployment, low wages, discouraged workers, and underemployment. Many of these communities have experienced painful plant shutdowns and declines in the number of available jobs. Individuals in loose labor markets often need to leave the area in order to find work. Programs to encourage more local jobs include public employment and private-sector job development. However, private-sector job-creation efforts account for many more new jobs than direct public jobs.

Most economists regard job creation as a primary purpose of local economic development strategies. Many state and federal grant programs employ job creation as an explicit program goal along with other important grant-selection criteria. Indicators of labor-market problems such as the unemployment rate are also criteria in state and federal project selection so that monies will tend to flow to areas with employment problems.

Fiscal Improvement.   Many municipalities encourage economic development in the expectation that new businesses will contribute more in tax revenues than the extra municipal services cost. Generally, land uses devoted to commerce and manufacturing generate net revenues for the city whereas middle- and lower-income residential property tend to cause public-service costs to increase by more than the tax revenues generated. Thus, communities seeking to strengthen their fiscal positions will usually attempt to attract either upper-income residential housing or businesses.

Fiscal-relief objectives often result in competition among localities within a metropolitan region. Unless tax-sharing agreements among neighboring communities exist, only the locality where a business actually locates will receive increased property tax revenues. (Some areas that have local income taxes may benefit if residents receive jobs in businesses located in nearby communities.) The job-creation benefits of a new or expanded business will be more diffused throughout the metropolitan area than the fiscal benefits. New jobs may be obtained by residents throughout a metropolitan area regardless of whether or not they live in the municipality in which the business located.

Physical Improvements.   Finally, many urban officials view economic development as a way to achieve physical improvements in their community. For instance, public officials may want to attract a new business at a particular corner of the downtown area in order to remove an existing eyesore or because too much vacant land in the downtown area creates an image of lack of progress. This motive is a remnant of the urban-renewal period of economic development when physical change was the principal criterion used to evaluate the success of economic development predictions.

Practitioners' Perspectives

Economic development practitioners include individuals working for chambers of commerce and other quasi-public agencies, economic development departments of governmental agencies, and private firms with strong interests in local economic development such as public utilities. Economic development officials should not be viewed as self-sacrificing public servants. Rather, the economic paradigm normally assumes that public and semipublic officials, like others in the economic process, attempt to maximize their utility. They want to perform so as to maintain their jobs, receive pay increases, receive perquisites, and so forth. In light of these motives, how would we expect economic development officials to behave?

Rubin (1988) interviewed economic development practitioners in order to better understand their perspective on economic development and how they performed their jobs. He concluded that practitioners operate in an environment in which their success in attracting businesses is determined by factors outside their control. In other words, economic development programs are only a partial consideration in attracting businesses; a community pursuing all the "right" economic development policies might still fail to attract new businesses or encourage others to expand. Consequently, practitioners adopt a "shoot anything that flies, claim anything that falls" attitude.

Economic development officials tend to employ a set of routinized activities that will allow them to assist businesses seeking to locate or expand in the area. Activities include computerized site-selection procedures, "one-stop" locational services, community information packages, tours for business officials interested in the area, and serving as a voice for business with government officials. Business needs become a checklist that helps transform a process with uncertain outcomes into a clearly defined set of activities. Thus, completion of tasks, such as providing information, identifying prospects, and printing brochures, may become more important than the outcomes of economic development.

According to Rubin, economic development practitioners become advocates for expanding business. They tend to encourage public-to-private transfer payments as incentives to business because business expansion is counted as a success to the practitioners regardless of the cost to the community. The probusiness attitude may also be encouraged because economic development practitioners often attend community events, such as ribbon-cutting ceremonies, along with local business elites. Although they are not on the same socioeconomic level with local business elites, they usually know them on a first-name basis and may identify with their interests.

Paths to Economic Development

Thompson and Thompson (1984) attempted to quantify the advantage in business location for five different types of economic activities. In so doing, they suggested five paths to economic development: (1) routine operations, (2) precision operations, (3) research and development, (4) central administration, and (5) entrepreneurship. Each of these paths requires different locational attributes; a city or region would benefit by analyzing how best to stimulate the region's economic growth by either nurturing those positive attributes that already exist in the region or by eliminating those that are detrimental. In addition, these paths are not mutually exclusive, but are sometimes substitutive, partly complementary, and often sequential.

Routine Operations

In mature industrial areas, routine operations are hampered by high local wages, fringe benefits, and unionization rates. Therefore, firms that perform routine operations would not be attracted to many declining industrial areas. For declining industrial areas seeking to attract routine operations, the authors suggest wage cuts, investment in education, outmigration assistance, or import substitution.

Precision Operations

Firms engaged in precision operations require a work force skilled in technology. However, mature regions tend to have a less mobile work force, many of whom are near retirement age. So these areas are in danger of losing their competitive edge in skilled labor. The public-policy directive should encourage young, skilled individuals to stay in the area by providing the environment that appeals to them.

Research and Development

Since this activity has received substantial press recently, the research and development path tends to be the one most often desired by development officials. To evaluate the area's potential, the authors would examine doctorates in science and engineering and total funds allocated to university research and development as the primary criteria.

Central Administration

According to the authors, one of the marks of advanced local economic development is an important role in central administration. To measure this, a "count" was taken of the *Fortune* first and second 500 firms that are located in the region. If there is an adequate number, then others will take advantage of the tertiary services provided within the region. One disadvan-

---

Paths to Economic Development (concluded)

tage of "heavy industry towns," however, is their bad track record for hiring women and minorities. If these opportunities are missing, the region will not be attractive to two-wage earners who are mobile, highly educated, and pursuing specialized careers.

Entrepreneurship

To cultivate entrepreneurship, the environment must be fertile for cultivating new businesses. The environment must foster innovation, creativity, and risk taking and have a source of capital. The critical question, according to the authors, becomes whether the costs of restructuring the local culture to stimulate entrepreneurship is justified based on the likely benefits. Many communities will find it difficult or impossible to create an entrepreneurial climate.

Finally, the author's contend that choosing regional development paths should be linked to state public policy. The state affects economic development when it allocates funds for university research, higher education, transportation, infrastructure repair, airports, etc. Although the economic development impacts are often unintentional, they will affect the state settlement patterns for years to come.

SOURCE: Wilbur R. Thompson and Philip R. Thompson, "Alternative Paths to the Revival of Industrial Cities," in *The Future of Winter Cities,* ed. Gary Gappert (Newbury Park, Calif.: Sage Publications, 1984), pp. 233–251.

SUBSIDY TOOLS

Local governments seldom involve themselves directly in the operation of market-oriented business. Yet, governments create conditions that influence the outcome of market forces. The most frequently discussed economic policy instruments are fiscal and monetary policies wielded by the federal government. These policies stimulate overall economic activity, although they are not normally targeted towards specific regions or specific businesses. In order to stimulate local business activities, localities have developed a vast array of policy instruments to provide subsidies or incentives, depending upon your point of view. Sometimes the subsidies are direct, although more often they are indirect or at least disguised. The purposes of this section are to provide a sense of the variety of subsidy possibilities and to discuss the prominent tools in some detail.

Prominent Subsidy Instruments

Although there are a large variety of subsidy approaches, most localities rely heavily upon a few well-known techniques. This section describes some of the major subsidies that are employed by local development officials. Many projects require more than one type of subsidy. Economic development officials frequently attempt to put together a subsidy package that meets the developers' requirements.

Tax Abatements.   A tax abatement is a waiver of taxes that would otherwise be due. Generally, tax abatements are given to real property or machinery and the tax waiver is limited to a specified numbers of years. For instance, a private developer may negotiate with city officials about building a new hotel. The city officials might provide the developer with an inducement by agreeing that the hotel will be exempt from property taxes for five years after construction.

A problem with property tax abatements is that, if they are overused, the community's taxable property base will shrink. If the tax base shrinks while revenue requirements remain unchanged, a higher tax rate must be applied to the remaining properties that have not been awarded abatements. Consequently, an overuse of tax abatements could result in an overall tendency to discourage business growth. Proponents of tax abatements may argue that existing properties really do not experience higher taxes due to abatements; because, in the absence of such incentives, the new businesses would not have located in the community in the first place. Therefore, there would not be an increased property base to tax. Partial tax abatements may be calibrated so that the taxes on a new facility will reflect the cost of additional services the city may have to provide while still providing a locational incentive.

States may provide corporate income tax abatements and investment tax credits. Firms may be allowed to deduct a percentage of their investment from their state corporate income taxes. Unlike local property tax abatements, which are normally negotiated between a business and local officials, most state abatement programs have predetermined qualification standards. Any qualifying business that satisfies the standards may receive the inducement.

Tax-Exempt Financing.   A locality may issue bonds that are exempt from federal and/or state taxes. The bonds can be sold in financial markets at below-market interest rates because the income from the bond is not taxed. The revenue raised through the bond sale can then be used to finance economic development projects. Since most business projects are run by private concerns, the advantage of the low-interest-rate borrowing is normally transferred to a private developer. For example, the city may borrow funds at 2 percent below the market rate and so be able to lend to a private developer at 2 percent below the market rate.

There are many variations on tax-exempt financing schemes. For instance, a public agency may agree to build a business facility and lease it to a private company while retaining ownership of the building. Navistar (formerly International Harvester) was induced to maintain a plant in Springfield, Ohio, because the state borrowed a portion of the $28 million needed to purchase the facility from International Harvester. The facility was then leased back to International Harvester at a below-market rent. Because of the low-interest-rate financing, the lease terms could be below what the tenant would have had to pay in the private market. The lease payments are usually earmarked to retire the bonded debt. When the bonds have been repaid, the tenant is often given an option to purchase the property at a nominal cost, say one dollar.

An interesting feature of the tax-exempt financing technique is that the cost of the subsidy (as distinct from the entire project cost) is borne by the federal taxpayers although the benefits accrue to localities and private businesses. The subsidy is paid for by the federal government in the form of lower revenues. This type of subsidy is referred to as a tax expenditure because it is not a direct expenditure. Because the tax-expenditure cost to the federal government increased rapidly in the early 1980s, limitations were placed on the use of the tax-exempt financing after 1988. State- and local-government debt has been divided into two categories—public- and private-purpose debt. Restrictions have been placed upon the tax-exempt nature of private-purpose debt, although not on public-purpose debt.

Loan Assistance.   Since financing is an important aspect of business-development decisions, localities have found that they can exert influence by providing developers with assistance in procuring loans. Loan assistance is particularly useful for new establishments that either lack access to traditional capital markets or are considered high risks. Loan assistance helps businesses in two ways. First, it may make it possible for a firm that otherwise could not obtain a loan to do so. Second, the interest cost of a loan may be reduced. There are three frequently used types of loan assistance: direct loans from local governments, loan guarantees, and second-mortgage assistance.

Direct loans may be financed from tax revenues, public employee pension plans, or other sources. Revolving loan funds have been set up so that money from loan repayments can be relent as part of an ongoing program. Program managers have strong incentives to use appropriate underwriting standards because if loans are not repaid, the program will self-destruct.

Through loan guarantees, governments agree to repay part or all of the loan in the event that the business borrower defaults. An advantage of loan-guarantee programs is that the community supplying the guarantee will not bear costs unless the borrower defaults. Thus, the locality can influence or leverage a great deal of private investment with small out-of-pocket expenses. Of course, agencies using a loan-guarantee strategy must assess risks carefully and attempt to maintain a reserve against defaults.

Second-mortgage assistance can help firms that have earning potential to repay a loan but lack the collateral necessary to secure a conventional loan. Most financial institutions will refuse to make loans equal to the full value of a property. Conventional lenders want an asset that they can attach and sell in the event of default. If lending institutions made loans equal to 100 percent of the value of property used as collateral and market changes subsequently caused the value of the property to decline, the lender could lose part of the loan. Therefore, lenders normally will make loans equal to less than 100 percent of the value of the property serving as collateral. In fact, banking regulations require loan-value ratios of less than 100 percent.

For instance, a new business may wish to purchase a building valued at $100,000, but lenders may be willing to extend a mortgage loan only equal to 70 percent of the building's value. State or local governments may help by providing a second mortgage equal to $30,000. In this case, a conventional lender could then more safely lend $70,000 secured by a first mortgage. In the event of default, the property serving as collateral would be sold. The first mortgage holder would have first claim on the proceeds of sale up to the amount of the first-mortgage debt. If funds remained after the first mortgage holder was repaid, the second mortgage holder would be repaid; and, if there were still funds remaining, the borrower (who defaulted) would receive the remainder. With reference to the above example, if a new business failed, its property would be sold to repay the loans. If the property sold for $90,000, the conventional lender would be repaid in full, $70,000, and the second mortgage holder would receive $20,000. Clearly second mortgages are more risky than first mortgages. Second mortgages are considered a type of "gap financing" because the public sector bridges the difference between the capital raised through the private sector and the amount need to finance the project.

Infrastructure Assistance.   Infrastructure is important to economic development because it provides the basis for physical development. Adequate regional infrastructures, including roads, sewers, and public buildings are a prerequisite for regional development. However, when discussing infrastructure assistance, most economic development practitioners normally refer to infrastructure designed to serve a specific business or location rather than projects that serve the entire community. Economic development can be stimulated by public funding of many costs related to property development.

Provision of facilities needed to accommodate a new plant probably accounts for the majority of state economic development funding. State and local governments frequently agree to provide basic infrastructure, such as access roads, water and sewers, treatment plants, parking garages, and rail spurs. Few major industrial facilities are built in the United States without some type of infrastructure assistance from state or local governments.

Write-Downs. Write-downs occur when the government sells property to a business at a below-market price. Many cities have land banks that include parcels of land purchased over a long period of time. Properties may have been purchased and cleared through power of eminent domain in an area of deteriorated and abandoned buildings. The objective of such land acquisitions is often to assemble a parcel large enough to warrant redevelopment. Economic development officials will normally hold these properties off the market until they are needed to attract a business compatible with the community's economic development plan. If a business is interested in the property, the price will be negotiated. The stronger the bargaining position of the prospective business, the lower the price will be. A major Honda Motor Company facility was induced to locate in Ohio partly because the state sold the land to the company for production as well as research facilities and a seven-mile automobile test track to the company at a significantly below market price. In some cases, a government will simply purchase the land a business needs and immediately resell it.

The value of property write-downs is difficult to measure because it is difficult to estimate the market value of properties sold by governments. The value of the write-down could be estimated easily if a property were purchased for, say, $1,000,000 and resold immediately for $750,000. In this case, the subsidy to the owner would be $250,000. Normally, the properties are acquired, improved by building infrastructure, and then resold after a substantial period. Thus, the market value at the time of final sale is obscured.

A Classification

The tools discussed in the previous section encompass the most popular and direct economic development instruments. However, they fail to reflect the variety of the economic development actions available to local governments. Several attempts have been made to classify the development tools of state and local governments. Sternberg (1987) developed a very useful double classification of economic development tools. Governments have a number of policy approaches that may affect a variety of business functions, such as production, personnel, finance, and marketing, that can receive assistance. Thus, we can envision a matrix with business functions on the side and types of assistance across the top.

Table 7–1 represents a matrix of policy instruments and business functions. Nine business functions are listed on the vertical axis, and the six types of policies affecting businesses are listed horizontally. Actions that can be employed by the federal government as well as state and local governments are shown. Specific development tools are listed in the cells. For instance, regulatory powers can be used to encourage land and facility acquisition through business-zoning actions (row c, column 4). Technology and managerial knowledge can be affected through regulations affecting patents, copyrights, patent pooling, and product standards (row d, column 4). Most of the regulations affecting technology are initiated at the federal level. However, state policies can shape market opportunities. For instance, many states have increased spending on university research in the hope of generating advanced-technology spinoffs.

The matrix developed by Sternberg is detailed enough to show many of the options open to state and local development officials. It illustrates the wide variety of development incentives and how broadly based many community development efforts are. However, even the classification of Table 7–1 is incomplete. Almost all state and local actions can directly or indirectly influence business success and, hence, local economic development prospects.

ECONOMIC DEVELOPMENT PROGRAMS

The previous section discussed specific tools. Most economic development programs employ a variety of tools. This section examines some of the major programs through which the individual tools operate.

Job Training and Partnership Act

Training programs are not a major tool for attracting or encouraging the expansion of business, but training programs can be used selectively to stimulate employment growth. Four types of manpower services are widely used. First, some on-the-job training programs provide wage subsidies for periods of time while workers learn skills. For instance, a firm hiring an electrical worker may receive a 50 percent wage subsidy for the time of training. Second, customized training operated through local training agencies will provide trained workers for specific businesses. Individuals will be interviewed and possibly hired by the client/business

TABLE 7-1 A Classification of State and Local Economic Development Policy Instruments

Business Functions	Types of Policy					
	(1) Provide Direct Subsidy	*(2)* Provide Indirect Subsidy	*(3)* Inform and Exhort	*(4)* Regulate	*(5)* Affect Crucial Industries and Institutions	*(6)* Shape Market Opportunity and Environment
(a) Financing	Financial incentives	Tax relief, depreciation allowances	Information on financing opportunities	Rules on audits, accounting, insurance, bankruptcy	Banking regulations	Controls of financial risk and markets, building LDCs
(b) Personnel	Subsidies for labor cost, in-house training, and municipal labor	Job training	Referral services, job counseling	Labor laws	Influence on educational institutions	Labor market policies, education
(c) Land and facilities	Land subsidies	Infrastructure	Inventories	Business zoning	Influence on real estate and construction industries	Spatial policy: CBD development, growth centers, industrial complexes
(d) Technology and managerial knowledge	Supply of ideas and expertise, support for in-house R&D	Economic statistics, economic monitoring	Technology transfer, industrial extension	Patents, copyrights, patent pooling, product standards	Development of communications networks	Support for basic research
(e) Labor-management relations	Discretionary involvement in labor relations	Community labor-management committees	Encouragement of new labor relations methods	Control of strikes and unions, plant closure notification		

(f) Operations	Raw materials subsidies, municipal purchase preferences	General municipal services	Introduction of new operational methods	Laws on labeling, advertising, consumer safety	Development of transport and communications industries	Strengthening the market for local products
(g) Acquisitions and marketing	Discretionary municipal services	Discriminatory municipal purchasing, export marketing	Promoting import substitution, and promoting export production	Regulation of externalities, inspections	Development of cooperatives and local marketing representatives	
(h) Motivation	Goodwill	Reduction in personal taxes	Boosterism	Nuisance controls, public safety	Encouraging institutions to develop local amenities	Developing community amenities
(i) Combined functions	Incentives packages	Incubation facilities	Publicity, ombudsmen	Regulatory promotion, streamlining, enterprise zones		Adjudication

Note: Other types of economic development policy: (7) Shape Market Structure, (8) Define and Limit Forms of Enterprise, and (9) Engage in Enterprise and Expand Government Employment. LDC = Local Development Corporation; CBD = Central Business District.

SOURCE: Ernest Sternberg, "A Practitioner's Classification of Economic Development Policy Instruments with Some Inspiration from Political Economy," *Economic Development Quarterly* vol. 1, no. 2 (1987), p. 155. Copyright 1987. Reprinted by permission of Sage Publications, Inc.

after receiving the customized training. Third, individuals may be given training in skills where potential labor shortages exist or may arise in the future. Officers of private companies are consulted in determining what skills need to be taught; however, trainees are not earmarked for specific employers. Finally, general skills, such as basic literacy or job-search skills, may be taught. Frequently, the hard-core unemployed lack the basic skills needed to take advantage of vocational training. The Job Training and Partnership Act (JTPA) is funded largely by the federal government. It is generally believed to be a successful program partly because the training has been focused on displaced workers—individuals who lost their jobs due to economic restructuring. Since displaced workers normally have better work habits than the hard-core (e.g., long-term) unemployed, training is often all the assistance they require. Also, the JTPA works through local private employers to determine the type of training that is most appropriate given local market conditions.

Incubators

Business incubators provide physical space and a nurturing environment for small businesses in their early, formative stages. Incubators are a system whereby new businesses share space as well as secretarial, marketing, management, and other services. Frequently, the space to house new businesses has been in previously vacant buildings that have been lightly renovated to provide low-cost space. Emphasis has been on providing small, flexible space. The renovation costs are usually publicly subsidized; consequently, rents are below market. However, about one third of incubators are privately owned, although they may still receive some public subsidies. The majority of tenants in incubators are in light manufacturing, office activities, or research and development.

The idea of small businesses sharing space and services is not new, but business incubators have expanded rapidly in recent years. In late 1986, there were over 200 incubators in the United States. The growth of incubators can be attributed to four factors. First, they provide a useful service for undercapitalized new businesses. Second, incubators fit local goals of encouraging job growth and reclaiming buildings that would otherwise be abandoned. Third, incubators are a suitable assistance program for small entrepreneurial businesses and for high-technology firms. Small, high-technology firms are viewed as particularly major job generators, so attracting them is a key development strategy in many communities. Finally, incubators can be structured in such a way that many local institutions can contribute. For instance, most incubators have university affiliations. Quasi-public foundations have helped establish incubators, and private firms have been willing to contribute consulting and other services, possibly hoping to build a paying client base after the "incubation" period.

Incubators have a mixed success record. New small businesses have a high failure rate regardless of whether they are located in an incubator or not. Furthermore, the rate of successful spin-offs of firms that have grown, left the incubator, and continued to grow is low. Nevertheless, incubator costs are relatively small, and it is difficult to determine how many business ventures would not have been attempted if incubator assistance had not been available.

Enterprise Zones

The enterprise-zone concept originated in England and was popularized in the United States as part of Reagan's urban policy. As originally proposed, enterprise zones were to be a federal program. Zones relatively free of government regulation and taxation would be designated in distressed urban areas. The idea behind enterprise zones was that government rules and regulations hinder business activity while a laissez-faire environment would stimulate business.

The enterprise-zone idea was particularly timely because it was proposed when many observers believed that concerns with the federal budget deficit outweighed the need to spend on urban programs and enterprise zones involved little or no out-of-pocket expenditures. Also, the enterprise-zone proposal was a solution consistent with the conservative philosophy of less government involvement in the economy. Furthermore, because the zones were to be located in the most distressed parts of distressed cities, the concept appealed to some advocates for the poor. Because tax reductions were an important feature, the program had a particular appeal to firms that anticipated large profits. Stuart Butler (1984) summarized the argument:

> The zone idea runs counter to the theory underpinning development strategy of most major American cities. Rather than engaging in the zero-sum game of "smokestack chasing" in an attempt to attract or retain large companies, the enterprise zone approach draws on recent evidence . . . to make the argument that cities should focus instead on stimulating small, new indigenous enterprises. This would be accomplished by "supply-side" tax and deregulatory policies. (p. 142)

Enterprise zones were extensively debated in Congress, but federal legislation languished. Some opponents feared that too much deregulation would result in sweat shops and porno strips. Others believed that enterprise zones would be so attractive that nonzone areas would to be unable to attract new business. Still other opponents felt that tax advantages available to business enterprise zones would not be very valuable to new businesses that might have small profits or losses in their initial years. A business earning zero profits normally has no federal tax obligation. In order to assure that enterprise zones would create jobs without exploiting employees or unduly subsidizing business, legislative proprosals became more complicated. As regulations increased, the laissez-faire aspect of the proposal was lost. To date, no federal enterprise-zone system has been established, although it continues to be proposed.

State and local governments did implement the enterprise-zone concept. The enterprise-zone idea was popularized at a time when state and local governments began to replace the federal government in providing local economic development leadership. Many states passed legislation to allow local governments to designate distressed or high-unemployment areas as enterprise zones. Localities took advantage of the legislation and established zones. Businesses located in enterprise zones received a variety of benefits, including training assistance, property tax abatement, and state income tax breaks. Currently, most major cities have enterprise zones. Because they are considered to have been effective, policy makers in many states are developing rural enterprise zones.

Free-Trade Zones

Free-trade zones (FTZs) reduce impediments to international trade. Tariffs and other import restrictions are a barrier to international commerce. These barriers are particularly detrimental to industries that import components from outside the United States and export finished products. Such firms may face higher costs than competitors in other countries who are not required to pay import duties. A free-trade zone provides a duty-free area; a product from abroad can be brought into a FTZ duty free. If the commodity is moved from the FTZ to somewhere within the United States, duties become payable only when the product leaves the FTZ. There are three important advantages to production in a free-trade zone. First, a firm that produces for domestic consumption may delay payment on imported items while they are in inventory. The advantage to the firm will equal the return that could be earned on the postponed tax. Second, if the imported components are manufactured and exported from the United States to another country, no duties are due. Finally, highly taxed items may be imported, fabricated into products that are less highly taxed, and then shipped. In this case, the tax is based on the fabricated product rather than the components.

Free-trade zones are not a high-profile local development program, although they are an important element in many local development strategies. They are particularly useful to localities seeking to strengthen the international linkages within their economies.

Most major cities have created FTZs around airports and harbors. As international trade becomes more important, the importance of FTZs can be expected to increase. However, if trade barriers are reduced, FTZs will become less important.

Urban Development Action Grants

The Urban Development Action Grant program (UDAG) was created to stimulate private investment in commercial, industrial, and neighborhood development projects. UDAG was predicated on the concept that many potentially useful projects face financial gaps. A large project may need a small amount of assistance relative to the overall project cost. Unless that gap can be bridged, the projects will not be undertaken. UDAG is designed to provide gap financing that some private developers require to make their projects successful.

UDAG is a discretionary program, because public officials determine whether or not to approve applications for funds. In contrast all a firm needs to do to receive advantages under the enterprise-zone approach is to locate in the appropriate area and meet other stipulated requirements. Once a firm has met the legal requirements, it is entitled to the enterprise-zone benefits.

The UDAG funding process is complex. For instance, a developer may wish to build a condominium complex in a deteriorating neighborhood, but some public assistance may be required. Projects must meet the "but for" requirement—"but for" the grant, the project could not be completed. Negotiations between HUD, the community, and private developers often occur before the project is deemed fundable. UDAG has often stimulated large amounts of private investment because the ratio of public to private investment is a grant-selection criterion. Other criteria include employment impacts on low- and moderate-income families, contribution to the tax base, and impacts on the community's physical condition.

Urban Development Action Grants have been popular with private developers and city officials. They have certainly encouraged city officials to learn the development process in order to negotiate with private developers. However, UDAG has been subject to two criticisms. Some opponents have suggested that there is too much discretion in project selection. Consequently, political officials may give grants to their cronies. A second criticism is that UDAG has overemphasized industrial and commercial projects at the expense of neighborhood development. Some have called UDAG the "Hotel Construction Relief Act" because such a large number of grants have been used to build downtown hotels. Because of these criticisms, the tight federal budget, and the prevailing philosophy that state and local governments should dominate local development policies, UDAG is being phased out.

Community Development Block Grants

While UDAG emphasized federal discretion in determining which projects should be funded, the Community Development Block Grants program (CDBG) features local discretion. Under the program, communities receive a grant from the federal government based upon indicators of need. The formula used to determine a community's share of CDBG funds is complicated in part because the formula was developed by political officials representing many regions with different needs. Local community development officials have the discretion to determine which projects should be funded as long as they conform to broad federal guidelines.

Economic development projects must compete with other community objectives for CDBG funds. In fact, economic development originally was not a significant component of the block-grant program. Most spending was on housing projects, infrastructure improvements, or social services. In the late 1970s, the regulations changed to encourage more economic development spending within CDBG. However, the percentage of funds designated for economic development has remained low.

There are several reasons for the relatively low priority given to economic development projects in CDBG. First, the low level of spending in the early years after economic development became an approved activity reflected the need to continue funding previous commitments in the area of housing and urban real estate projects. Second, the CDBG regulations required substantial targeting of benefits toward low- and moderate-income groups. Geographic targeting of poor areas of the city was often a means of achieving this end. These requirements were easier to meet through service-oriented programs rather that the economic development (ED) programs because beneficiaries of economic development programs tended to be difficult to determine. Third, public officials and citizens have preferred to channel CDBG funds to residential neighborhoods and public services that directly benefit citizens. Economic development projects are often at a political disadvantage when competing against other community improvement projects, because the benefits of economic development projects accrue directly to fewer individuals and the beneficiaries of jobs that may be created are hard to identify beforehand.

A conclusion from the analysis of the CDBG program is that while ED has become more important in community planning, ED functions remain one of many objectives from which local officials must choose. Given the institutional setting in which local CDBG funds are allocated, economic development does not appear to be the most pressing priority.

A THEORETICAL PERSPECTIVE: THE MARKET FOR JOBS

Governments directly and indirectly pay firms to locate or expand in certain areas. The "market for jobs" provides a conceptual framework for understanding the state and local economic development activity. This emerging market differs from the traditional job market where individuals and firms compete for labor services. In the market for jobs, cities, states, and other governmental entities seek to purchase jobs for their current or future residents.

Reasons for the Market for Jobs

A principal reason for the emergence of the market for jobs is changed public expectations regarding local economic development responsibilities. Job creation is now widely considered to be a responsibility of local officials. Hence, local politicians may receive benefits from successful participation in job-creation programs because success will lead to greater voter support. Politicians who fail to develop job-creation programs may be seen as not doing their job.

Economic dislocations are a second reason for the emergence of the market for jobs. The benefits of attracting jobs to an area increase with the extent of economic dislocations that have hit many industrial cities. Underemployed or unemployed workers in areas where employment has stagnated are willing to pay some amount of money to secure local jobs, given that mobility is costly. Theoretically, they should be willing to pay an amount up to the cost—both monetary and psychic—of relocating for a comparable local job. If a state or local government attracts employers, local employees who would otherwise have had to move or take less desirable local jobs receive benefits from job creation.

In the theoretical world of neoclassical economics, the labor market would function to reduce waste, lower production costs, and attract job-providing industries to the area. For instance, in most theoretical models, if the number of local jobs declined, wages would fall, and firms would find it cheaper to locate in a labor-surplus area rather than a full-employment area that would have higher wages. Prices of immobile nonlabor resources, such as rents, would also fall in a well-functioning market, further enhancing the attractiveness of the area to employers. However, in reality, minimum-wage laws, industrywide union contracts, and rigid wages prevent labor costs from falling significantly or quickly in labor-surplus areas. Likewise, family and cultural patterns give rise to rigidities that prevent the efficient operation of the labor market. For instance, the desire to live near one's family will retard migration. Many disadvantaged workers do not relocate because of high money costs, and others may be unaware of opportunities elsewhere in the economy. Additionally, public support programs are frequently tied to places rather than to people, and therefore, tie people to places. (Chapter 9 contains a more complete discussion of the place versus people prosperity issue.) In other words, an imperfectly functioning labor market exists.

Although local workers who gain employment in newly created jobs are the primary beneficiaries of the market for jobs, local property owners may also realize net gains from local job growth via higher property values, higher rents, or lower rental-vacancy rates. In addition, an increase in export jobs will have secondary employment and income effects. Job creation could also result in a larger base of taxable property so taxpayers as a group could benefit.

A Model of the Market for Jobs

Some economists argue that government involvement in locational decisions will be inefficient because the private market adequately reflects all relevant costs and benefits. Many local-labor-market models include assumptions of perfect knowledge, resources mobility, and no externalities. If such conditions were met in reality, public job-creation efforts would probably be inefficient—or efforts by one local group to capture benefits would be at the expense of others. However, Baum (1987) has shown that in an economy with market imperfections, such as national minimum-wage laws, public efforts to influence business locational decisions may be effective. This section shows that, under certain circumstances, the market for jobs can improve efficiency.

Figure 7–1 illustrates the market for jobs from the perspective of a single city. The community-benefits *(CB)* curve is a demand curve for jobs created during a given year. It represents the benefits to area residents of additional jobs. An example of benefits for a job would be if a local resident had an opportunity cost (i.e., an alternative job) of $25,000 but was able to get a job paying $30,000 because of local job-creation efforts. Benefits flowing to other members of the community could also be considered in the *CB* curve.

The area under the *CB* curve is the present value of the total benefits current residents receive from additional jobs. The value of an extra 200 jobs would equal the value of the first job (read off the *CB* curve), plus the value of each additional job up to and including 200.

Figure 7–1 is drawn to show the existence of positive social benefits to the community from the creation of up to 300 new jobs. It is certainly possible that the benefits curve for another community would indicate larger or smaller benefits from job creation depending upon local conditions. The greater the external benefits from new jobs, the higher the *CB* curve will be.

The model assumes all jobs are alike just as the traditional demand curve represents demand for a homogeneous product. This assumption may be modified by allowing that better jobs would shift the *CB* curve upward to the right. Poorer jobs would be represented by a lower *CB* curve.

The job-supply *(JS)* curve indicates that the higher the subsidy rate, the more jobs of a particular type will be created in the city. The subsidy is

FIGURE 7–1   A City's Market for Jobs

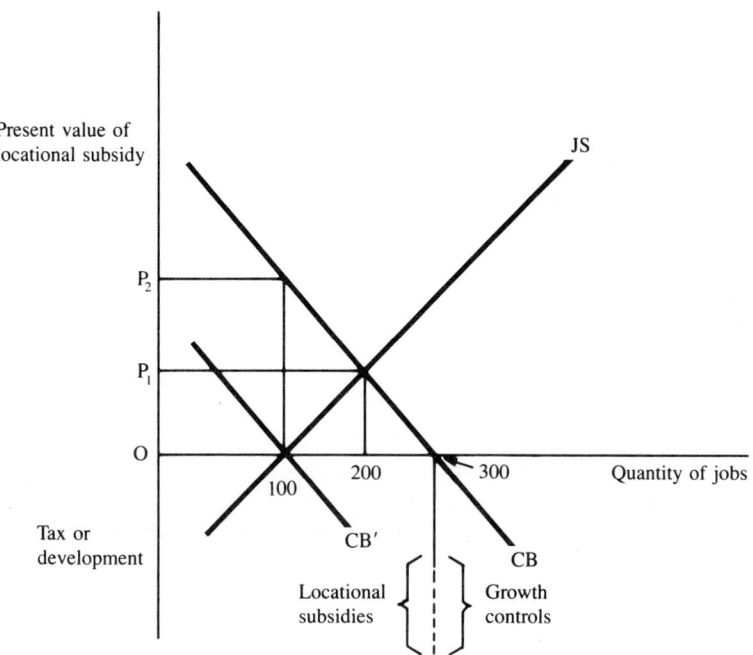

The *JS* curve represents the number of jobs that would be created at various subsidy levels. *CB* represents net community benefits from new jobs. In the absence of any subsidy program, only 100 jobs would be created. The region may choose to offer subsidy level P_1 and create a total of 200 jobs.

expressed as the present value of all future benefits to firms in order to facilitate comparison between a one-shot subsidy (such as a grant) and a subsidy over time (such as a five-year tax abatement).

If the city illustrated in Figure 7–1 maintained a neutral locational policy (no economic development subsidies or taxes), it would attract and maintain 100 jobs. To attract an additional job (the 101st job), the community would have to pay a slight subsidy (read off the *JS* curve) but residents would receive nearly P_2 benefits (read off the *CB* curve). Thus, it would make sense to provide subsidies to attract more jobs. The social optimum number of jobs for the community is 200 jobs. Only at a subsidy level of P_1 would community benefits and the public cost of an additional job be equal. In this case, it would make sense for the community to offer up to P_1 for the 200th job.

TABLE 7–2 Locational Payoff Matrix: Before Transfers

Parties to the Decision	Location A	Location B
Firm	10	0
Residents of A	10	0
Residents of B	0	35
Total benefits*	20	35

* Hypothetical, representing the present value of future benefits. The small numbers are used to illustrate the benefits. However, in reality, the numbers would be substantially larger.

Notice that the *CB* curve extends into the negative price range beyond 300 jobs. This might represent a situation in which urban residents were more concerned about the negative rather than the positive consequences of growth. If for some reason the *JS* curve shifted significantly to the right, a neutral locational policy could result in residents receiving costs rather than benefits from new jobs. Growth controls can serve as a "pricing" mechanism that discourages growth.

Each city or region is a distinct market so that community-benefits and job-supply curves will vary among cities. Notice that if the *CB* curve were sufficiently low (as might be the case in a region experiencing full employment), no local job-creation incentives would be justified. If the community-benefits curve were below *CB'*, growth controls would be appropriate because a neutral policy (no taxes or subsidies) would result in 100 jobs that result in costs (negative benefits) to residents.

In practice, no one has actually measured a community-benefits or job-supply curve. If they could be measured, economic development policies could be improved. However, even a conceptual understanding of the market for jobs will assist policy makers in understanding the increasingly important market for jobs.

Table 7–2 illustrates the locational choice in a context of competition between two cities. Assume a firm is to choose between locations in cities A and B, and the jobs created will result in net benefits to residents of both cities. The payoff to the firm for locating in A is $10 additional profit compared to that in B, the next best locational choice assuming no government locational subsidies. In both cities, additional jobs would produce third-party benefits for residents. City A residents receive $10 of benefits if the firm locates in A and no benefits if it locates in city B. For instance, if the firm were to locate in A, it may pay employees $100. The opportunity cost of those new employees might be $95, and local merchants might receive an additional $5 in benefits through extra sales. In this situation, employees and merchants would each receive an extra $5 in net benefits. The total local net benefits from locating at A would be $10 plus the profits to the firm. Residents of city B receive $35 of benefits if B is the locational choice.

The firm would locate the plant in city A in the absence of any side payments, although the total social benefits are larger in city B because of the spillover benefits to local residents. The firm could be induced to locate in city B only if it received a subsidy greater than $10. If city A offered no subsidy and city B offered $11, the firm would locate in city B. But if city A offered $10, city B would have to offer $21 to attract the jobs. A more adroit employer might be able to extract a $35 subsidy from city B before locating there, given that $35 represents that city's maximum willingness to pay. Although equity and distributional considerations are apparent, the market for jobs would be efficient if the plant is located in city B, whether the subsidy were $11 or $35. Hence, the market for jobs can provide an institution that establishes incentives appropriate to social payoffs.

Another example will show how the process of local competition could result in an inefficient use of resources. Suppose cities A and B were attempting to attract a firm that would be most profitable (ignoring any subsidies it might receive) if located in A. Also assume that there are no significant externalities associated with job creation in either city, but city B has an active industrial-attraction program. Under these circumstances, the firm might be induced to locate in B if the locational incentives were sufficient to offset the lower profits from selecting a second-best location. The location in B would be inefficient, however, and the inefficiency would have been paid for by the city's taxpayers. Residents of B paid more to attract the establishment than they received in benefits. (This analysis, however, does not consider the likely possibility that some individuals in B gained at the expense of taxpayers in general.)

The examples used in this section were hypothetical. The numbers could easily be changed to show how government involvement could be wasteful and inefficient. If local residents do not receive benefits from job-creation efforts or if areas that receive large spillover benefits from job creation are unable to compete successfully, local-government intervention may be inefficient. Furthermore, simply showing that the private market is inefficient does not lead to the conclusion that government involvement will increase efficiency. In fact, the next section discusses numerous cases where local job-creation efforts are likely to be inefficient.

DEVELOPMENT POLICY ISSUES

Local economic development policy is a controversial area because there is no clear consensus about the proper role of local governments in economic development. Furthermore, evaluations of local economic development practices have been inadequate to determine definitely which tools are effective. Economists prefer rigorous comparisons of costs and benefits in order to evaluate a program. Yet measurement of the benefits of economic development practices is difficult because they usually require an analyst to determine what market outcomes would have occurred in the absence of government intervention. The evaluation problem is compounded because analysts need to evaluate the appropriate policy mix, not just one program. The appropriate policy mix is likely to vary among regions. Consequently, while a few projects, particularly manpower training, have used the cost-benefit framework, most evaluations tend to focus on whether desirable outcomes were achieved or (even less informatively) whether funds were spent in desirable ways.

In the absence of a clear understanding of government's appropriate or most effective role, a number of development issues have emerged. This section explores some of the areas of controversy and illustrates uncertainties faced by policy makers in their efforts to develop appropriate regional policies.

Is Local Economic Development a Zero-Sum Game?

One of the criticisms of local economic development activities is that cities compete with each other without increasing the total number of jobs available. Consequently, whatever one community gains another community loses. An example of a zero-sum game occurs when a company announces that it will establish a facility in one of three or four cities and suggests that the ultimate site will depend heavily upon the size of the local incentive package. Zero-sum games are particularly likely to occur when communities within a particular metropolitan area compete for jobs. The *President's National Urban Policy Report* (1988), published by the Department of Housing and Urban Development, expressed concern over the zero-sum game aspect of economic development:

> At the federal level place specific economic development policies often do nothing more than tax one place to improve conditions in another. The wealth of both places is not greater and may actually be less than it might have been. (p. II-2)

Although local development efforts can result in zero-sum games, they do not always do so. In addition to merely allocating jobs, local incentive programs may provide incentives to create new jobs. Suppose a firm may have anticipated negative profits and, therefore, would not operate. However, suppose the externalities of job creation are so significant that they offset the private losses so that the firm's operations would generate net social benefits (without externalities, a firm operating at a loss would be inefficient). What factors could induce the firm to operate? If communities offer locational incentives, the value of the incentives may be sufficient to turn the potential business loss into a gain. Thus, jobs may actually be created. The local incentives would be efficient if the net social benefits from the job creation were greater than the cost of the local incentives.

Local development programs may also create jobs indirectly by building a set of community supports that encourage growth of existing businesses and the establishment of new businesses. A growth-oriented set of regional infrastructure, including good schools, entrepreneurial support, environmental quality, and adequate transportation systems, may increase a firm's efficiency and help create jobs. The benefits generated by these activities may outweigh the cost of the public programs. When this occurs, the increased efficiency refutes the zero-sum game criticism. However, since there are no direct subsidies, it is difficult to measure the effect of indirect job-creation efforts. Many local programs can help businesses add value to their products. When this is done, the extra value created by definition refutes the zero-sum game criticism.

Inefficiency and Oversubsidization

The existence of potential gains from local jobs is a necessary, although not sufficient, condition for efficient local job-creation programs. If economic development officials knew the nature of the community-benefits and job-supply curves shown in Figure 7–1, they would be better able to operate efficiently in the job-creation process. Unfortunately, Figure 7–1 represents a conceptual model and has not been quantified. Furthermore, because of conflicts of interest in the development process, officials may not always act in the community's interest. There are at least four important reasons why the market for jobs tend to be inefficient: (1) practical problems of collective action, (2) information asymmetry, (3) unspecified property rights, and (4) the operation of federal economic development programs.

Collective Action.   The ability of local governments to participate efficiently in the market for jobs is determined by how well the political process evaluates and responds to the external benefits of job creation. Most analysts agree that local governments respond imperfectly because of inherent limitations of the political process. A small group of highly interested persons can influence government more than a large group of moderately interested persons, because the small group has an incentive to bear the costs of influencing governmental action. Also, it is less costly for individuals represented by existing organizations to influence policy than it is for unorganized individuals.

A consequence of political-action characteristics is that cities are more likely to enter the market when new jobs offer external benefits to existing influential groups than when the benefits flow to politically unorganized groups. Thus, redevelopment projects that enhance the interests of major property owners and retail businesses are more likely to receive assistance than projects that lack influential beneficiaries. Also, existing establishments that threaten to reduce their work force are in a strong position to mobilize political support to secure a public grant. In contrast, small firms are less likely to muster the support needed to receive a special incentive.

The market is also likely to be affected by the strength or weakness of local politicians. Because the costs of an industrial location are generally paid in the politically distant future, a weak officeholder may have an incentive to overpay for a major industrial location. In their case study of a nearly $200-million locational subsidy package to General Motors, Jones and Bachelor (1984) reported that GM had an advantage negotiating subsidies with Detroit officials because local economic problems made state and local elected officials anxious to secure the plant. In this case, even a fairly popular mayor was unable to resist pressures to provide huge locational incentives.

Information Asymmetry. Information asymmetry arises when the circumstances surrounding a transaction are known by one party but not by the other participating party or parties. Such a situation can arise when one party deliberately provides distorted information to other parties.

Typically, all parties involved in a locational decision have incentives to provide selective or distorted information. For example, a firm trying to make a plant-closing decision may be forced to choose between two locations. The firm may have information regarding the two plants that it does not have to disclose to the cities that are offering to subsidize operations. This advantage provides the firm with bargaining power. The fact that many local economic development professionals become advocates for businesses contributes to the business's bargaining power.

Vaguely Defined Product. A third deterrent to efficient market operations is the poorly defined nature of the good (a "job") or poorly defined property rights. Although most negotiations over industrial location include corporate estimates of the number of jobs that will be created, firms do not guarantee specific numbers of job characteristics in exchange for locational grants. Often, temporary (construction) employment is included in the job estimates and seasonal low-paying jobs are not distinguished from better jobs. A Department of Housing and Urban Development (1982) study on urban development found that projections by grantees overstated by 29 percent the number of jobs that would be created by businesses receiving subsidies. Also, cities seldom attempt to elicit guarantees that the subsidized jobs will be provided for current residents.

Federal Subsidies.   A fourth factor that may reduce efficiency is federal programs that encourage cities to offer more for jobs than the benefits received or that subsidize cities competing against each other for the same jobs. Of course, federal assistance is appropriate when the federal interest in job creation transcends local interests, perhaps because of externalities received by other local areas in addition to the area that captures the jobs. But to be efficient, the federal programs must be carefully structured to avoid situations in which one city bids against another in a zero-sum game with federal dollars.

What Does a Job Cost?   One indication of an inefficient market is the presence of large variations in the product's price. Of course, the price of a job could vary even in an efficient market, owing to variations in job quality and externalities associated with jobs. Nevertheless, the cost of a job varies so much even within a local area that there can be little doubt that the market is inefficient.

Data on the cost of a job is fragmented and difficult to obtain. Lack of cost data is itself an indication of an imperfect market because well-functioning markets are characterized by buyers and sellers who know the prevailing price. However, the scattered evidence from major federal programs shows that costs per job range from over $300,000 per job created to as little as $5,000. (The cost of a job is the subsidy per job, not the capital-labor ratio.) The conclusion that there are wide cost variations is clear. The variation in the cost of jobs is accentuated because jobs created in small retail and service establishments receive no direct subsidy. Hence, the cost of an unsubsidized job is zero.

Subsidy Cost versus Value

An important dimension of economic development programs is how much of a subsidy actually reaches the intended party compared to the taxpayers' cost. Firms receive subsidies in a variety of indirect and often inefficient ways. The value of a tax abatement to a firm is fairly easy to determine. It is the present value of the tax savings. Low-interest loans and loan guarantees are more difficult to value precisely, because it requires an estimate of what rate the firm could borrow the funds at in the open market. Land write-downs may be costly, but they also limit choices of the firm, so it is difficult to determine how much the firm values the subsidized site compared to alternative locations. When packages, including several types of incentives, are compared, even industrial-development specialists will have difficulty determining which competing city is offering the most attractive net subsidy package. Two types of problems can cause the impact of subsidies to be diminished. First, the subsidy program may provide costly goods and services that are not highly valued by the locating firm. Second, unintended parties may capture some of the benefits.

Low-Valued Services. The most obvious instance of a poorly targeted subsidy is when a local community provides a service or infrastructure improvements that cost taxpayers more than they are valued by the firm the community is trying to attract. For example, suppose a region spends millions of dollars to beautify an industrial park. The better looks undoubtedly would be a plus in attracting firms and jobs. But, would firms value the beautification efforts enough to warrant the community's cost? (Of course, beautification programs provide benefits to residents as well, so one could argue that the marginal benefits to the community outweigh the costs.) If the community has a narrow goal of attracting a particular firm, the more directly the benefits are tailored to the firm, the greater the firm is likely to value the benefits.

Unintended Beneficiaries. Suppose a property owner had a parcel of land that he wished to develop as an industrial park and he convinced the city council that a tax abatement would be necessary to attract firms. Consequently, the city agreed to provide a tax abatement for any employer building a new facility in the industrial park. Prior to the availability of the tax abatement, the landowner might have asked $10,000 an acre. Because of the availability of the abatement, the demand for the land in the industrial park will increase. The owner may raise the price of the land. Thus, the landowner may capture part or all of the value of the tax abatement. In other words, not all of the abatement will accrue to the intended beneficiary, the industrial firm.

The use of tax-exempt industrial revenue bonds has been similarly analyzed. Suppose conventional loans are available at 16 percent interest and tax-exempt bonds yield 12 percent. Also, assume that the average purchaser of tax-exempt bonds is in the 30 percent marginal tax bracket. Table 7–3 summarizes the outcome from the alternative financing techniques.

Under the conventional financing techniques, the firm would have to pay $160,000 in interest annually on the $1,000,000 loan. However, the lenders would receive only $112,000 of that amount because, if they were in the 30 percent tax bracket, their tax obligation would increase by

TABLE 7–3   Alternative Financing on a $1 Million Loan

	Conventional Financing at 16 Percent Interest	*Tax-Exempt Financing at 12 Percent Interest*
Interest cost to firm	$160,000	$120,000
After tax to lenders	112,000	120,000
Tax payments	48,000	0
Tax expenditure under tax-exempt financier	—	48,000
Decreased cost to firm	—	40,000

$48,000. Under the 12 percent tax-exempt financing scheme, the government would have a tax expenditure of $48,000, but only $40,000 ($160,000 − $120,000) would benefit the firm they were trying to attract; the other $8,000 ($120,000 − $112,000) would benefit the lenders. In this case, the cost to the government is greater than the benefits to the firm.

Subsidy programs have been compared to carrying water in a leaky bucket. Some of the water will leak out on the way from the well to the destination just as some of the subsidy often goes to unintended parties.

Cost-Minimization versus Human-Capital Strategies

The majority of economic development tools are designed to reduce business costs and, hence, attract new industries to an area. Business-cost-reduction approaches have been criticized for three reasons. First, cost-minimization approaches may tend to attract branch plants of mature industries. Such facilities are a small component of local growth. Most growth is generated internally by existing businesses, and it is difficult to target cost-reduction benefits for existing businesses. In fact, existing businesses often pay (either directly or indirectly) for subsidies given to attract new firms. Second, it is extremely difficult for most regions in advanced countries to compete with locations in less-developed countries. Large multiplant companies are in positions to consider locations throughout the world. Third, local economic development strategies should attempt to increase local living standards, not just increase the number of jobs. A cost-minimization strategy might actually lead to lower per capita incomes for residents.

The human-capital strategy attempts provide businesses with a high-quality labor force. A high-quality labor force will attract activities that perform nonroutine operations such as corporate headquarters, skilled operations, and technologically oriented activities. Advocates of the human-capital approach contend that local residents will be better served by stimulating growth in these better-paying occupations. However, there is a danger that low-skilled populations could be left out of a development plan that valued only high-paying, high-skill jobs.

Warner (1989) conducted an empirical test to determine whether improvement in variables associated with cost minimization or variables associated with human-capital improvement best explained changes in per capita income among urban regions, between 1977 and 1984. He concluded that the human-capital approach is more effective in increasing average incomes. Although the specifics of Warner's empirical tests may be questioned, they indicate that regional development officials should not overemphasize cost-reduction programs at the expense of the human-capital strategy.

Discretionary versus Entitlement Subsidies

Discretionary policies provide local development officials with choices regarding the type or size of the incentive they may wish to extend to a particular business. UDAG is an example of a discretionary program because if local or federal officials believe a subsidy is unnecessary, then none will be given. Enterprise zones are an entitlement program because any firms that locate in a zone and meet other requirements will receive the incentive. Most business-incentive programs that operate through the tax system are entitlement programs.

The advantage of discretionary programs is that governments may avoid paying unnecessary subsidies or making unnecessary tax expenditures. The disadvantage of discretionary programs is that government officials must make decisions regarding the business potential of firms seeking subsidies. Can the firm succeed? How much of a subsidy is necessary? Government bureaucrats may not be able to make such decisions accurately. Entitlement programs create a business climate which all qualifying businesses can potentially exploit. Once the framework is established, government officials need not be directly involved in business decisions.

INTEGRATING URBAN AND INDUSTRIAL EMPLOYMENT PROGRAMS

Job-creation efforts have traditionally focused on both regions and industries. A city with a large portion of the work force employed in steel production might be helped as much by a program that gives tax credits to rehabilitate steel facilities as by an urban grant program. Because industry-oriented programs are sometimes viewed as alternatives to urban employment programs, this section briefly compares the two approaches. Urban programs and programs intended to assist particular industries address employment problems from complementary perspectives. The former are concerned with the geographic concentrations of unemployment, and the latter are concerned with unemployment or underemployment due to industrial shifts. Likewise, urban-oriented solutions involve creating location-specific jobs or encouraging individuals to move to places with job opportunities, whereas industrial approaches involve creating industry-specific jobs or training individuals for occupations that offer good job opportunities. Both approaches to policy are concerned with structural mismatches, and they address transitional problems that are traceable to wage rigidities and resource immobility. The similarities can be described in detail.

Structuralist

Both urban and industrial programs are structuralist solutions to unemployment. They both assert that macroeconomic policy by itself is insufficient because it does not solve the mismatch between jobs and potential employees. However, both approaches presume that the effectiveness of structural adjustments requires an adequate aggregate demand for labor. The *President's National Urban Policy Report* stated unequivocally that national economic health was a prerequisite for a successful urban policy (p. 1). Likewise, supporters of industrial policy believe that industrial policies are a poor use of resources in a general climate of stagnation.

Transitionalist

Both urban- and industrial-policy advocates are concerned about the need to mitigate transitional problems that have possibly been aggravated by the quickened pace of economic change. The *President's Urban Policy Report* (1984) stated that, although some cities (such as New York and Boston) have been transformed into service-based economies, other cities apparently need urban-oriented programs to help in the transition.

> Cities have had different degrees of success in dealing with their structural problems. The [Reagan] Administration has maintained several economic development programs to aid cities in adapting to these changes. (Department of Housing and Urban Development, *President's National Urban Policy Report* (1984), p. 72)

Similarly, industrial-policy proponents are concerned about the inability of workers to cope with the change from manufacturing to service and high-tech occupations (Blumenthal, 1983; Reich, 1983). They emphasized the need for industrial policy to facilitate the transitions that growth makes inevitable.

The transitionalist emphasis also reflects a fear that urban and industrial programs may institutionalize inefficiency by propping up obsolete activities. For instance, advocates of urban-oriented assistance recognize the danger of attempting to maintain a high level of employment in an area that no longer has a competitive advantage. If market forces are such that an employment decline is warranted, decline must eventually occur or assistance must be made permanent.

Wage Rigidities

Both urban and industrial approaches generally recognize that shifts in the demand for labor coupled with sticky, downward wages and prices contributed to unemployment. The prognosis of most theoretical models is that full employment could always be maintained if wages quickly adjust to any change in demand for the industry's or region's output. Put differently, unemployment is the direct result of the failure of wages to adjust. The failure of wages to fall, in turn, can be attributed to various institutional factors such as customs, union contracts, and minimum-wage laws. There is substantial disagreement, however, regarding whether wages *should* be more flexible.

Resource Mobility

In spite of the different reasons for the initial decline in labor demand, the failure of wages to fall sufficiently results in unemployment. As neither the urban nor industrial approach places much faith in falling wages or price to establish full employment, encouraging capital movements into the declining area (or industry) or encouraging labor to move out of the declining area (or industry) emerges as the main policy solution. If resources were perfectly mobile, no policy would be needed. However, opponents of government policies question whether government actions can improve the allocation of resources. In fact, some analysts oppose industrial policy on the grounds that government intervention will prevent resources from flowing to more efficient uses (Premus and Bradford, 1984, p. 58).

Inadequate resource (particularly labor) mobility contributes to the need for policy intervention in both spatial and industrial approaches. Urban policies are concerned with geographic immobility. Industrial policies are concerned with occupational immobility. Urban-oriented solutions to unemployment encourage individuals to locate in places of opportunity and seek to attract job-creating capital (or entrepreneurship) to either distressed or growth-potential areas. Industrial employment problems can be addressed by encouraging workers in declining industries to develop a different set of skills or by creating jobs that demand skills individuals already have.

Targeting

Among advocates of urban policy there has been a debate on whether assistance should be targeted towards expanding or declining cities. A similar division exists among industrial-policy advocates: Should assistance be targeted towards sunrise or sunset industries?

Individuals opposed to government involvement in either urban economies or particular industries contend that governments are poor vehicles for determining where investment should be directed (Weinstein, Gross, and Roes, 1985). Hence, they would generally oppose any targeting of assistance. Furthermore, the politics of government assistance tends to spread assistance rather than target assistance on a narrow group of regions or industries. For instance, the Model Cities Program and the Economic Development Administration were both intended to be narrowly targeted. Yet, the number of the sites eligible for model-cities assistance was 150 and the Economic Development Administration defined 88 percent of all U.S. counties as eligible for assistance under the Economic Development Act.

SUMMARY

Policies to encourage local development are an important part of U.S. economic history. Five periods of local development efforts are (1) the canal and railroad period, (2) the great city-building era, (3) the period of depression and war disruptions, (4) the era of federal efforts and, (5) the period of state and local predominance.

Motives for local development efforts include job creation, fiscal improvement, and physical improvements.

Prominent instruments for subsidizing businesses include tax abatements, tax-exempt financing, loan assistance, infrastructure assistance, and write-downs. These instruments and other assistance tools can be directed towards various types of business functions.

Most of the prominent tools can be used on an ad hoc basis, but they are important parts of economic development programs. The Job Training Partnership Act provides localities with federal funds to train workers. A trained work force can be an incentive to business development. Business incubators are an increasingly popular program intended to nurture new businesses. Enterprise zones have been initiated in many states to create areas of reduced taxation while free-trade zones are useful to communities seeking to strengthen their international trade. The Urban Development Action Grants program (UDAG) encourages public-private partnerships to stimulate investment. UDAG has been criticized because of political influence and an overemphasis on commercial projects and is likely to be phased out. The Community Development Block Grant program (CDBG) is a federally funded program that provides localities with resources that can be spent on a variety of needs.

When state and local governments provide incentives for firms to locate in their areas, they compete in a market for jobs. Public activity in local job creation has increased due to (1) a greater familiarity with business practice on the part of government officials, (2) economic dislocations, (3) public perceptions of local government's role in job attraction, (4) rigidities, and (5) resource immobilities in the labor market.

A model of community competition for jobs illustrates the conditions for encouraging and discouraging local job creation. It suggests that, if there are substantial local spillovers from job creation, localities may benefit by directly or indirectly subsidizing job-creation efforts.

Several important development policy issues were discussed. Economic development may be a zero-sum game if local governments compete for a fixed number of jobs. However, economic development incentives may also help create jobs. Nevertheless, local competition for job creation includes inefficiencies because of (1) political problems of collective action, (2) information asymmetry, (3) unspecified property rights, and (4) the role of federal programs. Often, the subsidy cost is greater than the value businesses place on the subsidies. Disagreements exist regarding the extent to which discretionary or entitlement approaches are preferable as well as the extent to which cost-minimization or human-capital strategies should be employed.

Finally, the relationships between urban and industrial approaches to job creation were discussed. Similarities between these two approaches include a focus on structural employment, the need to address problems of transition, and the role of wage rigidities and resource immobility in the preventing adjustments.

REFERENCES

Baum, Donald. "The Economic Effects of State and Local Business Incentives." *Land Economics* 3, no. 4, November 1987, pp. 348–60.

Benjamin, Robert Cook. "From Waterways to Waterfronts: A Public Investment for Cities 1815–1980." In *Urban Economic Development,* ed. Richard Bingham and John P. Blair. Beverly Hills, Calif.: Sage Publications, 1984.

Blair, John P. and David Nachmias. "Urban Policy in the Lean Society" in Blair and Nachmias (eds.). *Fiscal Retrenchment and Urban Policy.* Beverly Hills, Calif.: Sage Publications, pp. 11–42, 1979.

Blair, John P., Rudy Fichtenbaum and James Swaney. "The Market for Jobs." *Urban Affairs Quarterly* 20, no. 1, September 1984, pp. 64–77.

Blumenthal, S. "Drafting a Democratic Industrial Plan." *New York Times Magazine*, August 28, 1983, pp. 5–8.

Butler, Stuart M. "Free Zones in the Inner City." In *Urban Economic Development*, ed. Richard Bingham and John P. Blair. Beverly Hills, Calif.: Sage Publications, 1984, pp. 141–56.

Bradford, David F., and Henry H. Kelejian. "An Econometric Model of the Flight to the Suburb." *Journal of Political Economy*, May 1973, pp. 566–89.

Department of Housing and Urban Development. *The President's National Urban Policy Report 1988.* New York: Department of Housing and Urban Development, 1988.

Jones, Bryon D., and Lynn W. Bachelor. "Local Policy Discretion and the Corporate Surplus." In *Urban Economic Development*, ed. Richard Bingham and John P. Blair. Beverly Hills, Calif.: Sage Publications, 1984, pp. 245–67.

Levy, John M. *Urban and Metropolitan Economics.* New York: McGraw-Hill, 1985.

National Association of State Development Agencies; National Council for Urban Economic Development; and the Urban Institute. *Directory of Incentives for Business Investment and Development in the United States.* Baltimore: Urban Institute Press, 1983.

Premus, Robert, and C. H. Bradford. *Industrial Policy Movement in the United States: Is It the Answer?* Washington, D.C.: U.S. Government Printing Office, 1984.

Reich, R. *The Next American Frontiers.* New York: Times Books, 1983.

Rubin, Herbert J. "Shoot Anything that Flies: Claim Anything that Falls." *Economic Development Quarterly* 2, no. 3, August 1988, pp. 236–51.

Sternberg, Ernest. "A Practitioner's Classification of Economic Development Policy Instruments with Some Inspiration from Political Economy." *Economic Development Quarterly* 1, no. 2, 1987, pp. 149–61.

U.S. Department of Housing and Urban Development. *The President's National Urban Policy Report* (1984). Washington, D.C.: Department of Housing and Urban Development, 1984.

U.S. Department of Housing and Urban Development. *The President's National Urban Policy Report* (1988). Washington, D.C.: Department of Housing and Urban Development, 1988.

Warner, Paul D. "Alternative Strategies for Economic Development: Evidence from Southern Metropolitan Areas." *Urban Affairs Quarterly* 24, no. 3, March 1989, pp. 389–411.

Weinstein, Bernard L., Harold Gross, and John Roes. *Regional Growth and Decline in the United States.* 2nd ed. New York: Praeger Publishers, 1985.

Chapter Eight

Poverty and Antipoverty Programs

The three previous chapters address regional growth and job creation, the principal means for increasing living standards. Yet many individuals remain poor even in growing economies. The entire problem cannot be solved by job creation alone. Poverty is a traditional urban and regional topic because poverty is spatially concentrated. In fact, poverty was one of the first issues that focused attention on the need to spatially target economic policies for central cities and rural pockets of distress. Furthermore, poverty affects many other aspects of the spatial environment. Both poor individuals and areas with high concentrations of poor people have high incidences of social pathologies, and they frequently lack the resources necessary to adequately address the problem.

The first section in this chapter discusses conceptual and operational definitions of poverty. The extent of poverty and characteristics of the poor are the subject of the second section. Next, the principal causes of poverty are discussed. Because poverty is closely linked to lack of earnings, this section includes an examination of the labor market, especially labor market operation at the lower end of the pay spectrum. The fourth section describes the spatial dimensions of poverty, and antipoverty policies are described in the fifth section. The final section is a discussion of recent criticisms of welfare programs.

DEFINITIONS OF POVERTY

It is worthwhile to begin with a discussion of the definition and measurement of poverty. Conceptions of what being poor means affect how poverty is viewed and even whether it is considered a problem. Consequently, many policy debates hinge upon the definition of poverty. In this section, conceptual approaches to the definition of poverty will be described first and then the official U.S. definition of poverty will be discussed.

Conceptual Approaches

Three major conceptual definitions of poverty can be found in the literature: (1) absolute deprivation, (2) culturally or socially determined deprivation, and (3) relative economic position.

Absolute poverty is a concept in which a minimum real living standard (i.e., constant purchasing power) is established and anyone falling below that level is considered poor. When the focus is on absolute poverty, the poverty line should not change after the real living standard for poverty is initially set. However, since the absolute poverty line is expressed in dollars, it is necessary to adjust the poverty income threshold to account for price changes. Individuals favoring the absolute concept believe it is the most clear-cut definition of poverty. The official definition of poverty in the United States, as explained below, is based upon the absolute standard.

An alternative approach is to base the poverty level on societal norms at a given time and place. Individuals favoring cultural definitions of poverty point out that living standards once considered acceptable change as incomes increase. Therefore, the definition of poverty should reflect contemporary standards. The principal advantage of a culturally determined definition of poverty is that it reflects what average persons have in mind when they speak of being poor. Unfortunately, definitions that vary with time and place make comparisons over time or between countries less meaningful. Thus, it is not a good standard for measuring progress. Also, it may be very difficult to form a consensus about the level of income the society or the culture defines as poor. Many analysts, including Harrington (1984), have proposed a culturally flexible standard of poverty set at a level of income just sufficient to allow an individual to participate in "normal social life." Inability to afford birthday parties for children, an occasional recreational event or a restaurant meal, new clothes, and education are suggested indicators of poverty defined in cultural terms in the United States today. Lists of specific things that everyone should be able to afford makes the culturally determined definition of poverty a little more concrete. However, there is probably no strong consensus about exactly what is necessary for full participation in normal social life.

Some economists are concerned about relative poverty—the condition of the poorest portion of the population. Economists who focus on relative poverty are in fact concerned about the distribution of income. Increases in the proportion of income accruing to individuals in the bottom 20 percent would indicate reductions in poverty under this standard. An advantage of relative definitions of poverty is that it reflects the fact that individuals tend to feel poor when they are poor in comparison to others. Studies of how happy individuals feel indicate that relatively well-off individuals in poor countries consider themselves to be about as happy as relatively well-off individuals in wealthy societies.

Critics of purely relative definitions of poverty contend that it confuses the concept of poverty with inequality and it is logically impossible to eliminate a portion of the income distribution, such as the lowest 20 percent of the income distribution. Therefore, the concept of relative poverty is less helpful than other poverty definitions in policy development. However, policies can be designed to increase the resources of individuals in the lower portions of the distribution. Some Department of Housing and Urban Development programs, for instance, target funds for areas where residents have incomes below 80 percent of the median income in the region. Thus, in some cases, relative income concepts have been useful in developing policy.

Each of the three concepts of poverty provides a different perspective, but they are not necessarily inconsistent with each other. Initially, all three definitions could coincide, but over time they could grow apart. For example, suppose that in the early 1960s, $3,000 represented the threshold income for the absolute, culturally determined, and relative poverty definitions. Over time, however, the average income increased. Assuming that the income distribution did not change, the relative poverty threshold would increase along with the average income because the income of those in the bottom fifth would increase along with the rest of the population. The absolute poverty line, which may have been culturally influenced when it was set, will remain fixed. Therefore, a gap between it and the relative poverty thresholds will increase over time. How the culturally determined definition will change as average incomes increase cannot be determined theoretically. However, survey evidence as shown in Table 8–1 indicates that perceptions about what it takes to "get by" do increase as income increases. Public opinion polls indicated that $19,876 was the amount a family of four needed to "get by" in 1987 (Gallup, 1987).

The Official Poverty Definition

During the 1960s, the issue of poverty became a major national concern. As poverty issues became more important, so did the need to nail down the definition. The President's Council of Economic Advisors used a fixed definition of poverty, calculated as follows:

1. The U.S. Department of Agriculture determined the cost of an "economy food plan." It was the cost of foods that offer some variety and provided a balanced diet at minimum cost for families suffering temporary financial hardship. Clearly, it was a no-frills food budget. The cost of the economy food plan was calculated for various family sizes.

TABLE 8–1   Three Concepts of the Poverty Threshold: Family of Four

Year	Absolute Official Definition	Relative*	Social or Cultural†
1960	$ 3,022	$ 2,784	$ 3,884
1965	3,223	3,500	4,212
1970	3,968	5,100	6,552
1975	5,500	6,914	8,372
1980	8,414	10,286	13,000
1981	9,287	10,918	14,404
1982	9,862	11,200	15,392
1983	10,178	11,678	15,392
1984	10,609	12,489	15,360
1985	10,989	13,192	15,704
1986	11,203	13,886	18,148
1987	11,611	14,450	19,876

* Income below which a family would be in the lowest 25 percent of the income distribution.
† Response to question: "What is the smallest amount of money a family of four (husband, wife, and two children) needs to get by in this community?" (Gallup, 1987).

2. Since the average poor family spent about one third of their income on food, the cost of the economy food plan was multiplied by three to give the poverty income cut-off. Adjustments are made for farm families, since they can grow some of their own food. In 1963, this figure was $3,000 for a family of two adults and two children.

3. Each year, the poverty cut-off is revised to account for changes in the cost of living reflected by changes in the consumer price index.

The council's poverty threshold has been modified to account for family size and circumstances. Mollie Orshansky of the Social Security Administration identified 124 family types and calculated the appropriate budget for each family using methodology similar to that described above. Column 1, Table 8–1, shows the official definition of poverty as it has been adjusted for inflation over time for a family of four, two adults and two children. Table 8–2 shows the 1989 poverty level for various family sizes.

The official poverty line is considered an absolute poverty measure because, once set, it is adjusted only for inflation so it reflects constant purchasing power. However, the initial decision establishing the poverty line at three times the minimum food budget reflected the cultural stan-

TABLE 8–2 Poverty Standards, 1989

Size of Family	Poverty Standards
One member	$ 6,250
Two members	8,000
Three members	9,800
Four members	12,560
Five members	14,860
Six members	16,770
Seven members	19,100
Eight members	21,100

Note: The 1989 standards were estimated based on projected inflation.

SOURCE: Schiller, Bradley R. *The Economics of Poverty and Discrimination, 5th edition.* © 1989, p. 24. Reprinted by permission of Prentice Hall, Inc., Englewood Cliffs, New Jersey.

dards as well as political considerations in the United States at the time. The portion of family income spent on food falls as income increases. Therefore, if the poverty line had been established in an earlier period when families spent a higher portion of their income on food and then adjusted only for inflation, the poverty line would be lower than it is today. Conversely, if the same conceptual approach were used today, the threshold would be higher.

The official definition of poverty has been criticized because it fails to account for many in-kind transfer payments. A family with a money income below the poverty line could receive other assistance, including subsidized housing, food stamps, and Medicaid. When the value of these goods and services is included in income, the imputed income of some poor families would be increased above the poverty threshold.

A reason for excluding in-kind transfers from family income is that they are difficult to value. It may cost the government $500 a month to provide housing assistance to a poor family, but the family may not feel their welfare has been improved by $500 a month. Furthermore, a poor individual may become ill and receive say, $50,000 in medical care in a few months. Would such a subsidy make the individual rich?

Table 8–3 illustrates how the poverty rate would change if in-kind transfers were included. Notice that the overall poverty rate would have fallen from 13.6 percent of the population to 9 percent if the market value of food, housing, and medical benefits (excluding institutional expenditures) were included.

TABLE 8–3   Persons below the Poverty Line by Valuation Technique: 1986

Valuation Method and Type of Benefit	Percent Poor	Number (1000)
1. Current poverty definition (excludes noncash transfers)	13.6%	32,370
2. Market-value approach		
a. Including food and housing assistance	12.2	28,988
b. Including food, housing, and medical benefits (excluding institutional expenditures)	9.0	21,369
3. Recipient and/or cash-equivalent approach		
a. Including food and housing assistance	12.5	29,793
b. Including food, housing, and medical benefits (excluding institutional expenditures)	11.6	27,592

Persons as of March of the following year. Valuation techniques that are used to measure noncash benefits are as follows: (1) Market-value approach which is equal to the purchase price in the private market of the goods received by the recipient; and (2) recipient and/or cash-equivalent approach which is the amount of cash that would make the recipient just as well-off as the in-kind transfer or would reflect the recipient's own valuation of the benefit. For more information on the methodology, see source.

SOURCE: U.S. Bureau of the Census, *Estimates of Poverty Including the Value of Noncash Benefits: 1986*, Technical Paper 57.

A related problem is that no monetary value is attached to assets an individual may own, particularly cars and houses. Clearly, an individual is better off owning these assets than an individual with similar income who must pay rent and pay for public transportation. Thus, some analysts have suggested that imputed rental value of housing should be included as part of an individual's income.

POVERTY TRENDS AND CHARACTERISTICS

Throughout the 1960s, real income in the United States grew rapidly. Consequently, the number of persons below the poverty line declined and a more substantial drop occurred in the percentage of the population classified as poor. During the era of slow economic growth in the mid-1970s through the late 1980s, the number of persons below the poverty line increased slightly as did the percentage of the total population classified as poor.

The decline in the extent of poverty since the early 1960 has resulted in a change in the nature of the poverty population. Economic growth has helped raise many individuals who were slightly below the poverty line above that threshold. The individuals who were lifted from poverty by economic growth tended to be that portion of the poverty population most similar to the rest of society in terms of socioeconomic characteristics and their ability to work. As a result of freezing the official poverty threshold at a fixed absolute level, many individuals have moved out of poverty because their income increased along with everyone else's in a growing economy. However, an increasing portion of the remaining poor are less attached to the labor market and may have other pathologies associated with poverty, such as illness and illiteracy. Policies that may have worked for the marginally poor become less likely to be effective for the individuals who remain poor.

Who Are the Poor?

It is important to distinguish between the incidence of poverty and the portion of the poverty population having particular characteristics. The incidence of poverty is the probability that a family of a particular type will be poor. Table 8–4 shows the incidence of poverty in various categories using the official poverty definition. The high incidence of poverty among blacks and Hispanics is apparent. The portion of the poverty population with specific characteristics is also shown in Table 8–4. The fact that most of the poor are white and that nearly 40 percent of individuals in poverty are children is surprising to many who associate poverty almost exclusively with minorities or lazy workers.

Income Mobility.   Identification of the poor is complicated by income mobility, particularly among families near the poverty threshold. Poverty rates represent the average portion of individuals who are poor during the year. A poverty rate of 14 percent does not mean that the same 14 percent of the population was poor for the entire year. In fact, for many families, poverty status is temporary. They may be classified as poor some months, then their incomes may rise above the threshold, and then perhaps they return to poverty status depending upon events. Income mobility is particularly great among the poor who are willing and able to work. Levy (1976) observed that only 25 percent of individuals who were poor in 1967 were poor for five of the next six years. Over the period Levy studied, about 30 percent of poor families remained poor only about half the year, and only 45 percent of poor families remained in poverty all six years.

TABLE 8–4   Incidence and Structure of Poverty, 1986

	Incidence of Poverty	Percent of All Poor
Ethnic group		
White	11.0%	61.1%
Black	31.1	24.8
Hispanic	27.3	15.8
Age		
Under 6	22.1	14.8
6–17	19.6	25.0
18–24	15.6	12.8
25–44	10.2	24.1
45–64	9.1	12.6
65+	12.4	10.7
Region		
Northeast	10.5	16.1
Midwest	13.0	23.6
South	16.1	40.5
West	13.2	19.8
Employment status		
Employed	13.2	2.9
Unemployed	39.5	18.6
Total U.S.	13.6	

SOURCE: U.S. Bureau of the Census, *Estimates of Poverty Including the Valued Noncash Benefits: 1986,* Technical Paper 57; and author's calculations.

Women and Children.   The incidence of poverty is increasingly high for female-headed households. Writers have referred to the "feminization" of poverty to describe this trend. Over a third of all female-headed households is below the poverty line. Nearly three fourths of all the poor are adult women and children. School-age and preschool-age children have one of the highest incidences of poverty of any group. The poverty rate for children under six years old was 22 percent in 1986. Because families tend to move in and out of poverty, about 30 percent of children will be poor at some point in their childhood. Furthermore, as family size increases, the rate of poverty increases. For instance, in 1986, two-person families had a poverty rate of less than 9 percent, five-person families had a nearly 14-percent poverty rate, and families with 7 or more persons had a 32-percent poverty rate.

Family break-ups are strongly associated with the increasing incidence of poverty among women and children. Divorce and desertion are important causes of poverty. However, economic difficulties can also contribute to the growth of family break-ups and female-headed households. So, the relationship between family dissolution and poverty may be a chicken-egg problem. For instance, an unemployed family head is more likely to leave the family than an employed head and lack of money is a source of family tension. Therefore, like many other issues related to poverty, it is sometimes difficult to distinguish the cause from the effect.

The feminization of poverty has occurred during a period when women were moving into high-wage, professional jobs. Furthermore, the mean earning of women increased much more rapidly than men between 1975 and 1986. The success of women in high-wage occupations may be attributable to affirmative-action policies or cultural changes that the woman's movement created. However, not all women have been affected equally. Gains for women in the professional and managerial category increased more rapidly than other women workers (Wagman and Folbre, 1988) and have not offset the feminization of poverty.

The Ill and Traumatized.   A disproportionate number of the poor population have problems that limit their ability to participate in the labor market. Some health problems are straightforward and easily diagnosed, as in the case of retardation or visual impairment. Other problems are more subtle. For instance, mental problems, such as anxiety, will inhibit work but may go undiagnosed and untreated.

Health and poverty can form a vicious cycle. A poor person may be unable to afford adequate medical attention, which, in turn, may aggravate the problem. Furthermore, the U.S. Department of Health and Human Services reported that children of poor families have a variety of health problems, including higher incidences of low weight, hearing impairment, parasitic diseases, lead poisoning, and so forth. While no one knows the extent to which these health problems contribute to poverty in later life, it is reasonable to hypothesize that there is a relationship (Schiller, 1989).

The Aged.   The incidence of poverty among those over 65 is currently lower than the poverty rate for the U.S. population as a whole. Table 8–4 indicates that those over 65 have the second lowest poverty rate of any age group. The poverty rate among the aged has fallen dramatically in the past 20 years—partly because of increases in retirement benefits, including social security. The indexation of social security payments has been particularly useful to the elderly. In-kind social benefits, particularly Medicare, have also helped increase the living standards of the elderly, although these benefits are not reflected in poverty statistics that exclude in-kind transfers. By almost any standard, government policy has successfully reduced poverty among older Americans. However, older families are more vulnerable to economic changes than many other groups because their return-to-work options are limited. While some elderly families may have substantial savings, only about half of all aged families have savings of over $200.

Whether wealthy and middle-income elderly should receive as much public assistance as they do is a controversial question. On the one hand, many people feel that the elderly should not be required to deplete their savings or fall into poverty before becoming eligible for assistance. On the other hand, critics of programs for the elderly contend that many public programs protect the estates of the elderly for the primary benefit of their children and grandchildren. In other words, elderly-oriented antipoverty programs may perpetuate the existing distribution of wealth.

Minorities.   Blacks and other minorities have a much higher incidence of poverty than whites. Blacks are about three times more likely to be poor than whites. Hispanics have slightly less than twice the incidence of poverty as whites. Reasons for these differences in poverty rates include many types of discrimination, smaller inheritances, cultural background, and fewer parental gifts of such items as college education or the down payment on a house.

Wilson (1980) expressed a new and controversial view to explain black poverty. He contended that race is not as meaningful a category as it has been in the past. In documenting the "declining significance of race," Wilson argued that class characteristics, rather than overt racial discrimination, account for the lower economic achievement of blacks. Black immigrants to the United States are as successful as other immigrant groups, suggesting that factors other than race contribute to black poverty. Wilson (1985) concluded that "Any significant reduction in joblessness and related problems . . . requires a far more comprehensive reform than Americans have generally deemed appropriate" (p. 159). Wilson's critics have countered that overt racial discrimination still exists, although there can be little doubt that it is manifest in more subtle ways.

Working Poor.   The probability of a family with a full-time wage earner falling below the poverty line is less than 5 percent. The one-million-plus poor families with a full-time worker in the household are poor principally because of low hourly earnings. However, a substantial portion of the poor work either part-time or full-time. Over one half of all poor families have at least one member who works some of the time during the year. Such families are poor because of transient unemployment, underemployment, employment at low wages, or illnesses that prevent full-time work.

Danziger and Gottschalk (1986) found that two thirds of once poor households headed by someone who was not aged, disabled, or a single parent of preschool children were able to increase their income above the poverty threshold. This is a relatively high escape rate, although it does not preclude a lapse back into poverty. The main reasons these working-poor families escaped poverty were: a decrease in family size, additional family members working, receipt of nonearnings income, and welfare. It is also interesting that increases in earnings of the head of household were not among the main escape routes.

The working poor are likely to "bounce around" the poverty line—sometimes above, sometimes below—as circumstances alter their family size and earnings. Also, this group may be more sensitive to changes in employment opportunities because they have the ability to take advantage of improved employment opportunities. Harrington (1984, p. 111) described the working poor as part of a "large at-risk population . . . composed of unskilled, low-paid workers who are one recession, one illness, one accident away from being poor." Although only a small portion of working families earn below the poverty threshold at any one time, many more families earn below that level for temporary periods.

CAUSES OF POVERTY

This section discusses the causes of poverty. Like most social problems, there are a variety of reasons for poverty. These reasons often combine, so any attempt to explain all poverty by a single explanation is a reductionist fallacy. Furthermore, analysis of the causes of poverty has ideological and policy implications because theories about what causes poverty imply particular solutions. For instance, someone might reasonably argue that individuals are poor because they did not inherit money from their parents. Such an explanation of poverty may lead to policies involving inheritance taxes and transfers. Consequently, some disagreements over the causes of poverty may be rooted in ideological perspectives about what should be done.

Aggregate Economic Fluctuation

At any given time there are large numbers of families earning slightly above or slightly below the poverty threshold. Increasing the average income will raise many such families out of poverty, assuming the distribution of income does not change. Figure 8–1 depicts fluctuations in the percentage of the population with below-poverty incomes and the near poor with incomes equal to 125 percent of the poverty threshold. Poverty

FIGURE 8–1   Fluctuations of Near-Poor and Poverty-Level Population
(percent)

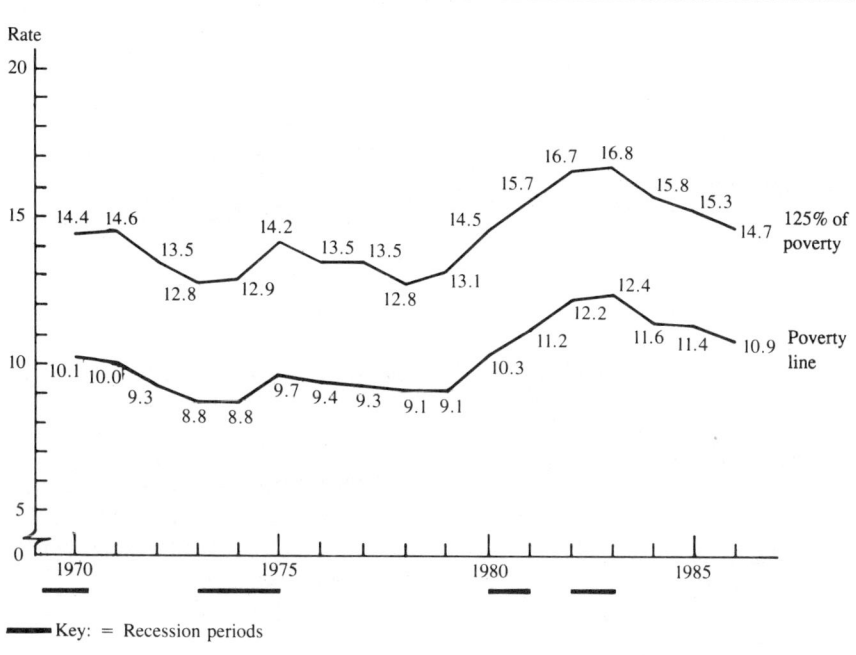

━━━ Key: = Recession periods

and near-poverty rates increased markedly during the recession between 1979 and 1983. As the nation entered a recovery phase, the poverty and near-poverty rates declined. Obviously, an increase in average income would not affect the poverty rate if the average increased only because individuals in the higher-income categories had increased incomes.

The poverty reductions flowing from an improved national economy are even stronger than would be anticipated by a proportional shift in average income. In fact, the poor benefit more from economic expansion and suffer more from economic downturns than the average person in the economy. Gramilich and Laren (1984) reported that a decrease in the unemployment rate will increase earnings among low-income families by two to four times the increase experienced by high-income families. Hill (1988) showed that regional variations in the portion of the population dependent on welfare are related to the unemployment rate. A 1 percent increase in the unemployment rate was associated with a 1.5 percent increase in the dependency rate.

Low Productivity

Conventional microeconomic theory leads to the conclusion that workers will be paid equal to the value of their marginal product in a well-functioning, competitive labor market. The value of the marginal product measures the amount of increased revenue to the firm from employing an additional worker. It is the value of the extra worker's contribution to a firm's revenues, holding other inputs constant. The concept may be expressed as:

$$VMP_i = MP_i \times MR \qquad (1)$$

where VMP_i = The value of the marginal product of the ith worker,
MP_i = The additional output produced by the ith worker (marginal product), and
MR = Marginal revenue attributable to a unit of extra output.

Accordingly, if the ith worker caused output to increase by five units and each unit of additional output sold for $2, the VMP_i would be $10. A firm would lose money if it paid a worker more than the VMP, because that would mean that the cost of hiring the worker was higher than the resulting revenue. But firms would be willing to employ additional workers as long as the value of the marginal product exceeded the wage. This theoretical relationship is the linchpin that links low productivity to low earnings and poverty.

Figure 8–2 illustrates the conventional view of how labor markets operate. The right-hand graph, (b), depicts the aggregate supply and demand while the left-hand graph, (a), depicts the situation for a single firm. The solid lines indicate conditions prior to any productivity improvements.

The firm's VMP curve, in (a), represents the extra revenue that the firm could earn if it hired an additional worker, holding other inputs constant. The VMP is the firm's labor-demand curve. As the number of employees increases, the value of the marginal product will fall for three possible reasons: (1) The law of diminishing marginal productivity states that after some point extra workers will contribute less to output than previously hired workers (remember, capital and land are held constant); (2) some producers may have to lower the product price in order to sell increased output; and (3) the first two reasons allow us to assume that all workers are equally productive—homogeneous. If we drop this assumption, then we discover a third reason why the VMP slopes downward— firms will hire the most productive workers first.

If the wage for the relevant class of workers is set by the market at $5 (see aggregate perspective in Figure 8–2(b)), the firm depicted in (a) would hire no more than 10 workers because the 11th employee would increase revenue by less than the wage.

FIGURE 8–2   Productivity Increase: Single-Firm and Aggregate Perspective

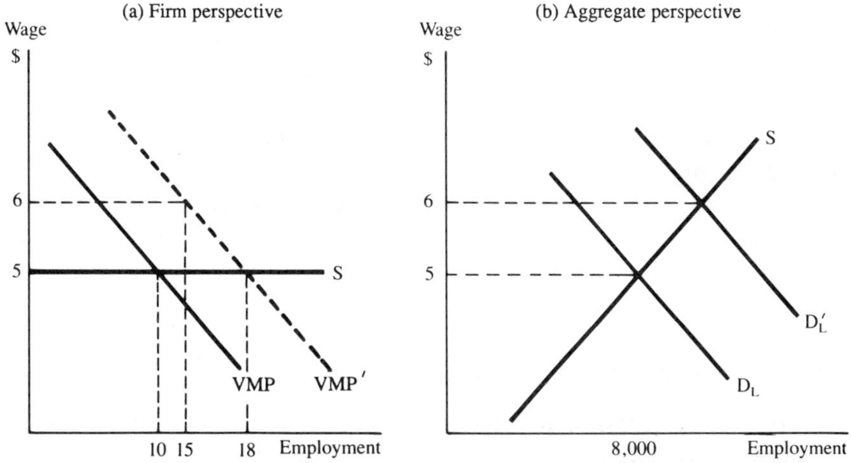

If the productivity of a class of labor increases, the wage will increase $5 to $6.00. A single, representative firm will consequently increase its demand for labor from VMP to VMP′ and increase employment from 10 to 15.

If productivity increases were to cause the VMP curve to shift upward to the right and the wage remained unchanged, the number of workers hired would shift from 10 to 18. This could represent the situation if the individual firm introduced a new method of production that causes the VMP of only its employees to increase. If the firm were a competitive employer in the labor market, its innovation would not significantly affect the overall demand. Hence, the market wage would remain $5.

However, if the productivity of a whole class of workers increased, it would be improper to assume that the wage rate faced by the firm would remain unchanged. The productivity increase of a whole class of workers would cause the aggregate demand for labor to increase, as shown by the shift from D_L to D_L'. Consequently, the wage rate would increase unless the aggregate labor supply were perfectly elastic. At the new, higher wage of $6, the firm would hire only 15 rather than 18 employees.

The model illustrated in Figure 8–2 examined the wage-determination issue for a group of workers. Individuals with VMPs below the prevailing wage would not be hired in that particular labor market. Although most economists agree that insufficient productivity contributes to poverty, it is not an ultimate explanation because it does not explain why some individuals have low productivity. An individual may have a low level of productivity or few marketable skills for several reasons, including low levels of innate physical or mental ability, laziness, illness, lack of education, poor work habits, or dysfunctional cultural traits. An individual may have acquired a highly specialized productive skill, but market shifts may have rendered such skills obsolete.

Most, but not all, individuals may enhance their productivity through education, training, or other means. How would the circumstances of individuals be affected if they increased their labor skills and hence productivity? The answer depends on which of several theories about how the labor market operates is applicable. Economists disagree about which theory best explains the link between individual productivity increases and income increases. There are a variety of labor markets, and some theories may explain the operation of some markets better than others.

Productivity Directly Recognized. An employer or supervisor within the firm will recognize and reward productivity improvement. In this case, greater productivity will result in greater pay without changing jobs or job categories. When compensation is on a commission or piecework basis, this case often applies.

Productivity Facilitates Job-Category Change. Workers within a particular class have similar skills and pay. If an individual's skills or productivity increase, they will move into another job class, such as from typist to secretary. The employee's wage in the new labor class will be higher than the wage being earned previously, reflecting the higher productivity.

Productivity Improves Place in Queue. Improved productivity will not affect an individual's particular class of labor or wage rate, but the more-productive workers will be more likely to be hired early and they will be among the last to be laid off. Hence, improved productivity may neither result in an increase in pay within a job class nor a change in job class. Nevertheless, productivity improvements may help an individual avoid the last-hired, first-fired syndrome.

Productivity Irrelevant. Some labor-market theorists believe that an individual's place in society is so constructed as to make pay impervious to productivity. Custom and tradition determine who is hired and what they are paid. According to this perspective, the job niche an individual fills determines pay. Increases in productivity alone may not allow individuals to change their niche. For instance, jobs may have customary promotion and advancement ladders and entry to a job ladder may require an appropriate social background. Even if individuals improve their productivity, increases in pay may be unlikely unless they are on an upward job ladder. Frequently, a college degree is required to get a job although job duties may not require a college degree. The secondary labor market where the poor and near poor are confined has few job ladders. Hence, productivity improvements do not lead to better pay within the job class. Furthermore, it is difficult to change job classes because of behavioral and other noneconomic requirements for jobs in the primary labor market.

The marginal productivity of workers is at least a part of the explanation in the first three cases. The fourth explanation views productivity as resting in the job, not in the employee. An ancillary idea is that background and status directly or indirectly (through education and so forth) determine access to jobs and therefore productivity. Accordingly, higher compensation associated with family background and education is not attributable to greater abilities or productivity but to the enhanced access to high-productivity jobs.

Market Barriers and Imperfections

Individuals with productive skills are often impeded from obtaining better-paying jobs by market barriers, even when such jobs are unfilled. Important types of market barriers include: lack of knowledge, geographic immobility, arbitrary discrimination, and wage rigidities.

Often, these barriers constitute market imperfections. When such imperfections exist, a rearrangement of resources can result in greater output. Other barriers exist because the costs of removing an employment barrier exceed the gains from a better employee-job match. For instance, suppose that if an unemployed, skilled electrician were to obtain an unfilled job, total output would increase by $3,000 monthly. However, one of the barriers described above prevented the match. If the barriers could be eliminated at a cost of less than $3,000 per month, the barrier would constitute a market imperfection. Since the removal of barriers caused by market imperfections can result in greater social output, the case for removing such barriers may be strong. Whether or not job barriers are market imperfections, they are important to understanding why many individuals cannot get better jobs.

Lack of Knowledge. Individuals may be earning a poverty wage because they do not know of better opportunities available to them, even though the cost of obtaining better knowledge may be low. Lack of knowledge can be a particular problem to poor workers lacking access to suburban labor markets where the opportunities are growing most rapidly. Lack of knowledge can also explain why individuals fail to acquire human capital. For instance, a high school student may not realize the loss in future income that results from dropping out. Poor counseling about future opportunities or a lack of role models to illustrate benefits of education undoubtedly contribute to lack of knowledge.

Many observers have presented evidence that blacks living in segregated areas of inner cities may lack information about jobs in the suburbs. Since job growth is fastest in the suburbs, this lack of knowledge can be a serious problem. Employment information services are designed to overcome information imperfections. However, information about most jobs is not widely disseminated.

Geographic Immobility.   The ideal labor market is usually described as an environment in which individuals can easily move from one area to another to take advantage of opportunities. However, some individuals may be bound to areas of low opportunity and, therefore, they will be unable to take advantage of opportunities elsewhere. For instance, unemployed workers may realize that better opportunities exist elsewhere, but they may be unable to relocate because of an inability to sell their houses, lack of funds to move, concern about losing welfare benefits, and so forth. Fear of losing welfare benefits that may tie a family to an area is a clear market imperfection. Factors that are often considered noneconomic, such as family and social ties to the community, may also raise the cost of relocation substantially. Illegal immigrants may feel tied to a job and area because of fear that their employers would report them to immigration authorities or that they would be conspicuous if they moved to another area.

Arbitrary Discrimination.   When an individual's opportunities are restricted or when pay is lowered for reasons that should be irrelevant to market processes, then discrimination can contribute to the problem of poverty. An individual may possess the skills and knowledge to do a job, but an employer may simply have a preference not to hire that person. Race, ethnicity, and gender are the main types of discrimination of concern to policy makers. However, cultural discrimination may also be a more subtle market imperfection. For instance, employers may believe they do not discriminate against blacks, but they may choose not to hire anyone with black diction or related mannerisms, even if such behaviors were irrelevant to doing the job. Discrimination against fat and/or ugly people may also affect a portion of the poor population.

Some free-market economists do not believe that discrimination would be a long-term problem in competitive economies. They believe that in a purely competitive labor market, employers would have to bear the cost of discrimination. For instance, if the most productive worker who applied for a job were black and the employer chose to hire someone else (indulging a "taste for discrimination"), then the firm would earn less profits than if the most qualified individual were hired. In such cases, employers bear a cost for discriminating. If discriminating employers sold their output in a perfectly competitive market and other firms did not discriminate, the higher cost of arbitrary discrimination would render the firm's product uncompetitive. Thus, arbitrary discrimination is a behavior that could not survive in a perfectly competitive economy in the long run.

In practice, however, the U.S. economy is not perfectly competitive, so there is ample room for discrimination. Managers and personnel officers of large private and public enterprises may discriminate at no cost to themselves in the short run. Even in the long run, discrimination may not noticeably affect the efficiency of the unit they manage. Many businesses have a degree of monopoly power, so a taste for discrimination may be indulged without creating a threat to the firm's existence from competitors. However, if a monopolist hires a less productive worker in order to satisfy a desire to discriminate, it will reduce profits. But most important, the concept of "the most qualified" job applicant has limited meaning for most positions. Although, theoretically, there may be one best worker, employers seldom find it useful to spend the resources to determine the best employee. Many, perhaps most, labor markets are characterized by an excess of nearly equally qualified prospective employees at the prevailing wage. To the extent that there are several persons equally capable of performing a job, there is potential to engage in discrimination at almost no cost to the employer. Wage rigidities discussed below contribute to the existence of an excess of qualified workers at the prevailing wage.

Wages Rigidities.   Impediments to the movement of wages can contribute to unemployment and poverty. Frequently, high-paying occupations maintain above-equilibrium wages through union rules, institutional customs, or political muscle. To the extent that the poor are locked out of these jobs, poverty escape routes are limited.

Minimum-wage laws are sometimes cited as examples of labor-market imperfections that hurt employment prospects of the poor. However, whether minimum-wage laws hurt or help the poor is a matter of debate. In order to understand the issue, assume that only poor or near-poor workers have minimum-wage jobs.[1] If the minimum wage were fixed by law at $3.35 per hour, then workers with productivity levels below that wage would be unemployed. Thus, lowering or abolishing minimum-wage laws would result in increased employment levels. Union contracts have similar consequences, although they fix the wage above the minimum.

---

[1] This assumption is, in fact, at variance with reality because many minimum-wage jobs are held by individuals in which other family members work in well-paying jobs. Of the nearly 4 million workers currently earning minimum wages, less than 10 percent are the head of a household below the poverty threshold.

However, many economists believe that the minimum wage may reduce poverty. A decline or removal of the minimum wage has two important consequences: one would tend to hurt the poor and the other consequence would help the poor. First, individuals earning at or near the minimum-wage level could experience a decrease in income. Not all minimum-wage workers would experience such a decrease, but some would. Second, previously unemployed individuals would get jobs at the lower wage. The total impact of a reduction in the minimum wage would depend upon which of the two countervailing tendencies is greatest—the decline in income or the increase in employment. The outcome in turn, depends upon how responsive employers' demand for labor is to a fall in the wage rate.

The impact of reducing the minimum wage can be analyzed with reference to Figure 8–3. Assume that only poverty-level families are affected by changes in the minimum wage. Although this is not a completely realistic assumption, a typical family supported by one full-time and one part-time worker both earning the minimum wage could easily be at or near the poverty level. The total income of minimum-wage level workers as a group would be $3.35 times the number employed. Employers would hire E at that wage rate. Total wages would equal $2.75 \cdot E'$ in the absence of a minimum wage. Which total income level is larger? The answer depends upon whether the percentage decrease in the minimum wage was larger or smaller than the percentage increase in employment.[2] If the elasticity of demand for labor is less than 1, then the total income from jobs that pay between the minimum wage and the equilibrium wage will decrease if the wage falls from $3.35 to $2.75.

Empirical evidence suggests that the elasticity of demand for labor is less than 1 (Hamermesh, 1986, p. 452). In other words, a 10-percent increase in the wage would result in a less than 10-percent decrease in the quantity of labor demanded. Consequently, a decline in the minimum wage would probably result in a decline in income of workers earning the minimum wage. Workers earning slightly above the minimum wage may also be adversely affected because wages in related markets could affect one another. However, the above discussion should not be interpreted to imply that the wage bill paid to minimum-wage workers should be the sole

---

[2] A simple formula for the elasticity of demand for labor is:

$$Ed = (\Delta E/E_1) \div (\Delta W/W_1)$$

where E is employment at the start of period, ΔE is the change in employment, and W and ΔW are the original wage and the change in wages. Thus, if the percentage change in the wage rate is greater than the percentage change in employment, the elasticity of demand will be less than 1.

FIGURE 8–3   The Effect of Minimum Wage

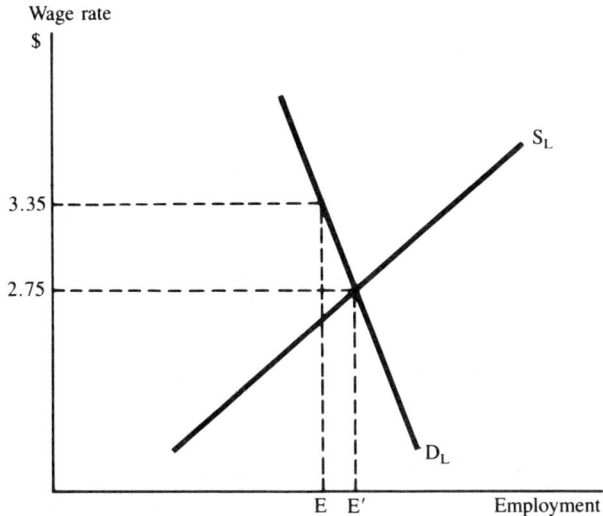

The effect of a decline in the minimum wage on the total wage bill depends upon the responsiveness of the demand for labor to a drop in the wage.

criterion in determining the minimum wage. Other factors such as which workers will lose their jobs if the minimum wage is increased and the effects on consumers must be considered in any such value judgement.

Cultural and Behavioral Traits

Most of the causes of poverty discussed above focused on the operation of the labor market. Poverty was attributed to the inability to sell labor in sufficient quantity or for a sufficiently high wage. This section examines cultural patterns that may complement labor-market perspectives. The poor may have a "culture of poverty" that contributes to and perpetuates poverty. This controversial view is that poverty can be attributed to the way the poor behave. One of the most important behavioral traits that distinguishes the poor, according to Banfield (1968), is time preference:

> At the present-oriented end of the scale, the lower-class individual lives from moment-to-moment. If he has any awareness of a future, it is of something fixed, fated, beyond his control: Things happen to him; he does not make them happen. Impulse governs his behavior either because he cannot disci-

pline himself to sacrifice a present for a future satisfaction, or because he has no sense of the future. (p. 53)

Banfield also attributed feeling of self-contempt and self-devaluation to lower-class individuals. Many psychologists believe that such feelings can result in self-destructive behavior that validates the feelings of low self-esteem. This dysfunctional attitude manifests itself in unsatisfactory work performance, lack of savings, wasteful consumption, and other behaviors that lead to poverty.

Family instability is a behavioral characteristic that has been seen as a cause of poverty. Moynihan (1965) stressed the association of poverty with female-headed black families. Since his initial description of the family structure–poverty link, the portion of female-headed households in the U.S. population has increased dramatically to about 20 percent of all families. Improvements in labor-market conditions may not benefit some female-headed households because family responsibilities prevent the mother from working. Other observers have suggested that female-headed households lack the essential male role models. The absence of a father or father figure is detrimental to the socialization of children (Guilder, 1981).

Welfare Dependency. Welfare dependency occurs when individuals become dependent on public support, thus, perpetuating poverty. Welfare dependency has been attributed both to growing up in environments where welfare is a way of life and to the incentive system created by welfare programs. It has been claimed that individuals raised in families receiving welfare view receiving public support as a normal and acceptable lifestyle. If a high percentage of the neighbors receive assistance, this view will be reinforced. Therefore, individuals may not try to become self-sufficient by taking advantage of educational, employment, or other self-help opportunities. Furthermore, being unemployed, receiving public assistance, or dropping out of high school are sources of shame in many middle-class communities. But, in urban poverty areas, such behaviors may not be viewed as deviant. Leaving school or bearing a child may be viewed as an early sign of independence and adulthood. Obviously, such psychological orientations can contribute to the problem of welfare dependency. Families that have received public assistance for more than one generation are often cited as examples where upbringing has encouraged welfare dependence.

The incentive system created by the availability of public assistance may also discourage work effort and, thus, help perpetuate poverty. Many critics of the welfare system claim that a woman will choose to have

TABLE 8–5 AFDC Payments by Family Size: Ohio, 1989 (single mother with children)

Number of Children	Monthly AFDC Payment	Marginal Revenue per Child
1	$263	—
2	321	58
3	397	76
4	464	67
5	517	53

SOURCE: Montgomery County, Ohio. Children and Family Services.

extra children in order to receive more state support. Table 8–5 shows the incentives for bearing extra children in Ohio. The increments do not appear to be sufficiently high to allow a surplus for a parent after paying normal child-care costs. Although welfare dependency is a widely expressed view of poverty's cause, empirical evidence in support of the proposition is weak.

A Critique   Critics of cultural and behavioral explanations of poverty suggest that they amount to "blaming the victim." The dysfunctional behaviors that constitute the culture of poverty are either (1) nonexistent or (2) necessary adaptations to poverty. Regarding the first point, most poor families have working members, try to help themselves, encourage their children to perform well in school, and, in general, behave as any other family. Furthermore scholars contend that the welfare status of children and parents are only weakly linked and that psychological orientations of welfare recipients do not differ from nonrecipients. Although some poor persons may have counterproductive behaviors, so do individuals in any income social class. Regarding the second point, the poor may use the welfare system just as the rich use the federal tax system. Thus, an individual may refuse work to retain medical coverage, but this is similar to physicians having conventions in the Bahamas to reduce their tax liabilities. The behaviors associated with poverty are often rational responses to a tough life situation.

Structuralist

A final set of explanations for poverty may be termed structuralist theories. This approach attributes poverty to the structure of the economy and suggests that poverty cannot be eliminated without major structural changes. Many Marxists express a structuralist view when they argue that a large pool of poor individuals depress wage levels, not only at the low end of the wage scale, but also in almost all jobs because differentials in pay must be maintained to encourage work effort and to reinforce the status of particular jobs. This perspective may be termed the "reserve army of the unemployed" function of poverty. The fear of becoming poor reinforces workplace discipline and, thus, increases output among the nonpoor. According to this view poverty is necessary to the functioning of the capitalist system.

Structuralists also point out that many social service institutions that support middle-income and upper-income families are based upon the existence of poverty. Along these same lines, many structuralists view antipoverty programs as serving a social-control function. The welfare system maintains downward pressure on wages, particularly at the low end of the income scale, and, on the other hand, creates jobs in the welfare bureaucracy for the benefit of middle-class members.

POVERTY'S SPATIAL DIMENSIONS

The spatial distribution of poverty is quite uneven. Table 8–6 indicates that regional variations in the rate of poverty are not large, although the South has the highest poverty rate at about 13 percent, and the Northeast has the lowest poverty rate, 9.1 percent. These differences, however, are small compared to intraregional differences. Table 8–7 shows that the incidence of poverty is greatest in central cities and nonmetropolitan areas. Within central cities, the poverty rate approaches 40 percent in areas designated "poverty areas"—census tracks in which 20 percent or

TABLE 8–6   Poverty Rates by Region, 1987

	All Races	White	Black	Hispanic
Northeast	9.1%	7.2%	26.3%	34.9%
Midwest	10.2	7.7	33.6	26.7
South	12.8	8.8	27.0	29.4
West	9.9	8.8	21.3	24.0

SOURCE: Calculated from *Current Population Reports,* series p. 60, no. 157, U.S. Department of Commerce, Bureau of the Census, 1988.

TABLE 8–7   Poverty by Type of Area, 1985 (in thousands)

Residence	Number of Persons	Percentage
All races		
Central cities	14,177	19.0%
Central-city poverty areas	7,837	37.5
Suburbs	9,097	8.4
Nonmetropolitan areas	9,789	18.3
Nonmetropolitan, Farm		12.6

Note: Poverty areas are census tracts in which 20 percent or more of the residents are below the poverty level. The standard errors for the figures in the table are high: 300,000 to 400,000, or 0.2 to 0.7 points in the rates.

source: National Research Council, "Committee Report," National Academy Press, Washington, D.C., 1988, p. 17.

more of the residents are below the poverty level. Nonmetropolitan poverty rates are comparable to central-city rates. The poverty rate for farm families is significantly lower than the overall nonmetropolitan poverty rate and probably reflects the considerable assets in the form of capital and land of farm owners.

Urban Poverty

Over 40 percent of poor persons live in central cities, and nearly 20 percent of all central-city residents are poor. Furthermore, within central cities, poverty has been increasingly concentrated in particular hard-core neighborhoods. Urban poverty has several characteristics that make it a unique and, thus far, an intractable social problem.

First, the high concentration of poor persons in one geographic area increases the potential that discontent will result in riots or other social disruptions. Second, the urban concentration of many poor persons may contribute to their political power because poor political districts can elect representatives and they may be in a position to influence the election of state and federal public officials. Political power can result in greater public attention and policy concern for the poor. Third, in major metropolitan areas, the poor often live near areas of affluence. A bag lady in Washington, D.C., was reported to have lived within a few hundred yards of the White House for years. Although most upper-income metropolitan residents live in income-segregated suburbs, they often work near poor areas. Negative spillovers from poverty areas threaten the lifestyle of affluent residents and depress nearby property values. The proximity of rich and poor may cause the wealthy to feel that they need a buffer and may cause the poor to feel more deprived because of their more clearly perceived, lower relative position. Finally, the cramped and crowded conditions of urban poverty often make poverty harder to bear. Urban poor are most likely to suffer negative spillover effects from the adverse behavior of other poor persons. Living conditions of the urban poor in many of the less-developed countries have been called the worst environments in the world because of the combination of poverty, crowding, and ugliness.

Several factors contribute to the concentration of poverty in central cities and to particular neighborhoods within central cities.

Migration. Central cities have been a point of departure for immigrants coming to the United States from abroad and for U.S. citizens who were forced out of agriculture, particularly during the era of agricultural mechanization. A large portion of these immigrants lacked skills needed to obtain high-paying jobs. These individuals have traditionally remained in cities as they learned skills needed to secure better-paying jobs. As their incomes rose, the migrants typically moved to the suburbs. Thus, central cities tended to attract families during the low-income phase of their earnings cycle. The role of cities in providing basic skills needed for upward mobility has been termed "the city as a sandbox." (Just as a sandbox is a training ground for children, the city trains workers in urban skills.)

Today, central cities are less likely to be seen as places to seek opportunity, but migrants continue to make their initial residence in cities, possibly because it is more difficult to search for appropriate housing and jobs in small towns and suburbs or because of beaten-path effects. Migration among the poor tends to be from one central city to another. Thus, there is little reverse migration to rural areas or suburbs that would reduce central-city poverty rates.

Employment Shifts. The employment base of central cities has grown very slowly during the 1980s relative to suburban areas. Slow job growth has hampered opportunities. Just as important, the composition of the urban employment base has shifted away from blue-collar manufacturing jobs towards both high- and low-skill service jobs. Manufacturing jobs tended to require little formal education while providing sufficient income to support a family's move into the middle class. Today, the urban job-growth areas that allow for a middle-class income tend to be in service occupations that require language, education, or social skills that many of the urban poor do not possess.

The gap between the educational attainment of central-city residents and the kinds of jobs available in central cities is contributing to a mismatch (Kasarda, 1985). Table 8–8 shows employment changes between 1959 and 1985 in industries classified according to the number of years of

TABLE 8–8 Central-City Jobs in Industries by Mean Education of Employees, 1962

City and Educational Mean of Industry	Change in Number of Jobs (000's)	
	1959–1970	*1970–1985*
New York		
Less than high school	−9	−504
Some higher education	320	268
Philadelphia		
Less than high school	−36	−187
Some higher education	70	51
Boston		
Less than high school	−1	−52
Some higher education	68	76
Baltimore		
Less than high school	−29	−75
Some higher education	31	34
St. Louis		
Less than high school	−11	−93
Some higher education	37	−1
Atlanta		
Less than high school	49	3
Some higher education	50	51
Houston		
Less than high school	156	219
Some higher education	85	224
Denver		
Less than high school	28	10
Some higher education	30	60
San Francisco		
Less than high school	12	19
Some higher education	56	80

SOURCE: John D. Kasarda, "Jobs, Migration, and Emerging Urban Mismatches," in *Urban Change and Poverty,* Michael G. H. McGeary and Laurence E. Lynn, eds. National Academy Press, Washington, D.C., 1988, p. 177. Reprinted from "Urban Change and Poverty," with permission from the National Academy Press, Washington, D.C.

schooling completed by the job holders in nine representative cities. Industries were classified based upon mean educational attainment in 1962. The implication is that, for most northeastern and north central cities, jobs in industries that had less than high school education requirements (in 1962) were declining significantly. The industries posting employment increases employed persons with average educational levels that included some higher education (junior college, postsecondary technical schools, college, etc.). Cities in the South and West tended to have job growth in industries where the average employee had less than a high school education, although the most rapid growth occurred in industries requiring some higher education. The pattern for all nine cities suggests that growth is predominantly in industries tending to hire individuals with some higher education. Similarly, poor children who are traditionally less well-educated are a greatly increasing percentage of all children and especially central-city children.

In contrast to the need for a better-educated central-city work force, demographic groups with traditionally low levels of educational attainment have increased their concentration in central cities. Several reports on the status of education indicate serious problems. A widely publicized report by the Carnegie Foundation (1988) stated:

> We are deeply troubled that a reform movement launched to upgrade the education of all students is irrelevant to many children—largely black and Hispanic—in our urban schools. In almost every big city, dropout rates are high, morale is low, facilities are old and unattractive, and school leadership is crippled by a web of regulations. (p. 2.)

Housing.   The nature of the urban housing stock contributes to central-city poverty concentrations. As metropolitan areas grow, expensive housing tends to be built on the fringe. The housing that the poor can afford has remained predominantly in central cities. Thus, within metropolitan areas, the poor can only afford housing in parts of the central city. Public actions, such as mortgage finance programs, transportation development, and land-use policies, all contribute to this phenomenon. Lack of available housing and/or knowledge of available low-cost housing also prevent families from returning to small towns or rural areas.

Housing discrimination against blacks and fear of discrimination have kept blacks out of suburban areas. Since blacks constitute a low-income group, racial discrimination has the effect of spatially concentrating poverty. Approximately 60 percent of the black poor live in central cities compared with only about 30 percent of white poor. Housing and employment discrimination combine with the lack of available job opportunities in central-city neighborhoods to aggravate the poverty problem. Policies dealing with this issue include improving the ghetto or integrating minorities into the suburbs. These alternatives are addressed in Chapter 11.

Public Services. The provision of public services, including charity and county hospitals, group homes, public transportation, and recreation facilities, may have the effect of attracting or retaining poor in the central city. This point is controversial because some policy analysts have suggested that urban social programs for the poor should be reduced in order to avoid poverty concentrations. However, there is little doubt that central cities have a disproportionate burden in providing poverty-oriented services compared to other cities in a metropolitan area.

Income Inequality

Within urban areas, the incidence of poverty appears to be increasing significantly in some areas while the affluent are locating in other areas. Hence, metropolitan areas are experiencing geographic inequality. Census tracts with high and increasing poverty rates are concentrated within urban areas. Furthermore, the 55 percent of the urban poor living in high-poverty census tract lived in seven large cities: New York, Chicago, Philadelphia, Baltimore, New Orleans, Detroit, and Newark.

In addition to the increased concentration of poverty within central cities, the gap in income between central cities and the surrounding suburbs is significant and has widened in recent years, as indicated in Table 8–9. The city-suburban gap appears to be largest in the Northeast, but it is significant everywhere. These geographic inequalities may create tensions in the future as metropolitan governments make decisions about where to spend funds and for what purposes.

There have been a number of theories about the relationship between income inequality and city size. Although generalizations regarding the impact of population growth on income distribution are empirically tenuous, four hypotheses have been offered to explain the relationship between size and inequality (Nord, 1980).

1. As city size increases, the occupational structure will change so that the gap between the skills of various members of the labor force increases. Consequently, income inequality will increase.

2. Individuals possessing monopoly power will benefit most from urban growth. Since the monopolists are likely to be high-income individuals originally, the effect of increased size will be to increase inequality.

3. Increasing city size is associated with larger average incomes, which tend to reduce inequality.

4. There will be a greater investment in human capital as urban size increases, thus reducing inequality.

The hypotheses do not allow for an overall conclusion regarding the size-inequality relationship, because they point in different directions—hypotheses 1 and 2 imply that increasing population size will increase

TABLE 8–9 Median Household Income by Type of Residence and Region, 1977–1983 (ratio of the local/national median)

Region	Total	All Nonmetropolitan	All SMSAs	SMSAs 1 Million +		SMSAs < 1 Million	
				Cities	Suburbs	Cities	Suburbs
United States							
1977	100%	87%	108%	87%	129%	90%	113%
1980	100	87	108	86	130	90	112
1983	100	85	107	87	131	91	112
Northeast							
1977	105	106	105	78	128	82	118
1980	103	101	103	76	125	83	117
1983	104	100	106	75	132	90	120
Midwest							
1977	105	90	115	86	140	94	123
1980	103	85	115	83	138	96	123
1983	101	86	109	85	131	89	118
South							
1977	91	79	103	93	129	89	103
1980	92	81	101	84	128	89	103
1983	93	78	105	88	135	89	107
West							
1977	103	91	107	95	120	93	107
1980	107	92	112	105	127	92	106
1983	106	92	111	103	127	97	103

SOURCE: U.S. Department of Commerce, Bureau of the Census, *Current Population Survey*, P-60, nos. 117 and 132, 1985.

inequality, while hypotheses 3 and 4 lead to the opposite conclusion. The empirical evidence is also somewhat mixed. It suggests that population growth may reduce inequality in small towns, but in large SMSAs growth may increase inequality.

Underclass

The "underclass" refers to the subgroup of poor who are permanently detached from the mainstream of social and economic life. The behavior of the members of the underclass has been described as deviant, anomic, fatalistic, apathetic, angry, and alienated. These attitudes contribute to the perpetuation of poverty and explain why some members of this population are potentially violent. Periods of high income from criminal activity are not uncommon for some members of the underclass, although the periods of transitory high income usually fail to establish conditions necessary for a higher, stable income.

Auletta (1982) and Harrington (1984) both developed classifications of the underclass. Their descriptions are not identical, but three general types stand out:

1. The passive poor, particularly female-headed welfare families and others dependent upon the welfare system, as well as some alcoholics and drug users.
2. Street criminals and hustlers, including prostitutes, drug dealers, and other members of the hidden economy.
3. The uprooted and traumatized, including bag ladies, the mentally ill, and drifters.

The "underclass" has never been a rigorously-defined concept, and only a minority of the poor are members of the underclass. However, because of their social detachment and the variety of other problems associated with the underclass, they are a special problem associated with urban poverty.

Rural Poverty

In the 1950s and 1960s, rural poverty was viewed as a more urgent problem than urban poverty. Hansen (1970) contended that rural poverty was a cause of migration to cities, thus contributing to congestion, pollution, and related urban problems. There is a clear link between urban problems and rural poverty. Although most of the discussion in this chapter has been devoted to central-city problems, rural poverty has unique aspects. In the United States, isolated rural areas such as Appalachia, predominantly black areas in the South, and western Indian reservations have higher poverty rates than central cities.

Moen (1989) suggested that it is more expensive to provide social services to scattered rural populations, so the rural poor often have few support services such as medical care. The rural poor also have even fewer economic opportunities than urban poor because of their isolation. Furthermore, the rural poor may be less visible, so rural poverty does not draw public notice as readily as urban poverty. However, Moen's analysis led to the conclusion that a better match between education and emerging employment opportunities is the best tactic for fighting poverty in the rural South.

ANTIPOVERTY POLICIES

Solutions to the poverty problem are many and varied. They range from benign neglect to programs calling for massive public intervention. For convenience, solutions will be discussed under six categories: (a) macroeconomic growth, (b) direct job creation, (c) education and training, (d) eliminating market imperfections, (e) income support, and (f) private charity.

No single approach will work for everyone who is poor. For instance, a job-creation program will not help individuals unable to work. For many individuals, elimination of poverty may require a combination of approaches. For instance, education and training efforts may be ineffective unless jobs are available at the completion of the programs. Furthermore, some poverty problems require immediate intervention because of clear and present need. However, permanent solutions are normally long-term in nature. Policy makers, therefore, are not concerned with the single best solution. The more important policy issue is what the best mix of policies is and how to implement that mix.

Macroeconomic Growth

The overall condition of the economy is perhaps the most important set of factors that determines the poverty rate. At any given time, there are many families on the margins of poverty and a change in the economy will move many such families into or out of poverty. The working poor particularly benefit by reductions in the unemployment rate because they are often the last hired and first fired. Furthermore, long-term economic growth has been the main force in raising everyone's living standards, including the poor. In the short run, economic growth alters the income distribution because it helps the unemployed more than those who already have jobs. Therefore, aggregate economic growth may be effective in reducing relative poverty (i.e., increasing the percentage of income going to the lowest one fifth) as well as absolute poverty.

Although growth will primarily improve living standards among individuals willing and able to work, growth also provides more revenues to finance other income-support programs. It is generally believed that, in a very slow-growth or stagnant economy, gains by one group must come at the expense of other groups. Thus, voters will be reluctant to increase social programs when it means actual reductions in living standards for the rest of the population (Thurow, 1984).

Economic growth is the poverty solution most favored by the conservatives in recent years. The *President's Urban Policy Report 1986* stated that strengthening the national economy was the key element in efforts to reduce urban poverty:

> The impact of economic recovery in cities . . . is reflected in the increased family income and reduced poverty of urban residents. The general improvement in the economy has been shared by the poverty population . . . as the economy continues its growth without inflation and as incomes continue to rise, there will be further opportunities for people, particularly poor people, to become permanently strong economically. (p. 25)

Direct Job Creation

One drawback to aggregate economic expansion as a poverty solution is that too much economic stimulation may cause prices and wages to increase in some sectors without sufficiently increasing the number of jobs available to the poor. For instance, during the 1970s, the entire economy was stimulated partly to create jobs for unemployed workers. As a result, wages and prices rose in bottleneck sectors, causing inflation. Direct job creation may avoid the inflationary risks of macroeconomic stimulation. With this approach, the jobs being created are targeted toward low-income individuals or toward regions with high poverty or unemployment rates. Ideally, the targeting will hold down potentially inflationary labor-demand increases in sectors that are at or near full employment.

Direct job creation has been implemented through subsidization of private-sector jobs and through public-sector employment. Subsidies for private-sector jobs are normally targeted towards unemployed workers, and the subsidy has normally been phased out after a training period. A role for the government as a last-resort employer is a frequently proposed direct job-creation program. Currently, the major direct job-creation efforts are state programs that require certain persons to work in exchange for welfare benefits. Job creation may be a secondary objective of many other governmental programs. For instance, some urban programs are not primarily intended to create jobs, but they have the positive consequence of creating jobs. The number of jobs created has been one of several criteria for project approval for some urban programs.

There are two major issues that have arisen in the evaluation of direct job-creation programs. First, are the jobs created worthwhile or are they merely busy work? Organizing useful work is a more difficult management task than may initially appear. Presumably, an organization's essential tasks are already being done prior to a new-job-creation program. Consequently, as new jobs are created, the new activity is likely to be of low priority from the perspective of agency decision makers. It is a short step from creating jobs of low priority to creating "make-work" jobs. If jobs do not produce useful goods and services, the job-creation program will not result in useful output and such programs amount to little more than reclassifying individuals from the unemployed to the employed category. Even worse, make-work jobs may create a cynical work atmosphere where jobs are not treated as important and poor work habits are tolerated by both supervisors and employees. The Comprehensive Employment and Training Act (CETA) included a public job-creation program that was widely criticized as "make work."

Second, it is often difficult to determine when jobs are actually being created or when one worker receives a job that would have existed without the job-creation program. This is termed the displacement issue. Because of the interdependence of the economy, it can be difficult to determine the extent of displacement. Suppose the federal government tried to create jobs by subsidizing a successful new furniture factory that hired 100 previously unemployed youth. Under such circumstances, it cannot be concluded that 100 new jobs were created because the expansion of the subsidized factory may have been at the expense of other furniture plants elsewhere in the country. Even within an organization, suspicion has been raised that subsidized employees have been hired under job-creation programs while the number of nonsubsidized jobs has been correspondingly reduced. When an organization is expanding, it is even more difficult to determine whether displacement has occurred because jobs created by an employment program might have been established in any event. Displacement is a particular problem when one person's employment simply results in someone else's unemployment.

Education and Training

Education and training programs are intended to increase the productivity and, hence, income of workers who are unemployed or employed in low-paying jobs. Education connotes broad-based efforts to improve productivity while training implies more direct assistance such as vocational programs and on-the-job training. In its broadest sense, education can be considered a long-term solution and may include programs for preschool children, such as Head Start.

Training. Currently, the Job Training Partnership Act is the main program for providing training to unemployed adults. The act authorized the creation of local Private Industry Councils (PICs) to determine how training can best match local labor-market requirements.

Education and training programs can be very useful in alleviating structural unemployment. Structural unemployment occurs when there are jobs available, but the unemployed are unable to qualify for the available positions. Education and training programs are less effective when the overall economy is performing at below the full employment level. If aggregate demand is so low that there just are not enough jobs to go around, unemployment will persist even if all potential workers are highly skilled.

Manpower training programs are somewhat easier to evaluate than other antipoverty programs because program costs are reasonably clear and the benefits can be calculated by measuring the increased earnings of individuals graduating from such programs compared to earnings of a control group. The earning in future years should, of course, be discounted to measure the present value of benefits. Thus, training programs can be evaluated on a cost-benefit basis. Many evaluation studies have registered mixed results. However, a few overall conclusions can be made:

1. Displaced workers—experienced workers with an employment history—are easier to place than long-term unemployed and inexperienced youth.

2. Very successful programs are difficult to replicate, suggesting that intangible factors such as the personality of a trainer or the quality of the individuals receiving training may be a significant and variable factor.

3. Individuals from the more disadvantaged groups—women and blacks—have the highest cost-benefit ratios.

4. Classroom training and on-the-job training have been about equally effective.

Academic Education. Among the long-run efforts to alleviate poverty, academic education may have a role equal to or greater than vocational training. Table 8–8 clearly indicates the trend towards employment in industries that have better-educated work forces. Yet, progress in improving educational achievements has been slow, particularly for poor children. *The President's National Urban Policy Report, 1988* concluded that: "The failure to educate adequately center city children is a shortcoming of such magnitude that many people have simply written off city schools as little more than human storehouses to keep young people off the streets" (p. 92).

The difficulty of the problem can be seen by comparing an outline of recommendations suggested by the U.S. Department of Education in *Schools That Work: Educating Disadvantaged Children* (Table 8–10) with the resources available to a typical school to accomplish these goals. Either existing resources are going to have to be allocated from elsewhere or substantial additional resources must be allocated.

Another approach to improving urban education is to restructure incentives so that schools will operate more like businesses and students or their parents will have greater choice in determining what schools they should attend. In particular, a school voucher system has been proposed whereby parents may send their children to the school they believe will serve them best. In theory, poor schools will not attract students, and therefore, the school will be required to improve to survive. Although variations on the voucher theme have been implemented, it is too soon to evaluate the programs.

Eliminating Labor-Market Imperfections

Market imperfections occur when the market does not behave as described by the competitive model. Efforts to overcome racial and gender discrimination are the most visible and controversial programs to eliminate market imperfections. Actions to eliminate discrimination have been initiated and pursued with varying degrees of effort at all levels of government and by private businesses. Efforts to improve market operations and reduce discrimination include outreach and widely advertised job notices to break up "old boy" networks, personnel review boards to overcome discriminatory results from certain tests, numerical goals, and, occasionally, quotas.

Discrimination is generally considered to be dysfunctional. However, some economists have argued that discrimination on the basis of race, gender, and other seemingly irrelevant factors may actually be efficient. They suggest that although these factors are irrelevant in and of themselves, they are associated or correlated with factors that are relevant. Therefore, a firm may minimize costs of selecting employees by using factors that are irrelevant by themselves but are correlated with relevant factors.

The effectiveness of efforts to reduce discrimination have received mixed evaluations. Some efforts have been perceived as reverse discrimination and have been very unpopular. Other critics of antidiscrimination efforts have contended that, because of aggressive efforts to advance blacks and women, programs have created the perception that all blacks and women in high positions are beneficiaries of affirmative action and would not have attained their positions if they had to compete on an equal basis. Even though such perceptions may be unsupported by evidence,

TABLE 8–10   Educating Disadvantaged Children

Schools

1. Mobilize students, staff, and parents around a vision of a school in which all students can achieve.
2. Create an orderly and safe school environment by setting high standards for discipline and attendance.
3. Help students acquire the habits and attitudes necessary for progress in school and in later life.
4. Provide a challenging academic curriculum.
5. Tailor instructional strategies to the needs of disadvantaged children.
6. Help students with limited English proficiency become proficient and comfortable in the English language—speaking, reading, and writing—as soon as possible.
7. Focus early-childhood programs on disadvantaged children to increase their chances for success.
8. Reach out to help parents take part in educating their children.

Parents, Guardians, and Communities

9. Instill in children the values they need to progress in school and throughout life.
10. Demand the best from children and show this concern by supervising children's progress.
11. Get involved with the schools and with children's education outside school.
12. Invest in the education and future success of disadvantaged children.

Local, State, and Federal Government

13. Ensure that education reforms make a difference for disadvantaged students.
14. Give local school officials sufficient authority to act quickly, decisively, and creatively to improve schools and hold them accountable for results.
15. Assess the results of school practices, paying special attention to the impact of reform on disadvantaged students.
16. Support improved education for disadvantaged students through supplementary and compensatory programs, leadership, and research.

SOURCE: U.S. Department of Education, *Schools That Work: Educating Disadvantaged Children* (Washington, D.C.: U.S. Department of Education, 1986), p. vii.

---

they affect the environment in which individuals operate. Of course, no serious affirmative-action plan has proposed promoting unqualified applicants, but the perception may create further problems.

Geographic immobilities can also create market imperfections. The federal income tax deduction of moving expenses is a type of mobility policy because it is intended to increase geographic mobility. Some federal efforts have also been directed toward improving the geographic mobility of unemployed workers living in distressed areas. Relocation assistance programs for workers who have lost jobs due to foreign imports have (The Trade Adjustment Act) been implemented, but at very modest levels of funding.

Income Support

The policies discussed thus far have emphasized improving the ability of individuals to earn income. The policies will help individuals who are willing and able to work. However, a substantial portion of the poor work already, but they remain poor because their earnings are insufficient. Many of these individuals may require more direct income assistance to eliminate their poverty. Furthermore, some individuals, including the disabled, elderly, and mothers with young children (although there is substantial controversy about the extent that women with young children should work), may have no viable wage earner in the household; therefore, transfers are their only source of income.

It is difficult to defend a sharp distinction between income-support programs and other governmental programs, because all governmental programs support somebody's income. Numerous programs support middle- and upper-class families, including Social Security and Medicare, which help the elderly of all income levels. Unemployment compensation and agricultural subsidies assist the wealthy as well as the poor. For purposes of our discussion, the focus will be on means-tested programs for which the recipient must have either low income and/or wealth (assets) to qualify. Table 8–11 shows some of the major means-tested programs. Means-tested programs are financed by a crazy quilt of federal, state, and local matching arrangements. Currently, the federal government pays about three quarters of the cost of means-tested programs. However, the percentages vary widely among programs.

The in-kind transfer programs are principally intended to help the poor. However, it is apparent that Medicaid, food stamps, and housing assistance all have well-defined and politically powerful producer interest groups that are also assisted by the programs. Medicaid programs support demand for medical services, food stamps (a program administered through the Department of Agriculture) supports food prices, and housing programs (run primarily by the Department of Housing and Urban Development) benefit the construction industry. The nonpoor political support helps maintain these programs in tough budget battles.

The largest cash-transfer programs are Aid to Families with Dependent Children (AFDC) and Supplemental Security Insurance (SSI). These programs are intended to support the most vulnerable among the poor. AFDC is probably the least popular of all of the income-support programs because the public believes that welfare mothers have large numbers of

TABLE 8–11   Major Means-Tested Welfare Programs

Program	Purpose
Aid to Families with Dependent Children	Designed to assist families with income insufficient to support their children. The family may or may not include a two-parent family depending upon state regulations.
Medicaid	Designed to provide medical care for elderly and disabled.
Food Stamps and National School Lunch Program	Both programs are designed to supplement the food budget of low-income families. The program also helps support agricultural prices.
Housing Assistance	Includes a variety of programs designed to provide minimum housing for low-income families.
General Assistance	Designed by states to provide assistance to individuals not eligible for other programs. For instance, a 35-year-old male indigent might receive general assistance.
Supplement Security Income	Designed to assist low-income blind, aged, or disabled.

out-of-wedlock children in order to support their expensive lifestyle. The term "welfare queen" is the term given to such women. The typical AFDC recipient family has two children. In spite of the political liability of the welfare-queen image associated with AFDC, it is impractical to separate assistance for children from family assistance. SSI primarily provides support for disabled workers and families of deceased workers.

In-kind versus Cash Transfers. Economists have long asked whether it is best to assist the poor through in-kind assistance or through money transfers of equal value. The traditional answer has been that cash transfers are preferable to in-kind support, assuming that: (1) the recipients are knowledgeable about what brings them utility and (2) the purpose of the transfer is to increase the utility of the recipients. The argument in favor of cash transfers is as follows. Suppose a poor person received $100 worth of food. Assuming the cost of the food to society were $100, then the government would be indifferent to the form of the subsidy—cash or in-kind. If transfer recipients received cash rather than $100 worth of commodities, they would either (1) spend all the cash on food or (2) spend it on other things, possibly including some food. With the cash they could do no worse than under the in-kind transfer program by spending all their income on food (option 1). If they used the cash to purchase any other combination of goods (option 2), the choice indicates it would make them better off than they would have been with $100 worth of food.

The rebuttal in support of in-kind transfers is based on two arguments. First, individuals may not know how to manage their money, and in-kind transfers may prevent spending on frivolities or harmful goods. Second, governments may attempt to achieve objectives other than maximizing the utility of program recipients. For instance, voters may feel better knowing that individuals have certain levels of food, housing, and medical care even if the recipient's utility is not as high as would be the case with a cash transfer. Assistance for producers of specific commodities is another objective of in-kind transfer programs. In-kind assistance may also help protect some children from unsound parental spending.

Child-Support Enforcement.   Part of the reason for the high incidence of poverty among women with children is that fathers have failed to pay child support even when they have been required by courts to pay support as part of separation or divorce settlements. Fathers of children born out of wedlock may have court-ordered support obligations as well. A problem has been that many fathers have defaulted on their obligations, and enforcement has not been strong enough to ensure support payments. States, under pressure from several federal mandates, have tightened and coordinated enforcement of child-support orders, particularly when the children are receiving public assistance. In many cases, support payments may be deducted directly from the parent's pay.

Robins (1986) presented empirical estimates to show that child-support enforcement may reduce welfare costs, but it is unlikely to have a major effect on either welfare dependency or poverty rates.

Guaranteed Annual-Income Plans.   Many observers have proposed guaranteed income plans as a strategy against poverty. Initially, flat guaranteed-annual-income plans were proposed. A threshold level of income was set according to family size. If a family earned below that amount, the federal government would transfer the difference to the family. For instance, if a family earned $5,000 and the guaranteed-annual-income level were $8,000, the government would transfer $3,000 to the family. The problem with this flat guaranteed income is that anyone who could earn near the threshold level would have little or no incentive to work, knowing the government would maintain family income at the threshold even if no one worked. Essentially, the "tax" or take-back rate on any earned income by families receiving assistance would be 100 percent.

The negative income tax (NIT) has been proposed as an alternative to the guaranteed income. NIT could provide an income floor and maintain work incentives. Under NIT proposals, individuals would be allowed to keep a portion of the extra income they earn. The marginal take-back rate, which was 100 percent under the flat system, can be reduced to some fraction of earned income.

Negative income tax proposals have three elements:

1. A guaranteed floor (F) or a level above which total income will be maintained.
2. A take-back rate (t) or a rate at which government transfers will be reduced per dollar of nontransfer income.
3. A break-even level above which government transfers will cease and the family will pay taxes rather than receive income support.

Once two of the three values are determined, so is the third. For example, if the income floor were $8,000 and the marginal take-back rate were 50 percent, then a family receiving a total $16,000 from nonguaranteed annual income sources would have the full $8,000 taken back.

An alternative way of expressing the plan is:

$$ATI = F + (1 - t)\,BTI \qquad (2)$$

where: ATI = After transfer income,
$\ F$ = Guaranteed income floor,
$\ t$ = Take-back rate, and
$\ BTI$ = Before transfer income (i.e., income from sources outside of the NIT plan).

Notice that the zero payment level occurs when ATI equals BTI. If F is set at $8,000, and t at .50, then when BTI is $16,000, ATI would equal $16,000 and the full value of the guaranteed floor would be taken back.

The guaranteed annual income has been strongly supported by both liberals and conservatives. One advantage is that it is simpler to administer than the variety of in-kind and other means-tested transfer programs. As the name implies, it could be administered through the Internal Revenue Service. It would also give the poor more choices about how to spend. If the NIT were to replace all the other income-support programs, then the net cost of the program could be politically acceptable. However, it is difficult to envision the NIT substituting for psychological, educational, and medical services provided by the government. Also, a federal NIT program would reduce the perverse relocation incentives and inequities in the state-managed assistance programs.

The arguments in favor of a negative income tax are strong. Both Presidents Nixon and Carter suggested a negative-income-tax type of plan as part of their welfare-reform proposals. However, the NIT has a major problem. Any proposal that has a guaranteed income floor near the poverty level and a reasonable take-back rate results in excessive transfers to families that are not poor. For instance, in our example, a $8,000 annual floor ($8,000 is significantly below the current poverty line for a family of four) and a 50 percent take-back rate (a very steep marginal tax rate) would result in transfers to families earning as much as $15,999 annually. Many voters would object to assistance to families earning that amount. Efforts to lower the income floor further below the poverty threshold, say to $5,000, would make the plan appear inadequate while take-back rates of over 50 percent would pose serious work disincentives.

The case for the negative income tax was further weakened by a series of experiments conducted during the 1970s (U.S. Department of Health and Human Services, 1983). Supporters of NIT believed that an income guarantee would not affect the willingness of recipients to work and would stabilize families (compared to alternative welfare programs where benefits increased if the father were absent). Experiments were conducted for a variety of benefit levels and take-back rates. The experiments showed that the guaranteed-income scheme reduced work effort and did not enhance family stability.

Private Charity: A Thousand Points of Light

Increases in private charity have been advocated as a means of ameliorating the negative impacts of recent reductions in antipoverty outlays. Charity has always been an important, although relatively understudied, aspect of the U.S. welfare support system.

Advocates of private charity claim that it is consistent with the free-market philosophy and involves the donor more directly. When local organizations give money, they are close to the situation, so they are more likely to know what is needed than when federal or state agencies run programs. While almost no one opposes private charity, many believe that it is too uncertain to be a reliable part of the social safety net.

CRITICISMS AND DEFENSES OF WELFARE PROGRAMS

Federal antipoverty programs have been challenged in recent years on two important counts. First, antipoverty programs have been criticized because they are believed to detract from the productive capacity of the economy. Second, many observers believe federal intervention has failed to alleviate poverty and it may even have aggravated the poverty problem.

Overall Economic Efficiency

Do welfare programs designed to assist the poor reduce the level of aggregate economic output and growth? Economists do not have a definitive answer to this question, although it is often the focal point of disagreements regarding the appropriateness of public assistance.

Economists have several theoretical reasons for believing that welfare spending will reduce economic output. First, redistribution of income will require taxing some groups in order to provide assistance for others. Increasing taxes may (although not necessarily) reduce work incentives. Second, potential welfare recipients may reduce their work efforts because of their belief that they will maximize their utility by not working and receiving government assistance rather than working. Incentives that may encourage individuals to act against the public interest have been termed the "moral hazard" problem. Finally, the higher taxes to finance public assistance may discourage, and thus reduce, economic growth. Other individuals might choose not to save and invest, knowing that the welfare system provided a safety net.

However, many observers deny the trade-off between greater economic output on the one hand and assistance to the poor on the other. As Schreiber and Clemmer put it (1982):

> It must be remembered that there is an efficient allocation of resources for every possible distribution of income among members of society. . . . It is both possible and desirable to achieve goals of equity and efficiency simultaneously. (p. 88)

During the 1960s and early 1970s, many public officials denied that the equity-efficiency trade-off was applicable. President Johnson, in particular, convinced citizens that welfare programs contributed to economic growth. It was then argued that many governmental programs designed to reduce poverty would actually increase national output in the long run and maybe even in the short run. Even the nonpoor could benefit from antipoverty programs because of their beneficial effects on efficiency. Training and education for structurally unemployed individuals would increase labor productivity. Nutrition programs for young children would improve their health and work skills in later life. Maintaining a stake in the U.S. economy for all could avoid the costs of crime and other problems associated with alienation. Rebuilding cities was a national goal because it was intended to improve the social infrastructure needed to boost productivity and create a better living environment for everyone. Training and education were viewed as long-run solutions to increase productivity. Even in the short run, public spending on welfare programs was seen as sustaining strong aggregate demand, preventing underconsumption that could retard economic growth and lead to recession.

However, as overall economic growth slowed, the rate of inflation increased, and the federal deficit began to grow, many observers become convinced that there was too much government spending in the economy. Antipoverty programs began to be viewed as a detriment to overall efficiency and to the living standards of the nonpoor. Government spending was seen as contributing to inflation. Inflation, in turn, created distortions, discouraged saving, and retarded economic growth.

Lower productivity also contributed to the economic slowdown. The belief that poor families would work more if welfare benefits were less adequate and that individuals in high tax brackets would increase their savings and investment efforts if marginal tax rates were lower was articulated by President Reagan. This provided a theoretical foundation for the proposition that support for the poor reduced opportunities for the non-poor.

Against this backdrop, the equity-efficiency trade-off was seen as a constraint on the scope of equity-oriented programs. The middle class began to believe that equity programs reduced their standard of living. Some policy makers argued that even the poor would be better off in the long run if the economy could grow faster, and to accomplish this goal, welfare spending would have to be cut.

As a counterpoint, Haveman (1986) attempted to quantify gains from antipoverty programs that accrued to the nonpoor. He concluded that "It would seem difficult to sustain the view that the Great Society initiative has imposed large net losses on the nonpoor. (p. 42)" But many of the impacts of antipoverty programs are hard to quantify, so Haveman's findings are subject to challenge.

Effectiveness of Antipoverty Programs

In addition to being the drag on economic growth and productivity, critics have claimed that the poverty program failed to alleviate poverty. The "War on Poverty" initiated during the mid-1960s was a highly visible effort to reduce poverty. However, the "war" failed to dramatically alleviate poverty. In some instances, it actually increased public awareness of the problem, leaving the impression that the problem was getting worse. Thus, it has been argued that the war on poverty was ineffective.

Supporters of antipoverty programs have challenged the contention that the war on poverty failed. Harrington (1984), one of the architects of the War on Poverty, even challenged the contention that there had in fact been a major effort to reduce poverty:

We must carefully document the fact that the radical and extravagant past . . . never existed. Instead, there was a decent, often timid and under-financed program that had two or three years of hope and well over a decade of impossible problems. (p. 37)

Supporters of the war on poverty also contend that success included the drastic declines in poverty among the elderly (through the Social Security Program) and the prevention of what otherwise would have been a major increase in poverty if the programs had not been in effect. Thus, in the absence of major social-welfare efforts, the rate of poverty would have been worse than the data indicate. Of course, "what would have been" arguments are usually difficult to prove.

Losing Ground. An influential critique of welfare programs has been developed by Murray (1984) in *Losing Ground*. He argued that social policies not only failed to eliminate poverty, but they actually made the problem worse. Efforts to provide more benefits for the poor merely produced more poor, he claimed. Notice that Murray's line of thought is consistent with Forrester's view (see Chapter 6) that cities are counterintuitive systems. Therefore, doing something to directly alleviate a problem may have a result the opposite of what was anticipated.

Murray's main evidence that antipoverty programs aggravate poverty was a correlation between the growth of welfare benefits and the increase in the number of persons receiving welfare. A similar relationship was described between the increased number of female-headed households and AFDC benefits. Murray also showed how a hypothetical couple with a child would have been better off in 1960 staying off welfare with the husband working. However, after changes in the transfer program, by 1980 they would have been better off if the husband left and the woman and child received a variety of other welfare benefits for which they would be eligible. In light of the incentives created by the welfare system, the poor, Murray contended, would behave as any other rational decision maker. That is, the family would break up and the woman would apply for and receive public benefits.

Once a family breaks up, it is more difficult for the woman and her children to climb back into the employment mainstream. Likewise, a man without a family may have less pressing ties to the work force. Thus, in Murray's view, the initial, well-motivated increases in social-welfare programs resulted in family break-up and the perpetuation of poverty.

Murray's data have been challenged by many critics. They pointed out that welfare benefits (in real terms) declined during the 1970s and throughout most of the 1980s, but welfare recipients still increased. Therefore, the correlation between increased welfare expenditures and the number of welfare recipients may be spurious. The supporters of poverty programs also contend that Murray's examples of instances where families would have been better off by going on welfare are carefully selected from the few states that had incentive systems that support his contention. However, they don't represent a realistic overall picture. The findings of Duncan, Hill, and Hoffman (1988), shown in the boxed section, challenge Murray's proposition that welfare causes dependency. The debate continues with both sides presenting statistical evidence that appears to support their case. Murray has struck a theoretical note that warrants consideration, although this thesis has not been proven.

Welfare Dependency: Some Conclusions

Duncan, Hill, and Hoffman reviewed recent literature to determine the extent of the unintended negative results of welfare. In a field where there is considerable speculation, their empirically based findings are welcome:

- "About thirty percent of recipients received welfare for one or two years. . . . The median length of receipt was less than four years. Clearly, long-term welfare usage characterizes only a minority of recipients."

- "Longer-term recipients account for the bulk of individuals receiving welfare at a particular time."

- "Among the recipients who when first on AFDC were 25 years of age or older and had previous work experiences and a high school degree, fewer than one in seven eventually received AFDC for as many as nine years. On the other hand, total duration of welfare receipt is quite long for younger, never-married recipients."

- "Divorce is the most common event associated with the beginning of a period of receipt."

- "That many brushes with the welfare system are short-lived indicates that receiving welfare does not lead inevitably to long-term dependency."

- "Evidence . . . indicates that income transfer programs do indeed reduce labor supply, but estimates vary widely as to the size of the effect."

- "Amounts of AFDC payments are found to have no measurable impact on births to unmarried women and only modest effect on rates of divorce, separation, or female head-of-household status."

- "Women, especially white women, who receive income from welfare feel less in control of their lives and are less oriented towards the future than those not receiving welfare."

- "The majority of daughters who grew up in highly dependent homes did not share the fate of their parents. Only one out of five of the daughters from highly dependent parental families were themselves dependent on AFDC in their early 20s . . . [However] there was a higher incidence of dependence on welfare among women with welfare backgrounds."

- "Programs aired at preventing initial receipt (for example, by reducing the number of out-of-wedlock births or increasing the number of 'at risk' children completing high school) have not proved consistently successful."

SOURCE: G. J. Duncan, M. S. Hill, and S. D. Hoffman, "Welfare Dependence within and across Generations," *Science* 29, January 1988, pp. 467–71. Copyright 1988 by the AAAS. Reprinted by permission.

Reducing the Welfare System. Even if welfare programs in fact do reduce work effort, abolishing them would not necessarily result in a reduction in poverty. Increased work effort may actually increase the rate of poverty. Figure 8–4 can help clarify this seeming paradox. Suppose welfare programs were reduced and consequently the labor supply among a particular class of labor increased from S to S'. The labor supply would increase principally in the lower end of the labor market affecting jobs that paid at or near the minimum wage.

On the one hand, if a minimum wage at MW is an effective floor on wages, then the increase in labor supply will not result in either an increase in the level of employment or a reduction in the wage rate. Unemployment, however, would increase. On the other hand, if the minimum wage were below the equilibrium wage in a particular market or if a minimum wage were not in effect, then the increase in labor supply would cause wages to fall but employment to increase. How much would wages fall and would the fall offset the increase in employment? If the demand for labor is relatively inelastic as some evidence indicates, then the total

FIGURE 8–4   Impact of an Increase in Labor Supply

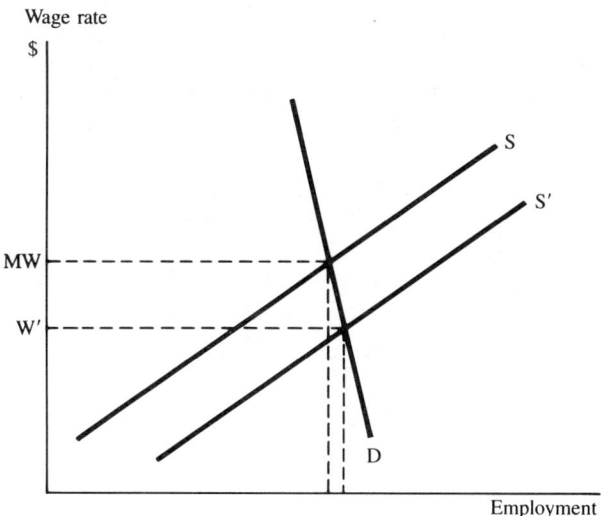

A reduction in welfare payments caused the supply of labor to increase from S to S'. The wage bill for the entire labor class would fall if the demand for labor were inelastic.

of all wages received by the class of workers would decrease. Thus, under some plausible circumstances, increases in labor supply would result in lower take-home pay to workers and increases in the rate of poverty.

Welfare Reform

The AFDC program has recently been reformed to address some of the disincentives problems. First, the bill requires work from welfare recipients. Part-time work is required for mothers (or fathers if the father is present) of school-age children. If the mother has a child who is not in school, there is a work option for which additional benefits can be earned. There is also an education program for teenage mothers. Again, additional benefits can be earned by participating in the program. Second, if an individual receives a job, their medical insurance benefits (Medicaid) will be continued for about six months. The purpose of this proposal is to avoid situations where the mother is actually worse off after getting a job than she would have been had she remained on welfare.

Critics have two concerns with the welfare-reform proposal. First, there is concern that a woman may move from welfare to work as long as the medical insurance benefits continue. Once the medical benefits expire, the woman may conveniently lose her job and return to public assistance. Thus, the intent of making welfare mothers independent may not be realized. A second concern is that the reform may make it easier for other individuals to go on welfare. Policy makers face a dilemma in this regard. Any changes that increase benefits to make it easier to get off public assistance may make it easier to get on public assistance in the first place.

Whether the welfare reforms actually reduce welfare dependency remains to be seen. However, it is doubtful whether the political process will ever result in a denial of benefits to children and their mothers or to individuals who are unable to earn a living. Consequently, policy makers are confronted with the problem of providing adequate public assistance for those who need it while avoiding undue incentives to receive assistance for those who can earn a living.

SUMMARY

The major conceptualizations of poverty are: (1) an absolute standard of deprivation, (2) a culturally or socially determined level of deprivation, and (3) relative economic position. The official U.S. definition of poverty is equal to three times the cost of an economy food plan. It is a fixed, absolute standard since it is adjusted only for increases in the Consumer Price Index.

The number of poor declined through the 1960s but rose again during most of the 1980s. Groups that have experienced particularly high rates of poverty include female-headed households with children, blacks and other minorities, and individuals living in central cities as well as in isolated rural areas. For most individuals, poverty is a transitory state. Families move out of poverty when their circumstances improve. For the underclass, however, poverty tends to be a permanent state.

There are a variety of interrelated reasons for poverty, and these include macroeconomic factors, lack of marketable skills, labor-market imperfections, cultural and behavioral traits, and the structure of capitalist economies. Analysis of the causes of poverty has ideological and policy implications because there is a bridge between theories about what causes poverty and feasible solutions.

Poverty is most pronounced in central cities and selected rural pockets. Factors contributing to central-city poverty include migration patterns, housing availability, discrimination, the distribution of public services, and a mismatch between skills and central-city job opportunities.

There are a variety of approaches to alleviating poverty. Macroeconomic growth and direct job creation help primarily by providing more jobs for the unemployed poor. Education and training programs can alleviate poverty by increasing the productivity of the poor, thus improving their chances of getting existing jobs or better-paying jobs. Eliminating market imperfections can also help the poor get existing jobs. Governmental income-support programs and private charity are also important weapons in the antipoverty arsenal. They can assist individuals who are unable to work.

Welfare programs are among the most controversial of public policies. Federal antipoverty programs have been challenged in recent years on two important counts. First, antipoverty programs have been criticized because they detract from overall economic efficiency. Second, critics claim the efforts have failed to alleviate poverty and may even have aggravated the problem.

REFERENCES

Auletta, Ken. *The Underclass*. New York: Random House, 1982.

Banfield, Edward C. *The Unheavenly City*. Boston: Little, Brown, 1968.

The Carnegie Foundation for the Advancement of Teaching. *An Imperiled Generation: Saving Urban Schools*. Pittsburgh: The Carnegie Foundation, 1988.

Danziger, Sheldon, and Peter Gottschalk, "Work, Poverty, and the Working Poor: Multifaceted Problem." *Monthly Labor Review,* September 1986, pp. 7–25.

————. "Earning Inequality, the Spatial Concentration of Poverty, and the Underclass." *American Economic Review,* May 1987, pp. 211–25.

Gallup, George, Jr. (1987). "Cost of Living," *The Gallup Report,* 248:2–4.

Gramilich, Edward, M., and Deborah S. Laren. "How Widespread Are Income Losses in a Recession?" In *The Social Contract Revisited,* ed. D. L. Dowden. Washington, D.C.: Urban Institute, 1984, pp. 160–70.

Gilder, George. *Wealth and Poverty.* New York: Basic Books, 1981.

Hamermesh, Daniel S., "The Demand for Labor in the Long Run" in *Handbook of Labor Economics.* Eds. Orley Ashenfelter and Richard Layard. Amsterdam: North Holland, 1986.

Hansen, Niles M. *Rural Poverty and the Urban Crisis: A Strategy for Regional Development.* Bloomington, Ind: Indiana University Press, 1970.

Harrington, Michael. *The New American Poverty.* New York: Penguin Books, 1984.

Haveman, Robert A. "What Antipoverty Policies Cost the Nonpoor." *Challenge,* January–February 1986, pp. 37–42.

Hill, Edward W. "Differences in Dependency Rates among States in 1985." *Economic Development Quarterly* 2, no. 3, August 1988, pp. 217–35.

Kasarda, John D. "Jobs, Migration, and Emerging Urban Mismatches." In *Urban Change and Poverty,* ed. Michael G. H. McGeary and Laurence E. Lynn, Jr. Washington, D.C.: National Academy Press, 1985, pp. 148–98.

Levy, Frank. "How Big Is the American Underclass?" University of California at Berkeley, 1976. Duplicated Report.

Moen, Jon R. "Poverty in the South." *Economic Review* 74, no. 1, January–February 1989, pp. 36–46.

Moynihan, Daniel Patrick. *The Negro Family: The Case for National Action.* Washington, D.C.: U.S. Government Printing Office, 1965.

Murray, Charles. *Losing Ground.* New York: Basic Books, 1984.

National Research Council, "Committee Report." Washington, D.C.: National Academy Press, 1988, pp. 1–66.

Nord, Stephen. "Income Inequality and City Size: An Examination of Alternative Hypotheses for Large and Small Cities." *Review of Economics and Statistics* 62, November 1980, pp. 502–8

Robins, Philip K. "Child Support, Welfare Dependency and Poverty." *American Economic Review* 76, no. 4, September 1986, pp. 768–88.

Schiller, Bradley R. *The Economics of Poverty and Discrimination, 5th edition.* Englewood Cliffs, N.J.: Prentice Hall, 1989.

Schreiber, Arthur F., and Richard B. Clemmer. *Economics of Urban Problems: An Introduction.* Boston: Houghton Mifflin, 1982.

Thurow, Lester C. *The Zero-Sum Society: Distribution and the Possibilities for Economic Change.* New York: Basic Books, 1980.

U.S. Department of Education. *Schools That Work: Educating Disadvantaged Youth.* Washington, D.C.: U.S. Department of Education, 1986.

U.S. Department of Health and Human Services, Office of Income Security Policy, *Overview of the Seattle–Denver Income Maintenance Experiment,* Final Report, May 1983.

Wagman, Barnet, and Nancy Folbre. "The Feminization of Inequality: Some New Patterns." *Challenge* 31, no. 6, November–December 1988, pp. 56–59.

Wilson, William Julius. *The Declining Significance of Race: Blacks and Changing American Institutions.* 2nd edition. Chicago: University of Chicago Press, 1980.

————. "The Urban Underclass in Advanced Industrial Society" in Paul E. Peterson (ed.). *The New Urban Reality.* Washington, D.C.: The Brookings Institution, 1985.

Chapter Nine

Interregional Resource and Commodity Flows

Regional economists have traditionally assumed that most resources were free to move among regions within a nation. In contrast, international trade theorists developed models in which factors of production were considered immobile between countries but commodities mobile. In more recent analyses, nations have been studied as regions in a larger global economy. Therefore, the theoretical distinction between regional and international economics has become blurred as international economists have come to appreciate the power and the assumptions of regional models. In practice, the distinction has also faded as groups of nations have formed multinational economic units in which both resources and commodities have relatively free movement. The European Economic Community is a prominent example of a region where economic relationships among countries are becoming more like linkages between regions in a single country.

First, this chapter presents two polar perspectives on interregional flows. One of these models assumes perfect commodity flows but resource immobility. The contrasting model assumes perfect resource mobility. Sections two, three, and four describe the movement of individuals, capital, and ideas, respectively. These sections include realistic discussions of mobility impediments. Finally, policy concerns related to mobility issues are discussed.

MODELS OF REGIONAL FLOWS

Two simple models of regional interaction are developed in this section. The first assumes that resources cannot move from region to region but commodities can. The second model is built on the assumption of perfect resource mobility.

Comparative Advantage

The theory of comparative advantage was developed to show that countries can benefit from trade. The principle of comparative advantage states that if resources cannot move between areas, then residents should specialize in commodities they can make relatively (not absolutely) efficiently. Relative efficiency is determined in terms of opportunity cost—the number of units of a commodity (or service) that must be foregone. It is unlikely that countries would have the same opportunity costs. If countries produce commodities in which they have a comparative advantage and then trade with other countries for other goods, the specialization and trade will benefit both countries.

One of the important implications of the theory of comparative advantages is that trade would still be beneficial even if one country could produce everything cheaper than all other countries. An example of an attorney and a secretary is frequently used to illustrate the theory. Suppose an attorney were better than the secretary at both law practice and typing. Even though the attorney could type faster than the secretary, it would still be more efficient for the attorney to concentrate on the practice of law and hire a typist. The attorney's comparative advantage is legal practice; the secretary's comparative advantage is typing.

An Illustration.   The example in Table 9–1 illustrates how specializing in the product of comparative advantage and trading for other products will increase income. Although the example is described in terms of countries, it is equally applicable to situations where resources are immobile between regions. It assumes that all costs are measured in terms of labor hours, transportation costs are zero, and the opportunity costs do not change as the output changes (constant costs).[1] Table 9–1 shows the amount of labor necessary to produce food and manufactured products in the region and in the rest of the world. Notice that, for simplicity, the rest of the world is being treated as a homogeneous region so large that the world price ratio will not be affected by the small region's output. The region can produce both food and manufactured products at lower labor costs than the rest of the world. However, the opportunity cost of a unit of food in region I is one half a manufactured product. That is, to produce a unit of food domestically, region I must forego one half a manufactured product. A unit of food costs three fourths of a unit of manufactured product in the rest of the world. Therefore, region I has a comparative advantage in food production.

---

[1] The assumption of constant cost is unrealistic but gives rise to a linear production-possibilities curve (see Figure 9–1) which simplifies the analysis.

TABLE 9-1 Production Requirements in Labor

Absolute Cost (necessary labor hours per unit)		
One Unit of	*Region I*	*Rest of World*
Food	1	3
Manufactured product	2	4
Opportunity Cost	*Region I*	*Rest of World*
Cost of one unit of food in terms of a unit of manufactured product foregone	½	¾
Cost of manufactured product in terms of food foregone	2	4/3

In order to determine the gains from specialization and trade, we will first compare production and consumption in region I before and after trade. In the absence of trade, the real wage for an hour's work in region I would be one unit of food or one-half unit of the manufactured product. The real wage in the rest of the world would be one-third unit of food or one-fourth unit of the manufactured output. Suppose region I had 6 million hours of labor available. The production-possibilities curve would be as pictured in Figure 9–1. In the absence of trade, the exact point of production (and consumption) would depend upon choices made by individuals within region I. For instance, they might choose to produce 4 million units of food and 1 million units of manufactured output as indicated by point a. In the absence of trade, the level of production would indicate the consumption possibilities as well.

Now suppose trade is opened between countries and transportation and other transactions costs are negligible. Relative prices in region I will equal relative prices in the rest of the world. Arbitrage will ensure the equalization of prices. Middlemen will buy products where they are cheap and resell them where they are expensive. Since manufactured goods are more expensive relative to food in region I, merchants will transport manufactured products to region I and they will ship food from there to the rest of the world.

Gains from trade can accrue to both residents of region I and to trading partners. Prior to trade, the production-possibilities curve would be identical with the consumption-possibilities curve. But, if region I trades with the rest of the world, the region's consumption possibilities will exceed production possibilities and consumption possibilities. To see this, suppose the region used all its resources to produce 6 million units of food and traded 2 million units of food for manufactured goods. The

FIGURE 9–1   Product and Consumption Possibilities

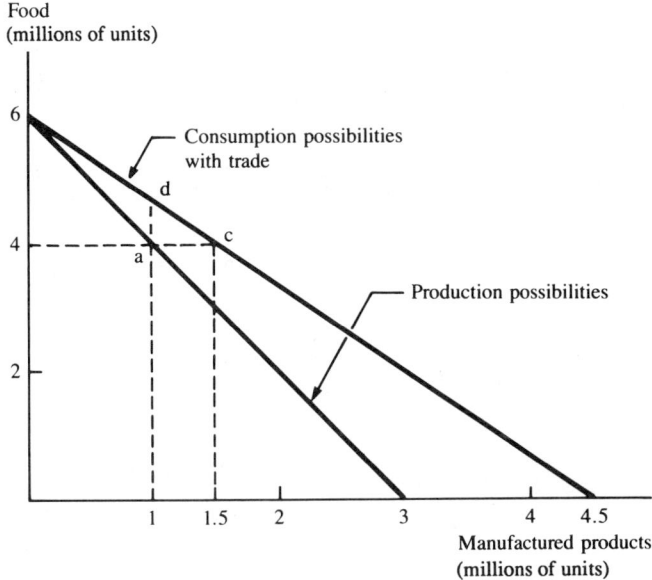

The production-possibility curve can differ from the consumption-possibility curve if trade occurs.

amount of manufactured products that could be purchased with the food would depend upon the terms of trade. Since it was assumed that the small region's output had a negligible effect upon world prices, the terms of trade would reflect the ratio of world prices. Therefore, the region would receive 1.5 million units of manufactured products in exchange for 2 million units of food, and consumption at point c becomes a possibility.[2] By similar reasoning, an entire consumption-possibilities line can be derived as shown in Figure 9–1. If residents of the region wanted to consume all manufactured products, they should produce all food and trade for 4.5 million units of manufactured products. If the point of production and consumption possibilities in the absence of trade were a, then trade could move the consumption-possibilities curve to a level where residents

[2] In the world economy, one unit of food would trade for three fourths of a manufactured product as implied by Table 9–1. Thus, 2 million units of food would trade for 1.5 million (2,000,000 × ¾) manufactured products.

of region I could consume more of both goods, as indicated by the points between c and d.

In the example, it was implicitly assumed that region I was too small to affect worldwide terms of trade. If the region were large, such as the United States or China, its entrance into world trade would alter the international terms of trade. The effect on the world terms of trade cannot be determined unless supply and demand conditions of the various participants are known. If the conditions of the competitive model apply, all parties to trade may benefit. Although this example was described in terms of one country and the rest of the world, the same principles would apply to opening a region to trade within a country.

By similar reasoning, trade can be shown to enhance the consumption possibilities of all regions that engage in trade. If each region specialized in producing its product(s) of comparative advantage, world output would be maximized. Furthermore, specialization could result in additional output if decreasing costs were assumed.

Heckscher-Ohlin Theorem.   The theory of comparative advantage states that countries (regions) should specialize in producing the commodities they produce relatively cheaply, but it does not indicate what goods and services would be exported. Heckscher and Ohlin hypothesized that if a country had a relative abundance of a particular factor of production, it would have a comparative advantage in the production of goods that require large amounts of the abundant factor. For instance, a region with abundant topsoil and rain could be expected to have a comparative advantage in agriculture products. Thus, although factors of production may be immobile, Heckscher and Ohlin envisioned a mechanism whereby the abundant factor of production would be mobilized as they become embodied in the dominant exports.

The commodity flows from trade will affect not only commodity prices but resource prices as well. A country with abundant labor will tend to have low wages (relative to the rest of the world) prior to trade. Export of labor-intensive products will increase the demand for labor and, hence, the wage. Labor-short countries will import labor-intensive products, thus taking pressure off labor demand, which, in turn, tends to lower wages for their workers. In a world of perfect knowledge and commodity mobility, the Heckscher-Ohlin theorem leads to the conclusion that commodity movements will result in equalization of factor prices. In this sense, commodity movements can be a substitute for resource movements.

Comparative Advantage Reconsidered.   The theory of comparative advantage and its complement, the Heckscher-Ohlin theorem, have been challenged because they may neither describe nor predict actual trade patterns. Empirical studies to determine whether countries export products that require a large portion of abundant inputs and import products that require resources that are scarce locally have not found the expected pattern of trade (Bowen et al., 1987). The empirical studies can be questioned on methodological grounds. Because there are so many types of labor, it may be inappropriate to lump all labor together as one factor and conclude that a country should either import or export labor-intensive products. Nevertheless, the lack of empirical evidence for the Heckscher-Ohlin theorem is discouraging.

One reason areas may not specialize in their comparative advantage is that the mechanism and institutions necessary for specialization may not exist. For example, suppose a land-abundant country had a comparative advantage in producing agricultural products. Yet, to take advantage of these opportunities, farmers needed to make a commitment to cash cropping. This may be alien to their tradition. Middlemen must come forward to buy the cash crops, perhaps advance money for purchase of new seed, export the cash crops, and import other products. The emergence of necessary middlemen may not occur.

If the laws, institutions, and customs necessary to support trade do not exist, extensive specialization and trade may not develop. Similarly, the growth of a comparative-advantage industry may require resource mobility between industries or activities within the region. For instance, if the export sector expands, resources must shift to the export sector and away from the local service sector. If customs or laws prevent workers from changing jobs or if inflexible wages discourage job switching, specialization for export will be restrained.

Finally, comparative advantage is a static theory. Some analysts believe nations should produce goods and services in which they may have a comparative cost disadvantage in the short run in order to develop a comparative advantage. Therefore, areas may establish tariffs, subsidies, and other public policies that are inconsistent with the static concept of comparative advantage. Protection from external competition so that a comparative advantage can be built is called the infant-industry argument.

Resource Mobility

The theory of comparative advantage was developed on the assumption that resources were immobile. While some resources may be regionally immobile, regional economists frequently use models built on the assumption of perfect resource mobility. Certainly, there are fewer im-

FIGURE 9–2   A Model of Resource Mobility

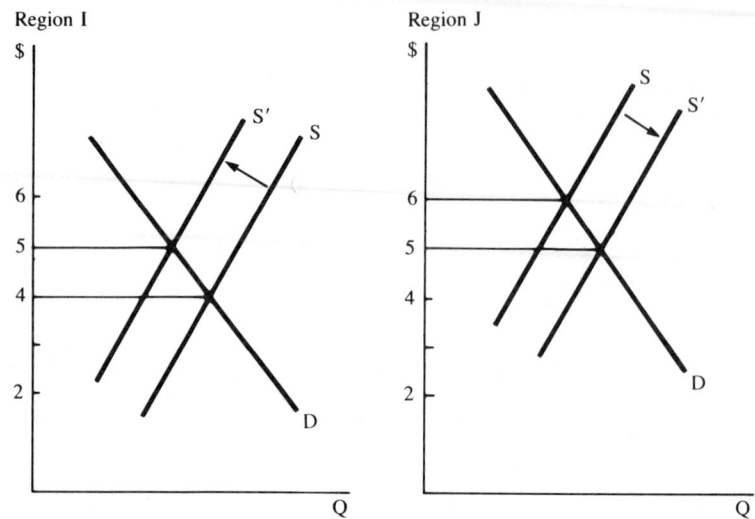

The resources in Region I are initially priced below the same resource in Region J. Therefore, resources move from Region I to J, decreasing supply and increasing the price in Region I. The supply increases and the price falls in Region J.

pediments to the movement of labor and capital between regions in the same country than to factor movement between countries.

In a world of perfect information and no relocation costs, factors of production would move to the region where compensation is highest. Figure 9–2 can be used to analyze resource mobility. Assume there are two regions and that compensation is initially $2 per unit greater in region J than in region I. (S indicates the initial supply curves.) The differential would induce resources to flow from region I to region J. When the compensation of the factor of production is equal at $5 in this example, migration will stop.

Next, consider how relocation costs will affect adjustment. A move would be worthwhile if the present value of future earnings in the destination region minus the relocation costs exceeds the present value of future earnings in the region of origin. In order to provide a sufficient incentive to relocate, relocation costs must be less than the present value of future extra returns that the factor could earn in J compared to I.

Figure 9–2 shows the supply curves shifting so as to eventually equalize factor prices because of the assumption of costless mobility. If resources relocation were costly, then the present value of the difference in compensation over the life of the factor of production would equal the relocation costs in equilibrium.

The adjustment process is not instantaneous, thus introducing an additional consideration. The higher factor returns in J will induce the resource to move from I to J. As the factor moves from I to J, the supply curve for the factor of production will shift to the right in J and to the left in I. Thus, factor returns in the low-compensation area will increase while they will decrease in the high-return area. Since the factor price gap is not constant but narrows during the adjustment process, it is difficult for a potential migrant to determine the value of future returns from moving to the high-priced region. In order to calculate whether it is worthwhile to move a factor of production to a higher-return region, the factor owner must not only know the current factor price differentials but also how the price differential will change in the future.

The shift in resources will benefit some abundant resource owners in the low-factor-price area and harm owners of that resource in the high-factor-price area. It is not possible to determine whether there will be more beneficiaries or losers from the relocation. It depends upon the number of workers originally in each region. However, the shift in resources will enhance total output, if resources are paid according to the value of their marginal product. Suppose the resources in our illustration have a higher marginal product in region J than in I as would be the case if the resources payment equaled the value of their marginal product. Hence, when resources are transferred from region I to J, the value of the output foregone in region I will be less than the increment to national output by employing the resource in J. Thus, gross national product will increase as the result of the movement of resources.

The model represented by Figure 9–2 does not show a demand response. In fact, a high resource price in one region could induce users of the high-cost resource to move out of the area. Hence, movements in demand may also help eliminate price differentials. For example, suppose labor and capital are the principal factors of production. Labor may relocate from a low-wage to high-wage region. But, simultaneously, capital may flow to the low-wage region in order to take advantage of the low-cost complementary input.

POPULATION AND LABOR MOVEMENT

The previous section was abstract in order to set forth the basic theory of commodity and resource flows. The simple factor-mobility model accurately describes important locational pulls. However, the assumption of perfect resource mobility hides many impediments to the movement of resources. This section and the two that follow examine in detail interregional flows of factors of production. The focus here is on interregional migration as opposed to movement within a local area.

Economics of Migration

The distinction between disequilibrium and equilibrium migration models is important. Disequilibrium models, the most common, assume migration is motivated by relative advantages or disadvantages that may exist among regions. For instance, higher wages in a region may encourage workers and their families to relocate to the high-wage region. Equilibrium models explain migration even when regional factor markets are in equilibrium. Migration can occur in response to lifestyle changes at key periods of life—at graduation, at marriage, before and after military service, after the birth of children, at retirement, and after the death of a spouse. At each of these "passages," the motive for relocating may be quite different. For instance, postgraduation moves are strongly associated with job prospects. The retirement move probably reflects quality-of-life factors. Moves associated with children and the death of a spouse may reflect family values. Graves (1979) showed that determinants of migration may vary significantly among age and racial groups. Consequently, migration studies that lump all demographic groups together will fail to reveal important variations among groups.

In disequilibrium models, wages and employment opportunities are perhaps the most obvious factors in labor movements. Migration is often analyzed in terms of push and pull effects. Migrants respond to the pull of jobs at high wages in the region of destination and the push of low wages or lack of employment opportunities in their own region. Evidence indicates that pull factors appear to be stronger locational determinants than push factors. Also, in the United States, job openings are probably more important than wage differentials in attracting immigrants. Greenwood et al. (1986) concluded that in an average year, the creation of two net new jobs in an area will attract one immigrant. Surprisingly, the pulling power of an additional job rises during an economic expansion and falls during a recession. Perhaps individuals are more willing to take risks during expansions. Furthermore, the pull of employment opportunities and higher wages attracts migrants to high-opportunity areas from both prosperous and distressed regions. Out-migration, however, appears to be less related to the push of low wages and poor employment opportunities than to the age distribution of the area's population.

Nonwage Factors.   Most empirical studies indicate that labor tends to migrate to high-wage or employment-growth areas, but nonwage factors also help explain migration. Imagine the factors besides wages that might influence a potential migrant's decision to relocate. First, fringe benefits as well as the basic wage rate would have to be considered. Many migrants are interested in the total compensation package, not just wages. Second, cost of living might have to be accounted for to reflect the fact that individuals desire a higher real compensation, not just a higher money wage. Both fringe benefits and differences in costs of living are relatively concrete concepts. More complex factors must also be considered.

The quality of life reflects a set of extremely important residential selection factors. Many individuals will accept a lower real wage in a location if the quality of life is better. Chapter 11 presents evidence that quality-of-life factors are embedded in the wage and discusses an economic approach to measuring quality of life.

Equalizing differentials refer to compensation differentials that will persist over time even if labor were perfectly mobile. For instance, an individual may be willing to accept 25 cents per hour less to enjoy the climate, quality of life, future opportunities, and so forth. Thus, the presence of equalizing differentials will prevent wage equalization.

In addition to quality of life, the future pay and promotion prospects may be as important as current pay. The kind of job also influences the choice. Furthermore, moves are a family affair, since many households have more than one wage earner. The earnings prospect for a spouse is an important consideration. Finally, potential migrants must not only explore wage differentials, but also the prospects of attaining a high-wage job in a new location. An area with a high wage rate but a high unemployment rate could be an unattractive site for a migrant.

The costs of relocation also enter the individual migrant's decision in a way that is more complicated than may appear. In a simple model, the relocation costs might simply be the cost of transporting one's possessions from one place to another. However, other monetary costs include the cost of selling a house and transaction costs of closing accounts, purchasing new license plates, and so forth. Nonmonetary costs include hassles, loss of proximity to friends and relatives, and lifestyle changes. In many cases, these factors may be more important than monetary costs. Uncertain prospects are another type of cost likely to be considered very significantly by risk-adverse individuals.

Although the individual's decision to migrate is complex, most of the factors described can be incorporated, at least conceptually, into a cost-benefit framework, because a monetary value can be assigned to nonmonetary costs and benefits. Table 9–2 illustrates major costs and benefits. Improved earnings prospects are one of the dominant components of the migration decision, so labor generally moves as described by the simple factor-price-equalization model. However, an understanding of the variety of additional factors that affect the decision to migrate may help explain instances where the simple factor-price-equalization model fails.

TABLE 9–2   Listing of Typical Factors that Comprise the Fourfold Cost-Benefit Mobility Matrix

Decision	Potential Costs	Potential Benefits
Migrate	**A** Transportation to new residence Uncertainty of finding employment Housing while seeking employment Food while seeking employment Clothing appropriate for employment Mistreatment by strangers Lack of social status Living in strange surroundings Need to use another language, improve speech Need to change customary dress, behavior, daily habits *(migration cost factors)*	**B** Higher rate of pay Employment of choice or preference Better education for children, self Better community service institutions More interesting, exciting social life Better race, ethnic, social conditions *(migration pull factors)*
Not Migrate	**C** Difficulties of finding local employment Lack of appropriate local recreation Excessive domination by family Unsatisfactory local social relations Unsatisfactory local institutions Unsatisfactory race, ethnic, political conditions *(migration push factors)*	**D** Inexpensive housing already available Inexpensive food Daily contact with family Daily contact with old friends, peers Living in familiar surroundings Social status assured Convenience of continued use of traditional speech, dress, customs Assured employment (for some) *(migration counterinfluences)*

SOURCE: Donald J. Bogue, "A Migrant's-Eye View of the Costs and Benefits of Migration to a Metropolis," in *Internal Migration: A Comparative Perspective,* ed. Brown and Neuberger (New York: Academic Press, 1977), p. 169.

Harris-Todaro Model.   Harris and Todaro (1970) developed a model to explain migration problems faced by some developing countries when people crowd into cities in spite of very high urban unemployment rates. It also explains the tendency of wage differentials to persist in spite of migration. They postulated that migration occurs when the actual wage in the area of origin is less than the *expected* wage in the area of destination. The expected wage is the actual wage times the probability of being employed. In the model workers assume their probability of employment is $1 - U$ where U is the unemployment rate. In other words, new residents believe they have the same probability of employment as current residents. If the wage rate were $10,000 annually and the unemployment rate were 20 percent, the expected wage would be $8,000.

In order to understand the Harris-Todaro model, assume a high-wage and a low-wage area. Also assume that wages in the high-wage region are institutionally fixed by law, union, or custom. Thus, urban wages will not decline in the face of substantial unemployment. If there were full employment in both regions, workers would migrate to the high-wage area. If the number of jobs in the high-wage area remained the same, unemployment would increase. Migrants are willing to trade off the risk of unemployment against the potential for higher wages. The additional migrant might find employment, but at the expense of another worker. Because of the higher unemployment due to migration, national product would fall. Workers would become unemployed rather than employed in low-wage (low-productivity) jobs. Nevertheless, the migration would be in the self-interest of the migrants, given their assumption about the probability of employment.

Figure 9–3 illustrates the Harris-Todaro model. The graph represents labor demand in a rural area and an urban area. The total labor supply is 100 workers. The labor force is divided between urban and rural workers. The labor demand curve represents the marginal product of additional workers.

In the textbook world of perfect labor markets, wages would equalize at $2 with 80 rural workers and 20 individuals employed in the urban area. However, assume that wages are fixed at $4 in the urban area. Employment in the rural sector would equal 80 workers at $2 per hour. If there were 20 workers in the urban area and only 10 were employed, the expected wage of $2 per unit (.50 × $4) would equal the wage in the rural area. Thus, in this example, equilibrium would occur with 50 percent unemployment in the urban area.

The Harris-Todaro model has three important implications: (1) migration to the high-wage area may fail to lead rapidly to wage equalization, (2) both wage rate and the level of unemployment may increase with city size, and (3) it may be difficult to prevent unemployment from rising in high-wage areas open to migration. The third implication is particularly

FIGURE 9–3   The Harris-Todaro Model

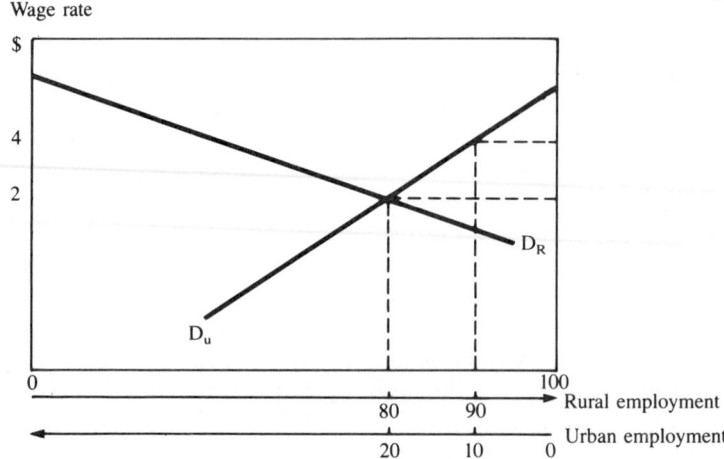

Migration may equalize the expected wage in the urban and rural areas. As a consequence, in equilibrium, there will be unemployment in the high-wage (urban) area.

important for urban planning in developing countries. However, within the United States, wages, particularly real wages, have fallen in many sectors. Even unions have ratified wage packages that provide decreased compensation. Thus, the implications of the model will be weakened to the extent that wages are flexible.

Gravity Models.   Migration flows are frequently estimated with a gravity model. Gravity models assume that migration between two regions increases in relation to the population of the region and decreases with distance between them. In the basic model, population represents the likelihood of a random individual leaving or migrating to an area. Distance is the main impediment. The following is an example of a simple gravity model:

$$M_{ab} = \frac{P_a P_b}{(D_{ab})^2} \tag{1}$$

where M_{ab} = Migration from A to B,
    $P_a P_b$ = Population in A or B, and
    D_{ab} = Distance between A and B.

The most obvious problem with the simple gravity model is that migration between the places would always net to zero. In order to avoid this outcome, other variables have been included to reflect opportunity differences. Differences in wage, income, and unemployment rates have been the most frequently used measures of opportunity differentials.

Another criticism of gravity models is that they are poorly specified because distance does not adequately measure difficulty of journey, particularly in an era of modern transportation, so travel time has been substituted for distance in some models. Social and political barriers, as well as uncertainty, are more important barriers. These factors are poorly correlated with distance. For instance, it is probably easier for a Texan to migrate to Oregon than to Mexico. So, although gravity models are used as empirical shortcuts, they do not reflect important theoretical factors that reflect opportunities and difficulty of journey.

Beaten-Path Effect and Intervening Opportunities.   One reason gravity models are sometimes inaccurate is due to the beaten-path effect. The beaten-path effect refers to the observed tendency of individuals from a particular area of origin to select the same destination. Often a few "pioneers" from an area will migrate first. Later, others, often relatives, will follow. Most migrants do not consider a shopping list of destinations. They do not ask, "Where among all possible places will I move?" Usually, they consider only one destination, often where their friends or relatives can provide job or housing information, or other help. Previously settled friends and relatives often also help support new migrants if necessary. Thus, by following a beaten path, migrants can lower money, uncertainty, and the social costs of relocating. The beaten-path effects help explain the concentrations of particular ethnic groups in particular cities. The concentrations of Polish in Milwaukee, Irish in Boston, or Cubans in Miami can be attributed to the beaten path.

In addition to lowering migration costs, the beaten-path effect has two other important implications. First, the flow of migrants may become self-perpetuating as migration costs fall and additional migration is stimulated. Second, the beaten path can be traveled both ways, so there is often a noticeable return migration. If economic prospects dim in the destination area or if migrants otherwise become disenchanted, large numbers may return to the place of origin.

Gravity models have also been modified to account for intervening opportunities. For instance, migration between one region and another may be less than a simple gravity model would project if there are regions of opportunities between the regions in the model.

Net and Gross Migration.   When economists first collected and analyzed data on migration, they were mainly concerned with net migration,

TABLE 9–3   Gross and Net Migration Flows and
Local Economic Conditions

		Out-Migration	
		High	Low
In-Migration	High	Low net migration	High net in-migration
	Low	Negative net in-migration	Low net migration

Similar net migration levels can occur through greatly different levels of gross migration.

the difference between in- and out-migrants. However, net migration patterns mask substantial differences in the level of gross migration because some individuals move into an area at the same time others move out.

Table 9–3 illustrates four different gross migration patterns: (1) high mobility—high in- and out-migration, (2) high in-migration, low out-migration, (3) low in-migration, high out-migration, and (4) low in-migration, low out-migration. Both the case of high in-migration/high out-migration and low in-migration/low out-migration could result in low net migration, but for very different reasons.

The high out-migration/high in-migration case results in significant cross-migration, which may be due to a combination of opportunities within the region and a footloose population base. Areas of opportunity may attract a highly mobile population. They may be young, without school-age children, or simply have a psychological propensity to move. They may be willing to move again if a slightly better opportunity in another region arises. Thus, regions with high opportunities may attract a mobile population resulting in cross-migration. Such regions will have high rates of population turnover.

Regions with low in-migration and low rates of out-migration will have low net population change. Areas with stable or declining economic bases may offer few opportunities for in-migrants, but they may have few push factors for those who have jobs. Perhaps the mobile population left in previous years. Many isolated, rural areas that have deteriorating economic bases have experienced both low in-migration and low out-migration. Those who remain may either have satisfactory jobs or are immobile either because of strong ties to the community, lack of a knowledge of opportunities elsewhere, or inability to take advantage of such opportunities. Recent studies indicate that demographic factors of a community are as important or more important than push factors (lack of economic opportunities) in determining out-migration.

A region with low in-migration/high out-migration could represent a low opportunity region with a highly mobile population. A region with a high proportion of 18–25-year-olds, but with declining employment opportunities, could be represented by this case. Net migration would be negative due to high out-migration and low in-migration. A region with low in-migration/high out-migration could eventually develop a pattern of low in-migration/low out-migration as initial out-migration results in a loss of the mobile population. Finally, the high in-migration/low out-migration case may be due to abundance of opportunities, while the existing population has low mobility characteristics. If enough footloose migrants moved into the area, and if they remained footloose, while opportunities remained high, the pattern represented by the region could evolve into a case of high in-migration/high out-migration.

Do Opportunities Equalize?   Even when migrants move to high-opportunity regions, there is disagreement over whether the population movements will actually reduce economic differentials between regions. Some analysts believe that migration will actually expand the differential between the high- and low-wage regions because migrants stimulate opportunities in the destination area. There are three major ways that migration may stimulate the economy of the destination region: (1) A larger and more diverse population will increase demand for employees to provide goods and services for the local populations. If the migrants are not in the labor force, such as retired individuals, the demand for labor may increase more rapidly than supply. (2) Greater economic activity may allow for greater agglomeration economies and productivity increases. This is substantial evidence that productivity increases as urban size increases. (3) The self-selective nature of migration may result in prosperous areas attracting more productive and enterprising individuals. If opportunity creators are among the migrants, they may contribute to further increases in labor demand.

In declining areas, the out-migration may further reduce economic opportunities. Migration is selective, so the population of a declining region often tends to become older, undereducated, and underskilled. Furthermore, the individuals left behind are likely to be less mobile. Thus, the area of origin may become a less attractive site for new economic activity. If wages are already low, the region may attract only low-wage employers. If wages in the declining region are high and rigid, the prospects of attracting additional firms are further reduced.

Gerking and Weirick (1983) determined that there have been persistent wage differentials among regions in the United States. However, these differentials are not entirely due to stimulative effects of immigration or to equalizing differences. Rather, regional wage and income differentials are largely attributable to the fact that regions have different economic functions and, therefore, have requirements for different labor skills. They found that each type of labor was paid approximately the same, regardless of region. High wages persist in some areas, because such regions have a high proportion of high-paying occupations in their industrial base. However, regional differences between persons in the same occupation tend to equalize. The findings of Gerking and Weirick support the theory that wage differentials are a major determinant of migration. However, in applying the theory, the heterogeneity of labor and occupations must be considered.

Efficiency of Migration. The simple economic model implies that migration will be efficient because migrants will move to areas of higher pay and higher productivity. Migration was inefficient in the Harris-Todaro model because migration increased the unemployment rate. The occurrence of significant cross-migration suggests inefficiency because, if regions are swapping movers, some of the relocations may be unnecessary. However, as explained above, cross-migration may be attributable to a mismatch between skills and the type of labor available in different regions. Substantial cross-migration may simply reflect the aggregation problem of lumping all labor together as a homogeneous factor of production.

One way of evaluating the effectiveness of migration is to examine whether individual migrants are better off after migration. Three approaches have commonly been used to evaluate benefits to individual migrants: (1) asking migrants if they are better off, (2) comparing migrants' earnings with the earnings of similar persons who did not move, and (3) examining social benefits, including externalities.

A survey by Lansing and Mueller (1967) found that the vast majority of migrants judged their moves to be either good ideas or very good ideas. Thus, individuals subjectively believe in the benefit from migration.

Studies also indicate that most migrants experienced an increase in earnings. However, simple income comparisons between the earning of migrants and the earning of seemingly similar individuals who did not relocate can be misleading because migration may be selective. Individuals who migrate could be expected to have higher incomes than those who did not migrate if migration correlates with greater desire or ability to advance. Nevertheless, empirical studies controlling for the measurable characteristics of the migrants, show that migration to areas of opportunity greatly improve earnings. It has also been shown that individuals who stand to gain the most from migration are the ones who migrate. Thus, the evidence indicates that migration improves the economic position of the migrant.

Hunt and Kau (1985) examined returns from migration for young male migrants. They found that repeat migrants experience a 13 percent annual wage increase. However, they found that one-time movers did not receive substantial benefits from migration. They concluded that multiple movers gain job search skills which help them in finding jobs in their new location. Inexperience precluded gains from a single move. Their findings imply that the efficiency of migration increases with experience.

The total social benefits of migration, including externalities, are more difficult to evaluate. Migration may be viewed as socially beneficial if higher migrant earnings reflect greater social output. However, the social effects of migration are difficult to assess because they require a judgment about the effect on residents in the place of origin and the place of destination as well as the effects on the individual migrant. For instance, a migrant from a declining area to an expanding area may cause greater demands on infrastructure, cause taxes to increase, and create additional congestion and pollution in the area of destination, while increasing the tax burden and imposing other costs on residents in the area of origin. Because of measurement problems, the efficiency of migration is much more difficult to evaluate when comparing marginal social costs and benefits.

Migration in the United States

Individuals are most likely to migrate in the mid-20s and early 30s age range as indicated by Table 9–4. At this age, they have generally completed school but are less likely to have established a household, a family, or local financial commitments.

Employed persons were less mobile than the unemployed. Although the data are not strictly comparable, individuals receiving public assistance have high interregional mobility rates and extremely high local mobility rates. Education also influences mobility. Persons with high educational attainment are more likely to relocate, particularly to a different county.

Moves within the same county or within the same MSA are primarily due to housing considerations and are not the focus of this chapter. Surveys consistently reveal that about half of interregional migration is due to job transfers or relocation for a new job.

Several important trends characterize U.S. migration patterns. Immigration from other countries to the United States was a major growth factor until about 1920. In recent decades, legal immigration has tended to reflect political events such as the Hungarian Revolution and the Vietnam War. Illegal immigration stimulated by economic difficulty in Mexico and political unrest in Central America has been a major factor in the Southwest. The largest flow of movers from aboard has been to metropolitan areas.

TABLE 9–4   Characteristics of Migrants in the United States: 1986–1987

	Percent Moving		Between States
	Within County	Within State	
All persons:	11.6%	3.7%	2.8%
Age			
15–19	10.8	3.3	0.7
20–24	21.7	7.6	.9
25–29	24.0	6.7	.8
30–44	21.1	3.9	.5
45–65	5.2	2.1	.2
65+	3.2	1.2	.1
Race			
White	11.2	3.8	.4
Black	13.8	3.3	.5
Hispanic	17.6	3.1	1.7
Education			
0–8 years	8.4	2.1	.5
High school—1–4 years	11.0	3.5	.3
College—1–3 years	11.9	4.4	.4
College—4 years or more	11.6	5.5	.7
Labor force status			
Employed	12.6	4.3	.4
Unemployed	17.0	10.7	.8
Type of settlement			
Central city	13.3	6.2	10.1
Suburb	9.5	6.2	9.5
Outside SMSA	8.9	6.9	8.9
Region of residence			
Northeast	7.7	4.4	.4
Midwest	10.7	6.0	.3
South	12.9	7.4	.3
West	14.5	7.9	1.0

SOURCE: *Geographic Mobility, March 1983 to March 1984,* U.S. Department of Commerce, Bureau of the Census, 1987.

There has been a consistent pattern of westward migration. California's rapid growth reflects the westward movement. It is also interesting to observe that blacks have constituted a disproportionately smaller portion of the westward migration, probably indicating the absence of a beaten-path effect. The Northeast and North Central regions have experienced net out-migration since about 1940. The out-migration has been

TABLE 9–5   Regional Migration Patterns in the United States: 1980–1987 (000s)

	Northeast	Midwest	South	West
In-migrants	3,249 (6.5%)	5,635 (9.5%)	9,527 (11.6%)	6,336 (13.2%)
Out-migrants	4,769 (9.6)	7,285 (12.3)	7,432 (9.1)	5,255 (10.1)
Net migration	−1,520	−1,650	2,085	1,081

(   ) = as a percent of 1985 population.
1986 mobility rate (includes regional moves): 12.6 (Northeast), 16.9 (Midwest), 20.1 (South), and 22.3 (West).

SOURCE: See Table 9–4.

particularly marked among whites. The trend accelerated in the 1970s, but leveled during the latter 1980s.

The gross and net migration flows for regions in the United States along with mobility rates are shown in Table 9–5. The South had the highest level of in-migration *and* the highest level of out-migration while the West had the highest *rates* of in- and out-migration. Both regions experienced above-average job growth during this period, high overall mobility rates, and in-migration due to life-quality reasons. The high out-migration may be explained by a population with a high propensity to relocate and/or economic restructuring in which some sectors declined while the region as a whole grew.

In contrast, the Northeast experienced net out-migration as the result of low out-migration but even lower in-migration. The Midwest experienced moderate in-migration but a very high rate of out-migration for a net negative migration pattern.

The growth of metropolitan areas is an important trend. Table 9–6 shows migration within the United States for central cities, suburbs, and

TABLE 9–6   In-Migrants, Out-Migrants, and Net Migration for Central Cities, Suburbs, and Nonmetropolitan Areas in the United States: 1986–1987 (000s)

New Residence in 1987	In-migrants	Out-migrants	Net migration
Inside MSAs	2,686	1,754	+932
Central cities	4,583	5,623	−1040
Suburbs	6,392	4,420	+1972
Outside MSAs	1,754	2,686	−932

SOURCE: See Table 9–4.

TABLE 9–7   Movers within and between Central Cities, Suburbs, and
Nonmetropolitan Areas in the United States: 1986–1987 (000s)

New Residence in 1988	Movers from Inside MSAs			Movers from Outside MSAs
	Total	Central Cities	Suburbs	
Central cities	14,100	10,606	3,494	1,089
Suburbs	16,743	4,795	11,948	1,597
Outside MSAs	1,754	828	926	6,920

SOURCE: See Table 9–4.

nonmetropolitan areas. The net gain of internal migrants for metropolitan areas occurred because the suburbs' net gains offset losses in central cities. The long-term phenomenon of in-migration to metropolitan areas from nonmetropolitan areas was disrupted during the 1970s. During that period, ex-urban counties—that is, counties bordering but not part of metropolitan areas—showed substantial in-migration. However, since 1980, the former pattern of net in-migration into metropolitan areas has been reestablished.

Suburbanization has been the most common residential growth pattern in this century. Table 9–6 indicates that suburbs were net population gainers compared with both central cities and areas outside MSAs. This population pattern reflects preferences for suburban living expressed in numerous opinion polls.

Table 9–7 also focuses on migration patterns within and between central cities, suburbs, and nonmetropolitan areas. An important feature of Table 9–7 is that most movers tend to relocate in the same type of area. For instance, of the approximately 14 million movers to the central cities, 10.6 million moved from another residence in the same city or from another central city. Only 3,494,000 moved into the central city from the suburbs, and only 1,089,000 moved into the central city from outside MSAs.

MOBILITY OF CAPITAL

Discussions of capital flows are often confused by the various meanings of "capital." In everyday use, capital often means money and assets that can be converted into money. But economists define capital as produced goods that can be inputs into further production. Accordingly, capital includes physical inputs into the production process, such as buildings, machinery, and also human capital. The amount of physical capital is usually expressed in monetary terms ("The machine is worth $100,000"), because money is a measure of value. So the distinction between money and real capital is easily blurred. The value of human capital can be expressed in terms of the increased value of increased earning power. For an individual, the distinction between money and physical capital may not always be important because an individual can convert some types of real capital into money by selling assets. However, a society as a whole cannot convert between capital and money.

Money capital is generally considered to be highly mobile among regions both domestically and internationally. Individuals and corporations can move accounts and transfer funds from financial institutions in one region to financial institutions in another region in a matter of minutes. Differences of fractions of percentage points trigger massive money capital flows from one region to another.

Economists are generally as concerned with real capital as they are with money accounts because real capital is one of the basic factors of production. It is combined with land, labor, and entrepreneurship. Real capital used in production is much less mobile than money. Buildings and some heavy machinery are almost place-bound, once created.

In spite of the limited mobility of some real capital, an individual may sell such an asset and transfer the proceeds to another region. So capital may be spatially mobile from the perspective of an individual even if the physical asset is immobile. Furthermore, since real capital is *valued* in money, the amount of capital invested in a region can shift quickly even when the real capital does move. For example, a facility that is operating efficiently may have high value based upon the income stream it generates. But, if the owner decides to abandon operations because the local environment is no longer suitable, the value of the physical assets could quickly drop to zero. Abandoned facilities may even have negative value if demolition costs are significant. Of course, if an alternative use for an abandoned facility were found, its value could be supported, but experience indicates that alternative uses often cannot be found.

In light of the various definitions of capital, three types of capital mobility can be identified. First, money capital can be transferred from one region to another either in exchange for goods and services or to finance real investment. Second, physical assets can be transported from one place to another, although the mobility of many physical assets is limited. Finally, the value of physical capital may change, reflecting changes in the economic environment.

Location and Expansion Decisions

Location and expansion decisions of firms are the most concrete way that money capital can be converted into physical capital. Construction of facilities in one region can also affect the value of facilities located elsewhere, as when a new plant renders an older factory obsolete. Locational decision criteria were discussed previously in Chapter 2. A facility can be developed in a region through outside investment even though little or no physical capital is imported. For instance, the owners of capital may believe that an electronics-component facility would be profitable in a region. Accordingly, they may hire local construction workers, purchase machinery made in the region, and hire a local work force. The real resources for each step could have come from local sources. In this case, the investment of money capital from outside the region resulted in an increase in physical capital even though no physical capital was imported into the region.

The value of a facility may be more or less than the amount of money spent to create the physical capital depending upon the value of the flow of net future income the facility is expected to generate. In a world of perfect knowledge among investors, competition for funds and for resources would ensure that the value of the facility would just equal the value of the money expended in construction. In reality, some investors spot opportunities overlooked by others and can create a capital asset that has greater value than the cost of producing it.

Obstacles to Capital Mobility

In theory, if capital were perfectly mobile and if investors were perfectly knowledgeable, rates of return among investments in different regions would be equal except for a risk premium in equilibrium. The proposition is difficult to test, however, because it is difficult to determine the extent of investment risk and whether markets are in equilibrium. When institutions such as bond-rating services or insurance programs exist, it can be shown that investments with similar risk ratings provide similar returns throughout the United States. For instance, equally risky municipal bonds or the rates on federally insured certificates of deposit vary over a small range regardless of the region. Likewise, major corporations have roughly similar access to funds regardless of the region of their headquarters or site of their proposed investment. The rise of large institutional investors, such as life insurance companies and pension funds, has contributed to greater capital mobility because these institutions can afford the costs of exploring investment opportunities throughout the nation and even internationally.

The pattern of past investment reduces options and, hence, the geographic mobility of capital. It would be very difficult for a company to simply write off a large plant in order to start from scratch a similar facility elsewhere, although such decisions have been made. Sunk costs are often considered to be irrelevant because decision makers should consider only marginal costs and benefits. Normally, the location of an existing facility will have lower marginal cost than an alternate site where no facility exists. However, there may be psychological costs that also prevent a business executive from declaring a previous location choice a failure.

The current capital stock of a region is a composite of many different vintages. Agglomerations of urban investment and clusters of related businesses influence the geographic distribution of new investment. Since businesses frequently depend upon investments of related firms, one firm may find it difficult to move away from its supporting infrastructure. Even if all the plants in an industrial agglomeration were owned by a single firm, the mobility of capital would be limited by the high cost of replicating the agglomeration elsewhere.

The historical investment pattern limits the geographic options but does not prevent new investment from seeking areas where returns are greater. However, many experts believe there are impediments that prevent investment from flowing to areas of highest returns, although the evidence that such impediments exist is debatable. The following are hypotheses about factors that limit the flow of capital to its area of highest return:

1. Lenders may be reluctant to extend loans to businesses located in the central city because they incorrectly perceive high risks of central-city investments. Racial bias against blacks and other minorities is considered to be linked with the failure of institutions to invest in minority-dominated sections of the central city.

2. Rural areas may fail to attract capital because they are underserved by financial institutions. Hence, it is more difficult for businesses to develop in rural areas. Special government programs such as the Farmers Home Loan Administration have been developed to stimulate the supply of capital to rural areas.

3. Firms may have a preference for reinvesting profits internally, rather than investing outside the company. The preference for internal investment may be due to better knowledge about in-house opportunities or a psychological preference for control. Hence, distressed regions with few profitable firms have less access to this source of funds.

4. Investors with small amounts of money have difficulty directly lending in distant regions because of high transactions costs. Investors need to be able to assess risks and may therefore avoid making loans to less-known companies when they cannot obtain adequate knowledge of the company. Such investors may participate in nationally marketed securities or they may limit their investments to the particular regions they know. This point is reflected in the belief that venture capital is not equally available in all regions.

INNOVATIONS AND IDEAS

Ideas and new ways of doing things are a major source of economic growth. Economists have traditionally been more concerned about innovations than inventions. Innovation is the economic application of a new idea, although the distinction may become blurred when the same person is both the inventor and innovator. Not only are innovations important to economic growth, but the rate at which innovations are copied, modified, and spread to other sectors of the economy influences economic progress.

At first glance, it may seem reasonable to assume that innovations would spread quickly and uniformly in a manner suggested by the competitive model. After all, ideas are weightless, so it is easy to assume they are costless to transport. As Borts and Stein (1964) said, "A new manufacturing process or a new machine is, under competition, available to all" (p. 81). However, numerous empirical studies have indicated resistance to innovation. The length of time between an invention and commercial application can span decades, and gaps of several years are common. More important for our purposes, there is a spatial pattern to the spread of ideas and innovations.

Spatial Diffusion

Innovations tend to originate in large metropolitan areas. The spread of innovations can be complex and differs depending upon the production process or the product being developed. However, in general, innovations tend to spread from metropolitan areas along a variety of paths.

Metropolitan Origination.   There are many related explanations for the dominance of metropolitan areas in the development of new ideas. Most explanations focus upon the needed variety of people, ideas, and resources that must be a part of or inputs to a new concept. The spread of innovations is similar for both products and production processes. Pred (1966), in a historical study of the spread of industrial innovations, used a supply and demand framework to explain the predominance of the metropolis in the innovative process. The quantity of innovations is greater in urban areas because both the supply of and demand for innovations are greater.

On the demand side, urban areas provide greater economic rewards for innovation because the market for new products and processes is more readily available. New products may capture only a small market share initially, so a large local market may be critical to achieving an adequate initial sales level. The larger demand for process innovation in metropolitan areas is due to the larger agglomeration of producers. A new production process may have applications in a variety of industries.

On the supply side, several factors make it easier to develop innovations in major urban areas. Metropolitan areas have a greater variety of support activities needed for innovations. Skilled engineering consultants, marketing firms, lawyers, intermediate manufacturers, venture capitalists, and other important contributors to the innovative process are all more readily available in metropolitan areas. Cities may also be the workplace of innovative elites and other individuals in key national information loops. Recently, policy makers in many urban areas are deliberately perusing strategies to enhance the supply of local innovations by encouraging incubators, inventors, entrepreneurial networks, and research parks.

Diffusion. New products and processes spread from the point of innovation in three distinct ways: (1) to nearby places in a radial pattern, (2) from one metropolitan area to similar areas, and (3) from larger to smaller places according to the central-place hierarchy.

First, there is a tendency for consumer-oriented innovations to spread in a radial pattern from the source of the innovation outward. Movement of an idea from the central city to suburban areas is an example of this diffusion pattern. The radial spread of innovations from a metropolitan center to other places is explained simply by proximity and resulting lower information costs. Innovations that depend upon personal, nonbusiness contacts are likely to have a strong tendency to spread in a radial manner.

Second, innovations move laterally among cities of roughly equal status in the urban hierarchy. For instance, an innovation may appear in Houston and Chicago at similar times. The availability of supporting services that stimulated original innovations in metropolitan areas make replication in similar metropolitan areas more likely. Particularly in the early stages of innovation, a supportive environment may be needed to replicate the original production process. For instance, it may be difficult to employ a new printing technology in a small town because it may lack the supporting services to deal with a breakdown. "Bugs" in production and marketing are likely to be encountered as the innovation spreads, and such problems can often be addressed more easily in urban settings. Also, communications and transportation systems between major cities in different regions are better than between a major city in one region and smaller towns in a different region. Therefore, the spread of innovations from one major center to another is expedited. In addition, the higher per capita incomes in metropolitan areas contribute to their early adaptation of innovations. Markets for income-elastic goods will first appear in metropolitan areas. Demand for income-elastic goods in smaller places will develop as income increases. The taste for something different—the taste for consumer innovation—is probably an income-elastic good.

Third, the diffusion of innovations from major metropolitan areas to smaller places in the major area's sphere of influence can be explained by economic linkages. Businesses are often organized along the same lines as the urban hierarchy. The central office, for instance, is frequently located in a major metropolitan area while regional and local offices are in hinterland locations. The business organizational hierarchy, in turn, affects the information flow. Thus, the corporate headquarters will tend to be the location of a company's first fax machine. If the innovations are successful, they may filter down to regional offices and later to local offices. Distribution channels for consumer products also reflect the hierarchy of places and information channels.

Implications for Regional Development

The tendency for larger metropolitan areas to be the site of innovation as routinized production tends to shift to smaller places in the urban hierarchy was central to the stages-of-growth theories of Thompson and Jacobs discussed in Chapter 5. The diffusion process, coupled with the tendency for products to grow rapidly in the early stages of their life cycle, has been termed industrial filtering. Figure 9–4 illustrates the time path of employment growth in a typical industry. The explanation for the shape of the industrial-growth curve centers on the fact that early in an industry's development absolute increases in output or employment will be large percentage increases. Furthermore, sales in the early stages include both new purchases and replacements, whereas in later stages only replacement production is needed.

Metropolitan areas tend to be the site of production early in the life cycle of a product or process. After a process is better understood and is broken into routine steps or after a market has been established for a product, a shift in the site of production to smaller towns often occurs. The large metropolitan areas have a higher proportion of fast-growth activities, but those activities spin off to smaller places. Accordingly, metropolitan areas will tend to lose a portion of their economic base to smaller cities.

Large cities may require a more highly skilled labor force because products in the early stages of development involve nonroutine production. The different skill requirements may account for the persistence of higher incomes in urban areas. Strategic investments in education, training, and a quality environment may help metropolitan areas attract and develop the skilled labor force needed for nonroutine operations. Larger cities may also explore ways to maintain activities that originate there and, hence, slow the filtering process. Conversely, smaller cities may consider how to speed up the filtering process so they can capture industries early in the product life cycle.

FIGURE 9–4   Employment Growth over Industrial Life Cycle

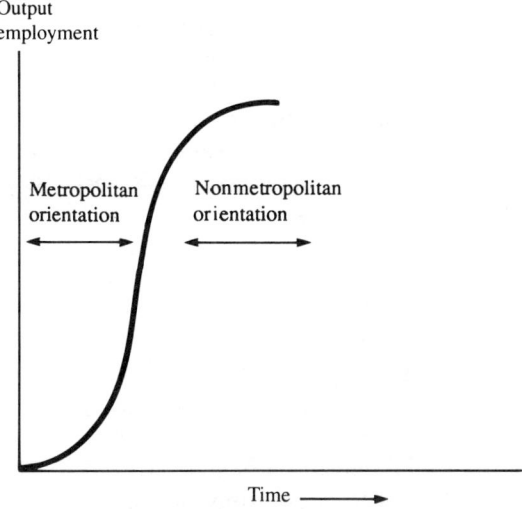

More-rapid growth occurs during the early stages of an industry's life cycle. As the industry ages, growth slows.

Recently, some policy analysts have questioned whether major urban areas can maintain their leadership in innovation if the site of production becomes too remote. Underlying this issue is the concern that, if research becomes too distant from the shop floor, researchers will lose their sense of purpose. Giese and Testa (1988) examined Chicago-area research and development firms. They concluded that metropolitan regions can retain their eminence as industrial research and development centers even as the manufacturing activities decline.

MOBILITY AND SPATIAL POLICY

Many policy areas involve mobility issues. Economists generally believe that the economy operates more efficiently when resources are mobile, so removing unnecessary barriers to mobility is often viewed as a way to improve performance. Furthermore, many social problems can be alleviated by allowing resources to move to places of greater opportunity.

Jobs to People versus People to Jobs

One of the perennial regional development issues is whether government policy should encourage job creation in high unemployment areas or whether individuals should be encouraged to move to where jobs already exist. Both moving jobs to people and moving people to jobs have been advanced as at least partial solutions to the problem of poverty discussed in the previous chapter. The issue presupposes the existence of a geographic mismatch between available jobs and workers. Table 9–8 provides a comparison of the two approaches.

The jobs-to-people approach dominated thinking about regional policy during the 1960s and was implemented through a number of regional commissions, such as the Appalachian Regional Development Commission. An example of the jobs-to-people philosophy was expressed by a presidential panel that stated that rural residents should have access to jobs without regard to race, religion, or *place of residence.* Most local officials in distressed areas favor the jobs-to-people approach because the areas they represent will tend to be beneficiaries of job-creation efforts.

Supporters of the jobs-to-people approach generally believe that people are so reluctant to move that the inducements—both carrot and stick—would have to be substantial before they would move. They also point out that push factors, such as high unemployment rates and low incomes, are poor predictors of out-migration. Therefore, "natural" market forces will not necessarily result in the efficient movement of people to jobs. Jobs-to-people advocates also contend that job-creating activity can create jobs in distressed areas at a low cost or with little or no loss of aggregate national output. In addition, Clark (1983) argued that only a jobs-to-people approach can support the stable communities and the social relationships "community" implies. Since community development is a legitimate end of economic policy, jobs to people can be justified even if it is not the most efficient way to establish full employment.

There is some evidence that indicates the reluctance of individuals to move. In determining the cost of relocating families in order to build an airport, a study group asked people how much over the fair market value of their house they would insist upon before agreeing to move. Respondents indicated they would voluntarily move only if they were paid an average of 140 percent of the home's value (The Roskill Commission, 1970). Similarly, Dunn (1979) found that residents of a small, rural community would accept a 14 percent wage reduction rather than relocate to avoid the wage reduction. Other groups that have been reported to place a high monetary value on community include older persons, blacks, low-income individuals, and people with friends and relatives in the area (Mills and Hamilton, 1989, p. 232).

The jobs-to-people approach has been criticized because it appears to place the welfare of places over the welfare of people. "We must do

TABLE 9–8   The People versus Places Controversy

Issue	People Prosperity	Places Prosperity
Rationale	Only individuals matter. Individual welfare is relatively independent of place condition	Places also matter. The welfare of individuals is relatively dependent upon place condition
Presumed efficiency effects	Not certain. Might increase GNP by improving labor force quality nationally	Inefficient. Lowers GNP if orthodox view is correct
Effects on interarea's migration	Probably accelerates it	Retards it
Strategy	Bottom up. May take a "worst-case-first" approach	Top down. May focus on places with most development potential (within eligible area)
Benefits to the poor	Undoubtedly some. Probably not as many as in other case	Clear and substantial benefits to the non-poor (see Box in Chapter 5)
Most obvious drawback	Does little to mitigate the social and psychological costs of economically forced migration. May do little to aid the survival of dying places	As a strategy to aid the long-term poor, it is at least partly defeated by labor force mobility and elasticity
Political support	Relatively weak, particularly if programs bypass local political structure	Very strong support from the political establishment of eligible areas
Relation to recent locational trends	No necessary conflict	Definitely swimming against the tide

SOURCE: John M. Levy, *Urban and Metropolitan Economics* (New York: McGraw-Hill, 1985), p. 150. Copyright 1985. Reprinted by permission.

something to help Dallas," an advocate of place prosperity might say. However, jobs-to-people strategies are really designed to help people where they live, not places per se.

The people-to-jobs approach has been the dominant approach in recent years, particularly as regional concerns have focused on big-city problems. A presidential commission report, *Urban America in the Eighties: Perspectives and Prospects* (1981) strongly rejected job-creation efforts in high unemployment areas. The report indicated that the federal government should facilitate structural and geographic shifts by encouraging migration to growing places. At the time the report was written, this meant encouraging migration to the oil regions of the Southwest and Far West. Efforts to create jobs in the distressed northern industrial cities were described as futile efforts to shore up an inefficient spatial distribution of resources.

The people-to-jobs approach assumes that the market allocates investments efficiently among regions so the government should not attempt to alter the pattern. Individuals are assumed to be highly mobile and jobs are not easily transferred from one region to another. Furthermore, advocates of the people-to-jobs approach suggest that even if the government attempted to stimulate development in declining regions, the efforts would probably fail because the governmental resources available for regional development are small compared to private investment.

If one accepts the people-to-jobs strategy, what policies follow? Many free market economists interpret the approach as implying that the government should not attempt to spatially target resources. The federal government should support private investment trends through infrastructure investment in growing areas, but should not use government spending to direct private investment. Other policy advocates suggest labor mobility programs to help the poor or unemployed relocate to opportunity areas.

As with many policy debates between polar alternatives, both positions have some merit and the extent to which one approach should dominate probably depends upon specific circumstances. Geographic mobility has and will continue to be a tool for individuals to improve their position. People to jobs is important and will continue to be, but it may not be a complete policy. Many individuals are very immobile, so they may resist relocation incentives. Furthermore, maintaining stable communities can be an end in itself. Therefore, a role for jobs to people should not be ignored.

Immigration and Capital Flows

Americans have an ambivalent attitude towards immigration. On the one hand, most citizens trace their heritage to immigrants. The Statue of Liberty asks for huddled masses yearning to be free, and excluding foreigners from the American "good life" is selfish. On the other hand, world population growth is so fast and conditions in much of the world are so far below the living standards in prosperous countries that the United States and other rich countries are unwilling to absorb everyone who wants to enter the country. Currently, immigration accounts for about half of U.S. population growth. The magnitude of individuals seeking entrance to the rich countries indicates both the strength of push factors and the great pull of opportunities. Economic analysis can only provide partial answers to many questions regarding immigration policy because the issues are so intertwined with value questions.

Immigration and Urban Regional Processes.   One theoretical approach to migration is to examine population size. It has been suggested that if labor were homogeneous, then immigration should be limited to the level that would maximize average domestic product. In effect, this population level would approximate maximum per capita income. This theoretical approach has been described as a "fun game that gets us nowhere" (Richardson, 1978, p. 73). There are two problems with the optimum-population-size approach. First, no one can empirically determine the optimum population level. Central-place theory implies a variety of optimum sizes depending upon function. Second, the assumption of homogenous labor masks many conflicts among the various types of labor and capital owners regarding the optimum level of immigration.

A simple supply and demand model of immigration can clarify conflicting interests regarding the migration issue. Suppose U.S. residents were divided into capital owners and laborers. As additional foreign workers enter the country, the rate of labor compensation would drop due to the increased labor supply. The lower compensation rate may cause some domestic workers to reduce their work effort. Specifically, work effort would decrease as wages fell if the domestic supply of labor were upward sloping. Thus, immigrant labor could tend to displace domestic labor. Because of the potential for lowering the wage rate of current workers, labor representatives tend to favor restrictive immigration policies. The competition between low-skilled native and foreign workers often results in conflict, particularly when economic competition is mixed with cultural or racial differences. Bloomberg and Sandoval (1982, p. 120) contrast the tensions along the California-Mexico border with the border shared by Detroit and Windsor, Ontario. Whereas the potential for conflict has led to strains and racial divisions in California, the commonality of interests and/or cultures has resulted in economic integration between Detroit and Windsor "almost as fully as if they were the same nation."

If capital and labor are complementary inputs (i.e., increased labor enhances capital productivity), then capital owners would welcome additional immigrant labor because the larger quantity of workers would tend to enhance the productivity of capital and depress wages. Undoubtedly, many employers recognize that they benefit from an increase in labor supply. The simple model helps explain why some employers and trade associations favor allowing large numbers of migrants into the United States and oppose sanctions on employers who hire illegal aliens. Many industries in the Southwest and the Farm Belt and some unorganized urban manufacturers are dependent upon labor from abroad.

There are several complications that limit the simple labor supply and demand approach. First, consumers may also benefit from high levels of immigration, if migration contributes to lower production costs. The lower wage rates may translate into lower production costs. The lower production costs may be passed on to consumers, particularly if the producers are under competitive pressure to keep prices low. Since workers are also consumers, it is necessary to balance these two effects to determine net benefits from migration for a particular labor group.

A second complication is masked by the assumption that labor is homogeneous. Since there are, in fact, many types of labor, the impact of immigration on wages and employment depends on the type of labor that enters the country and on whether labor markets are linked or segmented. The employment and wage implications of the simple model could be roughly accurate in the case of homogeneous labor if labor markets are linked. If labor markets are linked, wages of employees in sectors with few immigrant workers may be depressed because of the possibility of substitution among types of labor. However, many economists believe that labor markets are segmented. If labor markets were completely segmented, each market segment is unaffected by events in other markets. In this case, only the domestic workers who competed directly with immigrant workers would be adversely affected by immigration. Borjas (1987) presented empirical evidence indicating that immigrants are a substitute for some types of U.S. labor, but a complement to other types. Consequently, the overall affect of immigrant labor on earnings of the native born is small.

Evidence indicates that even if markets are segmented, the skills of migrants are so varied that few labor markets are unaffected by migration. About 40 percent of legal migrants are managerial or professional workers, and about 30 percent are operators, fabricators, and laborers. Consequently, there are no major labor groups protected from competition due to migration. However, the immigration mix is changing. The portion of unskilled and semiskilled immigrants is increasing. If illegal immigrants were included in the statistical estimates, the number of unskilled laborers would increase significantly.

Even if most immigrants were low-skilled workers, the simple supply and demand model fails to distinguish long- and short-run labor composition. The longer migrants are in the country, the more likely they will be to acquire the skills necessary to qualify for higher skilled jobs. Therefore, skilled workers will not necessarily be protected from competition from unskilled immigrants in the long run. (The potential for skill changes is even greater from an intergenerational perspective.) However, some economists who support the segmental perspective have marshalled evidence indicating that it is very difficult for a worker to move from one labor segment to another even accounting for intergenerational changes.

Finally, not all migrants are poor or unskilled. Many bring substantial capital and skills into the country when they migrate. In fact, most countries have immigration policies that make it much easier to gain entrance if the applicants have assets. British Columbia has experienced a construction boom due to the relocation of wealthy Chinese from Hong Kong. Thus, the stereotype of the impoverished immigrant with no way to earn a living but by selling labor is not always accurate. It may describe illegal migrations but does not fit the case of legal migrants where the United States is selective; generally insuring that migrants have a means of earning a living.

Illegal-Immigration Policy.   It is estimated that 40 million Americans compete directly with illegal aliens for jobs. The Immigration Reform and Control Act of 1986 is an attempt to restrict undocumented workers without disrupting industries that depend upon such workers. The highlights of this act are:

1. Sanctions on employers who knowingly hire undocumented workers. The sanctions increase depending upon the number of offenses.
2. A "guest worker" program for seasonal agricultural workers.
3. An increase in border-patrol funding.
4. A legislative program for workers who have resided in the United States since 1982.

In addition, U.S. political and military involvement in Central America has been justified on the basis that improved economic conditions in some countries will decrease the push factor and, hence, reduce illegal migration.

A permanent solution to the illegal-immigrant issue will be difficult to achieve because it is clearly in the interest of many residents of other countries to enter the United States and many U.S. citizens have an interest in hiring low-paid workers. The Immigration Reform and Control Act as well as other foreign-policy activities represent efforts to reduce the benefits of illegal migration and increase the penalties.

Foreign Ownership.   Recently, many observers in the United States have become concerned about the inflow of foreign-owned capital. The concern is new to the United States, but other countries have been concerned with issues of outside ownership for some time. For instance, some Canadians have long believed that U.S. residents own too much of Canada. Concern about the desirability of outside ownership has been a regional issue for some time. During the early 20th century, some individuals in the western United States expressed concern regarding the concentration of ownership by individuals and banks in the eastern United

States. Today, the issue is most pronounced at the level of the nation-region.

Tolchin and Tolchin (1987) suggested that foreign ownership of key industrial sectors threatens to dilute U.S. political sovereignty. Foreign ownership, they contended, may undermine the ability of the United States to control its own fate and defend its status as an economic power. Other observers have expressed the fear that the situation will degenerate to a point where important economic decisions are made abroad and U.S. workers become relegated to low-paying, routine jobs.

The concern about foreign investment was sparked by changes in the amount and pattern of investments. The United States became a debtor nation in 1986. The shock of this headline-grabbing change caused concern among many observers. However, some experts contended that the statistic was very sensitive to arbitrary accounting procedures and, therefore, not particularly meaningful. For instance, the appreciation of U.S.–owned assets abroad was not included.

Other observers contend that it does not matter to typical citizens whether the factory in which they work is owned by a capitalist living in another country or in a nearby suburb. It has further been argued that the fact that foreigners are willing to invest in a country indicates that the country is a secure place to invest. Thus, foreign investment indicates economic strength rather than weakness.

The flow of knowledge may be affected by ownership patterns. Managerial skills or other types of technical know-how may be transferred along with the investment. On the one hand, the information flow may be beneficial to the recipient region. For instance, Japanese automobile investments in the United States have undoubtedly contributed to the development of new management and production techniques on the part of domestic producers and have helped revitalize the automobile economy in the Midwest. On the other hand, foreign acquisitions may allow other nations to acquire technologies that will negate advantages of the target region.

It is doubtful that a general consensus regarding the desirability of foreign-direct investments can be reached. However, the opinion of most economists is that the free flow of capital across borders is desirable. In specific cases, the burden of proof rests with those wishing to restrict foreign investment.

SUMMARY

This chapter examined interregional resource flows. Polar theoretical models provided the initial perspective. On the one hand, if resources are immobile, but commodities are mobile, then regions will benefit by producing and exporting the product in which they have a comparative advantage. Commodity trade can be a substitute for factor mobility if regions export products that require a high proportion of the abundant factor of production. On the other hand, if resources are perfectly mobile, they will tend to flow from the low-return to the high-return area. If compensation reflects productivity, then the resource flow will increase total output.

Migration is the result of push factors in the place of origin and pull factors in the destination area. However, pull factors appear to be stronger migration determinants than the push factors. Most empirical studies indicate that labor tends to migrate to high-wage areas, but wages alone are inadequate to explain migration determinants. Migration will tend to equalize wages; however, in the presence of equalizing differences, wage differentials will persist.

The Harris-Todaro model described the tendency for workers to move to high-wage high-unemployment areas because the higher wage offsets the probability of unemployment.

Gravity models assume that migration between two regions increases in relation to population and decreases with distance between places. A major criticism of gravity models is that they are poorly specified, because they fail to reflect all of the factors that contribute to migration. The beaten-path effect illustrates how knowing individuals who have already migrated to an area may encourage additional individuals to migrate.

Capital is generally considered to be a mobile factor of production, although there are numerous obstacles to capital movement. In light of various definitions of capital, three types of mobility can be identified. First, money capital can be transferred. Second, physical assets can be moved. Third, the value of physical capital may change.

Patterns of the movement of innovations and ideas also affect economic development. Innovations tend to originate in metropolitan areas. The spread of innovations occurs: (1) across and down the urban hierarchy and (2) away from the innovative center in a radial pattern.

Interregional resource flows play an important role in policy questions. The issue of whether jobs should move to high-unemployment areas or whether people should move to where the jobs are may hinge on the relative mobility of labor and capital. Immigration policy is aimed at restricting international labor mobility without imposing an undue burden on families or on businesses that use migrant labor. Recently many commentators have expressed concern over the level of foreign investment.

REFERENCES

Bloomberg, Warner, and Rodrigo Martinez Sandoval. "Hispanic-American Urban Order: A Border Perspective." In *Cities in the 21st Century,* ed. G. Gappert and R. Knight. Beverly Hills, Calif. Sage Publications, 1982, pp. 112–32.

Borjas, George J. "Immigrants, Minorities and Labor Market Competition." *Industrial Labor Relations Review* 40, no. 3, April 1987, pp. 382–92.

Borts, George, H., and Jerome Stein. *Economic Growth in A Free Market*. New York: Columbia University Press, 1964.*

Bowen, Harry P.; Edward E. Leamer; and Leo Sveikauskas. "Multicountry Multifactor Tests of the Factor Abundance Theory." *American Economic Review*, December 1987, pp. 791–809.

Clark, Gordon L. *Interregional Migration, National Policy and Social Justice*. New Jersey: Rowman and Allanheld, 1983.

Dunn, L. F. "Measuring the Value of Community." *Journal of Urban Economics* 6, 1979, pp. 371–82.

Gerking, Shelby D., and William N. Weirick. "Compensating Differences and Interregional Wage Differentials." *Review of Economics and Statistics*, 1983, pp. 483–87.

Giese, Alenka and William A. Testa, "Can Industrial R&D Survive the Decline of Production Activity?" *Economic Development Quarterly* 2, no. 4, November 1988, pp. 326–38.

Graves, Philip E. "A Life-Cycle Empirical Analysis of Migration and Climate, by Race." *Journal of Urban Economics* 6, no. 2, 1979, pp. 135–47.

Greenwood, Michael J. "Urban Economic Growth and Migration: Their Interaction." *Environment and Planning* 5, 1973, pp. 91–112.

———. "Human Migration: Theory, Models, and Empirical Studies." *Journal of Regional Science* 25, no. 4, 1985, pp. 521–43.

Greenwood, Michael J., Gary L. Hunt, and John M. McPowell. "Migration and Employment Change: Empirical Evidence on the Spatial and Temporal Dimensions of the Linkage." *Journal of Regional Science* 26, no. 2, May 1986, pp. 223–34.

Hamermesh, Daniel S. "The Demand for Labor in the Long Run." In *Handbook of Labor Economics*, vol. 1, ed. Orley Ashenfelter and Richard Layard. New York: Elsevier-North Holland, 1986, pp. 429–68.

Harris, J. R., and M. P. Todaro. "Migration, Unemployment and Development: A Two Sector Analysis." *American Economic Review* 60, 1970, pp. 126–42.*

Hunt, Janet C., and James B. Kau. "Migration and Wage Growth: A Human Capital Framework." *Southern Economic Journal* 51, no. 3, January 1985, pp. 647–710.

Lansing, John B., and Eva Mueller. *The Geographic Mobility of Labor*. Ann Arbor, Mich. Survey Research Center, Institute for Social Research, 1967, p. 250.

Mills, Edwin S., and Bruce W. Hamilton. *Urban Economics*. Glenview, Ill.: Scott, Foresman, 1989.

Pred, A. R. *The Spatial Dynamics of U.S. Urban-Industrial Growth*. Cambridge, Mass.: MIT Press, 1966.

*Classics.

President's Commission for a National Agenda for the Eighties, *Urban America in the Eighties: Perspectives and Prospects*. Washington, D.C.: U.S. Government Printing Office, 1981.

Richardson, Harry W. *Urban Economics*. Hinsdale, Ill: Dryden Press, 1978, chapter 12.

Roskill Commission. "Report on the Third London Airport." London: Covenant of Great Britain, 1970.

Schreiber, Arthur F., and Richard B. Clemmer, *Economics of Urban Problems: An Introduction*. Boston: Houghton Mifflin, 1982.

Tolchin, Susan, and Martin Tolchin. *Buying into America*. New York: Times Books, 1987.

U.S. Department of Health and Human Services, Office of Income Security Policy. *Overview of the Seattle-Denver Income Maintenance Experiment: Final Report*. Washington, D.C.: U.S. Government Printing Office, May 1983.

Wagman, Barnet, and Nancy Folbre. "The Feminization of Inequality: Some New Patterns." *Challenge* 31, issue 6, November/December 1968, pp. 56–59.

Chapter Ten

Land Use

Urban observers recognize that land uses are segregated. Typically, about 30 percent of urban land is used for residential purposes, 10 percent for manufacturing, 5 percent for commercial activities, and 35 percent is devoted to other uses such as public buildings and vacant land. There are subcategories within the broader land-use divisions. For instance, residential housing is distinguished by the number of units in the structure, income of residents, and neighborhood ethnic characteristics. Areas of transition also exist where mixed uses are evident. Although a few planned communities deliberately blended different land uses, most land-use patterns evolved as the result of market forces regulated by government.

Previous chapters have tended to examine metropolitan areas as a whole, while occasionally discussing problems associated with particular parts of an area. This chapter describes how particular parcels of land are used and why they are used as they are. Just as important, the chapter shows how the economic factors that determine the use of individual parcels interact to generate land-use patterns. The first section describes theoretical aspects of rent and resource allocation. Next, we take a microscopic view of land use by examining the site-decision process for the use of a single parcel of land. The following section describes variations in the demand for land within the metropolitan area for a single activity. These sections combine to show why a single industry's and household's demand will fall as distances from the urban center increase. Next, competition among alternative land uses is introduced and a pattern of various land uses emerges. The fifth section examines changes in land-use patterns. Finally, political and institutional aspects of land use are discussed.

THE NATURE OF RENT

Rent is the return to land. The everyday meanings of rent and land differ from formal economic definitions. Technically, "land" is a natural factor of production, and, therefore, the supply of land is unaffected by price.[1] The quantity of land cannot be increased in response to higher prices or decreased in response to lower prices. Although we may speak of increasing "land" by such actions as clearing fields, such usage muddles several factors of production. A cleared field represents the combination of three resources—labor and capital used to clear the field and the original land itself. In addition to soil, "land" includes coal, sun, rain, and all other natural factors of production. Economists are careful to distinguish between land and property. A property is land and buildings. In formal economics, rent is the return to land. For convenience, we may refer to property rent as the return to land and capital improvement.

Determination of Land Rent

Rent is determined by the interaction of supply and demand for land as shown in Figure 10–1.

Notice that, unlike most factors of production, an increase in the price of land (rent) will not bring forth an increase in supply. The supply of certain types of land, such as commercial land, may be increased by market forces and by political decisions, such as zoning changes. However, additional land for one purpose must be at the expense of another type of land use.

Rent and Productivity. Business demand for land is based upon land's contribution to revenues. The marginal product of an extra unit of land (MP_i) is the physical output resulting from the use of an extra unit of land in the production process. If the firm sells its output in a competitive market, it will receive a constant price on each extra unit sold. Thus, a farm or firm would not be willing to pay more for additional land than the value of the increased output attributable to that land. Of course, they would like to pay as little as possible for the extra land. However, if there is competition among producers, they will outbid each other until the land rent equals the land's contribution to the firm's profits. When a firm sells in a competitive market, the product price is not affected by a firm's output. In this case, the demand for land is equal to the value of the marginal product, VMP. If all nonland inputs are held constant, the value of the marginal product may be expressed as the price of the output times the marginal product of an additional unit of land:

$$VMP_i = P_o \times MP_i, \tag{1}$$

---

[1] Land, what nature has endowed, is considered in fixed supply. We can get more arable land by applying labor and capital to the natural endowment; the endowment itself is not affected by human efforts.

FIGURE 10–1   Aggregate Supply and Demand for Land

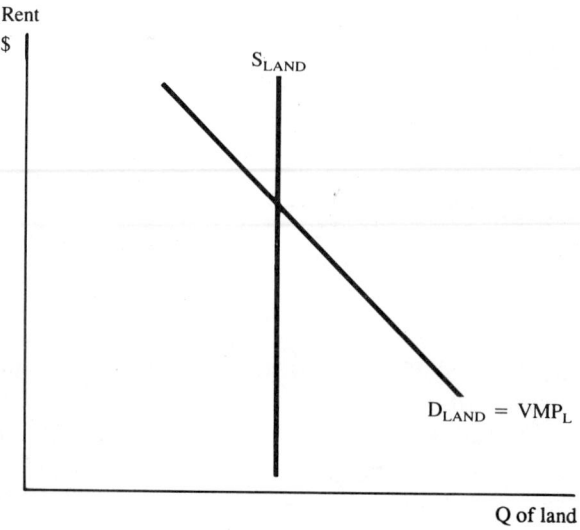

Land is fixed in supply. Consequently, changes in demand affect rent but not quantity.

where VMP_i = The value of the marginal product of the ith unit of land,
   P_o = The net price of output (after deducting transportation cost), and
   MP_i = The marginal product of the ith unit of land.

The VMP function declines as the quantity of land used in production increases because the marginal product of land falls as implied by the law of diminishing marginal productivity.[2] When the VMP is greater than the market rent for a unit of land, firms will employ more land, causing the MP and VMP to decrease. The VMP will decrease until it equals the rental rate.

If a firm has monopolistic power in the output market, the VMP of land will decline more rapidly than in the case of a competitive producer,

---

[2] The law of diminishing marginal productivity states that, as more units of a variable factor are combined with a fixed factor, output will increase but the increases will eventually taper off. If not for the law of diminishing marginal productivity, all food could be produced in a flower pot by adding more capital and labor.

because product price will fall as output increases. In addition, the decline in the marginal product of land will cause the *VMP* to fall. Thus, the *VMP* of land will fall for two reasons.

Ricardian Rent.   David Ricardo (1911) was one of the first economists to analyze land rent. Although his theory was designed to explain agricultural rent, it has implications for urban land markets. Ricardo believed the return to land was a residual. Since labor and capital had elastic supplies, they had to be paid competitive rates. Whatever was left after paying the mobile factors of production was the residual to land—rent.

Ricardo determined that various sites receive different rents because of varying productivity. Productivity of land was attributed to its fertility and its proximity to markets. (In urban markets, proximity is much more important than fertility.) The most productive land receives the highest rent because it has the highest residual, and marginal land on which the value of the crops just equals the cost of the nonland resources needed to produce and transport the output to market earns no rent. Ricardo believed that the most productive land would be cultivated first. Economic development and population growth cause agricultural prices to increase, thus causing additional land to be brought into production and rents on currently productive land to increase (p. 34).

> When in the progress of society, land of the second degree of fertility is taken into cultivation, rent immediately commences on that of the first quality, and the amount of that rent will depend on the difference in quality of the two portions of land. (Ricardo, 1911, p. 34)

Ricardo's view of land rent is illustrated in Figure 10–2. It shows costs and returns on three grades of land. The average- and marginal-cost curves show the costs of cultivation and transportation excluding land rents. The most productive parcel is site A as implied by the lower cost curves. Site C is the least productive parcel. Site A will be used if the price of the output is over $1.00. At this price, 100 units will be produced. However, since the value of the output will be just sufficient to cover nonland costs, the site will not earn rents. Only after price increases to $1.50 will site B be cultivated. At the higher price, rent on site A will then equal $60—the total revenue ($1.50 × 200) less nonland costs ($1.20 × 200). Because of low productivity, site C will not be used in production and, hence, will earn no rent. If price continues to rise above $1.50, site B will earn rents. Site C will not be used until price increases to $2.00.

As product price increases, output on land already in production also increases because additional units of capital and labor are combined with the constant quantity of land. Figure 10–2 shows the more productive site producing a higher level of output for each product price. This result is due to more intensive use as well as greater productivity per se.

FIGURE 10–2 Costs and Rents on Three Sites

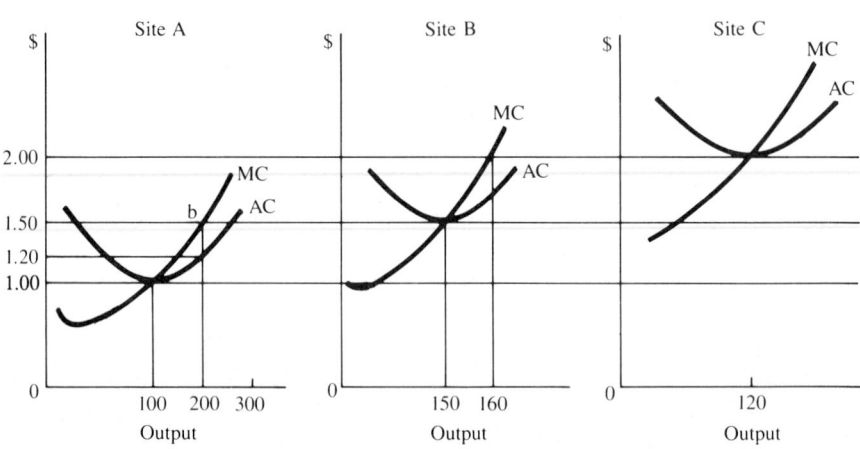

As the product price increases, (1) rent on land already in use increases, (2) output of land already in use increases, and (3) new land is brought into production.

Ricardo's analysis was originally used to explain the use of agricultural land, but it can also be applied to urban land use. Imagine that site A represents a parcel near the urban core. As demand for goods produced at the urban core increases, site A would be used more intensively and its marginal product as well as rent would increase. Eventually, outlying land would be brought into production because of the high rents earned by site A. In other words, outlying site B might be developed. However, the more-distant land would command a lower rent because its distance from the urban center increases the cost of doing business, thus lowering productivity. Furthermore, the more-distant site would be used at a lower level of intensity—combined with less labor and capital just as the less fertile agricultural land was used less intensively in the Ricardian model.[3]

---

[3] Rent is a payment above the amount necessary for society to secure the services of the factor of production. This fact has led some economists to use the term "rent" in a different context. Any factor of production can earn rent if it received above the minimum compensation necessary to cause the factor to be offered for use. For instance, suppose a popular rock group earns $100,000 for a performance. If they were not popular, they could only earn $10,000 and would perform for that amount. They would perform for any amount over $10,000. The difference between the $100,000 they receive and their next best opportunity, $10,000, has been termed "rent."

Of course, we all want to be paid above the minimum necessary to induce us to do what we're doing. So we try to capture "rents," possibly using the political system to do so. Consequently, some observers have called ours a rent-seeking society.

Is Rent Justified?

Henry George (1897) believed that, since the supply of land was perfectly inelastic, there was no justification for the landowner's return, and he questioned whether it was appropriate for landowners to receive compensation since they provide no useful economic activity. In order to capture the landowner's unearned return, George proposed a tax on land that would equal the entire rent that the landowner could receive if the site were put to its most profitable use. When Henry George wrote this, he anticipated that a single tax on the land would generate all the revenue governments would need. However, today only about 6.4 percent of income is estimated to be a return to land (Mills and Hamilton, 1989, p. 92), so it would not raise sufficient revenues. Yet, many economists believe that a land tax is a good idea and should be used to replace other taxes to the extent possible.

The advantage of George's scheme is that, unlike a tax on any other factor of production, a tax on land would not diminish the supply of land available. If the landowner chose to withhold the land from production or employ it in a suboptimal use, the tax equal to the maximum potential rent would still be due. For example, if the tax on site A in Figure 10–2 were $60, when product price was $1.50, the land would still be used to produce the same level of output, 200. The landowner would receive no rent, but a loss would be incurred if it were used in any other way. Therefore, the landowner would have an incentive to employ land in its highest and best use.

A land tax has theoretical merit, but in practice it is difficult to implement. First, a 100 percent tax on the value of land would be confiscatory. Most current landowners paid for their land, so taxing away all their rents would be unfair. A confiscatory tax would also be unconstitutional. Second, it is difficult for tax assessors to know what the maximum potential rent of land would be. For example, suppose that a farmer uses his land to grow corn. After deducting all the nonland costs, including the opportunity cost of the farmer's labor, the residual to land may be $500. However, the land tax should equal $500 only if there were no other uses that would generate a greater residual. If an alternative land use could yield a higher residual to land, a tax equal to 100 percent of market rent would to be larger. There are few, if any, tax assessors competent to make such judgments. Finally, opponents of a land tax have argued that it would be unfair to tax land rents and not tax the other forms of rent, such as talent, discussed in the previous section.

George's ideas have stimulated several more practical proposals. A tax on all or a high portion of the increase in land value has been proposed. Increases in land value are usually due to changes in the environment around the site—roads, population movements, other development—and are seldom due to anything the landowner may have done (other than perhaps influencing the political process). So, the argument goes, the landowner should not receive the benefits of land-value appreciation. Therefore, rather than taxing the total value of land, only the unearned increment should be taxed.

Other economists have argued that property tax structures should be revised so that a higher portion of the tax is allocated to land and a correspondingly lower portion is allocated to improvements. Following George's analysis, they believe that a tax on land will have no effect on resource-allocation decisions, but a tax on improvements to land (i.e., buildings) will discourage improvements. Most jurisdictions divide the assessed value of property into the value of land and the value of improvements. However, the same tax rate is usually applied to land and improvements. The expectation is that, by lowering the tax on improvements while increasing the tax on land, the same amount of revenue could be raised while reducing the disincentive to improve property. Tax-rate differentials between improvements and land are being applied in some cities, including Pittsburgh.

Rent and Value

Rent generated by land can be thought of as a flow of income. The sum of the (discounted) present value of the future rents equals the land value. In a perfectly functioning economy, the present value of future returns would also equal the sales price.

If land were expected to provide a constant return in perpetuity, the formula for determining value is:

$$V = \frac{R}{r} \text{ or } R = Vr \tag{2}$$

where V = Land value,

R = The periodic return (net of other costs such as property taxes), and

r = Appropriate discount rate.

Following Ricardo, R would be the residual to land after other factors of production have been compensated. The equation states that the periodic cost of holding land equals rent. If the only cost of holding land were foregone interest, r would equal the interest rates ($r = i$), and, in a competitive market, the rent would just equal the cost of holding the asset, (iV).

Equation 2 expresses the conceptual link between land values and the discount rate for assets having a constant and perpetual return. In practice, even agricultural property is not pure land—most agricultural land benefits from numerous capital improvements that have a limited life. Furthermore, the assumption of a constant return is unrealistic. In order to develop a more useful valuation model, an approach should (1) examine the value of property—land and capital—and (2) allow for fluctuating periodic returns.

The general formula for estimating property value is:

$$V = NOI_o + NOI_1/(1 + r) + NOI_2/(1 + r)^2 + \cdots \\ + NOI_n/(1 + r)^n \qquad (3)$$

where V = Property value,

r = Appropriate discount rate, and

NOI = Net Operating Income (income net of operating expenses, such as utilities, property taxes, and maintenance) in ith year, o indicating now.

Equation 3 is important because, when projects are being considered for development, estimates of future net operating income are combined with the discount rate to determine the value of the proposed property. The estimated value can be compared to the project's construction costs as a guide to the type of development that should occur. If the construction costs were subtracted from the estimated value of the property, the residual to land for developed properties would be determined.

In applying equation 3 to the case of, say, an apartment building, NOI would be the rents minus the operating costs, such as management, labor, and property taxes, etc. NOI_n might include a liquidation value. The discount rate, r, might also be adjusted to reflect costs other than the interest rate. For instance, in addition to the pure interest rate, the discount rate should be increased to reflect extra risk, depreciation, management effort, and so forth.

Alston (1986) examined factors that determined the value of U.S. farm land during a period of rapid inflation. On the one hand, the increase in expected inflation would tend to increase future sale prices (NOI_n), hence increasing value. On the other hand, inflationary expectations would increase the discount rate, tending to lower value. Alston concluded that expectations had a modest effect on land prices. The reason for the rapid appreciation during the period was primarily attributable to increases in net income.

Although the formula for converting future rents to present value is straightforward, application is often difficult. It is difficult to determine the appropriate discount rate, and forecasts of future rents are subject to error. Furthermore, if land is improved, it is difficult to separate the return that is due to capital and labor from the return due to land (unless the value of the improvements is already known). Nevertheless, valuation concepts expressed in equation 3 are important in determining how a particular site will be used.

SITE USE

What determines the land use of a particular site? Economists have focused upon two important determinants of land use: (1) highest and best use and (2) access. Both concepts are useful in understanding the development of a particular site as well as in establishing a basis for the land-development and planning process.

Highest and Best Use

The residual to land depends upon how the land is used. Clearly, the residual to land will be different if the site is used as a parking lot or a grocery store. The land use that provides the highest residual to land is the highest and best use. The most profitable, legal use of land is called the highest and best use.

The highest and best use is not necessarily the most socially desirable use because land uses entail considerable positive and negative spillovers. Construction of a supermarket in the middle of a rare downtown open space may be the most profitable use, but some might argue that it is not best in a social or ethical sense. However, the profitability of a particular land use is usually due to the fact that consumers are willing and able to pay for location in the form of higher prices for the goods sold at that location. Therefore, while private profitability and most socially desirable uses are not synonymous, they may be the same because the market for land reflects societal demand for products at particular places.

The most profitable use of land is seldom the most intensive or most highly developed use. A high-rise apartment is usually more valuable than a single-family house, but it will not necessarily be more profitable to construct high rises rather than single-family houses on vacant land. Low-density housing is built in many areas because (1) the cost of construction for a high rise is also greater than for a single-family dwelling and (2) rents per unit may have to fall in order to ensure adequate occupancy. If rents don't fall, higher vacancies may cause net revenues to decline. The second factor is apt to be particularly true for apartment units in areas with low population densities. The key question in determining highest and best use is: What use will provide the greatest return to land (residual) after construction and operating costs have been subtracted?

Table 10–1 employs hypothetical numbers to show the relationship between intensity of development, cost, and the return to land. Keep in mind that the values shown as "present value of income" could have been derived by an application of Equation 3. The economies of vertical construction are illustrated by the lower per story cost of the second level. However, construction costs per story start to increase after the second level because it is increasingly expensive to construct additional

TABLE 10–1 Highest and Best Use Determination

Intensity of Use (number of stories)	Present Value of Income	Present Value of Nonland Costs	Present Value Residual to Land
1	$ 200,000	$ 100,000	$100,000
2	400,000	175,000	225,000
3	575,000	300,000	275,000
4	750,000	525,000	225,000
5	900,000	775,000	125,000
6	1,000,000	1,250,000	−250,000

stories. At the same time, the present value of the property increases at a decreasing rate, reflecting the fact that per unit property rents might fall due to increased vacancies or the need to lower rents to avoid increased vacancies. The combined result of these forces causes the present value of land's residual to fall after the third floor. The present value of the return to the land is maximized at three stories. Hence, a building of three stories is the highest and best use.

The example illustrated the highest-and-best-use principle by examining different heights of a residential building. In all cases, the land use was residential. However, the same method applies to the choice among types of uses. For example, to determine whether a bakery or a three-story apartment would be the highest and best use, a similar calculation of the residual to land could be made.

Market mechanisms reinforce the tendency of land to be put to its highest and best use. For example, suppose an individual owns a parcel of land for which the most profitable use requires construction of a three-story apartment building (use 3 in Table 10–1). However, the owner of the property intends to build a one-story building (use 1 in Table 10–1). Perhaps the owner doesn't know a multistory structure is the highest and best use, or perhaps the owner lacks the financial or other technical skills necessary to develop a three-story apartment. The land could still be developed according to its highest and best use, because a developer might notice the vacant parcel (developers actively seek out such properties) and after analysis determine that a three-story apartment would be optimal. The developer could offer to buy the land for a maximum of $275,000. Since the residual to land is only $100,000 as a single-story building, there is ample bargaining range in which the two parties may reach a mutually satisfactory deal. Perhaps the original owner will sell the land and use the proceeds to purchase a property elsewhere on which a one-story building would be the highest and best use. If the owner knows the initial market value of the property, he would find it more profitable to sell the land and buy another lot rather than develop it as a one-story building.

If the real estate market were operating with perfect knowledge, there would be many potential buyers willing to pay a maximum of $275,000. Thus, competition would drive the price to exactly $275,000.

The discussion of the highest and best use has been about use of land prior to development. The highest-and-best-use principle also applies to changing preexisting structures. The use that will provide the greatest residual after additional capital costs, such as remodeling or demolition costs, have been subtracted from the total value of the renovated property is the highest and best use. This approach implicitly assumes that existing construction costs ("sunk" costs) must be paid even if the building is demolished. Table 10–2 illustrates how the owner of a gas station should analyze the modification of his property to either add a convenience grocery or to convert it into a body shop. The addition of a convenience grocery would cost more than the increase in the present value of the income generated by the improvements. Consequently, the gas station/grocery would not be a profitable land-use change. The conversion to a body shop is feasible because the present value of the increase income is greater than the cost of the improvements.

Accessibility

Access is the principal determinant of highest and best use in an urban environment. As the accessibility of land to urban goods increases, its productivity and, hence, value also increase. In fact, the locational choice involves a trade-off between access to a variety of other locations on the one hand and the cost of real estate at a given location on the other. The role of access as a factor in the evolution of cities has been recognized by Williams (1971).

> Urban locational decisions, indeed the very creation of cities, are the net product of many people trying to become more accessible to one another. The same process that creates cities continues after they are formed. (p. 30)

TABLE 10–2   Highest and Best Use of a Developed Property

Land-Use Conversion	Present Value of Income Change	Conversion Costs	Residual to Existing Property
Gas station (existing use)	0	0	0
Body shop	$52,500	$20,000	$32,500
Gas/grocery	10,000	15,000	−5,000

Pioneers in land economics viewed distance as a "social friction" that needed to be overcome. Friction, of course, is a metaphor for transportation and communication costs. As a general rule, the more accessible a location is to the positive elements in the environment, the more valuable it will be. However, different types of land uses call for access to different things. A commercial establishment may seek access to markets that make it easier (and cheaper) for customers to make a buying trip. Likewise, it is easier and cheaper for an establishment to deliver a product if its customers are accessible. As a result, land planners and developers recognize that the more accessible a location, the greater its profit potential. In addition to markets, businesses also seek access to a productive labor force, other businesses, and so forth. Households also desire access against others and to trade off overall access for larger lot size or lower cost per acre.

Proximity and access are not the same thing. Often, access is limited by social, political, and geographical barriers, in addition to distance. For example, in most suburban areas, individuals seek access to school districts. Political access explains why property values jump thousands of dollars from one side of a street to the other. The fact that housing prices in one school district are higher than in another means that families living in the more expensive houses will likely have higher incomes. This will reinforce the desirability of the school district because many parents like to have their children associate with children of higher-income families.

Some individuals relocate to improve access. Economists refer to this behavior as voting with your feet. However, such voting presumes families can afford to move. Often, poor households attempt to create access by political and social activities. For example, a group that lobbies city hall for a new park is, in effect, attempting to improve the access of neighborhood residents to recreational facilities.

Time and convenience are important elements of access. Modern transportation networks have made access as much a function of urban infrastructure—type of roads, availability of mass transportation, etc.—as of simple physical distance. There are also social dimensions to the accessibility concept. Fear of crime, for example, has caused many individuals to feel that areas in the central city are not accessible to them.

The Land-Development Process

This section builds upon land-use theory by showing the type of analysis that land developers use to determine highest and best use in a world where information is costly and imperfect. It provides an indication of how the hypothetical numbers in Tables 10–1 and 10–2 can be derived.

FIGURE 10–3   Steps in a Land-Use Study

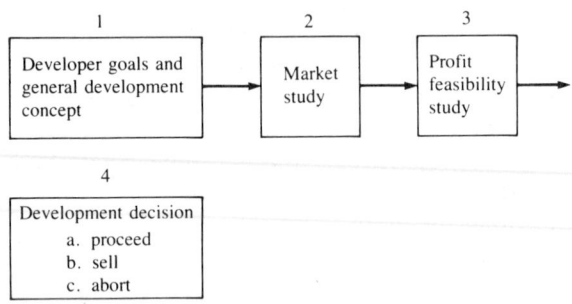

A typical land-use study will progress from questions that can be answered relatively easily and inexpensively to questions that are more difficult to address.

The amount of effort that goes into a land-use study depends upon the scope of the project and the value of the land. It would not be cost effective to evaluate every possible land use for a particular site. Some decisions are based only on hunches. For instance, a retailer may open a store simply because it is believed to be a good area and because space is available. However, major decisions are usually based upon careful analysis. Figure 10–3 summarizes the steps in a typical land-use study.

Developer Goals.   The developer normally initiates the land-development process. The developer's objective may be approximated by the desire to maximize profits, but routes to profit maximization include maximizing current cash flow, tax shelter, appreciation, personal use, or other factors. Income generation might be the goal of a retired investor, while a younger person might want to emphasize appreciation. Thus, developers normally determine their appropriate mix of objectives before focusing on particular real estate investments. During the early planning stages, a developer may have a site and wish to determine a better use for it or may have a general development concept and be seeking an appropriate site.

The initial concept should fit the developer's goals. For instance, construction of a new apartment complex may have good appreciation potential but it may not generate short-term cash flow. The development concept might simply be a rough idea that an apartment complex or an office tower would be profitable in a particular area. Preliminary architectural sketches may be drawn to illustrate the proposed concept, but the ideas are very tentative at this stage.

The Market Study. After a development concept has been tentatively identified, the analysis proceeds to the market study phase. The market study will help determine whether there is a market for the space under consideration and what potential impediments exist. The market study may also help the developer secure a loan, attract investors, or argue for public support, such as zoning changes or development incentives.

Suppose the general development concept is for an office building. The current and future market for the office space will be examined. The land-development researcher will usually develop a grid showing characteristics of existing offices in the area, including rents, occupancy rates, location, and amenities. This information will give the developer an idea of whether there is a current demand for additional space, the rental range that can be expected, and what features the development should include. Future employment will be forecast to determine whether the demand for office space will continue. Building permits will be examined to assess future increases in the quantity of space available.

The concepts of supply and demand are useful in market analysis even though supply and demand curves are seldom estimated. On the demand side, researchers normally assume that existing rents for similar projects, perhaps adjusted for inflation, will prevail. If the project is unique enough to command above- (or below-) average rents, the reasons for the above market rents should be strong. Market growth is also examined to provide an indication of how the demand curve will shift. Population growth is a good indicator of demand increases for residential and retail commercial properties. Demand for industrial and office space is harder to forecast because these land uses depend upon employment growth in specific industries. A target rental range for the proposed project is based upon the prevailing and future market conditions.

Supply-side factors include the planned new developments that may be indicated by building permits and other current activities. Current occupancy rates are used to determine whether there is an under- or oversupply at current rents. An estimated occupancy rate for the proposed development will be established based upon rent levels and the prevailing market conditions. If occupancy rates were generally low in the area, few developers would undertake a project even if rents were high, because such a market situation is likely to be temporary. The low occupancy rates will tend to depress rents. In this case, rents may be projected to grow slowly or fall.

Profit Feasibility. The market study should help the developer decide whether a development can be sold or rented within the target price range, but it does not assess whether the project will be profitable. This will be done in the feasibility study. In order to determine profitability, the present value of returns must be compared to the present value of the costs. The returns will normally be spread over the economic life of the property, say, 20 years. Most of the costs will be incurred in the year of construction, although maintenance, utilities, taxes, and possibly financing charges will be future costs. Income tax factors will also be incorporated in the feasibility analysis.

Usually, the initial economic analysis will be based upon quick and dirty assumptions. A pro forma statement, for instance, may show a static picture for a typical year. The static picture ignores variations in cost and revenue patterns that may occur over time. If initial pro forma calculations indicate the project could be profitable, more thorough analysis will be undertaken. The final cash-flow analysis will account for the timing of cash expenditures and receipts during construction and throughout the project's life.

Suppose at some stage the feasibility study indicates that the project will not be profitable. Rather than immediately abandoning the idea, the developer might redesign architectural features to reduce costs. Perhaps some features of the structure could be cut—the number of rest rooms in an office complex could be reduced or gingerbread detailing removed from a facade. Attempts to raise revenues will also be explored. Perhaps space could be rearranged to provide more rentable area. Interaction between the architectural and economic aspects of the plan will continue until a decision is made to abort or proceed with the project.

If the present value of the returns is equal to or greater than the present value of the project costs, the developer will earn or exceed the rate of return given by the discount or target rate. Therefore the project will continue towards development. Table 10–3 is a simplified cash-flow analysis of a project based upon equation 3. Although many of the details of a large-scale model are missing, the basic elements are present. It is based on several assumptions. The project is built in year 0 at a cost of $1.3 million. The immediate costs include land ($300,000) and building ($1,000,000). Income in the first year is projected to be $300,000, and property rents are assumed to increase 4 percent annually throughout the 20-year life of the project. Expenses are 45 percent of rents. Line 3 is the net operating income discussed in conjunction with equation 3. Although property taxes have been deducted from gross income to calculate *NOI*, additional calculations are necessary to account for income tax factors. Depreciation, an important tax shelter item, is $50,000 annually. The developer is in the 30 percent marginal tax bracket, so aftertax income will differ from the before tax income. The seventh row shows aftertax income.

The discounted value of the income flow is shown in row eight. The inventor's discount rate or target rate of return is 10 percent. Accordingly, the present value of the $130,500 after-tax income in year 1 is

TABLE 10–3   A Simple Cash-Flow Analysis

	Year			
	1	2	. . . .	20
1 Income	$300,000	$312,000	. . . .	$ 632,055
2 Operating expenses	135,000	140,400	. . . .	284,425
3 Net operating income	165,000	171,600	. . . .	347,630
4 Cost recovery	50,000	50,000	. . . .	50,000
5 Taxable income	115,000	121,600	. . . .	297,630
6 Change in taxes	34,500	36,480	. . . .	89,289
7 Cash flow after taxes	130,500	135,120	. . . .	258,341
8 PV cash flow after taxes	118,636	111,669	. . . .	38,401
9 Sum of present values on investment	$118,636	$230,306	. . . .	$1,425,738

[1] Increasing at 4 percent per year.
[2] Equal to 45 percent of line 1.
[3] Line 1 minus line 2.
[4] Depreciation at $50,000 annually.
[5] Net operating income less cost recovery.
[6] Taxable income × .30.
[7] Line 3 less increases in taxes.
[8] Line 7 discounted at 10 percent.
[9] Running total of line 9.

$118,636 ($130,500/1.10) and for year 2 it is $111,669 ($135,120/(1.10)^2). Row 9 is simply the sum of the present values for the current year and succeeding years.[4]

After 20 years, the sum of the present value of income is $1,425,738. The present value of the future net income discounted at 10 percent is greater than the project cost, which was assumed to be $1,300,000. Thus the venture would be profitable. If the discount rate were to increase to 15 percent, the present value of the project's net would be insufficient to justify the project.

The value of land is the residual value after accounting for other mobile factors of production used in the construction of the project. Since capital costs were assumed to be $1,000,000, the residual to land suggests a land value of $425,738 ($1,425,738 − $1,000,000). If the developer purchased the land for $300,000, as was initially assumed, he would have gotten a good deal. If other developers recognize that the present value of the returns indicated substantial profits are attainable, they might have been interested in the site, thus, driving the price up and decreasing

---

[4] This figure is determined by application of equation 3 for the appropriate number of years after adjusting for income taxes.

above-normal profits. If, on the other hand, preliminary feasibility analysis indicated that the present value of the returns was less than the present value of the costs (including estimated land costs), the developer would be in a strong position to negotiate the land price downward. Assuming the land market functioned well and assuming the developer had in fact identified the most profitable land use, the property owner would have no better offers.

The Development Decision.   After examining the market and profit-feasibility analysis, the developer will be in a position to determine how to proceed. If it is decided to go forward with the project, the market and profit-feasibility study may serve as a basis for securing a loan or attracting other equity investors. On the other hand, the investor may determine that the project is not feasible or profitable and abort the development. Other options include waiting until market conditions change or selling the plans to a developer who is interested in proceeding with the project.

SPATIAL VARIATIONS IN AN ACTIVITY'S DEMAND FOR LAND

Previous sections described the demand for a parcel of land. This section examines how a particular industry's demand for land varies over space. The central business district is assumed to be the most desirable location. Firms located at the urban center have maximum access to goods and services, and the center is the minimum-transportation-cost point for the metropolis. To further strengthen the pull of the metropolitan center, assume that wherever a commodity is produced it must be shipped to the urban center for export. For still greater simplification, assume that market access is the only relevant locational factor, so spatial variations in labor costs, taxes, public services, and so forth are equal everywhere in the area. Profits depend upon land costs and access to the metropolitan center.

An Industry's Demand for Land.   Why would a firm prefer a location at the center of the metropolitan area, the central business district (CBD)? Assume the CBD is a market center and the only transportation node in the metropolitan area. Some firms may simply be able to sell their products at a higher price because they are closer to their customers. Other firms will absorb delivery costs while selling at a uniform price, as would be the case of a competitive exporter of a product to other regions. For such a product, net price (price less transportation costs) will be greatest at the metropolitan center because it is the minimum-transportation-cost-point for the area as a whole. Thus, total revenue will be greatest at the metropolitan center for each quantity sold. Because we are assuming a uniform transportation surface, it follows that price per unit will fall the farther the firm is from the CBD. This situation is illustrated by the total-revenue curves shown in Figure 10–4(a).

Three separate total-revenue curves are shown in Figure 10–4(a). $TR_{d(1)}$ is the total-revenue curve for a location near the center of the city where price or net revenue is greatest, and $TR_{d(3)}$ is the total-revenue curve for a firm most distant from the center. The linear total-revenue curves implicitly assume that the firm is selling its output in a competitive market. This assumption aids the graphical presentation but does not affect the conclusions. Figure 10–4(a) also shows the total-cost curve for a typical firm. Because one of the outcomes of the model will be land rents at various distances from the CBD, the total-cost curve TC_{LR} excludes land rent but includes normal profits and all other business costs. The shape of the cost curve reflects decreasing costs at small levels of output, but eventually costs increase at an increasing rate.

The firm will maximize profits by producing at the output level where the difference between total revenue and total cost is greatest. As the firm's price increases due to better access, the profit-maximizing level of output will increase as shown in Figure 10–4(a). The higher price encourages firms to produce greater output even though marginal costs are increasing.

If the producer could secure free land at site 1, excess profits could be attained. The excess profits would equal the difference between total revenues and total costs at the profit-maximizing level of output or $100 ($600 − 500). Excess profits would be less at location 2, and no profits could be earned at location 3 because nonland costs equal revenues at the profit-maximizing level of output. However, competition for land will tend to eliminate excess profits from owners of establishments and transfer the benefits to landowners.

The Rent-Bid Curve.   All entrepreneurs in the industry would prefer locations near the urban center. However, competition for the preferable sites will cause rents to increase. The maximum rent an entrepreneur planning to use the land for the use implied in the cost curve in Figure 10–4(a) would be willing and able to pay for site 1, distance d(1) is $100. This is also the amount of excess profits that could be earned if rents were zero. The entrepreneur would still cover all operating constants, including normal profits. In Figure 10–4(b), $150 would represent the maximum land rent for the most accessible site. Competition among firms in the particular industry would ensure that the maximum rent an entrepreneur would be willing and able to pay would also be the minimum necessary to secure the site. Landowners will capture potential excess profits.

The difference between the total-revenue and total-cost (less rent) curves becomes the rent necessary to secure the site. The graph of the

FIGURE 10–4 Derivation of Rent-Bid Curve for an Activity

(a) Costs and revenue

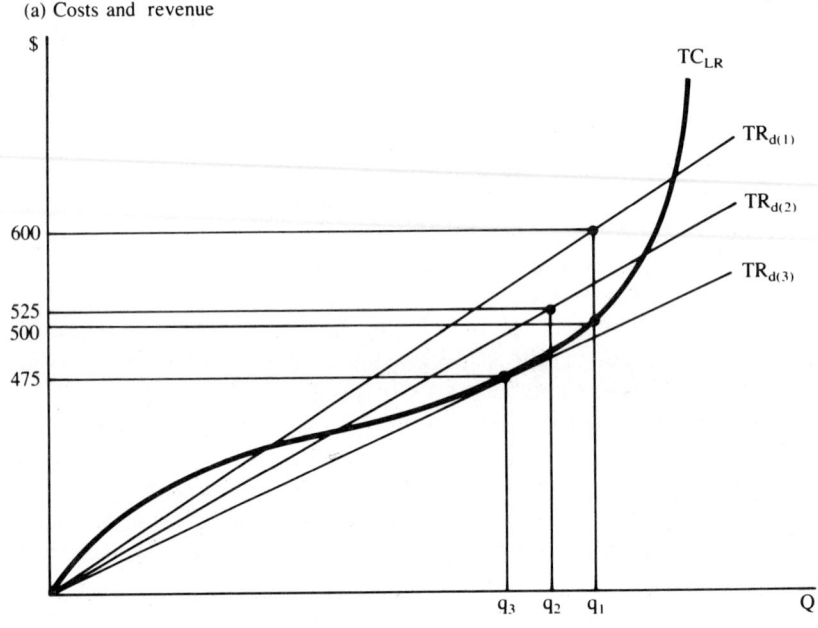

(b) A rent-bid curve

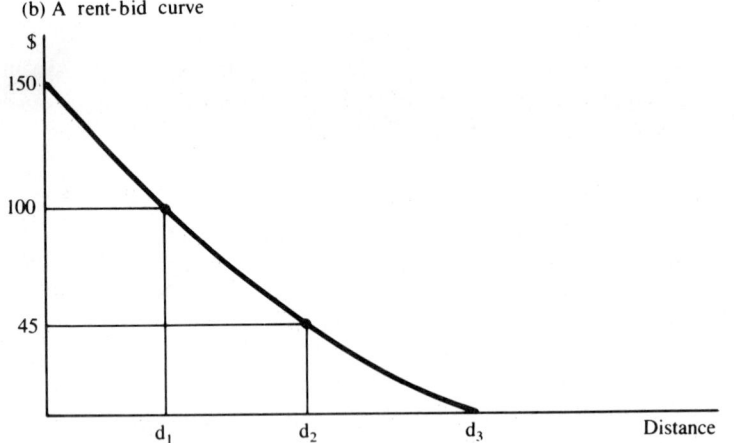

The maximum rent that a business would be willing and able to pay for a site is the difference between nonland costs (including opportunity costs in the case of property owned by the same person who owns the business) and revenues. Maximum rents at each location can be used to form a rent-bid curve.

maximum rents a firm in the industry would pay at various points is a rent-bid curve. The rent-bid curve corresponding to the revenue and cost data used previously is shown in Figure 10–4(b).

The rent-bid curve can also be thought of as a location-/rent-indifference curve because an entrepreneur would be indifferent between the high-rent, central locations and the low-rent, peripheral locations. Each combination results in normal profits but no excess profits.

The Shape of the Rent-Bid Curve.   For many activities, the rent-bid function will be convex from the origin as shown in Figure 10–4(b). In order to understand the shape of the rent-bid curve, suppose transportation costs were the only savings associated with a location at the center of the metropolis and that transportation costs increased linearly with distance. One might assume the rent-bid curve would be linear reflecting the transportation-cost savings. However, firms located near the center will employ land more intensively than firms located on lower-valued land at the periphery of the metropolis since input substitution is possible. A general principle of resource use is that the more valuable a resource, the more intensively it will be used. Since more labor and capital are used per acre, the nearer the site is to the CBD, the greater the marginal product per unit of land. The greater intensity of land use will be a factor increasing the rent for CBD locations. Therefore, land rent will increase at an increasing rate as distance from the CBD decreases.

Long-haul economies in transportation will also affect the shape of the rent-bid curve. A 5-mile trip to the urban core will cost more than half of a 10-mile trip because fixed costs are associated with both trips. Thus, the rent a firm would be willing to pay will fall more and more slowly as distance from the core increases. This is illustrated in Figure 10–5. As distance from the core increases, transportation costs increase, but they increase at a decreasing rate. Rent that would be offered at the most distant site is $1, the value of land in agriculture. The rent at all other sites equals the transportation-cost savings compared to the marginal site at the periphery. Total costs are $101 at all locations. Thus, rent bids fall as one moves away from the city center, but they fall at a slower and slower rate.

Other Attractions of the CBD for Businesses.   The assumption that market access and a central transportation point are the only locational pulls of the CBD may now be relaxed. There are other reasons why a firm would be willing to pay higher rents for a location near the center of a metropolitan area. Central locations provide access to inputs. Many activities, particularly in finance, law, and commerce, depend upon the ability to meet quickly with individuals in related fields. Face-to-face meetings are often necessary on short notice. Quick access is particularly

FIGURE 10–5   A Convex Rent-Bid Curve

Distance from CBD (miles)	Total Cost of Transportation	Maximum Rent	Total Cost of Transportation and Rent
0	$ 0	$101	$101
10	50	51	101
20	75	26	101
30	90	11	101
40	100	1	101

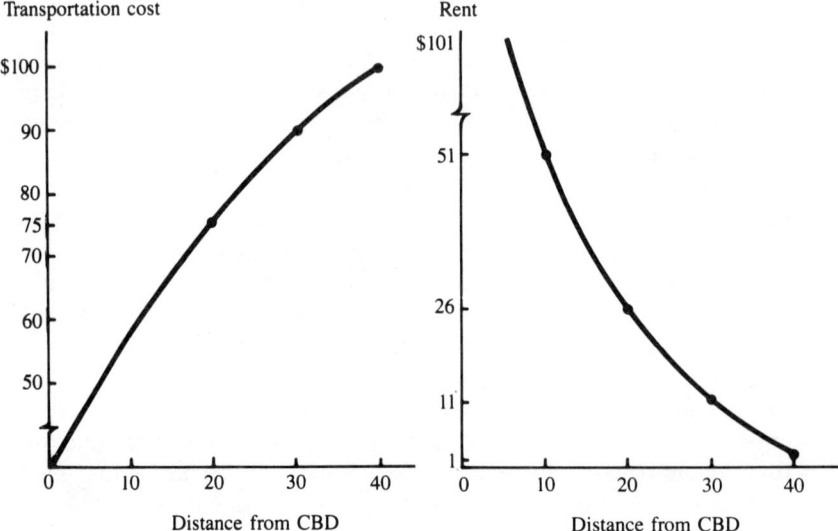

If transportation costs increase at a decreasing rate, the rent-bid curve will be convex.

important to sellers of short half-life ideas and information. Such activities are strongly oriented towards the center of the city.

Cultural and prestige factors are added considerations that attract certain businesses to the CBD locations. Firms realize that prestige is derived from being identified with a major downtown location. Furthermore, it is enjoyable to have a location close to good restaurants, civic activities, and cultural facilities.

An additional factor may detract from the CBD locations: Contrary to one of our preliminary assumptions, labor costs may not be equal at every location throughout the metropolis. Labor rates are often higher near the CBD. Such labor-cost variation tends to lower the rent firms would be willing and able to pay near core locations. Hence, the convexity of the rent-bid function may be reduced.

Interactivity Difference in Rent-Bid Curves.   The rent-bid curve represents the variations in rents that would occur for a particular activity. Each activity will have its own rent-bid curve reflecting the importance of sites at various points. The activity that bids the most money for the site will be the activity for which the site is used. Businesses such as financial and retail activities appear to have the steepest rent-bid curves (higher than other activities at the CBD). Financial activities probably need quick face-to-face communications. Retail establishments seek access to customers and also appear to prefer CBD locations. Generally, activities with steep rent-bid functions dominate centrally located sites. Why do some activities have steeper rent-bid curves than others? Several generalizations have been offered.

1. *Rates of Cost Change.*   Activities that face rapid increases in costs as they move from the maximum access point will have steeper rent-bid curves. Costs may increase because transportation costs, selling costs, input costs, or other factors increase.

2. *Need for Access.*   Activities that have a strong need for access will have steeper rent-bid curves than activities for which access is unimportant. Thus, the greater the number of daily face-to-face transactions per square foot of land, the steeper the rent bid curve will be.

3. *Ability to Substitute.*   Activities that cannot substitute other inputs for accesses afforded by central locations will have steeper rent gradients. Some activities have found that they can relocate away from the central access point and substitute other inputs, such as car phones, computers, etc., for face-to-face access. This ability flattens the rent-bid curve. Observers anticipate that further advances in communications technology will weaken the attraction of the CBD.

Household Demand for Land

Let us assume that households, like businesses, prefer access to the central business district in order to be near jobs. However, households seek to maximize utility rather than profits. Given the choice of two identical dwelling units, households would prefer the site with the greatest access. If we assume transportation costs are roughly equal in all directions around the core, households will prefer sites near the CBD and will pay higher rents for close-in locations. Thus, the household rent-bid curve will slope downward from the core. All along the household rent-bid curve, households will be indifferent between access costs/land rent combinations.

Figure 10–6(a) illustrates the relationship between transportation costs and site rents a household would be willing and able to pay at various locations. It is drawn on the assumption that households will pay a fixed amount for housing (excluding land rents), land rents, and transportation costs. (This assumption is relaxed shortly.) The price of housing (excluding site rents) is equal to $400 at all locations, as would be the case if the household consumed an equal quantity of housing and construction costs were equal throughout the metropolis. The transportation-cost curve reflects economies of distance so that savings from reducing a commute by one half are less than one half of the cost of the original trip. This perspective is consistent with most commuting situations. By moving towards the CBD, the household will lower transportation costs. If the total of housing costs (excluding site costs), land rents, and transportation costs are constant at $1,500, site rents would increase at distances closer to the CBD. Thus, assuming households would be indifferent between living further from the CBD and paying a lower land rent but higher transportation costs or living closer to the CBD and paying higher land rents but lower transportation costs, the area-designated site rent can be used to derive the rent-bid curve. A location at F would result in transportation costs of $800 ($1,200 − $400) and land rents of $300 ($1,500 − $1,200), while a location at D would result in transportation costs of $300 and site rents of $800. In Figure 10–6(b), the site rents are plotted against distance to derive the household rent-bid curve.

If the assumption that the household spends a fixed amount on housing (land and transportation costs) is dropped and replaced by the assumption that the household can substitute other goods for housing, the shape of the rent-bid curve will be altered. Under the restrictive no-substitution assumption, a move towards the CBD would leave households equally well off if the site-rent increase exactly offsets the decreased transportation costs. However, the household may substitute other goods for the relatively more expensive land. Hence, by substituting cheaper for more expensive goods, the household may be slightly better off by moving to the CBD if site costs exactly offset transportation costs. Yet, the rent-bid curve is supposed to show points of indifference between location and land rent. Hence, to account for the possibility of substitution, rents should increase faster than depicted in Figure 10–6(b), which is based only on transportation-cost differences. The substitution effect also explains the tendency of residential housing units to use land more intensively near the CBD.

This section ignored differences in households. In Chapter 9, important modifications to the model of residential choice will be introduced to

FIGURE 10–6 Household Locational Trade-offs

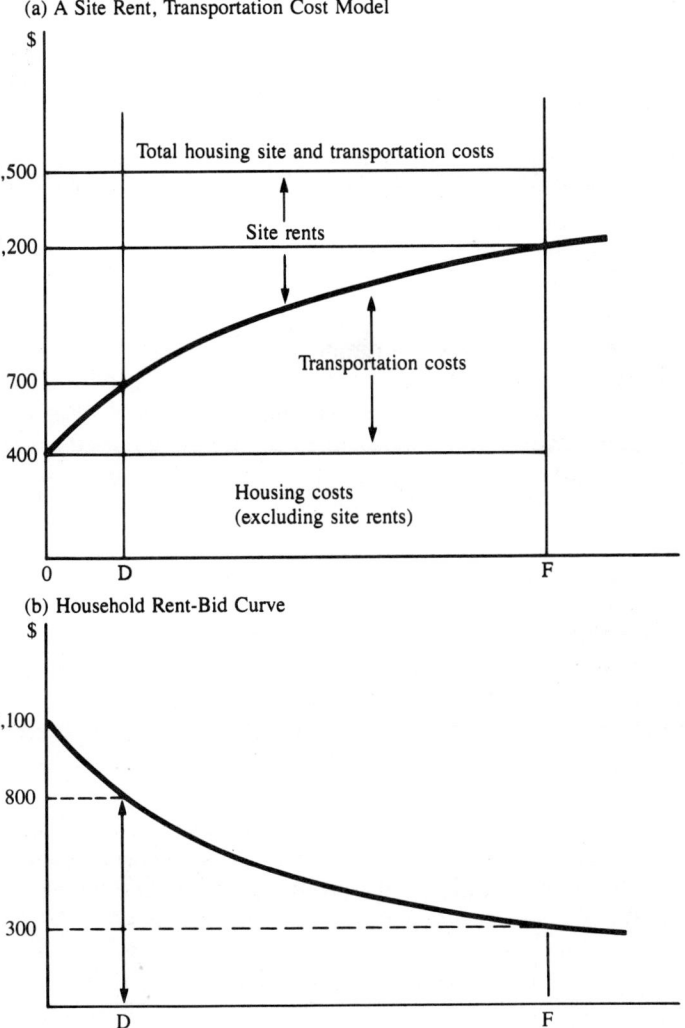

(a) A Site Rent, Transportation Cost Model

(b) Household Rent-Bid Curve

As a household moves closer to the CBD, it will be willing and able to pay a site rent equal to the transportation-cost savings.

account for income segregation of households and market imperfections, including racial segregation. The impact of urban "bads" which often repel residential locations from the CBD also will be analyzed.

COMPETITION FOR LAND AND LAND-USE PATTERNS

The previous section explained the downward slope of the rent-bid curve for particular activities. The activity offering to pay the highest rent at a particular point will establish the land use. This section shows how competition among various activities results in systemic land-use patterns. This section first describes the "standard urban model." Patterns of land use are based upon the assumption that the central business district is the transportation-cost-minimizing point and that transportation costs increase as one moves from the CBD in all directions. Later, assumptions are relaxed and more complicated patterns of land use are described. However, two key principles are always evident: (1) Activities seek access to urban goods, and (2) the activity willing and able to pay the highest rent for a site determines its use.

Von Thunen and the Concentric-Zone Model

Johann Heinrich von Thunen (1926) first developed a model of land-use patterns in an ideal region. He assumed an isolated state with a village at the center surrounded by uniform topography, climate, and soil. Thus, except for distance from the village, Von Thunen's model held constant all factors affecting land use. Practically all goods produced outside the village were consumed in the village.

Under these conditions, Von Thunen concluded that activities having high transportation costs per mile per acre of output would locate near the village. Outputs that can be transported cheaply would be produced further from the village. His ideal region reflected the technology of the day. Von Thunen believed land nearest the village would be used to produce products that require the most intensive interaction with the village, such as gardens, stall-fed milk cows, and chickens. Lands in the next zone should be devoted to activities such as forestry because the weight of the wood made it expensive to transport and wood for heating and cooking was needed everyday. Lands distant from the village would be used for activities that had low transportation costs, such as grazing cattle.

The concentric-zone model of land use can also be developed by comparing the rent-bid curves for individual activities. Since we assume an activity's demand is the same at all points equidistant from the CBD, one particular activity will outbid all other activities within a particular radius from the core.

FIGURE 10–7   The Concentric-Circle Model

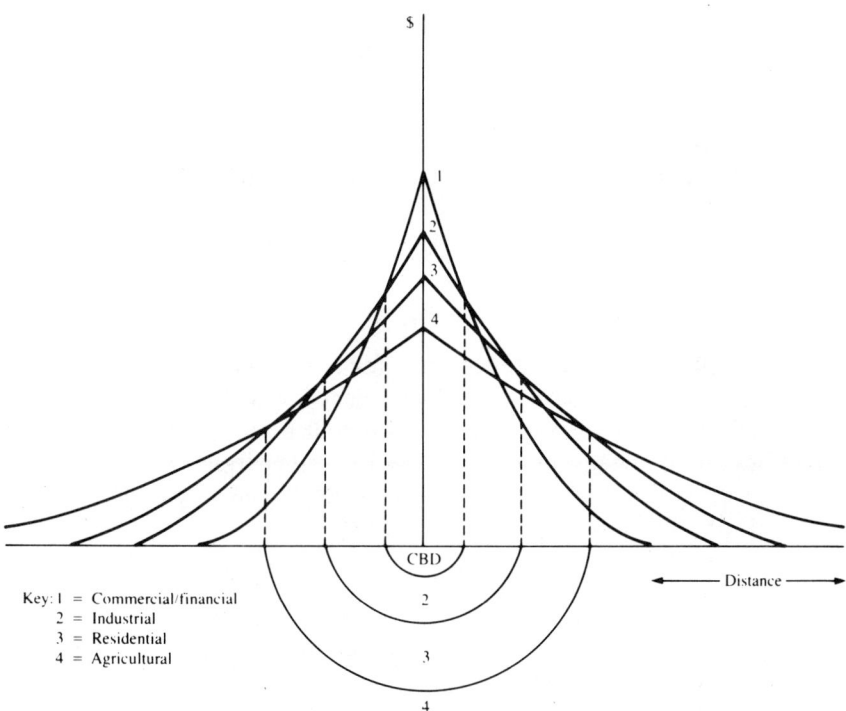

Key: 1 = Commercial/financial
     2 = Industrial
     3 = Residential
     4 = Agricultural

Competition among various activities may result in a concentric-circle pattern of land use.

The rent-bid curves for three activities are shown in Figure 10–7. For each activity, the rent-bid curve falls moving away from the center of the city, as explained in the previous section. Based upon the principle of highest and best use, the activities willing and able to pay the highest rent will determine the land use. If land is assumed to be homogeneous except for differences in access, land uses will form concentric circles around the core. Under certain circumstances, the same land use could occupy two distinct rings depending upon the slope of the rent-bid curves, although such a situation is not pictured in Figure 10–7. The points of the highest rent-bid curves at each location is called the rent gradient.

Ernest Burgess (1925) developed a stylized land-use pattern of concentric circles based upon empirical observation, thus supporting the theoretical predictions of the concentric-zone model. It is always satisfying when theoretically derived models match empirical observation. However, many urban economists believe the predictions of the concentric-zone model are unsatisfactory when compared to actual urban land-use patterns. The assumptions of a uniform transportation surface, spatially even distribution of resources, and infinite divisibility of land use are critical to the generation of the concentric-circle pattern. As these assumptions are relaxed, a more realistic picture of urban land-use emerges. Nevertheless, the concentric-circle model highlights the importance of access to the urban core and the ability to pay for that access. Also, the model is the basis of more complex models.

Roads and Axial Development

Recognition of the existence of highway systems requires modification of the concentric-circle model to reflect lower transportation costs along main arteries. Transportation costs will no longer be equal in all directions. A site near a main road may be further from the central business district than other sites, yet have better access. Since access, not proximity, determines the rent-bid function, the introduction of roads implies that each activity will increase its rent bid along the transportation route. Figure 10–8 is a land-use pattern that might exist if the assumption of equal transport costs in all directions were dropped from the concentric-circle approach. Rivers and other natural sources could be incorporated to show how other variations in transportation costs affect land use.

The doughnut city may be an emerging land-use form. As beltways around cities provide good access to the entire metropolitan area and as the area just a few blocks from the CBD is increasingly associated with urban blights, new development is becoming highly centered near the beltways. With the possible exception of the CBD, many central cities have experienced little development. Thus, large parts of the central city may become the hole and the beltway development will become the doughnut.

Hoyt (1939) believed that an axle model similar to Figure 10–8 was a good generalization of land-use patterns observed throughout the United States. Easier development in some areas of the metropolis resulted in less-symmetric land-use patterns than the one shown in Figure 10–7. He was also concerned about the dynamics of land use. As with the concentric-zone model, growth was viewed as radiating outward. Land uses are extended in the direction of easiest conversion. For example, if stable, high-quality residential use prevailed along one road and dilapidated housing was dominant along another road, then transitional commercial zones would be more likely to appear along the lower-quality residential road because of cheaper land-use conversion. Hoyt also argued that as the metropolitan area develops, activities that are pushed outward will

FIGURE 10–8   Roads and Axial Development

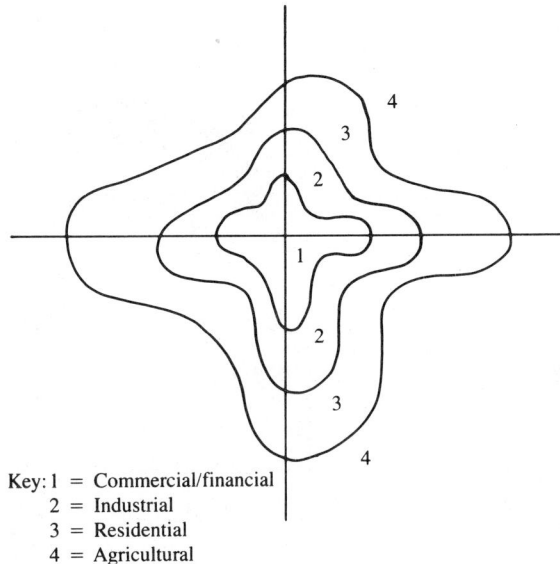

Key: 1 = Commercial/financial
     2 = Industrial
     3 = Residential
     4 = Agricultural

The imposition of a road system on the urban landscape may alter the access points and contribute to axial development.

relocate as near the previous location as possible, an idea that is a foundation of the invasion-succession model discussed later in this chapter.

The introduction of roads into the model also helps explain strip commercial development—commercial strips that dominate the row of buildings on either side of major roads. This pattern is often called "ribbon development," and it reflects the desire of many businesses for access to a stream of customers rather than a stationary customer base.

Agglomeration and the Multiple-Nuclear City

The multiple-nuclear city is perhaps the most sophisticated model of the modern metropolis. It recognizes that land-use clumps appear because of agglomeration economies within a single organization and among organizations. Intra-urban agglomeration is an important aspect of the CBD's attraction, and the same set of forces can cause subcenters to develop beyond the CBD. A medical complex of several blocks is an example of a specialized cluster. It would be ludicrous to suggest a hospital complex should exist in a narrow concentric circle around the CBD as

FIGURE 10–9   The Multiple-Nuclear City

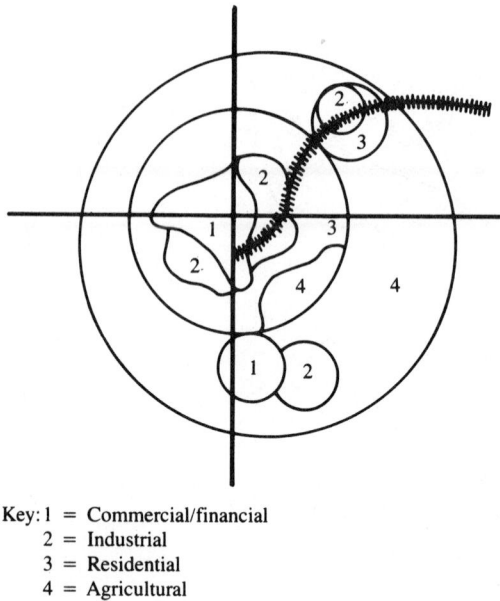

Key: 1 = Commercial/financial
     2 = Industrial
     3 = Residential
     4 = Agricultural
     ▦▦▦▦ Rail
     ───── Roads

Agglomeration economies and lumpiness will contribute to separate clusters of activity.

would be suggested by a literal interpretation of the concentric-zone approach. Agglomeration economics will also encourage clustering of groups of firms. Perhaps firms needing access to a railhead (and firms needing access to firms that locate near railheads) will form a cluster, and across town another cluster of manufacturing firms may form. Figure 10–9 illustrates the multiple-nuclear city.

Retail clusters are an important element of the multiple-nuclear city. As cities grow, access to the CBD becomes more difficult for families living near the periphery. Retail centers develop to serve the increasingly large suburban markets. Additional activity, such as office, entertainment, and residences, may develop around regional shopping malls, particularly if the transportation system is oriented towards the subcenter. As the metropolitan area expands, previously isolated communities may be brought into the metropolitan network. The enveloped communities will experience land-use changes, and they will develop into a subcenter within the metropolitan system.

Subcenters vary in size, ranging from small breaks in general decline in density to subcenters that dominate the land use for miles around and rival the CBD in many aspects.

Speculation

Large tracts of land are often maintained in low-density uses such as parking lots or golf courses while intensive development occurs nearby. Near the urban fringe, land is often used for agriculture while being held for speculative purposes. The owners may be speculating that the land will be suitable for a different use in the future and, therefore, land values will increase faster than the current interest rate. For instance, residential use may prevail in an area where unimproved lots sell for $20,000 per half acre. But an owner may believe that, if the land is not developed now, it will be worth more per acre than $20,000 plus the accrued interest on $20,000 in the future if it could be sold as part of a major subcenter.

Speculation usually involves differences of opinion about the future. If a current owner were prepared to develop housing on land, it might be sold to a speculator who believed a shopping center would be feasible in the future. Therefore, the land's value would rise more rapidly than the current interest rate and more rapidly than the current owner anticipates. Causes of differing opinions involve such factors as anticipated public improvements, the path of development, and the general state of the economy. The imperfect nature of the real estate market also contributes to speculative holdings. Consequently, land-use development is not smooth or incremental as implied by the model of axial growth. "Leap-frog" development will be observed.

Density Gradients

The density gradient shows density per unit of land at various distances from the urban center. Normally, density is greatest at the central business district and decreases as the distance from the CBD increases. An ideal density gradient representing a perfect concentric circle model would slope continually downward. A more realistic density gradient reflecting the multiple-nuclear model would have an overall downward slope but would include local peaks and troughs.[5] The central land is used

---

[5] The general shape of the density gradient is expressed by:

$$D_r = D_o e^{-br},$$

where D_r = Density at distance r,
D_o = Density at the urban core,
e = A constant, and
br = A slope factor.

more intensively in terms of both capital per acre and population per acre. In fact, the skyline is a rough representation of the intensity of capital per acre.

The density gradient is usually drawn for residential populations or for daytime population. Since the central business district has few residents compared to its daytime population of workers and shoppers, the distinction between residential and nonresidential density or day/night densities is important. Excluding hotel guests as residents, the residential gradient is volcano-like with a low point in the center. (One reason the crime rate appears so high in the central city is that the rate is usually calculated on the basis of residential population rather than daytime population.)

Larger cities have higher gradients. If population is held constant, several factors will cause the density function to flatten. They include:

1. Newer cities developed around the automobile tend to have flatter density gradients than older, "trolley-car" cities.
2. Higher-income groups are more likely to decentralize. Thus, cities with high-income populations will have flatter density gradients.
3. Low-quality central-city housing leads to lower density in the core of the city and, hence, a flatter density gradient.
4. Low manufacturing employment contributes to flatter rent gradients. American central cities have lower population densities than their European counterparts for many of the reasons cited above.

CHANGE AND GROWTH

Viewing the urban landscape as a static system impedes our understanding of what makes a city tick. Inertia is a strong force in land use. Transitions from one land use to another are usually slow. Typically, less than 3 percent of the housing stock is over a year old. Two major reasons for inertia are the long physical life of buildings and interdependence of land use. Most structures could last for hundreds of years. Changes in the urban environment generally cause buildings to be razed or converted to other uses, not physical deterioration of the structure itself. Locational interdependence among land uses creates a situation where one business would be reluctant to relocate unless many other activities in the neighborhood also relocated. The infrastructure that stimulates and supports development is particularly long-lived.

The Spreading of the Metropolis

Despite land-use stability, the CBD is declining in relative importance. Metropolitan areas are growing outward faster than they are growing upward. Regional shopping centers still lack the diversity and variety of the CBD, but the CBD's share of retail trade has dropped significantly in almost all cities. Accompanying the spreading of the metropolis has been a decline in the relative importance of the central city in terms of population and economic activity.

Suburbanization and exurbanization are manifestations of this trend. Density gradients and rent gradients have accordingly flattened. The emergence of a variety of metropolitan activity centers as represented by the multiple-nuclear model has been associated with the spreading of the metropolis. The reasons for the spreading out of the city are complex and nearly impossible to isolate, but a few key factors are within the scope of our discussion.

Growth.   Increased levels of population and economic activity will affect spatial structure. The spatial models can be dynamized by assuming that all rent-bid curves increase due to the increased demand for land. This process will lead to a pushing out and widening of the activity rings, called the invasion-succession model. The multiple-near model could be modified to include separates rates of growth among the CBD and the subcenters, so the impact of growth becomes less symmetrical overtime.

Figure 10–10 illustrates the process of invasion-succession. Growth caused the rent-bid curves for both commercial/financial (not shown in graph) and industrial activities to increase. The shift of the industrial rent-bid curve is shown as a movement from 2 to 2'. Thus, industrial activities claimed some previously residential land. Two zones of transition are also shown. In the first zone, land is changing from industrial to commercial-financial use. In the second zone of transition, land is changing from residential to industrial. Furthermore, newer land is being developed on the urban fringe. Because of the strength of inertia, land uses change very slowly. A zone could be in transition for over a decade.

Growth also creates problems for the CBD, because urban growth may not be symmetrical. Natural boundaries such as rivers or lakes may weaken the role of the CBD as the point of minimum transportation cost. Congestion and low-income zones of transition often separate the CBD from important suburban markets and sources of labor. Hence, growth tends to increase demand for land throughout the urban region, but the increases are greater at the periphery and near the subcenters than near the CBD. Hence, the rent-bid curve and density gradients tend to shift upward, but will also flatten.

Transportation Costs.   Suppose transportation costs decreased. The change would decrease the cost of access to the CBD for firms and households located in outlying areas. Firms or households that were initially

FIGURE 10–10   The Invasion-Succession Model

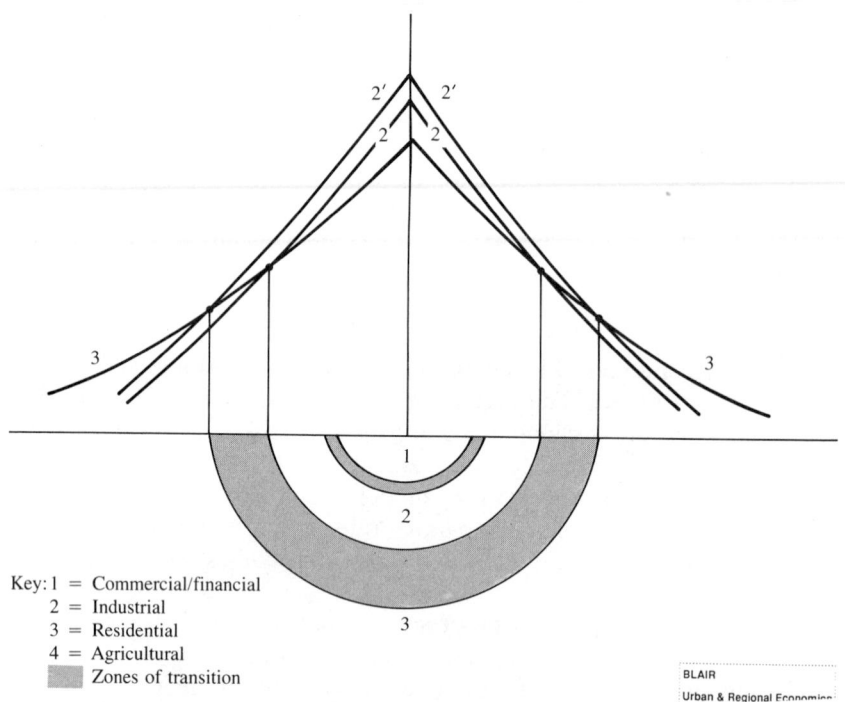

Key: 1 = Commercial/financial
     2 = Industrial
     3 = Residential
     4 = Agricultural
     Zones of transition

BLAIR
Urban & Regional Economics

Changing rent-bid curves will create zones of transition where alternative land uses will be mixed. Inertia could cause zones of transition to last for decades.

---

indifferent between a nearer-CBD, higher-rent site and a more-distant, lower-rent location would have their preferences tilt toward the more distant location. Thus, lower transportation costs will tend to flatten the density and rent gradients.

Parking has become a major transportation concern with the rise of the automobile. Suburban locations can provide parking considerably cheaper than CBD locations. Hence, businesses locating in "greenfields" may be able to provide parking more easily than CBD locations.

Production Techniques. Technologies that reduce the need for CBD access or increase the need for land will reduce the slope of the rent and density gradients. Cheap electric power and the development of the electric motor have tended to encourage horizontal, assembly-line production rather than production in a multistory plant. Thus, new facilities have required more land, which, in turn, has shifted their orientation towards outlying areas.

Many observers have speculated that computers would allow individuals to work at home rather than in the workplace. However they may have underestimated the need for face-to-face communication between worker and boss and the need for social contact among other individuals at work. Nevertheless, there is little doubt that telecommunication and computer technology have increased the potential for work at home. The effect of the new technologies has been to reduce the value of CBD access and lower the rent/density gradient.

New technologies are decreasing the need for clerical, typing, and related functions to be located near corporate-level decision makers. When information was kept on paper and transferred by hand, a decision maker had to be near the paper, as did the clerks and typists. Many firms are now finding it more efficient to relegate many "back office" functions to locations in the suburbs. Land is cheaper, and a suburban work force has developed that is difficult to attract to the city. The corporate headquarters is still tied to the CBD because executives and other officials still require face-to-face contact with each other and with other businesses.

Values and Image.   The value placed on access to the CBD and the goods available in the city have changed, thus, changing the urban land-use pattern. Families may prefer the single-family, detached house and the set of values associated with a suburban lifestyle relatively more now than in the past. This kind of value change would tend to flatten the rent-bid curve for housing and increase the radius of the metropolitan area. It could also encourage spreading of business. Not only will business follow markets and sources of labor, but some businesses may be affected by the same set of values as households. There is an as yet unresolved debate in the urban literature regarding whether jobs follow households to the suburbs or whether people follow jobs. Although one factor may eventually be shown to be more important than the other, both undoubtedly are operating in the city today.

Complicating real value changes is the changing image of the central city. In many metropolitan areas, the CBD is no longer seen as the urban apex. It is viewed as a place of abandoned buildings and the home of the indigent, blacks, porno stores, and criminals. In order to alleviate the problem, some cities such as Detroit and Atlanta have tried to separate parts of the CBD from the nearby zones of transition, but the "enclave" strategy has not been a complete success.

Incomes.   As incomes increase, families tend to spend an increasing proportion of their income on housing. They also may want to alter the kind of dwelling from multifamily housing, which is land intensive, to detached, single-family housing, which is land extensive. The best buys on single-family housing with large lots are distant from the CBD. In fact, such properties are rare in central cities. Thus, increasing incomes are associated with the spreading out of the city. The issue of location in housing choice will be discussed more completely in Chapter 11.

Evaluating Metropolitan Spread

The desirability of recent changes in metropolitan form has been questioned by many urbanists. Urban critics have occasionally disparaged the outward spread of the city. "Sprawl" is a pejorative term implying excessive outward growth.

Criticisms of Sprawl.   Observers at various times have argued that metropolitan spread is bad environmental management, bad aesthetics, and bad economics. Some critics argue that sprawl harms the urban environment, because land is used too extensively leading to the needless disruption of natural ecological patterns. Also, the resulting spatial distribution is inefficient because of the larger distances that must be traveled in the course of urban activities. The extra travel contributes to environmental pollution and excessive energy use. Critics also argue that the easier it is for the city to grow outward, the greater the rate of waste abandonment of intercity properties. Sprawl requires construction of new infrastructures as well as new housing and retail space. Critics of suburbanization and exurbanization also argue that too much land is taken from agriculture, so sprawl leads to higher food prices.

Another criticism is that sprawl contributes to an ugly urban environment with "ticky-tack" suburban housing in contrast to a more interesting urban landscape that characterizes more–densely built European cities.

Defense.   In reply, defenders of the spreading of the city contend that location is a matter of personal preference and market economics. If individuals believe that suburban life is better and are willing and able to pay for the extra land and related costs, then land should be put to its highest and best economic use. Similarly, if businesses find decentralized locations better to their needs, then they should be allowed to compete with other activities for the land. The market will allow land to be put to its most valued use. Furthermore, space for agricultural use can be made through irrigation, forest conversion, and so forth. The idea that urban development is using up land at a rate that could endanger our food supply is dubious (only about 10 percent of land in the United States is used for urban purposes).

Recap.   Individuals opposed to restrictions on urban sprawl seem to believe that the market is the best allocator of land and that government should not interfere in favor of one lifestyle (urban) over another (suburban) by restrictions on the use of land or the rate of development. On the other side of the argument are individuals concerned with the importance of spillover effects and land-use interdependence. They argue that private land-use decisions are often inefficient because they do not account for all the costs and benefits of a choice or because the preference for suburban and exurban living may be uninformed. Furthermore, central cities could also be made more attractive than suburbs if better policies were implemented.

The issue of urban sprawls is a question of balance rather than total cessation of outward urban growth or continued rapid outward growth. However, it does lead to the question of political regulation of land use.

REGULATION AND POLITICAL ASPECTS OF LAND USE

The previous sections primarily described economic factors affecting land use. Political forces also exert an important influence. In order to understand how market forces and public regulation interact, it will be useful to understand three important principles of land economics: the bundle-of-sticks analogy, the Coase theorem, and the problems of the commons.

The Bundle-of-Sticks Analogy

A variety of distinct rights are associated with a particular property. Lawyers use the analogy that the multitude of rights are like a bundle of sticks. The government has taken the sticks called police power, taxation, eminent domain, and escheat.

1. Police power is the authority of government to regulate use to enhance or preserve health, safety, and the general welfare. Building codes and zoning are the most important police powers.

2. Taxation affects the return that property generates. Property taxes can affect land use since they lower the return on a real estate investment. Some states allow agricultural land to be taxed at a lower rate than improved property. This differential discourages development and encourages urban sprawl. Income tax depreciation rules

TABLE 10–4   Valuation of Two of the Property Rights in a Commercial Building (in $000,000s)

Property Right	Value to Risk Taker	Value to Risk Minimizer	Maximum Value
Right to income from 10-year lease (safe)	$4.0	$6.0	$6.0
Right to income after 10 years (risky)	10.0	8.0	10.0
Total value	14.0	14.0	16.0

also affect land use by decreasing the tax burden on real estate earnings.

3. Eminent domain is the right of government to purchase property if its use is needed for a public purpose such as a road or a park. What constitutes "public purpose" has been a source of debate about land use. Should eminent domain be used by a city to accumulate land which is resold to developers to build private housing? When there is a defendable public purpose, courts usually approve of the use of eminent domain.

4. Escheat is government's right to all land for which there is no private owner. For instance, if someone dies without heirs, their property will be claimed by the government.

Zoning is probably the most significant determinant of land use among the governmental sticks in the property-rights bundle. In addition to the sticks, governments determine the location and timing of roads, sewers, parks, and so forth, which affect land use and the pace of development. Many communities have attempted to influence the use of property by regulating the type of infrastructure developed.

While recognizing the important sticks controlled by government, most property owners have the rights to use, rent, sell, and develop property subject to the government limitations. The sticks in the private-property-rights bundle may be rearranged so as to increase the value of the property. For instance, suppose a shopping center generates a certain return over the first 10 years of its existence because it is leased to a blue-chip tenant such as Sears. However, the return after the lease expires is less certain. The total value of the property could be increased by splitting the sticks so that risk-adverse individuals could purchase the certain income flow and risk takers could purchase the reversion.

Table 10–4 shows that while both groups place a higher valuation on the right to the larger amount of income after 10 years, the risk taker assigns a relatively higher monetary value to the less certain future income. The maximum that the risk taker would pay for the entire property is $14 million. Likewise, the risk minimizer places a value of $14 million on the combined rights in the property. It would be worthwhile to split the ownership rights by selling the 10-year lease to the risk minimizer for $6 million and selling the rights to the benefits of the property 10 years hence to the risk taker for $10 million. By dividing the real property rights, the value of the combined property rights could be increased from $14 million to $16 million.

This illustration is not as complicated as a more realistic example. Real estate professionals have developed extremely complicated techniques for selling components of the property-rights bundle. Furthermore, different attitudes toward risk are not the only factors that cause individuals to value the rights associated with real estate differently. For example, one individual might place a higher premium on capital-gains income than another. Variation in the time preference for money is also an important reason why investors may want to split ownership rights. Finally, there are more rights involved than merely right to income. For instance, rights to use condominiums are split among individuals over a yearly period in some resort areas.

The Coase Theorem

An externality or spillover effect exists when one individual's activities impose uncompensated costs on other parties or provide free benefits for them. Activities that impose costs on others are called negative externalities. Suppose the owner of a tract of land decides that the greatest return can be derived by constructing a noisy and polluting foundry on it. The foundry will cause the residential character of the neighborhood to deteriorate and property values of existing homes to decline. In terms of property rights, we might ask: Should the owner of the foundry have the right to use the property in such a way as to create negative externalities for neighboring properties?

The foundry example illustrates an important and general principle of land use. The property use that maximizes the owner's return may not be desirable from an overall social perspective, because the owner may not consider the externalities imposed upon others. The desire to reduce externalities is a major reason for zoning. However, it is not feasible to eliminate all externalities. Particularly in an urban area, properties are so interrelated that almost any change in land use will have some repercussions for owners of other properties. Thus, zoning attempts to eliminate blatant negative externalities, but not all externalities.

Coase (1960) argued that, if property rights were clearly defined and freely transferable (two big ifs), then property could always be put to the most socially valued use even without zoning. His reasoning was that the market will allocate property rights to the individual who places the highest monetary value upon them. If all individuals affected by land use change could "bid" on how the land should be used, externalities could be eliminated without zoning.

The example of the polluting, noisy foundry can be resurrected to illustrate Coase's point. Let the "right to build a foundry" on property A be a distinct and transferable property right. Assume that the owner of site A on which the foundry was proposed valued the use as a foundry at $1,000 more than the next-best, nonpolluting alternative. Suppose also that the owner of the adjacent residential property would receive a negative value of $5,000 on the use of site A as a foundry. On the one hand, if the property right to specify whether the foundry could be built on site A were given to the owner of site A, the neighboring residential owner would be willing to pay up to $5,000 to prevent the foundry. He might offer to pay, say, $3,000 to the neighboring landowner to give up the right to build a foundry on site A. The owner of site A would accept the offer since she places a value of only $1,000 on the right to use the land as the site of a foundry. If, on the other hand, laws were such that the consent of neighbors had to be obtained before a property could be put to a polluting use, then the owner of site A would have to get her neighbor's consent before she could build the foundry. Given the initial value the foundry planner placed upon the right to construct and operate a foundry, she would be unwilling to pay the neighboring resident enough to obtain his consent. Thus, regardless of whether the foundry developer or the neighboring resident initially had the right to determine if a foundry could be constructed, the foundry would not be built if property rights are clearly defined and marketable.

Suppose the monetary values placed upon foundry use had been reversed. The resident placed a negative $1,000 value on the neighboring foundry and the foundry planner placed a positive $5,000 value on the foundry use. Regardless of who had the initial property right to determine whether the foundry could be constructed, the market would operate. If the foundry developer had to obtain the resident's consent in order to construct the foundry, she would be willing to pay him up to $5,000. The resident would agree to accept any amount over $1,000. Thus, the parties could strike a deal and the foundry would be constructed. If the foundry developer were initially given the right to use the property for whatever purpose she pleased, then the resident would be unwilling to pay the $5,000 minimum price necessary to purchase an agreement from her not to construct a foundry and the foundry would be constructed.

The Coase theorem has been used to imply that public regulation may not be necessary as long as the property right that causes spillovers can be purchased. Neighbors could then pay the owner not to use the property in

TABLE 10–5   The Coase Theorem Illustrated

	Initial Distribution of Land-Use Right	
	A has right to impose negative spillovers on B	B has right to refuse or allow spillovers
A values right to offend > B values removal of offense	No exchange, B suffers and spillovers and is not compensated for A's actions	A purchases the right to offend B. B is compensated for the consequences of A's actions
A values right to offend < B values removal of offense	B purchases from A a promise not to offend	No exchange. A is denied right to offend

a way that adversely affects them. However, there are two additional points that are important for understanding the relationship between the transferability of property rights and the role of government. First, while the ultimate use of property may not depend upon the initial allocation of property rights (i.e., the right to determine whether the foundry may be built), the distribution of wealth is affected. Zoning, thus, provides some property owners protection from nuisance land uses. Second, if negative externalities affect many property owners, then the cost of organizing and bargaining might be extremely, even prohibitively, costly. Coase stressed that when many parties are harmed by an action, transactions costs may be too high for the market to function effectively. Zoning and other regulations reduce the transactions cost of protecting residential and other land uses.

The Problem of the Commons: Free-Rider Problem

Inefficient use of land can result from poorly defined property rights, as illustrated by the "problem of the commons." England prior to 1700 had a property system in which pasture land was owned in common. All individuals in a specified area had the right to graze their sheep on the common land. No one was excluded and no one had the right to exclude others.

The problem with the English common-property-rights system was that no individual had an adequate incentive to conserve land. For example, suppose that a farmer decided to double his flock from 6 to 12. One of the most important costs of such a decision is the extra grass that a larger flock consumes. If the land were owned individually, the owner would consider this cost before expansion. But, from the perspective of an individual using commonly owned land, the grazing costs would not be considered particularly important because they would be shared with the other users of the commons; if the common land were owned jointly by 10 farmers, then a farmer expanding his flock would bear only one tenth of the increased grazing costs. Yet, if the farmer had increased his flock, there would have been less grass left for the sheep of other individuals. Consequently, the group paid the costs of the expansion, but the farmer who expanded his flock received all of the benefits from his increased flock size.

Naturally, every farmer viewed the situation in the same way. They realized that it was in their individual interest to expand the size of their flocks and proceeded to do so. The problem was that when all farmers attempted to increase their flocks the pasture area was not large enough to support the increase. The sheep ate so much grass that the field could not replenish itself. The commons was overgrazed.

The solution to the problem of the commons is to redefine property rights to reflect individual costs and benefits of land use. For example, rather than saying that anyone may use the commons property as much as they want, the property right might be redefined to give each farmer the right to graze no more than a given number of sheep.[6] Alternatively, the commons might be subdivided so that each farmer has a clearly defined area upon which other farmers may not trespass. After partition, any farmer who wanted to increase his flock could still do so, but the cost of overgrazing would be borne by that individual alone.

The commons problem is a special case of externalities, because the division of real property rights among numerous individuals creates a divergence between costs and benefits borne by an individual and social costs and benefits. The large group–shared ownership situation is not uncommon in modern urban society. For example, an urban neighborhood can be viewed as a commons area.

Table 10–6 shows payoffs (net of improvement costs) as a function of the maintenance of the property and the maintenance level of the neighborhood. It can be used to analyze the problem of the commons in an urban setting. Table 10–6 shows four possible outcomes which may occur depending on whether the individual and the group maintain or do not maintain property. Assume the individual cannot affect the group out-

---

[6] Enclosure of the commons was also motivated by the redistribution of wealth that occurred as some individuals gained control of increasingly valuable land.

TABLE 10-6   The Problem of the Commons

Individual Choice	Group Behavior (N–1 individuals)	
	Maintain Property	*Not Maintain Property*
Maintain Property	$10,000 G $500 I	$0 G –$1000 I
Not Maintain Property	$ 9,000 G $1,000 I	$0 G $0 I

I = Individual payoff.
G = Group payoff.

come. Therefore, the self-interested individual would receive the highest payoffs net of improvement costs by not maintaining the property, regardless of what the group does. To understand why, suppose an individual is considering whether or not to spruce up the property's exterior. On the one hand, if the group maintains the neighborhood, the individual would receive a greater payoff by not maintaining ($1,000 rather than $500). The higher net gain would be due to the spillover benefits from being in a nicer neighborhood without incurring any of the maintenance costs—a free-rider situation. On the other hand, if the rest of the neighbors fail to improve their properties, the individual would also be better off not improving his property ($0 rather than –$1,000). Regardless of whether the group (rest of the neighborhood) maintains or does not maintain their properties, the individual's payoff will be greatest by not maintaining the property.

   If all property owners in the neighborhood view the situation similarly (as might realistically be the case), no one would maintain their property. Consequently, the lower right-hand cell—no maintenance— would represent the equilibrium. From the perspective of the group, this result is suboptimal. The optimal payoff is the upper left cell. If the process of undermaintenance continues, the neighborhood would become a slum, just as the commons became an ecological disaster. Even international problems, such as those concerning ocean fishing rights, can be understood as a variation on the problem of the commons. Zoning and building codes can be helpful in overcoming some of the problems of shared ownership in the urban environment.

Zoning and Its Critics

The need for zoning is widely accepted. But zoning is not without its critics. Bernard Siegan (1970) suggested that zoning is an unnecessary encumbrance upon the operation of the free market. He contended that Houston, Texas, is an example of a city that developed without zoning laws. Yet Houston is pleasant, and the location of residential next to commercial property has not resulted in incompatible land use. As in most cities, industries in Houston locate near the major highway and railways and do not invade residential areas. In Houston, however, these locations are more the result of market economics than zoning regulation (although there were other land-use controls available to public planners). In place of zoning, developers of large tracts of land sold property but restricted the deed of sale. They required all future owners to restrict the use to functions compatible with the rest of the subdivision. The deed restrictions made it easier to sell the sites initially and improved resale value.

The argument that private contracts could replace or at least reduce the need for land-use regulations would not be particularly appealing if individuals were satisfied with zoning regulations. However, there are at least six specific criticisms of zoning:

1. There is an opportunity for graft, corruption, and inefficient political deals. Since the approval of a zoning variance can be worth hundreds of thousands of dollars to a major real estate developer and can have significant monetary value even to a small landowner, the potential for corruption is obvious. Charges of outright graft are frequent. Just as important as direct bribery are the more subtle conflicts of interest, since members of zoning boards are usually active in other aspects of a local economic and political system.

Mills (1989) showed that zoning encourages landowners to attempt to have their properties zoned in socially inefficient ways and suppresses potential net social gains because it is often difficult to rezone a property. Because large social costs can be imposed through improper implementation, the benefits zoning is intended to achieve may be lost. Mills proposed that some of the inefficiencies of zoning could be overcome by providing options for the sale of zoning rights as implied by the Coase theorem.

2. Changing land use becomes difficult. Land use ought to change with changing circumstances. However, zoning and the bureaucratic and legal structure associated with it often prevent redevelopment of an area when, for example, a change from residential to commercial land use is needed. Furthermore, it is often more difficult

for a small landowner to change the zoning regulations than it is for large developers or corporations with political connections.

3. Zoning may inflate land costs. Zoning restricts the amount of land available for certain uses. Residents often create political pressure to limit industrial, commercial, and multifamily residential land. This effectively limits the supply of land for such purposes and artificially raises the price of industrial and commercial land. In addition, limiting housing density by requiring large lots or large houses increases the price of housing.

4. There are aesethetic and social shortcomings of zoning. Architectural critics sometimes claim that suburban tract housing is dull and monotonous. Yet the standardization is at least partly a result of zoning. Furthermore, there have been charges that zoning contributes to social and racial segregation, since blacks tend to have lower incomes than whites and zoning drastically decreases the likelihood that a person who cannot afford to own a house or who can afford only a modest house will live next to an upper- or middle-income individual.

5. Public planners make mistakes. The free market will occasionally err. The result will be an inefficient or socially harmful land use. But the officials who plan, often without the aid of "market signals," also make mistakes. Critics of zoning argue that public officials may be more likely to misallocate land than developers. Furthermore, the government planners' mistakes may be more harmful because they are large-scale mistakes. Simply because a market failure exists in the private sector does not necessarily mean public intervention will make the situation better.

6. Exclusionary and fiscal zoning occur. Many communities attempt to zone out the poor by prohibiting all but very expensive housing. Other communities allow only such construction that will generate more tax revenues than it will cost to service the property. Hence, apartments with three or more bedrooms and trailer parks are excluded from many communities because they will generate less in revenues than a single-family house. However, the large number of bedrooms implies that the tenants will have school-age children, and families with children tend to be high-cost residents, particularly because of the associated educational expenses.

Legal challenges to growth controls have been based on the idea that growth controls increase housing prices, thereby excluding lower-income households. Zorn et al. (1986) have shown that communities can use zoning effectively to control growth without unduly excluding low-income families. However, often exclusionary zoning is the goal and growth control only the excuse.

Developments in Land Regulation

During the 1950s and 1960s, the public construction of infrastructure drove the suburban zoning process. Frequently, land developers captured substantial windfalls by influencing local governments to extend city services to areas they owned. They also obtained zoning changes to allow for more intensive development. These public actions enhanced the value of the property of the developer, although at taxpayers' expense. The public expense associated with private development can be indirect and after the fact. For example, a new development might increase congestion on existing roads, thereby creating a need to widen them at a later date.

Currently, planners are more careful about how decisions to extend public infrastructure are made. Frequently, they negotiate some type of quid pro quo before allowing a zoning change, particularly if the change will require public expense. For instance, they may require developers to set aside property for recreation areas or schools before recommending a new residential project. They may require developers to bear all or part of the public infrastructure costs associated with a new development.

Linkage. Linkage programs have carried the idea that current city residents should receive compensation for the costs of development a step further. Linkage programs are attempts to require developers to provide support for unrelated development as a condition for permission to develop their original program. The logic of linkage programs is that certain areas of a city, such as the central business district, are desirable development sites. However, residents living in other parts of the region, such as city residential neighborhoods, will not benefit from the development. Hence, permission to develop in some areas must be linked to projects that can benefit residents living elsewhere. It has also been argued that new downtown development causes indirect negative consequences for current residents and linkage programs can help compensate for these adverse impacts. For instance, new office development may encourage white-collar employees to live downtown. In doing so, they drive up rents and displace current residents.

Typically, a developer may wish to build a downtown project. Particularly in fast-growth areas, the demand for office space is strong. However, before allowing construction, the city may require the developer to commit to actions such as employment guarantees, high-quality building design, residential housing projects, transportation services, or other activities that may be unrelated to the project under consideration.

Flexibility. There also has been a trend toward providing developers more flexibility in meeting legal requirements and avoiding overly homogeneous development. Public land planners are currently modifying the way they regulate to give private developers and market forces more leeway while maintaining some control over externalities.

Transferable development rights are one technique that has been used to avoid congestion. Traditionally, land-use planners have specified the maximum number of apartment units each proposed building may have. A developer could apply for a zoning change and each change was evaluated on a case by case basis. The transferable-development rights technique provides a way of regulating density in an area, but also allows greater scope for market forces. Community officials may simply rule that within a particular district the number of units (or number of floors) may be no more than N. The rights to build apartment units will be distributed among landowners according to an equitable formula. Perhaps each acre could be assigned the right to 10 residential units. If a landowner wants to build a project with more units than he was originally assigned, the extra development rights could be purchased from another landowner. Thus, the overall density of an area may be controlled consistent with the available city infrastructure without rigid zoning.

Planned-unit developments (PUDs) allow developers to propose a comprehensive plan for an area that may mix single-family housing, multiple-family housing, commercial land use, and even industrial use in a single development. "New town" developments are large-scale applications of PUDs.

Floor-area ratio is a technique that limits the ratio of total floor area to the area of the lot. If an area were regulated with a floor-area ratio of one, an individual may construct a one-story unit on the whole lot, a two-story unit on half the lot, a four-story unit on one fourth of the lot, and so forth. Density is controlled, yet private developers have more flexibility than they would have under many zoning laws.

Environmental-Impact   Concerns.   Environmental-impact   statements (EISs) are required by both state and federal governments. Most large development projects require a careful analysis of projects to ensure that the variety of direct and indirect impacts of a project are examined. EISs do not require a full cost-benefit analysis for two reasons. First, it is too difficult to accurately measure many of the costs and benefits. Secondly, public planners are less concerned about private costs and benefits. They generally focus directly upon community impacts.

The concept of environmental impact has been interpreted broadly. In the words of the Council on Environmental Quality (1972), an EIS should:

> utilize a systematic, interdisciplinary approach which will insure the integrated use of natural and social sciences and the environmental design arts in planning and decision making which may have an impact on man's environment. (p. 5)

Thus, a project's impact on crime, poverty, and employment should be as much a part of the EIS as the effects on birds and water quality.

There is no formula for constructing an EIS. The nature of the project should dictate the questions that require attention. The EIS for a small subdivision will be significantly different than an EIS for a regional suburban shopping center. However, the Council on Environment Quality (1972) has described an eight-step procedure that may serve as a skeleton around which an EIS may be structured:

1. A description of the present conditions is an appropriate starting place and should include physical, social, and aesthetic features of the area. A detailed description of the entire environment would not be appropriate. Features to be discussed later in the report and that may be controversial should receive the most attention at this stage.

2. The description of the proposed project should be adequate to allow a careful assessment of the environmental repercussions by agencies that will evaluate the project. Maps showing the project's relationship to the community and the region should be included.

3. The probable impact of the proposed action can be tied closely to the description of present conditions. Because so many factors conceivably can be included in an impact statement, a checklist might be useful simply as a reminder of what sorts of impacts might be important. The Department of Housing and Urban Development has suggested 14 areas that ought to be included: (1) geology, (2) soils, (3) special land features, (4) water, (5) biota, (6) climate and air, (7) energy, (8) services, (9) safety, (10) physiological well-being, (11) sense of community, (12) psychological well-being, (13) visual quality, and (14) historic and cultural resources.

4. Probable adverse environmental impacts that cannot be avoided or that would be adverse to the environmental goals of the nation or community should be described next. This step requires a value judgment concerning what impacts are adverse. Also, some distinction must be made between significant and insignificant ad-

verse effects. For instance, would the filling of a mosquito-infested swamp be considered an adverse impact? Is the probable extinction of the snail darter (a small fish) significant? Real estate projects should be particularly sensitive to social impacts, such as congestion, as well as the damage caused by solid- and liquid-waste disposal to ecosystems.

5. The review of alternatives to the proposed project requires the responsible party to "study, develop, and describe appropriate alternatives to recommend courses of action in any proposal which involves unresolved conflicts, concerning alternative uses of available resources" (Sec. 102 (2) (D)). Normally, reviewing agencies believe this step is critical because it serves to avoid premature foreclosure of options that might be less disruptive. Alternative real estate proposals include adjusting the size of the project and varying the mix of units (to decrease density), building designs, and landscape possibilities.

6. The sixth step should distinguish between the short-term and long-term impacts. This requires the analyst to assess the project from the perspective stated in the legislation. Each generation should act "as trustee of the environment for succeeding generations" (Sec. 101 (b)). The time dimensions vary from very short-term construction disruption, to short-term effects (such as temporarily increased erosion), to permanent changes in the natural or social environment. The long-term impact forces policy makers to think beyond the projected economic life of a project.

7. Irreversible impacts and irretrievable losses should be documented. They are effects that will be very difficult to obviate once the project has been approved. Topsoil that is destroyed during development on agricultural land is an irretrievable loss; the commitment of public resources to support a development—police, roads, etc.—is, for most practical purposes, an irreversible commitment. This section should not simply reiterate impacts discussed in previous sections. Rather, the focus should be on resource use.

8. Finally, a discussion of problems and objections raised by other governmental agencies as well as private organizations should be included. The council suggests that this might best be developed near the end of the review.

The discussion in this section has not exhausted the possible types of land-use controls, but rather illustrated a trend toward greater reliance on market forces while maintaining control over negative spillover effects from incompatible land uses.

SUMMARY

This chapter surveyed land use. Land is paid according to its productivity. In the case of urban land, productivity is a function of access to goods in the environment. Rent is the residual to land after the other factors of production are compensated. Land is fixed in supply, not created by human efforts, so some economists have maintained that the return to landowners is unearned and should be heavily taxed.

The highest and best use of land is the most profitable use subject to legal restrictions. Access is an important determinant of highest and best use. A land-use study is frequently conducted to determine the appropriate use of a site. The culminating step in a land-use study is a cash-flow analysis to determine the present value of the future returns from a project. If the discounted present value of the returns is greater than the project cost, the project will be undertaken.

Political as well as economic factors influence land use. Zoning is the primary tool used to regulate land use, but not the only tool. Zoning is intended to reduce land-use spillovers. However, zoning has been criticized for being both ineffective and inefficient. The current trend is to allow developers more flexibility within the regulatory limits.

Individual development decisions result in land-use patterns. The simplest model of the city is the concentric-circle model. More complicated models can be developed by introducing roads, agglomeration economies, and speculation.

However, all major land-use models of urban development are based upon the idea that firms bid among each other and the highest bidder (subject to legal restrictions) determines land use. The rent gradient peaks at the center of the metropolis and slopes downward reflecting the desirability of CBD access. However, the multiple-nuclear model allows for subcenters of activity and density.

Land-use patterns are changing in response to urban growth, changes in transportation costs, production technology, values, incomes as well as other factors. The invasion-succession model describes growth as a process where one land-use area overlaps another area creating zones of transition, as well as growth, at the urban fringe. Currently, the outward spread of the metropolis is a major land-use trend.

REFERENCES

Alonso, William. *Location and Land Use.* Cambridge, Mass.: Harvard Univ. Press, 1964.*

Alston, Julian M. "An Analysis of Growth of U.S. Farmland Prices, 1963–1982." *American Journal of Agricultural Economics* 68, no. 1, February 1986, pp. 1–9.

Barlowe, Raleigh. *Land Resources Economics.* 2nd ed. Englewood Cliffs, N.J.: Prentice Hall, 1972.

Barrett, G. V., and John P. Blair. *How to Conduct a Real Estate Market and Feasibility Study.* 2nd ed. New York: Van Nostrand Reinhold, 1988.

Burgess, Ernest W. "The Growth of the City" in R. Park ed. *The City.* Chicago: University of Chicago Press, 1925.

Coase, Ronald. "The Problem of Social Costs." *Journal of Law and Economics* 2, 1960, pp. 1–44.*

Council on Environmental Quality. *The Third Annual Report.* Washington, D.C.: U.S. Government Printing Office, August 1972.

Hardin, Garrett. "The Tragedy of the Commons." *Science* 162, 1968, pp. 12243–48.*

Heilbrun, James. *Urban Economics and Public Policy.* 2nd ed. New York: St. Margin's Press, 1981, chapter 6.

George, Henry. *Progress and Poverty* (1897). Reprint. New York: Robert Schalkenbach Foundation, 1954.*

Hoover, Edgar M., and Frank Giarratani. *An Introduction to Regional Economics.* 3rd ed. New York: Alfred A. Knopf, 1984.

Hoyt, Homer. *The Structure and Growth of Residential Neighborhoods in American Cities.* Washington, D.C.: U.S. Government Printing Office, 1939.

Mills, David E. "Is Zoning a Negative Sum Game?" *Land Economics* 65, no. 1, February 1989, pp. 1–12.

Mills, Edwin S., and Bruce W. Hamilton. *Urban Economics.* 4th edition. Glenview, Ill.: Scott, Foresman, 1989, Chapter 6.

Ricardo, David. *Principles of Political Economy and Taxation.* London: J. M. Dent and Son, 1911.*

Siegan, Bernard. "Non-Zoning in Houston." *Journal of Law and Economics* 13, 1970, pp. 71–113.*

Von Thunen, Johann H. *Von Thunen's Isolated State.* Peter Hall ed. London: Pergamon Press, 1961.

Williams, Oliver P. *Metropolitan Political Analysis: A Social Access Approach.* New York: The Free Press, 1971.

Zorn, Peter M.; David E. Hansen; and Seymour I. Schwartz. "Mitigating the Price Effects of Growth Control: A Case Study of Davis, California." *Land Economics* 62, no. 1, February 1986, pp. 46–57.

* Classics.

Chapter Eleven

Housing and Neighborhood Development

Chapter 10 described factors that determine land use. This chapter focuses on housing, the land use that most directly affects the welfare of families. The National Housing Act declared that: "The general welfare and security of the Nation and the health and living standards of its people require . . . the realization . . . of the goal of a decent home and suitable living environment for every American Family." The National Housing Act indicates that American housing goals go beyond providing the biological minimum necessary level of shelter.

The private, albeit government-influenced, housing market, is the primary mechanism used to provide housing in the United States. Accordingly, a substantial portion of this discussion examines the operation of housing markets. Government policies are also explored in depth. The first section describes some fundamentals of residential property transactions including characteristics of housing supply and demand. The second section describes the relationship between housing and the aggregate economy. Residential choice is linked to neighborhood-change models in the third section. U.S. housing conditions and problems are discussed in the fourth section, followed by an analysis of U.S. housing policy.

FUNDAMENTALS OF HOUSING ECONOMICS

An understanding of market forces is a valuable analytical tool, but it is also important to realize that theory is sometimes a rough model of reality, not an exact description, so mechanical applications of theory can lead to incorrect conclusions. Nevertheless, supply and demand factors shape the housing market. Accordingly, supply and demand and other economic models will be described so as to reflect real estate realities.

Housing Supply and Demand

Supply and demand analysis is useful in understanding forces that affect the housing market. Figure 11–1(a) illustrates a traditional supply and demand curve for housing. The equilibrium price and quantity of housing are determined by the intersection of the supply and demand curves. Figure 11–1(b) shows fuzzy supply and demand curves which may be a more accurate representation.

"*Ceteris paribus*," or "other things equal," assumptions are necessary to allow the equilibrium price and quantity to remain stationary. Supply and demand curves represent the behavior of producers and consumers. However, their behavior is stable with respect to price and quantity only when all relevant variables other than price and quantity are held constant. The most common factors that must be assumed constant in supply and demand analysis of housing are shown in Table 11–1.

The *ceteris paribus* assumptions are not strictly met in reality, but that does not diminish the usefulness of supply and demand analysis. Paradoxically, it is the violation of the assumptions that makes the model useful. When any of the factors assumed to be constant change, the relevant supply or demand curves will shift. Thus, it is changes in the *ceteris paribus* assumptions that give predictive power to economic

FIGURE 11–1.   Two Models of the Housing Market

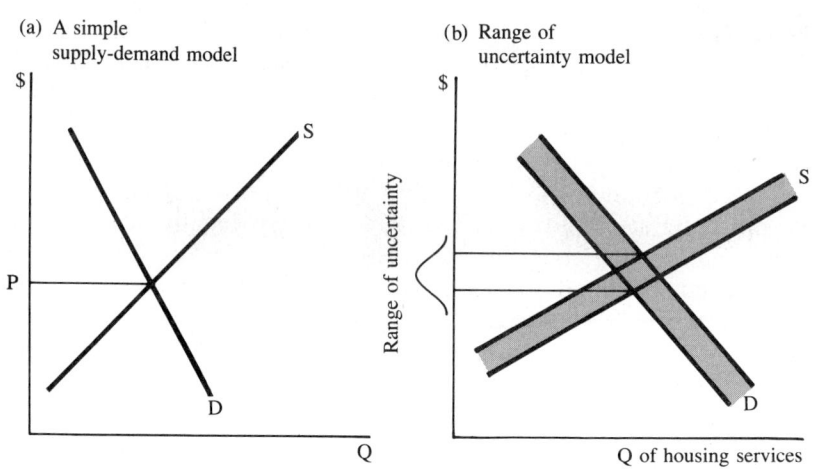

(a) A simple
    supply-demand model

(b) Range of
    uncertainty model

The traditional supply and demand presentation implies that a single, observable price will emerge. In reality "fuzzy" supply and demand curves might be used to illustrate the range of uncertainty.

TABLE 11-1. Important *Ceteris Paribus* Assumptions

General	*Specific Real Estate Example*
Demand	
1. Price of other goods	Price of home fuel
2. Consumers' tastes and preferences	Recent importance of family rooms
3. Size of the market	Number of families in a city due to factory relocation
4. Incomes of consumers	Incomes in a city or employment
5. Expectations	Inflation changes beliefs about future housing prices
Supply	
1. Price of inputs	Price of lumber, tools, etc.
2. Number of producers	Number of building contractors
3. Conditions of technology	Advances in factory fabrication of homes or plastic plumbing (where legal)

models. For instance, if an increase in income were anticipated while other important factors remained relatively stable, housing prices could be projected to increase.

Quantity.   The horizontal axis traditionally measures the quantity of a homogeneous product per period of time. When the housing market is being studied, it is obvious that houses are usually very dissimilar. So what does the quantity axis measure? We cannot study housing without distinguishing large from small units. The problem of distinguishing between large and small houses could be solved by defining the quantity axis as "square feet of housing" rather than as "one housing unit." However, this approach does not solve the measurement problem because the quality of equal-sized houses differs widely. Some housing units are well designed and appointed with luxury features, while others are little more than large boxes. Location itself ensures that no two properties will be exactly alike. A house represents a bundle of goods including the structure itself, the lot, various benefits of the location, and other factors. The concept of housing as a bundle of goods is developed further in the next section.

In order to finesse the problem of what is being measured on the quantity axis, economists have assumed that housing can be defined in terms of "units of housing services." A mansion might contain five units of housing services while a small apartment might contain only half a unit of housing services. The level of housing services contained in a dwelling unit can vary with design, location, and other features. The neighborhood environment and local public services that residents may receive can also be considered part of housing services. Although the method of measuring the units of housing services is complex and has been widely criticized, it is conceptually sound (Bartik, 1988).

Price.   Price is also a slightly more complicated concept when applied to housing. In order to understand the concept of housing price, first distinguish between the stock of housing and the flow of housing services derived from that stock. A house (stock) represents a flow of services over a period of years. The price of the housing stock is the sales price; the price of a periodic flow of services is the rental price. If the focus of analysis is on the supply of rentable housing, the price axis, the vertical axis, may best be defined as rent. If purchase of the housing stock is of concern, then the vertical axis may be sales price. However, conversion between rent and sales price is straightforward. The value of a house is the discounted present value of rents. In a well-functioning market, value will equal sales price. Therefore, it is conceptually easy to move between rent and sales price. If rents rise, sales prices rise (assuming factors such as maintenance cost and expected life of the property do not change). If housing prices rise, monthly payments increase. The relationship between the flow of income and sales price may be expressed using the same formula that was used in Chapter 10 to estimate property values:

$$SP = R_0 + \frac{R_1}{(1 + r)} + \frac{R_2}{(1 + r)^2} + \frac{R_n}{(1 + r)^n} \qquad (1)$$

where SP = Sales price (assumed to equal value),

R_i = Net rent (excluding associated expenses) the property could command in year i. R_n includes liquidation price and R_0 is rent due now,

r = Applicable discount rate, and

n = Holding period.

Variations of equation 1 are used by real estate appraisers in determining the value of income-producing properties. In the case of owner-occupied properties, it is necessary to impute the rental value of the housing service. The imputed rent is the monetary value of the periodic flow of benefits from the property that could be attained if rented.

The discount rate used to convert a periodic flow of net rents into housing value is an important part of the equation. The higher the discount rate, the lower will be the value of the property for a given level of net rent. The discount rate measures the cost of holding a unit of capital in the form of housing for a year. The discount rate would normally be higher than the rate on a comparable risk-maturity bond because of the need to extract a premium for management, depreciation, and other factors. At times, it might be appropriate to decrease the discount rate to account for anticipated appreciation (Mills and Hamilton, 1989, p. 190).

Hedonic Pricing[1].   Hedonic pricing models segment the housing-services bundle into detailed components and use statistical techniques such as regression to determine the marginal value of each component. The value of the entire housing bundle can then be determined by aggregating the value of various components. This section is intended to provide an overview of hedonic pricing, not to show the detailed statistical mechanics of the approach.

The essence of hedonic pricing models can be summarized in equation 2 which states that price is a function of housing characteristics:

$$P = f(C_i) \tag{2}$$

where P = Price

C_i = The ith characteristic (i.e., size, access, number of baths, etc.)

Equation 2 is a general functional form. When the function is specified, the coefficients associated with each variable express the value of that characteristic, holding all other characteristics constant.

For instance, if value were determined only by the square footage of the apartment and the number of bedrooms, the hedonic equation might be:

$$PR = a + b_1 \text{ (sq. ft.)} + b_2 \text{ (bedrooms)} \tag{3}$$

where PR = Property rent per month,

a = Intercept term,

sq. ft. = Number of square feet of space,

bedrooms = Number of bedrooms, and

b_1, b_2 = coefficients

Using regression techniques, the value of a_1, b_1, and b_2 could be determined. Suppose the regression technique resulted in the following equation:

$$RR = 75 + .40 \text{ (sq. ft.)} + 2.0 \text{ (bedrooms)} \tag{4}$$

Then, a 3-bedroom, 1,000-square-foot apartment would be expected to rent for $481 [75 + ($.40)(1000) + ($2)(3)]. The model not only provides

---

[1] This section may be skipped without loss of continuity.

TABLE 11–2. Determinants of Monthly Rents

	Regression Coefficient*
Intercept	2.44
Size (in square feet)	.421[x]
S1—extra bedroom for studio apartment	.050[xx]
S2—extra bedroom for medium-size unit	.068[x]
S3—extra bedroom for larger-size unit	.101[xx]
Age (in years)	.020[xx]
Condition (subjective, above or below average)	.032[xx]
Patio (yes or no)	.043[x]
Electric paid (yes or no)	.181[x]
Bathroom (extra beyond standard)	.027[xxx]
Fireplace (yes or no)	.071[xx]
Dishwasher (yes or no)	.078[x]
Children (allowed or not)	−.043[x]
Distance to downtown Phoenix	.148[xx]
Distance to major expressway	−.022[x]
Swimming pool (yes or no)	.078[xx]
Tennis (yes or no)	.017
Sauna (yes or no)	−.005
Hot tub (yes or no)	.014
Exercise room (yes or no)	.042[xxx]
Barbecue (yes or no)	−.001
Pool table (yes or no)	−.018

$R^2 = .81$
$W = 291$

* Shows the contribution of marginal increase in each variable on rent. For instance, an extra square foot will add 42 cents per month to rent, other things equal. X = .99, xx = .95, xxx = .90 confidence level.

SOURCE: Karl L. Guntermann and Stefan Norrbin, "Explaining the Variability of Apartment Rents," *American Real Estate and Urban Economics Association Journal* 15, no. 4, 1987, pp. 321–39.

information on the value of the housing bundle, but it also shows the marginal value of the components. For instance, an extra bedroom adds $2 per month to the rent, holding the apartment size and all other factors constant.

Actual price models are much more complex than the simple, linear, two-independent-variable model illustrated by equation 2. A study by Guntermann and Norrbin (1987) provides a more realistic example. They used a hedonic pricing model to estimate apartment rents for private development in the Phoenix metropolitan area. The results of the regression are shown in Table 11–2.

Not surprisingly, size is the dominant variable. Rents increase by about $.421 per additional square foot of living area in the unit. Notice that the signs on some of the coefficients are not what might be expected. Barbecues and pool tables (in the clubhouse) detract from rents. However, since these findings are not statistically significant, we can only conclude that they are not very important in the housing bundle. The appendix to this chapter shows how hedonic pricing models have been used to analyze metropolitan quality of life.

Market Comparison.   The market-comparison approach has long been used by real estate practitioners to estimate value. Although the market-comparison approach lacks the statistical rigor of the hedonic price model, it is based upon the same concept—housing is a bundled goods.

The four steps in the market-comparison approach are illustrated in Table 11–3 (Barrett and Blair, 1981). First, examine the subject property for which price is to be estimated. Relevant characteristics of the subject property may be described. Second, collect data for three or more comparable properties that have been sold and have known sales prices. Third, adjust the sales prices of the comparables to reflect the price they would have sold for if they had the characteristics of the subject property. If a comparable property is better than the subject property in some respect, then the sale price of the comparable should be decreased. If a comparable property is worse than the subject on a particular feature, then the comparable's price is adjusted upward. Usually, judgement and experience are used in making adjustments. Finally, the values of the comparable properties are averaged to provide an estimate of value of the subject property.

Uncertainty, Market Imperfections, and Competition

In perfectly competitive markets, such as the New York Stock Exchange or commodity exchanges, prices are set by impersonal market forces. Every buyer or seller is a price taker. Real estate transactions are fundamentally different from the competitive markets. One important difference between housing markets and competitive markets is that buyers and sellers can only guess the price for which a particular property will sell. Another important difference between real estate and competitive markets is that while there are generally hundreds of buyers and sellers in any real estate market at any given time, there may be only one or two sellers and only a few buyers for any particular type of property. Thus, each actor in a real estate market has some ability to affect price.

Because of the nature of real estate markets, price is seldom known before an actual sale has been made. From the point of view of buyers and sellers, the equilibrium price for a particular class of property in a given

TABLE 11-3. The Market-Comparison Approach to Value: Grid Analysis

Improvements	Comp A	Comp B	Comp C	Subject Property
Sale price	$56,000	$53,500	$48,000	?
Time of sale	Recent 0	1 year ago +$2,700	18 months ago +$3,500	Now
Location and neighborhood conditions	Better −$5,000	Worse +$5,000	Worse +$3,000	Average
Architectural style	Worse +$500	Better −$1,000	Worse +$250	Good
Total square feet	2,500 square feet −$7,000	Same 0	Same 0	2,300 square feet
Kitchen size and design	Better −$500	Same 0	Same 0	Average
Heating and air conditioning	Same	Same	Same	Electric
Number of rooms	8 0	7 +$3,000	8 0	8
Number of baths	2 0	1½ +$1,300	2 0	2
Type of construction	Better −$1,200	Better −$700	Better −$1,500	Poor
Physical condition	Same 0	Better −$1,000	Worse +$1,200	Average
Garage and other outbuildings	Same	Same	Same	1½ car garage
Lot value difference	Worse +$500	Equal 0	Equal 0	Average
Indicated value	$43,300		Overall rating $54,450	

Correlated value of subject property   ($43,300 + $62,800 + $54,450) ÷ 3 = $53,517 area may be better visualized as a range, rather than as an exact point. Figure 11–1(b) shows a modified supply and demand graph for a select type of real estate such as three-bedroom, one-and-one-half-bath ranch houses in the Saville subdivision.

The supply and demand curves in Figure 11–1(b) are fuzzy and a range of uncertainty is indicated because any one individual who decided to sell will affect supply, and there is no way to be certain ahead of time exactly how many similarly priced properties will be for sale. Likewise, demand for narrowly defined types of property can be affected by the behavior of any single purchaser.

The Role of Bargaining.   The uncertainties introduced into the search for a market price have important implications for real estate. Bargaining becomes a prerequisite to successful real estate dealings. In a perfectly competitive market, it is seldom worthwhile to bargain because there are many alternative buyers and sellers at the equilibrium price. However, in real estate transactions, it is necessary to bargain, not only because price is uncertain, but also because other factors besides price (such as closing and occupancy dates, items to be included in sale—rugs, draperies, and so on—and earnest money deposits) must also be determined. Often, a party will trade off more or less money for a less or more convenient occupancy date.

The Role of Specialists.   Uncertainties and the bargaining process partially explain the role of real estate specialists and middlemen. Loan officers, appraisers, and market analysts help decrease the range of uncertainty in a particular transaction. Improved knowledge is particularly important to institutions making real estate loans secured with only a small down payment. Uncertainty is also a significant problem in dealing with multimillion-dollar properties, where a small percentage error can mean a loss of tens of thousands of dollars. Because of such uncertainties, the appraiser's job is to estimate the most probable sales price under normal "arms-length" bargaining.

Appraisers are specialists at examining the real estate market and determining property value. There are three principal techniques used to estimate value: (1) the market approach, (2) the cost approach, and (3) the income approach. Each of the three approaches is grounded in economic theory. These approaches are summarized in Table 11–4. The extent that an appraiser will rely on one or another estimation technique depends upon data available and theoretical suitability.

Brokers play an important role in the bargaining process in several ways. First, by making a property known to more buyers, brokers can increase contacts with interested individuals and provide informed estimates of the parties' maximum prices to their clients. Finally, given the

TABLE 11–4. Approaches to Estimating Housing Values

The Market Approach

Theoretical foundation: If good information exists, prices of similar properties will be similar due to competition among buyers and sellers.

Technique: Actual sales prices of previously sold units are adjusted upward or downward to make the prices of the previously sold units comparable to estimated value of the subject property. For instance, if a property that did not have a garage sold for $60,000, then the estimated sale of an identical property that had a garage might be $67,000. See equation 2.

Most frequent use: Single-family houses in established areas with recently sold, comparable properties are best suited for valuation by this technique.

The Income Approach

Theoretical foundation: The present value of a property will equal the discounted value of future benefits. See equation 1.

Technique: Assign to the future the benefits that will flow from the property. Determine the appropriate discount rate and discount future benefits.

Most frequent use: Income-producing properties, such as rental apartments and shopping centers, are best valued using this approach.

The Cost Approach

Theoretical foundation: In a well-functioning market, competition will eliminate excess profits. Therefore, the sales price of a new house will equal the cost (including normal profit). The sales price of an existing property will equal the cost less adjustment for depreciation.

Technique: Use cost estimates to determine the construction cost and make adjustments for depreciation. Add the cost when new less depreciation to land value.

Most frequent uses: New properties or special-purpose properties such as schools, churches, or public buildings.

---

many details that are negotiated as part of a real estate contract, brokers can be effective bargaining agents for the client, helping to bring about a satisfactory trade-off between price and other items.

Housing Demand

Substantial research has been devoted to estimating the demand for housing. One of the simplest demand functions is:

$$Q = A + b_1P + b_2Y \qquad (5)$$

where Q = Units of housing services demanded,
P = Price per unit of housing services,
Y = Income, and
A, b_1, b_2 = Parameters.

The price elasticity of demand for housing can be estimated by examining the value of b_1. Most recent studies indicated a short-run price elasticity for housing is less than 1 in absolute value. In other words, a 1 percent increase in price will result in less than 1 percent decrease in the quantity of housing demand. The income elasticity of demand for housing can be derived from the b_2 parameter. Quigley (1979, p. 378) summarized a variety of empirical studies and concluded that the income elasticity of demand was about 0.7 to 0.9 with respect to long-run, permanent income. This means that a 1 percent increase in income will result in a slightly less than 1 percent increase in housing services.

Although the aggregate income elasticity of demand is about slightly less than one, it varies among income groups. Ihlanfeldt (1982) found that as incomes rise, the income elasticity of demand rises. The income elasticity for low-income households is between 0.14 and 0.62, and the elasticity for high-income households is between 0.72 and 1.10. Furthermore, the income elasticity of demand for housing quality is greater than the elasticity of demand for space. Thus, as incomes increase, a larger portion of increased expenditures will be oriented towards better quality rather than more square feet of housing space (Olsen, 1973, p. 990; Mayo, 1981).

Housing Supply

Empirical studies of the supply curve for housing are scarce. Changes in supply can be attributed to two sources: (1) new construction of dwelling units by builders and (2) adjustments to the existing stock of housing. However, because the existing stock of housing is substantial, new construction and adaptive adjustments can affect only a small portion of the housing stock in a given year.

A fundamental characteristic of the adjustment process is that elasticities of both supply and demand increase with time. It takes more time to increase the supply of housing than most kinds of goods. The concept of time explains why the supplies of housing and other types of real estate are often visualized as inelastic. It generally requires at least two years to complete a major development project and, thus, increase the supply. One year is a common time period for the completion of a single-family residence. Consequently, in the short run, price will be more responsive to changes in either supply or demand. Over longer periods, the quantity of housing services will mitigate price changes.

New Construction. New construction generally adds units to the upper end of the housing market. For instance, in 1986, the median price of a newly constructed home in the United States was $92,000 compared with $80,300 for an existing house. Table 11–5 shows regional and metropolitan variations in housing prices.

TABLE 11–5. Median New and Existing House Costs for Single-Family Homes in 1987–88 (by city, in thousands of dollars. Areas are metropolitan statistical areas (MSAs) except as indicated)

METROPOLITAN AREA	1987	1988, 2nd quarter	METROPOLITAN AREA	1987	1988, 2nd quarter
United States, all areas............	85.6	88.9	Memphis, TN-AR-MS..................	75.0	76.8
Akron, OH PMSA........................	57.1	60.1	Miami-Hialeah, FL PMSA.............	81.1	83.5
Albany-Schnectady-Troy, NY........	86.4	91.1	Milwaukee, WI PMSA.................	70.5	75.3
Albuquerque, NM........................	82.6	81.6	Minneapolis–St. Paul, MN-WI	80.5	84.3
Anaheim–Santa Ana, CA PMSA	167.3	204.0	Nashville, TN............................	75.5	78.3
Baltimore, MD...........................	81.1	87.3	New York–Northern New Jersey–		
Baton Rouge, LA	67.8	64.5	Long Island, NY-NJ-CT CMSA...	183.5	194.0
Birmingham, AL	71.6	76.5	Oklahoma City, OK....................	62.3	56.9
Boston, MA PMSA.......................	177.2	182.9	Omaha, NE-IA	59.0	58.7
Buffalo–Niagara Falls, NY CMSA...	56.7	64.8	Orlando, FL...............................	76.2	77.7
Chicago, IL PMSA	90.8	99.3	Philadelphia, PA-NJ PMSA	97.0	101.9
Cincinnati, OH-KY-IN PMSA	66.1	69.6	Phoenix, AZ..............................	80.9	79.1
Cleveland, OH PMSA	68.1	69.9	Portland, OR PMSA	64.2	64.9
Columbus, OH	68.7	73.4	Providence, RI PMSA..................	121.4	130.4
Dallas–Ft. Worth, TX CMSA	89.2	85.5	Riverside/San Bernardino PMSA	98.7	104.9
Denver, CO PMSA	88.9	83.4	Rochester, NY	72.5	73.7
Des Moines, IA...........................	55.6	58.2	St. Louis, MO-IL........................	74.3	79.5
Detroit, MI PMSA........................	65.6	72.3	Salt Lake City–Ogden, UT...........	69.4	66.9
Ft. Lauderdale–Hollywood–			San Antonio, TX..........................	70.2	65.2
Pompano Beach, FL PMSA	79.6	79.2	San Diego, CA	129.2	142.6
Hartford, CT PMSA......................	157.4	169.0	San Francisco–Oakland–San		
Honolulu, HI	186.0	198.7	Jose, CA CMSA	171.3	196.3
Houston, TX PMSA......................	65.9	63.5	Seattle/Tacoma CMSA.................	82.6	93.6
Indianapolis, IN	62.5	66.7	Syracuse, NY.............................	68.9	74.9
Jacksonville, FL..........................	65.1	67.4	Tampa–St. Petersburg–		
Kansas City, MO-KS	69.8	71.9	Clearwater, FL........................	63.8	65.5
Las Vegas, NV	77.0	77.9	Tulsa, OK.................................	65.7	65.0
Los Angeles–Long Beach, CA			Washington, DC-MD-VA..............	114.2	131.2
PMSA	147.7	175.9	West Palm Beach–Boca Raton–		
Louisville, KY-IN	51.7	54.1	Delray Beach, FL	102.6	94.8

	UNITED STATES	NORTHEAST	MIDWEST	SOUTH	WEST
New Construction	92,000	125,000	88,300	80,200	95,700
Existing	80,300	104,800	63,500	78,200	100,900

SOURCE: U.S. Department of Commerce, *Statistical Abstract*, U.S. Government Printing Office, Washington, D.C., 1988.

The construction industry, including housing construction, is much more sensitive to changes in the business cycle than other industries. For instance, the number of privately owned housing starts dropped 35 percent between 1973 and 1975 and increased by nearly 60 percent between 1982 and 1983. Variations have been even more dramatic in some local economies.

Practices in the industry make it relatively easy for general contractors, subcontractors, and laborers to exit and enter the industry. The housing construction industry is primarily composed of relatively small firms that hire independent contractors to do selected parts of construction rather than firms carrying carpenters, electricians, and so forth on their payrolls. Although general reliance on subcontractors can be more costly, the construction industry is so unstable that developers are reluctant to have a large, permanent work force or to invest heavily in equipment.

Time Cost and New Construction.   The time constraint on supply is caused by economic as well as physical factors. It might be physically possible to construct a major complex of buildings in a few months, but doing so would be prohibitively costly. Overtime payments would be required, and extra funds would have to be spent on coordination and backup materials to ensure that no bottlenecks occurred. The developer would have to purchase readily available inputs and would not have time to shop for the least expensive materials. On the other hand, the longer a project takes, the greater will be the interest costs for construction financing. The interest on the money borrowed to lay the foundation will be a higher figure if the project takes two years to build than if it takes only one year, because the loan can be repaid only after the building is completed and sold. As interest costs rise, developers want to shorten the completion time of a project. Thus, the optional amount of construction time may be thought as a trade-off between coordination costs, which decrease over longer time periods, and the opportunity costs of tying up land and capital.

Adaptive Adjustment.   In addition to new construction, changes to the housing stock can be made through adaptive adjustments. Adaptive adjustments account for much of the short-run elasticity of housing supply. Such adjustments can usually be made more quickly than adjustments through construction of new units. The principal mechanisms for adaptive adjustment are remodeling existing dwelling units and conversion of buildings. Conversion includes changes to or from residential use (i.e., conversion of a warehouse to a multifamily apartment) as well as the separation of one dwelling unit into two or more units. Owners and renters can change the quantity of housing services provided by a particular dwelling unit through maintenance, repair, alteration, and so forth. For instance, a family that wants a larger home may add a room or two to their existing house or convert an attic into an apartment for a mother-in-law. Changes in existing residential units are more likely in a tight housing market where purchase of a different home is difficult. Financial reasons, such as the desire to maintain a low-interest-rate mortgage may also encourage individuals to choose an adaptive adjustment rather than new construction.

Table 11–6 indicates the importance of adaptive adjustment compared to new construction. The first row shows the number of housing units in existence in 1980. The second row shows the number of units in

TABLE 11-6. Changes in Composition of the Housing Stock (000s of dwelling units)

	United States	Metropolitan Areas	Central City	Metropolitan Areas but Outside Central City
1. 1980 stock	89,292	30,389	25,836	33,067
2. 1980 stock existing in 1973	70,725	22,388	22,451	25,886
3. New construction	13,119	5,198	2,104	5,817
4. Conversions*	5,448	2,803	1,281	1,364
5. Total additions	18,567	8,001	3,385	7,181
Conversions as a percent of total additions	29%	35%	39%	19%

* Estimated as a residual of row 5 minus row 3. Includes conversions from nonresidential use and the separation of one dwelling unit into two or more.

SOURCE: *1980 Census of Housing: Components of Inventory Change*. Data found in Edwins Mills and Bruce Hamilton, *Urban Economics*, 4th ed. (Glenview, Ill.: Scott, Foresman, 1989).

1980 that were in existence in 1973. The difference between the two represents the total additions to the housing stock between 1973 and 1980 as shown in row 5. Data on the number of housing units newly constructed is shown in row 3. If we assume none of the housing units constructed between 1973 and 1980 were lost, then the difference between the total additions and the number of newly constructed units would equal the number of units added through conversions as shown in row 4. Not surprisingly, metropolitan areas outside the central cities had the lowest rate of change due to adaptive adjustment. However, in central cities, conversions accounted for nearly 40 percent of the housing stock change, and in metropolitan areas, 35 percent of the change was attributed to conversion. Table 11–6 only addresses changes in the number of units. It does not reflect other aspects of adaptation, such as quality changes that increase housing services, so it understates the extent of adaptive adjustments.

Adaptive adjustments are often associated with neighborhood transition and filtering, discussed in detail later in this chapter. When a lower-income group moves into a neighborhood, the quality of housing stock may deteriorate. For instance, the previous income group may have been willing and able to spend $1,000 per year on maintenance, but the lower-income groups may spend only $600. However, due to the subdivision of living space, the quantity of housing services may increase (i.e., single-family units subdivided into duplexes). Conversely, when a neighborhood goes through a gentrification phase, the number of housing units may decrease as apartment buildings are converted to single-family residences but the quality of each housing unit may increase. The key point is that through adaptive adjustments changes in the supply of housing can occur without new construction.

Interaction of Construction and Adaptation

Both new construction and adaptation are important to the adjustment process. However, it takes considerably longer to change housing conditions through new construction than through adaptation. Nationally, new construction adds only about 2 to 3 percent per year to the housing stock. Figure 11–2 illustrates the interaction between adaptive adjustment and new construction. The long-run supply curve S_L represents the quantity of housing services that developers would be willing and able to provide if they had time to construct new units. The short-run supply curve S_{SR1} represents the quantity of housing services that could be provided if the number of units were set at the level indicated by the corresponding point on the long-run supply curve but there was sufficient time for adaptation—remodeling, conversion, and so forth.

FIGURE 11–2   Long- and Short-Run Supply Curves

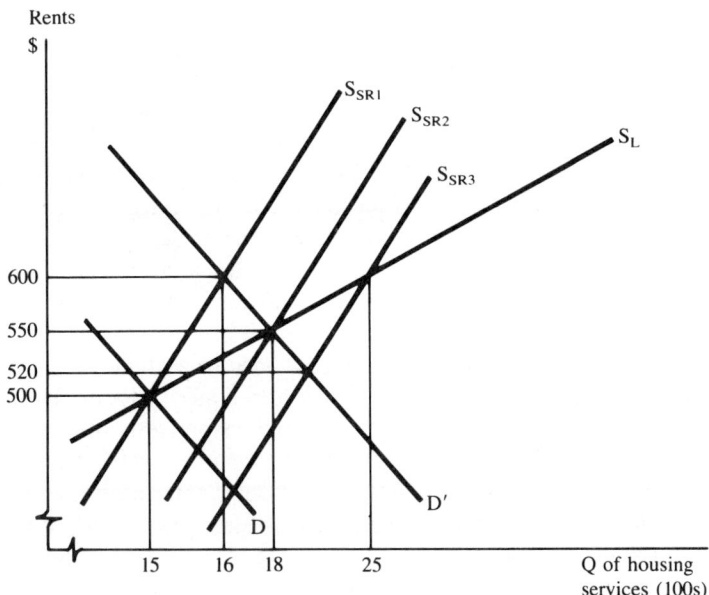

The short-run supply of housing services is relatively inelastic because only adaptive adjustments are possible. New construction adds to the housing supply in the long run, making it more elastic.

There is only one quantity of housing services that is consistent with both the long-term behavior of builders and short-run adaptive behavior. This level is shown along the long-run supply curve, S_L. Let the short-run supply curve represent levels of housing services that could be provided with the stock of housing units represented by the corresponding point on the long-run supply curve. At the price-quantity combination $500 and 1,500, the housing stock implicit in short-run supply curve S_{SR1}, is also consistent with the long-term behavior of producers. Residential building activity will be maintained at a level just sufficient to replace units demolished. But at $500 per month rent and quantity 1,500, there is no incentive for producers to increase the overall housing stock.

In order to better visualize the adjustment process, assume that housing demand increases from D to D' causing price to rise. How will suppliers of housing services respond? Initially, additional housing services will become available through conversions from other uses. Adaptive adjustment explains the slight elasticity in the short-run supply curve. This increase in housing services is shown in Figure 11–2 as a movement from 1,500 to 1,600 units. Rents are $600. However, this short-term increase is only part of the adjustment process.

At a rent level of $550, producers would be willing and able to offer 1,800 units of housing services in the long run. Over the long term, the most efficient way to expand the housing supply will include new construction. The 300 additional units represent the extra housing units that producers would like to make available through new construction. The provision of 1,800 units of housing services requires a larger total housing stock than is implied by the short-run supply curve, S_{SR1}. S_{SR2} represents the new short-term supply curve that would exist after producers increased the housing stock. Rents would equal $550 and the housing market would again be in long- and short-run equilibrium.

Rydell (1982) examined the supply response to a change in demand. His findings are consistent with the stock-adjustment model. He found that when demand increases the initial supply response is dominated by adaptive adjustments. However, within three years, construction of new units accounted for the bulk of supply response. The extent of the response depends upon the vacancy rates in the market. If the initial vacancy rate were 4 percent, a 3 percent increase in demand would result in a 4 percent increase in price in the short run and a less than 1 percent increase in the quantity of housing services consumed. At higher vacancy rates, the price increase is smaller and the effect on the quantity of housing services consumed increases.

An implication of both the model and Rydell's research is that changes in price may be more significant than changes in quantity in the short run. Therefore, developers can easily miscalculate future market conditions if they fail to consider the additional construction that the short-term higher prices will induce. Construction activity has a tendency to shift from boom to bust, particularly if overly optimistic views about the rate of increase in demand are widespread. For instance, when the 1974 recession hit, Florida and Georgia were among the most affected states in the country because their economies had been fueled by a major construction spurt. Atlanta had dozens of partially-filled office buildings, and Florida had hundreds of unsold condominiums and thousands of unemployed carpenters, masons, crane operators, and developers.

The problem of overbuilding can be illustrated with the aid of Figure 11–2 using the concept of short- and long-run housing supply. Assume that initially the demand and supply of housing are in equilibrium, at a rent level of $500 and a housing stock of 1,500 units. Since the stock of housing that determines the short-run supply is consistent with the long-run desires of developers, new construction is just sufficient to replace demand. Suppose next that demand shifts from D to D'—rents will initially increase to $600 where demand intersects S_{SR1}. At a rent level of

$600, developers will feel that it is profitable to rent 2,500 units and may make plans to expand the stock of housing accordingly. However, if many developers decide to construct major subdivisions, the housing-stock increase could shift the short-run supply curve to S_{SR3}, and price consequently would fall to $520 per month (where S_{SR3} intersects D'). If rents do not fall, that is, if they are "sticky in a downward direction" and remain at $600, then housing units will remain vacant. In this example, 900 units (2,500 − 1,600) would be vacant. Overbuilding will have taken place. Construction may cease until the vacancy rate declines and price rises to a level that justifies additional construction.

Over time, vacancy rates will decline as a result of two factors. First, in most areas, demand will increase gradually. Often, when overbuilding occurs, units will remain idle as owners maintain above-equilibrium rent. Meanwhile, demand gradually increases, and eventually the surplus real estate is absorbed. Second, existing stocks will decrease, largely through the adaptive-adjustment process.

The demand curve also becomes more elastic the longer the time period allowed for adjustment. If price rises "overnight," many customers of real estate—both businesses and households—will find it more convenient simply to pay higher rents rather than move to new locations and use less space. Over time, however, behavior will change. Shopkeepers will evolve ways of using less space, possibly by conserving inventory, or perhaps some store owners will go out of business. Households may start purchasing space-saving appliances and furniture, or they may leave the area and move to a lower-cost locality. While consumers may not change behavior immediately, these long-term adjustments will eventually decrease demand or slow increases in demand.

HOUSING AND THE AGGREGATE ECONOMY

The housing sector is more sensitive to changes in the aggregate economy than the average industry for at least four reasons. First, housing is sensitive to expectations about the future. Since the purchase of a new house or even moving into a different apartment represents a long-term commitment, individuals are reluctant to upgrade their housing standards unless they believe they can afford to on a permanent basis. When individuals are optimistic about future income, they are more willing to accept long-term financial obligations associated with improved housing services. Lenders' expectations are similarly affected, so they are more inclined to reject loan applications in times of pessimism. Second, housing is a durable and flexible good, so many housing needs that arise due to changed circumstances can be accommodated in the housing units individuals are currently using. Third, housing demand and supply are both sensitive to the interest rate. Interest rates often peak when the economy is near the business-cycle peak and, thus, housing tends to lead the economy downward. Finally, because of the many small construction firms in the industry, there is relatively easy exit, so excess capacity can be absorbed into other activities more easily.

In addition to being sensitive to the business cycle, housing is a leading sector. Housing construction starts to decline prior to the aggregate economy and turns up before the rest of the economy. Part of the explanation for the timing of the housing cycle is related to the reasons housing is cyclically sensitive. Expectation and the impact of interest-rate changes affect the housing sector earlier than they affect the average industry. In addition, housing is a large part of the economy. Thus, declines in housing will have a ripple effect on the rest of the economy.

Housing in an Era of Inflation

During the early and mid-1970s, the economy experienced fairly high and generally unanticipated inflation. During that time, individuals owning real estate experienced substantial gains. There are three reasons why housing has been a good investment during periods of inflation:[2] (1) appreciation, (2) leverage, and (3) expectations.

Appreciation.   Why does the resale price of housing increase when the resale price of other goods—appliances, clothing, cars, etc.—normally decreases in price? First, there is a well-established resale market for housing. Used goods that lack an established market may carry a secondhand stigma or require greater search costs on the part of buyers. But a more important reason for the appreciation potential of housing is its long economic life, or, to say the same thing in another way, its low rate of depreciation. As a house ages, it loses value due to deterioration, functional obsolescence (older houses may not have two-story foyers), and changes in the surrounding neighborhood. However, these changes occur so slowly that a typical property will lose only 2–3 percent of its value annually due to these factors. Inflation has been greater than the rate of deterioration, so the net effect has been that most residential units have increased in value. For instance, a property may be worth $100,000 at the start of the year. In a world of no inflation, depreciation might cause values to fall by 1 percent to $99,000. However, if a 5 percent inflation factor is applied to the real value at the end of the year, the property value would increase to $103,950.

---

[2] In addition to inflation, another reason that demand for housing was strong during the period is because the "baby boom" generation was in the family-formation stage and, thus, in the housing market.

Leverage.   Leverage is critically important to understanding why housing can be a good investment during inflationary periods. Most real estate is purchased with the use of borrowed funds. The first-time buyer may make a down payment of, say, 10 percent on the price of a house and borrow the remainder. Investors in multiple-family structures may have higher down-payment requirements, but they still borrow the bulk of the money used to finance their investment. The value of a property minus the amount owed is called the owners' equity. Inflation not only allows home purchasers to repay loans in cheaper dollars, but more importantly, inflation increases the value of the property without affecting the amount owed. Hence, the equity holder receives the full benefit of the inflationary price increase while investing only a portion of the money needed to purchase the property.

An example will illustrate the working of leverage. Suppose an individual purchased a $100,000 home with 10 percent of the purchase price as a down payment and $90,000 borrowed (secured by a mortgage) from a lending institution. The initial situation would be:

Property value	$100,000
−Mortgage debt	−90,000
= Equity	$ 10,000.

Assume the property appreciated 5 percent during the year. Also, assume for simplicity that during the year the homeowner paid interest on the mortgage debt but did not repay principal. Assume the interest, taxes, and other expenses just equaled the monetary value the homeowner received from living in the house. At the end of the year, the situation would be:

Property value	$105,000
−Mortgage debt	−90,000
= Equity	$ 15,000.

Equity increased 50 percent, an excellent rate of return. Most of the books on how to make millions in real estate advise investors to be highly leveraged when values are increasing.

Expectations of Appreciation.   A final factor that drove housing prices during the latter part of the 1970s was the expectation of future price increases. As individuals saw prices increase, they anticipated future increases and, hence, increased their demand for housing stock, although not necessarily their demand for housing services. When this happens, the anticipated increases become capitalized in current prices. In terms of equation 1, R_i was defined as the rent (net of associated expenses) the property could command as well as the liquidation value. Expectations would affect the R_i terms.

The Financial Sector.   Although the era of unanticipated inflation was beneficial to home buyers, the mortgage-lending industry was hurt. Many lenders were stuck with loans on which they were essentially earning zero or negative real interest. Real interest is the nominal interest rate adjusted for inflation. For instance, if they were earning 7 percent interest on the loans they made while inflation was 12 percent, the real interest was negative 5 percent. To make matters worse, they had to pay competitive rates to keep their deposits, and individuals with low-interest mortgages were reluctant to sell their houses and extinguish their mortgages (a factor that also had the consequence of reducing labor mobility).

In order to protect themselves in the future, lending institutions have initiated important changes. One of the most notable is that borrowers are given incentives to accept variable-rate mortgages. Variable-rate mortgages link the interest rate borrowers pay to an increase in market interest rates, so if interest rates increase in the future, the mortgage payments will increase.

Housing and the Fight against Inflation

In the late 1970s, fighting inflation became a principal goal of macroeconomic policy. A big part of the battle against inflation was a Federal Reserve tight-money policy that resulted in high interest rates. The effect of higher interest rates was dramatic and affected both new construction and existing home sales. In 1977, the number of new housing starts began to decline, and the decline was particularly sharp between 1980 and 1982 when mortgage rates were at record highs in the 15–16 percent range. (The author was moving from Washington, D.C., to Dayton, Ohio, during this period and can attest to the problems caused in trying to sell one home and buy another during that period.)

Purchase of existing housing units did not drop as dramatically as the newly constructed units, but sales peaked in 1978, and by 1987, housing sales had yet to reach the 1978 level. Because of the significant impact on housing, many industry advocates said housing bore an unfair share of the inflation fight. But, as explained at the outset of this section, housing has always been a volatile sector.

Mortgage interest rates have fallen since the peak periods of 1980–83. However, many economists believe real interest rates are as important as nominal rates for housing investment. As interest rates have declined, so has inflation, so real interest rates have remained at historic high levels and so have continued to adversely affect the level of housing construction.

RESIDENTIAL LOCATION AND NEIGHBORHOOD FORMATION

The choice of where to live is an individual decision shaped by larger social forces. Individual decisions have the cumulative effect of forming recognizable neighborhoods. This section describes the processes that result in the social and economic similarity of neighborhood residents. The models discussed in the sections will have implications for neighborhood change.

The Filtering-Down Theory

The filtering-down theory explains how different socioeconomic groups come to occupy particular neighborhoods. The theory was originally put forward by Burgess (1952) to explain his observations about Chicago, where higher-income households moved farther from the city center and slightly lower income groups occupied the vacated housing.

As incomes among a high-income group rise, their demand for housing increases. The extent of the increase depends upon the elasticity of demand for housing. Some individuals will be able to satisfy their increased demand for housing best by buying newly constructed houses. The newly constructed house will likely be located further from the heart of the city where vacant land is available. It is usually cheaper to build on vacant land than to bear the opportunity cost (i.e., the remaining value), demolition, and clearance expenses on a site with existing buildings. Furthermore, inner-city lots are generally too small to accommodate preferences of upper-income households.

The filtering process depends upon what happens to the houses vacated by the families that purchased newly constructed homes. There are three likely possibilities:

1. No filtering. Families of similar economic backgrounds might purchase the vacated houses. In this case, there would be no change in the economic status of the neighborhood. The filtering process will not be effective in increasing the supply of housing to lower-income groups.

2. Complete filtering. Suppose that families of comparable incomes were not interested in moving into the vacated properties at the price the initial occupants paid, although the quality of the housing unit had not deteriorated. In this case, the price of housing in the neighborhood would fall and the house would be affordable to lower-income households. The house could be described as filtering down to lower-income families. This second case is the clearest example of how poor families may benefit from the filtering process.

3. Filtering and adaptation. Houses will often undergo some adaptive change when they filter to a lower-income group. One important reason for the change in the housing stock is that lower-income groups may be unable to afford the same levels of maintenance as the previous higher-income group. Also, lower-income groups may wish to use houses in different ways, such as using a building to handle more people than previously. The vacated property could be altered by lowering the level of maintenance or by other types of adaptive adjustment. In physical terms, the lower maintenance levels might be reflected in houses that were in need of paint, had cracked windows, and so forth. Some adaptation will result in lower-quality housing services, although the quantity of housing services provided in a neighborhood may increase if properties are used more intensively. In this case, the housing units in the neighborhood filtered to a lower-income group, but whether the housing services increased would depend upon the extent of the adaptive adjustment. If the decline in housing quality is slight, the adaptive filtering will probably lead to better housing for the lower-income group.

The three possibilities describe what might happen to an individual house. If the focus of analysis is on the neighborhood, possibilities 2 and 3 will change the socioeconomic composition. To the extent that adaptation occurs, the physical characteristics of the neighborhood will also change.

The filtering theory does not necessarily require a growth pattern in which lower-income groups move outward from the central city. For instance, the filtering process could operate equally well if we assumed that new houses were being built along major urban corridors or radiating outward from more than one urban subcenter. Furthermore, the filtering process need not start at the top of the income scale. If middle-income families move into newly constructed housing, the filtering process can start with the income group just below the movers.

Initiating and Perpetuating the Process. Why do higher-income groups move from the neighborhood in the first place? What initiates the filtering process and keeps it going? Most filtering models assume the process is initiated by individuals moving outward from the center of the city as their incomes increase. This process is part of the trade-off model described below. In addition, Little (1980) suggested that the filtering process may be touched off by "mobile externalities," such as congestion, noise, or fear of crime, that move outward from the urban core. These externalities may trigger the relocation process. Low-income and minority populations are viewed as a negative externality by many upper-income families. As the supply of low-income housing in the inner city is diminished through deterioration and demolitions or as additional low-income families move into the urban area, pressures to move outward increase.

After a certain concentration of a group has moved into a neighborhood, the filtering process may quicken. Racial transition of neighborhoods is sometimes characterized by a tipping point. Evidence indicates that when a neighborhood reaches a point where between 20 to 30 percent of the population is black, the neighborhood becomes stigmatized as a black area and the speed of racial change is accelerated. The same concept probably applies to neighborhood transition in general. For instance, once a neighborhood becomes identified as working-class rather than middle-class in the minds of buyers and sellers, the transition may accelerate.

Blockbusting and redlining are two other responses that may initiate or perpetuate the process of neighborhood transition. Blockbusting refers to real estate activity whereby brokers encourage whites to sell at a low price by preying on fears that blacks are taking over their neighborhood. The real estate dealer either hopes to purchase properties cheaply from whites and resell the properties to blacks at a substantial profit or simply to turn over properties to earn commissions.

Redlining refers to the practice by lending institutions of withholding mortgage financing from potential buyers in neighborhoods that are undergoing economic transition to a lower-income group. If mortgage funds are not available, the price of housing will tend to fall, speeding the process of change. Insurance companies have also been accused of redlining by refusing to insure (or charging higher premiums for) houses in certain areas or refusing to provide automobile insurance for residents in those areas.

There are laws against some forms of blockbusting and redlining. However, both may occur in subtle ways. A broker may intimate that a racial change is occurring without being explicit (e.g., "the character of the area isn't what it once was"), or a lending institution may place barriers to a potential borrower in a redlined area that are difficult to detect. Although both blockbusting and redlining are frequently proposed theories that stimulate neighborhood transition, the extent that they actually affect neighborhood transition is unknown.

Another factor that can speed the rate of neighborhood change is the level of maintenance. Galster (1987) investigated the decision of homeowners to repair and maintain their houses. He found that both sociological and economic factors affected the upkeep decision. Social factors include the solidarity of the neighborhood and the expectation that it might deteriorate. A neighborhood going through the filtering process may have a social environment that discourages reinvestment. Economic factors include the potential for capital gains. The expected capital gains from a maintenance investment is affected by the anticipated appreciation and the expected length of tenure. If individuals plan to move in the near future or if they anticipate declines in property values, there will be less investment.

Porell (1985) showed that when landlords reside in the building they rent, they tend to maintain property better than absentee landlords. By implication the findings also suggest that when landlords live in the neighborhood, they will better maintain rental units. If landlords move from the neighborhood in the course of the filtering process, the quality of the housing stock may fall, quickening the filtering process.

Implications.   There are several important implications of the filtering analysis. First, the model explains the tendency of income groups to segregate. Higher-income groups will seek better housing, thus, freeing their existing units for lower-income groups. The model suggests that poor families must live in lower-quality, used housing. Although used housing does not have to be low quality (someone remarked that the Queen of England lives in a used house), new construction tends to occur at the upper end of the market.

Second, the model explains the observation that housing quality occasionally deteriorates during the process of neighborhood change. Lower-income families have lower demand for housing services. Adaptive adjustment will bring the quantity of housing services in line with demand.

Another implication of the filtering-down theory is that household location will be determined by the kind of housing available and the potential for the housing stock to be altered through adaptive reuse. In this sense, the filtering theory is supply-oriented.

The filtering-down theory also has an important policy implication. The housing of the poor may be improved if new construction is encouraged for the upper and middle classes. However, this process will help low-income families only if the new housing units the poor occupy as the result of filtering are less expensive than previously and do not deteriorate to the level of housing they previously occupied.

Olsen's (1969) model of the filtering process indicated that in the long run the price of a unit of housing services would be determined by the cost of production. Therefore, in the long run, the housing stock would evolve through disinvestment to the level residents could afford to construct and maintain. Unless they were willing and able to pay the cost of additional housing services, their housing standard could not be improved. Hence, filtering could not improve the housing standards of low-income groups in the long run. However, in the case of housing, the "long run" is generations, so filtering may indeed result in better housing for trailing groups.

Weicher and Thibodeau (1988) provided empirical evidence that filtering improved housing conditions of low-income groups and that it was quantitatively an important mechanism. They found that about one less substandard housing unit was occupied during the 1970s for each new housing unit built during the 1960s. Although the ratio of reduced substandard occupancy to new construction will change depending upon market conditions, their findings suggest that filtering is an important way to increase the supply of housing services to trailing groups. Whether it is more effective to improve the housing conditions of the poor directly rather than relying upon the filtering process is an issue that remains subject to debate.

The Trade-Off Model

The trade-off model explains the predominance of high-quality housing on the city perimeter in terms of the trade-off between access to central locations and household demand for space (Muth, 1969). The model is based on the assumption that as incomes rise the rate at which households are willing to substitute access for cheaper land changes.

Space versus Access.   The model starts with the proposition that the rent-bid curve (see Chapter 10) slopes downward, moving away from the central city. The negative slope is due to the greater access to urban goods available closer to the central city making such land more valuable. Picture a household at location M in Figure 11–3. The location at M represents the optimal trade-off for the household between access to the cen-

FIGURE 11–3   Space versus Access as Income Rises

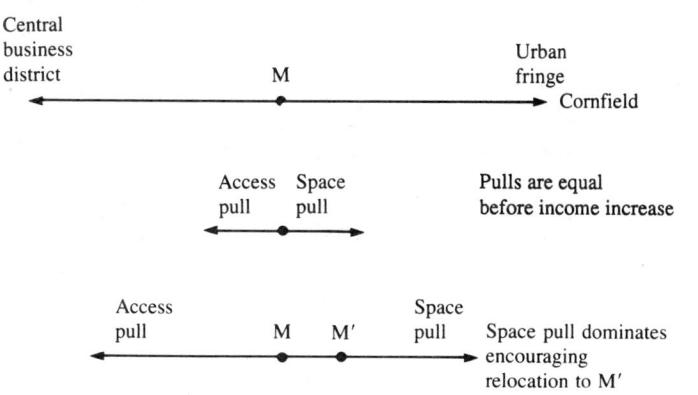

Initially, the household is in equilibrium. As income increases, the household will relocate because the desire for more space plus the cheaper land near the fringe is stronger than the increased pull of the desire for better access.

tral city, on the one hand, and lower land costs, on the other. Each household has two factors to consider in choosing its location. One consideration is the amount of space that it prefers. The larger the amount of space the household desires, the farther from the city center the household will tend to locate, all other things being equal. Second, costs of travel into the city must be considered. Travel costs include the out-of-pocket costs and opportunity costs of foregone activities while traveling. Empirical studies have shown that time costs of commuting are valued at about 25 percent of the traveler's hourly wage. These opposite pulls determine the slope of the individual access/price trade-off curve.

As the income of the family located at M increases, the household will want more land. The higher the elasticity of demand for land, the stronger the tendency to move away from the central city where land is more expensive. However, the increased income will also increase the opportunity costs of commuting, tending to favor a location closer to the center city. The desire for more land will tend to tilt the locational choice towards the periphery. The increased opportunity cost of travel will tend to orient the optimal location towards the city's center where access is best. Which pull will dominate cannot be determined theoretically.

Evidence in the United States indicates that the outward movement effect is much greater than the travel-cost effect. Therefore, neighborhoods of higher-income families are more likely to locate in the metropolitan area's outer ring. Many South American and European countries have not experienced the tendency of families to move farther from the city center as incomes increase. The contrast suggests (not surprisingly) that the trade-off is affected by attitudes regarding the value of nonwork time and preferred living accommodations.

Trade-Offs in the Multiple-Nuclear City.   There are increasingly multiple points within a metropolitan area that represent points of substantial access. The central business district is no longer the controlling access point in most major metropolitan areas. During the past twenty years, jobs have shifted from the central city to suburban locations, so the assumption of minimum transportation costs at the CBD are unrealistic for most families. The CBD remains the site of the plurality of jobs, but many large business agglomerations exist throughout most metropolitan areas.

In light of the new realities of urban form, the trade-off theory should be modified to describe households as examining trade-offs between a variety of jobs and residential locations. Within limited areas, land costs may actually decline, moving toward the central city. However, the generalization that preferences for increased space are more easily attainable at the urban fringe remains valid, particularly if newly constructed housing is desired.

The Cultural-Agglomeration Model

The filtering and the trade-off models explain the emergence of neighborhoods with similar incomes. Cultural factors are also important in neighborhood formation. People often believe they will find congenial friends or mates (or mates for their children) if they live near people like themselves. Thus, neighborhoods of individuals with similar social characteristics will form based upon social desires and agglomeration economics.

The services that some ethnic groups desire may be provided economically only if economies of scale can be achieved. Therefore, groups may form neighborhoods around stores that reflect their buying patterns. Aged individuals may congregate in neighborhoods that provide health services, while families in the child-rearing stage may be overrepresented in a neighborhood with recreational facilities and good schools. Ethnic groups may form neighborhoods around a church. The changing demographic composition of a neighborhood portends a change in the services available in the area. In addition to the forces that draw like groups together, there are discriminatory processes at work that tend to isolate poor and minority families.

Socially homogeneous neighborhoods have been criticized. Sarkissian (1976) has argued that greater socioeconomic diversity in neighborhoods would: (1) help promote a stable social mix of community leaders, (2) provide alternative role models for individuals in the lower class, (3) encourage artistic diversity, (4) encourage cultural cross-fertilization, (5) increase opportunities for the poor, (6) reduce social tension, (7) avoid residential instability, and (8) help prepare residents for life in a diverse world. The desirability of neighborhood diversity has been recognized and encouraged in some local development programs. However, the forces tending to segregate households along income and racial lines continue to be strong.

The Tiebout Model

Tiebout (1956) developed an informative model that describes the relationship between local government programs, taxes, and housing prices. His model represents an ingenious and useful application of the fundamental concepts of supply and demand. The Tiebout model is normally considered part of the public finance literature because it emphasizes the role of government services as a main attraction and taxes as a major detractor in creating neighborhood amenities. The model is discussed here because it also has implications for neighborhood change. In fact, in a metropolitan context, a small suburb is similar to the neighborhood as a reference point. There are four necessary postulates of the model:

1. A house purchased in a particular area embodies a bundle of services that vary depending upon government activity. For instance, the housing services in a particular neighborhood may or may not include garbage collection, adequate police service, friendly neighbors, and quality public schools. These government-related services are in addition to the private housing services of the shelter and land. The model can be extended to include nongovernmental amenities that neighborhood residents receive, such as prestige, sociable neighbors, and quiet.

2. Individuals form preferences for an area based upon the public services and other features of the external environment as well as the private services of the house.

3. Different levels of service provisions will often result in different tax burdens among municipalities. Other things equal—that is, assuming equal service levels—the higher the tax burden, the smaller will be the housing demand in a jurisdiction. Negative features of the neighborhood, such as unsafe conditions, higher insurance premiums, and pollution, can be treated similar to increased taxes in their affect on property values.

4. Individuals differ in their preference and willingness to pay for private housing services and also for the goods associated with housing in a particular neighborhood. In other words, some individuals will be willing and able to pay different amounts for packages of neighborhood amenities and disamenities.

In order to understand the implications of the Tiebout model, assume that the legislative body in a small suburb voted to construct a major sports facility to include tennis courts, swimming pools, and a gymnasium with an indoor track, weight rooms, and sauna. The facility would be available free to community residents only. Property taxes would increase by an average of $100 per household per year to finance the project. The tax boost includes maintenance as well as repayment of bonds issued to support construction. How will the change in the amenity-disamenity mix affect housing prices and the characteristics of individuals living in the neighborhood?

First, some residents will be deterred from living in the area because the higher taxes are more of a burden to them than the value they place upon the sports facility. In other words, they would no longer be willing to pay as much as they previously would have paid for a house in the same area. Demand among this group will decrease. Conversely, other individuals will be attracted to the municipality because they value the services of the sports complex more than they object to the extra taxes. Thus, some individuals will move out of the suburb to avoid the high taxes while others will move into the area because they want access to the complex.

The process of housing adjustment is best illustrated by the supply and demand model. Assume there are two groups of individuals that we shall term "sports nuts" and "misers." The sports nuts are willing to pay for the extra facilities while the misers are not. The responses can be analyzed by reference to Figure 11–4. Prior to the sports complex construction, the demand by the two groups may have been similar. Thus, the pre–sports complex demand curve D_1 in Figures 11–4(a) and 4(b) is the same for both the sports nuts and the misers. After the increase in services and taxes, however, the demand for housing in the area increases among sports nuts and decreases among misers. The isolated effect of the sports nut is to increase prices from $500 to $600 per month. The isolated effect of the misers is to decrease housing prices from $500 to $400. The combined effect depends upon which group has the largest shift in demand. Figure 11–4(c) is drawn on the assumption that the sports-nut effect outweighs the miser effect. Hence, housing prices rose to $580. Of course, the combined outcome could have resulted in lower property values; it depends upon tastes and preferences.

The adjustment process is also accompanied by spatial rearrangement of households. The misers will sell their property in order to both avoid higher taxes and capture the higher prices that the sports nuts are willing to pay. When they sell their properties, they will move to an area providing a better service/tax mix for their preferences. Sports nuts, on

FIGURE 11–4   The Tiebout Model

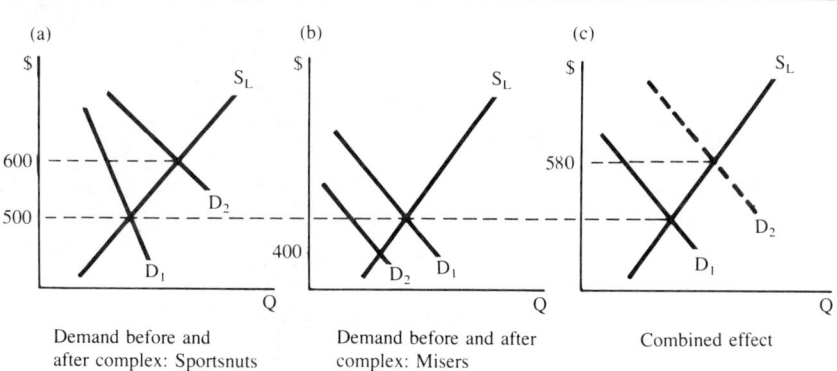

(a) Demand before and after complex: Sportsnuts

(b) Demand before and after complex: Misers

(c) Combined effect

The public improvement made the community more desirable for some residents, but the higher taxes to finance the improvements made the community less desirable for others. The combined effect cannot be determined theoretically although in this example the net effect was to increase property values.

the other hand, will move into the suburb. In Tiebout's words, spatial arrangement amounts to "lumping together of all similar tastes for the purpose of making joint purchases" (p. 417). Individuals "voted with their feet" for the combination of amenities and disamenities they preferred.

The Tiebout hypothesis has been tested on several occasions. Oates (1969), for instance, found that, *ceteris paribus,* "property values would be higher in a community the more attractive its package of public goods" (p. 960). Oates was the first to show that property tax increases tend to be capitalized into the current value of property. School expenditures exert a particularly significant positive impact in the municipalities examined by Oates. Clotfelter (1975) has documented spatial rearrangement as a result of school desegregation using the Tiebout model as the basic theoretical framework. Jud and Bennet (1986) showed that school quality has been a significant factor in shaping interurban locations, even holding racial composition constant. Differences in property insurance have also been shown to affect housing prices (MacDonald et al., 1987).

An important implication of the Tiebout model is that individuals select areas that provide their preferred mix of services and taxes. Better services and lower taxes will increase housing demand within the area. Individuals will express their preferences by attempting to move into the district—a process termed "voting with their feet." If property values increase more than property values in nearby jurisdictions, one may infer that a possible reason may be that local officials are providing a desired mix of taxes and services. Some observers have suggested that relative changes in housing prices be a measure of the performance of public officials. However, nongovernmental actions, such as establishment of an attractive shopping center nearby or a neighborhood escort service for the elderly, will also change the amenity-disamenity mix.

The Aggregate Economic Fallout Model

Hill and Bier (1989) developed a model of neighborhood change that links changes in the economic base, discussed in Chapter 5, to neighborhood formation. Changes in the national economy may affect particular local sectors and these impacts are in turn translated into changes in neighborhood characteristics. Their model suggests that neighborhoods have identifiable links to occupations and industries in the local economy. For instance, one neighborhood may have a disproportionate number of residents who are blue-collar workers in an automobile plant. Another neighborhood may be composed primarily of high-income professionals in the service sector, such as lawyers and bankers. A lay-off in the automobile plant is likely to result in deterioration and lower property values in the neighborhood linked to the auto sector. Neighborhoods with occupational-industrial mixes that are not linked to the auto sector would be affected only indirectly. Hill and Bier use data from Cleveland to show that both the positive and negative effects of industrial and occupational changes in the local economy spilled into neighborhoods where workers lived, affecting poverty levels and housing costs.

Recap of Neighborhood-Change Models

The five models of neighborhood formation and change are consistent with each other. In fact, they complement one another. The filtering model best explains the adaptive adjustments that occur during neighborhood change. The trade-off model explains why wealthy families lead the suburbanization movement and create a process that allows filtering to occur. The concept of mobile externalities also shows how pressures from within the urban center can create pressures for wealthy families to move outward. The concept of social agglomeration helps explain different social and ethnic characteristics of neighborhoods of similar income. The Tiebout model shows how neighborhood characteristics affect housing prices and how individuals vote with their feet for neighborhood characteristics and public services associated with a property. Neighborhood characteristics are also affected by macroeconomic forces. Although in some instances one model may have more explanatory power than another, each model provides an important perspective on neighborhood development.

U.S. HOUSING CONDITIONS

Housing is a good of special importance. Not only do most families spend a large portion of their income on housing, but housing is central to most people's conception of the good life. Where people live helps define who they are in the eyes of others and even in their own eyes. This section explores U.S. housing conditions and problems.

Housing Trends

Housing conditions have generally improved over time. This is particularly true of objective measures of housing quality. However, there is less evidence that individuals are more satisfied with their dwellings. Four particularly important areas are housing adequacy, affordability, homeownership, and the homeless.

Adequacy. Most objective measures of housing adequacy indicate that housing conditions have greatly improved since the National Housing Act proclaimed housing a national priority. The improvement has been

TABLE 11–7 Housing Characteristics of New, Privately Owned,
Single-Family Houses (percent)

	1970	1980	1987
Floor area (square feet)			
Under 1,200	36%	21%	14%
1,200–1,599	28	29	27
1,600–1,999	16	22	22
2,000–2,399	21	13	16
2,400+	21	15	21
Bedrooms			
2 or less	13	17	21
3	63	63	58
4 or more	24	20	20
Bathrooms			
1 or less	32	18	10
1½	20	10	7
2	32	48	45
2½+	16	25	38
Parking			
Garage	58	69	74
Carport	17	7	3
No garage or carport	25	24	18

Average floor area (square feet): 1,500 (1970), 1,740 (1980), and 1,905 (1987).

source: U.S. Bureau of the Census and U.S. Department of Housing and Urban Development, *Construction Reports,* series C25, Characteristics of New Housing, 1987.

steady and can be attributed more to overall economic growth than to housing policies.

The number of dilapidated units, units lacking plumbing, or overcrowded units (over 1.1 persons per room) has fallen to such an extent that they are no longer a serious problem. Less than 3 percent of all metropolitan households lived in units lacking some plumbing facilities. However, there are a greater percentage of inadequate units among renters and rural populations than for homeowners in metropolitan areas.

The number of square feet of housing, number of bathrooms, parking provisions, and the number of bedrooms are relevant indicators of housing quality today. Recent trends in these indicators are shown in Table 11–7. Significant improvement is evident in every category except the number of bedrooms. The reason for the small decline in the number of bedrooms while the size of housing units increased may be attributable to smaller household size. In particular, the increase in two-bedroom units undoubtedly reflects the boom in retirement communities.

Affordability.   Although the quality of housing has improved, problems of affordability have not improved. In 1981, 54 percent of the population paid more than 25 percent of household income for housing. The affordability problem is most severe among metropolitan, low-income populations. Of the very low-income families, about 70 percent live in adequate housing, but they pay over 30 percent of their income for rent.

Four factors have contributed to the housing affordability problem. First, throughout most of the 1980s, housing costs rose faster than incomes. This is particularly true of ownership costs. Contributing to the cost increases has been an escalation in urban land costs. In 1949, land was 11 percent of the cost of a new home compared to approximately 25 percent today. Second, the quality of housing has improved and the size has increased, so one could expect costs to increase. Third, household sizes have fallen. As fewer people live in a household, there will be fewer earners per household, so the ratio of housing expenses to income should increase. Fourth, high interest rates throughout most of the 1980s caused monthly payments to increase for both new homeowners and renters.

A long-standing rule of thumb has been that families should budget about 25 percent of their income for housing. The finding that there are more families spending above this ratio is one of the reasons for the affordability concern. However, an inflexible rule will not account for individual circumstances. As aftertax household income increases, discretionary income increases on an almost dollar-for-dollar basis. If households choose to spend the extra discretionary income on housing, then the percent of income going to housing will increase. But the increase will not necessarily represent an affordability problem. For instance, would a family earning $250,000 have an affordability problem if they were spending half of their income on housing? They certainly would have plenty left over after housing expenses to live nicely.

Homeownership.   Homeownership has been viewed as an element that helps stabilize neighborhoods and society. Neighborhoods are believed to benefit from high rates of home ownership because homeowners allegedly care more about property maintenance and appreciation. Therefore, they will be more inclined to keep up the neighborhood. Furthermore, society as a whole is believed to be more stable because homeowners have a financial stake in the system. As a result of the link between homeownership and stability, some observers have suggested that a "social compact" existed in which the government has placed a high priority on increasing homeownership.

The 1980 census indicated that homeowners were 65.4 percent of all households. The long-term trend had been upward. However, since 1980, the rate of homeownership has dipped or leveled. In 1988, the home ownership rate was 63.7 percent. The decline in ownership has been most pronounced among households headed by young people, while the ownership rate among older households has actually increased. The causes for the decline in homeownership rates include many of the factors contributing to the affordability problem. Furthermore, the up-front costs of homeownership have become a critical barrier. Home prices have risen faster than incomes, and the percentage of income needed to set aside for a downpayment has grown.

The ownership issue may not be a problem at all according to some analysts because the advantages commonly associated with homeownership may not exist. Homeowners may not be better citizens, care more for their neighborhoods, or be less likely to participate in free-rider behavior by leaving neighborhood improvements to others than renters.

Homelessness.   The problem of the homeless is one that has recently become a major feature of housing concerns. The number of homeless is not known. Estimates range from 250,000 to 300,000, and most observers agree that the number of homeless has increased. "Deinstitutionalization" of individuals who would previously have been placed in mental institutions or jail has contributed to the problem. For instance, in the 1960s, about 40 percent of all arrests were for vagrancy, public intoxication, or disorderly conduct. Today, such crimes account for only 20 percent of arrests as such deviant behaviors have been de facto decriminalized among street people. Providing housing may not be a complete solution because most of the homeless have other problems. One survey (Rossi and Wright, 1987) found that 40 percent of the homeless were alcohol abusers, 16 percent were drug abusers, and 33 percent were mentally ill. The homeless also tend to be very poor and isolated from family and friends.

Currently, provisions of very short-term assistance are made through night shelters or dormitory housing. Even these stop-gap measures are costly. However, rather than initiating new programs, many conservatives have suggested that government and its programs may make matters worse.

Segregation

Residential segregation is an obvious characteristic of most American cities. Blacks and other minorities are hurt by housing discrimination in several important ways. First, their housing choices are limited. Blacks and other groups tend to be confined to areas that may not suit their housing preferences. Second, blacks and other minorities may have less access to jobs on the metropolitan periphery. In many areas, service jobs are expanding most rapidly in the subcenters away from the CBD. Housing segregation may reduce job opportunities for groups locked into inner-city locations due to discriminatory housing patterns. The geographic segregation may raise job-search costs for suburban jobs, particularly because most jobs are obtained through informal referrals from other employees or signs posted in stores. Furthermore, it has been speculated that housing segregation contributes to the difficulty a member of a minority group has in attaining suburban clerking jobs because there will be fewer minority customers. Third, confinement of minorities in inner-city neighborhoods may also contribute to higher travel costs if a suburban job is obtained.

Mechanisms of Segregation.   The existence of segregated housing markets does not prove housing discrimination. Housing segregation could result from factors other than discrimination. For instance, the relatively low incomes of black families and other minority groups could also account for a significant amount of segregation as low-income households locate in areas of low-quality housing.[3] However, income differences would not account for the segregation of low-income blacks from low-income whites. The degree of racial discrimination is much greater than would be anticipated based on income. Furthermore, an implication of the social-agglomeration model is that segregated neighborhoods could result from a voluntary process. However, several empirical studies have shown that blacks are more segregated than other ethnic minorities, a finding that suggests racial differences are recognized in the operation of housing markets.

There are several mechanisms of segregation. First, blacks may fear moving into white neighborhoods because they are uncertain how they will be treated. They may fear being isolated from neighborhood activities or being the object of racial attacks. Second, landlords and home sellers often deliberately discriminate. Although discrimination on the basis of race is illegal, subtle forms of discouragement can have the effect of maintaining all-white neighborhoods. For instance, landlords may quickly rent to whites if they believe a black family is going to consider the same rental unit. Negotiations over lease terms can be a mechanism for discrimination if softer or more flexible terms on such matters as occupancy, pets, children, security deposits, and so forth are accorded to white applicants. Third, brokers and new real estate salespersons can steer minority buyers into areas already dominated by the particular minority group and

---

[3] The lower incomes of blacks could, in turn, be attributed to discrimination.

fail to inform black buyers of homes for sale in white areas. Although salespersons have defended themselves by saying they try to show buyers houses in neighborhoods where the buyers would want to live, the effect is to maintain housing segregation.

Several studies by the Department of Housing and Urban Development examined practices of racial discrimination. Black couples and white couples responded separately to the same housing advertisements (Yinger, 1986). Black couples experienced some form of discrimination when responding to 27 percent of the advertised vacancies. The extent of discrimination was higher in the case of rental housing than owner-occupied housing. The primary mechanism appears to be that housing agents promote their economic interests by abiding by the racial prejudice of current or potential customers. Another study in Dallas (Department of Housing and Urban Development, 1979) found that Hispanics were likely to experience the same level of discrimination as blacks.

Do Blacks Pay More?   Historically, most empirical studies indicated that blacks pay more for comparable housing than whites. However, the findings of more recent studies are ambiguous. Some show that blacks pay more than whites for comparable housing while others fail to find a difference. One reason for the ambiguous empirical finding is the difficulty of measuring a standard unit of housing services. Another, more optimistic explanation is that state and federal open-housing policies have been effective in eliminating some (although few would say all) housing discrimination.

Some students find it perplexing that blacks may pay a premium for housing in light of the low-quality housing that a high proportion of blacks inhabit. Within most cities, there is a frontier of racial transition. As blacks move into racially mixed neighborhoods and whites move out, the supply of housing available to blacks increases and should accordingly decrease in price. This perspective suggests that blacks would pay less than whites for housing. However, other factors can explain the frequent empirical finding that blacks pay more.

The black population has been growing faster than the population as a whole. Thus, the increasing demand for housing in black areas has put upward pressure on prices. If whites near the black-white frontier resist moving and the mechanisms of segregation are effective, blacks are thwarted in efforts to expand their housing supply. The result of the increase in demand and the limitations on the expansion of housing available to blacks has been to confine the majority of blacks to a disproportionally small part of the housing market, thus, increasing their housing costs.

Although most of the empirical studies have focused on housing for blacks, the same model may apply to other minority groups that have suffered discrimination. Enforcement of equal-housing laws and changes in social attitudes may have diminished the problem in recent years.

HOUSING POLICIES

Housing is considered a merit good. It could be provided by an unsubsidized market so some individuals may argue that there is little need for government involvement in the housing market. However, housing has such an important influence on individual welfare and the nature of the community that government involvement to improve housing conditions is generally considered a legitimate activity. Housing-assistance programs have been undertaken for households of all income levels and by all levels of government.

Over the years, four types of subsidies have appeared and reappeared in various forms: (1) Special tax benefits, (2) mortgage assistance, and (3) low-income assistance. In addition, zoning and other land-use controls as well as more indirect federal actions, such as macroeconomic interest-rate policies, have affected housing.

Tax Benefits

The largest housing program is the deductibility of mortgage interest and local property taxes from federal income taxes. Individuals can avoid paying taxes on the income spent on mortgage interest and property taxes for their home. Since mortgage interest and property taxes are major expenses of homeownership, the tax benefits can be substantial. For instance, for each dollar spent on these deductible items, an individual in the 28 percent marginal tax bracket will pay 28 cents less in federal taxes than would have been due had the tax deduction not been available.[4] Because most state income tax laws are modeled after the federal tax, states also support homeownership through state income tax policies.

The mortgage-interest deduction has been considered unfair because many individuals believe it violates the tax principle that equals (in all relevant tax respects) should be treated equally. A renter and a homeowner who have equal incomes and are equal in all other respects except for homeownership should pay the same amount of taxes according to this principle. However, because of the federal tax expenditure to encourage

---

[4] This statement is based on the assumption that the individual would itemize deductions whether or not the housing deductions were taken.

TABLE 11–8 Savings Due to Deductibility of Mortgage
Interest and Property Tax Deductions*

	Homeowner	Renter
Adjusted gross income	$75,000	$75,000
Nonhousing deductions	10,000	10,000
Deductible housing expenses	7,000	0
Taxable income	48,000	65,000
Tax liability (at .28)	$16,240	$18,200

Tax savings due to homeownership $1,960.

* Assume these individuals are equal in all respects including the quantity of housing services received during the year. The only difference is the owner/renter status.

homeownership, the homeowners will be able to deduct interest and property tax expenses that the renters will not, even if these expenses are embedded in their rent. Hence, individuals who are equal in all circumstances will pay different amounts of taxes. Table 11–8 illustrates the tax advantage from homeownership. The individuals have equal adjusted gross incomes, but the homeowner has $17,000 of deductions compared to $10,000 for the renter. Hence, the homeowner's tax liability is less by $1,960.

Similarly, an individual who owns a home outright receives value from the use of the home which could be expressed as the imputed value of rent that would have to be paid for a comparable dwelling. These housing services are an in-kind income but are not taxed. In some countries, rent on homes is imputed and taxed. (Notice that it would not be correct to tax interest and property tax payments *and* tax the imputed value of the rent because in that case the tax would be levied on a legitimate expense of earning income.)

The problems with housing tax expenditures are well understood. Consequently, several attempts have been made to modify the current treatment of mortgage interest and property tax deductions. Although some minor changes were made, no fundamental changes have been implemented for two reasons. First, homeowners are a very strong political interest group since over half of U.S. households own their homes and many nonhomeowners aspire to ownership. Second, the value of residential property already reflects the homeownership tax deductions. The deduction has encouraged homeownership and supported higher prices than would otherwise be the case. Repeal of these tax breaks would decrease the demand for owner-occupied housing and impose capital losses on current homeowners. Recent reductions in the marginal tax rate have indirectly reduced the size of the homeownership tax expenditure, so the issue is less acute than it was several years ago.

Generous cost-recovery rules and other tax provisions are used to stimulate some residential units. Without getting bogged down in details, the role of accelerated depreciation can best be understood by distinguishing between (1) cost recovery, which is the amount an income property owner may deduct from rents to account for the declining value of the property, and (2) the actual decline in the value of the property. The actual value decline is a legitimate expense of doing business. However, if a property owner can deduct costs in excess of actual depreciation, then current-year taxes will be lower than otherwise. When this tax advantage exists, it will encourage construction of income-producing properties. Most income-producing properties can be written down at a faster rate than the true rate of depreciation. Hence, there is some tax-related encouragement for most types of income-producing properties, including rental apartments. Currently, especially rapid rates of cost recovery are allowed for some types of low-income housing.

Mortgage Assistance

Normally, a buyer makes a down payment and borrows the balance of the money needed to buy the house. In 1987, 57 percent of homeowners had mortgage debt, and the average ratio of loan to purchase price for a home purchase was 75 percent. The federal government, and to a lesser extent state governments, has attempted to increase the supply of funds available to home buyers by increasing the supply of funds that financial institutions can lend and by making mortgage loans more secure for the lenders. Government mortgage operations also have the effect of reducing interest rates and, thus, making homes more affordable. Mortgage assistance has taken two principal forms: (1) mortgage loan guarantees and insurance, and (2) secondary mortgage market operations.

Mortgage Loan Insurance and Guarantees.   The most notable and successful mortgage-assistance program is the Federal Housing Administration's (FHA) mortgage-insurance program. Under this program, the federal government insures the lending institution against default by the borrower (home buyer). The borrower pays a fee for the insurance which protects the lender. The loan program is calibrated so that if a potential home buyer provided a modest down payment the federal government would insure a mortgage for up to 97 percent of the value of the property. Thus, a lender could make a mortgage loan requiring only a 3 percent down payment and a 97 percent FHA insurance policy. The lender would have very little risk in the event the borrower defaulted. The portion of the property that can be insured decreases as the value of the property increases. Thus, expensive properties will require higher down payments if the lending institution is to be fully insured. The Veterans Administration has a VA loan-guarantee program that also reduces lender risk by guaranteeing repayment of a large portion of loans in the event of default.

The FHA loan-insurance program enabled many families to purchase housing with modest down payments and contributed to the post–World War II expansion of the suburbs. Because the FHA insurance program has operated in an era of generally rising housing prices, defaults have been few. Individuals who cannot afford mortgage payments normally sell their property, repay the mortgage loan, and pocket the difference between the sale price and the outstanding mortgage debt. Even when defaults occurred and properties were sold in foreclosure sales, most of the mortgage loan outstanding was recouped, so losses were small.

The FHA insurance program was so successful that it has been one of the federal government's few profit centers—the insurance premiums were greater than the payouts in spite of high default rates in some inner-city areas, until 1989 when inner-city defaults caused payments to rise. Private mortgage-insurance companies have entered the loan-insurance industry because they saw how successful the FHA program was.

In order to continue to make mortgage money available to homeowners, the FHA has approved the use of new types of mortgage instruments such as:

1. Shared equity mortgages, in which investors share the monthly mortgage payment in return for a share of the tax benefits and the equity of the home at the time of sale.

2. Graduated payment mortgages, that allow payments to increase so they are low in the early years of the mortgage and increase as homebuyer income is anticipated to increase.

3. Adjustable-rate mortgages, that allow the interest rate to fluctuate, reflecting market conditions.

Secondary Mortgage Operations. The primary mortgage market refers to the exchange between the home buyer (borrower) and the financial institution (lender). However, lenders frequently sell pools of mortgages to other institutions in the secondary mortgage market. For instance, a local bank may pool $2,000,000 of mortgages and sell these mortgages to a pension fund. The mortgage pools will sell for more or less than the face value of the mortgage notes depending upon whether the prevailing interest rates have fallen or risen between the time the loan was originated and the time of sale in the secondary market. Normally the local institutions will continue to service loans by collecting payments, monitoring escrow accounts, and so forth, in exchange for a service fee. The homeowner (borrower) may not know the mortgage has been sold.

The secondary market stimulates homeownership because it provides additional funds for local financial institutions to lend. Thus, home buyers are indirectly linked to national capital markets. Accordingly, mortgage interest rates are lower than they would be in the absence of secondary mortgage operations.

The federal government has taken several actions to stimulate the secondary mortgage market. First, the presence of standardized mortgage insurance, such as FHA mortgage insurance, has greatly reduced the risk to buyers in the secondary market because they do not need to evaluate the worth of the property securing the mortgage. In the event of default, the mortgage is insured and if the value of the property is less than the amount owed, the insurer will cover the difference. Second, the federal government has chartered institutions such as the Federal National Mortgage Association (FNMA or Fannie Mae), the Government National Mortgage Association (GNMA or Ginnie Mae), and the Federal Home Loan Mortgage Association (FHLMA or Freddie Mae) to provide liquidity to the housing market.

The Three Markets.   Three markets normally influence the sale of a property. They are: (1) the sale of the property itself, (2) the primary mortgage market, and (3) the secondary mortgage market.

Figure 11–5 illustrates the participants in each of the three markets and how each party may benefit from the secondary mortgage market.

Low-Income Assistance

Analysts often distinguish between supply- and demand-side assistance. Supply-side assistance stimulates housing by encouraging new construction and housing rehabilitation whereas demand-side assistance provides low-income families with assistance to pay for housing. Neither demand- nor supply-side programs are funded at a level sufficient to provide subsidies for all eligible recipients. Consequently, most housing programs have long waiting lists. A two-year wait to receive housing assistance is not uncommon.

Supply-Side Assistance.   Public housing has traditionally been the mainstay of the supply-side approach to housing low-income families. Under public housing-assistance programs in the 1950s and 1960s, the federal government would fund the construction of usually large apartment complexes to house the poor. Many of these projects were well maintained and were considered successes. However, traditional public housing fell into disrepute during the late 1960s as some of the buildings became uninhabitable due to crime, vandalism, and other by-products of the social pathologies associated with poverty. Problems were aggravated

FIGURE 11–5   The Three Real Estate Markets

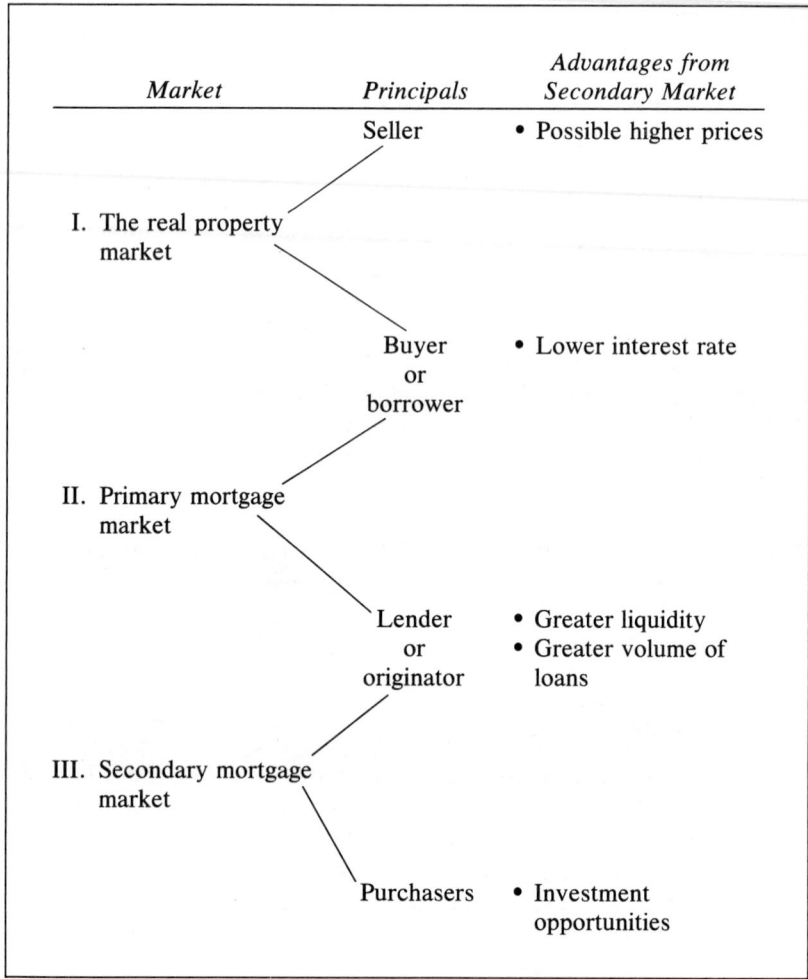

The three real estate markets interact. Consequently, the secondary market may generate benefits for participants in the real property market.

because of difficulties in evicting residents even when their behavior created serious disruptions for other residents and lack of funding for rehabilitation.[5] Public housing also contributed to segregation because many

---

[5] Currently, HUD is making a major effort to evict disruptive tenants and secure public housing projects from potentially disruptive persons, such as drug dealers or users.

units were located in black areas of cities and the residents of the projects themselves were predominantly black.

Today, construction of low-income housing units has been reduced to a trickle, units are much less concentrated, and programs have created economic and ethnic integration. The Section 8 new-construction program allows developers to receive federal assistance for their projects by agreeing to set aside units for low-income families within an otherwise "market-rent" housing complex. Although problems of high-density development have been addressed, the popularity of new construction as a solution to the housing needs of the poor has continued to decline because it is more costly to house a poor family in a newly constructed unit than in an existing unit.

Housing-rehabilitation programs are designed to take advantage of the existing housing stock in both central cities and rural areas by upgrading existing units. Rehabilitation grants or low-interest loans have been used to bring units up to appropriate standards. When rehabilitation programs are used by landlords to improve their rental property, the owners must agree to make the units available at rents affordable to low-income families.

Demand-Side Assistance.   Demand assistance was the cornerstone of the Reagan administration's low-income housing-assistance program. The Section 8 existing program and the voucher program are the principal means of assisting families through the existing housing stock. The programs are similar because they both allow recipient families to shop for housing that suits them. Under the Section 8 program, families receiving assistance may select from eligible existing units and rent cannot exceed a certain level (called "fair market" rent). The "reasonable rent level" varies with the area.

Under the voucher program, a family is able to select a rental unit and the government guarantees payment to the landlord for a portion of the rent. HUD pays the difference between 30 percent of the family's adjusted gross income and fair market rent. The family is free to spend more than the reasonable rent level if it so chooses, although it must pay the difference between the rent level and the federal subsidy from family income.

Housing Policy Debates

Problems with U.S. housing-assistance programs have been widely discussed. The principal controversies are discussed in this section. Several policies tend to dominate most of the debate about reform. The issues are described here as polar positions in order to make the distinctions as sharp as possible. However, policy makers often must select the appropriate middle ground.

Rent Control versus Market Forces. The role of rent control in local housing policy is a perennial issue. Several cities have enacted rent controls. Tenant groups in many cities where rents have increased rapidly have pressured their local legislators to enact controls. Rent controls take many forms. In some cities, rents are allowed to increase at a given amount per period. Often, the controls are lifted when one tenant moves and a new base is established. Even within a city, some units may be rent controlled while others are not, depending on the time, the location, and the conditions of construction.

In spite of the variety of rent controls, the issue is generally analyzed by the simple supply and demand curve shown in Figure 11–6. The market rent per unit of housing services is $400 per month. However, the rent is controlled at $300 per month. Consequently, more housing services are demanded at the controlled price than building owners are willing and able to supply.

The arguments for rent control are generally based on equity. Proponents of rent control argue that tenants may be exploited if building owners are allowed to raise rents according to what the market will bear. The reasons for rent increases are frequently attributed to neighborhood or

FIGURE 11–6 Rent Control

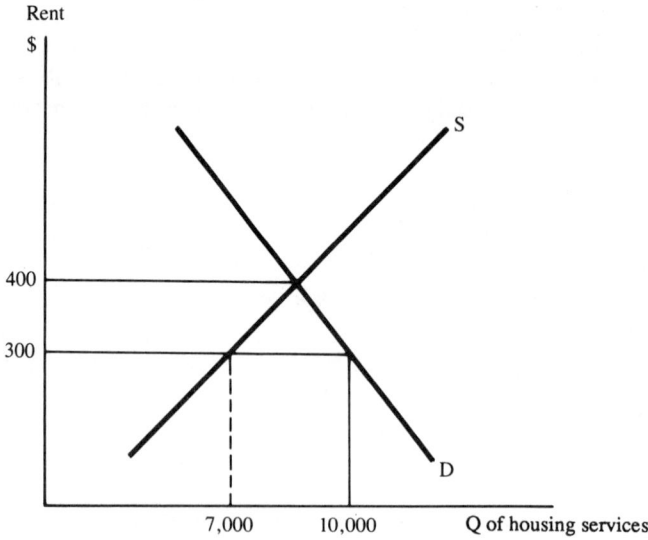

The controlled rent of $300 per month will result in a shortage of 3000 units of housing services.

communitywide factors as opposed to actions of individual property owners. Therefore, tenants, as part of the community, might be as entitled to some of the benefits of increased community desirability as much as property owners. Furthermore, the buildings subject to control are already in existence and were built based upon rent expectations in a previous period. Consequently, rent-control proponents view rent increases (above increases needed for tax and operating cost factors) as windfalls. Luger (1986) has shown that there are instances in which rent controls serve the interests of a majority of the voters, so rent controls may make political sense.

Opponents of rent control believe that rent controls are inefficient. They point out that if rents are prevented from increasing, property owners will reduce the housing stock. The housing supply will shrink until the supply is consistent with the lower-than-market rents. Mechanisms for decreasing the quantity of housing services include: (1) reducing maintenance levels, (2) abandonment, (3) providing fewer amenities, and (4) lower rates of new housing construction.

Furthermore, the problem of rationing will remain. If rents are below the equilibrium, building managers will have to select incoming tenants. Criteria for choosing which tenants will occupy below-market-rent properties could include race and a willingness to pay kick-backs to the managers (an under-the-table means of raising rents).

Measures to skirt the intent of rent controls may also be attempted. Landlords may convert rental units to condominiums or tear down a building that is under rent control in order to construct a building that is either not subject to controls or is subject to a less restrictive set of controls. Instances of property owners deliberately cutting heat or vandalizing their own buildings in order to encourage tenants to leave have been reported. Moorehouse (1987) has shown that landlords have lowered the benefits tenants receive from rent control by reducing housing maintenance and other techniques. However, some benefits continue to accrue to tenants even after 25 years of rent control.

Proponents of rent control have argued that many abuses can be avoided by a well-designed and administered rent-control law. However, most economists oppose rent controls because of the inherent inefficiency and because the administrative costs needed to prevent abuses are substantial.

Income Support versus Housing Assistance.   One of the classic arguments in welfare economics is that individuals would be better off receiving cash grants rather than an equal-valued amount of in-kind transfers. Consider a family receiving $100 per month as a rent supplement. The traditional argument is that if the family were given $100 in cash rather than a housing grant, they would be better off. At the very least, the family would continue to spend the money on housing, so they would be no worse off. If they choose to spend the funds to purchase an alternative mix of goods, then they must be better off since each individual is the best judge of his own welfare (and as a corollary, parents are the best judges of their children's welfare). Therefore, if the purpose of housing programs is to improve the lot of the families they are designed to serve, income rather than housing subsidies of various types should be given.

The rebuttal to the superiority-of-cash-transfers argument is that while individuals may know what is best for them, they may not know what is best for society. Substandard housing is not only an undesirable (and possibly the most visible) manifestation of poverty, it may also create other social problems such as arson, street crime, homicide, and so forth. Thus, aid designed to alleviate housing conditions is intended to help ameliorate problems in the larger society as well as to help the direct recipients. The argument about cash grants versus strings-attached transfers is a variant of the more general question of how much discretion recipients of aid should be allowed. The trend in housing policy has been toward greater discretion in choice of housing, but the argument that cash is preferable to housing assistance has not been accepted as policy.

A housing experiment conducted by the Department of Housing and Urban Development indicated that the income elasticity of demand for housing among low-income families is quite low, in the 0.3 to 0.4 range. Thus, if given a cash grant, only a small percent of the grant would likely be spent to upgrade the housing of the recipient. Even if housing vouchers are provided, households will substitute the voucher for what they otherwise would have spent on housing and use money they would otherwise have spent on housing for other purposes.

In practice, it is very difficult to prevent families from substituting other goods for housing. For instance, suppose a family was spending $200 per month on housing prior to receiving assistance. The government then provides a $100 per month housing subsidy. If the family moves to a $225 per month unit, then $75 of the housing assistance will be used for nonhousing assistance. The substitution could occur even if the government assistance were provided in the form of a $100 voucher that could be used only for housing.

Supply versus Demand Strategies. Should governmental low-income housing programs be designed to increase the supply of housing available to the poor, or to increase the ability of the poor to purchase housing services? Figure 11–7 represents the choice. The demand subsidy tends to raise prices as well as increase the quantity of housing supplied. The supply strategy lowers prices and simultaneously operates to increase quantity. Thus, many analysts have supported supply-side assistance because it may avoid rent increases. However, the Experimental

FIGURE 11–7   Supply versus Demand Assistance

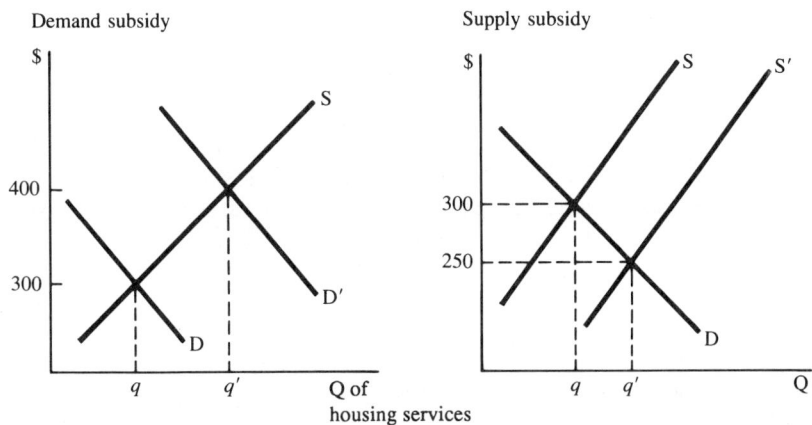

In the short run, demand-side assistance tends to increase price while supply-side increases tend to lower rent.

Housing Allowance Program indicated that providing demand-side assistance to low-income families has only a small impact on rents.

Directly increasing the housing stock lowers rents. How will future private housing production be affected? Subsidized construction could simply displace unsubsidized production, so direct government stimulus could have no effect on overall stock. Alternatively, if, as many argue, the low- and moderate-income market is separate from the private market, and if attainable profits are insufficient to warrant private construction for low-income families, then direct public construction will not displace private activity. The extent of displacement of private production will also vary, depending upon the current unemployment rate in the building trades. The higher the unemployment rate, the less likely it is that the displacement will be immediate. However, public construction, even if initiated during a period when the resources would otherwise be unemployed, could still displace future private construction.

Many analysts have advocated housing policy to encourage demand stimulation among moderate- and middle-income families in order to lubricate the filtering process. As middle-income families move into newly constructed units, additional housing will be available to the poor. Thus, the filtering process will increase the supply of housing in the low-income housing market.

Public versus Private Construction and Ownership.   If low-income programs are to emphasize construction, should the projects be built and owned by governments or by the private sector with government subsidies? Unfortunately, proponents on either side of this issue can provide examples of mismanagement and fraud to illustrate failures of both public and private construction. Likewise, there are sterling examples of good public and privately subsidized housing. The distinction between public and private, however, is not always clear. For instance, cooperatives, nonprofit church groups, and limited-profit corporations are nongovernmental institutions that are not profit maximizers. But the record of these groups is also spotty.

Concentrated versus Scattered-Site Housing.   The initial concept of public housing placed great emphasis upon the cost reductions that could be achieved through economies of scale in the production and operation of large-scale developments. Thus, large-scale high rises, were constructed. Such projects housed thousands of people. Yet the concentration of the very poor into dense developments led to problems. Crime, for instance, became rampant in many projects. Repairmen and even fire and police employees became afraid to enter some buildings. Fear stimulated the cycle of deterioration. Social critics claimed that the concentration of poor in these environments made it difficult for families to break the cycle of poverty. The failure of concentrated public housing is symbolized by the destruction of a large housing project in St. Louis that had to be demolished after only 10 years of existence because crime and vandalism had rendered it uninhabitable, or at least unmanageable.

Ghetto Dispersal versus Ghetto Improvement.   The problem of housing segregation has led many policy makers to argue that policies should strive to disperse the large concentrations of blacks in the inner city. If assisted housing were more integrated, blacks would have better opportunities to secure jobs in suburban areas and would have lower travel costs if they obtained suburban jobs. Furthermore, if more blacks were represented in currently nearly all-white areas, employers would be less likely to discriminate against blacks in hiring practices. Provisions of subsidized housing in the suburbs and enforcement of fair-housing laws have been the primary tools to encourage housing desegregation.

An alternative policy approach has been termed the gilded ghetto. Some observers believe that dispersing blacks and other minorities to the suburbs would not open up significant job opportunities because discrimination in hiring practices would persist. Furthermore, dispersal of black populations throughout the metropolitan area would likely weaken black political strength. Assuming voters are more likely to vote for someone of the same race, blacks would have a difficult time being elected if a metropolitan area were spatially integrated. However, black political control of urban ghetto's voting is virtually assured. Thus, blacks are more likely to be assured of some representation in city, state, and national legislatures.

Dwelling-Unit versus Neighborhood Development.   Closely related to the previous issue is the question of whether the focus of policies should be to improve the house or to improve the larger environment in which the low-income families live. The condition of housing units among the poor has improved dramatically since the 1940s, yet there has been little improvement in the public perception of the "problem" of slums. The home itself may be but a small part of the environment. Social programs to eliminate crime, provide recreation, and clean up neighborhoods may be equally important.

SUMMARY

The housing market can be analyzed using traditional supply and demand concepts. However, care must be taken to understand what the supply and price represent. It is useful to describe the quantity axis as "units of housing services" rather than a physical quantity. Price may be expressed as sales price of a stock of housing or as rent for a periodic flow of housing services. By discounting the present value of rents, one can compare rents and sale prices.

The hedonic pricing model splits the housing-service bundle into detailed components and uses statistical techniques, such as regression, to value each of the components. The hedonic pricing model may be represented in functional form as:

$$P = f(C_i)$$

where P = Price and C_i = The ith characteristic. Characteristics that affect price include features of the property itself as well as characteristics of the surrounding area. The market-comparison approach is a "quick and dirty" application of the hedonic pricing perspective.

Real estate markets are imperfect—characterized by few buyers and sellers and imperfect information. Consequently, bargaining is an important part of real estate transactions and specialists are needed to assist buyers and sellers. There is also a range of uncertainty regarding price.

Changes in the supply of housing can be attributed to new construction and adjustments to the existing housing stock. Elasticity of supply is greater in the long run than in the short run because of the greater potential for new construction. Short-run changes occur primarily through adaptive adjustment. Because of long lags in the adjustment process, developers can miscalculate future market conditions resulting in overbuilding or higher than normal vacancy rates.

Housing is affected by changes in the aggregate economy. During an era of unanticipated inflation, homeowners may benefit due to appreciation, leverage, and expectations of inflation. During the 1970s, these factors benefited many homeowners but worked to the detriment of mortgage lenders.

Five complementary models of neighborhood formation were described. The filtering model stresses that as incomes rise, upper-income groups tend to purchase new housing on the urban periphery. The houses vacated become available to lower-income groups. The trade-off model emphasizes the space versus access trade-off. As incomes increase, the pull of cheaper space near the urban fringe increases more than the pull towards the central business district. Social forces drive the cultural agglomeration model as individuals with similar tastes and backgrounds often live in the same areas. The Tiebout model describes the process in which individuals "vote with their feet" in order to live in the neighborhood that provides the best combination of housing units, neighborhood amenities, public services, and housing prices. Improvements in neighborhood amenities, public services, and taxes become capitalized into property values. Finally, the aggregate economic fall-out model links neighborhood change to large economic activity.

The physical condition of U.S. housing has steadily improved, although concerns about homeownership, affordability, homelessness, neighborhood quality, and racial segregation remain.

Providing tax breaks for homeowners is the mainstay of U.S. housing policies. The federal government also provides mortgage assistance through loan-insurance and loan-guarantee programs and by providing liquidity to the secondary mortgage market. Low-income-housing policies have emphasized demand-side assistance in recent years.

Many policy analysts have been dissatisfied with current low-income-housing assistance programs. Issues include: (1) income support versus housing assistance, (2) supply versus demand assistance, (3) public versus private construction and ownership, (4) concentrated versus scattered-site housing, (5) ghetto dispersal versus gilding, (6) dwelling-unit versus neighborhood development, and (7) housing support versus income assistance.

APPENDIX: HEDONIC PRICING AND THE QUALITY OF LIFE

The importance of the quality of economic life has been discussed at various points thus far. It is an industrial-location factor, and it is also a residential-location factor. Early studies measured the quality of life based upon surveys. Individuals were asked to rank and weigh the value of various amenities and disamenities. Based upon such surveys, metropolitan areas and individual neighborhoods could be compared. The quality-of-life index for a region could be expressed:

$$QLI_j = \sum_{i=1}^{n} A_{ij} V_i \tag{1}$$

where QLI_j = Quality-of-life index for region j,
$\quad A_{ij}$ = Quantity or level of amenity factor i in region j, and
$\quad V_i$ = Value placed upon amenity i.

The value of an amenity factor (V_i) could be positive or negative. For instance, sunshine is an amenity and, thus, would be valued positively whereas particulate matter in the air would be a disamenity and would carry a negative value. Accordingly, areas with high levels of highly valued amenities and low values for disamenities would have a high QLI.

Although survey data may reflect opinion, relative values of various amenities are more difficult to assess. The majority of individuals surveyed may say that congestion is a disamenity. But what are they willing to give up to relieve congestion? Although surveys may reflect opinion, economists normally prefer to use values reflected by market activity. Although surveys are useful, many individuals have difficulty estimating the actual monetary value of amenities such as sunshine, and economists normally prefer to use values reflected in the market. Market values represent actual behavior regarding the selective worth of amenities.

In order to better quantify amenities' values, economists have used hedonic pricing techniques. Rosen (1974) suggested that a location is a bundle of wages, rents, and amenities. Individuals will trade off among elements in the bundle. For instance, someone may accept lower wages and pay higher rents in order to live in an amenity-rich area. Roback (1982) showed that interregional differences in amenity differences are reflected in land rent differences and/or wage differences. If individuals are in spatial equilibrium—that is, if they have no incentives to move and if the local housing and job markets are in equilibrium—then the premiums or discounts accepted by individuals in their wages and rents will reflect the value they place on amenities associated with an area. Amenities should decrease wages and/or increase housing costs while disamenities should be associated with the higher wages and/or lower housing costs, other things equal.

Blomquist et al. (1988) developed two hedonic models to explain differences in rents and wages. Their sample consisted of over 34,000 housing units in 253 countries. The housing equation expressed housing expenditures as a function of characteristics of the housing unit (age of structure, number of units at an address, number of baths, and so forth) and 16 county amenities shown in column 1 of Table 11A–1.

$$HE = f(CIH_1 \ldots CIH_n, A_1 \ldots A_{16}) \tag{2}$$

where HE = Monthly housing expenditures,
$\quad CIH_i$ = Characteristics of the individual housing units, and
$\quad A_i$ = Level of 16 county-level amenities.

TABLE 11A–1 Linearized Parameter Estimates, Full Implicit Prices, and
Quality-of-Life Index Components

Amenity Variable (wage sample mean and unit of measurement)	Monthly Housing Expenditure Equation*	Hourly Wage Equation†	Full Implicit Price‡
Precipitation (32.0 inches per year)	−1.047	−.0144	$23.50
Humidity (68.3 percent)	−2.127	.0065	−43.42
Heating degree days (4,326 per year)	−.0136	−.0001	−.08
Cooling degree days (1,162 per year)	−.0760	−.0002	−.36
Wind speed (8.89 miles per hour)	11.88	.0961	−97.51
Sunshine (61.1 percent of possible)	2.135	−.0091	48.52
Coast (.330, = 1 if county on coast)	32.51	−.0310	467.72
Violent crime (647 per 100,000 population per year)	.0434	.0006	−1.03
Teacher-pupil ratio (.0799 teachers per pupil)	635.3	−5.451	21,250.00
Visibility (15.8 miles)	−.8302	−.0026	−3.41
Total suspended particulates (73.2 micrograms per cubic meter)	−.5344	−.0024	−.36
NPDES effluent discharges (1.51 county)	−7.458	−.0051	−76.68
Landfill waste (477 hundred million metric tons per county)	.0095	.0001	−.11
Superfund sites (.883 per county)	13.42	.1069	−106.07
Treatment, storage, and disposal sites (46.4 per county)	.2184	.0013	−.58
Central city (.290, = 1 if residence in central city)	40.75	−.4537	645.02
R^2	.6624	.3138	

TABLE 11A-1   (concluded)

---

* The dependent variable is actual or imputed monthly housing expenditures. Control variables which are included in the housing hedonic regression, but which are not reported include: units at address, age of structure, stories, rooms, bedrooms, bathrooms, condominium status, central air, sewer, lot size exceeds 1 acre, renter status, and renter interaction terms for each of these variables.

† The dependent variable is annual earnings divided by the product of annual weeks worked and usual hours per week. Control variables which are included in the wage-hedonic regression, but which are not reported include: experience (age-schooling-6), experience squared, gender interaction with experience and experience squared, race, gender, gender interaction with race, marital status, gender interaction with marital status, gender interaction with children under 18, schooling, disabled, school enrollment status, dummies for 5 of 6 broad occupation groups, and percent of industry covered by unions.

‡ The full implicit price is the sum of the annual housing expenditure and wage differentials. To obtain an annual household full implicit price, the housing coefficients are multiplied by 12 (months per year) and the wage coefficients are multiplied by (1.54)(37.85)(42.79), the product of the sample means of workers per household, hours per week, and weeks per year.

SOURCE: Glenn C. Blomquist, Mark C. Berger, and John P. Hoehn, "New Estimates of the Quality of Life in Urban Areas," *American Economic Review,* March 1988, pp. 89–107.

Similarly, the wage equation reflects both individual workers' characteristics (age, education, race, etc.) and the same 16 county-level amenities used in the housing equation.

$$W = f(IWC_1 \ . \ . \ . \ IWC_n, A_1 \ . \ . \ . \ A_{16}) \tag{3}$$

where W = Hourly wage rate,

IWC_1 = Individual worker characteristics, and

A_i = Level of the 16 amenities.

The amenity parameter estimates for both the housing and wage equations are shown in Table 11A-1. The parameter estimates for characteristics of the individual housing units (CIH_i) and individual worker characteristics (IWC_i) were calculated but are excluded from the table.

Humidity is an example of a disamenity. Row 2 of Table 11A-1 indicates that housing prices fell ($2.127 per month) and wages increased ($.0065 per hour) in an area for each percent increase in humidity. On the other hand, the teacher-pupil ratios caused rents to increase and wages to fall, indicating that individuals were willing to accept higher rents and lower wages to live in areas with a higher teacher to pupil ratio, presumably indicating a better quality of education.

For some amenities, the values given by the housing equation and the wage equation are inconsistent. For instance, monthly housing expenditures decrease by $7.458 per effluent discharger, suggesting it is a disamenity. But it also decreases the wage rate by $.0051 per hour, suggesting the presence of effluent dischargers is an amenity. In order to determine whether effluent dischargers is an amenity or disamenity, it is necessary to determine whether the wage or the housing effect is larger. The addition of the housing and wage variables will also allow a value to be set on each amenity.

TABLE 11A-2   Quality-of-Life Index Values for Large Metropolitan Areas

Metropolitan Area* (1980 SMSAs)	Quality-of-Life Index (1979 dollars)†
Denver–Boulder, Colo.	$1,197.96
San Diego, Calif.	980.83
Phoenix, Ariz.	870.69
Anaheim–Santa Ana–Garden Grove, Calif.	803.49
Nassau–Suffolk, N.Y.	687.80
Los Angeles–Long Beach, Calif.	667.64
Tampa–St. Petersburg, Fla.	191.57
San Francisco–Oakland, Calif.	139.55
Riverside–San Bernardino–Ontario, Calif.	135.46
Philadelphia, Pa., N.J.	9.21
Washington, D.C., Md., Va.	5.08
Newark, N.J.	−11.48
Atlanta, Ga.	−25.74
Seattle–Everett, Wash.	−124.18
Cleveland, Ohio	−190.62
Pittsburgh, Pa.	−330.90
New York, N.Y., N.J.	−369.20
Minneapolis–St. Paul, Minn., Wis.	−372.20
Dallas–Fort Worth, Tex.	−399.70
Baltimore, Md.	−422.70
Chicago, Ill.	−822.80
Houston, Tex.	−948.40
Detroit, Mich.	−968.00
St. Louis, Mo., Ill.	−990.10

* Listed are 24 standard metropolitan statistical areas (SMSAs) with a 1980 population exceeding 1.5 million. The 1980 definition of an SMSA is used. Boston, Mass., and Miami, Fla., are omitted because sufficient data were not available to estimate the parameters for the quality-of-life index (QOLI). The mean QOLI for the 24 SMSAs is −11.95.
† The differences in index values represent the annual premiums households are willing to pay for differences in amenities in different metropolitan areas. The values reported are taken from a study by Berger et al. (1987) that ranks 185 metropolitan areas by quality of life.

SOURCE: Berger, M. and Blomquest, G. C. "Income, Opportunities and the Quality of Life of Urban Residents," in (eds.), M. G. H. McGeary and L. E. Lynn, *Urban Change and Poverty*. National Academy Press, Washington, D.C., 1988.

Column 4 of Table 11A-1 shows the sum of the annualized housing expenditure and wage differentials. In order to annualize the housing coefficient, the monthly differential is multiplied by 12. In order to annualize the wage coefficient, the hourly differential is multiplied by the average number of hours worked per year. The annual amenity value is determined by (1) changing the sign of the housing differential (to show a positive value for the amenity) and (2) adding the annualized values for housing and rent to provide the estimate of amenity value shown in column 4 of Table 11A–1. For instance, in the case of effluent dischargers, it is not surprising that the housing effect (which indicated a disamenity) outweighs the wage differential. The results indicate a marginal amenity value of $76.68 for water effluent discharges. The value of the central city amenity factor is interesting. Central city housing expenditures are lower than elsewhere in the metropolitan areas as are wages of central city residents. However these appear to be the result of other factors in the hedonic models. When the value of living in the central city is isolated, that is, when other amenities are held constant, central city residence has a positive amenity value of $113.

Column 4 shows the implicit price for each quality of life indicator. The implicit price represents V_1 (monetary value of an amenity) in equation 1. Since the level of each amenity factor is known for each county in the study, a quality of life index can be constructed through the application of equation 1. The estimated value of each of the 16 amenity factors was multiplied by that amenity's level in each metropolitan area and the results summed.

Table 11A–2 shows the quality-of-life index for several major metropolitan areas (Berger and Blomquist, 1988, p. 96). Whether the results are consistent with popular expressions of where the areas with a high quality of life are will be left to others to decide. The main point is that Blomquist and his associates illustrated a technique allowing quality-of-life comparisons between counties. In order to compare quality of life among neighborhoods within a county, a similar technique could be used but the variables indicating life quality would have to reflect factors for which neighborhood-level data is available and the wage variable might not be useful because a metropolitan area is usually a single geographic labor market.

REFERENCES

Barrett, G. V. and John P. Blair. *The Foundations of Real Estate Analysis.* New York: Macmillan, 1981.

Bartik, Timothy J. "Measuring the Benefits of Amenity Improvement in Hedonic Price Models." *Land Economics* 64, no. 2, May 1988, pp. 172–83.

Berger, Mark C., and Glenn C. Blomquist. "Income, Opportunities and the Quality of Life of Urban Residents." In *Urban Change and Poverty,* ed. M. G. H. McGeary and L. E. Lynn. Washington, D.C.: Committee on National Urban Policy, National Research Council, 1988.

Blomquist, Glenn C.; Mark C. Berger; and John P. Hoehn. "New Estimates of the Quality of Life in Urban Areas." *American Economic Review,* March 1988, pp. 89–107.

Burgess, Ernest W. "The Growth of the City." In *The City,* ed. R. Parks, E. Burgess, and C. McKenzie. Chicago: University of Chicago Press, 1952.

Clotfelter, Charles T. "Spatial Rearrangement and the Tiebout Hypothesis: The Case of School Desegregation." *Southern Economic Journal* 24, no. 2, October 1975, pp. 263–71.

Galster, George C. *Homeowners and Neighborhood Reinvestment.* Durham, N.C.: Duke University Press, 1987.

Guntermann, Karl L., and Stefan Norrbin. "Explaining the Variability of Apartment Rents." *American Real Estate and Urban Economics Association Journal* 15, no. 4, 1987, pp. 321–39.

Hill, Edward W., and Thomas Bier. "Economic Restructuring: Earnings, Occupations and Housing Values in Cleveland." *Economic Development Quarterly* 3, no. 2, May 1989, pp. 123–34.

Ihlandfeldt, Keith R. "Property Tax Incidence on Owner-Occupied Housing." *National Tax Journal* 35, 1982.

Jud, G. Donald, and D. Gadar Bennet. "Public Schools and the Pattern of Intraurban Residential Mobility." *Land Economics* 62, no. 4, November 1986, pp. 362–70.

Little, James T. "Contemporary Housing Markets and Neighborhood Change." In *Residential Mobility and Public Policy,* ed. W. A. V. Clark and E. More. Beverly Hills, Calif.: Sage Publications, 1980, pp. 126–49.

Luger, Michael. "The Rent Control Paradox: Explanations and Prescriptions." *Review of Regional Studies* 16, no. 3, Fall 1986, pp. 25–41.

MacDonald, Don N.; James Murdoch; and Harry L. White. "Uncertain Hazards, Insurance and Consumer Choice." *Land Economics* 63, no. 4, November 1987, pp. 361–71.

Mayo, S. K. "Theory and Estimation in the Economics of Housing Demand." *Journal of Urban Economics* 9, 1981, pp. 190–211.

Mills, Edwin S., and Bruce Hamilton. *Urban Economics.* 4th ed. Glenview, Ill.: Scott, Foresman, 1989.

Moorehouse, John C. "Long-Term Rent Control and Tenant Subsidies." *Quarterly Review of Economics and Business* 27(3), pp. 6–24.

Muth, Richard F. *Cities and Housing.* Chicago: University of Chicago Press, 1969.

Oates, Wallace E. "The Effects of Property Taxes and Local Public Spending on Property Values: An Empirical Study of Tax Capitalization and the Tiebout Hypothesis." *Journal of Political Economy* 77, 1969, pp. 957–70.

Olsen, Edgar. "A Competitive Theory of the Housing Market." *American Economic Review* 59, 1969, pp. 612–21.

————. "The Demand and Supply of Housing Services." In *Handbook of Regional and Urban Economics,* ed. E. Mills. New York: Elsevier-North Holland Publishing, 1973, pp. 989–1022.

Porell, Frank W. "One Man's Ceiling Is Another Man's Floor: Landlord Manager Residency and Housing Conditions." *Land Economics* 61, no. 2, May 1985, pp. 106–18.

Quigley, John M. "What Have We Learned from Housing Markets?" In *Current Issues in Urban Economics,* ed. P. Mieszkowski and M. Straszhen. Baltimore: The Johns Hopkins Press, 1979, pp. 389–90.

Roback, J. "Wages, Rents and the Quality of Life." *Journal of Political Economy* 90, pp. 1257–278.

Rosen, S. "Hedonic Markets and Implicit Prices: Product Differentiation in Pure Competition." *Journal of Political Economy* 82, 1974, pp. 34–55.

Rossi, Peter H., and James D. Wright. "The Determinants of Homelessness." *Health Affairs* 6, issue 1, Spring 1987, pp. 19–32.

Rydell, C. P. "Price Elasticities of Housing Supply." Rand Report, r-2846-HUD. Santa Monica, Calif.: The Rand Corporation, 1982.

Sarkissian, Wendy. "The Idea of Social Mix in Planning: A Historical Review." *Urban Studies* 13, no. 3, October 1976, pp. 27–38.

Tiebout, Charles. "A Pure Theory of Local Public Expenditure." *Journal of Political Economy* 64, 1956, pp. 416–24.*

U.S. Department of Housing and Urban Development. *Measuring Racial Discrimination in American Housing Markets*. Washington, D.C.: U.S. Department of Housing and Urban Development, 1979.

Weicher, John L., and Thomas G. Thibodeau. "Filtering and Housing Markets: An Empirical Analysis." *Journal of Urban Economics* 23, 1988, pp. 21–40.

Yinger, John. "Measuring Racial Discrimination with Fair Housing Audits: Caught in the Act." *American Economic Review,* December 1986, pp. 881–93.

* Classic.

Chapter Twelve

Transportation Systems

The importance of access to the location of firms and households has been a major focus of the discussion of land use and housing choice. The urban transportation system is one of the primary determinants of access. Consequently, an understanding of the transportation system can contribute to our understanding of the working of the urban economy.

The field of regional economics developed largely because traditional economic theory often ignored the consequences of transportation costs. Yet transportation is an essential component of modern economics, accounting for as much as 20 percent of national output. This chapter examines several important transportation issues. The first section describes some of the ways transportation affects the spatial distribution of economic activities and analyzes the impacts of transportation systems. The second section explores economic characteristics of transportation systems and shows how these characteristics affect operations. The third section examines the demand for transportation services. The nature of demand and the characteristics of transportation systems have implications for optimal pricing systems and other policies discussed in the fourth section. The final section examines policy issues.

IMPACTS OF TRANSPORTATION ROUTES

The impacts of transportation routes and travel costs are pervasive. A discussion of all the consequences of new transportation systems is beyond the scope of this section, although many effects have been alluded to elsewhere in the text. However, as a first cut in describing these impacts, it may be useful to distinguish between transportation factors that affect the relationships among urban areas and intrametropolitan impacts that affect the relationship between areas within a region.

Intermetropolitan Impacts

The urban hierarchy is supported by established transportation and communications networks, and new transportation systems tend to be established on the base of existing trade and travel patterns. Therefore, new transportation systems generally reinforce the existing relationships among regions and cities within regions. When all roads led to Rome, each new road reinforced Rome's preeminence in the world.

Although the general tendency is for new transportation systems to reinforce the existing urban hierarchy, there are notable exceptions. It is practically impossible to create major changes in interregional transportation systems without disturbing the urban hierarchy in some way. Some areas will inevitably benefit more than others when new roads or other transportation systems are built. The development of new transportation modes often contributes to a realignment of trading patterns. Interregional transportation is so important to regional prosperity that until after World War II, state and local economic development efforts concentrated predominantly on improving transportation linkages with other areas.

In colonial and post–colonial America, port cities were critical links to European markets. New York, Boston, and, later, New Orleans benefited from port development. Furthermore, most of the important inland cities were on natural waterways. Cincinnati was an early interior trading center because of its strategic location on the Ohio River, while St. Louis and other Mississippi River cities depended upon the water transportation and the natural transshipment functions (unloading and reloading) necessary for goods crossing the continent.

The construction of the Erie Canal in the early 1800s contributed to the emergence of Erie, Pennsylvania, and New York as the key transshipment points between the western agricultural markets and the East Coast. The Erie Canal also contributed to both Chicago's and Cleveland's strength as port cities. Many smaller communities experienced economic growth due to their links with other canals.

The railroad era had a major impact on regional development patterns. Baltimore was the first city to use public funds to help finance a railroad. The success of the Baltimore–Ohio Railroad encouraged other cities to subsidize railroads that would link them to markets or resources. Chicago, Kansas City, and numerous smaller cities grew because of access to rail transportation. Railroads became a key to determining the hinterland of major metropolitan areas.

The development of interstate highways increased the access of smaller communities to major urban centers and also increased the access of major urban areas to each other. The highway transportation system and the development of technology that facilitated the transportation of goods by trucks added flexibility to the distribution process and greatly increased the number of potential transshipment points. However, areas that were not included in the modern interstate system have been disadvantaged. The first national road (now U.S. 40) connecting the East to St. Louis was overshadowed by the construction of new interstate highways, particularly I70, which runs parallel to U.S. 40. The numerous abandoned villages, motels, restaurants, and gasoline stations along U.S. 40 illustrate the negative impact interstates can have on places left out. Large parts of Appalachia were left out of the highway boom that followed World War II. Partly because of their isolation, they became "islands of poverty" in an otherwise rapidly growing economy during the 1950s and 1960s. One of the major strategies to stimulate development in the Appalachian region was a massive highway construction effort to link key cities in Appalachia with the existing interstate system.

Currently, air travel is creating new sets of linkages. The availability of air travel has become an important locational factor for many businesses, especially where executives or sales personnel (employees with high opportunity costs) must travel quickly and on short notice. Regions that have become hubs for one or more major airlines have benefited. Atlanta and Dallas–Fort Worth are examples of regions that have made air transportation a major component of their economic development plans.

Observers have speculated that, in the future, high-speed rail may connect major urban areas, although current studies suggest that interurban passenger service is not cost effective. If high-speed urban rail services were to be established, we could speculate that economic activity would be stimulated in the newly linked metropolitan regions, while the areas bypassed would lose economic activity. In addition, a new rail system would strengthen the rail head area within the cities included in the network.

Intraurban Impacts

Transportation systems link the parts of a metropolitan area and create patterns of access to urban goods and protection from urban bads. The controversy associated with the location of transportation routes is a perennial feature of urban politics. The importance of transportation systems in determining personal comfort income and property values has been widely recognized. Access affects the overall productivity of the region, land use, property values, and the shape of the metropolis. Of course, these factors are related, but it is instructive to examine how transportation affects each.

Productivity. Metropolitan regions have been compared to machines. If the metaphor is useful, the transportation system can be considered the oil that lubricates the machine. The aggregate regional perspective is important because the differential impacts of changes in the transportation system on various parts of the region are often discussed so vigorously that the net regional impact can be forgotten. For example, a beltway will usually attract business away from core areas and towards beltway areas. Therefore, representatives of innercity areas may oppose construction of a suburban highway system. But the beltway may also increase economic activity and productivity in the region, and many inner-city residents may benefit, either directly or indirectly, from the increased scope of activity.

Land Use.   Almost any change in a region's transportation system will result in altered land-use patterns. A new highway linking rural roads with major arteries into the city may set the stage for residential development in rural areas. Commercial development normally occurs first at major intersections or near entrance and exit ramps. After an area has become more heavily populated, additional commercial development may appear in strips along major roads. Eventually an intersection may develop into a major subcenter if access is sufficient to justify a commercial agglomeration.

Public transportation, such as buses and subway trains, also affects land use. Numerous studies have shown that capital investment and population density increase near major pickup and departure points. Many of the station stops on the Washington, D.C., Metro system have evolved into major subcenters within the metropolis largely because of housing demand on the part of individuals wanting to live near the station and the development of commercial establishments to serve the large neighborhood population as well as commuters from elsewhere.

Land-Value Impacts.   Transportation changes have both positive and negative property-value impacts. Positive impacts normally occur when sites become more accessible. One of the most dramatic instances of transportation changes increasing property values is the increased land values near the Washington, D.C. subway stations. Land values have skyrocketed at sites near major airports in recent years. Bus and commuter train stops are used as selling points for residential and commercial properties. However, the positive price effects of public-transit nodes diminish rapidly with distance and become very small beyond a short walking distance. Transportation-cost savings from being located near a transportation node can be capitalized into the present value of land.

Gunterman and Norrbin's (1987) model of rent determinants (see the discussion on hedonic pricing in chapter 11) showed that access to major expressways was associated with higher rents, holding other things equal. Since rents influence property values for income-producing properties, their model implies that apartments with access to expressways will be more valuable. Access to major highways may be even more critical to the value of commercial land.

Negative property-value impacts occur from the noise, air, and visual pollution that are associated with transportation corridors. Flight paths, for example, reduce property values due to noise pollution. Residential properties that are near limited-access highways may also experience property-value declines. Such neighborhoods may experience extra noise and pollution; yet the limited-access feature of the highway may not afford better access. Transportation changes can also make some sites less accessible. For instance, highway and rail lines can cut across neighborhoods so that one side has very poor access to the other side.

As metropolitan areas develop, new roads open land and support development at the urban fringe. Since residents of the new fringe properties usually travel towards the central city (although not necessarily to the central city) to reach activity points, they will tend to travel through already developed areas, thus increasing noise, congestion, and pollution in areas closer to the major activity centers. In this regard the transportation-development process tends to hurt older areas' existing neighborhoods.

Urban Form.   The growth of an urban area requires transportation changes that link the urban core to the periphery. The long-term lowering of transportation costs has encouraged decentralization. Urban density is lower than would be the case if transportation costs had not decreased. Lower transportation costs have been considered a major cause of urban sprawl. However, the causes of decentralization include personal values, income, zoning, land costs, escape from central-city pathologies, and population growth, as well as lower transportation costs. The increases in gasoline prices during the 1970s had a negligible long-term effect on the rate of suburbanization.

Improved public transportation has an ambiguous effect on the central business district. On the one hand, the CBD becomes more accessible as transportation improves and, as a result, may be a more attractive business location. On the other hand, better public transportation may encourage downtown workers to live further from the central city. Thus, central-city retail and related establishments will lose important market segments. Some observers have found that central city properties are enhanced slightly when public transportation is improved, indicating a weak relationship. However, even very major public-transportation improvements are unlikely to affect suburbanization today, because few commuters use public transportation. Table 12–1 shows that slightly less

TABLE 12–1 Distribution of Metropolitan Workers: By Workplace, Place of
Residence, and Travel Mode, 1975

*Workplace, Residence, and Travel Mode**	*Percentage of Workers Using Travel Mode*
City workplace	
City resident (34.8 percent)†	
Travel by car	74.0%
Travel by transit	16.7
Suburban resident (19.5 percent)†	
Travel by car	89.3
Travel by transit	9.7
Suburban workplace	
City resident (8.1 percent)†	
Travel by car	93.0
Travel by transit	5.6
Suburban resident (37.7 percent)†	
Travel by car	90.9
Travel by transit	1.8

* Other travel modes not shown (such as bicycling, walking) would bring total in each workplace-residence category to 100 percent.

† Percentages shown are share of total metropolitan workplace-residence category. People working at home and people working or living outside metropolitan areas are excluded.

Kenneth A. Small. "Transportation and Urban Change," in *The New Urban Reality,* ed. Paul E. Peterson (Washington, D.C.: The Brookings Institution, 1985), p. 209.

SOURCE: Author's calculations from the U.S. Bureau of the Census, *Current Population Reports,* series P-23, no. 99, "The Journey to Work in the United States: 1975" (Government Printing Office, 1979), table F.

than 17 percent of central-city residents working in the central city use public transportation. The smallest category of transit users is suburban residents working in the suburbs. Among this group, less than 2 percent travel by transit.

Although transportation policy changes are unlikely to reverse the decentralization trend, they can influence where decentralization occurs. Expansion of highways along certain axes will influence the outward development path. The placement of intersections, entrance-exit ramps, and public-transit stations may influence commercial and industrial centers.

CHARACTERISTICS OF
TRANSPORTATION SYSTEMS

In this section, various cost and supply characteristics are examined as well as unique characteristics of demand for transportation services. Although the major transportation systems have many characteristics in common, the automobile will be in the spotlight because of its importance. Other transportation systems will be discussed in comparison.

Fixed, Variable, and Marginal Costs

Most transportation systems are characterized by high fixed costs and low marginal costs when the system is operating below capacity. Of course, not all transportation systems have high fixed costs. Bicycle commuting has low fixed costs but high marginal costs in terms of time, effort, and risk. Fixed costs do not change as output changes. In the case of automobile travel, fixed costs include the cost of the automobile and the cost of the road system. Fixed costs include costs to the individual driver and costs to the public. Fixed costs are often expressed in terms of the annualized payments required to finance the construction costs of the facilities. Not only are fixed costs high, but they have depreciation periods that span decades. Automobiles are durable goods, and road systems are intended to last for generations. Variable costs are costs that can be terminated in the short run. If individuals stopped driving, they might be able to cancel their automobile insurance. For public transportation systems, the cost of labor needed to operate a facility could be an example of a variable cost. Marginal costs are the costs of transporting an extra passenger or driving an extra mile. Particularly, if the concern is the cost of transporting an extra person on an existing route or of shipping an extra pound of a commodity, the marginal costs are very low. However, if a transportation system is operating at capacity, say, the highway is congested, the truck is fully loaded, or all the seats on the plane are taken, the marginal costs may be very high.

Shutdown Analysis. One of the implications of the combination of high fixed costs and low variable, as well as marginal, costs is that transportation systems will continue to be used even if the benefits (measured by price) are below average cost. The automobile is a particularly important case of a transportation system with relatively low marginal costs and high fixed costs. The automobile purchase, provision of a garage, and so forth are fixed costs. Insurance and license fees are major variable costs since they must be paid if you plan to drive. Gasoline and time are the major marginal costs of driving. Therefore, once an individual has made the outlays necessary to purchase a car, there is less incentive to econo-

TABLE 12-2   The Shutdown Decision

	Shutdown	Continue Operation
Revenues	$ 0	$ 2,000
Fixed costs	100,000	100,000
Variable costs	0	1,000
Losses	100,000	99,000

mize on extra trips. A car may be necessary for some purposes, so it may have a high average cost per mile. However, once having purchased the car, the marginal cost of using it for other purposes will be relatively low.

Managers of public transportation systems will be reluctant to shut down transportation facilities because of the cost structure. A profit-maximizing firm will shut down when revenues no longer cover variable costs. However, it would continue operations even if it did not make a profit as long as revenues covered variable costs. In this case, continuing to operate would at least minimize losses. The excess of revenue over variable costs can contribute towards the fixed costs, even if they cannot cover all of the fixed costs.

Table 12-2 illustrates why a transportation provider would continue operations even when making a loss. Assume an airline with $100,000 of fixed costs is considering whether to shut down or continue operations. If the airline shuts down, its revenues would be zero and its losses would be equal to the fixed costs, $100,000. Assume it costs about $1,000 to add an extra flight. In the case of an airline, the variable cost might reflect the cost of fuel and extra labor costs. In the case of other shippers, the variable cost might reflect extra wear and tear or extra fuel usage. If the firm shuts down, its losses will equal the fixed costs of $100,000. However, if it operates and earns only slightly more than the variable costs, its losses will be reduced. In Table 12-2, losses would be $99,000 if operations were continued.

Planning.   Because the fixed overhead of many transportation systems depreciates slowly, the planning horizon for highways and most other transportation systems may extend 25 to 50 years into the future. Railroads have operated at a loss for many years because it was difficult to shed fixed investment. The problem is compounded when an industry, rather than a firm, experiences excess capacity. A single firm may shed excess capacity by selling facilities to other firms in the same industry. It is more difficult for the industry to shed excess capacity because particular facilities may be useless in other industries.

In a high-fixed-cost/low-marginal-cost situation, average costs will decline with increased usage over a considerable range because the averaging of fixed costs will lower per unit costs. Hence, average costs tend to be lower on routes with higher traffic volume up to the point where capacity is reached and congestion becomes a problem.

Peaking and Cost.   Urban transportation systems are characterized by sharp peaks of use during the time individuals are going to and from work. A similar peaking pattern applies to airlines. The critical implication of this fact is that the extra or marginal cost of accommodating additional travelers at off-peak times is relatively low but the marginal cost of accommodating extra travelers at peak times is high. For instance, a bus may travel between two points all day. During off-peak hours, the cost of an extra rider may be zero. Since the bus is committed to the route, an extra off-peak rider will not appreciably increase labor, fuel, capital, or other costs. (Notice that the term "cost" refers to the extra resources required, not to the fare paid by the passenger.) During peak hours, the bus may be full. The cost of transporting an extra rider during these peak periods may be quite high because it could require purchase of an extra bus and hiring a driver.

Marginal costs can increase sharply after a transportation system has reached its capacity for two reasons: (1) extra users may require expensive additions to system capacity, such as an extra lane on a highway, and (2) extra users create congestion that imposes costs (time, discomfort, and so forth) on other users.

Line-Haul and Terminal Costs

Most transportation systems have two distinct sets of costs. Line-haul costs are the costs of moving people, commodities, or information. Terminal costs occur at both ends of the line in the form of loading or unloading costs.

Terminal costs are particularly significant in commuter transportation. Pickup costs, or costs of collecting passengers, are high for suburban morning commuters using public transportation because of the wide area from which riders are drawn. The pickup cost is particularly high when time and convenience are considered. The automobile has low pickup costs for commuters. Buses have low unloading costs because of the concentration of workplaces in the central city. Automobiles have relatively high unloading costs due to the need for parking in high-density locations during the day.

Time and Money Costs

Costs are frequently measured in terms of out-of-pocket expenses. However, most economists recognize that time costs are also important, particularly in transportation decisions. In fact, time-costs savings are the reason for most transportation improvements. Airplanes, electronic communications, and high-speed rail systems are examples of innovations that offer major time-cost advantages even though out-of-pocket costs may be higher than competing modes. Walking has almost no out-of-pocket costs, but it is very expensive in terms of time.

Time costs are particularly important for the transportation of people. In fact, people are one of the most expensive "things" to transport, largely because of time costs. Empirical studies indicate that commuters value travel time at 25–30 percent of their wage when choosing between a quick but expensive route (say a tollway) and a longer but cheaper route. However, time costs of individuals traveling during work hours might be equal to the hourly wage from the employer's perspective.

The importance of time and money costs in determining the appropriate mode of transportation can be seen in a hypothetical example. The example uses reasonable data although it has been adjusted to show a commuter indifferent between taking a private car or using public transportation. The individual lives eight miles from the workplace and can commute by car at an out-of-pocket cost of 15 cents per mile or by public transit at a total cost of $1.00. It is assumed that the individual would own a car in any case, so no capital costs of the auto are included. The individual values time costs at $5.00 per hour. This example assumes that the cost of a unit of time riding the bus and driving are equal. Some people enjoy driving and will have a lower driving time cost than public-transportation time cost. Other individuals may enjoy reading on the bus, playing cards with fellow commuters on the train, or use travel time to work. Such individuals will place a lower time cost on public transportation than driving. The example ignores these differences. However, it should be noted that individuals appear to place higher costs on time spent walking than on time spent riding a bus, and the lowest cost on automobile travel (Domencich and McFadden, 1975).

Table 12–3 indicates that the total costs of the trip by the two modes of transportation are equal. Time cost is the largest cost component. As income increases, the value of time will increase and tilt the travel decision toward private autos.

The individual preference for the private auto also will be strengthened by several factors not reflected in Table 12–3. First, the time cost of unanticipated delays is probably higher than anticipated travel time. Thus, if the bus is delayed or full, the time cost of the unanticipated delay

TABLE 12–3   Costs of a Two-Way Urban Commute during Rush Hour

		Private Auto	*Private Transit*
1.	Miles	8	8
2.	Minutes	25	45
3.	Auto operating costs at 15¢ mile	$1.25	n.a.*
4.	Transit fare	n.a.	$1.00
5.	Parking cost	1.40	n.a.
6.	Time cost at $5.00 an hour	2.10	3.75
7.	Total cost	$4.75	$4.75

* n.a. = Not applicable.

could be more costly. For instance, unanticipated delay could cause you to miss a meeting. Second, the auto's flexibility allows the commuter to take alternative routes in the event of anticipated blockages in traffic flow. The extra flexibility is also useful when there is a need to combine trips, for example, to purchase something on the way home, or when the commuter must leave work in midday. Third, if the public transportation system requires any transfers, the time costs in the example will increase substantially. Therefore, public transportation is seldom competitive in low-density areas where transfers are required.

Time costs are important to the transportation of commodities as well as people. Costs of holding inventories, possible spoilage, or market obedience are time sensitive. The advent of just-in-time (JIT) inventory-control systems has increased the importance of time costs in the transportation of commodities. JIT methods emphasize maintenance of low levels of inventories. The smaller the stock of inventories, the lower the holding costs. However, before a firm can implement a JIT system, it must be assured of access to inventories when they are needed. Shortages must be replaced quickly, particularly if they create bottlenecks that can affect an entire plant.

Air Pollution Externalities

Most transportation systems are sources of pollution. Air, noise, water, and visual pollution are all associated with transportation. However, air pollution is the type of pollution of most concern to transportation planners and environmentalists. The energy conversion in internal combustion engines is the largest source of air pollution. Straszheim (1979) estimated that the cost of automobile pollution during the 1970s was between .50 and .80 cents per mile. However, recent legislation and regulations have reduced the air pollution of automobiles.

The Clean Air Act authorized the Environmental Protection Agency to implement programs to ensure that motor vehicles and airplanes avoid undue air pollution. In comparison to cars and trucks, railroads are not a significant source of pollution, although railroad pollution is regulated through the Department of Transportation.

Congestion Externalities

Congestion is a form of externality that can affect all transportation modes, but is of critical concern to highway users. An extra individual using a transportation route may increase the travel time of every other person using that route. The number of trips along a certain road depends upon the number of cars on the road at any time and the average speed. As density increases beyond a certain point, speed falls because slower drivers create bottlenecks. In addition, speed reductions will be necessary to avoid accidents as congestion increases.

Exponential Cost Increases.   External costs of congestion may increase at an exponential rate as congestion increases because additional cars on an expressway increase both the number of delays and the number of individuals affected by the delays. This relationship may be illustrated with a simple model (Baumol, 1967). Let the number of delay-causing events (DCE) be proportional to the number of cars on a particular route: $DCE = cn$. This situation would be the case if delay-creating mishaps were randomly distributed. Thus, the number of delays will be cn, where c is the proportion of cars creating delays and n is the number of travelers. The number of persons affected by a single delay (PA) will equal some fraction, k, of the cars on the road at any time $PA = kn$. In this model, the number of persons experiencing delay, PED, will equal the number of delay-causing events (cn) times the number of persons affected by each delay event (kn). Thus,

$$PED = kncn, \text{ or} \tag{1}$$

$$PED = kcn^2.$$

The number of persons affected by delay increases exponentially as the number of travelers increases. The exponential increase in congestion costs is a general urban problem because the number of pollution-causing events and the number of victims both increase with population.

An Externality Model.   Figure 12–1 provides another perspective on the congestion problem. Automobile travel is the most important instance of congestion; however, the model can be applicable to other transportation forms as well. The number of cars using a strip of road during a

FIGURE 12–1 Benefits and Costs of Travel under Congestion

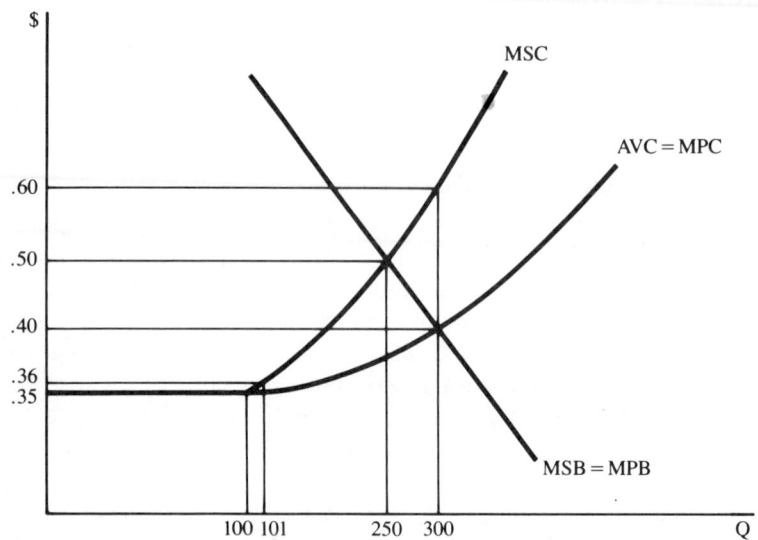

Congestion causes a divergence between marginal private and marginal social costs. Optimum usage is 250, but in the absence of extra road charges, 300 trips/minute will be made.

particular period of time is measured on the horizontal axis. The average-variable-cost curve is horizontal at low levels of output because the variable costs approximate the marginal costs (time, gasoline, auto wear and tear, etc.). Wear and tear on the road are ignored. The average-variable-cost curve eventually slopes upward because congestion will increase travel time.

The private costs that an extra driver will accrue from using the road will approximate the variable costs of all the other users. In other words, the expected vehicle operating costs and the time costs will be the same for the last person to decide to use the road during the given time as for the typical driver. A driver considering whether to use the road will consider the average time it takes to drive the distance as part of the marginal cost. Since the expected travel costs an additional driver will incur will equal the average costs of all other drivers and road wear and tear are assumed to be negligible, the marginal private cost (MPC) to an additional driver will approximate the average variable costs (AVC) for all users. The MPC curve represents the costs that an individual will consider in determining whether to travel the road at the relevant time.

The social costs of an extra car on the road are measured by the marginal social cost (MSC) curve. The MSC curve is above the AVC curve for levels of usage above 100 trips per minute because each additional drive imposes delay costs on all users. In order to see why the MSC may be above the MPC when 100 cars are using the road, suppose the 101st car increases costs from 35¢ to 35.1¢ per trip. The MPC of the 101st driver will be 35.1¢, but the MSC will include the 35.1¢ cost to the extra driver *plus* an extra .01¢ (one hundredth of a cent) for each of the other 100 drivers. Thus, the marginal social cost of the 101st driver would equal 36.1¢ (35.1 + (100 × .01)). When 300 cars are on the road, an additional car will impose 60 cents of costs on society but the private costs will be only 40 cents. Hence, externalities will equal 20 cents. Congestion begins to occur beyond 100 in Figure 12–1, the point where marginal social costs exceed congestion.

If use of the highway were free to drivers except for their operating costs, drivers would use the road until the marginal private benefits are equal to the marginal private costs. Therefore, the road will be used for up to 300 trips. However, the socially optimum level of use would be 250 trips, where the social cost of an extra trip would just equal marginal social benefits. Pricing models to reduce the number of trips to an optional level are discussed in the next section.

Peak-Time Congestion.   The problem of road congestion almost always occurs during selected time periods (Straszheim, 1979; McConnell-Fay, 1986). For instance, an expressway may be congested only during rush hours. The same length of road or bus route can be congested during some periods and operate with excess capacity during other periods. The issue of time congestion adds an extra dimension to the question of where a new transportation facility is necessary to alleviate congestion. If a road is congested for only a few hours a week, some observers might consider it congested but others would not.

Downs's Law

New roads tend to become congested quickly. Road improvements often have smaller effects on congestion than anticipated based upon preconstruction traffic flows. The situation is sometimes termed "Downs's law of peak hour congestion" because Anthony Downs suggested that traffic on commuter expressways tends to rise to meet road capacity.

There are four reasons why traffic on new or improved commuter roads tends to increase. First, commuters may switch from old routes to improved routes. Thus, if route A is improved to accommodate the existing level of traffic, commuters using other routes will switch to route A and cause congestion. In equilibrium, travel costs (including time) will equalize among competing routes. Second, individuals may switch modes. Some commuters may have taken public transportation, but a new or improved road may induce them to switch to private automobiles. A third source of additional traffic may come from individuals who were previously deterred from commuting at peak hours. They may have come to work early and/or left late. Many individuals may have been nearly indifferent between traveling at peak or off-peak times. If travel times decrease even slightly, additional peak-time commuting will occur. The first three factors will occur relatively quickly. The fourth factor may be a longer-term impact. A road may also create new points of origin, such as housing developments, and new destinations. The additional destinations will add to congestion.

Down's observation has three important implications. First, improvements in transportation capacity should be planned on the basis of the likelihood that such improvements will also result in an increase in traffic levels. Improvements that are designed to meet only current usage levels will quickly be congested. Second, because of the large number of individuals who will shift travel to peak-hour times, it may be very costly to avoid peak-hour congestion. It may be wise public policy to allow peak-hour congestion if the costs of delays or other ways of eliminating delays (such as staggered commuting times) are less than route-construction costs. Third, if a previously congested road is improved, the point of congestion may be moved from the route itself to the route's entrance and exit points or elsewhere. Therefore, transportation planners should examine the potential for new bottlenecks in other areas.

Demand Elasticities

The demand for a particular mode of transportation at a given time may be expressed as:

$$T_d = f(MC, TC, Y, PS) \qquad (2)$$

where T_d = Amount of travel demanded,
MC = Money costs,
TC = Time costs,
PS = Price of substitute transportation systems, and
Y = Income.

The demand equation could apply to either the private automobile or to public transportation. In order to assess the responsiveness of travel demand to each of the independent variables in the demand equation, it is useful to estimate elasticities. An elasticity shows the responsiveness of the amount of travel demanded to changes in the independent variables.

Thus, the price elasticity of demand would be:

$$PED = (\%\Delta T_d)/(\%\Delta MC) \qquad (3)$$

where PED = Price elasticity of demand,

$\%\Delta T_d$ = Percentage change in the number of trips, and

$\%\Delta MC$ = Percentage change in money costs.

It is reasonable to expect that as both time and money costs increase the quantity of trips will decrease. Hence, we would expect a negative elasticity for these features. (Since quantity and price normally move in opposite directions, the negative sign is sometimes ignored, but we will not follow that practice here.) It is also reasonable to assume that as the price of substitutes decreases (increases) the level of trips by the mode represented by the demand function will decrease (increase). Hence, a positive cross-elasticity coefficient is reasonable. The income elasticities of demand are more difficult to determine, particularly for public transportation. As incomes increase, individuals may take more rides, hence a positive elasticity coefficient. But, as income increases above a certain level, a family may substitute a car for mass transportation, in which case the income-elasticity coefficient for public transportation would be negative.

Elasticity coefficients are important not only because they reveal the direction of the response an independent variable will have on the quantity of trips but also the magnitude.

The price elasticity of demand for transportation tends to be inelastic; that is, the number of trips is unresponsive to a change in price. One reason for the general inelasticity of travel demand is that transportation demand is derived from the desire for other goods and services or the requirements of going to and from work. Therefore, travel costs are a relatively small part of a package. A large increase in transportation will have only a small impact on the delivered cost of most goods. Likewise, a commuter's 50 percent increase in the costs of traveling to work may cause take-home pay to fall by less than 10 percent.

While the demand for transportation in general is relatively inelastic, the demand for particular types of transportation or the demand of particular customers may be very elastic if close substitutes are available. For instance, a transport company may have a very elastic demand because of the competitive nature of the industry. For some commodities over certain routes, barge and rail transportation may compete with each other, so both transportation modes will have elastic demands. Elasticities are important guides to business policy because they show how effective changes in price can be in affecting behavior. Table 12–4 shows the responsiveness of public and private demand for transportation to money costs, time costs, and income. Representative elasticities from various

TABLE 12–4 Demand Elasticities for Private and Public Transport

	Money Costs	*Time Costs*	*Income Elasticity*	*Cross-Elasticity*
Private transportation	Low to moderate −.49* −.35[†] −.87[‡]	Moderate or responsive − .82* − .27[†] −1.02[‡]	Low .27	Unresponsive—statistically insignificant
Public transportation	Low −.55[†] −.33[‖]	Moderate to very responsive −1.85[†] − .593[#]	Unresponsive −.03[§]	Unresponsive—statistically insignificant .07[†]

* Domencich, et al. (1972), for work trips.
[†] Burk K. Burright (1984).
[‡] Domencich, et al. (1972), for shopping trips.
[§] U.S. Department of Transportation (1977), for moderate-income families.
[‖] U.S. Department of Transportation (1977), based on current ridership in 263 cities.
[#] Domencich, et al. (1972), includes line-haul and waiting time.

studies are included in Table 12–4. There are significant variations because the studies differed regarding time, place, purpose of the trip, and so forth. Therefore, the elasticities have been characterized in terms of the degree of responsiveness to emphasize that the existing empirical studies provide a range of possibilities.

In general, both public transportation and private automobiles are unresponsive to money costs, although shopping trips are moderately responsive to cost increases. A 1 percent decrease in money cost will result in an increase in travel of less than 1 percent. However, demand is more responsive to changes in time costs than to changes in money costs.

Most of the money and time cost elasticities in Table 12–4 represent short-run responses. The results for longer time periods would be more elastic because individuals would have more time to adjust. For instance, if bus fares were reduced, a commuter might continue to drive to work until a new car was needed. Then the commuter might decide to forego a new car and take the bus. Furthermore, as incomes change behaviors regarding demand will change; so while market-derived elasticities may be accurate on the average, they may be inaccurate for certain segments of the population. Therefore, policy makers should avoid drawing implications about the demand responsiveness of poor inner-city residents based upon elasticities that are averages of all income groups.

There are several policy implications implied by the elasticity studies. First, the income elasticity of private transportation and the negative income elasticity for public transportation suggest that reliance on private transportation will increase if incomes continue to increase. Second, efforts to increase usage of public transportation systems by decreasing price are likely to be unsuccessful. If prices are cut and ridership does not increase or increases only slightly, revenues will fall, requiring larger public subsidies. Third, since usage of public transportation is more responsive to decreases in time costs, cutting travel time will be more effective than policy changes that decrease money costs by the same percentage. Time saving from better residential collection could be particularly effective because some studies have shown that time spent waiting has a higher cost to individuals than time spent traveling.

PRICING ISSUES

In a perfectly competitive economic system, the optimum price would emerge from the interaction of producers and consumers. In competitive equilibrium, the producer's costs of providing an extra unit of transportation services would equal the benefits from the services provided. This is another way of saying that marginal social costs would equal marginal social benefits if there are no spillover effects. In reality, the provision of transportation services seldom resembles the competitive model. Therefore, there are a number of situations where inappropriate pricing of services results in inefficiency. Transportation services could be provided more efficiently if pricing were more effectively employed.

Pricing under Conditions of Excess Capacity—Short Run

One pricing problem associated with both private automobile and public transportation is that the marginal cost to the transportation authority of allowing an extra car on the road or an extra person on the bus is nearly zero. Optimum-pricing theory implies that no one should be excluded from a trip if they value the trip more than the marginal cost. In the case of a bus trip, for example, an extra rider would not increase costs to the bus company because the bus would travel whether there were n or $n + 1$ passengers. Yet, fare changes will reduce ridership, resulting in a loss of social benefits without a compensating reduction in social costs.

Figure 12–2 illustrates the problem. For easy exposition, assume time costs to riders are zero. The fixed cost of the system is large, but the marginal cost is small. That is why the marginal cost is below the average

FIGURE 12–2 Pricing under Conditions of Decreasing Costs

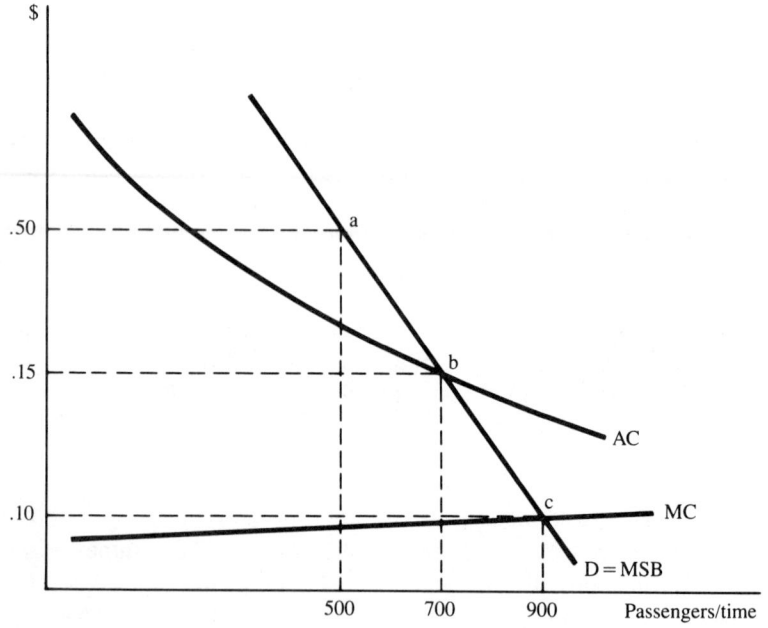

Price-quantity combinations that will maximize profits, point a, or cover costs, point b, will result in suboptimal usage. The socially optimal quantity of passengers of 900, point c, can be achieved at price $.10.

cost. In the case of an extra bus rider, the marginal cost would reflect the fuel needed to transport the extra weight, extra wear and tear, and congestion. Since the marginal cost is below the average cost over the relevant range, average cost continually declines. The decline in average cost reflects the averaging of the large fixed cost over additional riders.

What price and service level should result from the situation depicted in Figure 12–2? Once the price is set, the service level will be determined by the demand, so any equilibrium ridership level will have to be a point on the demand curve. Let us consider the advantages and disadvantages of price-quantity combinations a, b, and c, where a is the profit-maximizing point, b is the break-even level, and c is a situation where total revenues are less than total costs, so the agency providing the service is losing money.

Profit Maximization.   At point a, profits for the transportation provider would exist since at the indicated ridership level average revenues exceed average cost. The marginal-revenue curve is not shown, but if it were, it would intersect marginal cost at passenger level 500. Let point a indicate the profit-maximizing price-quantity combination. The problem with the 50 cent price is that the marginal rider (the 500th passenger) values an additional trip at 50 cents, but the cost of providing the marginal trip is only 10 cents. Hence, if social welfare could be increased by increasing ridership, net social benefits would increase by 40 cents ($.50 − $.10). Increased ridership could be attained by lowering price. However, lowering price could also lower profits for the transportation provider.

Break-Even Analysis.   At the price-quantity combination indicated by point b, total revenue would equal total cost (both equal $.15 × 700). The transportation provider would cover all costs, but profits would be zero. In comparison with point a, the net social benefits are greater at point b, reflecting the extra ridership at relatively low social costs. However, one could still argue that a further increase in ridership would not increase social benefits since MSB > MSC at 700.

MSC = MSB.   In the case represented by point c, net social benefits will be maximized. Let price be set at 10 cents, the marginal cost. Ridership would increase to 900. This level of ridership is socially optimal because the demand curve (marginal social benefits) equals marginal social costs. The problem with solution c is that revenues will not cover costs. Therefore, some kind of subsidy will be necessary to cover costs or in some cases a fixed-fee "access permit" could be used to cover costs while maintaining a low marginal cost for those who paid the fixed access fee. Although the socially optimal level of service is provided, the taxes needed to finance the subsidies could create distortions elsewhere in the economy. Nevertheless, this case is often used to justify subsidies for transportation systems.

Price Discrimination.   The three previous cases assumed that all riders paid the same price and there was no price that would encourage the optimum ridership while covering costs. However, the socially optimal level of ridership could be achieved and the revenues may be sufficient to cover costs if different prices are charged to different passengers. For instance, relatively high prices could be charged to those who are willing and able to pay "full fares," while a 10 cent fare could be charged to individuals who would not otherwise use the system.

There are several techniques used by transit systems to price discriminate. Monthly passes and discounts to seniors and school-age children are examples. However, these price-discriminating techniques are imperfect because they still result in the exclusion of some potential passengers who would be willing to pay their marginal costs, but are unwilling to pay full fare.

Pricing under Conditions of Congestion—Short Run

Beyond a given level of usage, excess capacity will be dissipated and congestion will occur. Congestion can cause the marginal cost of traveling to exceed the average cost. An extra rider will pay the average cost, but, because of the delays and other disamenities of crowding, the marginal cost of the extra rider will be higher than the average cost. Although the problem of congestion is common to most transportation modes, the problem is especially significant for expressways during rush hours.

The problem of congestion is illustrated in Figure 12–3. The main difference between Figure 12–3 and Figure 12–2 is that Figure 12–3 shows averages and marginal costs increasing due to congestion. In fact, Figures 12–2 and 12–3 could represent the same stretch of road or the same public transportation route at different levels of usage. As explained previously, the cost to the individual, the marginal private costs, are approximately equal to the average cost of other users. In the case of an

FIGURE 12–3 Pricing under Conditions of Congestion

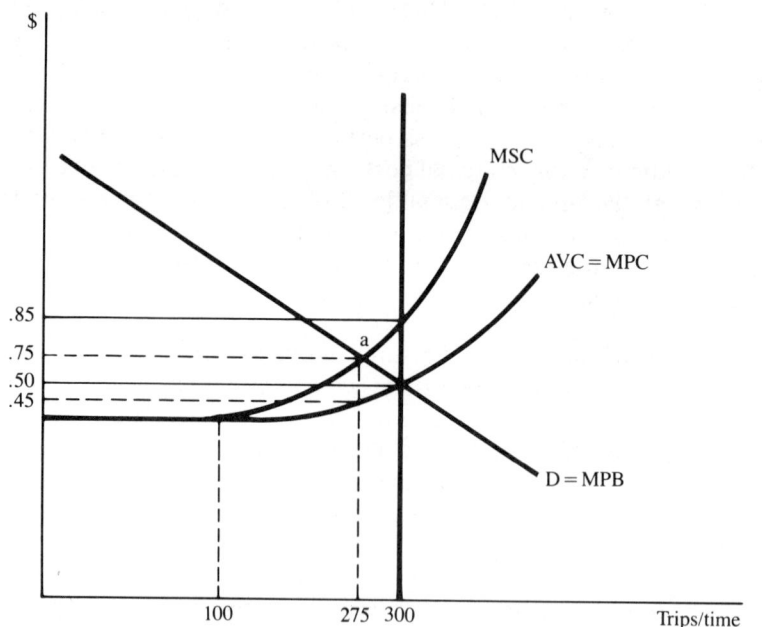

A toll of 30 cents will raise the total cost of a trip to 75 cents. At that cost, 275 trips will be made.

expressway user, these costs would include operating costs, depreciation, and time costs. As service usage increases beyond 100, congestion causes average costs to increase. Marginal social costs are greater than marginal private costs for service levels beyond 100, reflecting the congestion externality.

The benefits to the extra travel are assumed to be the only benefits from trips. Therefore, the marginal private benefits and the marginal social benefits are equal. Since the marginal private benefits (MPB) equal the maximum an individual would be willing and able to pay for a trip, the MPB curve also represents a "demand" curve.

The equilibrium traffic flow in the absence of any special congestion price would be 300, determined by the intersection of the average cost (which is the marginal private cost) and demand. At that level, the marginal traveler will impose congestion costs of 35 (85¢ − 50¢) cents on each traveler in addition to the private costs of 50 cents.

A toll of 30 cents would be appropriate in this case. The toll would increase the marginal costs for all users and would reduce the number of travelers. Reductions in the number of trips from 300 to 275 would reduce social costs by more than the reduction in social benefits. Hence, net social benefits would increase as the number of travelers dropped. The intersection of MSC and MSB at point "a" indicates the optimum level of travel, 275 trips. Reductions in service levels beyond 275 would result in decreases in social benefits greater than the cost savings.

Pricing for Added Capacity—Long-Run Adjustments

The previous case of short-run pricing assumed that the system's capacity was fixed. However, transportation planners are often concerned with whether the capacity of a transportation system should be changed. In the case of automobiles, roadways are the dominant component of capacity. Buses, airlines, trains, and subways have other types of fixed costs that limit capacity. The principle used to determine the optimum size is that capacity should be added to the point where the costs of adding capacity exceed the benefits.

Traditional Model.   Pricing can be used to reduce road usage and, hence, alleviate congestion as explained in the previous section. Congestion can also be reduced by expanding system capacity. In fact, if the costs of adding capacity are constant (expanding capacity and ridership by the same percentage does not increase average cost) then an optimum congestion toll will be sufficient to cover the capital costs of expanding capacity. Kraus (1981) has provided empirical evidence suggesting that construction costs per lane mile are constant as the number of lanes

FIGURE 12–4   Tolls to Finance Expansion

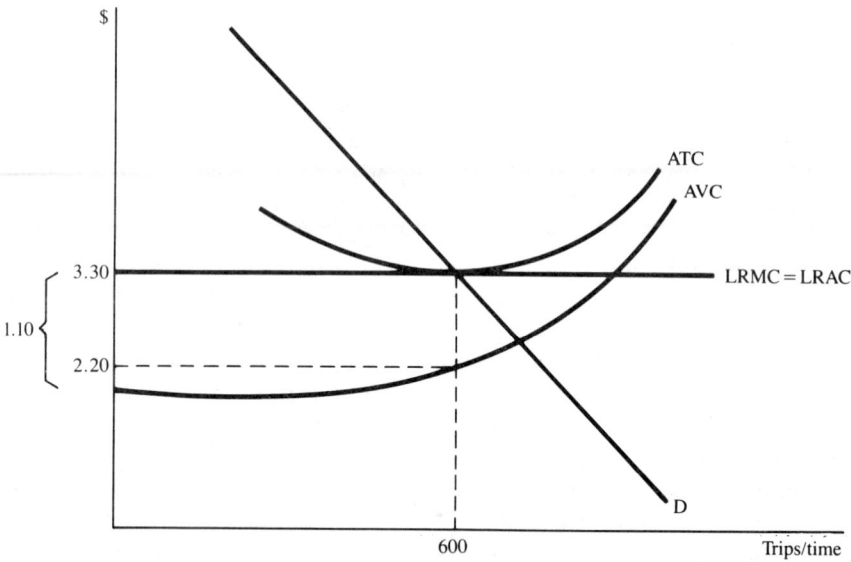

A toll of $1.10 would generate enough revenues to cover the capital costs.

increases, indicating that the assumption of constant costs is realistic—capacity can be doubled by doubling costs.

Figure 12–4 illustrates a situation in which a toll serves two functions simultaneously; that is, the toll helps eliminate congestion and finances the capital costs. The LRAC and LRMC curve represents the long-run average and marginal costs. It includes both the private costs of travel and the capital costs. The LRAC and LRMC is horizontal, reflecting the assumption of long-run constant costs. The average-cost (ATC) curve represents the short-run average cost for a road built to provide 600 trips per period. This cost includes private money and time costs as well as costs of providing capacity. The average-variable-cost (AVC) curve represents the private money and time costs for travel on a system designed to service 600 trips per period. The difference between the ATC and AVC represents capacity costs. Average capacity costs fall as the number of trips increase because the fixed-capacity cost is spread over more trips. This is represented by the narrowing of the gap between the ATC and AVC curves. Average variable costs increase rapidly when the number of trips per period exceed 600 due to time costs associated with congestion.

A toll that would limit the number of trips to 600 would also finance the capital costs of the transportation system. When 600 trips are provided, the AVC (the private costs) would be $2.20. If $2.20 were the total cost paid by travelers, the number of trips would exceed 600. A toll of $1.10 would increase costs to travelers to $3.30 per trip and reduce the number of trips to 600. Also, the toll of $1.10 would cover the capacity costs. Average capacity costs would be the difference between the average variable costs and the average total costs, or $1.10. That amount is also the difference between AVC and ATC at level 600 trips. Total capacity costs per period and the total revenues from tolls would equal $660 ($1.10 × 600).

The Benefit-Cost Approach.   Benefit-cost analysis is an alternative way of examining the need for additional transport capacity. Chapter 13 presents a detailed discussion of benefit-cost techniques. In essence, the analyst compares the marginal social benefits and the marginal social costs of a project. A necessary condition for adding capacity would be that benefits exceed the costs.

Compared to the traditional analysis, there is an important advantage to a benefit-cost study of transportation capacity decisions. All external benefits and costs are included (at least conceptually) in benefit-cost studies. The benefits should include the monetary value of (1) benefits to new travelers who previously used other routes, (2) benefits to users of existing transportation systems who will experience less congestion due to diverted traffic, and (3) benefits to new travelers who would not have traveled to particular destinations in the absence of a new route. Costs from noise and air pollution and other externalities should also be included.

THE POLITICAL ECONOMY OF TRANSPORTATION

Transportation represents an interesting combination of public and private production. For instance, cars are privately owned while the roads they travel on are public. Almost every transportation mode is influenced by public-sector decisions. This section starts with a discussion of major federal transportation programs followed by a discussion of alternative proposals—some new and some quite old.

Federal Transportation Programs

Federal programs assist both highways and public transportation in cooperation with state and local governments. The substantial federal presence in transportation provision reflects the importance of transportation to the nation and the need to coordinate state and local efforts.

Highways and Bridges.   The highway system is managed through a division of responsibility in which states and localities maintain owner- ship and primary responsibility for maintenance. States and localities also initiate new projects subject to Federal Highway Administration ap- proval. The federal government provides support through matching grants that vary depending upon the type of project.

Federal-aid highways are divided into four categories:

1. Interstate highway system. These limited-access routes connect major cities and industrial areas and are subject to the highest standards. The interstate system consists of about 43,000 miles of road—1 percent of the nation's total—and carries 20 percent of all traffic. About one quarter (10,600 miles) of these 43,000 miles are in urban areas.

2. Primary system. This is a system of interconnected roads important to interstate, regional, and state traffic, including rural arterial routes and extensions into and through cities. Excluding the interstate highways, the primary system consists of 257,000 miles of roads—7 percent of the U.S. total—but carries 29 percent of the nation's traffic. About 31,900 miles are in urban areas.

3. Urban system. This is a system of urban arterial and collector routes, exclusive of urban extensions of the primary system. It includes about 137,000 miles of roadways—4 percent of the U.S. total—and carries about 22 percent of total U.S. traffic.

4. Secondary system. This is a system of rural, major collector routes designed to provide access to rural residents. It includes about 397,000 miles of highway—just over 10 percent of the U.S. total—and carries about 22 percent of total U.S. traffic.

Spending levels for major categories are shown in Table 12–5.

An emerging issue is the need to increase maintenance spending for both the interstate system and primary highways. Estimates are that more than 75 percent of the system will need rehabilitation by 1990 (Ross, 1988). Ross concluded that the federal-state-local system of finance and maintenance must adjust the balance between new construction and maintenance in order to better maintain existing infrastructure.

Urban Mass Transportation Administration (UMTA).   Assistance for mass transit is provided through a $3 billion annual program of federal grants for public transportation. UMTA has two funding mechanisms, discretionary and formula. The discretionary mechanism requires locali- ties to compete for funds on the basis of their needs and their proposal. It is funded through the federal motor-fuels tax, and is used for major capital improvements, such as new rail systems, modernizing existing rail sys-

TABLE 12-5   Total Capital Spending of the Federal-Aid Highway Program*:
1982–1986 ($ billions)

Year	Interstate		Primary	Secondary	Urban	Total Highway Aid	UMTA
	Con-struction	4R†					
1982	$3.0	$0.5	$5.8	$1.1	$1.5	$11.9	$3.6
1983	3.1	1.3	7.0	1.1	1.7	14.2	3.7
1984	2.9	2.4	8.1	1.2	1.9	16.5	3.4
1985	2.5	3.2	8.5	1.3	1.9	17.4	3.1
1986	4.0	2.0	9.3	2.0	2.1	19.4	3.1

* Includes highways, bridges, and engineering costs, but not right-of-way costs.
† Resurfacing, restoration, rehabilitation, and reconstruction.
SOURCE: *The President's National Urban Policy Report (1988).* U.S. Department of Housing and Urban Development, Washington, D.C., 1988.

tems, and major bus purchases. The formula program, which accounts for about two thirds of UMTA funding, is used for routine capital replacement, direct subsidy of operating expenses, and a rural transportation program funded through the states. UMTA has been especially hard hit by recent budget cuts as is evident in Table 12–5.

Pricing and Rationing

One of the primary implications of the congestion model is that pricing could be used to better ration transportation services and provide an income source. Efficient pricing would require that charges for using roads should vary with particular routes and with the time of travel. Keeler and Small (1977) developed a method for measuring the appropriate fees for road usage during various time periods.

Pozdena (1988), using the Keeler-Small methodology, estimated that during peak travel times in the San Francisco Bay area a congestion tax of 65 cents per mile on major urban highways would be required to equalize marginal social costs with marginal social benefits as represented by point a in Figure 12–3. The congestion tax would be less for suburban and fringe highways. Even during off-peak hours, a fee of 3–5 cents per mile would be required on all locations. Most metropolitan areas have far less congestion than the San Francisco area, so it is reasonable to assume congestion charges would be significantly less elsewhere. Nevertheless, Pozdena's work provides a rough indication of the level of fee that might be required to reduce congestion to an economically optimal level.

Even though techniques exist for measuring optimal congestion fees, pricing in the public sector is frequently constrained by policy consider-ations. Voter-consumers may resent price increases. In the case of con-gestion fees, they may believe they are being forced to pay for something they previously received for free. However, there are several techniques that can potentially improve the efficiency of urban transportation.

Automatic Vehicle Identification.   Vickrey (1963) has suggested that Automatic Vehicle Identification (AVI) is a technological solution that could make efficient road pricing possible. Actual prices could approxi-mate the theoretically efficient levels. He proposed that each car should be equipped with an electronic device that would set off sensors placed at important intersections. A computer could record the time a car passed a certain point. Transportation planners could develop an appropriate set of prices so that it would cost more to use congested roads than less-congested facilities. Automobile owners could be billed monthly based upon where and when they drive.

The proposal for road charges based on time of day and place is a radical departure from the current system. However, such a system is technically feasible. Estimates of installation costs are less than $50 per car. An AVI-like system is in use in San Diego to charge passengers using the San Diego–Coronado Bay Bridge. Denver is planning a $1 billion beltway to be financed partly by tolls. Electronic express gates will read special identification signals transmitted from cars. Drivers with the trans-mitters will not have to stop, and the car owners will be billed automati-cally.

The Denver plan shows that AVI-like systems have potential. How-ever, there are important impediments to their widespread use. The basic hostility of voters being charged for something they may believe they get for free (i.e., paid from taxes) will create resistance. Also, the public may have concerns about privacy. Many drivers do not want records kept about where they drive. Consequently, the political realities indicate that the chances of adopting an AVI system on a large scale are practically nil. Since the best allocation system is not feasible, policies tend to establish second-best conditions.

Tolls.   Tolls on key bridges or strips of highway serve a function similar to automatic vehicle identification (Williams, 1981). However, tolls have three disadvantages. First, the cost of toll collections is high, particularly because bottlenecks occur at collection points, increasing travel time. The Denver plan may reduce collection costs if widely adopted. Second, entrances and exits must be spaced in coordination with the toll booths. Consequently, entrances and exists tend to be far apart on many toll roads, limiting flexibility. Third, toll roads do not normally vary prices to reflect time-of-day congestion. If only travelers adding to capacity could be charged, the rationing of roads would be as selective as if both peak and off-peak users were charged, but political objections would be reduced.

Parking Policies. Parking policies include restricting the availability of space either through high parking fees or shortages. Most observers believe there is potential to better regulate traffic, particularly in downtown areas, through careful parking policies. The practice of employers providing free parking for their employees contributes to congestion. Higher parking fees in congested areas will reduce the number of cars in those areas. However, parking policies alone will not solve the congestion problem.

The use of parking charges or restrictions has several drawbacks. First, failure to provide adequate parking may actually increase congestion in downtown areas if it encourages "cruising" by individuals looking for parking spaces. Second, parking fees are not related to distance traveled; yet, long-distance commuters normally cause more externalities than short-distance commuters. Third, downtown merchants want cheap, available parking for their customers. Shoppers are resistant to parking fees, so merchants are an effective lobby group against increased parking fees. Unfortunately, when parking is free or very inexpensive, merchants or employees often use the spaces all day, thereby denying shoppers parking. Fourth, parking fees do not deal directly with the problem of peak-use congestion on major commuter roads. Shoppers often enter and leave the central business district during off-peak hours. Furthermore, parking fees will not discourage travel through downtown areas that adds to congestion.

Some analysts have suggested that an automatic vehicle identification system could be integrated with parking spaces so place and time-of-day rate differences could be reflected in parking fees as well as road usage charges. For instance, an experiment in Madison, Wisconsin, imposed a $1 surcharge on cars parked in garages between 7:00 and 9:00 AM and left for more than three hours. The surcharge succeeded in decreasing traffic volume during peak hours.

Gasoline Taxes. If driving were the only use of gasoline and if all vehicles received equal mileage per gallon, then gasoline usage would be proportional to miles driven. Therefore, gasoline taxes are sometimes considered an appropriate, indirect technique for taxing individuals who use roads. The gasoline taxes are often "hidden" in the pump price, thus enhancing their political acceptability.

However, the gasoline tax fails to discriminate among users, so they do not effectively discourage congestion or charge users who cause additional capacity to be added. Major urban arteries are more congested than others. Yet, gasoline prices cannot be designed to differentiate between users of congested and uncongested roads. If service stations in congested areas were required to charge higher taxes, the price differentials would probably be sufficient to encourage individuals living in congested areas to buy gasoline elsewhere. Furthermore, gasoline prices cannot be adjusted to reflect time-of-day congestion.

Subsidized Public Transit.   Automobile congestion could be reduced if more individuals used public transportation. Therefore, some economists have advocated lowering public-transportation charges as a way of reducing automotive congestion. According to those who advocate this approach, fares should be particularly low during rush hours to discourage the use of private automobiles.

The subsidization of rush-hour fares may seem like an ironic solution. Simple theory suggests that rush-hour fares on public transit should be higher than off-peak fares since transit systems usually operate near capacity during rush hour. However, the economic principle known as "the theory of the second best" implies that if one part of the economy is operating inefficiently (i.e., private automobile use is too high) then a nonoptimal price in another part of the system may have a counterbalancing effect and actually improve overall efficiency. Thus, a price that may appear perverse if we examine only the public-transportation system may be reasonable if the scope of analysis is expanded to the entire transportation system. However, because we subsidize both roads and public transportation, there exists the likelihood that policies may encourage "over-commuting."

In practice, the extent of automobile travel has not been significantly diminished by lower public-transit rates for two reasons. First, transit use is not very responsive to price changes (see Table 12–4). Second, the extent of public transit use is so small compared to the use of private automobiles that even a larger percentage increase in transit use would result in a small decrease in automobile use. Thus, while increased usage of public transportation may have a small effect on automobile usage, it is unlikely that even the elimination of mass-transit fares will cause a major decline in automobile congestion (Mehay, 1985).

Public-Transit Alternatives

Several alternative systems for public transportation have been implemented or proposed. It seems probable that no single solution to urban transportation problems will emerge. Rather, solutions will involve combinations of transportation modes. The automobile will be the predominant carrier, but mass transit will still be necessary to relieve congestion, reduce air pollution, and to provide transportation to those who lack either the ability or income to drive a car. Transportation planners have developed several alternative transportation systems.

Commuter Rail Systems.   Fixed-rail systems are an established part of urban transportation. Light rails are similar to street cars. Newer systems such as the Washington, D.C. Metro and San Francisco's BART (Bay Area Rapid Transit) are especially fast, quiet, and attractive. They run longer distances between collection and distribution points than traditional public-transportation systems. Commuter rail systems usually provide parking lots near suburban stations so that commuters may drive from their homes to the transit points. Rail systems work best when downtown employment sites are concentrated.

The advantage of the concentrated collection and distribution points is that the collection and distribution process of most traditional bus services often requires at least one transfer. Transfers are a major cause of delays, particularly unanticipated delays when connections are missed. The concentration of stations eliminates this source of delay and can make public-transport time competitive. Since many suburban commuters have two cars in the family, the short-run marginal cost of driving to the suburban stations is low.

Fixed-rail systems are expensive. It is especially costly to acquire rights-of-way after urban development has occurred. Consequently, new systems will require almost full subsidization of construction costs in addition to some operating-cost subsidies. Even excluding the capital subsidies, the operating cost of the BART system was 2¢ per passenger mile more than the bus. Given the current budgetary outlook, it is unlikely that any metropolitan area will undertake a fixed-rail system in the future (*President's National Urban Policy Report (1988)*, pp. IV–26). Some analysts, however, believe that a fixed-rail system may be useful for interurban transportation. In such cases, trains can achieve high speed, and per mile costs of acquiring rights-of-way are lower than intrametropolitan use. An UMTA study indicated that there are many instances where the revitalization of interurban rail systems may be cost-effective (*President's National Urban Policy Report (1988)*, pp. IV–22).

Express Buses.   Express buses have very few collection or distribution stops in order to reduce travel time. Like the fixed-rail systems, express-bus systems often include suburban parking facilities to avoid transfers. Some highways include express-bus lanes so that bus riders can travel faster than commuters in private automobiles. Express-bus systems are more flexible than rail systems. They can piggyback on existing road systems, and the number of buses on a particular route can be adjusted quickly.

Jitneys, Small Buses, and Gypsy Cabs.   Jitneys are small buses or vans normally operated by owner-operators. They can provide more-flexible service than traditional bus systems. For instance, a jitney may schedule routes with more convenient stops for its customers or the drivers may provide boarding or deboarding services for mobility-impaired individuals. The extra time required to provide such services will not disrupt the schedule on a small route as much as it would disrupt a larger route. Furthermore, jitneys often "fill in the cracks" underserviced by metropolitan transit authorities. Walters (1982) described various possibilities in which small buses or vans may be more efficient than either cars or normal-sized buses.

Gypsy cabs are often operated illegally and are an important part of the urban underground economy. Most cities regulate taxis in such a way that the quantity of taxi services that individuals would be willing and able to provide is greater than the demand at the prevailing (usually regulated) fares. Taxi services are limited by restrictions on both the number of firms and the number of taxis. There are twice as many taxis per capita in cities without restrictions than in the minority of cities with restrictions (Rosenbloom, 1972). Cabs have historically been regulated in the interest of the licensed operators. The limitation of services has been particularly detrimental to the poor and minorities (Mehay, 1985).

Liberalizing the regulation of jitneys and gypsy cabs may be particularly beneficial to the poor. Poverty-stricken areas tend to be underserviced by the legitimate taxi services, partly because drivers fear crime when operating in some low-income areas. Furthermore, the low rates of automobile ownership render residents of lower-income neighborhoods more dependent on alternative transportation systems. In fact, the poor may use taxis—an expensive form of transportation—more than the middle class because the poor have such a low incidence of automobile ownership. The dependence of the poor on expensive taxi services will be increased if bus service is poor or nonexistent. Finally, since gypsy drivers are often poor, restrictions on their use will also be regressive.

Privatization and Deregulation

Reducing restrictions on jitneys and gypsy cabs is a step in the deregulation process. Individuals who favor further privatization of traditional public-transportation systems suggest that efficiency would be increased if the private sector were allowed to provide services normally provided by government. Many analysts have suggested that private companies could provide bus service more efficiently. But, since bus service normally must be subsidized, how could private firms be interested? In order to encourage privatization, some metropolitan transit agencies have allowed private contractors to bid on particular routes. They submit the minimum payment they would require in order to operate a particular route. The private company may be allowed to keep the fare, but the fare will continue to be regulated by the transit agency. Safety and other service dimensions are also regulated.

Proponents of privatization claim that it can reduce costs by 30–60 percent. A major reason for the savings is that drivers in private systems are paid considerably less than drivers in public systems. Fort Wayne hired nonunion labor to drive some of its routes and reduced the hourly wage (including fringe benefits) from the $18.95 paid to public employees to $8.50 for private contract drivers. More-efficient work rules associated with privatization have also been cited as a source of savings.

The deregulation movement is often associated with privatization because the theoretical underpinning of both groups is less government involvement in the economy. Deregulation began in the mid-1970s, especially at the federal level. In general, most economists believe that deregulation has increased the efficiency of the transportation sector. Those who want to deregulate the transportation sector point out that, while the goals of deregulation appear worthy, in practice, regulatory agencies often become captured by the industry they are intended to regulate. For instance, regulatory critics point out that the Interstate Commerce Commission regulated carriers in a way that greatly reduced price competition. Also, where deregulation has occurred, prices have tended to fall.

In the near future, transportation will probably continue to be regulated to some degree for at least three reasons. First, bureaucratic agencies tend to be self-perpetuating. Even as some regulations are dropped, new regulations will be promulgated. Second, the externalities associated with many types of transportation will require some regulation. Finally, information costs about safety are too high for the average consumer. Consequently, safety regulations appear to be necessary.

SUMMARY

Transportation issues are critical to urban and regional economies. Transportation changes affect economic prospects of metropolitan regions and the distribution of activity within regions. Changed transportation systems will affect productivity, land use, land values, and urban form.

There are several important characteristics of urban transportation systems. The high ratio of fixed costs to marginal costs helps explain why managers are reluctant to shut down transportation systems and why the planning horizon extends so far into the future. Marginal costs are especially low at off-peak times, but they may be quite high during peak hours. Costs may also be divided into line-haul and terminal costs and into time and money costs.

Externalities characterize most types of transportation. In addition to the various types of pollution, congestion is an important externality. Congestion tends to expand exponentially as traffic volume increases because extra trips both increase the number of people subject to delay and the number of delays. Downs's law of peak-hour congestion explains that it is difficult to eliminate congestion because road improvements attract more travelers.

The responsiveness of travel to changes in price, time, and income can be expressed as elasticities. The money, price elasticity for both public and private transportation is inelastic. The fact that demand for transportation is derived from the demand for other goods and services is one reason for the low demand elasticity.

A pricing issue associated with excess capacity is how to encourage extra riders. Since extra riders have near-zero marginal costs, it is efficient to encourage extra ridership. Yet, if price is lowered to reflect marginal cost, the revenues will fail to cover average costs.

When transportation systems are congested, pricing can be a tool to reduce congestion. Price should equal marginal social costs to ensure the optimum usage. Pricing can also be used to allocate additional system capacity. The principle used to determine the optimum size is that capacity should be added to the point where the cost of additional capacity exceeds the benefits.

Pricing techniques derived from economic theory are seldom implemented without modifications to accommodate political realities. Although road pricing through automatic vehicle identification systems is feasible, it is not politically acceptable. Tolls, parking policies, gasoline taxes, subsidized public transit, other public-transit alternatives, and privatization represent different approaches to achieving a more efficient transportation system.

REFERENCES

Baumol, William J. "The Macroeconomics of Unbalanced Growth: The Anatomy of Urban Crisis." *American Economic Review* 573, June 1967, pp. 415–26.

Dickey, John W.. "Urban Transportation." In *Urban and Metropolitan Economics,* ed. John M. Lewy. New York: McGraw-Hill, 1985.

Domencich, Thomas, and Daniel McFadden. *Urban Travel Demand.* Amsterdam: North Holland, 1975.

Domencich, Thomas; Gerald Kraft; and S. P. Vallete, "Estimation of Urban Passenger Travel Behavior: An Econometric Demand Model," in M. Edel and

J. Rothenberg, eds. *Readings in Urban Economics*. New York: Macmillan, 1972, pp. 464–65.

Downs, Anthony. "The Law of Peak-Hour Expressway Congestion." *Traffic Quarterly* 16, 1962, pp. 397–409.

Goldberg, Michael, and Peter Chinloy. *Urban Land Economics*. New York: John Wiley & Sons, 1984, chapter 16.

Guntermann, Karl L., and Stefan Norrbin. "Explaining the Variability of Apartment Rents," *Journal of the American Real Estate and Urban Economics Association* 15, Winter 1987, pp. 321–40.

Heilbrun, James. *Urban Economics and Public Policy*. 3rd ed. New York: St. Martin's Press, 1987, chapter 8.

Keeler, Theodore E., and Kenneth A. Small. "Optimal Peak-Load Pricing, Investment and Service Levels on Urban Expressways." *Journal of Political Economy* 85, 1977.

Knows, Marvin. "Scale Economies Analysis for Urban Networks." *Journal of Urban Economics* 10, January 1981, pp. 15–22.

Kraus, Marvin. "Scale Economies Analysis for Urban Highway Networks." *Journal of Urban Economics,* January 1981, pp. 15–32.

Lago, Armando M; Patric Mayworn; and J. Matthew McEnrow. "Transit Fare Responsiveness to Fee Changes." *Traffic Quarterly* 35, January 1981, pp. 99–119.

McConnell-Fay, Natalie. "Tackling Traffic Congestion in the San Francisco Bay Area." *Transportation Quarterly* 46, 1986, pp. 159–70.

Mehay, Stephen L. "Urban Transportation Problems and Policies." In *Urban Economic Issues: Readings and Analysis,* ed. S. Mehay and G. E. Nunn. Glenview, Ill.: Scott, Foresman, 1985.

Pozdena, Randall J. "Unlocking Gridlock." *Federal Reserve Bank of San Francisco Weekly Letter,* December 1988, pp. 1–5.

Rosenbloom, Sandi. "Taxis and Jitneys: The Case for Deregulation." *Reason* 3, February 1972, pp. 12–17.

Ross, Catherine. "Transportation Infrastructure: Current and Projected Needs" in ed. J. M. Stein, *Public Infrastructure Planning and Management,* Beverly Hills, Calif.: Sage, 1988, pp. 149–64.

Small, Kenneth A. "Transportation and Urban Change." In *The New Urban Reality,* ed. Paul E. Peterson. Washington, D.C.: The Brookings Institution, 1985.

Straszheim, Mahlon R. "Assessing the Social Costs of Urban Transportation Technologies." In *Current Issues in Urban Economics,* ed. Peter Meiszkowski and Mahlon Straszheim. Baltimore: The Johns Hopkins Press, 1975.

U.S. Department of Housing and Urban Development. *The President's National Urban Policy Report (1988)*. U.S. Department of Housing and Urban Development, Washington, D.C., 1988.

U.S. Department of Transportation, Office of the Secretary. *Public Transportation Fare Pricing.* NTIS, Springfield, Va., 1977.

Vickrey, William S. "Pricing in Urban and Suburban Transport." *American Economic Review,* May 1963, pp. 452–65.

Walters, Alan. "Externalities in Urban Bases." *Journal of Urban Economics* 2, 1982, pp. 60–72.

Williams, Stephen F. "Getting Downtown: Relief of Highway Congestion Through Pricing." *Regulation,* March–April 1981, pp. 45–50.

Chapter 13

Metropolitan Government
and Finance

Government organization has significant implications for urban and regional economies. Many countries, including the United States, have a federal system of government. In the United States, the levels of government are often divided into federal, state, and local. However, such divisions can be misleading because there are many different types of local governments with overlapping jurisdictions. For instance, a water district may serve an entire city and half of the remaining county, while a school district may serve only part of a city. The picture is further complicated because state and municipal governments differ in the type of functions they perform. In some states, the city government is primarily responsible for functions like education, while elsewhere independent school districts bear such responsibilities. Also, local governments function with varying degrees of assistance from states. Multistate regions, such as the Tennessee Valley Authority, also perform important governmental functions. The U.S. federal system has been described as a "crazy quilt" because of the patchwork nature of local governments.

The concern of this chapter is the operation of regional governments ranging from state governments to geographically small special-purpose districts. Special emphasis is given to problems of metropolitan governments, and central cities in particular.

GOVERNMENTAL FUNCTIONS IN A
SPATIAL CONTEXT

Musgrave (1959), in a classic analysis of federal government functions, concluded that government has three basic functions: maintaining a stable economy, providing an adequate distribution of income, and insuring the appropriate production of goods. Accordingly, he divided the federal government into the stabilization, distribution, and allocation branches. These conceptual branches have become a standard way of classifying federal government activities. The same framework can be used to understand the functions of state and local governments.

Stabilization and Growth

The primary tools used by the federal government to encourage economic stability and growth are monetary and fiscal policies. The conventional wisdom is that state and local governments have only limited roles to play in stabilization policy. Therefore, the stabilization and growth functions should be left to the federal government.

One reason for the conventional view is that state and local governments lack the resources to stabilize the national economy. A single state cannot tax and spend on a scale large enough to affect the national economy significantly. Another reason that stabilization policy has traditionally been left to the federal government is that local economies are so interdependent that any increase in local spending will quickly leak out of the local economy. (That is to say, the multipliers are small because of large marginal propensities to import as discussed in Chapter 5.) Therefore, the stimulative benefits from local deficits will quickly be lost to the local economy. The lack of respending within the local economy is reflected in small local mulitpliers. A type of free-rider problem would exist if stabilization policy were left to local governments. All governments would receive benefits from fiscal stimulation of other governments, but the costs would be borne primarily by the spending jurisdiction. Finally, state and local governments lack the authority to significantly influence the money supply.

In practice, many localities do engage in a type of local stabilization and growth policy, but not by using budget deficits to stimulate spending or surpluses to reduce inflation. As pointed out in Chapter 7, local and state governments have attempted to stimulate economic growth by targeting taxes and spending on particular sectors of the local economy. Through highly targeted subsidies and tax breaks, local governments are taking a more aggressive interventionist role in local stabilization and growth activities. However, no local governments engage in national stabilization efforts. Accordingly, we can conclude that state and local governments play a role in encouraging economic development, but they use spatially targeted subsidies and/or incentives rather than aggregate fiscal-policy to accomplish the goal.

Distribution

The distribution branch refers to governmental activity designed to ensure the appropriate distribution of income. It is generally believed that income-distribution activities should be a function of the federal government. If a state or local government attempted to tax the rich and redistribute the proceeds to the poor, an influx of poor and an exodus of wealthy families could be anticipated. Accordingly, the wealth base to support the redistribution would decline and the policy would fail. Furthermore, local redistribution efforts could be unfair because they would violate the principle that individuals of equal income should receive equal net fiscal residuum (taxes minus government benefits) regardless of where in the country they live.

In practice, state and local governments have a variety of redistribution programs. Many local services are provided primarily because they help the poor. The most widely discussed welfare program is Aid to Families with Dependent Children (AFDC), which is principally a state program although it receives federal monies. Many analysts have contended that state differences in AFDC payments influence the potential recipients' choice of residence. Counties and other local governments have general relief programs, food pantry programs, and so forth, so there are variations in benefit levels even within a metropolitan area. The state and local governments could continue to finance redistribution programs without encouraging relocation if state and local governments coordinated benefits. Nevertheless, the concern that local redistribution programs will result in an influx of individuals seeking to take advantage of those programs and an exodus of the individuals paying more than the benefits they receive is an important limit on local redistribution efforts.

The distribution branch activities are conceptually distinct from the allocation branch activities. While the allocation branch determines the type and quantities of goods that the government should produce, these decisions should be based on the appropriate income distribution established by the distribution branch. In the conventional framework, the allocating branch should not attempt to redistribute income by distorting the type or quantity of public goods produced.

However, in practice, state and local governments are continually mixing distribution and allocation functions. For instance, there are many services that are financed by tax dollars, yet they are received more or less equally by everyone in the district. The cost of the service falls disproportionately on the wealthy, since they tend to pay more taxes.[1] Therefore, many goods and services provided by local governments tend to redistribute income even when the purpose of the local program is not redistributive.

---

[1] Taxes are regressive, proportional, or progressive according to whether they take a lower, proportional, or higher percent of income as income rises. The wealthy generally pay more taxes in absolute dollars under each type of rate structure.

Allocation

The allocation branch deals with the good-providing functions of government. State and local governments probably have their greatest role in the allocation of resources. Three types of goods provided are pure public goods, good with externalities, and merit goods.

Pure Public Goods.   Pure public goods can be consumed by one person without diminishing the consumption of that same good by anyone else (i.e., the marginal cost of an extra consumer is zero) and the exclusion of potential consumers is not feasible. If goods have either of the characteristics of a pure public good, the private market will not provide the good in optimal quantities. If the marginal cost of an additional person consuming the good were zero, then no one should be excluded because they could not pay. But if no one paid, how would production be financed? If nonpayers could not be excluded from consuming the commodity, why should anyone pay?

National defense is a classic example of a pure public good. Everyone consumes the same amount of national defense, and nonpayers cannot be excluded. If national defense were financed privately, rational individuals (in the economic sense of utility maximizing) would refuse to pay because their individual contribution would not affect the level of services received. This is a typical free-rider problem. National defense is a national public good.

There are also goods that have characteristics of "publicness" only within the confines of a smaller geographic area, such as police or fire protection. Within a jurisdiction, everyone may receive similar benefits regardless of whether or not they pay. For instance, streets that are safe for taxpayers are also safe for nontaxpayers. It is also often impractical to exclude nonpayers from many types of amenities, such as a riverfront walkway. Accordingly, governments must provide public goods if they are to be provided at all (and force individuals to pay through the coercive means of taxation). But in what quantities?

Figure 13–1 provides a framework for determining the quantity of a public good that should be produced. Let the good be shared among the only three citizens in a community whose demand curves are shown. The individual demand curves are added vertically to determine the aggregate demand curve. If, for instance, 500 units were produced, each citizen could consume 500, unlike most goods where one person's consumption detracts from the quantity another person can consume. The vertical summation of the individual demand curves represents the monetary value placed upon an extra unit of output by all three citizens. Given the marginal cost, the optimal quantity is 500, where the marginal valuation (vertical sum of the demand curves) equals the cost of producing an extra unit, $4.50.

FIGURE 13–1   Demand for a Pure Public Good

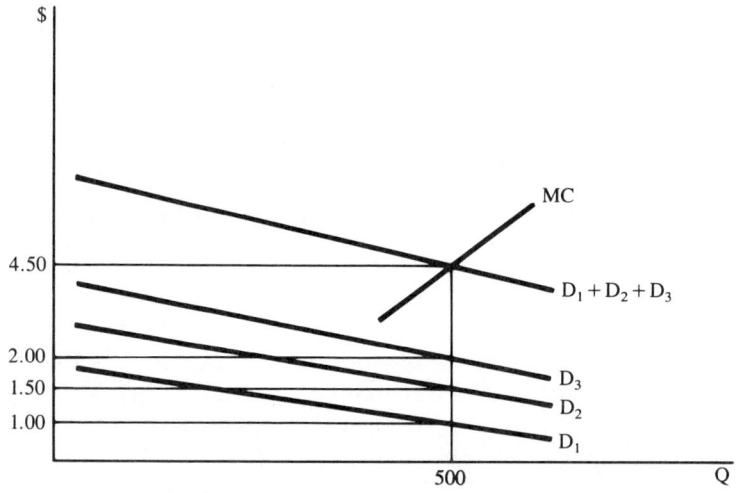

The aggregate demand for a public good is the vertical summation of individual demand curves.

While the optimum quantity of output is 500, public authorities will probably not price the commodity in a way that reflects the values that each citizen places upon the output (i.e., the individuals represented by D_1, D_2, and D_3 pay $1.00, $1.50, and $2.00, respectively). Governments lack mechanisms to induce voters to reveal the true monetary value they place upon extra units. Therefore, the cost will usually be financed according to individual tax liabilities.

The Tiebout Model Again.   The Tiebout model was described in some detail in the discussion of neighborhood change. It also has important implications for the allocation branch. In fact, Tiebout developed his model to show that citizens do have a mechanism for expressing their preferences for public goods. It is hard to determine citizen preferences for pure public goods. Because of the lack of excludability, individuals have no incentive to reveal their preferences for such goods.[2]

Tiebout showed that if local governments provided goods that were pure public goods for residents within the jurisdiction but from which

---

[2] Technically, voting schemes that would force citizens to reveal their preferences have been developed (Tideman and Tullock, 1976). But such schemes are not practical.

nonresidents could be excluded, a mechanism for revealing preferences for pure public goods would exist. Specifically, individuals would move to communities that provided their preferred mix of governmental services and taxes. Individuals would vote with their feet.

Obviously, individuals can best vote with their feet when relocation costs are zero, a condition not met in reality. The conditions necessary for citizens to vote with their feet are more closely approximated in the context of residential choice within a metropolitan area than in the context of interstate or international locational choice.

Eberts and Gronberg (1989) used the Tiebout model as the framework to examine the hypothesis that if local governments were forced to compete with one another, they would operate more efficiently. Inefficient governments would be constrained by citizens voting with their feet. They found that the greater the number of general-purpose governments within a metropolitan area, the smaller the share of personal income given to government. In other words, competition among general-purpose governments constrains local public spending.

Externalities. Goods with externalities (spillovers) are another instance where allocation branch involvement may be necessary to ensure that the proper quantity of goods is produced. Externalities may either be positive or negative. Positive externalities provide benefits to third parties, whereas negative externalities impose costs on third parties. The market will tend to underproduce goods that have positive externalities and overproduce commodities with negative externalities. Furthermore, externalities may be produced by either production or consumption processes.

Figure 13–2 illustrates two cases of externalities. Figure 13–2(a) represents a negative production externality. The only beneficiaries in consumption are the parties that purchase and consume the commodity. Thus, the demand curve (which reflects private valuation of the marginal unit) equals the marginal social-benefit curve. However, the production of the commodity imposes costs on other members of society, yet only the private costs are reflected in the supply curve. If the price were $5, the producer would be willing and able to produce 300 units. However, 300 units are greater than the socially optimal amount. The optimal level of production would be 200, where the marginal social cost equals the marginal benefit. The marginal social cost exceeds the marginal social benefit for all units produced beyond 200. In this case, the task of the allocation branch would be to reduce the level of output the market would provide. Taxes, discharge fees, regulation, and redefinitions of property rights are among the techniques that could be used to reduce the level of output to 200.

Figure 13–2(b) illustrates a good that generates positive externalities in consumption, such as a flower garden. The marginal social benefit from

FIGURE 13–2   Negative and Positive Externalities

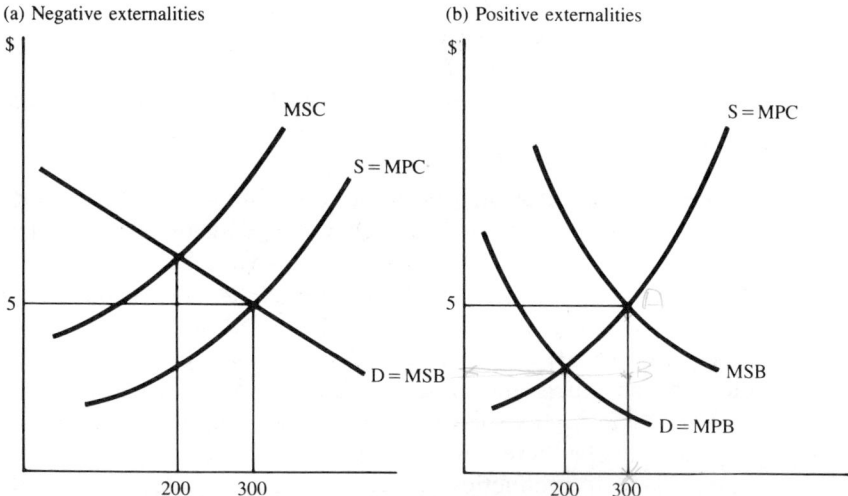

(a) Negative externalities

(b) Positive externalities

Goods with negative externalities tend to be overproduced by the market. Goods with positive externalities tend to be underproduced by the market.

the flower garden will be greater than the private benefit because nonpayers will enjoy the benefit of viewing the garden. However, the effective demand for flower gardens will depend only upon the benefit received by the party paying for the garden. Thus, reliance solely on the market will result in the actual level of output (200) being less than the optimal level (300).

The market will not account for the spillover benefits. Subsidies, regulation, and alternative definitions of property rights may be used by the allocation branch to increase the output of goods with positive spillovers.

An important drawback to the use of the externality concept as a guide to resource allocation is that almost all goods have some externalities. Therefore, almost any kind of government intervention can be justified on the basis of an externality.

Local governments face two kinds of externalities. First, they must deal with externalities that occur strictly within their jurisdictions. For instance, a crowded shopping area may impose negative externalities on nearby residents. Second, local and regional governments must address externalities that spill over to or from neighboring jurisdictions. For instance, jurisdiction A could allow a large shopping mall to be constructed on A's side of the boundary separating A and B. Jurisdiction A's actions could create externalities in the form of congestion, noise, and air pollution for residents of jurisdiction B. Problems of interjurisdictional spillovers often require methods for coordinating local actions such as grants or regulations imposed by higher governmental units. The use of grants to encourage activities with positive externalities and withholding grants to discourage regional externality activities are discussed later in this chapter.

Merit Goods.   The provision of merit goods by public intervention in the market economy is controversial. They are goods or services considered so meritorious that the market will not provide them in the optimal quantities. Higher education may be an example of a merit good. The private benefits from higher education may be sufficient to ensure that education will be provided in optimal quantities, but, because society values education so much, the allocation branch may encourage additional production. Merit goods do not necessarily generate externalities, so some scholars believe there is no justification for government intervention to stimulate their production. They believe the concept of merit goods is elitist because the market would provide the optimal amounts of such goods by traditional economic criteria. But other individuals believe that additional quantities of certain goods should be provided.

An Institutional Approach to Governmental Functions

The institutional approach to describing governmental functions is an alternative to the conceptual approach that dominates economic thinking. The institutional approach employs historical analysis to examine how and why governmental functions emerged. Goods may be provided by government because of historical values, political necessity, and so forth. The institutional approach may explain why some activities undertaken by the government have very weak theoretical justification, while other activities that theory would suggest should be undertaken by government are not. An institutionalist approach examines what goods are provided by various levels of government. In contrast, Musgrave's conceptual approach provides a framework for discussing what types of activities ought to be undertaken by various levels of government.

SIZE AND SCOPE OF LOCAL GOVERNMENTS

The discussion regarding governmental functions addressed the issue of the proper scope of government, but it did not directly discuss the appropriate size of local governments. This section explores two perspectives on governmental size. The traditional approach to optimal size has been to examine the economically efficient (lowest cost) size of production to determine the appropriate size of government. More recently, however, decision-making costs have been viewed as the most important consideration in determining governmental size.

Economies and Diseconomies of Scale

Some economists have argued that the appropriate size for a local government should be the population size that will allow the government to provide services at the lowest average cost. Suppose the average cost with regard to population resembled the curve in Figure 13–3. The average cost of services declines until the population is about 50,000 and starts to increase after the city size is over 100,000. Thus, the optimal city size could be considered to be between 50,000 and 100,000 people. The generally flat-bottomed portion of the curve is consistent with numerous empirical studies.

There are three serious problems regarding the minimum-cost approach. First, Oates (1969) and others have shown that costs are influenced by the type of people being served. "For public safety, for example, a given input of police services will be associated with a higher degree of safety on the streets the less prone are the members of the community

FIGURE 13–3   Average Cost of Government Services

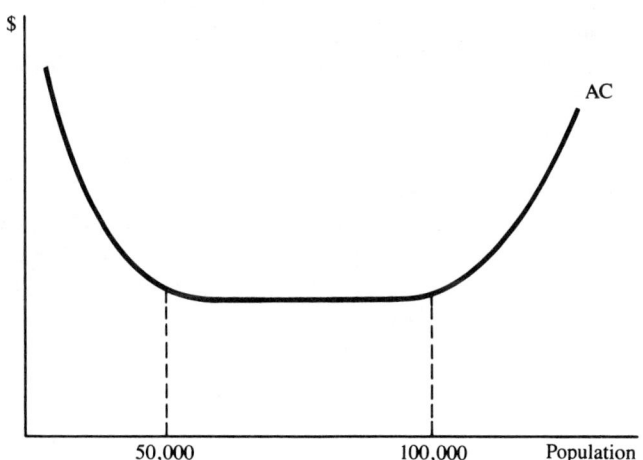

The cost of providing a basket of governmental services declines until a population size of about 50,000 is reached and increases after a population size of about 100,000 is reached.

to engage in the crime'' (Oates, 1969, p. 959). Likewise, the more able and highly motivated the pupils in a certain school, the greater may be the potential for independent study. Hence, the optimum class size or the need for special educational services may depend upon the type of students.

A second criticism of the minimum-cost approach to optimal city size is that it fails to recognize that governments perform many functions, from managing airports to providing social services. The relationship between average cost and population may be different for each function. Consequently, the lowest-cost population size depends upon the number and type of services provided by local governments. Thus, local governments in states that assign many functions to local governments could have different average-cost curves compared to local governments in states that assign few functions. Similarly, some countries have strong national governments, and cities are correspondingly assigned fewer functions. Given the various assignments of functions, it is inappropriate to generalize about the optimum size of all local governments.

A third drawback with the minimum-cost approach is that it fails to recognize that communities may purchase selected governmental services from other cities. For instance, a small city may enter into an agreement with another jurisdiction to pay a part of the cost of the fire department in return for fire protection. Since local governments do not have to produce all the services they provide, low average production costs need not be a factor in determining optimum government size. To continue the fire-protection example, the large city may have been large enough to generate substantial economies of scale in fire protection. The small city may receive the benefits of the scale economies by purchasing fire protection at a cost that reflects the scale economies.

Lakewood, California, implemented a deliberate policy of acting as a demand coordinator for the purchase of services rather than producing directly. The city manager searches for the lowest prices and buys many services from other cities as well as from private contractors. (The privatization of public services will be discussed in detail later.) The economies of scale that do exist can be captured by the lowest-bid producer willing to sell the services to Lakewood. Lakewood produces services only if the city can produce the service at a lower cost than others are willing to sell or if the function is integral to the city, such as legislative decision making. Just as purchases of services allow a small city to capture production economies, diseconomies of scale will not necessarily limit city size. Services for large cities may be purchased from a variety of producers at prices reflecting appropriate economies of scale.

Some observers object to ''Lakewood plan'' arrangements because they believe that certain functions must be produced, as well as provided, by the local government. For instance, it might be difficult to contract zoning laws or other legislative functions. The critical point, however, is that the theoretical link between optimum size and economies of scale is tenuous in light of the ability of local governments to contract for services.

The discussion of optimal governmental size should be distinguished from a substantial literature on optimal size of urban agglomerations. The discussion of optimal government size uses a minimum-cost approach. Literature on the optimal size of an urban area is primarily concerned with the external economies and diseconomies that accrue as the size of the entire area (which could include several governments) changes and affects the real income level of residents.

Decision-Making Costs

Another approach to local government size is to examine the decision-making ability of citizens as size changes. Do decisions reflect citizen preferences and are the costs of reaching a decision low? There are three aspects of decision-making costs: (1) preference mismatches, (2) decision-making effort, and (3) intergovernmental spillovers.

Preference Mismatch.   If the set of goods and services provided by government does not match the preferences of residents, then a preference mismatch exists. Preference mismatches are a necessary cost of public action. The larger the political jurisdiction, the greater the number of citizens who will be dissatisfied with the mix of public services and taxes. The mismatch between preferences and governmental performance is a political externality. Reducing political externalities reduces this aspect of decision-making costs.

What government size best satisfies the preferences of voters? The most efficient size for satisfying individual preferences would be a government serving only one person. In this case, an individual's preferences can be accommodated exactly. However, because of the nature of governmental functions, outputs must be shared, so, one person/one government is not feasible.

Preference-mismatch costs of local governments vary with the homogeneity of the population. Voting theory suggests that the preferences of the median voter will dominate decisions. In order to see this, imagine a single-dimensional issue such as the number of city police to hire. Let $n - 1$ equal the number of voters who want to hire more than 10 police officers and let $n - 1$ equal the number of voters who prefer less than 10 police officers. Let the median voter favor hiring exactly 10. The distribution of voter preferences is shown in Figure 13–4(a). Anyone running for office advocating hiring 9 or fewer police officers wold lose to a rival candidate advocating hiring 10. The latter candidate would receive at least one more vote (assuming everyone voted). Conversely, anyone advocating hiring 11 or more police officers would lose to a candidate advocating 10 officers.

Next, assume that if the actual level of service exceeds or falls short of an individual's preference by a given percent, they become dissatisfied. The greater the gap between the service level and the preferred level, the greater the dissatisfaction. The extent of dissatisfaction is a decision-making cost. In Figure 13–4(a), the citizens have relatively homogeneous preferences for the level of service provision as indicated by the small spread of opinion. Consequently, more persons are seriously dissatisfied in the population represented by Figure 13–4(b).

Figure 13–4 helps explain why dissension is much greater in some areas or over some issues than others. Areas and issues where preferences are diverse are likely to experience high levels of dissatisfaction.

Citizen Effort and Governmental Scope. Decision-making costs are also influenced by the effort or resources required to make wise decisions. Consequently, the decision-making effort depends upon the number of issues voters are expected to decide. On the one hand, proliferation of many jurisdictions usually makes decision-making harder because voters must know more potential officeholders. On the other hand, if there were only one general-purpose government, specific issues might not get the attention they deserve. Citizens would vote for representatives who would reflect their preferences only on some issues. High-profile issues, such as abortion or drug control, might dominate voter attention, while issues like the need to separate garbage might not receive attention.

Thus, in attempting to minimize decision-making costs, the scope of government should balance the ability of voters to express their opinions on specific issues with the higher information costs that would exist if a separate representative or unit of government existed for every set of public issues.

Intergovernmental Spillovers. The potential for intergovernmental spillovers is another factor that can determine the appropriate size and scope of local government. These externalities occur when one governmental unit imposes costs on (or provides services to) residents of another jurisdiction.

For example, if one government provided excellent police protection, crime may be deterred in nearby communities. Consequently, residents of neighboring jurisdictions benefit from actions of a nearby government. Conversely, if a jurisdiction provided poor public health services, adjacent jurisdictions may suffer adverse consequences. Obviously, the larger the political jurisdiction, the fewer the intergovernmental spill-

FIGURE 13–4 Preference Distribution in Homogeneous and Heterogeneous Communities

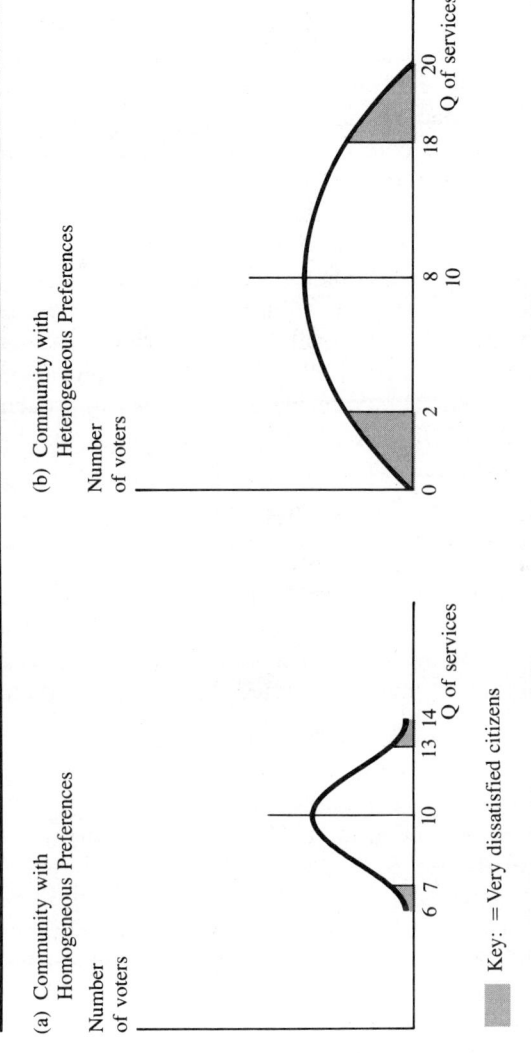

(a) Community with
Homogeneous Preferences

Number
of voters

6 7   10   13 14
                Q of services

(b) Community with
Heterogeneous Preferences

Number
of voters

0   2   8   18   20
                10   Q of services

Key: = Very dissatisfied citizens

The preference of the median voter is the most likely outcome of a democratic political process. The match between preferences and outcomes will be closer in a community of homogeneous preferences.

overs. However, larger governmental units may increase the preference-mismatch problem.

The suburban–cental city exploitation thesis is based upon the idea of intergovernmental spillovers. The thesis is that suburban residents benefit from the services provided by the central city, but they do not pay their fair share of the cost. For example, suburban residents use central-city roads but do not pay central-city property taxes. Because so many suburban residents work in the central city, they use many central-city services during the day. Suburban residents also use cultural and recreational facilities often found in the central city. Accordingly, the charge has been made that suburban residents exploit residents of the central city.

Neenan (1972) tested the exploitation thesis. He adjusted the benefits suburban residents received by their assumed willingness to pay for the service. High incomes were associated with high estimates of willingness to pay. Neenan concluded that the suburban residents exploited central-city residents. However, his approach has been criticized because of the attempt to measure and place a dollar value on the utility suburban residents received from central-city services. A simpler approach has been suggested by Ramsey (1972). He argued that central-city exploitation existed if the value of the following equation was negative:

$$EC = (CRSR - CCSSR) + (CSSCR - SRCR) \tag{1}$$

where EC = Exploitation coefficient,
   CRSR = City revenues collected from suburban residents,
   CCSSR = Cost of city services consumed by suburban residents,
   CSSCR = Cost of suburban services consumed by city residents, and
   SRCR = Suburban revenues collected from central-city residents.

The Ramsey approach assumes that both central-city residents and suburban residents may receive spillover benefits for which they do not pay. Greene et al. (1976) failed to find exploitation in their analysis of Washington, D.C. However, Washington, D.C. is a unique city because it receives large federal support to help support costs of federal employment in the city. In fact, generalizations about whether suburbs exploit central cities or vice versa cannot be supported by existing empirical studies. However, in specific cases where exploitation exists, it creates important costs for central cities.

It has also been alleged that central cities have become dumping grounds for many economically dependent individuals. Hence, some central-city residents are also exploited because they must deal with the numerous pathologies of individuals excluded from the suburbs. If you believe that drug control and education are regional rather than strictly local responsibilities, then it may follow that suburban jurisdictions should share the costs of these pathologies.

Possibly because the issue is hard to resolve empirically, the exploitation thesis has become highly politicized. Ideological predilection has become an important determinant of whether many observers believe central-city exploitation occurs. Potential central-city exploitation is often an argument in support of metropolitan consolidation efforts. The possibility of suburban–central city exploitation also has implications for intergovernmental fiscal relations and the extent that central cities should benefit from intergovernmental grants.

INTERGOVERNMENTAL GRANTS

The crazy quilt of intergovernmental relationships provides a background for understanding the role of intergovernmental grants. This section presents the rationale for intergovernmental grants followed by a discussion of the types of intergovernmental grants and their effect on the behavior of other units of government.

Reasons for Intergovernmental Grants

Two reasons are generally given for intergovernmental grants. First, there is a need to adjust for spillover effects in order to improve the efficiency of government resource allocation. Second, some intergovernmental grants are necessary to rectify fiscal disparities among jurisdictions. Grants to rectify fiscal disparities have both equity and efficiency objectives, since unequal fiscal treatment may result in inefficient relocation of households. Because grants are used to coordinate activities of smaller units of government, grants almost always flow from larger units of government to smaller units.

Efficiency and Spillovers. Externalities among local governments are common. For instance, excellent parks in one jurisdiction may be used by residents of another jurisdiction. In this case, nonpayers will receive a positive externality. Economic theory suggests that when positive externalities exist, the good in question tends to be underprovided. When negative spillovers are present, the good tends to be overproduced.

Figure 13–5 can be used to illustrate the problem. Let D_A represent the (vertical) summation of demands (marginal valuations) for a public service among residents of the providing jurisdiction. D_A was derived by the process illustrated in Figure 13–1. It shows the sum of the values residents of jurisdiction A place upon a marginal unit of the good. For instance, if 325 units of the public good are being provided, residents would place a value of $260 on the 325th unit.

However, this public good provides an externality for residents of a nearby jurisdiction. Perhaps the "good" is a public park, that is used by

FIGURE 13–5   Externalities among Jurisdictions

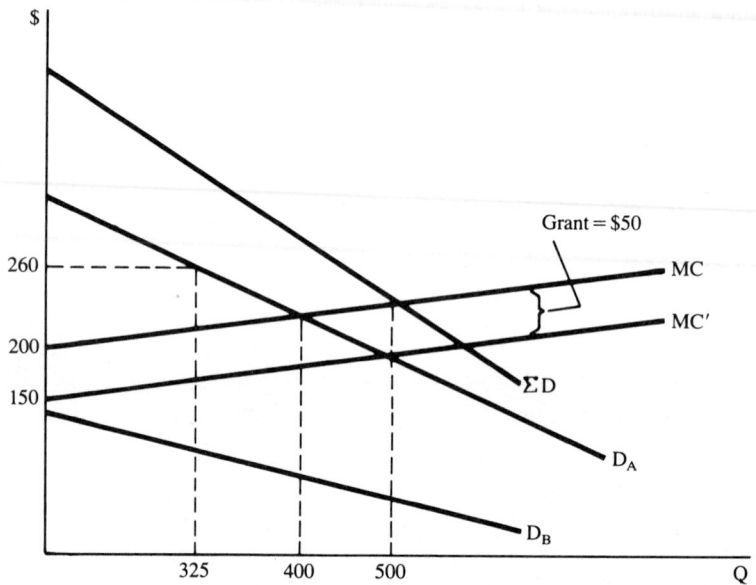

Externalities among jurisdictions can cause underproduction. A matching grant may lower the cost to the providing jurisdiction and cause output to increase.

residents of jurisdiction B. D_B represents the marginal valuation of residents from nearby jurisdiction B for parks in jurisdiction A, holding other things equal.

In order to determine the optimal level of output from the point of view of the society (i.e., the two jurisdictions) as a whole, benefits to residents in both jurisdictions A and B should be considered. Thus, in order to determine the combined level of benefits, D_A and D_B must be added, providing ΣD. Notice the demand curves were added vertically to reflect the fact that one group's use of the park does not diminish consumption of any one else's. (This implies no crowding or congestion costs.)

The optimal level of output is 500, where the sum of the two demand curves equals the marginal cost, MC. When determining the level of output, however, only the demands of residents in the providing jurisdiction A count. Residents of B have no way of expressing their demand for a public good in the providing jurisdiction; the providing jurisdiction has no way of forcing nonresidents to pay for the use of the park (assuming costs of collecting a user fee are too high). Hence, the locality would provide only 400 units. In other words, in the absence of any intervention, a suboptimal level of the public good would be provided, because no one would take the benefits to nonresidents into account.

Intergovernmental transfers can be used to stimulate jurisdiction A's output. Perhaps a federal grant of $50 per unit of the public good produced could be given, thereby reducing jurisdiction A's marginal cost to MC'. Consequently, output would increase to 500. (Figure 13–5 is based on the premise that the grant was financed without affecting the demand for the local service in either jurisdiction as might be the case if it was financed by taxes that significantly lowered aftertax income in A.) The $50 grant will encourage the providing jurisdiction to provide the optimal output.

Jurisdictions can also be encouraged to reduce negative externalities through the use of intergovernmental grants. For instance, grants for sewage improvements reduce the water pollution that affects downstream communities. Expressed differently, we could say that water purification carries positive externalities and a grant to increase purification efforts will increase the level of this output.

Equity. A second reason for intergovernmental transfers is to ensure that unequal burdens are not placed on individuals living in jurisdictions with different taxing abilities. Often, poor districts with small tax bases must impose higher tax rates on their residents and yet the district collects less total revenue than more affluent communities.

Suppose individuals A and B earn equal incomes, but A lives in a rich city and B lives in a poor city. Further assume that their tastes and preferences are the same and taxes are proportionate to income. Given the assumptions, it would be advantageous to be a resident of the wealthy community because the local tax burden would be smaller. To receive the same services, B would pay more taxes than A. This situation violates the tax principal that "equals should be treated equally." Thus, transfers to ensure that A and B receive equal fiscal residuum may be appropriate.

Furthermore, given the potential disadvantageous tax treatment of B, an incentive would exist for B to relocate to the richer community. There are two potential efficiency problems that arise from the fiscal incentive to live in a wealthy jurisdiction. First, political jurisdictions may attempt to exclude lower-income families. Fiscal zoning, in which zoning standards are so high that only wealthy people can afford to live in the area, will accomplish this end but may result in inefficient resource use. Excessive income segregation could also result in increased social problems. Second, the provision of public services is often characterized by congestion costs. Migration could increase costs in the richer jurisdiction and increased congestion could reduce the quality of services.

Types and Consequences of Intergovernmental Grants

Frequently, economists distinguish between matching grants in which the size of the grant depends upon the level of local spending and lump-sum (fixed amount) grants. Another typology is between categorical grants that must be used for a particular purpose and block grants that can be used for a wide range of purposes.

Matching and Lump-Sum Grants.   The amount of intergovernmental transfers depends upon the level of the recipient government's spending in the case of the matching grant. The lump-sum grant is a fixed amount. In order to compare matching and lump-sum grants, assume that the transfers are not financed through taxes on residents in the recipient area. Thus, we are examining only the effect of the grant, excluding how the grant was financed.

Matching grants have two effects that tend to encourage the grantee to increase spending on the service being supported by the grantor. First, the matching grant will lower the relative price of the activity being encouraged. This is called the substitution effect. Second, an income effect exists because the grant will increase the revenue and, hence, the spending ability of the jurisdiction receiving the grant. The recipient jurisdiction will tend to spend more on all activities, including the target activity. However, in the case of lump-sum grants, local spending ability will increase (income effect), but there will be no substitution effect. While the grant may be directed towards a particular activity (e.g., a $10 million grant to support education), relative prices will not change. Hence, a local government could simply reduce its own source outlays on the target activity and use the grant to maintain existing activity levels.

Matching grants are more likely to encourage spending on the activity the grantor has targeted than lump-sum grants. Since the matching grant has the effect of lowering the relative price of the target activity, city officials are likely to provide more of the lower-priced activity. Bell and Bowman (1987) compared the consequences of matching and lump-sum grants given by the state of Minnesota to cities. They found that matching grants are most stimulative and even cause local taxes to increase so that the localities may take advantage of the match. Lump-sum grants increased the level of local services, but did not influence the level of taxes.

Figure 13–6 illustrates the stimulative effects of matching grants compared to lump-sum grants.[3] Let AB represent the jurisdiction's original budget line. If all income were spent on other public activities, $20 million would be the maximum amount that could be spent. If nothing

---

[3] The next few paragraphs are intended to illustrate the stimulative effects of a matching grant compared to a lump-sum grant. They may be skipped without loss of continuity.

FIGURE 13–6   Matching and Lump-Sum Grants

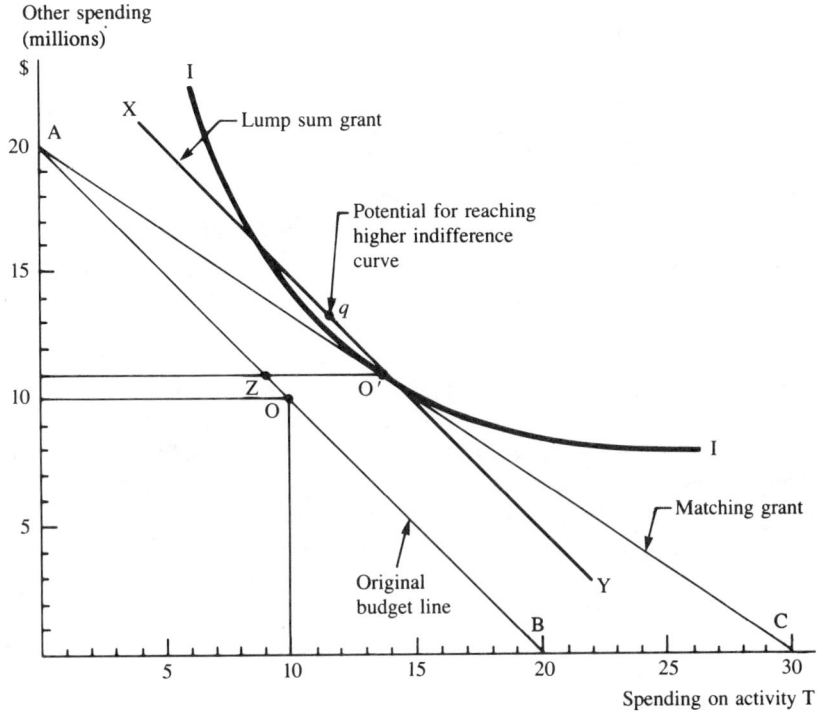

Matching and lump-sum grants will affect a jurisdiction's choice set differently.

were spent on other activities, $20 million could be allocated towards the target activity, T. Let point 0 ($10 million on each activity) represent the combination of spending that would occur in the absence of intergovernmental transfers. Now let us introduce a matching grant whereby a higher level of government matches local spending 50 cents on the dollar. The matching grant will cause the budget line to shift outward from A, as shown by AC. The greater the public expenditure, the greater the grant.

In order to determine the spending level after the matching grant, an indifference curve must be introduced.[4] An indifference curve shows the various levels of spending that would leave residents equally satisfied. The indifference curve I–I indicates that residents are equally satisfied

---

[4] How individual preferences can be aggregated into an indifference curve is a technical issue beyond the scope of this text.

with various levels of spending on other goods and the target good. Indifference curves are dense everywhere (they cover the graph), but only one is shown. Indifference curves above I–I indicate more satisfaction than the level indicated by I–I, whereas indifference curves below I–I indicate less satisfaction.

The spending level after the matching grant has been introduced would be point 0', because that would place residents on the highest possible indifference curve given the new budget line. The size of the transfer would be Z0', since that amount represents the extra spending that would occur if other spending were at the level indicated by Z on the original budget line.

Next, let us compare the matching grant with a lump-sum grant of equal size. A lump-sum grant would cause the jurisdiction's budget line to shift outward, parallel to the original budget line, as shown by XY. The parallel shift is due to the fact that a lump-sum grant will increase the area's spending ability for both activities equally. To ensure that the lump-sum grant is of equal size, the budget line would have to pass through point 0'.

A new level of consumption could be point q, putting local residents on their highest possible indifference curve. Point q differs from point 0' in two important respects. First, the lump-sum grant provided greater satisfaction for residents of the recipient jurisdiction. This is because the community has more spending flexibility. Second, there is less spending on the targeted activity under the lump-sum grant than under the matching-sum grant.

The theoretical analysis of spending effects indicates that matching grants may be the preferred type of transfer if the grantor government wants to stimulate an activity. An activity that generates positive spillovers for residents of other jurisdictions might be a candidate for a matching grant. However, if the purpose of the transfer is to equalize fiscal abilities without interfering with local decision making, the lump-sum grant may be preferable.

Fiscal Illusion and Flypaper Effects. Grants are financed by taxes so they cannot increase the average community's spending ability (and may even lower spending ability due to administrative costs). Conventional theory suggests the effect of a lump-sum tax and lump-sum transfer of an equal amount would result in a lowering of the initial budget line (the tax effect) and a restoration to the original position (the grant effect). Ultimately the budget line would not change so spending patterns should not be altered. However, empirical analysis indicates that when a higher unit of government provides lump-sum grants financed by a tax of equal amount, local expenditures tend to increase. The stimulative effects of such a grant have been explained by the fiscal illusion effect, on the one hand, and the flypaper effect, on the other.

Some economists believe that grants may create a fiscal illusion, causing residents or their representatives to believe that the marginal cost of public services is lower than it really is. A project may be supported if citizens are told it will be paid through a federal grant rather than local taxes. Another explanation of the stimulative effect is that grants give bureaucrats more control over resources, and bureaucrats prefer spending rather that reducing taxes. Although there are no illusions about the source of the grant, dollars tend to stay where they are put. This explanation has been termed the flypaper effect.

Categorical and Unrestricted Grants.   Categorical grants are transfers the granting agency earmarks for a rather narrow range of spending purposes. For instance, a state road-improvement grant would have strictly limited purposes. Categorical grants may be either lump sum or matching. In contrast, unrestricted grants may be spent on a variety of purposes, so they will not tend to stimulate one type of spending program over another. Consequently, the recipient jurisdiction has more discretion in determining how to spend the unrestricted funds. However, the term "unrestricted" should not be taken literally, because no grant is totally unrestricted. One of the most well-known unrestricted grants was general revenue sharing whereby the federal government provided funds for state and local governments. Federal revenue sharing was terminated in an effort to reduce federal spending. There are, however, a variety of states that share revenues with local governments.

Advocates of unrestricted grants believe that the smaller units of government are closer to the problem and best know how to spend the funds to satisfy local needs. Furthermore, a dollar of unrestricted funds is worth more to the recipient jurisdiction than a dollar that must be spent in a particular way. One of the hallmarks of Reagan's federalism was the reduction of intergovernmental transfers while giving local governments more spending discretion. The explanation was that the same level of benefits could be achieved with smaller, but less restricted, grants. The return of authority to state and local governments has been termed "devolution."

Opponents of unrestricted grants have argued that they merely reshuffle money rather than accomplish any clearly defined goal. Furthermore, the administrative costs of sending money to Washington and then back to state and local governments is high. However, unrestricted grants may improve fiscal equity if they return more funds to the poorer jurisdictions than they take.

Restricted grants can be very fungible. For instance, a city may receive a $100,000 transportation grant. The local budget authorities could reduce the amount of local tax revenues earmarked for transportation by $100,000 and use the grant in its place. Thus, the grant failed to stimulate spending on transportation.

In practice, the distinction between categorical and unrestricted grants is sometimes ambiguous. For instance, the Community Development Block Grant allows communities some discretion regarding how the grants are to be spent, although there are broad purposes that should be accomplished with the funds.

LOCAL FISCAL GOVERNMENT ACTIVITIES

There have been three pronounced trends in local government revenue sources: First, there has been rapid growth of intergovernmental revenues since the 1960s, particularly among larger cities. Although recent federal programs have attempted to cut back many intergovernmental grant programs, they have succeeded only in slowing the rate of growth. Second, state and local revenue sources have become more diverse. Historically, the property tax was the province of local governments, state governments relied primarily on the sales tax, and the federal government relied upon the income tax. In recent years, states have increasingly turned towards income taxes. Local governments, particularly city governments, have instituted new sales and income taxes and deemphasized the property tax. Finally, local governments are relying more heavily on user fees to finance services. Currently, smaller cities rely more heavily upon user fees than larger cities. Table 13–1 highlights some of these important trends.

Table 13–2 shows spending patterns for city governments. Perhaps the most notable feature of Table 13–2 is the consistency of the relative shares of each category. While total city spending increased nearly 60 percent between 1980–86, the share of each category remained relatively constant. Social service spending increased its share from 10.7 percent in 1980 to 13.5 percent in 1987. This may reflect a response to federal cuts (in real terms) in social service programs.

Guidelines for Evaluating Taxes

This section first discusses general criteria for evaluating taxes. Although there are numerous standards for evaluating taxes, the principal criteria are efficiency, equity, and revenue elasticity. This discussion is followed by a detailed analysis of the property tax and briefer discussions of sales taxes, income taxes, and user fees.

Tax Efficiency.   Traditionally, economists have considered an efficient tax to be one that did not alter outcomes of private economic activity unintentionally. An income tax, for instance, can be considered inefficient because a high income tax may encourage some individuals to work less. A head tax, on the other hand, will not distort the work/leisure

TABLE 13–1 City Revenues

Year	Total Revenue (in millions)	Federal Grant	State Grant	Property Tax	Sales Tax	Income Tax	Other Tax	Charges Miscellaneous	Utilities
1960	$14,915	3.1%	12.5%	27.9%	6.5%	n.a.*	3.8%	27.5%	18.7%
1970	32,704	4.1	18.9	27.5	7.6	n.a.	6.2	20.2	15.5
1975	59,744	9.8	21.8	21.7	7.8	n.a.	6.2	18.9	13.8
1980	94,862	11.5	16.8	17.8	8.3	n.a.	6.4	22.9	16.3
1981	105,431	10.7	16.1	17.3	8.5	4.3	2.2	23.7	17.2
1982	115,416	9.5	16.4	16.8	8.8	4.3	2.1	24.7	17.4
1983	124,861	8.5	15.8	16.7	9.0	4.2	2.1	25.9	17.8
1984	134,376	7.7	15.3	16.4	9.3	4.4	2.4	26.6	17.9
1985	147,672	6.5	15.8	15.9	9.3	4.5	2.5	27.8	17.7
1986	158,885	6.2	15.5	15.8	9.3	4.4	2.6	28.9	17.3
1987	169,814	5.0	15.5	16.0	9.2	4.7	2.7	29.9	17.0

* n.a. = Not available.

SOURCE: U.S. Bureau of the Census, *City Government Finances*, various years.

TABLE 13–2 General-Fund City Expenditures (noncapital)

Year	Total (in millions)	Education	Social Services	Public Highways	Safety	Housing/ Community Development	Government	Other
1970	$ 22,093	18.1%	18.3%	6.3%	21.5%	1.8%	6.8%	27.2%
1980	58,195	15.3	10.7	6.1	23.7	3.4	7.8	33.0
1981	63,485	15.0	11.5	6.0	23.8	3.6	7.8	32.3
1982	69,239	14.1	12.0	6.0	24.1	3.6	8.1	32.1
1983	73,342	12.8	14.0	6.1	24.8	3.6	8.2	30.5
1984	79,463	12.6	14.3	6.0	24.6	3.4	8.3	30.8
1985	85,855	12.6	14.7	6.1	24.8	3.6	8.4	28.8
1986	92,845	12.6	14.0	6.2	24.9	3.6	8.5	30.2
1987	100,283	12.8	13.5	6.0	25.1	3.4	8.5	30.7

SOURCE: U.S. Bureau of the Census, *City Government Finances*, various years.

choice because the taxpayer cannot escape the tax by working less. However, some taxes may deliberately distort prices in order to correct for other imperfections in the economy. Hence, a tax on a polluting product may be efficient even it if alters existing incentives.

There is a saying that "an old tax is a good tax." Once the market has adjusted to a tax, it may be more disruptive to remove an existing tax and replace it with a theoretically more efficient tax. The old tax–good tax principle implies that stability is an important efficiency characteristic.

Tax Equity.   The main criteria for judging the fairness of a tax are: (1) the ability to pay and (2) the benefits-received principle. The ability-to-pay principle asserts that taxes should be levied based upon a person's ability to pay. Equals should be treated equally and unequals should be treated unequally. Since income is a major indicator of ability to pay, the principle is usually interpreted as implying that high-income families should pay more taxes.

The benefits-received principle links tax payments to benefits received from governments. The benefits-received principle is most useful in situations where benefits of the government program accrue directly to the recipient and where the value the recipient places on the good is easily determined. A motor fuel tax is based upon the benefits principle since it is assumed that the use of motor fuel represents use of roads. Direct user charges for public services, such as garbage collection, are an increasingly popular form of user fees.

Tax Shifting.   Tax shifting must be considered when examining equity. The determination of tax equity is difficult because the person who actually pays the tax to the government may be able to pass the tax forward to consumers or backwards to producers. If a tax can be passed to someone other than the initial payer, the tax is said to have been shifted. The party that actually has a reduction in income because of the tax bears the "tax incidence."

Figure 13–7 illustrates the shifting process. Suppose S_1 and D represent the original supply and demand curves prior to the imposition of a tax. Then a fee on taxi trips between two zones equal to $1 per trip is imposed. Assume that cab drivers are responsible for collecting the tax. The initial effect of the tax will be to reduce the supply of taxi trips at each price the consumer pays. This is shown by the backward shift of the supply curve to S_2. The new equilibrium price will be $2.75. In this case, 75 cents of the tax has been shifted forward to the consumer because they pay 75 cents more than before the tax, and 25 cents is shifted backward to the driver. Often, the fare might be expressed "$1.75, plus $1 tax." When expressed this way, it appears the consumer is bearing the full incident, but, in reality, the price of the taxed service drops, forcing the producer to bear part of the burden.

FIGURE 13–7   Tax Shifting

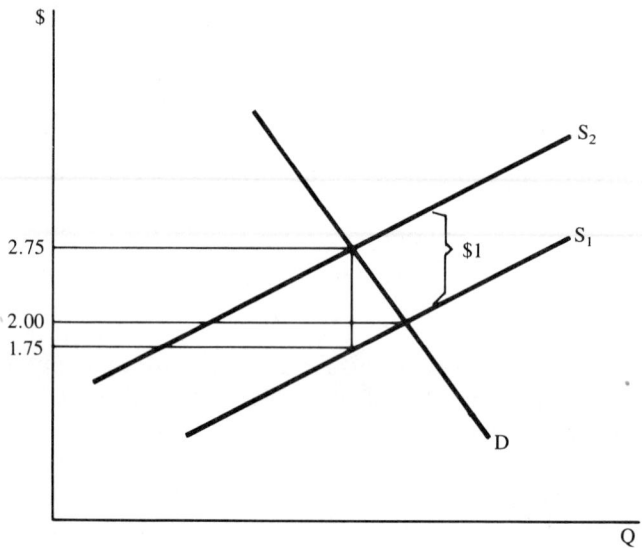

Out of a $1 tax, 75 cents will be shifted forward. In this example, 25 cents will be shifted backwards. The extent of shifting depends upon the elasticities of supply and demand.

The relative elasticities of supply and demand determine the extent of shifting. If consumers have an inelastic product demand (i.e., prices can be increased without consumers significantly decreasing their purchases), producers will be able to shift a high portion of the tax forward to consumers; but, if consumer demand is elastic, producers will have difficulty passing taxes forward. Similarly, if the product being taxed has an inelastic supply, as would be the case if the resources used in production had few alternative uses, the tax would tend to be shifted backwards to producers. Producers with greater options would tend to avoid the tax and it would be shifted to consumers. Shifting prospects have important implications for metropolitan taxing policies. Suppose a small jurisdiction imposes a sales tax on a particular type of store which consumers could easily avoid if they shop at competitive stores outside the taxing jurisdiction. Since consumers have elastic demands for products sold within one specific jurisdiction in a metropolitan area, (they can always go elsewhere) it is difficult for owners to shift the tax to consumers. Thus, the incidence will fall on the owner of the store's resources. On the other hand, a metropolitan wide sales tax is more likely to be shifted forward to consumers. Since consumers have fewer nontaxed options, their demand will be less elastic.

Supply elasticity is also an important determinant of tax shifting. Factors of production with elastic supplies can move to untaxed areas, whereas immobile factors of production cannot avoid the tax. Building upon the previous example of a sales tax, if shop owners were mobile and able to relocate to an untaxed district, they could escape the tax.

Revenue Elasticity. Another important characteristic of taxes is their revenue elasticity, their elasticity with respect to growth in the economy. One measure of tax-revenue elasticity is:

$$RE = \frac{\text{Percentage change in tax revenues}}{\text{Percentage change in national income}} \qquad (2)$$

Most communities want a tax base that increases at least proportionally to national income. However, they also desire a revenue source that is stable during economic downturns, because local expenditures are difficult to reduce during downturns. Often, these two goals conflict.

Property Taxes

Property taxes are an important source of local government revenue. Because of the historical importance of property taxes and because of their effects on urban development, more attention will be devoted to the property tax than to other tax-revenue sources.

Calculating the Property Tax Bill. The tax bill on an individual property is the product of two processes. First, the value of the property is determined in the assessment process. Assessed value (value for tax purposes) is usually less than market value, a custom that probably reduces the number of complaints an assessor receives. Individual tax bills may be appealed to special boards and to the courts.

The calculation of the tax rate is the second component of the tax determination process. Each governmental unit determines the total revenues that need to be raised through the property tax. This amount divided by the total value of taxable property in the district equals the tax rate for the governmental unit. An individual's tax bill normally represents claims by several tax jurisdictions, such as a school district, city, conservation district, and county. Each jurisdiction applies a separate rate to the assessed value of a particular property. Figure 13–8 illustrates the property tax process.

Efficiency. The property tax has been considered inefficient because the higher taxes discourage property improvements. For instance, a

FIGURE 13–8   The Property Tax Collection Process

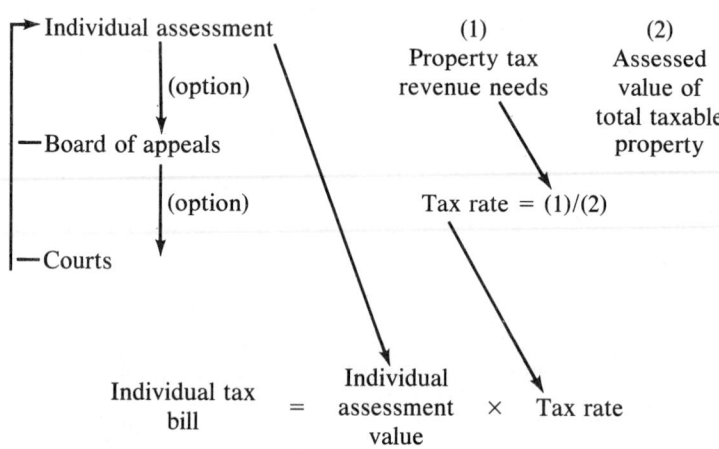

The individual tax bill is determined by the assessed value of each property times the jurisdiction's tax rate.

property owner may be reluctant to improve the appearance of a building fearing an increase in assessed value. Of course, the increased taxes will not discourage all improvements, but there may be many instances where they discourage development.

The inefficiency of the property tax is aggravated by the fact that property improvements provide positive spillovers, particularly in high-density urban areas. One individual's decision not to improve a property will tend to reinforce a neighbors' decisions not to improve their property.

Attempts to improve the efficiency aspect of the property tax include: (1) taxing land (which cannot be improved) at a higher rate than structures, (2) creating tax-incremental districts where increases in local revenues due to improvements are respent in the tax district, and (3) providing tax abatements for property improvements.

Equity.   Is the property tax fair? The property tax is considered one of the least-fair taxes. It is considered to be regressive because the poor pay a higher portion of their income on housing. The tax is hard to justify on the basis of ability to pay since a rich person with few real estate assets may not be taxed. Assessment practices vary, so owners of equal-value properties within the same district often pay different taxes. It may encourage communities to zone out low-income housing because low-valued housing does not generate sufficient tax revenues, thus, encouraging income segregation. However, before we can make a final judgement on the progressivity of the property tax, issues of shifting and incidence must be examined.

Property Tax Shifting.   The literature on property tax shifting is often divided into the traditional and revisionist views. Advocates of both views agree that land taxes cannot be shifted because the supply of land is inelastic. Their analyses differ, however, regarding the impact of taxes on structures. Since structures constitute the bulk of real estate value, the disagreement is important. The traditional view considers the property tax as a tax on real estate in a particular district. The revisionist view examines the repercussions of the property tax on capital markets, since most real property is a form of capital. These different approaches result in different conclusions regarding who bears the burden of the property tax.

1. The Traditional View.   The traditional conclusion is that property taxes on structures cannot be shifted to tenants in the short run because a tax increase will affect neither the supply nor the demand. Hence, the tax will not cause rents to increase in the short run. Landlords frequently explain to tenants that rents must be raised because of "last month's property tax increase." Consequently, some observers incorrectly believe that the tax is actually passed to tenants in the short run. However, the traditional view is that in cases like this, landlords would have increased rents in any event—they would charge equilibrium rents—and the property tax increase is simply used as an excuse. Thus, in the short run, landlords, not tenants, bear the burden of the property tax.

In the long run, the jurisdiction's tax increase will reduce the supply of property from what it would have been. New construction may be reduced and existing properties may not be maintained as well. Hence, the supply curve will decrease, causing rents to rise until the rate of return on local property is equal to the rate of return on property elsewhere in the United States. Thus, in the long run, tenants bear the burden of property tax increases.

By similar reasoning, commercial property owners may not be able to shift the burden of the property tax in the short run, but the tax may be passed to local consumers or owners of resources used in business in the long run. Suppose the owner of a commercial property attempts to pass a property tax increase forward to tenants who own a business. If the businesses were in a competitive industry in a local market, the owners must either raise prices to cover the property rent increases or go out of business. If some of the firms went out of business or left the area, supply would decrease and prices increase, providing the mechanism for shifting the tax on business property to consumers. If a competitive situation did not exist originally, some local firms may have been earning excess profits due to monopoly power prior to the tax increase. These firms may not have better capital investment opportunities outside the area. Therefore, it may not be profitable to relocate in order to avoid the tax, even in the long run. In this case, the owners of the resources used in the business will bear the tax. If labor and capital are mobile, the incidence is likely to fall on the entrepreneurs with monopoly power. Finally some firms may sell their products in competitive national markets. If the jurisdiction in which such firms were located pursued a tax policy that resulted in rents increasing, the business would be unable to pass the tax forward. Since it was a competitive industry, it would be earning only normal profits. Hence, a property tax–induced rent increase would force the firm to relocate, shift the incidence to the immobile factors of production (i.e., lower wages for workers) or go out of business.

2. The Revisionist View.   The revisionist view is the same as the traditional analysis of shifting in the short run. However, revisionists contend that a nationwide tax on structures would be borne by capital owners in the long run. The revisionist reasoning assumes that the aggregate supply of capital is inelastic because savings are not affected by the rate of return. In other words, the supply of savings is inelastic. If a property tax increase caused capital to be withdrawn from real estate and invested elsewhere, the rate of return on other investments would fall. Since the aggregate supply of capital is assumed to be inelastic, the total supply of capital will not change. Thus, owners of capital bear the burden of the property tax in the long run.

In the long run, property tax rate differentials between jurisdictions will decrease the supply of real estate in the higher-taxed districts. However, tenant mobility will make it difficult for property owners to shift the tax burden forward to tenants. Capital will leave a higher-tax jurisdiction until the local rate of return equals that in the rest of the United States. The mobility of both households and capital will enable both to escape the higher tax rates. The jurisdiction's higher property tax will be borne by the only immobile factor—land. Land rents will decline.

A nationwide tax on business structures would rest on capital for the same reason that a tax on residential structures rests on capital. However, different tax rates between jurisdictions may rest on either capital owners, consumers, or workers, depending upon their relative mobility. To the extent that product demand is inelastic, a portion of the tax on business structures may be passed forward to consumers. However, if the firm sells in a competitive national market, then it will be unable to pass the tax forward. It may also be possible for the property owners to shift the tax backward to immobile factors of production, such as land or certain types of labor.

Revenue Elasticity.   The property tax is income inelastic. Thus, the property tax base tends to be more stable than the aggregate economy. In times of aggregate economic expansion, local governments are often pinched between rapidly rising prices and demand for services, on the one hand, and a slowly rising property tax base, on the other. Such a fiscal problem might be solved by increasing property tax rates, but, of course, the rate increases are politically unpopular.

Sales and Excise Taxes

Sales-related taxes account for about 15 percent of local revenues, although there are great variations among states. A sales tax that covered all spending would probably be regressive because the poor spend a higher portion of their income than the wealthy, who save a higher portion. However, most states exempt certain purchases from the sales tax in order to reduce the burden on the poor. All states exempt rent, most states exempt drugs and medical services, and many states exempt food and clothing. However, the more exemptions, the less efficient the tax because spending will be distorted to non taxed goods. Therefore, there is a trade-off between equity and efficiency. The sales tax is based on the ability-to-pay rather than the benefits-received principle.

Sales tax revenues tend to increase proportionally to income, so revenues expand as regional economies expand. They are also easy to administer and relatively inexpensive to collect.

Income and Payroll Taxes

State and local governments have increasingly been turning to income and payroll taxes as revenue sources. State governments tend to rely on income taxes that are modeled after the federal tax. Payroll taxes are more common among local jurisdictions. Payroll taxes are assessed on earnings at the place of employment. Thus, central cities benefit from payroll taxes because employees who work in the city but live and shop in suburban communities will pay the central-city payroll tax.

Payroll taxes are justified on both ability-to-pay and benefits-received criteria. With regard to the ability-to-pay standard, city income and payroll taxes are seldom progressive (that is, tax as a percentage of income does not increase with income), but they do require that higher-income earners pay more. With regard to the benefits principle, it has been argued that individuals use public services where they work as well as where they live. Therefore, the payroll tax has a benefits component, although the level of benefits individual workers receive is not linked directly to their tax liability.

Neither state nor local governments have high or very progressive tax rates because they must calibrate their tax rates based upon jurisdictions that also compete to attract business activity. Ohio recently decreased the progressivity of its income tax because officials were convinced that high-paid business decision makers avoided locating businesses in the state because of its high personal tax rates. Likewise, many New Yorkers believed an exodus of businesses from New York to Connecticut was attributable to the high New York income tax rate combined with the absence of a payroll tax in Connecticut.

User Charges and Fees

User charges have grown rapidly during the 1980s. They are consistent with the benefits-received principle since they require the users of a service to pay all or part of the cost of the service. Sometimes, "sliding scale" fees are used that link the user charge to income. Thus, an ability-to-pay standard also can be applied to user fees. The recent popularity of user fees can be attributed to four factors. First, they help ration public services and, thus, alleviate pressures to produce more. When a good or service is free, it tends to be used until consumers receive no more utility from an extra unit. Second, user fees can help reduce congestion. By increasing the user fee, usage can be reduced. Well-designed user fees can also be used to spread usage away from peak-use times. Third, user charges provide decision makers with information regarding citizen valuation of goods and services. If a small user fee causes usage to fall drastically, policy makers may conclude that most users place a low value on it. Finally, user charges are a revenue source. Since many communities face tight budgets and political pressures to increase spending, additional revenue sources are usually welcome.

However, there are important limitations to user fees. Principally, user charges are generally only appropriate for goods that could be provided privately. Thus, public swimming pools and other recreation facilities are susceptible to user charges. However, goods with characteristics of nonexcludability are not suitable for collection of user fees. Also, services and transfers designed to correct for problems of income distribution are not suitable for user-fee financing. Often, local governments face stiff opposition when they impose user fees because of a type of fiscal illusion. Some citizens believe they will have to pay for something they previously received for "free." The political problem of establishing user fees is aggravated by the fact that users of some services where user fees could be applied are a well-defined group that can lobby effectively to avoid charges for their services.

REASONS FOR FISCAL PROBLEMS

This section examines fiscal problems among local governments. First, the meaning and measure of fiscal stress is discussed. Next, several major ideas about causes of fiscal stress are presented. The reasons for fiscal stress are generally complementary rather than mutually exclusive explanations.

Measuring Fiscal Stress

There are two approaches to measuring fiscal stress. The "funds flow" approach identifies city-government fiscal or budgetary characteristics. This approach implies that the causes of fiscal stress can be traced to budget management. If a budget is poorly managed, any city, no matter how wealthy, could experience fiscal stress. Measures of fiscal stress include current account surplus or deficit as a percentage of revenue and average debt service costs as a percentage of total revenues. These and related fiscal measures have been combined into rather complicated indexes.

The "socioeconomic" approach employs demographic characteristics in association with governmental fiscal measures. This approach implies that an area's fiscal health can be determined by comparing resources and needs. Needs are determined by socioeconomic characteristics such as community income, infrastructure age, population change, and per capital income. The level of spending needed to bring the local government to a certain norm, such as a U.S. average, is compared to the ability to support that norm such as community wealth or income. Thus, areas with a high ratio of needs to resources will have high fiscal stress regardless of the area's budgetary deficit or surplus.

There is substantial evidence that the condition of a local economy affects the level of fiscal stress. Bradbury and Ladd (1985) examined the revenue-raising capacity of large cities between 1970 and 1982. They found that adverse changes in the local economies, such as job losses, filtered through the tax system and had deleterious effects on the ability of cities to finance public services with their own resources. Almost 30 percent of large, central cities experienced declines in fiscal capacity in the 1970s. Cutbacks in federal assistance during the 1980s undoubtedly aggravated the problem. Although improvements in fiscal capacity can be expected as local economies improve, Bradbury and Ladd concluded that localities need more flexibility in creating revenue-raising instruments.

Both measures of fiscal stress can be useful depending on the nature of the problem. The socioeconomic approach is more useful to measure the ability of local governments to support service needs or to deal with their internal problems. The ratio of needs to resources is likely to change more slowly than flow-of-funds measures because demographic trends and spending needs are more stable than line items in an annual budget. The funds-flow approach might be most useful if the concern is a fiscal crisis such as a jurisdiction's inability to meet short-term obligations. Even a city composed of wealthy families could experience short-term fiscal problems because the local public sector can have a deficit even when the private sector is growing.

There is significant variance among states regarding the responsibility of local governments and their access to revenues. Consequently, analysts should be careful that measures of fiscal stress account for interstate differences in fiscal responsibilities.

Productivity and Baumol's Disease

Baumol (1967) viewed the inherent nature of local government services as a contributing reason for fiscal problems. He argued that many local governmental activities are service intensive and, therefore, are less likely to benefit from cost-saving technologies. For instance, law enforcement technologies are unlikely to replace police officers. In his model, goods and services are divided into: (1) technologically progressive activities and (2) activities that are not susceptible to substantial productivity increases. The first type of activities were called progressive and the second type, which Baumol believed constituted most public activities, are nonprogressive. Baumol contended that the most important reason for an increase in productivity is that capital and knowledge can be substituted for labor for some activities. For other activities, labor is practically the end product, so it is difficult to increase labor productivity. The division of goods and services into only two sectors is procrustean, but it is a useful classification for his purposes.

Baumol assumed that wage differentials (adjusted for skills and working conditions) between the two sectors would remain about equal. If the differential temporarily increased, workers would move into the higher-wage sector until the initial wage differences were reestablished. Baumol also assumed that the wages of workers in the progressive sector would rise based upon increases in productivity.

Wage and Price Effects.   As productivity in the progressive sector increases, wages will increase. Since workers in the nonprogressive sector can substitute for workers in the progressive sector (at least in the long run), nonprogressive wages will also increase. In the progressive sector, the wage increases will not cause prices to increase because the wage increases will be offset by increases in productivity. However, in the nonprogressive sector, the wage increases will not be matched by productivity increases, so prices will rise.

Table 13–3 illustrates the situation. In Period 1, wages in the two sectors are equal, $10 per labor unit. Assume for simplicity that labor is the only cost and that the output is sold in a competitive market. Prices are determined by dividing the price of a labor unit by the output pro-

TABLE 13–3   Baumol's Disease

	Period 1			Period 2		
	Wage	Units of Output per Labor Unit	Price	Wage	Units of Output per Labor Unit	Price
Progressive sector	$10	20	$ .50	$20	40	$ .50
Nonprogressive sector	10	10	1.00	20	10	2.00

duced by a unit of labor. Accordingly, prices are 50 cents per unit in the progressive sector and $1 in the nonprogressive sector in Period 1. In Period 2, productivity and compensation doubled in the progressive sector, so prices remained the same. However, in the nonprogressive sector, both wages and prices doubled. Wages doubled because of the wage increases in the progressive sector. Prices increased because there was no productivity increase to accompany the compensation increase. Notice that if wages remained constant in both sectors, the relative price of the output in the nonprogressive sector would still increase.

Implications.   Baumol believed that public sector services tended to be nonprogressive because it is difficult to apply technology to many areas of social services. There is a fixed or nearly-fixed ratio of service providers to recipients. For instance, a public school teacher may find it difficult to increase class size beyond 20 students. The ratio of pupils per teacher may be increased slightly by using computers and other educational technology, but the scope of such productivity enhancements is limited. Yet, if teachers' pay is to remain in line with compensation in other occupations, the per pupil cost of education will rise. If local governments provide a disproportionate share of nonprogressive services, there will be a tendency for taxes to increase or for local governments to face fiscal crisis. The increased productivity in the progressive sector will provide society with the extra wealth to continue to be able to purchase nonprogressive services, but Baumol's point is that government cost increases should be expected. Understanding the reasons for the tendency of urban governmental costs to increase may diminish some voter opposition to tax increases. Nevertheless, governments should look for opportunities to use technologies to minimize costs in those areas where such adaptations are possible.

Federal Mandates and Regulations

Mandates are responsibilities imposed on one level of government by another. Normally, the federal government, the judiciary, or state governments impose duties on local governments. Mandates may be required directly or as a condition for receiving aid. In either case, local governments are usually effectively forced into actions that may increase costs.

It has been estimated that local governments face over 1,200 federal mandates. Obviously, a discussion of the pros and cons of the various mandates is well beyond the scope of this chapter. However, a sampling of a few mandates is informative:

Davis-Bacon Act.   Wages paid for public construction must be at the prevailing wage.

The Rehabilitation Act of 1973.   Prevents federal-grant recipients from discriminating against the handicapped in service provision, causing significant expenditures to provide access and otherwise make facilities usable to the handicapped. School districts have been notably affected by this provision.

Equal Employment Opportunity Commission Hiring Procedures. Hiring guidelines have added to personnel administration costs.

The Environmental Protection Agency.   The federal courts have frequently required local governments to undertake costly waste-management and water-management projects.

The Department of Transportation.   Regulations on handicapped access have caused costly changes in urban transportation systems.

In order to alleviate problems of imposed costs on local governments, the federal government has started to weigh the benefits of a regulation against its costs and to consider alternative means for achieving the objective at lowest possible cost. Perhaps regulatory agencies should have a "cost-imposition budget" limiting the dollar amount of costs they can impose on local governments.

Underfunded Obligations

It is often appropriate to set aside some current revenues for obligations that will occur in the future. If adequate provisions are made for future obligations, they can be paid without borrowing or without sharp tax increases. However, if such obligations become due and the community lacks sufficient reserves, then a fiscal crisis could result.

Reserves are necessary to provide for the repair and improvements of pubic roads, buildings, sewers, and other infrastructure. Several studies have indicated that state and local governments are not adequately setting aside reserves for infrastructure needs. Starting in the mid-1960s, capital spending by state and local governments started to decline, particularly for capital maintenance in large cities. For the United States as a whole, Kaplan (1988) projected a $400 billion shortfall between revenues set aside for infrastructure repair and upcoming needs. The shortfall is the result of an unwillingness to raise taxes, other budgetary pressures, and lower-than-anticipated government revenues.

Infrastructure maintenance can be deferred, but, eventually, bridges will become unsafe, roads will require major repairs, or sewers will leak and collapse. Then, cities must either borrow to make the necessary repairs (borrowing may affect the community's credit rating) or close the particular facility.

Public employee pensions are another underfunded obligation in many communities (Ferris, 1987). Cities provide pension plans for their employees, often in lieu of increased current compensation. But they have not fully funded the pension obligations, so they do not have sufficient money saved to pay the pension obligations they have incurred. Therefore, as employees retire, city governments must finance pension obligations from current revenues. The demographics of public employment suggest that pension obligations will increase in the future and contribute to urban fiscal problems.

Perverse Incentives: A Public-Choice Perspective

Public choice is a branch of economics that studies decision-making processes in the public sector. The public-choice perspective provides insights about governmental institutions and incentives that help explain behavior that leads to fiscal crises. Proponents of this theoretical view of the public sector have supported many efforts to bring competitive forces into government.

The view that public officials are altruistic in contrast to the selfish motives that dominate the private sector is naive. The naive view may be supplemented by the contention that public officials know what is good for their community better than the typical citizen. In contrast, the public-choice perspective is that everyone acts in their self-interest, regardless of whether they are in the public or private sector.

In the ideal competitive market, forces ensure that individuals in pursuit of their self-interests will behave in the public interest as if they were led by an "invisible hand." But where is the invisible hand in government? The public-choice approach suggests that governmental incentive systems should be designed to simulate an invisible hand and make the self-interests of government officials better coincide with the public interest.

Elected Officials. Rather than trying to achieve the public good, elected officials may use their office to maximize their own self-interest, subject (usually) to legal constraints. Since "self-interest" is too broad a concept to be useful in predicting behavior, many public-choice economists assume that public officials seek to maximize their chances of being reelected or of gaining higher office. Frequently, politicians will enhance their chances of being reelected by doing what is in the public interest, but this is not always the case.

The public-choice perspective explains the tendency to underfund anticipated future obligations. Most political leaders have short-term policy horizons, maybe lasting only until the next election. Therefore, they are understandably reluctant to set aside money to meet an obligation that will become due in 15–20 years. From their perspective, it is better to use the resources to provide benefits to voters today and let future officials concern themselves with obligations of the more distant future.

Also, the public-choice perspective explains the power of narrow special-interest groups. Most citizens are uninformed and/or don't care about the outcome of most public decisions. For instance, only a few of the residents of a neighborhood would care whether new equipment were installed in a playground. Yet members of a special-interest group (in this case, those with small children) may feel strongly about that decision. Their votes and campaign contributions may hinge on the outcome of that single issue. In order to maintain office, it may behoove politicians to decide issues in favor of special-interest groups.

Bureaucrats. Bureaucrats may also have perverse incentives. Bureaucrats may seek more pay, better perquisites of office, or hassle-free work environments rather than better serving the citizens. Also, public employees operate under looser constraints than employees in profit-seeking firms because (1) public outputs are often difficult to measure, (2) responsibility for performance is often vague ("buck passing" is likely), and (3) there is no bottom line to measure success. Public agencies have been shown to produce some outputs at higher costs than their private-sector counterparts, providing some evidence of public inefficiency.

In addition to a tendency to be inefficient, public employees may have incentives to expand services beyond the level desired by most citizens. After all, most people would rather be director of an agency with a $10 million budget and 50 employees than an agency with a $100,000 budget and a secretary. Consequently, bureaus lobby legislatures for more funds and new programs. Essentially, they become another special-interest group.

Public workers also constitute an important voting block that would probably support higher pay and better working conditions for local government workers. Gramlich (1976) viewed the voting power of New York

City employees to command better compensation as a factor that contributed to New York's fiscal crisis. He pointed out that:

> If each (city government employee) was married, lived in the city, and had one close friend or relative who would vote alike on city issues, conceivably 1,350,000 votes, 30 percent of the entire voting age population and roughly half the probable number of voters, could be marshalled in favor of making some concessions to . . . unions. (p. 417)

Cumulative Decline

Fiscal problems can lead to cumulative decline. For instance, a city facing a small fiscal problem may have to raise taxes or lower spending in ways that reduce the attractiveness of the community. As attractiveness diminishes, individuals may relocate to another city. The potential to relocate due to local fiscal policies is greater in metropolitan areas than in isolated cities, because, in metropolitan areas, it is much easier to change residences without changing jobs. Thus, the tax base will shrink, leading to more revenue loss and/or service cutbacks.

Service cutbacks may cause property values to fall, aggravating fiscal problems in several ways. First, individuals purchase houses with some hope of building equity through appreciation. If property values fall, this expectation of appreciation could be diminished, causing further decline in real estate prices. Second, the decline in property values may cause tax rates to increase. If revenue requirements are unchanged and there are no compensating increases in other revenues, then the tax rate would have to increase in proportion to the decline in the tax base. Third, the drop in property values may cause the composition of the community to change. Particularly, if lower-income groups that required expensive public services moved into the city, the demographic change would add to the fiscal stress.

Population declines can also contribute to cumulative fiscal distress even if demographic changes do not occur. Many of the costs of urban infrastructure are fixed, regardless of population size. The maintenance costs of sewers and roads, for instance, will vary little with population size. Yet most local revenue sources depend upon population size. Tax revenues may decline more rapidly than the expenditures required to provide desired services. Thus, the fiscal problems will increase, leading to further population loss.

Cumulative decline is not inevitable, and many cities have stabilized their fiscal position after a major fiscal crisis. The choices made by political leaders and other public groups may halt successive rounds of service cuts or tax increases. The health of the private-sector economy can also help avoid cumulative decline if there are business expansions that compensate for the initial fiscal shortfall. Nevertheless, there is a danger that, once a local fiscal unit raises taxes or cuts services, it may be on a slippery slope of decline.

FISCAL STRATEGIES AND TOOLS

Many areas face substantial fiscal pressures. Often, annually balanced budget requirements further reduce local options. The federal deficit and fiscal strain in many states have made increases in intergovernmental revenues an unlikely source of additional funds. Consequently, local governments are looking for alternative solutions. This section describes some of the fiscal strategies and decision-making tools being used by local governments.

Privatization and Shedding Responsibilities

Many individuals consider private-sector activities to be more efficient than public operations. The private sector has been shown to provide some services at a lower cost than governments. If the private sector is in fact more efficient than government, citizens may be better served if private businesses delivered services traditionally provided by governments. Even if efficiency were not a concern, financially pressed governments might want to shed some activities and let them be provided by businesses if an effective demand for the service exists. In addition to shedding responsibilities, local governments have attempted to act more like private producers.

Local governments have relied more heavily on user fees that are similar to private sector prices. Governments can act more like private organizations if agencies change appropriate prices. Privatization can also be achieved when local governments contract with private firms to provide a service the government previously provided. For instance, a school district may contract with a private institution to provide special testing services. Private organizations have been hired to provide services such as school lunches, transportation, and safety services. Franchises have been used to privatize public services. A local government may grant the right to provide certain services to private producers. The private provider may charge the public for the services although the price and conditions are regulated by the terms of the franchise agreement. Several states use a franchise system to collect fees for automobile license plates.

Voucher systems allow the government to pay for a stipulated service level, but the choice of provider is left to the individual. The voucher will support a minimum level of service, and if recipients wish to spend in excess of the voucher amount, they may do so with their income. The individual is responsible for arranging for the services, and the service will normally be produced by a private source. Food stamps are the most well-known type of voucher, and, recently, the federal government has provided housing assistance through a voucher. President Bush has proposed using vouchers in education. Although vouchers are not widely used by local governments, their popularity is increasing.

Traditionally, local governments have relied upon volunteers to provide many services, and the interest in using volunteers is increasing. The use of volunteers in schools, social service agencies, and other organizations has been viewed as a way to expand services at modest costs. Recently, the concept of volunteerism has been expanded as governments have negotiated formal arrangements with businesses—*public-private partnerships*.

Intergovernmental Rearrangements

Several types of intergovernmental rearrangements have been suggested to relieve pressures on local governments. These include reassignment of functions, regional tax-base sharing, and annexation.

Reassignment of Responsibilities.   The reassignment of responsibilities is a solution that usually involves shifting the financial burden upward where the ability to pay is perceived to be greater. There are two limiting problems, however. First, as fiscal responsibility shifts upward, there is a tendency for control to shift upward, too. Yet many programs are best controlled and administered at the local level where opportunities and needs can be seen more clearly. Thus, the ability to shift programs upward is hindered by the propensity to lose local control. Second, higher units of governments may not necessarily have greater fiscal ability. After all, the state's taxable base is ultimately equal to the sum of the individual areas that make up the state.

Tax Sharing.   Under tax sharing, increases in metropolitan taxes are shared among local jurisdictions. For instance, suppose industry and the property tax base is growing in a northern suburb while the central-city tax base declines. Under a tax-sharing system, the growing district might turn over a certain percentage of the increase in taxes to the central city as well as to other local jurisdictions.

Tax sharing has been supported for at least three reasons. First, employment growth often depends upon a variety of regional factors including a vibrant downtown. Expenditures of the central city often make the entire region more attractive to industry, so the central city should benefit from growth that occurs elsewhere in the region. Second, the central city and older suburbs tend to be the residence of many low-income families. Thus, they become responsible for what is often considered to be a regional responsibility. Third, tax sharing may reduce the zero-sum game aspect of intrametropolitan competition among jurisdictions attempting to enlarge their tax base. Such competition has resulted in such generous tax abatements that even jurisdictions with increasing employment and industrial tax bases fail to increase their revenues.

Annexation.   Many communities have attempted to solve fiscal problems through annexation. If a city annexes industrial or commercial areas, it may expand its tax base by more than the cost of providing services to the annexed area. Likewise, annexation of undeveloped land can provide sites for the growth of future taxable property.

Unfortunately, few central cities can benefit from annexation. Most central cities are surrounded by incorporated suburban cities, and it is usually difficult to annex an incorporated area. Furthermore, many suburban areas resist annexation by major cities because of the poor image and other problems that central cities have. However, annexation is a possible way that isolated towns or suburbs near the metropolitan fringe may alleviate fiscal problems.

Fiscal-Impact Studies

City planners often have the responsibility of evaluating proposed housing developments to determine their desirability. A community may wish to discourage some types of development if the costs to the community, such as the public infrastructure that may be necessary, outweigh the benefits. Of course, the costs and benefits may include other factors besides the impact on the treasury, but fiscal impacts are usually a primary consideration.

Fiscal-impact analyses are useful for forecasting the effects of development projects on an area's fiscal health. They vary greatly in scope and detail. However, there are certain steps that are common to most fiscal impact studies. A formula developed by Muller and Dawson (1972) provides a basic framework:

$$NFI = W - (X + Y) \tag{3}$$

where W = The present value of development-linked revenue,
$\quad\ X$ = The present value of development-linked operating expenditures,
$\quad\ Y$ = The present value of development-linked capital expenditures, and
NFI = Net fiscal impact.

Although the net fiscal-impact formula is very clear conceptually, in practice it is usually difficult to estimate the various components. A brief analysis of the three variables that determine net fiscal impact will illustrate how the formula may be implemented.

Estimating Revenues.   Local revenues can be divided into property tax revenues, sales tax revenues, income tax revenues, intergovernmental transfers, and user charges/fees. Separate calculations may be made for each type of revenue. The importance of specific types of revenue sources will vary from district to district.

Residential developments are likely to generate most revenue through the property tax. The approximate value of new residential properties will be known when a fiscal-impact study is undertaken because developers normally know the price range of houses in their development. Therefore, increased property tax revenues are relatively easy to estimate by multiplying the effective tax rate by the increase in the tax base. Revenues from sales taxes and income taxes may be more difficult to determine because they depend on shopping and work patterns. However, based upon shopping and employment patterns of existing residents as well as the income levels that could be assumed based upon the value of the properties, reasonable estimates may be derived. Intergovernmental transfers depend primarily upon population size and the number of school-age children, although other factors may enter some grant formulas. Since family size can be estimated from the type of residential development proposed, roughly accurate estimates of intergovernmental revenues may be obtained.

Property tax revenues from commercial developments are also fairly easy to estimate based on the value of the proposed development stated in the zoning request or building permit. Local payroll tax revenues may also increase to the extent employment increases. Sales taxes will increase to the extent sales increase. An analyst must be careful to adjust revenue estimates if increased sales or employment come at the expense of other local businesses.

Estimating Operating Expenditures.   A major difficulty in measuring operating expenses is that costs may remain fixed when usage increases by a small amount, so that marginal costs are near zero. Such might be the case for small increases in road use. Other governmental services may face sharply increasing marginal costs as demand increases, as might be the case if new roads were required to accommodate development related traffic increases. In the absence of reliable data on marginal cost, analysts often assume that the marginal cost of public services made necessary by a new development will equal average cost.

Operating expenses for residential developments may be analyzed by considering whether demand for governmental services: (1) is concentrated among low-income households, (2) increases with income, (3) changes with the size of the units constructed, and (4) varies in other relevant variables. Estimates of likely expenses may be improved by examining the type of project being proposed. Operating expenses of commercial enterprises may be estimated based on average costs of similar businesses in the area.

Estimating Capital Expenditures.   Capital expenditures caused by new development include: (1) facilities linked directly with the proposed project, such as sewer lines or fire stations, (2) facilities that would have been constructed regardless of the new development, but in which new residents will share, and (3) facilities that will have to be constructed because of the new development but which will be shared by other residents. Theoretically, only the marginal costs of a new development are relevant. However, marginal costs are seldom the basis for evaluating a development's capital costs, because they are difficult to determine and may differ from citizens' concepts of fair-share burden. In practice, the new project is normally assigned the entire cost in the first instance. In the second case, the new development may not be charged for any of the costs or an average cost may be assigned. In the third case, the development is often assigned a disproportionate share of the incremental costs.

Benefit-Cost Analysis

Benefit-cost analysis is a decision-making tool that can be used to improve governmental decision making by going beyond narrow fiscal impacts and examining a broader range of costs and benefits. It attempts to measure the social costs and social benefits of public projects. If the benefits outweigh the costs, then the presumption is that the community would be enhanced by the project. If, on the other hand, the costs exceed the benefits, then the aggregate value of the resources required to build a project is greater than the benefits placed upon the output. The former case is intended to be the public-sector equivalent of a profitable business venture, and the latter case is the counterpart to an unprofitable business.

The formula central to benefit-cost analysis is:

$$B/C = \sum_{i=0}^{n} B_i \bigg/ \sum_{i=0}^{n} C_i \qquad (4)$$

where B/C = Benefit cost ratio,

$\displaystyle\sum_{i=0}^{n} B_i$ = The sum of the discounted value of social benefits (0 = present year), and

$\displaystyle\sum_{i=0}^{n} C_i$ = The sum of the discounted value of the social costs.

The concept of benefit-cost analysis is simple: measure and compare the benefits and costs. Yet there are conceptual difficulties and implementation problems. Social costs and benefits will differ from private costs and benefits if there are spillover effects or externalities. The private costs of producing a commodity are costs to the producer. Additionally, a social cost might include the effects of pollution on residents near the factory. Social costs include both private costs and spillover effects.

The inclusion of all benefits and costs in the decision is the key element in understanding the differences between benefit-cost analysis and the private decision-making process. However, the comprehensive perspective creates an implementation problem, since the consequences—both good and bad—that stem from a project are too numerous and often too small to measure.

Steps in Benefit-Cost Analysis.   The discussion of potential difficulties of benefit-cost analysis suggests that benefit-cost studies should be structured and implemented to avoid potential abuses. The steps in a benefit-cost study may be briefly summarized:

1. Describe the Nature of the Project.   This step is necessary because the purposes of benefit-cost studies are not always the same, and the purposes may affect methodology. Benefit-cost analysis can be either a decision-making tool or an evaluative tool. For example, one study may answer the question, "Should the school be built?" and another, "Should the school have been built?" There may also be relevant constraints that will affect the outcome or nature of the study. For example, a budgetary constraint may prevent analysis of a bigger project that might appear better.

2. Delineate the Set of Choices.   Benefit-cost analysis is not feasible for comparing all governmental projects. In describing the choice set, the analyst should specify alternative projects being considered. In the simplest case, where only one project is being considered, the issue may be whether the benefit-cost ratio is greater than a certain level. The choice will become more difficult if projects are mutually exclusive or otherwise interdependent.

3. Describe the Benefits and Costs of the Project.   This step and the next are possibly the most difficult in the analysis. The benefits and costs should include not only direct but also indirect impacts. The analyst might even choose to discuss "speculative effects," so that those factors that might or might not result would at least be mentioned. One of the significant lessons learned from evaluations of federal urban programs is that unintended and unanticipated effects often turn out to be more significant than planned impacts.

An important dimension of the description of the costs and benefits is the time period in which they occur. The further in the future the costs and benefits take effect, the less weight they will be given.

4. Estimate the Monetary Value of the Costs and Benefits. Techniques and examples for estimating social benefits include:

- The benefits of a road can include time savings valued at the traveler's hourly wage in addition to direct transport-cost savings.
- The value of mass-transit facilities includes the benefits to automobile drivers, who will save time because mass-transit facilities reduce driving time.
- Public housing benefits have included the estimated value of crime prevention.
- The value of public parks and other recreational facilities has included the price paid for admittance to similar private facilities, plus the value of travel time saved because of the nearness of the facility.
- Surveys have been used to determine what individuals might be willing to pay.
- The increased property values of land near public improvements have been a measure of benefits of parks.
- Flood-control projects have included the value of the increase in agricultural output.

Of course, there are still significant estimation problems with attempts to quantify elusive outcomes. All attempts to estimate value are subject to criticism. Some analysts prefer simply to list or set aside some qualitative benefits.

5. Select a Discount Rate. The selection of the discount rate for government projects is a controversial aspect of benefit-cost analysis. Since most government property development projects involve large, current expenditures and provide a flow of benefits over many years, a low discount rate increases the net present benefits and, hence, also increases the number of projects that can be justified. Among the possible discount rates that can be used are these:

- Private rate of return, because it represents the opportunity cost of capital used in the project.
- A rate slightly lower than the private rate of return, to adjust for the risk of public projects.

- The rate at which government borrows.
- A rate that reflects appropriate concern for future generations.

There is yet to be a final resolution of the discount-rate issue. While the conceptual problems inherent in this step may be great, a rate is usually selected based upon rates in effect at the time of the study.

6. *Discount the Costs and Benefits.*   The first five steps are preliminary to the actual calculation. Once the appropriate benefits, costs, and discount rates are established, this step is mechanical.

7. *Perform Sensitivity Analysis.*   While not always necessary, repeating the fifth and sixth steps with different assumptions will provide an indication of how sensitive the results are to changes in the discount rate or in values placed upon some intangible benefits. If the results are sensitive to small changes in, say, the value of time savings resulting from construction of a road, then doubt will be cast on the project.

8. *Describe Conclusions and Caveats.*   Many benefit-cost studies leave the impression that, if the benefit-cost ratio is greater than 1, it is obvious that the conclusion should be to construct the project. However, if a result is sensitive to the discount rate, or to one of the variables that the analyst could only roughly estimate, then the conclusion would be in doubt. There could be a discussion of how the inclusion of qualitative variables may have affected the analysis. Furthermore, because of budget constraints, the cutoff point for government projects may be a benefit-cost ratio greater than 2 rather than greater than 1. In addition, funding a project with the highest benefit-cost ratio may not maximize the difference between the total benefits and total costs. Consequently, the reasoning behind any cutoff point should be discussed.

Conceptual and Implementation Issues.   The theoretical justification for benefit-cost analysis is that when a project's benefits outweigh project costs, net social wealth will increase. With the increase in social wealth, the government could redistribute income so as to make at least one person better off without making anyone worse off (called a Pareto move). Society may decide not to redistribute income because they prefer the existing distribution; but as long as everyone can be potentially better off, the project should be undertaken. The final distribution of income will be a decision implemented by the distribution branch. On scientific grounds, there is no basis for preferring one distribution to another. Thus, benefit-cost analysis is based on efficiency rather than equity criteria.

One method for dealing with the distributional issue is to assign different weights to various income groups. Thus, $1 of benefits or costs to a low-income family could be weighted by a factor of 1.2 or 1.7. Whatever the weight (even if all are weighted equally), the analyst is making a value judgment, not a scientific judgment. Some writers have suggested a "balance sheet" approach whereby the benefits and costs that accrue to individuals in different income categories are separated.

Several criticisms of benefit-cost analysis have been discussed in the literature. One criticism is that all the costs and benefits cannot be counted. Since almost every action sets off numerous second, third, and greater-order consequences, tracking down and valuing all the ramifications are impossible. While this criticism is true, benefit-cost studies should attempt to count the costs of the major consequences. An analyst may have to assume that unforeseen or remote costs and benefits balance out.

A second criticism has been that the governments cannot afford to undertake all projects for which the benefit-cost ratios are greater than 1. Consequently, another standard must be developed to select among projects. Most analysts recognize this point. As a result, benefit-cost studies are more appropriate as a guide to an agency selecting among similar projects than as a guide to a legislature trying to allocate funds among very different projects, such as health and road maintenance. A small agency may also lack the resources to undertake all projects with positive benefit-cost ratios, but it could have a decision-making rule requiring benefit-cost ratios of over, say, 1-5, before a project could be undertaken.

The presence of intangible costs and benefits presents another problem. It is nearly impossible to place a monetary value on some activities. Frequently, critics suggest that since we can't place a value on a human life, benefit-cost studies are not appropriate to projects where such issues are involved. Some observers contend that the very act of putting a price on something reduces its value. Proponents of benefit-cost studies counter this point in two ways. First, society often places value on human life. Second, some benefits and costs that cannot be valued may be set aside so the benefits of, say, raising the speed limit from 55 to 65 miles per hour could be expressed as "$1 million in net savings but at the expense of X extra deaths per year." Thus, the decision makers are still left with the decision regarding how to handle the trade-off. The inability of benefit-cost analysis to value some benefits and costs is another reason why benefit-cost studies are better suited to evaluations of similar projects than to determining funding levels among very different departments.

Finally, benefit-cost studies remove decisions from the political decision makers and place them in the hands of technocrats. When benefit-cost techniques are employed, citizens lose the ability to engage in debates and affect outcomes. It is true that benefit-cost studies can be used to "snow" people and make a political decision appear to be only a technical decision. However, this abuse can be avoided in well-implemented studies.

SUMMARY

Many countries have federal systems of government whereby responsibility for regional and urban issues rests with governments at a variety of levels. National governments have the dominant influence in stabilization activities, because local governments lack the capacity to control overall levels of economic activity. Distribution functions are also difficult to implement at the local level, because migration between governmental jurisdictions may negate efforts to transfer income from one group to another. However, some redistribution does occur at the local level. Most state and local government activities are designed to influence the allocation of resources. Allocation activities include the provision of public goods as well as adjusting market outcomes for externalities and merit goods.

Many observers examine economies of scale to determine the appropriate size of local governments. More recently, economists have claimed that decision-making costs should be the key factor in determining government size. Local governments can purchase services from elsewhere, so there is no need to have a government large enough to achieve economies of scale. Three important aspects of decision-making costs are preference mismatches, decision-making effort, and intergovernmental spillovers.

Intergovernmental grants are used to improve the efficiency in the allocation of goods that spill over from one jurisdiction to another. They are also used to encourage fiscal residuum equity. There are a variety of types of intergovernmental grants that can be used to influence how a government reacts to a grant from another unit of government.

Taxes have been evaluated according to their efficiency, equity, and revenue elasticity. Shifting is important to the analysis of equity. The property tax is an important source of local government revenue. Unfortunately, the property tax does not score well on any of the three criteria. Issues of shifting and incidence of the property tax were discussed.

Urban fiscal problems include fiscal stress, lack of productivity increases in the provision of public services, federal mandates and regulations, underfunded obligations, perverse incentives, and cumulative decline. Strategies and tools for improving local government decisions include privatization, annexation, fiscal-impact studies, and benefit-cost analysis.

REFERENCES

Bell, Michael E., and John H. Bowman. "The Effects of Various Intergovernmental Aid and Local Own-Source Revenues: The Case of Property Taxes in Minnesota Cities." *Public Finance Quarterly* 15, no. 3, July 1987, pp. 282–97.

Baumol, William J. "Macroeconomics of Unbalanced Growth: The Anatomy of Urban Crisis." *American Economic Review* 57, 1967, pp. 415–26.

Eberts, Randall W., and Timothy J. Gronberg. "Can Competition among Local Governments Constrain Government Spending." *Economic Review* 24, no. 1, 1989, pp. 2–9.

Ferris, James M. "Local Government Pension Funds and Their Funding: Policy Issues and Options." *Review of Public Personnel Administration* 7, no. 3, Summer 1987, pp. 19–24.

Gramlich, Edward. "The New York City Fiscal Crisis." *American Economic Review* 66, May 1976, pp. 415–29.

Greene, Kenneth V.; William B. Neenan; and Claudia D. Scott. "Fiscal Incidence in the Washington Metropolitan Area." *Land Economics* 52, 1976, pp. 13–31.

Kaplan, Marshal. "Infrastructure Needs Assessment: Methodological Problems and Opportunities." In *Public Infrastructure Planning and Management.* ed. J. M. Stein. 1988, pp. 35–39.

Lovell, Catherine H., and Charles Tobin. "The Mandate Issue." *Public Administration Review* 41, May–June 1981, pp. 318–331.

Muller, Thomas, and Grace Dawson. *The Fiscal Impact of Residential and Commercial Development.* Washington, D.C.: The Urban Institute, 1972.

Musgrave, Richard A. *The Theory of Public Finance.* New York: McGraw-Hill, 1959.

Neenan, W. B. *Political Economy of Urban Areas.* Chicago: Markham, 1972.

Oates, W. E. "On Local Finance and the Tiebout Model." *American Economic Review,* 1969, pp. 957–71.

Ramsey, D. D. "Suburban-Central City Exploitation Thesis: Comment." *National Tax Journal* 25, 1972, pp. 599–604.

Rhoads, Steven E. *The Economist's View of the World: Government, Markets, and Public Policy.* Cambridge: Cambridge University Press, 1985.

Tideman, T. Nicolaus, and Gordon Tullock. "A New and Superior Process for Making Public Choices." *Journal of Political Economy* 84, no. 6, 1976, pp. 1145–59.

Chapter 14

Urban Economics, Planning, and the Future

Economics, futures studies, and urban planning are important parts of the process of policy development. Urban planners need reasonable estimates regarding the likely course of future events in order to anticipate needs and develop policy responses. Economics is near the heart of planning processes because planners are interested in economic outcomes, economic methods are used in the planning process, and economic factors constrain what can be done. The influential planner George Sternlieb described the importance of economic issues and methods to planners when he said, "In a word we have all suddenly become economists" (1986, p. 154). Many applied urban economists work closely with planners. Planners, in turn, are influenced by their opinions about the future. In practice, it is often difficult to determine whether someone engaged in planning or policy development has an academic background as an economist, planner, or futurist or in some other field.

Futurists and planners have learned a great deal from economists. But economists can also learn from futurists and urban planners. This chapter is intended to sample the ways futurists and urban planners view urban and regional economic development. It should stimulate thought, speculation, and wide-ranging thinking about urban futures and how to influence the course of future events.

FUTURIST PERSPECTIVES

The process of thinking about the future is frustrating because nobody knows the future. Yet, decision makers want to know what the future holds and they want to affect the future. Therefore, most decisions require at least implicit assumptions about the future. Consequently, some type of futures analysis is almost unescapable. Our decisions about the future course of events often have an implicit assumption—the future will be pretty much like today. That assumption is usually sufficient, but not always. We often look back on events and realize that they could and should have been anticipated.

Futurists, like economists, are careful not to imply that they can "predict" the future. Rather they use words and phrases like, "trend analysis," "scenarios," "forecasts," and "projections" when describing what the future might be like.

Futurist thinking is diverse, and, therefore, a few generalizations will be used to illustrate the futurist perspective. This section examines four areas that illustrate the futurist perspective.

Concern with Values and Attitudes

Economics has been called the science of values. Choice is the observable reflection of values, yet economists generally take individual values as given. For example, the utility function is usually the starting point for analysis. Thus, economists are generally concerned with how individuals behave given a set of values. Futurists are concerned with changing values. They ask what value changes are likely to occur and how those changes may affect the way we live.

Two types of theories of value change are popular. Value-conflict/synthesis theories suggest that in the course of time value conflict will be recognized. These value conflicts will create political and personal agitation. Eventually, one of the values will prevail or a third value that rationalizes the conflicting values will emerge. The choices made by individuals as well as social institutions will change to reflect the value shift. A classic example of conflicting values was the existence of slavery (and, today, discrimination) in the United States, a country that professed that "all men are created equal." The conflict between these two values created a "house divided," and new institutions, laws, and behavior emerged. In many urban areas, there are similar conflicts. For instance, citizens favor neighborhood preservation, but that value can conflict with individuals' rights to use property as they please. A weakness of the value-conflict theory is that conflicting values are not uncommon. But the theory provides no satisfactory explanation of when the conflicts will be widely viewed as a problem or will result in reconciliation.

The second view is that values are functional, and values will change if they no longer serve the individual or society. For instance, the right of private property is functional, because (among other things) it contributes to economic efficiency. However, the value of private property has had to give way when it conflicted with other social goals. Taxation requires individuals to give up their private property, yet some taxation is necessary for social maintenance. A weakness of the functional theory is that there may be a "meta-value" that determines what is functional and what is not functional. For instance, private property may not be valued in and of itself, but its value may depend upon the importance attached to economic well-being—the meta-value.

Individuals studying value shifts may monitor surveys of public opinion and social trends in order to anticipate value changes. Futurists are also aware that scientific discoveries and policies shape values as well as reflect current values.

Several possible value changes that may affect urban development could result from the leisure-income trade-off, the importance of friends and family, attitudes toward race and gender, and communal versus individual consumption.

Leisure-Income Trade-Off.   If individuals become more interested in leisure activities, the importance of the city as a place for consumption will increase relative to its importance as a site of production. Efforts to protect the quality of life reflect a greater concern for the consumption city relative to the production city.

Importance of Friends and Family.   The high level of mobility in U.S. society in part reflects a preference for monetary success, even when it requires moving from family and friends. A value change, whereby individuals placed a greater importance on friendship and other stable social relationships, could decrease interregional mobility. In response, the neighborhood might become a more important urban building block. Public policy could tilt towards a jobs-to-people approach relative to the people-to-jobs approach. However, technological changes in transportation and communications could make it easier to maintain relationships over distance. So the tendency towards increased population mobility could continue in spite of such a value shift.

Attitudes toward Race and Gender.   Sargent (1980) argued that the central city has been identified with masculine pursuits and imagery such as aggression, energy, power, and danger. This imagery has contributed toward the desire to separate home life from the central city. As the life pursuits of men and women become more similar, the environments they use may become less differentiated by economic and domestic functions.

Race relations are one of the most distinguishing characteristics of U.S. cities. They contribute toward political tension and other urban problems. Increased respect for individuals regardless of race (or ethnicity) would affect urban life. It would increase the access individuals have to parts of the urban environment that are currently considered out of bounds because of subtle or not-so-subtle social barriers. On the other hand, a variety of negative consequences could be anticipated if racial attitudes deteriorate and urban areas became more segregated.

Communal versus Individual Consumption. Americans tend to value privacy and individual consumption more than shared consumption. Sharing common areas was a concern that had to be addressed before condominiums were widely accepted. Urban living offers numerous sharing possibilities. It might be economical for neighbors to share a lawn mower or even take turns mowing combined lawns. Local governments might provide more semipublic goods if joint consumptions were valued more highly (e.g., more public or club facilities and fewer private swimming pools). The possibilities for joint consumption are many, but U.S. citizens today prefer private consumption. A significantly different urban environment could be imagined if shared consumption were more highly valued.

Technological Change

Technological change refers to new ways of organizing activity. Technology does not have to be embodied in a machine. For instance, the reorganization of a plant so that employees became more efficient could reflect a change in technology even if no new machines were used. Futurists are concerned with the impacts that technological changes can have. In fact, technological forecasting is a strong subarea of futures studies. Futurists are concerned not only with what new technologies may be developed but how they will affect society.

Coates (1982) has described five important ways that new technologies may affect urban development.

1. Technologies can affect the hierarchical relationship among regions. The growth of agribusiness and the decline of the family farm changed the relationship among rural service centers. Declines in transportation costs have expanded the hinterland of major metropolitan areas. Increases in economies of scale have tended to centralize the urban hierarchy, while several new technologies have tended to diminish the importance of centralization of production. Central-place theory is a useful tool to help anticipate how technological change will impact the system of cities.

2. Technological change will affect the internal structure of cities. Electricity helped create the nocturnal city and the elevator. Both factors contributed to increased density. The automobile, on the other hand, contributed to decentralization. The cellular phone will add mobility and thus affect urban structure. More recently, advances in technology have made possible the creation of urban megastructures, such as domed stadiums, which have affected the organization of urban regions.

3. Technological innovations will develop in response to urban

problems. Flood-control technologies have made construction possible in previously unbuildable areas, including New Orleans and other coastal cities. Many current urban problems could be alleviated through technological change that can be anticipated today. New technologies that will alleviate environmental and energy problems can be anticipated. Although technological developments will undoubtedly present solutions for many serious problems, most futurists believe it is unwise to simply assume that a "technology fix" will negate the need to anticipate alternative solutions. Economists similarly warn that behavioral changes may be more efficient solutions to problems than technological innovations.

4. Technology has effects through what is displaced. New technology usually replaces something else. Technological changes that replace certain types of work continue to be examples of this route to change.

5. Technology will interact with other trends to create changes that are difficult to anticipate. In the past, the technology of food production and the trend toward two-income households have interacted to stimulate the fast- and frozen-food industries.

Systems Orientation

Like economists, futurists have a systems orientation. They realize that because of the interrelatedness of subsystems a change will have repercussions on many variables. "You cannot change just one thing," a systems thinker once quipped. Futurists usually assume a more open system and they often take a global perspective than economists. Even in general-equilibrium analysis, economists usually limit their analysis to a few variables, such as prices and quantities. Although no one can examine all of the changes that spring from an event, futurists try to track a wider variety of the repercussions because they are less limited by boundaries of academic disciplines. The futurists' examination of a wider scope of variables has at least one notable drawback. The approaches used by futurists are usually less rigorous than the tight deductive models common in economics.

Related to the systems perspective is the realization that most changes can create additional problems that are often unanticipated. Would public policy have been as supportive of the automobile had decision makers anticipated costs including 50,000 deaths annually, hundreds of thousands of injuries, billions of dollars of property damage, urban sprawl, oil dependency, and unwanted pregnancies? Of course, the benefits of the automobile may still outweigh the costs, but even desirable changes have some undesirable impacts.

Hamrin (1974) listed some important "problems of success":

1. Prolonging the life span results in regional overpopulation and problems of old age.
2. Highly developed science results in hazards of mass destruction.
3. Automation of work results in dislocated workers.
4. Advances in communication and transportation result in pollution, information overload, and vulnerability of a complex society to breakdown.
5. Efficient production systems result in dehumanization of some work.
6. Affluence results in increased energy use and pollution.
7. Satisfaction of basic needs results in revolutions of "rising expectations."
8. Expanded choice results in counterproductive and destructive applications of technology, including terrorism and fear of "insane" nations.
9. Economic growth results in inequality between rich and poor countries.

The fact that improvements bring more challenges is reflected in science fiction writer Isaac Asimov's observation that there are no happy endings in history, only crises that have passed. The same concept is embedded in the thinking of most economists who recognize the elusiveness of happiness—the problem of virtually unlimited human wants and limited resources.

Nevertheless, the idea of progress has been embedded in the world view of most Westerners since the 1700s. History tends to be viewed as a movement from a less desirable state towards a more desirable state. This perspective is shared by futurists with few exceptions.

Importance of Timing

Economists recognize the importance of time in forecasting. Anyone can correctly forecast an economic expansion or recession. Eventually such an event will occur. But such forecasts do little good unless the forecast explains when the event will occur. Futurist writers often are not precise about the timing of events when they describe qualitative or speculative trends. (Futurists are more speculative than economists.)

The future has been categorized as follows: (1) immediate future—starting now and generally extending up to 1 year in the future, (2) near-term future—1 to 5 years in the future, (3) middle-range future—5 to 20 years from now, (4) long-range future—20 to 50 years from now, and (5) the far future—more than 50 years from now. Economic forecasts tend to be in the immediate future. Planners for government and business tend to operate in the near-term and middle-range future. Futurists tend to focus on the middle-range future and the long-range future. Predictive power of our descriptions of the future decreases as thinking shifts from the immediate to far future.

Futurists are very sensitive to how rapidly change occurs, and many futurists believe that the rate of change is accelerating. Furthermore, if a society makes a particular project a high priority, it can often be accomplished quickly. For instance, it required only four years to develop the nuclear bomb once the decision had been made to give that goal a high priority. Eight years after President Kennedy announced the goal of reaching the moon, we were there. Of course, the scientific knowledge base for accomplishing these goals took centuries to develop. Yet, at the time the goals were announced, most people considered them unattainable in the near future.

PLANNING PERSPECTIVES ON POLICY

Planning is an established profession. Planners need the ability to understand what the future could be (called an image of the future), the ability to understand how the future could be different, and the ability to describe the means to achieve desirable futures.

The term "planner" frequently connotes an urban land-use planner. However, land-use planning is only one type of planning activity. Near-, middle-, and long-range planning have become an important function in both public and private sectors. Private firms, such as real estate development companies, engage in planning. Almost all major corporations engage in some type of strategic planning. Public agencies, such as the Department of Defense, use planners to help accomplish a variety of goals. A social service agency or a transportation authority might use a planner to develop goals and strategies for specific activities. The discussion below is primarily concerned with urban planning in the public sector; however, the principles are applicable to private planning as well.

The Planning Process

Most planners agree that the planning process is important because it serves as a mechanism for participants to think about the future. The process is generally considered to be more important than the document or "plan" that results from the process. Numerous regions initiated "Urban 2000" projects in which citizens discussed the likely future of their communities. Some of these efforts resulted in the hiring of a consulting firm to write a plan which was filed and forgotten. Many cities devote considerable effort to futures analysis and planning because of the belief that the more citizens think about the future of their community, the more well-informed and valuable their political participation will be. A "second-best" plan that has widespread community support may be preferable to a technically superior plan imposed from the outside that lacks broad-based support.

Figure 14–1 illustrates a generic planning process. The principal steps are (1) goal articulation and projections, (2) intervention choice, and (3) implementation. Goal articulation requires a vision of what the city should look like at some time in the future. Future goals should be based on a realistic understanding of what is possible rather than a wish list. Interventions are required to alter likely outcomes. Finally, the implementation process should feed back into the plan so it can be updated to reflect changing circumstances.

Goals and Projections. Many cities have master plans that set future goals. Historically, urban master plans have been strong in describing physical development goals, such as where the new shopping centers, sewage treatment facility, and other developments will be. They have been weak in describing social goals, such as what the future crime rate should be.

FIGURE 14–1   The Planning Process

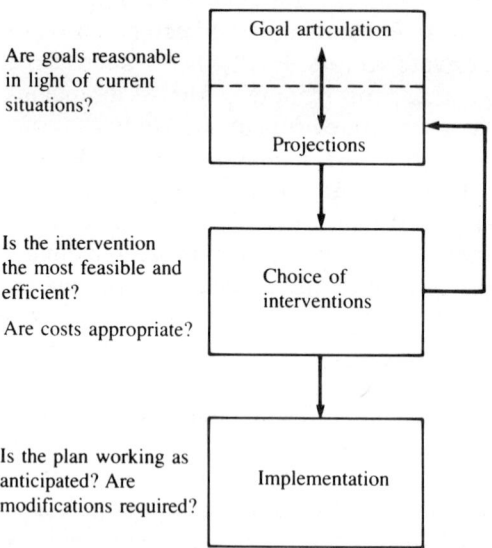

The planning process may include feedbacks so that goals may be revised or new interventions selected.

Goals must be developed from a base of where the community is, where it will be if current trends continue, and the resources available to affect change. Goals should be realistic. Consequently, planners need to understand and analyze the community before or simultaneously with the development of goals. Data gathering and analysis are an important part of the process of selecting goals and making projections. Specific features of the data collection process may include conducting a community economic inventory to determine local strengths and weaknesses.

The selection of the most appropriate goals is more difficult in public than in private planning. Private companies often have a clear goal—profits or stockholder wealth. Public agencies have a variety of goals that reflect competing interests within the community. For instance, the goal of open space could conflict with the goal of industrial employment growth.

In addition to determining where the community is now, it is important to determine where the community will be if current events run their course. How well can analysts predict the future? Some things can be predicted very well, such as community demographic composition. Other elements of the urban future are easy to predict because local officials control the outcome. For instance, the land-use pattern might be predictable if a particular land-use pattern were of a high political priority. However, most aspects of the urban future are neither easy to predict nor are they controllable.

Comparing goals with projected outcomes in the absence of deliberate interventions is necessary to determine whether intervention is necessary. Frequently, goals must be changed if they are unrealistic in view of the existing situation and the nonintervention projections.

Selection of Interventions.   What changes could be made to alter the course of events in order to achieve desired goals? There are many ways to achieve particular ends, and planners usually consider a variety of interventions to achieve particular goals.

A first step in selecting interventions is to determine whether proposed interventions are feasible. Can the intervention be implemented given the community value, political patterns, budget constraints, and national trends? A proposal that cannot be implemented is seldom useful. It is also necessary to determine whether the intervention will actually bring about the desired goal. Like a less-than-adequate dosage of medication, some policies may be insufficient to accomplish the tasks. Consequently, if the resources are not available to complete the task, it may not be worth undertaking in the first place. Many proposed interventions may be rejected at this stage.

Since an end can be achieved through a variety of interventions, the planning process should select one of the various feasible interventions.

Criteria for evaluating interventions can include which intervention (1) is most likely to produce the desired outcome, (2) is least costly, (3) has the lowest risk of negative outcomes, and (4) contributes to other desirable outcomes. Selecting among feasible interventions can be complicated because some interventions may affect more than one planning goal. Therefore, an intervention that is less efficient in achieving one particular goal may be preferred because it helps achieve other goals.

Implementation.   Many, many plans have failed because planners have not been concerned with "marketing" the plan to the community or with implementation. The plan may sit on the shelf, or unanticipated snags may result in scrapping the plan. Not surprisingly, plans tend to become less useful the older they are. Many planners believe that a plan should be updated regularly (a plan should be a process). These rolling plans require a link to the implementation process so the plan can be modified to reflect unanticipated events or implementation problems. A 10-year plan might require revisions every two years. The fact that a plan must be modified to reflect changes in the environment does not mean the initial plan was inadequate.

A suboptimal plan may be better than a technically "best" plan if the suboptimal plan has the support of the individuals involved in implementation. During implementation, cooperation of many persons is required. An excellent plan introduced in an uncooperative environment will probably be sabotaged. Unanticipated events normally require changes in a plan, and these same changes provide opportunities for the individuals charged with implementing the plan to undermine it. The more broadly based the planning process, the more likely that individuals responsible for implementing the plan will support it. Of course, some plans must be introduced in situations where the implementors are hostile, as might be the case in a corporate takeover. In this case, implementation can be very difficult.

Planning and Policy Paradigms

In developing images of the future and community goals, most analysts have a perspective about the kind of future that is likely and desirable. These images help shape the planning process. For instance, if a planner has a basically optimistic worldview, he or she may envision the future of pleasant cities. On the other hand, "dystopian" pictures of the future have been described by a number of influential futurists. Lewis Mumford, one of the first urban futurists, was optimistic in *The Culture of Cities* (1938), but changed his view in later works.

A paradigm is a reflection of the spirit of thought. Different models may be incorporated within a paradigm. Gappert (1982) has described four paradigms that affect the way we view urban futures and, consequently, affect urban planning.

The technocratic perspective is concerned mainly with rationality and efficiency. Individuals with this perspective suggest that the city will develop efficient social arrangements for consumption and production. A typical question asked by individuals with the technocratic perspective is "Will the buses run on time?"

The utopian perspective suggests that improvements can be achieved by the proper application of knowledge, resources, and good intentions. It attempts to define very clear patterns that will characterize the future city. They might develop an urban plan in which buses would be unnecessary. Expressions of this perspective include the urban experimens in solar energy, urban gardening, and "appropriate" technologies. Conversely, a dystopian perspective emphasizes undesirable human tendencies.

The pragmatic humanistic paradigm is concerned with the quality of human behavior and is less concerned about technical change. It recognizes that behavior can increase the efficiency of urban activities. The importance of urban leadership and political coalitions in developing a satisfactory future are emphasized. Planners with this perspective would plan with a goal of ensuring that the bus driver, as well as the passengers, were polite.

Strategic reconstructionists emphasize the development of large-scale projects that may create or exploit new opportunities. Planners oriented toward this perspective might ask whether the subway would link the central business district to the new jetport.

Common Themes in Economic Development Plans

Economic development planning has significantly increased in importance in the past 10 years. Today, large- and medium-sized cities have either economic development plans or they have a strategic plan in which economic development is a major part. Numerous consulting firms specialize in economic development planning, and many states provide financial assistance for such planning. There is a wide variety of economic development plans, reflecting differing regional resources and opportunities and differing philosophies of the planners.

Blakely (1989) suggested that the nature of plans reflects the economic circumstances and community interests (including, presumably, potential conflicts of interest) that initiated the planning process. He identified four types of plans depending on (1) whether the plan was designed

TABLE 14–1   Types of Local Economic Planning

		In Response to	
		Opportunities	*Threats*
Historic or Future Orientation	Reactive	Recruitment planning	Impact planning
	Proactive	Strategic planning	Contingency planning

to take advantage of opportunities or respond to threats and (2) whether the plan was reactive or proactive. Accordingly, a two-by-two matrix shown in Table 14–1 can be used to describe the types of local economic plans.

Recruitment planning, in Blakely's model, represents efforts to take advantage of emerging opportunities by attracting firms in new or fast-growth industries. For example, once it became evident that many industries had locational requirements that could be satisfied best if space in industrial parks were available, many communities began planning for the development of such facilities. *Impact planning* occurs only after a community has experienced an economic setback and there is a realization that "something needs to be done." Both recruitment and impact planning represent reactions to past events.

Strategic and *contingency planning* are intended to anticipate events and appropriate responses. Contingency planning involves developing appropriate responses to anticipated threats. A danger of contingency planning is that plans to deal with an adverse economic situation could lead to the expectation of decline, leading to a self-fulfilling prophecy. For instance, if economic discussions were dominated by how the region would respond to the loss of a mill, potential suppliers to the mill might be deterred from locating there because they believed the planners knew the mill was going to close. Strategic planning is comprehensive and long range. It examines emerging external opportunities and includes plans to take advantage of such opportunities.

The goals of economic plans often take one of two forms. Some plans emphasize process goals. In other words, the goals are to change the economic environment so as to make the locality attractive to businesses. For instance, improving community infrastructure, the tax environment, or the quality of life may help attract and retain businesses. The success of a plan is then judged according to whether the environment was enhanced. Other plans contain ultimate outcome goals such as "create 5,000 new manufacturing jobs.'' One drawback of plans that include very specific outcome goals is that it may be difficult to determine whether specific jobs are attributable to local efforts or whether they are fortuitous.

Allardice and Giese (1987) examined the economic development plans of states in the Seventh Federal Reserve District. They found four common themes in the reports. Of particular importance was decreased emphasis on industrial recruitment (''smokestack chasing'') and more emphasis on helping firms and industries already in the area. This change in approach is often justified by the fact that most new jobs are created by expansions of existing facilities rather than new start-ups or relocations. Second, while strengthening technology continues to be important, there is a realization that the high-tech sector will account for only a small percentage of future jobs. The key point stressed in recent studies is the application of advanced production processes and product innovation to traditional activities. Thus, Michigan's emphasis on robotic technology follows from the increased importance of robotics in automobile production. Third, the reports analyzed by Allandice and Giese indicated a trend towards cooperative coalitions between governments, universities, labor, and business. Universities are frequently assigned roles in stimulating the transfer of technology. Finally, international trade is being incorporated into regional planning strategies. Not only are planners suggesting strategies for encouraging exports abroad, but attraction of investment from abroad is an important feature of development plans.

Most of the recommendations identified in the state plans are also reflected in local plans (Fosler, 1988). In addition, local plans often target specific industries with special potential and provided suggestions to market the community or improve the city's image.

Plans are often put away and forgotten. But, increasingly, they call for the creation of an ongoing organization to monitor implementation, while specific tasks are assigned to appropriate organizations. For instance, a university-based group might monitor and update the plan through annual reports, while a preexisting group such as the Chamber of Commerce might be charged with the task of enhancing the metropolitan area's image. Special ongoing committees of key public and private individuals might also be assigned tasks called for in the plan.

PLANNING AND FUTURES STUDIES TOOLS

The tools that economists bring to the study of urban futures are powerful. They include econometric modeling, forecasting, shift-and-share analysis, input-output analysis, and other techniques previously described in this book. Perhaps most important, economists should have the ability to build models and deduce outcomes from a set of assumptions. There are some tools that have been useful for understanding future events that are unfamiliar to many economists. This section describes three tools that can be used in the planning and futures analysis—delphi forecasting, scenario development, and gaming.

Delphi Forecasting

Delphi forecasting is useful in developing answers about future events for which technical knowledge is required and where judgment is an important ingredient. The delphi technique is a way of combining the opinions of experts while allowing some feedback and discussion. In order to illustrate the use of the delphi forecast, suppose you wish to know if and when a new regional airport will be necessary.

First, a questionnaire might be sent to a group of experts asking when or if a new airport will be needed. An explanation of their reasoning and their degree of confidence might also be requested. After the responses have been tabulated, the results would be sent to the panel of experts and the question asked again. In the second round, the experts would be able to reevaluate their original forecasts in light of the opinion and information given by other experts. For instance, one expert might have said a new regional airport would be required by 1995 because of traffic-control problems. Another expert might have replied that new technologies in traffic control would relieve the congestion problem without the need for an additional facility. Faced with the new information, the individual who thought the airport would be needed in 1995 might revise the estimate to, say, 2005. The second-round projections would be informed by the results of the first round. Generally, the expert opinions will converge after successive rounds as indicated by Figure 14–2.

The delphi technique is quite versatile. The rounds can be conducted by mail, by phone, face to face, by computer network, or by other means. The moderator can instruct the panel to accept certain assumptions as given so that various alternatives can be explored. For instance, an assumption about regional population growth could be built into the question regarding the need for a new regional airport. Cross-impact analysis can be combined with futures analysis so that the impacts forecast in one set of delphi conferences can be used as assumptions in other delphi studies or to ensure that events projected in various studies are consistent.

Two significant dangers of delphi forecasting should be noted. First, situations where the results represent an averaging of ignorance should be avoided. The usefulness of an expert panel will be negated if the questions are about things with which the respondents are unfamiliar. However, the experts need not have similar backgrounds. In fact, it may be useful to include experts in a variety of fields in some forecasts. Second, a domi-

FIGURE 14–2   Convergence of Opinion in a Delphi Forecast

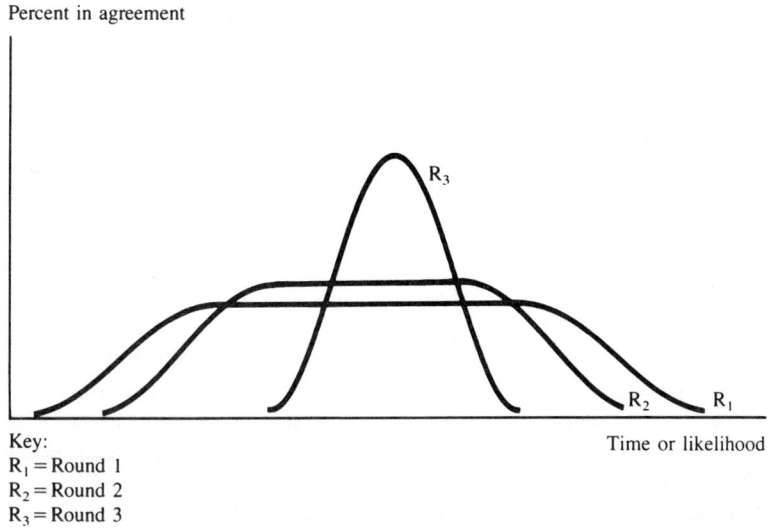

Percent in agreement

Key:
R_1 = Round 1
R_2 = Round 2
R_3 = Round 3

Time or likelihood

During a successful delphi forecast, the opinions of experts will tend to converge.

nant personality can sometimes force individuals to conform to an opinion simply to avoid being contrary. The moderator should be particularly careful not to dominate the expert panel.

Games

Games are characterized by the assignment of a role to various participants. Individuals behave as they believe they would given their role. The game should be structured so that the participants face constraints similar to the situation being simulated. An urban game might include such roles as mayor, land developers, factory owners, and factory workers. A game master would create a situation and set parameters. As the game proceeds, the players might make demands on each other, form coalitions, or negotiate particular outcomes. The games are useful in helping players grasp the complex interactions that might be involved in real-life situations. The rules of the game might be changed to determine how the outcome would differ under different situations.

Games have been a major tool in military planning. War games often involve actual soldiers, but they can also be played in a more abstract setting. Military games played at think tanks, such as those at the RAND

Corporation, help demonstrate the problems with a strategy of "massive retaliation" and help demonstrate the need for flexible responses in addition to all-out war.

Scenarios.   A scenario is a plausible story. It is a description of a series of events that the writer could imagine happening. Although scenario writing appears simple, the technique can be quite useful. If the details of how an event could occur cannot be plausibly described, it is an improbable event. For instance, if no one can imagine the series of events that would lead to the development of an enclosed football stadium, then that event is unlikely to occur. Similarly, if the only events that can lead to the development of an enclosed stadium are improbable, then the end result is also improbable. Conversely, if the occurrence of an event can be described as the logical outcome of a series of likely intermediate events, higher probability should be given to the scenario. Often when a historian looks back on an event, the steps that led to it appear logical and predictable. With hindsight, it may appear that a scenario of the future could have been written easily.

Scenario development seems simple because we are so familiar with the technique. Many novels are scenarios. Samuelson's correspondence theorem suggests that it is not sufficient to say that a condition can be achieved; we must also show how it can be achieved. A scenario is a way of describing how a future state can be achieved. Developing a plausible scenario that leads to a nonobvious conclusion about the future is a difficult but valuable exercise.

ALTERNATIVE URBAN FUTURES

How will the city change over the next 20 years? It is hazardous to project too far into the 21st century because there are many critical unknowns. Technology seems to be extending life, and revamped communications are driving changes in production technology. Lifestyles are also changing rapidly. In spite of the changes that are occurring, many urbanists believe that much of the future is already determined.

The history of urban change indicates that the shape of the metropolis changes slowly. Most of the urban infrastructure in place today will be in place in 50 years. The principal innovations in transportation and communications can be accommodated within the framework of existing structures of roads, tracks, and harbors. Major physical changes that do occur are more likely to be at the urban fringe than at the core, because there is more room for development at the fringe. More urban subcenters can be anticipated, but central business districts are likely to remain almost exactly where they are. Similarly, historical evidence indicates that the urban hierarchy only changes slowly.

In spite of the difficulties of describing the future urban economy, several tantalizing images can be developed that represent likely cases of urban development in the middle-range future. In my opinion, elements of each of the urban futures described in this section are likely to occur within a single city; they are not mutually exclusive. Nevertheless, some cities are more likely to closely approximate particular vignettes than others. These outlooks are important because they reflect extrapolations of trends that are likely to continue, and, consequently, they have implications for urban planning and policy today.

Decline Economies

Many of the urban futures discussed above are predicated on the assumption that the manufacturing base of older northeastern and north central regions will continue to decline. Therefore, the urban economy will evolve into something other than the traditional industrial region. Some areas are making the transitions from manufacturing to services and other activities successfully. But suppose the erosion of manufacturing continues and opportunities for restructuring fail to appear. This image of the future might be referred to as the decline economy.

In the absence of new opportunities, a small decline in employment or the quality of life could snowball into a cumulative deterioration. Closure of some major plants or industries could result in the loss of agglomeration economies, resulting in further plant closings. The fiscal impacts of more public service needs and fewer resources would also aggravate the decline. Migration patterns could leave the region with an older, less-skilled, and immobile population. Residents could become increasingly dependent upon state and federal transfers. Budget deficits at the federal level and fiscal problems in many states will make major outside assistance less likely.

Bradbury, Downs, and Small (1982) examined the problem of declining central cities and concluded that it is likely that population decline will continue for at least the next decade or two. Policies that could reverse the declines would require more resources than are practical, and moderate programs are unlikely to reverse the situations. Although the simulations by Bradbury et al. were for central cities, some metropolitan areas face similar problems.

Physically, the landscape of a decline economy would be distinguished by abandoned buildings and deteriorating infrastructure. High incidence of mental and physical health problems may be a social characteristic. The political climate may be characterized by conflict as interest groups fight over a fixed or shrinking pie.

Individuals who believe the decline economy is a likely event may suggest that city planning should emphasize adapting to a smaller size.

Efforts to reduce urban infrastructure, avoid major new commitments, and cut public employment gradually through attrition might be suggested. However, a policy of planned shrinkage is unlikely to be politically popular and, thus, not likely to be implemented.

Youngstown, Ohio, is an archetypical example of a decline economy. In 1977, steel-mill closings put 5,000 people out of work immediately. Ripple effects permeated the local economy contributing to additional shutdowns. To date, the community has not regained the jobs lost. As Buss and Redburn (1983) stated:

> An economic crisis drains vitality from a community slowly in a thousand small ways. It alters the underlying economic structure. . . . It does not produce a sudden, sharp break with the past. (p. 215)

Knowledge-Based Cities

The advent of the global economy will drive major changes in urban economies. Knight (1987) suggested that urban regions will prosper by gaining international preeminence in a specialized cluster of knowledge-based activities. These activities are also likely to be service oriented because production of things tends to shift to lower-cost, rural production sites. Governance of technology will be the primary activity of knowledge-based cities.

Knowledge-based cities will replace manufacturing-based economies as manufacturing-based economies replaced agriculture:

> Industrial metropolises gained prominence as agriculture and manufacturing was mechanized, as markets were expanded and as rural areas were depopulated. Now, with the advancement of science, the improvement of communication and the annihilation of distance, the globe is shrinking. Improvements in communications and increases in the knowledge content of goods and services are rapidly eroding the locational advantages previously enjoyed by manufacturers in industrial areas. Consequently the future of older industrial metropolises is now in question. (Knight, 1987, p. 53)

The concept of knowledge-based economies is a natural extension of the industrial filtering modeling in a more rapidly changing economy. The rapid rate of spin-offs makes it more important that successful cities pioneer new products and processes.

The hinterland for the knowledge-based cities will be the world. A knowledge-based city will be characterized by strong transportation and communications linkages with the world. International airports, satellite dishes, campuslike research parks, and a buzz of foreign languages might be physical characteristics of knowledge-based regional economies. Linkages among world-class cities will increase in importance. The social atmosphere might be characterized by a cosmopolitan outlook, including a tolerance for new or different ideas and lifestyles.

Knowledge-based economies will need to attract and retain talented individuals who, because of their abilities, will have opportunities in a variety of locations. Therefore, knowledge-based cities will need to have a strong amenity base, including recreation, cultural, and educational outlets.

Menlo Park, California, the Research Park Triangle area of North Carolina, Boston, and New York are examples of knowledge-based economies.

There is a general uneasiness in the minds of planners about development of knowledge-based cities because the services that are produced—knowledge, administration, advice, culture, and so forth—are intangible. Likewise, the ties that bind a knowledge-based business to a region are often intangible. A manufacturing plant has an image of stability. A knowledge-based enterprise may be housed in an ordinary-looking office, so it may lack public visibility and appear footloose. However, if knowledge-based activities depend upon agglomerations of individuals doing similar research, they may be quite stable. Furthermore, it may be quite costly to move key individuals. In many cases, the costs of relocating a knowledge-based enterprise may exceed the costs of relocating a manufacturing plant.

Leisure Cities

Leisure cities represent another future development path. U.S. citizens are starting their work life later and retiring earlier than previously. They are also living longer. Thus, a greater portion of life is spent outside the work force. Furthermore, vacation spending is an income-elastic good, so as incomes increase, individuals are spending proportionally more on recreation. The growth of convention business will also contribute to the rise of the leisure city, since conventions are often viewed as company-paid or at least tax-deductible vacations. There may also be a value shift toward the accumulation of experiences and away from the accumulation of things. Thus, the rise of the leisure city has been anticipated.

Examples of the leisure city today include Orlando, Florida; Reno, Nevada; and Sun City, Arizona. Many cities that have other economic bases are pursuing development paths that strengthen their appeal as recreation or tourist centers. Nashville and New Orleans depend upon recreation dollars.

Irregular Economies

Individuals in some urban areas may earn an increasing portion of their income in nontraditional ways, including:

1. Illegal activity—unlicensed businesses, prostitution, drugs, and so forth.

2. Legal activity made illegal by hiding income—yard work, baby sitting, flea market sales, and so forth.

3. Public transfers—welfare, scholarships, social security, and so forth.

4. Private transfers—charity, support from parents, and so forth.

5. Household business—shade-tree mechanic, direct sales, and so forth.

These income sources can be lumped into what has been called the irregular economy.

The increasing pace of change tends to create dislocated workers, particularly in manufacturing-based regions. The mainstream economy will be able to absorb most of the dislocated workers, but not all. Dislocated workers will undoubtedly seek new jobs in traditional occupations. However, there may be serious skill mismatches because the abilities and attitudes required in the fast-growing service sector are different from those required in the manufacturing sector. Impediments to smoothly operating formal markets, such as mobility limitations and sticky wages and prices, will compound the adjustment problem. A wider spectrum of residents will be attracted to the irregular sectors. Retirees, increasingly healthy in retirement (many urban residents may be forced into early retirement due to structural changes), may seek to supplement their income in the irregular economy. Accordingly, we may speak of the irregular economies of cities.

The export-base theory implies that the irregular economy will not dominate a region's activities. Most irregular activity tends to provide services to other local residents rather than earning import dollars. Consequently, a region with an economic base only dependent upon the irregular sectors is unlikely. However, irregular economies may become a substantial part of many urban economies.

Neighborhoods

Several observers have suggested that neighborhoods will become more important building blocks in the urban economy. Cities that are considered to have strong neighborhoods include Denver, Seattle, Washington, D.C., Milwaukee, and Cleveland. Nearly every major city has a neighborhood system that is generally recognized throughout the metropolitan area. Neighborhoods are less well-delineated in the suburbs, although small suburbs may constitute a neighborhood since they are relatively homogeneous.

Strengthening of neighborhood is often associated with the need for resource conservation. Energy shortages may encourage individuals to live, work, and shop nearby. Food shortages may encourage intensive use of urban land for agricultural purposes which will require neighborhood-based organizations. Materials shortages may be addressed through neighborhood-based conservation centers. Conservation of the existing housing stock is integral to neighborhood preservation.

Neighbors are valued and so neighborhoods tend to be valued. Grassroots democracy usually requires a neighborhood base, and individuals often feel they are linked to the larger metropolitan region through their neighborhood. Many organizations have neighborhood bases, such as senior citizens groups, political organizations, day-care centers, and food cooperatives. Efforts to accomplish the goals of these organizations will strengthen neighborhoods.

Neighborhoods also provide security, and they often represent defensible areas in which individuals feel safe. Strong neighborhoods could develop in a city characterized by internal conflicts if neighborhoods represented strong political interest groups. Neighborhoods often provide the spatial analog to ethnic conflict. Consequently, cities in racial conflict could develop strong neighborhoods that serve to exclude outsiders.

SUMMARY

The planning process and the future of urban regions were the focus of this chapter. Urban economists, planners, and futurists work closely together in the planning process. Most decisions require at least some assumptions about the future, so some type of futures analysis is essential for policy development. Economists should be familiar with the thinking of futurists and planners because they often work together.

Futurists avoid suggesting that they can predict the future. They describe likely events if certain trends prevail. Futurists have diverse points of view; yet there are common threads in their analysis. Futurists are concerned with value changes, technological developments, the interrelatedness of social and ecological systems, and the importance of timing.

Planners need to be able to understand future possibilities and the ability to describe the means to achieve desirable futures. Planners in both the public and private sectors frequently rely upon economic methods. Most planners believe the planning process is as important as a final document or plan. The planning process can be a vehicle for thinking about the future. A three-step planning process would include (1) the development of goals and projections, (2) selection of interventions, and (3) implementation. In developing future images and goals, most analysts have perspectives about the kind of future they believe is likely and/or desirable. Delphi forecasting can be used to help understand the future by drawing upon expert opinion. Games can be used to simulate the possible course of events. A well-structured game includes realistic constraints on the behavior of the participants. Scenarios are descriptions of events that could evolve from the current flow of events. If the evolution of an event cannot be plausibly described, it is improbable.

The history of urban change indicates that urban form and the urban hierarchy change slowly. Yet, the many urban economies are going through a transition from a manufacturing orientation to something else. The something might be captured by models of decline economies, knowledge-based economies, leisure cities, irregular economies, and neighborhood-based economies. Elements of each of the urban futures described in this section could occur within a single urban region.

REFERENCES

Allardice, David R., and Alenka S. Giese. "Economic Development Efforts in the Seventh District." *Economic Perspectives* 11, September–October 1987, pp. 32–37.

Blakely, Edward J. *Planning Local Economic Development: Theory and Practice*. Newbury Park, Calif.: Sage, 1989.

Bradbury, K. L.; A. Downs; and K. A. Small. *Urban Decline and the Future of American Cities*. Washington, D.C.: Brookings Institution, 1982.

Buss, Terry F., and Steven Redburn. *Shutdown at Youngstown: Public Policy for Mass Unemployment*. New York: State University of New York Press, Albany, 1983.

Coates, Joseph F. "New Technologies and Their Urban Impact." In *Cities in the 21st Century*, ed. G. Gappert and R. Knight. Beverly Hills, Calif.: Sage Publications, 1982, chapter 10.

Fosler, R. Scott. "Economic Development: A Regional Challenge for the Heartland." *Economic Review* 73, May 1988, pp. 10–19.

Gappert, Gary. "Future Urban America: Post Affluent or Advanced Industrial Society?" In *Cities in the 21st Century*, ed. G. Gappert and R. Knight. Beverly Hills, Calif.: Sage Publications, 1982, chapter 1.

Hamrin, Robert. "The Coming Transformation in Our View of Knowledge." *The Futurist* 8, no. 3, June 1974, pp. 15–20.

Knight, Richard V. "Governing the Post-Industrial Metropolis—Building the Global City." Paper presented at the Conference on Global Cities, Milan, Italy, February, 1987.

Mumford, Lewis. *The Culture of Cities*. New York: Harcourt, Brace, and Company, 1938.

Sargent, Susan. "Masculine Cities and Feminine Suburbs." *Signs* 5, 1980, pp. 93–108.

Shostak, Arthur. "Seven Scenarios of Urban Change." In *Cities in the 21st Century*, ed. G. Gappert and R. Knight. Beverly Hills, Calif.: Sage Publications, 1982, chapter 4.

Sternlieb, George. "Grasping the Future." In *New Roles for Old Cities*, ed. E. Rose. Brookfield, Vt.: Gower Publishing Company, 1986, chapter 14.

Index

C

G

Q–R